D1524967

LIBRARY

Gift of

The Bush Foundation

WITHDRAWN

Reflections on Reality

A

BOOK

The Philip E. Lilienthal imprint honors special books
in commemoration of a man whose work
at the University of California Press from 1954 to 1979
was marked by dedication to young authors
and to high standards in the field of Asian Studies.
Friends, family, authors, and foundations
have together endowed the Lilienthal Fund,
which enables the Press to publish under this imprint
selected books in a way that reflects the taste and judgment
of a great and beloved editor.

Reflections on Reality

The Three Natures and Non-Natures in the Mind-Only School

Jeffrey Hopkins

Dynamic Responses to Dzong-ka-ba's
The Essence of Eloquence: Volume 2

UNIVERSITY OF CALIFORNIA PRESS

Berkeley Los Angeles London

The publisher gratefully acknowledges the generous contribution to this book provided by the Philip E. Lilienthal Asian Studies Endowment of the University of California Press Associates, which is supported by a major gift from Sally Lilienthal.

University of California Press
Berkeley and Los Angeles, California

University of California Press, Ltd.
London, England

© 2002 by
The Regents of the University of California

Library of Congress Cataloging-in-Publication Data

Hopkins, Jeffrey.
Reflections on reality : the three natures and non-natures in the mind-only school : dynamic responses to Dzong-ka-ba's the essence of eloquence : II / Jeffrey Hopkins.
p. cm.
"A Philip E. Lilienthal book."
Includes bibliographical references and index.
ISBN: 0-520-21120-0 (alk. paper)
1. Tsoṅ-kha-pa Blo-bzaṅ-grags-pa, 1357-1419. Legs bśad sñiṅ po.
2. Vijñaptimātratā. 3. Dge-lugs-pa (Sect)—Doctrines. I. Title.
BQ7950.T754 L4337
2002
294.3'420423—dc21 2002016645
CIP

Printed in the United States of America
9 8 7 6 5 4 3 2 1

The paper used in this publication meets the minimum requirements of the American National Standards for Information Sciences—Permanence of Paper for Printed Library Materials, ANSI Z39.48-1984.

BQ
7950
.T754
L4337
2002

071503-5280 T8

Contents

Preface

This book presents an introduction to and analysis of many facets of the first two sections of Ḏzong-ka-ḇa's[a] *The Essence of Eloquence,*[b] the Prologue and the section on the Mind-Only School. In six parts, it

- places reactions to Ḏzong-ka-ḇa's text in historical and social context by examining the tension between allegiance and rational inquiry in monastic colleges and the inter-relationships between faith, reason, and mystical insight
- presents the religious significance of the central doctrine of the Mind-Only School, the three natures of phenomena
- examines in detail the exchange between the Bodhisattva Paramārthasamudgata and Buddha in the seventh chapter of the *Sūtra Unraveling the Thought* concerning the three wheels of doctrine and the three natures
- documents the markedly different view on the status of reality presented by the fourteenth-century scholar-yogi Shay-rap-gyel-tsen[c] of the Jo-nang-ḇa[d] order as well as criticisms by Ḏzong-ka-ḇa and his Ge-luk-ḇa[e] followers
- fleshes out Tibetan presentations of the provocative issue of the relationship between two types of emptiness in the Mind-Only School and comparison with how the topic of two emptinesses is debated today in America, Europe, and Japan, thereby demonstrating how the two forms of scholarship refine and enhance each other (these discussions continue in the three Appendices)
- demonstrates the types of reasonings establishing mind-only used as means to overcome a basic dread of reality.

My annotated translation of these sections in Ḏzong-ka-ḇa's text is to be found in the first volume of this series, *Emptiness in the Mind-Only School of Buddhism.*[1] It is in four parts:

- A historical and doctrinal introduction
- A translation of the General Explanation and the Section on the Mind-Only School in *The Essence of Eloquence* with frequent annotations in brackets, footnotes, and backnotes
- A detailed synopsis of the translation that re-renders the text, with additional information, in more free-flowing English

---

[a] *tsong kha pa blo bzang grags pa,* 1357-1419.

[b] *drang ba dang nges pa'i don rnam par phye ba'i bstan bcos legs bshad snying po;* Peking 6142, vol. 153.

[c] *dol po pa shes rab rgyal mtshan,* 1292-1361.

[d] *jo nang pa.*

[e] *dge lugs pa.*

- A critical edition in Tibetan script of these sections in *The Essence of Eloquence.*

The third volume, *Absorption in No External World,* examines a plethora of fascinating points on these same sections of Ḏzong-ka-ḇa's text raised in six centuries of Tibetan and Mongolian commentary through:

- identifying the teachings in the first wheel of doctrine
- probing the meaning of "own-character" and "established by way of its own character"
- untangling the implications of Ḏzong-ka-ḇa's criticisms of the Korean scholar Wonch'uk, and
- treating many engaging points on the three natures and the three non-natures, including (1) how to apply these two grids to uncompounded space; (2) whether the selflessness of persons is a thoroughly established nature; (3) how to consider the emptiness of emptiness; and (4) the ways the Great Vehicle schools delineate the three natures and the three non-natures
- contrasting these presentations by Tibetan scholars with others in America, Asia, Europe, and so forth.

The aim is to bring to life scholastic controversies in order both to stimulate the metaphysical imagination and to show the non-monolithic nature of the interpretations of the followers of a seminal figure.

Please see the Preface in volume one for a lengthy expression of gratitude to the many Tibetan and Mongolian scholars who have aided me on this project over the last eighteen years. I also wish to acknowledge the assistance of the Jo-nang-ḇa scholars L̄o-drö-gyel-tsen[a] of S̄ay[b] Monastery in Am-do Province, Tibet, presently residing in Taipei, and Ken-ḇo Tsul-trim-dar-gyay Rin-ḇo-chay[c] of Lung-ḡya[d] Monastery in Ga-day, Go-lok[e] in Am-do Province.

Jeffrey Hopkins
University of Virginia

---

[a] *blo gros rgyal mtshan,* born 1938.

[b] *bswe,* located in the district of Nga-wa (*rnga ba*).

[c] *mkhan po tshul khrims dar rgyas rin po che,* born 1962.

[d] *lung skya.*

[e] *dga' bde 'go log.*

Technical Notes

It is important to recognize that:

- citations from volume one, *Emptiness in the Mind-Only School of Buddhism,* are indicated by "*Emptiness in Mind-Only*" with a page reference; notes within those citations are not repeated in this volume;
- footnotes are marked "a, b, c..."; backnotes are marked "1, 2, 3...." References to texts are mostly given in the backnotes, whereas other information, more pertinent to the reading of the material at hand, is given in the footnotes. Footnote references in italics indicate that the note includes a linkage to an issue treated in volume three, *Absorption in No External World;* those issues are arranged in numbered sequence, and thus references to them are by issue number;
- full bibliographical references are given in the footnotes and backnotes at the first citation in each chapter;
- for translations and editions of texts, see the Bibliography;
- citations of the *Sūtra Unraveling the Thought* include references to the edited Tibetan text and French translation of it in consultation with the Chinese by Étienne Lamotte in *Saṃdhinirmocanasūtra: L'Explication des mystères* (Louvain: Université de Louvain, 1935) and to the English translation from the *stog* Palace edition of the Tibetan by John C. Powers, *Wisdom of Buddha: Saṁdhinirmocana Sūtra* (Berkeley, Calif.: Dharma, 1995). There is also a translation from the Chinese by Thomas Cleary in *Buddhist Yoga: A Comprehensive Course* (Boston: Shambhala, 1995), in which the references are easily found, as long as chapter 7 of Lamotte and Powers is equated with chapter 5 of Cleary as per the Chinese edition that he used (see *Emptiness in Mind-Only,* Appendix 2, p. 457ff.). Passages not cited in D̄zong-ka-b̄a's text are usually adaptations of Powers's translation as submitted for his doctoral dissertation under my guidance;
- I have translated the term *drang don* (*neyārtha*) sometimes as "interpretable meaning" and other times as "requiring interpretation," or a variant thereof. There is no significance to the multiple translations other than variety and clarity, the latter being to emphasize that the scripture requires interpretation;
- the names of Indian Buddhist schools of thought are translated into English in an effort to increase accessibility for non-specialists;
- for the names of Indian scholars and systems used in the body of the text, *ch, sh,* and *ṣh* are used instead of the more usual *c, ś,* and *ṣ* for the sake of

easy pronunciation by non-specialists; however, *cch* is used for *cch,* not *chchh.* In the notes the usual transliteration system for Sanskrit is used;

- transliteration of Tibetan is done in accordance with a system devised by Turrell Wylie; see "A Standard System of Tibetan Transcription," *Harvard Journal of Asiatic Studies* 22 (1959):261-267;
- the names of Tibetan authors and orders are given in "essay phonetics" for the sake of easy pronunciation; for a discussion of the system used, see the technical note at the beginning of my *Meditation on Emptiness* (London: Wisdom, 1983; rev. ed., Boston: Wisdom, 1996), 19-22. The system is used consistently, with the result that a few well-known names are rendered in a different way: for example, "Lhasa" is rendered as "Hla-sa," since the letter "h" is pronounced before the letter "l"; and
- an English-Tibetan-Sanskrit glossary will be given at the end of the third volume, *Absorption in No External World.*

PART ONE:
BACKGROUND

1. Monastic Colleges: The Tension between Allegiance and Inquiry

Standing at my window, peering into the very black night, I tried to locate the source of the shouting voice. For nights I had heard it—proclaiming a memorized text—not the expected poetry, but prose. The intensity of the voice was intriguing, loud, and seemingly strained, yet continuing for hours. He was forcing himself to shout!

I had fallen asleep many nights not quite listening to the voice—there was so much noise almost all day at the college (one long-term visitor said that it was like living in the midst of a kindergarten) that this seemed easy to ignore—but now I was paying attention. I could not put it aside; I wanted to locate it.

I was staying in the guest house of the Shar-dzay[a] (East Point) College of Gan-den[b] (Joyous) Monastic University in Mundgod in N. Kanara of Karnataka State in south India. The Tibetan refugee community had resettled monastic and lay groups in Mundgod. The Shar-dzay guest house lies near the boundary between it and the Jang-dzay[c] (North Point) College of the same monastic university—with an alleyway between them that serves not as a passage between the two colleges but as an invisible wall keeping students from straying into the rival college. With buildings so close on three sides, the voice seemed to come, at different times, from all of them.

I gave up peering into the darkness and lay down on my bed, occasionally able to put together phrases, still trying mentally to place the voice now here, now there, now in Shar-dzay, now in Jang-dzay. Phrases gradually formed into clauses, and meaning began to emerge—it suddenly dawned on me that this was Dzong-ka-ba's *The Essence of Eloquence.*[d] My first teacher of Tibetan Buddhism, Geshe Wangyal—from Astrakhan, a Kalmuck Mongolian area where the Volga River empties into the Caspian Sea in *Europe* no less—had reported that as a young man in Hla-sa (during his thirty-five-year stay in Tibet) he had memorized the text, though I was never sure whether this meant the entire book or the initial section on the Mind-Only School.[e] In English, a translation of the entire text without explanatory commentary would take about 250 pages; of the section on Mind-Only, about 90.

This was what was nightly being etched into my mind—Dzong-ka-ba's very complicated rendition of Indian Buddhist presentations of schema for

---

a *shar rtse.*

b *dga' ldan.*

c *byang rtse.*

d The text was written in 1407-1408; see Robert A. F. Thurman, *Tsong Khapa's Speech of Gold in the Essence of True Eloquence* (Princeton, N.J.: Princeton University Press, 1984), 88.

e *sems tsam pa, cittamātra.*

interpreting what the tradition holds to be Shākyamuni Buddha's many and various teachings over forty-five years of preaching. Shākyamuni had become enlightened at age thirty-five around 528 B.C.E.[a] and spent the rest of his life, until age eighty, teaching disciples of vastly different interest, disposition, and understanding, adapting what he said to their capacities. Thus, his teachings seem contradictory on the surface but actually are not; one needs to realize a hierarchy of views and how realization of the lower ones serves to promote understanding of the higher. At least this is the in-house rationale for the contradictory variety in Buddha's teaching; others have viewed it as the technique of a devil to confuse and capture the minds of persons! As a contemporary Chinese scholar from Taiwan called "the master," now living outside of Washington, D.C., advised a friend and me several years ago through his interpreter, "The Master says to avoid the I-Ching and Buddhist philosophy; they absorb the mind in endless entanglement."

D̄zong-ka-b̄a attempts in this book to present *three* very different Indian Buddhist scholastic formats for organizing Buddha's diverse teachings into a coherent whole—how this is done in the Mind-Only School,[b] in the Middle Way Autonomy School,[c] and in the Middle Way Consequence School.[d] The complexity of his text, often cryptic in its brevity and shifts of topic, is renowned among D̄zong-ka-b̄a's followers (called the Ge-luk-b̄a[e] order) as the foremost text on the view of emptiness in the eighteen volumes of his collected works, consisting of 210 separate texts. Their imaginations have been captured for the last six centuries as they have tried to discover (or construct) the coherence that D̄zong-ka-b̄a saw in each of these three strategies for formulating order in what otherwise is, to say the least, bewilderingly complex. D̄zong-ka-b̄a's work is seen, at once, as an avenue to approach reality and as an opportunity for an elaborate game of constructing his thought. For these scholars, the main thrust of their education while at the monastic university is not toward confirmation in meditative experience of the vision of their founder but an attempt to render the content of his vision in a consistent verbal presentation; serious meditation, for the most part, comes later in solitary retreat. This procedure is justified from the basic Buddhist trilogy of first **hearing** the doctrine (which includes getting the words straight in memory), then **thinking**, which includes realizing its meaning, and finally **meditating** on what has been realized; still, the educational system takes so long that I wonder whether the physical

[a] The dates are in accordance with the Southern Buddhist tradition. In Tibet, the time of Shākyamuni's enlightenment is placed much earlier.

[b] *sems tsam pa, cittamātra.*

[c] *dbu ma rang rgyud pa, svātantrikamādhyamika.*

[d] *dbu ma thal 'gyur pa, prāsaṅgikamādhyamika.*

[e] *dge lugs pa.* The sect probably was originally called the "Joyous Way" (*dga' ldan pa'i lugs*) after the monastic university called "Joyous" (*dga' ldan*) established by D̄zong-ka-b̄a in 1409.

demands of meditation can be met once the time of isolated meditation begins in one's late forties or early fifties.

The endeavor at the monastic university for those who enter the rigorous series of classes (and not all do, since many do not have the capacity or the endurance) is to rediscover (or create) the wholeness of Ḏzong-ka-ḇa's system of meaning without the slightest internal contradiction. This is done with the assumption that the founder's many works themselves are devoid of the slightest internal contradiction, that they fit together in all aspects in complete harmony. The cryptic nature of many of Ḏzong-ka-ḇa's statements leaves room for considerable interpretive creativity that is bounded, to some extent, by his many clear pronouncements. I say "to some extent" because the game allows for positing the founder's *actual* thought, despite his words, behind what otherwise may seem to be a clear statement. Nothing is left paradoxical; the assumption of consistency dictates the reformulation of the presumed thought behind seemingly incomplete or inconsistent statements.

The framework of the game is transmitted from generation to generation through a teacher's remarking at some point fairly early in a student's training, "It is amazing how there is not the slightest internal contradiction in all of the works of the Foremost Precious One (Ḏzong-ka-ḇa)!" and then, shortly thereafter, confronting the student with an apparent inconsistency as if the student were the origin of the original proposition that there was no inconsistency. A great deal of cultural transmission, as I see it, is accomplished through identification with one's superiors, and, in this case, the identification is forced through the teacher's operating within a presumption of a shared perspective. Transmission also is accomplished through a far less satisfying identification with the *aggressor*—the teacher makes an outrageous demand that shocks the student and calls forth unacceptable counter-aggression, which the student hastens to avoid recognizing by identifying with the teacher and then, when the chance arises, pressing the same outrageous demand on a more junior student. The student thereby becomes the inflicter of his teacher's aggression! A story from my childhood will suffice to communicate the process. Out under the elm tree where my dog was tied, my mother—for reasons now not remembered—scolded me somewhat vehemently; I immediately turned around and upbraided the little dog unmercifully. (I still remember my mother staring at me awestruck.) This sequence of identifying with the hated aggressor and thereby shifting the object of aggression away from oneself provides a psychologically complex bonding that is built on the dangerous foundation of anger and separation from oneself—denying one's own anger and identifying with a person angry at oneself. As a mechanism of cultural transmission, it serves to transmit the outrageous demands of many cultural forms with violent rigidity. A result can be that when students of *The Essence of Eloquence* find what honestly seems to be an inconsistency in Ḏzong-ka-ḇa's presentation and thus fail to find the presumed harmony, they feel guilt at questioning the basic assumption of coherence, thereby endangering the bonding with the teacher. Or they decide that their intellect is inadequate to the task and adopt a superficial, often vehement, repetition of the basic presumption of non-contradiction.

Other students (or even the same students at other times) somehow manage their way through this difficult situation by developing an esthetic delight in the game of ferreting out inconsistencies and *attempting* to explain them away. Since the game is not played individually but is highly social, performed in the company of classmates and fellow scholars in daily sessions of debate, the highly satisfying intellectual and esthetic delight that is shared between two students when a particularly artful re-presentation of the founder's thought is put together is the stuff that perpetuates the process. To my sight, it creates an adherence to the process that is far stronger than even the sometimes violent effects of identification with the aggressor. Such moments of beauty, shared with other participants, are at the heart of the educational system in these monastic universities. As in any university, these are the experiences on which teacher and student thrive. The intense nature of the Tibetan system—built as it is on intimate contact with a teacher and on rigorous debate twice daily—provides many opportunities for such esthetic epiphanies to dawn.

The power of mutually supportive appreciation—as the very sustenance of the enterprise—may explain in part the structure of Tibetan universities. Around Hla-s̄a there are three large monastic universities—Gan-den (Joyous, so called because the Joyous Pure Land is the abode of Maitreya), Dre-b̄ung[a] (Rice Mound, said to be called this because its founder Jam-ȳang-chö-jay[b] announced, "I will build a monastic university like a mound of rice and retreat hermitage above it for myself shaped like a mouse ready to eat the rice, the latter being called Mouse Hermitage), and S̄e-ra[c] (Rain of Hail, said to be called this because its founder Jam-chen-chö-jay[d] announced, "I will build a monastic university like a rain of hail and a hermitage above it for myself like the sun melting the hail, the latter being called Sun Hermitage). Gan-den University, located about an hour and half east of Hla-s̄a by land cruiser (40 km), was founded in 1409 by D̄zong-ka-b̄a himself eight years before his death.

The two scholastic colleges of Gan-den University, S̄har-d̄zay and Jang-dzay, which came to be the basic organizational units of D̄zong-ka-b̄a's monastic university, were founded by two of his disciples. They are the primary

---

a *'bras spungs.*

b *'jam dbyangs chos rje;* the monastery was founded in 1416 (Victor Chan, *Tibet Handbook: A Pilgrimage Guide* [Chico, Calif.: Moon, 1994], 145). The story is from the late Ge-s̄hay L̄o-sang-w̄ang-chuk, the first top-ranked ge-s̄hay after the reinstitution of the annual prayer festival in Hla-s̄a.

c *se rwa.*

d *byams chen chos rje;* the monastery was founded in 1419; the story is from the late Ge-s̄hay L̄o-sang-w̄ang-chuk. Others, including Chö-drön Rin-b̄o-chay, say that it gets its name from a low bush which surrounds much of the monastery.

functioning units of the university, with their own administrations, their own faculty, and their own textbooks.[a] It would be like having two departments of physics, philosophy, and so forth, with separate sets of deans, on opposite sides of the lawn which is at the heart of the University of Virginia designed and built by Thomas Jefferson. Instead of one Rotunda at the end of the lawn, each college—shall we call them East Range and West Range, these being the names for the two rows of buildings behind those on the lawn—would have its own Rotunda as an assembly hall; thus, there would be three Rotundas. Everything else would be in duplicate, with the general University of Virginia being merely an administrative unit that, by nature, could not unite the two parts.

Factionalism is indeed encouraged, with far more going on between the colleges of the Ge-luk-b̄a order than between it and other sects. The Ge-luk-b̄a sect that formed among D̄zong-ka-b̄a's followers is, therefore, by no means monolithic in its views, for the basic adherence is to one's college, which is in competition with other colleges. Students are inculcated with the greatness of the author of their textbook literature—the authors being viewed, like D̄zong-ka-b̄a, as incarnations of Mañjushrī—the deity that is the manifestation of the wisdom of all Buddhas—or as reincarnations of great figures of Indian Buddhism, and so forth (Jay-d̄zün Chö-ḡyi-gyel-tsen[b] is considered actually to be an incarnation of Mañjushrī, and Jam-ȳang-shay-b̄a[c] is an incarnation of the late fourth-century and early fifth-century Indian sage Buddhapālita[d] who, in the distant future, will be the chief general when the troops from Shambhala come to relieve the world of the scourge of barbarism and to inaugurate an age of such great devotion to Buddhism that there will be no other significant religions). Young students are told story after story about the greatness of the author of their textbook literature such that, as one lama said about the years of his early studies (probably during his twenties), he considered the members of the other colleges to be as bad off as non-Buddhists! (What could be worse!) Nowadays, some refugee parents leave their children in the monastic university to be raised at the expense of the colleges, only to remove them in their late teens or early twenties to go to work and provide for the family. When an abbot related this to me, I expressed my shock at the parents' using the monastic

---

[a] Eventually, the Jang-d̄zay College came to adopt the textbook literature of Jay-d̄zün Chö-ḡyi-gyel-tsen (1469-1546), who wrote sub-sub-commentaries on Maitreya's *Ornament for Clear Realization,* Dharmakīrti's *Commentary on (Dignāga's) "Compilation of Prime Cognition,"* and Chandrakīrti's *Supplement to (Nāgārjuna's) "Treatise on the Middle."* The S̄har-d̄zay College came to adopt the textbooks written by Paṇ-chen S̄ö-nam-drak-b̄a (1478-1554) on the same three texts. Paṇ-chen S̄ö-nam-drak-b̄a also wrote commentaries on Vasubandhu's *Treasury of Manifest Knowledge* and Gunaprabha's *Aphorisms on Discipline,* but they are not taken as primary.

[b] *rje btsun chos kyi rgyal mtshan,* 1469-1546.

[c] *'jam dbyangs bzhad pa,* 1648-1722.

[d] C. 470-540?

colleges as means to support their children, and he agreed that it was bad but that it had its good side, since it creates an economic base of support outside the monastery that has a determined loyalty to the former monk's college. It was apparent that he valued the benefits over the disadvantages.

It is clear that the many differences on points of doctrine expounded in each college's textbooks are used not only for intellectual and spiritual stimulation but also for sociological and economic advantages—helping to establish group identity and a sense of uniqueness that justifies promotion of that group and receipt of donations. The loyalty generated by such dynamics often obscures the straightforward pursuit of knowledge and creates an added tension for knowledge-oriented persons. Still, the situation is multi-sided, for although in a debate between two students the defendant usually *must* uphold the position of his college's textbook author, the challenger—usually from the same school—*must* make this task as difficult as possible, and he easily becomes enamored of the sensibleness of his own attack. (I say "he" and "his" because in Tibet women, for the most part, were long excluded from the halls of intellectual pursuit, though this situation is now slowly beginning to change.)[a] There being considerable emphasis on winners and losers, students—through the role of challenger—develop elaborate arguments against their own textbook literature. The resolution of this conflict is, for many, a bifurcation of viewpoint—a more public one that manifests as strong adherence to the textbook author's positions and a more private one that is highly critical. The Tibetan scholars with whom I have studied over the last thirty-nine years all seem to have these two sides to varying degrees; one lama, a fine scholar with penetrating insights into larger issues but sometimes failing ascertainment of minor points, was so oriented to the public side that on issues of intense disagreement between the monastic textbooks he acted as if there was no disagreement at all, unless I brought it up—almost never would he even lay out the positions of other colleges. It seemed that he wanted me to think that his college's viewpoint was the only one! In his more private moments, he could reveal the difficulties involved in a particular position, but hardly ever with deference to another college's textbook author.

Another lama, however, would take me through the positions of t̄hree of the main textbook authors (the two given above and Jam-ȳang-shay-b̄a, who authored the textbook literature of the Go-mang,[b] or Many Doors, College of Dre-b̄ung Monastic University), though almost always within the context of showing the superiority of view in his own college. The variety of opinion with which he was fluent was indeed impressive, often causing me to melt in admiration, but then upon mentioning the name of the opposing college in the same

[a] For valuable insights into Tibetan Buddhism and feminism, see Anne Carolyn Klein, *Meeting the Great Bliss Queen: Buddhists, Feminists, and the Art of the Self* (Boston: Beacon Press, 1994).

[b] *sgo mang.*

monastic university, he would suddenly turn his head to the side and spit on the floor! I never ceased to be horrified at this, my disgust magnified, no doubt, by the fact that the floor was covered with a rug! Never mind spit on the floor, one should not spit on a rug! (My loyalty to my mother easily dominated my newfound loyalty to my lama.) Sitting in hateful conflict at his feet, I was appalled at these not infrequent displays of parochial partisanship, directed, of course, at the rival college, located just forty paces from his own (when I got to Tibet I counted off the number of steps it took between the assembly halls of the two colleges). He would repeat that the textbook literature of the other, third college—not in his own monastic university—was indeed not so bad, even quite good, but that the textbooks of the rival home-group were pathetic. Pituey! Since we were renting the house, I cautioned him against spitting on the rug, and he got so that he only made the noise of spitting. Still, he was a grand personality with an incredible capacity to convey the complicated architecture of a worldview, largely through well-timed repetition of key issues and positions. Sometimes the repetitions seemed boringly and excruciatingly unnecessary, but eventually when I challenged myself to produce what he was about to say, I would find that I could not quite do it, and thus I would hang on his every word in order to do so. The kindness of his untiring repetitions was considerable. Indeed, one of his intentions was to indoctrinate me such that I would become a follower of his college's textbook literature, but the benefits that I gained from his repetition of focal issues far outweigh the disadvantages.

Particularly insidious, however, was the fact that, despite my wrenching hatred of his partisanship and my consequent determination not to assume his viewpoint on the rival college's worth, when I finally began studying that other college's texts, I found that I uncontrollably viewed them to be pathetically inadequate, even though I had not yet read a word. During my study of their texts I was, over and over again, amazed that scholars of this college could make interesting distinctions. Despite being *conscious* of my hatred at his partisanship, my identification with my old friend was such that, contrary to my own heartfelt and repeated intentions in pained intensity, I came to be imbued with a mental version of spitting on the floor.

That Tibetan scholars and administrators appreciate the power of such indoctrination explains, in part, the busy schedule of a monastic college. Here I was in the Shar-dzay College in south India, falling asleep in the midst of the voice's shouting a memorized text, and I would awaken in darkness the next morning to the sound of a congregation of monks praying. With a full schedule of prayers—for hours—interspersed with classes and debate sessions, the monks are kept busy all day and a good part of the night. Exposed to this unending scenario of activity for two months, my secularly indoctrinated view of monks as lazily living off the wealth of the populace was reduced to ash.

Quite contrary to the partisanship of the above-mentioned lamas was another who showed a deep appreciation of the textbook literature of the same three authors, often even preferring another college's viewpoint to that of his own. It strikes me that the strength of his college in the bureaucracy that has developed in India allowed him this freedom. Dre-b̄ung Monastic University is divided into four colleges—one tantric and three for the study of the Five Great Books of sūtra Buddhism;[a] of these three, L̄o-s̄el-l̄ing College (Lucid Intelligence)[b] dominates the bureaucracy in the refugee community in India. A network of appointments—initiated with the appointment of one scholar—of persons from the same college (it, of course, being impossible to find competent scholars to fill such posts from another college!) practically guarantees that, when visiting an office, one can safely assume that its holder is from this college, just as currently in Tibet, one of the colleges of S̄e-ra Monastic University, the Jay[c] (Separatist) College, similarly dominates the general, supposedly inter-monastery offices. This particular scholar, since he was a refugee from L̄o-s̄el-l̄ing College living in India within the comfort of knowing that the transmission of his college's literature was secure, could afford to be open-minded, the solidity of his college allowing for non-commitment. Still, his openness was not sanctioned by his colleagues, and I was often moved both by his true quest for knowledge and by his ability to articulate in public, so to speak, this non-partisanship.

A scholar from L̄o-s̄el-l̄ing's rival college, Go-mang, sometimes seemed to be quite non-partisan. Over lunch in New Jersey around 1964, he held forth on the importance of non-partisanship, moving several lamas from different colleges and sects and myself with a pluralistic appeal based on appreciation of common purposes, but he finished by saying, "Still, there is something extraordinarily different about Jam-ȳang-shay-b̄a's texts!" A pall of sickening partisanship descended over the table.

A final story will complete the picture. The monastic colleges are further broken down into "house units" (which are associated with the region from which students come—and thus promote another level of parochialism—and which sometimes are very large). These, in turn, are broken down into "families" if there are enough members. The smaller units provide effective means of addressing the needs of particular students—sufficiently small so that students are cared for with concerned attention. Since these units are primarily social—

---

a See *Emptiness in Mind-Only*, 9-12.

b *blo gsal gling.*

c *byes.* In May, 2001, Chö-drön Rin-b̄o-chay, a member of the Jay College from Kam Province, reported that the Jay College receives its name from a statement made by a statue of one of the sixteen Foe Destroyers in the Mantra College of S̄e-ra Monastic University when the to-be-founder of the Jay College, the Omniscient L̄o-drö-rin-chen-s̄eng-gay (*kun mkhyen blo gros rin chen seng ge*), arrived at S̄e-ra from Dre-b̄ung Monastic University. The statue spontaneously leaned forward, stretching his head clearly outside his niche, extending his right arm in greeting with palm upward, and said, "Has the separatist, having separated, arrived?" (*byes pa byes nas phebs lags sam*).

not having their own textbook literature—they are not the primary units of identification, and thus monks, for the most part, would find it unthinkable to give their house or family unit when asked, in a general situation, where their identity lies. In 1972, at a time when I had studied with three scholars from the same house unit of Go-mang College of Dre-b̄ung Monastic University, called Ham-dong (which is so large that it has its own sizable temple in Tibet), I was staying in a bungalow on the hill above Dharmsala for several months. One day, I was visited by a scholar who happened upon my place by mistake; after we talked for a while, he remembered having heard of me and, assuming that my allegiance was with the Go-mang College, asked, "Are you Go-mang?" Now, although I am a Buddhist, I do not consider myself a Ge-luk-b̄a, never mind any unit smaller than that. So, thinking of a pithy reply, I answered, "No, I am Ham-dong!" He was stunned, trying to make sense of my identifying with such an unsuitable unit; he did not see that this was just what I was suggesting he was doing.

Such centrality of allegiance is reminiscent of a warrior's oath of fealty to his chieftain in Anglo-Saxon England (I studied Anglo-Saxon in college); the warrior's identity was so totally bound to the tribe that, if he outlasted his chieftain in battle such as by being knocked unconscious and taken for dead by the enemy, he was left psychologically homeless, as is depicted in the poem *The Wanderer*.[a] This type of loyalty to one's chieftain, therefore, was used by Christian missionaries as a model for loyalty to God, the eternal chieftain. The implication in *The Wanderer* (in its final Christianized form) is that secular loyalty is to be superseded by religious loyalty to a higher leader. What is so surprising in these Ge-luk-b̄a universities is that the seemingly higher loyalties are replaced by lower ones—allegiance to Buddha is replaced by allegiance to a college. Indeed, the author of the textbook literature is seen as a Buddha of this era, but the form that the allegiance takes, with its biased rejection of other colleges, does not allow such apologetic. A good deal of my shock, no doubt, comes from my own historical position of living at a time when national, ethnic, and religious parochialisms are obviously driving the world to its own destruction and from my perception that such factionalism must be overcome for our survival. Nevertheless, parochial factionalism in Tibetan Buddhism is deeply at odds with its own professed cardinal doctrine of universal compassion and the call for assuming responsibility for the welfare of all sentient beings, certainly including the members of the neighboring college.

Still, I do not wish to create the impression that such parochial bias completely taints the enterprise of scholarship and spiritual development in these universities, for it does not. Rather, I wish to point out the tension present in a multi-aspected situation. The inculcation of parochial bias is often consciously used to establish a mode of operation, much like a stage facade, that sets a scene

[a] My translation is "The Wanderer: An Anglo-Saxon Poem," *Virginia Quarterly Review* 53, no. 2 (1977):284-287. Ezra Pound translated the companion poem "The Seafarer."

in which other activities take place. It brings an energy to study and to debate, a focus for students not yet moved in a universalistic way. The inculcated sense of the unique value of one's college and the awesome responsibility of being a member of this club charges a course of study during which profound understanding and spiritual progress that run counter to this parochialism can be made. Adherence to a college often becomes, as a student matures, an operational mechanism that alternates—sometimes in self-consciously humorous contradiction—with penetrative insights into the weaknesses of a host of philosophical positions of the otherwise favored author.

Let me illustrate the point. One of the most rewarding periods of my life was three weeks of daily classes with the last great Inner Mongolian scholar at Tibet's Go-mang College of Dre-b̄ung Monastic University, in Tibet during the summer of 1987. When he returned to Go-mang in 1985 (after spending twenty years repairing watches in Hla-s̄a and taking food to his teacher who was imprisoned for seventeen years for refusing to denounce the Dalai Lama—his teacher said it would better to take care of his future lives by not lying than to lie and live more comfortably for a short while during the rest of the present life), only three students were studying the textbook literature of Go-mang College—that authored by Jam-ȳang-shay-b̄a. In the summer of 1987, fifty students were studying with him. His task was to build up a group of scholars who would take on the responsibility of serving as caretakers of Jam-ȳang-shay-b̄a's stances. He was seeking the same with me, but his manner of doing this was to subject Jam-ȳang-shay-b̄a's positions to unblinking analysis, riddling both sides of a questionable stance with flaw after flaw, to the point where one could understand that the enterprise of caretaking was to be done from within a frank perception of those weaknesses, not with the fragile perspective of anxiously seeking to hide them. I was particularly impressed with his attitude, given the situation of his being the sole person left to re-create—out of the rubble of the Chinese Communist destruction of intellectual challenge—the beginnings of the study of the curriculum of a college that formerly had three thousand members.

These colleges drew students to Tibet from a vast area of Inner Asia. Since the takeover, Tibet amounts to about 25 percent of the land mass of China. (The Chinese government has absorbed at least one-third of Tibet into Qinghai, Gansu, Sichuan, and Yunnan Provinces such that the current map of Tibet makes it appear much smaller than it is. In China, it is commonly held that the influence that the Mongolian and Manchurian emperors had in Tibet from the sixteenth century to the beginning of the twentieth was somehow Han Chinese power or at least a case of a minority within a single nation assuming rule over the nation, but this is a myth fabricated by Sun Yat-sen.) The Tibetan cultural region goes far beyond Tibet, stretching from Kalmuck Mongolian areas near the Volga River (in Europe where the Volga empties into the Caspian Sea), Outer and Inner Mongolia, the Buriat Republic of Siberia, as well as Bhutan,

Sikkim, Ladakh, and parts of Nepal. In all of these areas, Buddhist ritual and scholastic studies are conducted in Tibetan. Young men came from throughout these vast regions to study in Hla-s̄a, usually (until the Communist takeovers) returning to their native lands after completing their studies.

Even with the pool of students so large, it is, at first glance, surprising that Hla-s̄a, having a population of only around twenty-five thousand until 1950, could support three large monastic universities in its vicinity and be the cultural center of such a vast region. That it could support such a vast population of monks (at least twenty thousand) is due to its being a center of pilgrimage and thus of offering and also to the large landholdings of the monastic institutions.

As mentioned earlier, the first of these Ge-luk-b̄a centers of learning was Gan-den University, founded by D̄zong-ka-b̄a in 1409, with two colleges: S̄har-d̄zay, which adopted the textbook literature of Paṇ-chen S̄ö-nam-drak-b̄a,[a] and Jang-d̄zay, which adopted that of Jay-d̄zün Chö-ḡyi-gyel-tsen. Two of D̄zong-ka-b̄a's students started other institutions, closer to Hla-s̄a but still on its outskirts, which developed into even larger monastic universities—Dre-b̄ung (which was officially allowed to have 7,700 monks but had more), founded in 1416, and S̄e-ra (officially 5,500 monks), founded in 1419, the year of D̄zong-ka-b̄a's death. The two most influential of Dre-b̄ung University's four colleges are L̄o-s̄el-l̄ing, which, along with S̄har-d̄zay at Gan-den University, follows the texts of Paṇ-chen S̄ö-nam-drak-b̄a, and Go-mang, which first used the textbooks of Gung-ru Chö-jung[b] but later, at the beginning of the eighteenth century, adopted those of Jam-ȳang-shay-b̄a, thereby marking the close of the phase of choosing basic textbooks, the colleges keeping their basic texts until the present. Dre-b̄ung also has a third but not nearly so important scholastic college, Day-ȳang (Blissful Melody?),[c] that uses the textbook literature of the Fifth Dalai Lama.

At S̄e-ra University—which is located at the foot of a mountain on the north side of Hla-s̄a valley within sight of the Dalai Lama's winter palace, the Potala—the Jay College, like Jang-d̄zay at Gan-den University, uses the textbook literature of Jay-d̄zün Chö-ḡyi-gyel-tsen, and the M̄ay[d] (Lower) College, so called because it is lower on the mountain, uses the texts of Ke-drup-d̄en-ba-dar-gyay.[e]

In other parts of Tibet, D̄zong-ka-b̄a's student Gen-dün-drup[f] built a large monastery to the west in Shi-ḡa-d̄zay in 1445, called D̄ra-s̄hi-hlün-b̄o (Mount Luck).[g] It came to have one mantric and three philosophy colleges—

[a] *paṇ chen bsod nams grags pa.*

[b] *gung ru chos 'byung / gung ru chos kyi 'byung gnas.*

[c] *bde dbyangs.*

[d] *smad.*

[e] *mkhas grub bstan pa dar rgyas,* 1493-1568.

[f] *dge 'dun grub,* 1391-1475.

[g] *bkra shis lhun po.*

Tö-sam-l̄ing,[a] Ḡyil-kang,[b] and S̄har-d̄zay.[c] (Gen-dün-drup received the name Paṇ-chen from an erudite Tibetan contemporary, Bo-dong Chok-lay-ñam-gyel,[d] when he answered all of the latter's questions.[e] The successive abbots of D̄ra-s̄hi-hlün-b̄o Monastery, who were chosen for term appointments and were not viewed as reincarnations of Gen-dün-drup, were then each called "Paṇ-chen." Gen-dün-drup himself came to be retroactively called the First Dalai Lama when the third incarnation in his line, S̄ö-nam-gya-tso,[f] received the name "Dalai"[g] from his Mongolian patron and follower, Altan Khan, in 1578. Then, in the seventeenth century the Fifth Dalai Lama[h] gave D̄ra-s̄hi-hlün-b̄o Monastery to his teacher, L̄o-sang-chö-ḡyi-gyel-tsen,[i] who, as the fifteenth abbot of the monastery, came to be called Paṇ-chen. After his death "Paṇ-chen" became a title for his reincarnations when the Fifth Dalai Lama announced that his teacher would reappear as a recognizable child-successor.[j] In this way Gen-dün-drup served as the source for both titles—Dalai Lama by way of reincarnation and Paṇ-chen Lama by way of his title as abbot of D̄ra-s̄hi-hlün-b̄o Monastery.) Two other large Ge-luk-b̄a monastic universities were founded in the east:

- at Ḡum-bum[k] (D̄zong-ka-b̄a's birthplace) in the late sixteenth century, which has four monastic colleges—medical, tantric, Kālachakra, and philosophical, with the last using the textbook literature of both Jay-d̄zün Chö-ḡyi-gyel-tsen and Jam-ȳang-shay-b̄a
- at D̄ra-s̄hi-kyil[l]—called L̄a-brang[m]—founded by Jam-ȳang-shay-b̄a, which has six colleges: four for tantric studies (Lower, Kālachakra, Hevajra, and

---

a *thos bsam gling.*

b *dkyil khang.*

c *shar rtse.*

d *bo dong phyogs las rnam rgyal,* 1375-1451.

e "Paṇ-chen" means "great scholar" from the Sanskrit word *paṇḍita* meaning "scholar" and the Tibetan word "chen po" meaning "great."

f *bsod nams rgya mtsho,* 1543-1588.

g *tā lai.* This translates the Tibetan *rgya mtsho* ("ocean") in his name, *bsod nams rgya mtsho* ("ocean of merit").

h 1617-1682.

i *blo bzang chos kyi rgyal mtshan,* 1567?-1662.

j The title also was applied retrospectively to his teacher's two previous incarnations even though they did not belong to the D̄ra-s̄hi-hlün-b̄o Monastery, and thus the new incarnation became the fourth in the line.

k *sku 'bum.* It has three colleges: for philosophical studies (*mtshan nyid*), for tantric studies (*rgyud pa*), and for medical studies (*sman pa*).

l *bkra shis 'khyil;* according to the late Ge-s̄hay Tup-d̄en-gya-tso (*thub bstan rgya mtsho,* oral communication) of the Tibetan Buddhist Learning Center, Washington, New Jersey, the monastery gets its name from the name of a spring at its site.

m *bla brang.*

Upper),[a] one for medical studies,[b] and one for philosophical studies[c] which, like Go-mang at Dre-b̄ung, uses Jam-ȳang-shay-b̄a's textbooks.

Two tantric colleges (in addition to tantric colleges at Dre-b̄ung, S̄e-ra, and so forth) were erected in the Hla-s̄a area, and hundreds of middling and small monasteries devoted to the Ge-luk-b̄a order were established throughout Tibet. Within roughly two hundred years, the sect had become an important political force, such that with the help of the Mongolian potentate Gu-shri Khan, the Fifth Dalai Lama, a Ge-luk-b̄a lama from Dre-b̄ung Monastic University who had been born in a N̄ying-ma-b̄a (Old Translation Order) family, assumed power as head of the government around 1640. He ruled from the Gan-den Palace at Dre-b̄ung University until the Potala was sufficiently completed. After the death of the Fifth Dalai Lama, the Regent pretended for twelve years that he was alive so that he could finish the building. The lineage of Dalai Lamas maintained a position of varying degrees of authority until the Chinese takeover in 1959.

The Ge-luk-b̄a educational system so captured the imagination of Tibetans that their universities attracted a large number of boys and men whereupon they became a political force, made much stronger after the Fifth Dalai Lama gained wide political power. Largely supplanting the S̄a-ḡya[d] (White Earth) Order, which had spread the influence of Tibetan Buddhism in Mongolia, Ge-luk-b̄a gradually provided the main mode of religious education and became the dominant cultural force in the Tibetan cultural region. Hla-s̄a, with its large Ge-luk-b̄a universities, became the cultural, religious, educational, liturgical, medical, and astrological focus of much of Buddhist Inner Asia. The ecclesiastical power of appointment was limited largely to the area around Hla-s̄a, but an even greater influence was exercised by a complex system of education, devotion, meditation, and cultism, the pattern for which was set by several brilliant leaders, fostered by an educational system open to all classes, over several centuries. One reason why the monasteries were open to all levels of society probably was simply that the colleges needed members, and, as the Inner Mongolian scholar mentioned above put it, one reason why so many persons entered the monastic universities was to escape the stultifying work (and the social rigidity) on the estates of noble families. These forces—combined with a respect for scholarly achievement and despite a hierarchy of governmentally recognized lamas privileged from birth—yielded the result of social and intellectual advancement for persons from low classes. Several of my Tibetan teachers testify to the fact that a person from any class could ascend to the very top of the intellectual hierarchy through winning debate run-offs—first on the college level,

[a] *rgyud smad/ dus 'khor/ kyai rdor/ rgyud stod.*

[b] *sman pa.*

[c] *rmad byung thos bsam gling.*

[d] *sa skya.*

then on the university level, and finally in the inter-university national competition, emerging as cultural heroes. (I do not mean to suggest that this openness to advancement of persons from all classes entirely overcame the deleterious influence of politically, socially, and economically motivated identifications of reincarnations. Nor do I wish to suggest that the system of recognizing reincarnations was entirely corrupt.)

2. Faith, Reason, and Mystical Insight

It was February, and the heat in south India was starting to be oppressively debilitating such that during the day I would lie on my wooden bed on a thin cotton mattress, tape recorder on my chest, speaking a translation of Dzong-ka-ba's *The Essence of Eloquence*, sentence by sentence into it. Outside, during the brightness of the ever-warming day, there was the noise of long sessions of debate between small groups of students, some of the debates being on issues in that text. Also, in the blackness of the night the voice still kept shouting the same text, allowing me to recognize more and more of the beginning section on how the Mind-Only School classifies Buddha's teachings into those that are definitive—in the sense that they can be accepted literally—and those that are interpretable—in the sense that they require interpretation since they cannot be accepted literally. This differentiation into the interpretable and definitive is the structure through which Dzong-ka-ba presents the school's delineation of emptiness, or selflessness, realization of which is held to be a key to psychological transformation.

In the course of study of the Five Great Books[a] that are the basic curriculum in Ge-luk-ba colleges, Dzong-ka-ba's *The Essence of Eloquence* becomes the focus during the second year of study of the first Great Book, the coming Buddha Maitreya's *Ornament for Clear Realization*.[2] This occurs at the point where the late eighth-century Indian scholar Haribhadra—in his *Clear Meaning Commentary*,[3] which is used as an avenue to approach Maitreya's text—introduces the topic of reasonings proving emptiness, specifically the reasoning that phenomena do not exist as their own reality because of not ultimately being one or many, singular or plural. The mode of study with long, elaborate, and intricate debates mirrors a dominant posture of the Ge-luk-ba dedication to intellectual confrontation through reasoning.

Modes Of Doctrinal Training

In general, Ge-luk-ba doctrinal training can be divided into two types based on a division of texts into sūtra and tantra—both attributed to be Shākyamuni Buddha's teachings that were committed to writing even many centuries later. The term "sūtra" can be used to refer to tantras, but here in the division of all of Buddha's scriptures into the mutually exclusive categories of sūtra and tantra, it refers, roughly speaking, to those texts that are not based on the practice of deity yoga.[b] "Tantra," on the other hand, refers to texts and systems whose

[a] For a discussion of this curriculum, see *Emptiness in Mind-Only*, 9ff.

[b] Here I am following Dzong-ka-ba's presentation of the difference between sūtra and tantra in his *Great Exposition of Secret Mantra* (*sngags rim chen mo*) as found in H.H. the Dalai Lama, Tsong-ka-pa, and Jeffrey Hopkins, *Tantra in Tibet* (London: George Allen and

primary practitioners can employ deity yoga. In deity yoga, practitioners meditate on themselves as having the physical form not of an ordinary person but of a supramundane deity, an *embodiment* of the highest levels of wisdom and compassion.

Training in the systems that formed around sūtra-style teachings can be further divided into more practically oriented and more theoretically oriented modes of study. Both modes are concerned with both theory and practice, but the style of the former directly addresses particular meditation practices and behavior modification, whereas the style of the latter is primarily concerned with countering wrong ideas with scholastic arguments that, although they can be employed in meditation, are framed around critiques of issues largely in the format of debate—refuting others' errors, presenting one's own view, and then dispelling objections to it. Both systems are based on focal Indian books and Tibetan texts, the latter being either explicit commentaries on the Indian texts or expositions of their main themes or of issues that arise when juxtaposed with other material.

The more practical system of study is aimed at making coherent and accessible the plethora of practices that were inherited from India and are the topics of critical study in more theoretical texts. In the Ge-luk-b̄a sect, the more practical system of study centers on:

1. D̄zong-ka-b̄a's *Great Exposition of the Stages of the Path,*[4] which calls itself a commentary on the *Lamp for the Path to Enlightenment*[5] by the eleventh-century Indian scholar Atisha (who spent the last twelve years of his life in Tibet) but is much more
2. A commentary by one of D̄zong-ka-b̄a's two chief disciples, Gyel-tsap Dar-ma-rin-chen,[a] on the Indian text *Engaging in the Bodhisattva Deeds* by the eighth-century scholar-yogi Shāntideva.[6]

The more theoretical system of study centers either on a comparative analysis of systems of tenets, both Buddhist and non-Buddhist, or on the Five Great Books

Unwin, 1977; reprint, with minor corrections, Ithaca, N.Y.: Snow Lion, 1987). D̄zong-ka-b̄a presents the difference between the Great Vehicle sūtra system (called the Perfection Vehicle) and the tantra system in terms of what the four classes of tantra (Action, Performance, Yoga, and Highest Yoga) present as the path for their **main** intended trainees. In this way, he is able to posit deity yoga as the central distinctive feature of tantra, even though a majority of the tantras included in the class of Action Tantra do not involve deity yoga, since, as he puts it, those Action Tantras that do not involve deity are not intended for the **main** intended trainees of that class of tantra. One would expect that the **majority** of Action Tantras would be for the **main** intended trainees of Action Tantra, but in D̄zong-ka-b̄a's presentation they are not. Therefore, the mere presence and absence of the practice of deity yoga cannot serve as the feature distinguishing a particular text as tantra or sūtra, for it serves only to distinguish those two in terms of the practices of their *main* intended trainees. This is why I have used in the qualification "roughly speaking."

[a] *rgyal tshab dar ma rin chen,* 1364-1432.

of Buddhist India. The comparative analysis of philosophical (and psychological) schools is based on Tibetan presentations of several non-Buddhist Indian schools but primarily on what came to be classified as the four schools of Indian Buddhism (to be discussed in chapters 3 and 4). The large Ge-luk-b̄a universities use presentations of the four schools of tenets only as side-studies—choosing as their main focus a curriculum structured around the Five Great Books of Buddhist India, which are the basis of an elaborate curriculum for sūtra study that begins around age eighteen and lasts for twenty to twenty-five years. The debates that I was hearing from my prone position while translating D̄zong-ka-b̄a's *The Essence of Eloquence* were drawn from the Tibetan textbooks of S̄har-d̄zay College on these Indian treatises, as well as from the daily lectures by the monks' teachers.

Throughout the long course of study in a monastic college, ***reasoned*** analysis is stressed to the point that a surprising tradition of even avoiding attending lectures outside of this curriculum has developed. Some scholars advise that students involved in this training should forgo lectures even on D̄zong-ka-b̄a's presentation of the stages of the path to enlightenment—the foundation of the more practically oriented system of study—or on his presentation of the tantric stages of the path in his *Great Exposition of Secret Mantra.*[7] These are to be avoided as distractions from immersion in the school's curriculum. (In India, this exclusivistic tradition is dying out, whereas in Tibet it still lives.) Despite this macho immersion in their own style of learning, students nevertheless maintain (1) daily practice of tantric rites that revolve around visualizing oneself as a deity, (2) participation in cultic rites on the university, college, and house level to appease and gratify individual protector deities associated with those units, and (3) devotional assemblies centered around deities such as Tārā, a goddess of great importance throughout the Tibetan cultural region. Nevertheless, students are not allowed, in their own devotions and ritual recitations, even to ring bells, despite the fact that bell and vajra (diamond scepter) are central tantric ritual objects.

Because of the long training period in sūtra studies, the strong, more hidden, and perhaps even dominant tantric side of the Ge-luk-b̄a sect is often unnoticed by those with only a casual acquaintance with Tibetan Buddhism. Indeed, many Ge-luk-b̄a scholars become proficient in tantra; after taking the highest degree in sūtra studies, called Ge-s̄hay,[a] a monk can proceed to a tantric college,[b] the two prime ones in Hla-s̄a being the Tantric College of Upper Hla-s̄a and the Tantric College of Lower Hla-s̄a (other tantric colleges are housed at universities such as S̄e-ra and Dre-b̄ung in separate facilities). Both tantric colleges have as their main purpose the study, transmission, and practice of the

---

[a] *dge bshes / dge ba'i bshes gnyen.* Literally, the term translates as "virtuous friend," a spiritual guide.

[b] Monks whose commitment is largely to ritual may enter at any time.

Guhyasamāja Tantra, through the extensive commentaries of Nāgārjuna,[a] Chandrakīrti, and Ḏzong-ka-ḇa, who are also prime sources for sūtra study.

Underlying the program of religious immersion through doctrinal, devotional, ritualistic, and meditational means is a commitment to reason and its harmony—albeit in a preparatory way—with the most profound religious experiences of compassion, wisdom, deity yoga, and manifestation of the fundamental innate mind of clear light. Even in meditation, great stress is put on ***analytical*** meditation, in which reasoning is used to develop and enhance the experience of central doctrines. For instance, in developing compassion, meditators employ reflective reasoning on the beginningless course of the round of birth, aging, sickness, and death to bring home on a level of intense feeling the consequent implication that all beings—both intimate and alien—having been born beginninglessly, have been in every possible relationship with oneself. Intimacy is chosen over alienness through recognizing the commonly observed predominance of intimacy such that, when, for example, a loved one becomes temporarily insane and attacks oneself with a knife, the response is to relieve the person of the weapon and then, instead of attacking in return, to attempt to restore the person to his or her senses. This ***reasoned*** model of intimacy is adopted as the mode of relationship with all beings—friends, enemies, and neutral persons alike—through gradual meditation on each and every acquaintance individually, using the force of reasoned and deeply felt realization developed by the channeled force of meditation. Relationships are thereby restructured.

The meditation then proceeds to apply the rationale that, since every living being has been close, everyone has extended great kindness to oneself, which, based on the commonly observed fact that we feel a sense of debt toward those who have extended help, leads to development of an intention to repay that debt incurred over the beginningless cycle of lives. This leads to love (the wish that they have happiness and the causes of happiness) and compassion (the wish that they be freed from suffering and the causes of suffering). These attitudes form the basis for ***realizing,*** based on the reason of others' kindness extended over many lifetimes, that it is indeed ***suitable*** for one to take on the burden of ensuring their happiness and freedom from pain. This high-spirited intention leads to reflection on one's own situation in cyclic existence, unable to control one's own destiny and thus unable to help others on such a vast scale. This realistic appraisal, in turn, leads to the realization that enlightenment ***must*** be attained by reason of the fact that it is endowed with the two qualities that are needed most for assisting others on a vast scale—thorough knowledge of all possible techniques to help others improve their situation and intimate knowledge of others' dispositions, interests, and predisposing tendencies, such that the appropriate technique can be matched with the particular person.[8] This

[a] Contemporary European, American, and Japanese scholars for the most part identify the tantric Nāgārjuna as a different person. I am here reporting a common Tibetan view.

reasoned understanding that enlightenment must be attained culminates in the development of a decision to attain highest enlightenment for the sake of others.

Since this series of attitudes runs counter to the desire, hatred, and bewilderment that have become ingrained over countless lives, superficial reasoning is not sufficient; reasoned understanding must be brought—through repeated exploration of its foundations and implications—to the point where it is felt so deeply that it profoundly affects the ideational structure underlying selfish and self-centered behavior. In these ways, the process of reasoning is used to develop and enhance basic feelings that are recognized as part of common experience:

- One uses the commonly observed sense of love for close relatives and friends as the model for identifying all beings as having, in former lives, been in a close relationship with oneself.
- One uses the naturally noticed predominance of love for close beings, even when they become mad and attack oneself, as the justification for emphasizing closeness over alienness.

Such reliance on unreasoned, observed experience accords with a basic posture that all reasoning meets back to common experience. When stating the individual sub-reasons for the main reason, the process eventually must end with observable experience as the floor of the process; otherwise, the process of stating sub-reasons to prove the former reasons would never end, and the thesis could never be realized. Simply put, the fundamental perspective is that from observed experience reasoned conclusions can be drawn; this is why reasoning in this tradition is often not a disembodied, uncontextualized, merely formal exercise. As the current Dalai Lama says in his *Key to Middle Way:*[9]

> With respect to a non-conceptual wisdom that apprehends the profound emptiness, one first cultivates a conceptual consciousness that apprehends an emptiness, and when a clear perception of the object of meditation arises, this becomes a non-conceptual wisdom. Moreover, the initial generation of that conceptual consciousness must depend solely on a correct reasoning. Fundamentally, therefore, this process traces back solely to a reasoning, which itself must fundamentally trace back to valid experiences common to ourselves and others. Thus, it is the thought of Dignāga and Dharmakīrti, the kings of reasoning, that fundamentally a reasoning derives from an obvious experience.

This is a natural philosophy that makes appeal not to the superior insight of high beings (though such is central to other aspects of the religion) but to one's own observations and power of reasoning. The process recognizes and is built on the potential for re-formation of mind, and thus of character, through engaging in analytical meditation that is enhanced in psychological power through alternating analysis with stabilizing meditation, the latter involving fixing the mind one-pointedly within an attitude that has been developed to the point of palpable insight.

Reasoning—brought in this way to the level of faith that is founded on the conviction of valid realization—is said to provide a much sounder basis for transformation than even the moving faith inspired by contact with advanced persons, locations, or doctrines. The latter is called the faith of clear delight[a]—a temporary clearing of the muddied waters of the mind, providing an openness that can lead to an aspiration for such states, called aspiring faith.[b] Despite the immense value of these two types of faith as motivators toward a spiritual path, they are said to be less powerful in the long run than faith aroused from well-reasoned and, therefore, deeply felt conviction—this type of faith being called the faith of conviction.[c] As the Dalai Lama says:[10]

> There are many stages in the improvement of the mind. There are some in which analysis of reasons is not necessary, such as when trusting faith alone is to be cultivated single-pointedly. Not much strength, however, is achieved by just that alone. Especially for developing the mind into limitless goodness, it is not sufficient merely to familiarise the mind with its object of meditation. The object of meditation must involve reasoning. Further, it is not sufficient for the object to have reasons in general; the meditator himself/herself must know them and have found a conviction in them. Therefore, it is impossible for the superior type of practitioner not to have intelligence.

The weakness of temporary inspiration is overcome through conviction derived from valid reasoning enhanced by intense concentration. (The line between conditioning to what is unfounded and conditioning to what is certified with valid reasoning is admittedly difficult to determine.)

Similarly, in developing wisdom penetrating to the reality of falsely appearing phenomena, reflective reasoning is used in an intricate process of analytical meditation directed toward realizing the incorrectness of consent to the false appearance of phenomena as if they exist in their own right. The aim of reasoning into reality is to overcome one's own *innate* misconception of the nature of phenomena and not just to defeat rival systems, despite the fact that much of the reasoning is presented in theoretical texts as if its aim were the latter. Meditators seek to come to experience and feel the impact of the reasonings learned in theoretical studies, the basic observation (or assumption) being that our afflictive emotions are built on misoriented ideas, not uncontrollable instincts that are endemic to the mind. Defilements of mind are seen as peripheral to the basic entity of consciousness, which is unaffected in its essence by the afflictive

---

a *dang ba'i dad pa.*

b *'thob 'dod kyi dad pa.*

c *yid ches kyi dad pa.* This type of faith is said to be induced by valid cognition (*tshad mas drang pa*).

emotions of lust, hatred, bewilderment, belligerence, enmity, jealousy, laziness, pride, and so forth. Since this basic nature of mental purity is what allows for transformation of mind and body into the exalted mind and body of a Buddha, it is called the matrix of One Gone Thus,[a] the Buddha lineage,[b] the basic constituent.[c]

Also, analytically derived realization of the emptiness of the duality of subject and object or of the emptiness of inherent existence constitutes the first step in practicing deity yoga, which involves using a wisdom consciousness realizing emptiness as a basis for compassionately manifesting oneself—to one's own mind—as an ideal person, wise and actively compassionate, a deity. The compassionately motivated wisdom consciousness itself is the mental "stuff" imaginatively used to manifest in form as a deity in an indivisible fusion of wisdom and compassion. The symbol of this indivisible fusion is a vajra, the Tibetan word for which is *dor-jay* (*rdo rje*), which literally translates as "foremost of stones," a diamond. In earlier times, diamonds were considered to be unbreakable (they are still used industrially to cut other substances), and thus a diamond symbolizes a fusion of compassion and wisdom that cannot be affected by afflictive emotions.

Within continuous divine appearance in imagination, an additional practice, aimed at enhancing the power of the wisdom consciousness realizing emptiness, can be utilized. In Highest Yoga Tantra, stabilizing meditation is performed on essential points within the body (at the point between the brows, the throat, the heart, the solar plexus, the base of the spine, and inside the sexual organ) in order to induce subtler levels of consciousness that are at the root of grosser levels of mind and thus more powerful. When such subtle levels are manifested, they are utilized to realize the same emptiness of inherent existence that had been realized earlier. When one does this with the most subtle consciousness, the fundamental innate mind of clear light,[d] it is said that the wind,[e] or perhaps energy, associated with this most subtle consciousness is used as the substantial cause for appearing in an *actual* divine form, without further need for the old coarse body except as a vehicle for teaching others.

This most subtle consciousness is the same as the clear light of death that is said to terrify ordinary beings, since they fear annihilation when it manifests. Ordinary beings are so identified with superficial states that the transition to the deeper involves even fear of annihilation; when the deeper states begin to manifest, we panic, fearing that we will be wiped out and, due to this fear, swoon unconsciously, unable to utilize this most subtle and most powerful level of mind for anything, never mind realization of the nature of reality. As the late

a *de bzhin gshegs pa'i snying po, tathāgatagarbha.*

b *sangs rgyas kyi rigs, buddhagotra.*

c *khams, dhātu.*

d *gnyug ma lhan cig skyes pa'i 'od gsal gyi sems.*

e *rlung, prāṇa.*

eighteenth- and early nineteenth-century Mongolian scholar Nga-w̄ang-ke-drup[a] says in his *Presentation of Death, Intermediate State, and Rebirth,*[11] at the time of the clear light of death, ordinary beings generate the fright that they will be annihilated. Since the clear light of death is the same clear light that is at the basis of all mental states, the basic fear is of one's own innermost nature.

This psychology suggests that ordinary conscious life is concerned with only the gross or superficial, without heed of more subtle states that are the foundation of both consciousness and appearance, not knowing either the origin of consciousness or the basis into which it returns. Much of the Ge-luk-b̄a system of education can be viewed as aimed at overcoming this fear of one's own most basic nature. The fear-inspiring aspect of its manifestation accords with the often described awesomeness and sense of otherness that much of world culture associates with types of profound religious experience. From this Buddhist perspective, the fact that this awesomeness is one's own final nature suggests that the otherness and fear associated with its manifestation is not part of its nature but due to our shallowness. These are functions of misconception of the basic nature of the mind, specifically the sense that afflictive emotions subsist in the nature of the mind and the consequent identification with them such that when their own basis starts to manifest, the fright of annihilation is generated.

In the N̄ying-ma, or Old Translation, Order of Tibetan Buddhism, an accomplished yogi's experience of fundamental mind is called "being set on mother's lap."[b] The joy and sense of at-homeness that a child feels when (in a happy mood) he or she is set on mama's lap is an analog to highly developed yogis' sense of joyful naturalness when they identify in experience their own basic nature. (The analogy recalls, of course, Freud's descriptions of drives to return to earlier pleasant states and of his "insight" into the meaning of the infant Jesus on Mary's lap as a depiction of a basic unconscious thrust of the religious enterprise. For Freud, these insights undermined the claims of religions, whereas, for me, it still is to be decided whether the metaphors are using the religions or the religions are using the metaphors.[c]) The at-homeness of the

---

a *ngag dbang mkhas grub,* 1779-1838; also known as *kyai rdo mkhan po.*

b *ma pang bu 'jug.*

c Consider, for example, Jung's description of the search for wholeness as disguised in the form of incest:

> Whenever this instinct for wholeness appears, it begins by disguising itself under the symbolism of incest, for, unless he seeks it in himself, a man's nearest feminine counterpart is to be found in his mother, sister, or daughter.

The Collected Works of C. G. Jung (Princeton, N.J.: Princeton University Press, 1971, second printing 1974), vol. 16, 471 (the latter number refers to the paragraph number, used for coordination between editions). Taken Jung's way, the image of the mother indicates a yearning for wholeness, which is naturally associated with the mother because of warm childhood experiences. Thus, the primary motivating force is the striving for wholeness; the fundamental innate mind of clear light when experienced by one who has overcome the initial, distorted fear and sense of annihilation suggests that this fundamental mind is, in a sense, most common, most ordinary. In fact, in N̄yingma literature, it is indeed called "ordinary mind."[a] In this way, the sacred (or an aspect of the sacred) is both awesomely other (when initially experienced) and the fundamental stuff of ordinary existence.

In these highly systematized Tibetan systems, preparatory practices serve to undermine the fear and the sense of otherness usually associated with the manifestation of fundamental reality. In the Ge-luk-b̄a order, particular emphasis is put on *reasoned* investigation brought to the level of profoundly moving experience as a principal means of accomplishing the destruction of fear. With such deeply felt rational penetration of the actual status of phenomena, it is then possible to perform non-analytical stabilizing meditation on focal points within the body in order to induce manifestation of increasingly subtle levels of mind. In this way, D̄zong-ka-b̄a's followers have a highly developed view of the compatibility of reason and deep mystical insight, expressed in a system of education, meditation, ritual, and prescriptions for behavior.

This worldview—a perspective on the nature of human (and other) beings and their potential for development through reasoning and meditation—explains the main reason for D̄zong-ka-b̄a's composition of his *The Essence of Eloquence,*[b] the focus of which is how emptiness is delineated through reasoning in the Mind-Only, Autonomy, and Consequence Schools. His aim is to develop the capabilities of reasoning and to identify, in intimate detail, emptiness as presented in these systems, realization of which undermines reifications of phenomena upon which an emotional life contrary to one's own basic reality is built.

Consonant with this emphasis on the compatibility of reasoning and profound transformative experience is the Ge-luk-b̄a presentation of all phenomena, both conventional and ultimate, within the rubric of being validly established, despite being empty of even a speck of being established by way of their own being. Conventional phenomena are not canceled, or invalidated, by realization of ultimate reality—only a falsely ascribed reification of them is. This is done by showing that the Middle Way reasonings explained by the Indian scholar and yogi Nāgārjuna (about 200 C.E.) refute not phenomena but a reified status.

When these reasonings are used in meditative analysis, an object such as one's body is not found, and thus one might think that therefore the object is understood not to exist, and many interpreters of Buddhism from both the inside and the outside have indeed made this conclusion.[12] After all, this

feminine image is the medium of its expression.

[a] *tha mal pa'i sems.*

[b] I do not intend to suggest that there are not other factors, sociological and otherwise, in his composition.

analytical consciousness that does not find objects is the best, the ultimate of all valid consciousnesses, and, if it does not find objects, how could they be posited to exist? However, Ge-luk-b̄a scholars clearly make the distinction that not analytically finding objects refutes only that objects exist in the concrete way in which they so palpably appear, not their very existence. The reasoning consciousness does not refute the existence of a nominally existent object that is merely imputed in dependence upon its basis of imputation—the collection of its parts. Through this distinction, the emptiness of inherent existence is shown to be compatible with dependent-arising, described as the existence of phenomena in dependence upon (1) causes and conditions that produce them, or (2) their parts, or (3) a conceptual consciousness that imputes them. As a consequence of this thoroughgoing view of the compatibility of emptiness and phenomena, this sect of Tibetan Buddhism, so influential in the Tibeto-Mongol-Himalayan world, not only limits the scope of the conclusions that can be drawn from ultimate analysis but also does not disavow all analysis of conventional phenomena, attention to detail being hallowed as consistent with understanding the final mode of subsistence of objects.

This estimation of the compatibility between knowledge of diverse manifestation and knowledge of the one taste of phenomena as empty of their own self-instituting principle is expressed in diverse ways. Great emphasis is put on:

1. The process of epistemological verification of objects
2. Tantric meditations of imagining oneself as an intricately described deity inside an elaborate mansion often with many (even seven hundred) finely identified companions—a mandala (the paintings being two-dimensional depictions of a three-dimensional palace and surroundings)
3. Extremely intricate artistic designs in butter (even sixty feet high) used as offerings, said to be more finely done in the Ge-luk-b̄a sect than in other orders of Tibetan Buddhism
4. A culture of scholarship that revolves around debate on highly complex issues and exposition of subtle doctrinal distinctions
5. Clear expositions of the process of tantric initiation even during an initiation ceremony
6. Elaborate devotional rituals.

Though these features are not unique to Ge-luk-b̄a, together they are a cluster of qualities difficult to find in the other orders of Tibetan Buddhism to the extent that they are emphasized in Ge-luk-b̄a.

A downside of such elaborate attention to the details of appearance is that profound meditative experience can be postponed indefinitely in order to meet the demands on time and energy that such intricate and sustained attention to appearance requires. In prematurely trying to mimic the state of Buddhahood in which realization of emptiness and realization of all appearances are fused, many abandon the difficult meditative pursuit of emptiness and devote themselves to elaborating detail. This is to great advantage in the development of conceptual systems that expound on both cardinal and minor doctrines of Buddhist India—thereby providing a system of education attractive to the intellect of hundreds of thousands of Inner Asians over the last seven centuries. This highly developed attempt to extend conceptual description into areas which other forms of Buddhism consider best left unexplained also yields a rich source of thought for those outside of the Tibetan cultural sphere—conceptual stances founded on fairly straightforward logic that cancel the sense of paradox (or nonsense) that many cannot avoid feeling in the face of many Buddhist attempts to explain doctrines and realizations, even if these are expressions of profound intuitive insight.

The conceptual immersion that results from pursuing such a highly thought out form of Buddhism can yield, if one does not take such conceptualization to be an end in itself, insights into seemingly unfathomable postures of other Buddhisms and, indeed, of other religions. It is my conviction that, if one pursues a particular religion far enough, its strengths—and especially its weaknesses—become so evident that one can begin to appreciate why another system prefers to take a different fork in the conceptual road. With this attitude, there is no fear of entrapment in pursuing the intricate maneuverings spawned in the colleges of Tibet. Indeed, such an attitude allows for a sense of humor, relieving the pressure—at least for the time being—of making decisions of right and wrong and allows one to notice internal resonance and lack thereof when facing the material. My own survival over thirty-seven years of such study has, I have sometimes thought, been due to a frequent, forthright acknowledgment of my reactions and feelings, ranging from sheer delight and upliftment, to insights into my character, to cynical disappointment, to snide disparagement, and even to inward screams of suffocation as I perceived my Tibetan and Mongolian teachers as stuffing me with doctrine as if they were stuffing sausage.

From noticing that some scholars become defensively insistent on the importance of their work in order to hide from their own perception that they have wasted their time on trivia, I have tried to distinguish the woods from the trees and not force on others the excruciating trials that I have had to undergo to understand topics that turned out to be minor indeed. Thus, even though in our travels in the succeeding chapters we shall spend a great deal of time with the trees in order to find the woods, I shall try not to pretend that what is not central is central.

In the debate format that is at the heart of this Tibetan system of education, interest and even esthetic delight can be generated whether the particular debate is on a central or a peripheral issue. That such attention to minor issues is encouraged can be a sign of addiction to conceptual meanderings but is, more likely, a frank recognition that from detail a broad picture begins to dawn. Immersion even in unsolvable problems involves such command of the central issues that major issues become the background, the floor, the foundation of the intellectual and spiritual pursuit, taken from the level of unfelt abstractions out there in the world of discourse to the gritty level of everyday experience—the material of life. Thus, what seem at first to be dry abstractions—especially as contrasted with the immediately psychologically evocative terminology in the original order of Tibetan Buddhism, the N̄ying-ma or Old Translation Order—become vividly relevant in a palpable way.

PART TWO: *RELIGIOUS SIGNIFICANCE OF THE THREE NATURES OF PHENOMENA*

3. Bondage and Release: Ignorance and Wisdom

Presentations Of Tenets: Structuring A Worldview

In the Ge-luk-b̄a order of Tibetan Buddhism, D̄zong-ka-b̄a's *The Essence of Eloquence* is considered to be the mother of a genre of literature called "presentations of tenets."[13] This genre mainly refers to delineations of the systematic schools of Buddhist and non-Buddhist Indian philosophy. Focal topics and issues of these schools are presented in order to stimulate metaphysical inquiry—to encourage development of an inner faculty that is capable of investigating appearances so as to penetrate their reality. Thus, in this context philosophy is, for the most part, related to liberative concerns—the attempt to extricate oneself and others from a round of painful existence and to attain freedom.

The basic perspective is that afflictive emotions—such as desire, hatred, enmity, jealousy, and belligerence—bind beings in a round of uncontrolled birth, aging, sickness, and death and are founded on misperception of the nature of persons and other phenomena. When a practitioner penetrates the reality of things and this insight is teamed with a powerful consciousness of concentrated meditation, the underpinnings of the process of cyclic existence can be destroyed, resulting in liberation. Also, when wisdom is further empowered through the development of love, compassion, and altruism—and the corresponding actions of generosity, ethics, and tolerant patience—the wisdom consciousness is capable of achieving an all-knowing state in which one can effectively help a vast number of beings.

Because of this basic perspective—namely, that false ideation traps beings in a round of suffering—reasoned investigation into the nature of persons and other phenomena is central to the process of spiritual development (though it is not the only concern). Systems of tenets primarily are studied not to refute other systems but to develop an internal force that can counteract one's own *innate* adherence to misapprehensions. These innate forms of ignorance are part and parcel of ordinary life. They are not just learned from other systems, nor do they just arise from faulty analysis. Thus, the stated aim of studying the different schools of philosophy is to gain insight into the fact that many of the perspectives basic to ordinary life are devoid of a valid foundation. This realization leads the adept to replace invalid assent to deceptive appearance with well-founded perspectives. As was mentioned earlier (p. 4), the process is achieved through (1) first engaging in *hearing* great texts on such topics and getting straight the verbal presentation, (2) then *thinking* on their meaning to the point where the topics are ascertained with valid cognition, and (3) finally *meditating* on the same to the point where these realizations become enhanced by the power of concentration such that they can counteract innate tendencies to assent to false appearances.

Since it is no easy matter to penetrate the thick veil of false facades and misconceptions, it became popular in the more scholastic circles of India to investigate not just what the current tradition considered to be the best and final system but also the so-called lower systems. Systematic study provided a gradual approach to subtle topics so as to avoid confusion with less subtle ones. Also, in Tibet, because of the need to get a handle on the plethora of Buddhist systems inherited from India, the genre of presentations of tenets comparing the views of the different schools of thought assumed considerable importance. That the primary concern was indeed with developing the capacity to appreciate the profound view of a high system of philosophy is evidenced by the amount of time actually spent by students probing the workings of the so-called lower schools. Since the philosophies of those schools were appreciated, they were studied in considerable detail.

The main Indian precursors of the genre were texts such as the *Blaze of Reasoning*[14] by Bhāvaviveka (500-570? C.E.)[15]—and the *Compendium of Principles*[16] by the eighth-century scholar Shāntarakṣhita, with a commentary by his student Kamalashīla. Both Shāntarakṣhita and Kamalashīla visited Tibet in the eighth century and strongly influenced the direction that Buddhism took there. In Tibet, the genre came to be more highly systematized, the presentations assuming a more developed structure.[a] Some of these texts are long; for instance, a lengthy text entitled *Treasury of Tenets, Illuminating the Meaning of All Vehicles*[17] was written by the great fourteenth-century scholar L̄ong-chen-rap-jam[b] of the N̄ying-ma order of Tibetan Buddhism. It appears that D̄zong-ka-b̄a's *The Essence of Eloquence* was written in reaction to presentations like those of L̄ong-chen-b̄a.[c] Again, in reaction to D̄zong-ka-b̄a's writing, the great fifteenth-century scholar D̄ak-tsang S̄hay-rap-rin-chen[d] of the S̄a-ḡya order wrote a long text entitled the *Explanation of "Freedom from Extremes through Understanding All Tenets": Ocean of Eloquence,*[18] detailing D̄zong-ka-b̄a's "contradictions." D̄ak-tsang's text in turn gave rise to the most extensive text of this genre in Tibet; refuting D̄ak-tsang's account of D̄zong-ka-b̄a's contradictions but also incorporating much of D̄ak-tsang's text, Jam-ȳang-shay-b̄a (1648-1721) wrote the *Explanation of "Tenets": Sun of the Land of Samantabhadra Brilliantly Illuminating All of Our Own and Others' Tenets and the Meaning of the Profound*

---

[a] For more discussion on this genre of Tibetan literature, see Katsumi Mimaki, *Blo gsal grub mtha'* (Kyoto: Université de Kyoto, 1982), 1-12; and David Seyfort Ruegg's foreword to Geshé Ngawang Nyima, *Introduction to the Doctrines of the Four Schools of Buddhist Philosophy* (Leiden, 1970).

[b] *klong chen rab 'byams / klong chen dri med 'od zer,* 1308-1363.

[c] D̄zong-ka-b̄a's main opponent is the fourteenth-century scholar-yogi S̄hay-rap-gyel-tsen; see Part 4.

[d] *stag tshang lo tsā ba shes rab rin chen,* born 1405.

[Emptiness], Ocean of Scripture and Reasoning Fulfilling All Hopes of All Beings, also known as the *Great Exposition of Tenets.*[19] This text is replete with citations of Indian sources but is written, despite its length, in a laconic style (unusual for him) that can leave one wondering about the relevance of certain citations. Perhaps this was partly why the eighteenth-century Tibetanized Mongolian scholar J̄ang-ḡya Röl-b̄ay-dor-jay[a]—whom Jam-ȳang-shay-b̄a, then an old man,[b] helped to find as the reincarnation of the last J̄ang-ḡya—composed a more issue-oriented text of the same genre entitled *Clear Exposition of the Presentations of Tenets: Beautiful Ornament for the Meru of the Subduer's Teaching.*[20]

After Jam-ȳang-shay-b̄a passed away, his reincarnation, Ḡön-chok-jik-may-w̄ang-b̄o,[c] became J̄ang-ḡya's main pupil. In 1733 Ḡön-chok-jik-may-w̄ang-b̄o wrote an abbreviated version of these texts, entitled *Presentation of Tenets: A Precious Garland.*[d] Authors such as Ḡön-chok-jik-may-w̄ang-b̄o chose to write concise texts so that the general outlines and basic postures of the systems of tenets could be taught and memorized without the encumbrance of a great deal of elaboration. Sometimes, the brevity itself makes the issues being discussed inaccessible, but, at minimum, it provides a foundation for students, who can memorize the entire body of the text and use it as a locus for further elaboration. The aim is to provide an easy avenue for grasping issues that revolve around the nature of persons and phenomena.

A medium-length presentation of tenets that also treats the other schools of Tibetan Buddhism in a biased fashion was written by J̄ang-ḡya's biographer and student, who was also a student of Ḡön-chok-jik-may-w̄ang-b̄o, Tu-ḡen L̄o-sang-chö-ḡyi-nyi-ma.[e] His text is called *Mirror of Eloquence Showing the Sources and Assertions of All Systems of Tenets.*[21]

The number of texts testifies to this genre's having captured the attention of several important authors as a means to stimulate the metaphysical imagination and thereby to penetrate the veil of false appearances.

---

[a] *lcang skya rol pa'i rdo rje,* 1717-1786. A Tibetanized Mongolian born in what is presently the Am-do Province of Tibet, currently the Qinghai Province of China, he is also known as the Second J̄ang-ḡya Hu-tok-tu (*hu thog thu*), using the Mongolian for *sprul sku.*

[b] Jam-ȳang-shay-b̄a himself had been tutored by the previous J̄ang-ḡya, Nga-w̄ang-l̄o-sang-chö-den.

[c] *dkon mchog 'jigs med dbang po,* 1728-1791.

[d] *grub pa'i mtha'i rnam par bzhag pa rin po che'i phreng ba.* In this sub-genre of brief Presentations of Tenets are earlier texts such as the *Presentation of Tenets* by Jay-d̄zün Chö-ḡyi-gyel-tsen (1469-1546), the *Ship for Entering the Ocean of Tenets* by the Second Dalai Lama (1476-1542), the *Presentation of Tenets, Sublime Tree Inspiring Those of Clear Mind, Hammer Destroying the Stone Mountains of Opponents* by Paṇ-chen S̄ö-nam-drak-b̄a (1478-1554), and the *Condensed Essence of All Tenets* by J̄o-nay-b̄a Drak-b̄a-shay-drup (*co ne ba grags pa bshad sgrub,* 1675-1748). For a list of other such brief texts, see the bibliography (XLVI, and so forth) and introduction (5-12) in Katsumi Mimaki, *Blo gsal grub mtha'.*

[e] *thu'u bkvan blo bzang chos kyi nyi ma,* 1737-1802.

Format Of Presentations Of Tenets

D̄zong-ka-b̄a's *The Essence of Eloquence,* despite focusing on the single topic of what is definitive and what requires interpretation in Buddha's word, served as a prime source in the Ge-luk-b̄a order for presentations of tenets structured around a series of topics in each of the schools. Bringing a high degree of clarity and opening the way for easy cross-comparisons, these presentations, though themselves stemming from D̄zong-ka-b̄a's works, became the context in which his complicated exegesis is both viewed and tested for coherence. Thus, as a tool for appreciating how his text was absorbed in Tibetan culture, let us apply the format of a typical presentation of tenets, that by Ḡön-chok-jik-may-w̄ang-b̄o, to the Mind-Only School, the first school that D̄zong-ka-b̄a treats. His exposition of issues central to the school will thereby be placed in its larger context in the Ge-luk-b̄a educational system.

Ḡön-chok-jik-may-w̄ang-b̄o presents the principal tenets of Indian schools, both Buddhist and non-Buddhist; first he treats six renowned non-Buddhist schools briefly and then focuses on the four Buddhist schools and their main sub-schools. In the order of their presentation (the list of Buddhist schools represents an ascent in order of estimation), these are:

Non-Buddhist Schools

Vaisheṣhika[a] and Naiyāyika[b] (Particularists and Logicians)
Sāṃkhya[c] (Enumerators)
Mīmāṃsa[d] (Analyzers or Ritualists)
Nirgrantha[e] (The Unclothed), also known as Jaina[f]
Lokāyata[g] (Hedonists)

Buddhist Schools

Lesser Vehicle (*hīnayāna*)[h]

---

a *bye brag pa.*

b *rig pa can pa.*

c *grangs can pa.*

d *dpyod pa ba.*

e *gcer bu pa.*

f *rgyal ba pa.*

g *rgyang 'phan pa.*

h The term "Lesser Vehicle" (*theg dman, hīnayāna*) has its origin in the writings of Great Vehicle (*theg chen, mahāyāna*) authors and was, of course, not used by those to whom it was ascribed. Substitutes such as "non-Mahāyāna," "Nikāya Buddhism," and "Theravādayāna" have been suggested in order to avoid the pejorative sense of "Lesser." However, "Lesser Vehicle" is a convenient term in this particular context for a type of tenet system or practice that is seen, in the tradition analyzed in this book, to be surpassed—but not negated—by a higher system. The "Lesser Vehicle" is not despised, most of it being incorporated into the "Great Vehicle." The monks' and nuns' vows are Lesser Vehicle, as is much of the course of study in Ge-luk-ba monastic universities—years of study are put into the topics of

Great Exposition School[a]
Eighteen sub-schools
Sūtra School[b]
Following Scripture[c]
Following Reasoning[d]
Great Vehicle (*mahāyāna*)
Mind-Only School[e]
Following Scripture
Following Reasoning
Middle Way School[f]
Autonomy School[g]
Consequence School[h]

Notice that Gön-chok-jik-may-wang-bo (and all other Ge-luk-ba scholars) rank the Middle Way School higher than the Mind-Only School, although the Indian adherents to Mind-Only ranked their own school as the highest.

The division of Buddhist philosophy into four schools is itself largely an artificial creation. The so-called Great Exposition School is a collection of at least eighteen schools that never recognized themselves as belonging to a single, over-arching school. Also, their tenets are so various (some prefiguring Great Vehicle schools) that it is extremely difficult to recognize tenets common to all eighteen; rather than attempting to do so, Tibetan systematizers set forth representative tenets as explained in the root text of Vasubandhu's *Treasury of Manifest Knowledge*[22] as if these constituted the general tenet structure of such an over-arching system, even though they are merely typical of assertions found in these eighteen schools. This pretended amalgamation of many schools into one is a technique used to avoid unnecessary complexity that might hinder the main purpose of this genre of exegesis—the presentation of an ascent to the systems considered to be higher. Hence, in the Great Exposition School there is a wide variety of opinion, a range of views some of which differ greatly from those found in a short general presentation such as that by Gön-chok-jik-may-wang-bo. Strictly speaking, even the name "Great Exposition School" should be

Epistemology (*tshad ma, pramāṇa*), Manifest Knowledge (*chos mngon pa, abhidharma*), and Discipline (*'dul ba, vinaya*), all of which are mostly Lesser Vehicle in perspective. ("Lesser Vehicle" and "Low Vehicle" are used interchangeably in this book.)

a *bye brag smra ba, vaibhāṣika.*
b *mdo sde pa, sautrāntika.*
c *lung gi rjes 'brangs, *āgamānusārin.*
d *rigs pa'i rjes 'brangs, *nyāyānusārin.*
e *sems tsam pa, cittamātra.*
f *dbu ma pa, mādhyamika.*
g *rang rgyud pa, svātantrika.*
h *thal 'gyur pa, prāsaṅgika.*

limited to followers of the *Mahāvibhāṣhā* (*Great Exposition*), a text of Manifest Knowledge[a] by Vasumitra that was never translated into Tibetan.

Also, the division of the Sūtra School into those following scripture and those following reasoning is highly controversial as it is found only in Ge-luk-b̄a scholarship.[23] The former are said to follow Vasubandhu's own commentary on his *Treasury of Manifest Knowledge,* in which he indicates disagreement with many assertions of the Great Exposition School as presented in his root text. The latter—the Proponents of Sūtra Following Reasoning—are said to be followers of Dignāga and Dharmakīrti, who (despite the fact that Dignāga and Dharmakīrti do not assert external objects) assert external objects—objects that are different entities from the consciousnesses perceiving them. Again, neither of these groups saw themselves as sub-divisions of a larger school called the Sūtra School.

Similarly, the two sub-divisions of the Mind-Only School are those following scripture, who depend on the writings primarily of Asaṅga and his half brother Vasubandhu (after the latter converted to Asaṅga's system), and those following reasoning, who depend on what is accepted to be the main system of Dignāga's and Dharmakīrti's writings. Again, it is unlikely that these two groups perceived themselves as being sub-schools of a larger school even though Dignāga was a student of Vasubandhu, and Dharmakīrti, though not a direct student of Dignāga, sought to explicate Dignāga's works. For, as far as I have been able to determine, neither Dignāga nor Dharmakīrti cites Asaṅga or Vasubandhu as sources. Rather, the groupings are the result of later schematizations that are based on similarities between their systems and that are committed to the dictum that there are only four schools of tenets.[b]

Also, the names of the two sub-divisions of the Middle Way School—the Autonomy School and the Consequence School—were, as is clearly admitted by D̄zong-ka-b̄a and his followers, never used in India. Rather, these names were coined in Tibet in accordance with the (infrequent) mention of autonomous syllogisms in the works of Bhāvaviveka and Chandrakīrti.[c]

---

a *chos mngon pa, abhidharma.*

b One reason for insisting that there are only four schools of tenets is to leave no room for the Great Middle Way propounded by S̄hay-rap-gyel-tsen.

c For a discussion of the Tibetan origins of the names of the sub-divisions of the Middle Way School, see:

- Katsumi Mimaki, *Blo gsal grub mtha'* (Kyoto: Université de Kyoto, 1982).
- Katsumi Mimaki, "The *Blo gsal grub mtha'*, and the Mādhyamika Classification in Tibetan *grub mtha'* Literature," in *Contributions on Tibetan and Buddhist Religion and Philosophy,* ed. Ernst Steinkellner and Helmut Tauscher (Vienna: Arbeitskreis für tibetische und buddhistische Studien, 1983), 161-167.
- Peter della Santina, *Madhyamaka Schools in India* (Delhi: Motilal Banarsidass, 1986).
- Jeffrey Hopkins, "A Tibetan Delineation of Different Views of Emptiness in the Indian Middle Way School: D̄zong-ka-b̄a's Two Interpretations of the *Locus Classicus* in

Thus, the very format of the four schools and their sub-divisions does not represent a historical account of self-asserted identities but is the result of centuries of classification of systems in India and Tibet based on certain shared assertions. The purpose of the schematization is to give the emerging scholar a handle on the vast scope of positions found in Indian Buddhism.

In Tibet, students are first taught this fourfold classification, without mention of the diversity of opinion that it conceals. Then, over decades of study, they gradually recognize the structure of such presentations of schools of thought as a technique for gaining access to a vast store of opinion through focusing on topics crucial to certain Indian authors. The task of then distinguishing between what is clearly said in the Indian texts and what is interpretation and interpolation over centuries of commentary becomes a fascinating enterprise for the more hardy. The devotion to debate as the primary mode of education provides an ever-present avenue for students to challenge homegrown interpretations and affords a richness of critical commentary within the tradition that a short presentation of tenets does not convey. Given this situation, the format of four schools can be seen as a horizon that opens a way to appreciate the plethora of opinions, not as one that closes and rigidifies investigation. It serves as a framework for interrogating texts such as D̄zong-ka-b̄a's *The Essence of Eloquence* in order both to tease out its implications and to create interpretive conundrums absorbing the mind in attempts to maintain the hierarchy of systems.

Topics In Presentations Of Tenets

In Ḡön-chok-jik-may-w̄ang-b̄o's text, each Buddhist school is treated under four major topics, the last having numerous sub-divisions.

1. Definition[a]
2. Sub-schools
3. Etymology
4. Assertions of tenets

Chandrakīrti's *Clear Words* Showing Bhāvaviveka's Assertion of Commonly Appearing Subjects and Inherent Existence," *Tibet Journal* 14, no. 1 (1989):10-43, although the printing contains egregious typographical errors.

- Kodo Yotsuya, *The Critique of Svatantra Reasoning by Candrakīrti and Tsong-kha-pa: A Study of Philosophical Proof According to Two Prāsaṅgika Madhyamaka Traditions of India and Tibet,* Tibetan and Indo-Tibetan Studies 8 (Stuttgart: Franz Steiner Verlag, 1999).

[a] A definition (*mtshan nyid, lakṣana*) in this system is not a verbal description; it is the actual object, viewed in one way as being the meaning (*don, artha*), whereas the definiendum is the name (*ming, nāma*). In another way, the definition is viewed as a "defining property" that characterizes an object. For a thoroughgoing discussion of this topic, see Georges Dreyfus, "Some Considerations on Definition in Buddhism: An Essay on the Use of Definitions in the Indo-Tibetan Epistemological Tradition," M.A. thesis, University of Virginia, 1987.

Assertions on the basis
  Objects: the two truths, and so forth
  Object-possessors (that is, subjects)
    Persons
    Consciousnesses
    Terms
Assertions on the paths
  Objects of observation of the paths
  Objects abandoned by the paths
  Nature of the paths
Assertions on the fruits of the paths

Let us relate these briefly to the Mind-Only School, drawing on presentations of tenets by Jam-ȳang-shay-b̄a,[24] his reincarnation Ḡön-chok-jik-may-w̄ang-b̄o,[25] and J̄ang-ḡya Röl-b̄ay-dor-jay.[26] Since our purpose, like that of a brief presentation of tenets, is general orientation, the many source quotes in Indian treaties as well as related issues and problems will be left for later.

Definition Of A Proponent Of Mind-Only

A person propounding Buddhist tenets who asserts the true existence of impermanent phenomena but does not assert external objects.

Sub-schools

- Followers of Scripture, that is, followers mainly of Asaṅga's Five Treatises on the Grounds[27]
- Followers of Reasoning, that is, followers mainly of Dignāga's *Compilation of Prime Cognition*[28] and Dharmakīrti's Seven Treatises on Prime Cognition

Etymologies

- They are called "Proponents of Mind-Only"[a] because they propound that the three realms—Desire Realm, Form Realm, and Formless Realm—are truly established as only mind.
- They are called "Proponents of Cognition"[b] because they propound that all

[a] *sems tsam pa, cittamātrin.*

[b] *rnam rig pa, vijñaptika / vijñaptivādin.* The central term *vijñaptimātra* has been translated differently by almost every scholar who has touched the topic. A list of translations used by nine American, Asian, and European scholars will suffice to illustrate the variety:

"perception-only": Stefan Anacker in *Seven Works of Vasubandhu* (Delhi: Motilal Banarsidass, 1984)

"ideation-only": Wing-tsit Chan in "The Thirty Verses on the Mind-Only Doctrine," in *A Sourcebook in Indian Philosophy,* ed. S. Radhakrishnan and C. A. Moore (Princeton,

phenomena are of the nature of fifteen cognitions.[a]

- They are called "Yogic Practitioners"[b] because they delineate the practice of the deeds of the path from the yogic point of view or the four grounds of

N.J.: Princeton University Press, 1957), 333-337

"mere representation of consciousness": Thomas A. Kochumuttom in *A Buddhist Doctrine of Experience* (Delhi: Motilal Banarsidass, 1982)

"ne sont rien qu'idée" (*vijñaptimātra*): Étienne Lamotte in *La Somme du grand véhicule d'Asaṅga,* reprint, 2 vols., Publications de l'Institute Orientaliste de Louvain 8 (Louvain: Université de Louvain, 1973)

"mere denominations" (*prajñaptimātra*) as used in Asaṅga's *Grounds of Yogic Practice:* Lambert Schmithausen in "On the Problem of the Relation of Spiritual Practice and Philosophical Theory in Buddhism," in *German Scholars on India,* 235-250, Contributions to India Studies 2 (Bombay: Nachiketa, 1976), 238

"nothing but cognition" (*vijñaptimātra*) as used in the *Sūtra Unraveling the Thought:* ibid., 240

"pure information": Robert A. F. Thurman in *Tsong Khapa's Speech of Gold in the Essence of True Eloquence* (Princeton, N.J.: Princeton University Press, 1984), 239.19

"pure consciousness": ibid., 233.9

"consciousness-only": Yoshifumi Ueda (for more discussion of Ueda's interpretation, see Appendix 2, p. 520ff.) in "Two Main Streams of Thought in Yogācāra Philosophy," *Philosophy East and West* 17 (January-October 1967):162, and so forth

"conceptualized thing" as in "(the object of *vikalpa* are all consciousness-only [*vijñaptimātratā*]), that is, for one whose mind is *vijñāna,* the object known is a conceptualized thing, and not the object as it really exists": ibid., 163

"representation-only": Alex Wayman in "Yogācāra and the Buddhist Logicians," *Journal of the International Association of Buddhist Studies* 2, no. 1 (1979): 67, 68, and so forth; for more discussion of Wayman's interpretation, see Appendix 1, p. 506ff.

"only representation," or "just conceptualization": Janice D. Willis in *On Knowing Reality: The Tattvārtha Chapter of Asaṅga's Bodhisattvabhūmi* (New York: Columbia University Press, 1979; reprint, Delhi: Motilal Banarsidass, 1982), 34 and 36 (for more discussion of Willis's interpretation, see Appendix 3, p. 525ff.

"nothing but conceptualization": ibid., 28-31

In the traditions of scholarship following Ḏzong-ka-ḇa, it is clear that the term refers to mind-only involving a lack of external objects; see chapters 18-20.

For a provocative and thorough article on this term, see Bruce Cameron Hall, "The Meaning of Vijñapti in Vasubandhu's Concept of Mind," *Journal of the International Association of Buddhist Studies* 9, no. 1 (1986):7-23. Hall faults all translations and does not give one of his own, but provides important context for the term within Indian culture. He (14) cogently explains that *vijñaptimātra* does not imply a subjective or absolute idealism in which mind is the final reality. See also Kochumuttom (*A Buddhist Doctrine of Experience,* 6 and 197-219) for a cogent presentation that emptiness of the duality of subject and object—and neither mere representation of consciousness nor its equivalent mind-only—is the final reality. That the emptiness of difference in entity between subject and object is the final reality accords with most Ge-luk-ḇa scholarship on this issue; for divergent opinions within Ge-luk-ḇa, see p. 246ff.

[a] For a listing of these, see p. 436ff.

[b] *rnal 'byor spyod pa pa, yogācāra.*

yoga:[29] the yogic ground realizing the selflessness of persons, the yogic ground observing mind-only, the yogic ground observing thusness, and the yogic ground dwelling in non-appearance.

Assertions Of Tenets

The topics considered under the heading of "assertions of tenets" reveal the soteriological orientation of the inquiry. These are divided into three categories—presentations of the basis, the paths, and the fruits of the path. The presentation of the basis refers to assertions on classes of phenomena, which provide the *basis* for practicing the spiritual *paths,* which, in turn, produce attainments, the *fruits of the path.* It is clear from this ordering that a principal reason for philosophical learning about phenomena is to enable spiritual practice that can transform the mind from being mired in a condition of suffering to being enlightened in a state of freedom.

The general structure of basis, paths, and fruits takes its lead from the emphasis in texts of the Middle Way School on three coordinated sets of twos:

1. Two truths—conventional and ultimate—which are the basis
2. Two practices—method (that is, motivation and its incumbent deeds) and wisdom—which are the paths
3. Two Buddha Bodies—Form Bodies and Truth Body—which are the final fruits of the path.

According to Great Vehicle systems of tenets, taking as one's basis conventional truths, one practices the paths of method—love, compassion, and the altruistic intention to become enlightened as well the compassionate deeds that these induce—in dependence upon which one achieves the fruit of the Form Bodies of a Buddha. Also, taking as one's basis ultimate truths, one practices the paths of wisdom—especially the realization of the final status of persons and phenomena, their emptiness—in dependence upon which one achieves the fruit of a Truth Body of a Buddha. This threefold format—which finds its main expression in the Middle Way School—supplies the structure for the genre of presentations of tenets for both the Lesser Vehicle and the Great Vehicle.

Within the section on the basis, the emphasis—found in Tibetan presentations of tenets—on the two truths in all four schools derives from the fact that the two truths are a prime subject in the tenets of what is considered to be the highest school, the Middle Way School. As the late eighteenth- and early nineteenth-century scholar, Gung-tang Ḡön-chok-d̄en-b̄ay-drön-may[a] (hereafter called Gung-tang), who was the chief student of Ḡön-chok-jik-may-w̄ang-b̄o, says,[30] the prime way that the Great Exposition School and the Sūtra School

[a] *gung thang dkon mchog bstan pa'i sgron me,* 1762-1823. For a brief biography, see E. Gene Smith, *University of Washington Tibetan Catalogue* (Seattle, Wash.: University of Washington Press, 1969), 1:81-82.

delineate the meaning of the scriptures is by way of the four noble truths, whereas the Mind-Only School accomplishes this through the doctrine of the three natures, and the Middle Way School, through the doctrine of the two truths. Thus, the emphasis on the four schools' delineations of the two truths derives from the system that this tradition has determined to be the highest, the Middle Way School. This is not to say that the two truths are not important topics in all four schools, for they are; rather, the two truths are not *the* central topic in the other schools in the way that they are in the Middle Way School.

Thus, in the genre of presentations of tenets, the very structure (basis, paths, and fruits) and the choice of some topics (such as the two truths) clearly do not arise from prime concerns within each school but are brought over from focal issues in other schools, particularly those considered to be higher. That topics of prime concern in the "higher" schools dominate to some extent the presentation of the tenets of all four schools is natural, given that the main aim is to draw readers into realizing the impact of the views of those systems.

Basis

The topic of the basis is treated in two parts—objects and object-possessors, or subjects. Objects, in turn, are treated in Ge-luk-b̄a texts presenting the Mind-Only School under two rubrics—the three natures (which is the school's own primary topic) and the two truths (which, although apparent in the school's texts, is not the central topic). For these two topics, let us use the exposition in the *Clear Exposition of the Presentation of Tenets* by the eighteenth-century Mongolian scholar J̄ang-ḡya Röl-b̄ay-dor-jay, also known as Ye-s̄hay-d̄en-b̄ay-drön-may.[a]

---

[a] *ye shes bstan pa'i sgron me.* J̄ang-ḡya's biography illustrates the many roles that lamas often play—child prodigy, disseminator of the religion, political go-between, priest to the ruler, monastery leader, yogi and magician, teacher, and learned scholar. See Jeffrey Hopkins, *Emptiness Yoga* (Ithaca, N.Y.: Snow Lion, 1987), chap. 1, which, in turn, was drawn from E. Gene Smith's introduction to Collected Works of Thu'u-bkwan Blo-bzang-chos-kyi-nyi-ma (Delhi: N. Gelek Demo, 1969), vol. 1, 2-12, and from a brief biography put together at my request by the late Ge-s̄hay Tup-d̄en-gya-tso. The material was further amplified and explained by Ke-d̄zün-sang-b̄o Rin-b̄o-chay (*mkhas btsun bzang po rin po che*), who was visiting the University of Virginia under the auspices of the Center for South Asian Studies. Both Gene Smith and Ge-s̄hay Tup-d̄en-gya-tso were condensing Tu-ḡen L̄o-sang-chö-ḡyi-nyi-ma's long biography of J̄ang-ḡya, found in the first volume of his Collected Works, which is 414 pages (827 sides) in length and is divided into twenty-five chapters. Another biography of J̄ang-ḡya, authored in 1787 by his younger brother Chu-sang Nga-w̄ang-tup-d̄en-w̄ang-chuk (*chu bzang ngag dbang thub bstan dbang phyug,* born 1736), found at the beginning of the supplementary volume of the Peking edition of J̄ang-ḡya's Collected Works, has been translated by Hans-Rainer Kämpfe in *Ñi ma'i 'od zer / Naran-u gerel: Die Biographie des 2. Pekinger Lcaṅ skya-Qutuqtu Rol pa'i rdo rje (1717-1786),* Monumenta Tibetica Historica 2 (1) (Sankt Augustin: Wissenschaftsverlag, 1976). For an illuminating review article of this work, see Samuel M. Grupper, "Manchu Patronage and Tibetan

Objects: Three Natures

Objects are divided into the three natures: other-powered natures, imputational natures, and thoroughly established natures.

Other-powered nature. With respect to other-powered natures[a] Jang-ḡya says:[31]

> An other-powered nature is a thing that arises from causes and conditions. Why is it called other-powered? Because it is produced from causes and conditions that are other than it. Or because it is produced without its own power to remain for other than one moment. Or because it is produced from the seed which is its own respective internal latency.

Other-powered natures are phenomena under the influence of something other than themselves—their own causes and conditions. Since that is so, they themselves do not have the power to stay for even a second moment, even though they often can generate an object that is similar in type to them. Beings who have not trained in the doctrine of emptiness see other-powered natures such as bodies, minds, tables, chairs, and houses falsely as if they were under their own power and thus could remain. However, since they are under the influence of the force of causes and conditions outside of themselves, they cannot remain even for another moment. On a more profound level, those causes and conditions are predispositions, internal seeds, etchings on the mind by former perceptions which, when activated, produce appearances and the consciousnesses that pay attention to them. One such seed brings about the appearance of the object and the appearance of the subject, much as in a dream.[b]

Imputational nature. Subject and object appear to be different entities—distant and cut off—but are not. Jang-ḡya gives the example of a magical display:[32]

> When a magician casts the mantra of illusion on a pebble or stick, even though that stick does not exist as a horse or an elephant, it appears in the form of a horse, elephant, and so forth. In the same way, these other-powered natures are not established in the manner of the object and the subject being distant and cut off, but—by the power of conceptuality of the unreal—subject and object appear to be distant and cut off.

Buddhism during the First Half of the Ch'ing Dynasty," *Journal of the Tibet Society* 4 (1984):47-75. Grupper presents the view that the Manchu allegiance to Tibetan Buddhism during the first half of the Ch'ing dynasty was genuine and not just a technique for holding the loyalty of the Mongolian nobility.

a *gzhan dbang gi ngo bo nyid, paratantrasvabhāva.*

b For a discussion of the mechanics of perception without an external object impinging on a consciousness, see p. 217ff.

For instance, a tree falsely appears to be distant and cut off from the eye consciousness apprehending it. The tree exists, but not how it appears to exist as an external object. In Jang-gya's example, during a magical display created by putting a salve on a small object such as a pebble or a stick and using a mantra that affects the eye consciousness of all present, including the magician, a pebble appears to be a horse but is not. Similarly, a tree appears to be distant and cut off from an eye consciousness perceiving it but is not; nonetheless, it seems external through the power of unreal ideation.[a] In this context, "unreal ideation" is not present conceptuality thinking, "This is a different entity from my eye consciousness"; rather, through past repeated naming of objects, predispositions were established for the false appearance of objects, distant and cut off from the perceiving subject even in raw sensation. The (false) establishment of object and subject as separate entities is called an imputational nature,[b] the second of the three natures.

Another principal type of imputational nature is the establishment of a phenomenon by way of its own character as the referent of a conceptual consciousness or of a word.[c] About this, Jang-gya says:[33]

---

[a] *yang dag pa ma yin pa'i kun tu rtog pa / yang dag min kun rtog, abhūtaparikalpa;* for a discussion of this term, see *Emptiness in Mind-Only,* 307.

[b] *kun btags pa'i ngo bo nyid, parikalpitasvabhāva.*

[c] *rang 'dzin rtog pa'i zhen gzhir rang gi mtshan nyid kyis grub pa;* also, *gzugs gzugs zhes rjod pa'i sgra 'jug pa'i 'jug gzhir rang gi mtshan nyid kyis grub pa.* Although in other works I have translated *zhen yul* as "referent object," I now use "conceived object." This is to provide separate terms for the difference between (1) a form's being a conceived object of a conceptual consciousness (*gzugs sogs rtog pa'i zhen yul yin pa*) and (2) a form's being a referent of a conceptual consciousness (*gzugs sogs rtog pa'i zhen gzhi yin pa*), as the latter is meant when discussed in the context of the object of negation in selflessness. Jik-may-dam-chö-gya-tso (*Port of Entry,* 550.4, 554.6-555.1) says:

> A form's being a conceived object of a conceptual consciousness [means] that a form is taken as the object of the mode of apprehension apprehending form by way of being conceived [that is, thought about] by a conceptual consciousness (*gzugs gzugs 'dzin rtog pas zhen pa'i sgo nas 'dzin stangs gyi yul du byas pa*). However, a form's being a referent of a conceptual consciousness [means] that a form appears to a sense consciousness as a basis for the affixing of names and terminology from the side of its [that is, the form's] own mode of abiding, without depending on the association of conventions by terms and conceptuality, whereupon a subsequent conceptual consciousness also adheres to such an appearance and takes it to be a basis of conceiving—with regard to the form—"This is a form." (*dbang shes la gzugs sogs ming brda 'jug pa'i gzhir sgra rtog gis tha snyad sbyar ba la ma ltos par rang gi sdod lugs kyi ngos nas song bar snang zhing rjes kyi rtog pas kyang snang ba de ltar du zhen nas gzugs la 'di gzugs so zhes zhen pa'i gzhir byed pa*)

As Jik-may-dam-chö-gya-tso (*Port of Entry,* 550.4, 555.2-555.3) proceeds to point out, neither a form's being a conceived object of a conceptual consciousness nor a form's being a referent object of a conceptual consciousness is established by way of their own character but the way each is not so established differs greatly:

> These are called imputational natures because they are only factors imputed by names and terminology[a] and do not exist there by way of their own character as they are imputed to so exist.

A non-existent imputational nature of a body, for instance, is that it is established by way of its own character as an object expressed by words for entities and attributes and as the referent of thoughts about entities and attributes. This imputational nature is closely related with the other imputational nature, being a separate entity from the consciousness apprehending it.[b]

Those are non-existent imputational natures. An existent imputational nature of the table is its being a referent of a term or conceptual consciousness, without the qualification that it is **established by way of its own character** this way. Thus, there are two types of imputational natures—existent and non-existent.

Thoroughly established nature. For instance, the emptiness of a tree's or a body's establishment by way of its own character as the referent of a conceptual consciousness or of a term and the emptiness of its being a separate entity from the consciousness apprehending it is a thoroughly established nature,[c] the third of the three natures. As Jang-ğya says:[34]

> The reason why such is called a thoroughly established nature is that (1) it is an object of observation by a path of purification, (2) it does not change into something else, and (3) it is the supreme of all virtuous phenomena.

A path of purification must observe something the realization of which will remove obstructions dependent on unfounded misperceptions. Hence, such an object—emptiness—is thoroughly established. It is permanent in that it does not change moment by moment. Also, a wisdom consciousness that realizes it is the supreme of all virtuous phenomena, due to which the thoroughly established nature is **called** the supreme virtue, even though it is not an actual virtue.

> Since a form **is** a conceived object of a conceptual consciousness, a form's being the conceived object of a conceptual consciousness exists, and since the factor of its being the conceived object of a conceptual consciousness is only posited by conceptuality, this factor is posited as not established by way of its own character. The meaning of form's not being established by way of its own character as a referent of a conceptual consciousness is that:
>
> - A form is a referent of a conceptual consciousness not through the force of its own thingness but in dependence upon the association of conventions by way of term and conceptuality.

[a] "Terminology" here is taken as referring to conceptuality in order to avoid redundancy with "names."

[b] The topic of the relationship between the two types of non-existent imputational natures and their respective emptinesses is treated at length in Part 5, 393ff.

[c] *yongs su grub pa'i ngo bo nyid, pariniṣpannasvabhāva.*

The three-nature theory is used in two ways. The prime mode is, as explained above, its application as three aspects, so to speak, of each and every phenomenon—the object itself is an other-powered nature that is the basis of the false imagination of the imputational nature and is the basis of thoroughly established nature, the emptiness of that imputational nature. In this way the three natures can be applied to each and every phenomenon.

The other use of the three-nature theory is to categorize the entire range of phenomena into three separate groups. As Ḡön-chok-jik-may-w̄ang-b̄o says:[35]

> The Proponents of Mind-Only assert that all objects of knowledge are included in the three natures. This is so because they assert (1) that all compounded phenomena are other-powered natures, (2) that the real natures of all phenomena [emptinesses] are thoroughly established natures, and (3) that all other objects of knowledge are imputational natures.

Indian, Chinese, and Tibetan scholars have devoted considerable attention to the usage of the three natures in this secondary way as a rubric to categorize all phenomena, since there are intriguing problems with the schema when it is set alongside the primary application of the three natures as a rubric that can be applied to each phenomenon. The seventh-century Chinese scholar Hsüan-tsang, after traveling to India, made use of ten Indian commentaries on Vasubandhu's *Thirty Stanzas on the Establishment of Cognition-Only* in his own commentary, the *Ch'eng wei-shih lun.* In that composition, he devotes a short section to just this type of problem; thus, we can understand that, at the latest, in seventh-century India the conundrum that still occupies Tibetan scholars had begun. Hsüan-tsang,[36] reflecting the Indian tendency to view one topic in many lights, takes a multiple approach, whereas Ge-luk-b̄a scholars look for the single category in which a permanent phenomenon such as uncompounded space can be assigned, whether elegantly or inelegantly. They decide that it is an existent imputational nature, since, lacking production, it cannot be an other-powered nature and it obviously is not a thoroughly established nature. However, it is difficult to work out how the prime usage of the theory applies to uncompounded space—namely, if the three natures can be applied to each and every phenomenon, what is the other-powered nature of uncompounded space? We will return to this briefly later (see p. 182).[a]

Objects: Two Truths

The format of the two truths—conventional and ultimate—also has a liberative directionality. As a definition of a conventional truth[b] J̄ang-ḡya gives:[37]

---

[a] See the index entries under "uncompounded space"; see also *Absorption,* #139-143.

[b] *kun rdzob bden pa, saṃvṛtisatya.*

a conventional phenomenon that, upon observation, is suitable to generate afflictive emotions.[a]

This definition is built around the opposite of the first reason why an emptiness is called a thoroughly established nature—"it is an object of observation by a path of purification." Rather than removing obstructions through observing them, conventional truths, for the most part, increase defilements and obstructions. In the all-inclusive division of existents into the two truths, these are all objects except emptinesses.

Conventional truths are existents other than the final reality of phenomena; they appear in a deceptive aspect with a false status, assent to which induces suffering. This perspective also is evident in equivalents of conventional truth—falsity,[b] deceptive phenomenon,[c] and that whose mode of appearance and mode of abiding are discordant.[d] Conventional truths appear to be separate entities from the consciousnesses perceiving them and appear to be established by way of their own character as the referents of their respective conceptual consciousnesses and terms, whereas they are not. There is a conflict between how they appear and how they are. This disparity is a central message of both the three natures and the two truths.

There are two types of conventional truths—other-powered natures and existent imputational natures. Non-existent imputational natures are not included in the two truths simply because they do not exist, and existents are what are divided into the two truths.

Conversely, the definition of an ultimate truth[e] is:[38]

a phenomenon that is a final object of observation purifying obstructions through taking it as an object of apprehension and meditating on it.

Equivalents of ultimate truth are:[39]

- thusness,[f] so called because whether Buddhas arise or not it permanently abides thus without changing

---

[a] Perhaps due to the objection that pure conventional truths, such as non-conceptual wisdom of meditative equipoise, are not objects of observation suitable to produce afflictive emotions, Jang-ḡya (*Presentation of Tenets,* 174.8) gives another, more carefully worded definition of a conventional truth: a phenomenon that is not a final object of observation purifying obstructions through taking it as an object of apprehension and meditating on it.

[b] *brdzun pa, mṛṣā.*

[c] *bslu ba'i chos.*

[d] *snang tshul gnas tshul mi mthun pa.*

[e] *don dam bden pa, paramārthasatya.*

[f] *de bzhin nyid, tathatā.*

- limit of correctness (or limit of reality),[a] so called because of not being perverse
- signlessness,[b] so called because in it the signs of the proliferations of duality are ceased
- ultimate object,[c] so called because it is the object of the activity of Superiors' exalted wisdom of meditative equipoise
- element of attributes,[d] so called because of being that through meditation on which the attributes of a Superior[e] are generated.

The ultimate is reliable due to its unchangeability; it is non-deceptively good in that paying attention to it both removes obstructions and generates marvelous qualities. The doctrine of the two truths, built on that of the three natures, calls practitioners away from the ensnaring allurements of most phenomena and toward correction of basic error.

From among the three natures, other-powered natures and existent imputational natures are conventional truths, and thoroughly established natures are ultimate truths. Thus the rubric of three natures is not more expansive than that of the two truths; nevertheless, through the category of non-existent imputational natures it explicitly calls attention to the misconceived status that is superimposed on phenomena, thereby leading to suffering and limitation of knowledge.

---

a *yang dag mtha', bhūtakoṭi.*

b *mtshan ma med pa, animitta.*

c *don dam, paramārtha.*

d *chos dbyings, dharmadhātu.*

e *'phags pa, āryan;* someone who has cognized emptiness directly and thus has risen above the state of a common being.

4. Transformation

In a presentation of tenets, the exposition of objects within the section on the basis provides the context in which spiritual paths effect transformation into the liberations that are the fruits of those practices. Persons mainly enact these practices through mental adjustment, and thus before presenting the paths and fruits, presentations of persons, consciousnesses, and terms are given under the heading of object-possessors, since persons possess objects, consciousnesses are aware of objects, and terms express objects.

Object-Possessors

Persons

One might wonder why there is a section on persons if Buddhist schools advocate a view of selflessness. In Ge-luk-ba delineations of the schools of Buddhist India, the term "self" in "selflessness" refers not to persons but to an over-reified status of phenomena, be these persons or other phenomena. Consequently, even though it is said that in general "self,"[a] "person,"[b] and "I"[c] are equivalent, in the particular context of the selflessness of persons "self" and "person" are not at all equivalent and do not at all have the same meaning. In the term "selflessness of persons," "self" refers to a falsely imagined status that needs to be refuted, whereas "persons" refers to existent beings who are the bases with respect to which that refutation is made. All four Buddhist schools, therefore, hold that persons exist; they do not claim that persons are mere fictions of ignorance.

The schools hold differing opinions on the nature of the person. According to Ge-luk-ba scholars, all except the Middle Way Consequence School posit something from within the bases of imputation of a person—usually either mind or the collection of mind and body—as being the person. In contrast, the Consequence School holds that, even though a person is imputed in dependence upon mind and body,[d] the person *is* neither mind nor body nor a collection of mind and body, since it is just the I that is imputed in dependence upon mind and body. Following the lead of Chandrakīrti, recognized by most as the founder of the Consequence School, Ge-luk-ba scholars identify how in the other schools some factor among the five aggregates (forms, feelings, discriminations, compositional factors, and consciousnesses) is considered to be the person when sought analytically from among its bases of imputation. According

---

a *bdag, ātman.*

b *gang zag, pudgala.*

c *nga, ahaṃ.*

d In the Formless Realm, a person is imputed in dependence only on mind.

to Ḡön-chok-jik-may-w̄ang-b̄o's *Precious Garland of Tenets:*

- The Proponents of the Great Exposition, in general, hold that the mere collection of the mental and physical aggregates is the person.
- Some of the five Saṃmitīya Sub-schools of the Great Exposition School maintain that all five aggregates are the person (although the absurdity of one person being five persons would seem difficult not to notice).
- Another Sub-school, the Avantaka, asserts that the mind alone is the person.
- In the Sūtra School, the Followers of Scripture assert that the continuum of the aggregates is the person.
- The Sūtra School Following Reasoning maintains that the mental consciousness is the person.
- The Mind-Only School Following Scripture holds that the mind-basis-of-all[a] is the person.
- The Mind-Only School Following Reasoning asserts that the mental consciousness is the person.
- Both the Yogic Autonomy School and the Sūtra Autonomy School assert that a subtle, neutral mental consciousness is the person.

For the most part, the delineation of what these schools assert to be the person is a matter of conjecture and not reporting of forthright statements in these schools' own texts. Though it is clear that most of these schools (if not all) accept that persons exist, it is often not clear in their own literature that they assert that something from within the bases of imputation of a person is the person. Rather, as presented in Vasubandhu's commentary on the ninth chapter of his *Treasury of Manifest Knowledge,*[40] persons are merely asserted to be non-associated compositional factors[b] and thus an instance of the fourth aggregate, compositional factors, without a specific identification—of any of the five aggregates that are a person's bases of imputation—as the person.

Also, it is safe to say that there is not a single line in Indian Mind-Only literature explicitly asserting that the mind-basis-of-all is the person. Rather, such a notion is deduced from the fact that the Mind-Only School Following Scripture (that is to say, the followers of Asaṅga) asserts that the mind-basis-of-all travels from lifetime to lifetime carrying with it the karmic predispositions established by earlier actions. However, Bhāvaviveka, the founder of the Autonomy School, openly asserts that the mental consciousness is the person, when, in response to a challenge, he says that, if the opponent is attempting to

a *kun gzhi rnam par shes pa, ālayavijñāna. Laya* means "basis"; it is derived from the Sanskrit verbal root *li,* which means "providing support or basis." *A* is taken as meaning "all." *Vijñāna* means "consciousness." The verbal root *jña* means "know"; *-na* is an ending that means "way" or "means"—the means of understanding; *vi-* means "individually" or "in detail." The term is often translated as "storehouse consciousness."

b *viprayuktasaṃskāra, ldan min 'du byed.*

establish for him that consciousness (that is, the mental consciousness) is the person, the opponent is proving what is already established for him,[41] but aside from this one scant line there seems to be no other evidence in his writings. In sum, the Ge-luk-b̄a emphasis on identifying, for each of these schools, what, from among the five aggregates, is the person comes from their acceptance of Chandrakīrti's claim to a ***unique*** assertion that nothing from among them is the person.

Consciousnesses

The Mind-Only School Following Scripture is renowned for its assertion of eight consciousnesses—two more than the usual six:

1. Eye consciousness, apprehending colors and shapes
2. Ear consciousness, apprehending sounds
3. Nose consciousness, apprehending odors
4. Tongue consciousness, apprehending tastes
5. Body consciousness, apprehending tangible objects
6. Mental consciousness, apprehending the five sense objects and other phenomena
7. Afflicted intellect,[a] mistakenly conceiving that the I substantially exists
8. Mind-basis-of-all, serving as a repository for all seeds of perception.

The afflicted intellect mistakenly conceives the mind-basis-of-all to be a self-sufficient person. Hence, it is responsible for the misconception of a self of persons, whereas the mental consciousness is responsible for the deeper misconceptions that subject and object are different entities and that objects are established by way of their own character as the referents of their respective conceptual consciousnesses and verbalizing terms.

Every sentient being has a mind-basis-of-all (or a partially purified continuation of it called a fruitional consciousness)[b] the primary function of which is to serve as the basis connecting karmic cause and karmic effect. The mind-basis-of-all persists even through states in which consciousness is seemingly absent, such as deep sleep and meditative states of cessation, and thus can serve as

[a] *nyon mongs can gyi yid, kliṣṭamanas.* For an extensive exposition of D̄zong-ka-b̄a's presentation of the afflicted intellect, see Gareth Sparham, *Ocean of Eloquence: Tsong kha pa's Commentary on the Yogācāra Doctrine of Mind* (Albany, N.Y.: State University of New York Press, 1993), 107-121, 143-151.

[b] *rnam smin rnam shes, vipakavijñāna.* For extensive expositions of D̄zong-ka-b̄a's presentation of the mind-basis-of-all, see Sparham, *Ocean of Eloquence,* 51-105, 124-142; and Joe B. Wilson, *The Meaning of Mind in the Mahāyāna Buddhist Philosophy of Mind-Only (Cittamātra): A Study of a Presentation by the Tibetan Scholar Gung-tang Jam-b̄ay-ȳang (gung-thang-'jam-pa'i-dbyangs) of Asaṅga's Theory of Mind-Basis-of-All (ālayavijñāna) and Related Topics in Buddhist Theories of Personal Continuity, Epistemology, and Hermeneutics* (Ann Arbor, Mich.: University Microfilms, 1984).

an enduring basis for the infusion, maintenance, and fruition of seeds established by actions.

The mind-basis-of-all is described from four viewpoints:

- Its **entity** is non-defiled and neutral. Due to not being accompanied by afflictive mental factors such as desire, hatred, ignorance, and jealousy, it is non-defiled. It receives infusion of seeds by both virtuous and non-virtuous actions, and thus it must be neutral, that is, neither virtuous nor non-virtuous.

- Being a consciousness, it must have **objects of observation**, which are the five senses and the objects of the senses. Also, even though the seeds, or latent predispositions, are not actually its objects of observation, they are *called* such because they produce appearances of objects and consciousnesses perceiving them.

- Even though a mind-basis-of-all is a consciousness with objects of observation, its **aspect** is constituted by the fact that it does not notice its objects, nor can it draw another consciousness into noticing them.

- Being a consciousness, it must be accompanied by mental factors called **concomitants**, which are the five omnipresent factors—feeling,[a] discrimination,[b] intention,[c] mental engagement,[d] and contact.[e] The feeling that accompanies the mind-basis-of-all is only neutral (that is, neither pleasure nor pain). Also, since a mind-basis-of-all does not notice its objects, discrimination in this case is merely a non-confusion of its objects. Similarly, the intention that accompanies a mind-basis-of-all is merely the movement of the mind to its object and thus is more like attention, although it is non-retentive attention.

The primary function of the mind-basis-of-all is to serve as a repository of seeds, or predispositions, including those that simultaneously produce an apprehending-subject and an apprehended-object, thereby accounting for the appearance of objects without external phenomena impinging on consciousness. It also is the substratum for naturally inhering potencies for liberation (see below, p. 58).

A principal focus of the tenets concerning consciousness is to identify the different types of minds in terms of misapprehension and correct apprehension. In the Ge-luk-b̄a system of education, this phase is usually associated with study of the Sūtra School Following Reasoning, but J̄ang-ḡya puts this section in the

---

[a] *tshor ba, vedanā.*

[b] *'du shes, saṃjñā.*

[c] *sems pa, cetanā.*

[d] *yid la byed pa, manaskāra.*

[e] *reg pa, sparśa.*

Mind-Only School, most likely because its origins are found in Dharmakīrti's *Commentary on (Dignāga's) "Compilation of Prime Cognition,"* the basic system of which is said to be the Mind-Only School Following Reasoning and because J̄ang-ḡya began composition of his *Presentations of Tenets* with the Mind-Only chapter. The purpose of this phase of study is to provide a psychological structure for therapeutic paths that cause a practitioner to proceed gradually from misconceived notions about the nature of persons and other phenomena—that induce suffering—to states of mind that can counteract innate misconceptions. The liberative directionality of the enterprise informs the course of the discussion, the main interests being to distinguish correctly perceiving from improperly perceiving consciousnesses and to identify the difference between conceptual and non-conceptual consciousnesses. The latter, when they realize the thoroughly established nature, are sufficiently powerful so that they can overcome obstructions to liberation from cyclic existence and from obstructions to the omniscience of full enlightenment.

There are seven stages in the process. First the person has unwavering conviction that other-powered natures are established by way of their own character as the referents of their respective conceptual consciousnesses and that subject and object are different entities; this stage is called **wrong consciousness**[a]—one is overwhelmed with adherence to the imputational nature. Then, through hearing about the thoroughly established nature—the ultimate truth, emptiness—adherence to the imputational nature weakens a little, and the person merely suspects that other-powered natures are established in accordance with the imputational nature; this stage is called **doubt not tending toward the fact.**[b] Reflection turns this state into doubt tending toward both what is and what is not the fact, the suspicion that other-powered natures both are and are not established in accordance with the imputational nature; this is called **equal doubt.**[c] Then, study turns this state into **doubt tending toward the fact**;[d] the practitioner suspects that other-powered natures are not established by way of their own character as the referents of their respective conceptual consciousnesses and that subject and object are not different entities.

Further hearing, study, and meditation on the thoroughly established nature brings the person to a conceptual understanding of emptiness that can be generated through the processes of inference but is not yet inference because it is not incontrovertible. This level is called **correctly assuming consciousness**[e]

---

a *log shes, viparyayajña.* Defined as "a cognition that is mistaken with regard to its object of engagement." The definitions are drawn from Lati Rinbochay and Elizabeth Napper, *Mind in Tibetan Buddhism* (London: Rider, 1980; Ithaca, N.Y.: Snow Lion, 1980).

b *don mi gyur gyi the tshom.* Doubt is defined as "a cognition that by its own power has qualms in two directions."

c *cha mnyam pa'i the tshom.*

d *don gyur gyi the tshom.*

e *yid dpyod, *manaḥparīkṣā.* This is defined as "a cognition which, although it adheres

and can (1) be unreasoned, (2) be based on a bogus reason, or (3) have a correct reason that has not been ascertained. Then, through penetrating a correct reason proving the thoroughly established nature, the practitioner gains a conceptual incontrovertible realization that other-powered natures are not established by way of their own character as the referents of their respective conceptual consciousnesses or that subject and object are not different entities. This level is called **inference.**[a] An image or concept of the non-affirming negative that is an other-powered nature's mere absence of establishment in accordance with the imputational nature appears to the practitioner, and the thoroughly established nature is incontrovertibly ascertained. Thus, the "appearing object"[b] of an inference is a conceptual image, or "meaning-generality,"[c] of the thoroughly established nature, whereas the conceived object,[d] or object of engagement,[e] is the thoroughly established nature itself. Hence, although the realization is "conceptual," this does not mean that the mind is discursively going over the reasoning—the state is the result of successful reasoning, a full-fledged explicit realization of the thoroughly established nature, emptiness.

Then, through a meditative process to be described below (p. 55ff.), conceptual understanding turns into **direct perception**[f] of the thoroughly established nature. Even the image of emptiness disappears; the subject (the wisdom consciousness) and the object (the emptiness of duality) are like water put in water, undifferentiable. Ge-luk-b̄a scholars maintain that, in fact, the wisdom consciousness is not the thoroughly established nature, and vice versa, but their difference is not noticed in this special state. In order to preserve the dictum that all consciousnesses are impermanent and that emptiness is permanent, they make the distinction that the thoroughly established nature is realized in a non-dual manner but it is not being realized that the thoroughly established nature is wisdom or that wisdom is the thoroughly established nature. Other systems in both Tibet and China prefer to speak of reality as both emptiness and wisdom. For Ge-luk-b̄a scholars, the wisdom consciousness is a pure other-powered nature that is **called** a non-perverse thoroughly established nature but is not an actual thoroughly established nature. As Ḡön-chok-jik-may-w̄ang-b̄o says:[42]

one-pointedly to the phenomenon that is its principal object of engagement, does not get at an object with respect to which superimpositions have been eliminated."

a *rjes dpag, anumāna.* Defined as "a determinative cognition that, depending upon its basis, a correct sign (that is, reason), is incontrovertible with regard to its object of comprehension, a hidden phenomenon."

b *snang yul, *pratibhāsaviṣaya.*

c *don spyi, arthasāmānya.*

d *zhen yul.*

e *'jug yul, pravṛttiviṣaya.*

f *mngon sum, pratyakṣa.*

> Although non-perverse thoroughly established natures [such as a Superior's wisdom of meditative equipoise directly realizing emptiness] are stated as a division of thoroughly established natures, they [actually] are not thoroughly established natures. This is because they are not final objects of observation by a path of purification through observation of which obstructions are extinguished.

That which purifies obstructions when it is taken as an object of meditation is just a non-affirming negative—the absence of the establishment of other-powered natures in accordance with the imputational nature.

Once direct perception of the truth is attained, a practitioner must re-enter this state again and again (see p. 55ff.). The concern here is with mapping out possible progress from error, which induces suffering, to incontrovertible cognition, which undermines misperception.

Terms

The word loosely translated here as "term"[a] literally means "sound." Assertions on sounds assume considerable importance in Buddhist tenet systems, since they provide an avenue for discounting non-Buddhist assertions that the sounds of the Vedas are eternally authoritative. Buddhist systems emphasize that sounds do not of their accord express their meanings but are arbitrary conventions. (Nevertheless, in seeming contradiction, Buddhists praise Sanskrit as more fundamental, since it is the language of the gods; also, the Mantra, or Tantra, systems use Sanskrit syllables and phrases as if the sounds themselves commanded their meanings.[b])

In addition to the general Buddhist assertion that terms are arbitrary, the Sūtra School Following Reasoning, based on Dharmakīrti's *Commentary on (Dignāga's) "Compilation of Prime Cognition,"* asserts that the explicit object of verbalization by a term is not the object itself but a "meaning-generality"[c] of the object. In addition to this, the Mind-Only School asserts that objects are not established by way of their own character as the referents of their respective conceptual consciousnesses and terms. Thus, the topic of terms and in what fashion they express objects comes to be crucial to the Mind-Only School's assertions on the thoroughly established nature and hence is of liberative concern.

In order to draw students into the topic of terminology and communication, presentations of tenets divide sounds in general into two types, those arisen from elements conjoined with consciousness such as the voice of a sentient being and those arisen from elements not conjoined with consciousness

---

a *sgra, śabda.*

b To counter this, Gung-tang offers the opinion that in Buddhism the meanings of mantras must be contemplated as the sounds are repeated.

c Roughly speaking, this is a generic image.

such as the sound of a river. Both of these are divided into sounds that intentionally do and do not indicate meaning to sentient beings. It is easy to understand that:

- the spoken expression "house" is a sound arisen from elements conjoined with consciousness that intentionally indicates meaning
- the sound of a spontaneous hiccup is a sound arisen from elements conjoined with consciousness that does not intentionally indicate meaning
- the sound of an ordinary running brook is a sound arisen from elements not conjoined with consciousness that does not intentionally indicate meaning.

More unusual is the assertion that there are sounds that are arisen from elements not conjoined with consciousness but intentionally indicate meaning; a frequently cited instance is the sound of the great drum in the Heaven of the Thirty-Three that itself conveys the messages of impermanence and so forth. Another instance is the words of doctrine taught by trees rustled by a Buddha's extraordinary powers.

Paths

Having drawn a general outline of objects and subjects—the basis—a presentation of tenets describes the spiritual paths that are based on the three natures and two truths and are implemented in order to remove defilements. The clear light nature of the mind makes purification of obstructions possible. As Dharmakīrti's *Commentary on (Dignāga's) "Compilation of Prime Cognition"* says:[a]

> The nature of the mind is clear light.
> The defilements are adventitious.

"Adventitious" here does not mean "uncaused"; it indicates that the defilements do not subsist in the very nature of the mind. Since desire, hatred, and ignorance do not subsist in the entity of the mind, the nature of the mind is clear light, and thus the defilements can be removed without destroying the mind.

The clear light nature of the mind persists in the sense that its continuum exists forever—that is to say, while one is afflicted and while unafflicted. It has no beginning and no end in time. It may seem surprising that a system

---

[a] Chap. II, 208cd:

sems kyi rang bzhin 'od gsal te//
dri ma rnams ni blo bur ba//.

(Varanasi, India: Pleasure of Elegant Sayings, 1974), vol. 17, 63.11. The Sanskrit is:

prabhāsvaramidaṃ cittaṃ prakṛtyāgantatro malāḥ.

See Swami Shastri, *Pramāṇavarttika of Āchārya Dharmakīrtti* (Varanasi, India: Bauddha Bharati, 1968), vol. 3, 73.1.

emphasizing suffering as much as Buddhism does should also have a doctrine of a basic goodness or fundamental purity of the mind, but such a foundation is needed for the radical transformation of the condition of suffering into a state of freedom. The basic error of misapprehending other-powered natures to be established in accordance with the imputational nature can be removed through realizing and becoming used to the thoroughly established nature.

Liberation—whether release from cyclic existence or the great liberation of Buddhahood—is from a state that needs healing and to a new, healed state of release. The Buddha is viewed as like a doctor with the medicine of doctrine for the diseased practitioner. The state of release from suffering and finitude is a time of life without error, without distortion, of markedly increased effectiveness. The distortion from which release is sought is not limited to temporary attitudes of desire and hatred but is systemic, an ingrained misconception contrary to ultimate reality.

The systemic distortion is understood as having two aspects. One is the conception that persons substantially exist in the sense of being self-sufficient. The other, more fundamental one is the appearance—even in raw sensation—of subject and object as different entities as well as conceptual assent to that false appearance, that is to say, agreement with the way the subject and object appear as if distant and cut off. Also included is the appearance of objects as if established by way of their own character as the referents of their respective conceptual consciousnesses and verbalizing terms as well as conceptual assent to this appearance. The first set of defilements are called afflictive obstructions, preventing liberation from cyclic existence, and Hearers and Solitary Realizers (to be discussed below, p. 57) mainly meditate on the selflessness of persons in order to overcome the afflictive obstructions. The second is called obstructions to omniscience, preventing the all-knowing state of Buddhahood. Since Bodhisattvas are primarily motivated to help others, they mainly want to remove the obstructions to omniscience, since they prevent subtle knowledge of others' minds and full knowledge of liberative techniques.

Thus, not just desire and hatred are afflictions or distortions; ignorance is the basic bondage, the basic systemic distortion. From it, and entirely dependent upon it, the other systemic distortions arise, seeming to be in the fabric of life but actually not. The only counteragent is wisdom. Although discussion, dialogue, and argument can be important aspects of gaining wisdom, realization that arises from such is not sufficient; a powerfully concentrated mind is necessary. Gaining a wisdom consciousness that can serve as an actual antidote to the obstructions depends upon developing one-pointed concentration. Then the practitioner alternates such fixed concentration with analytical meditation so that eventually the one, rather than harming the other, serves to induce a greater degree of the other. The achievement of this is called a meditative stabilization that is a union of calm abiding and special insight. Still, this level of spiritual development is not sufficient as long as the understanding is conceptual—that is to say, as long as the thoroughly established nature is seen through the medium of a conceptual image, a meaning-generality. By repeated meditation, the meaning-generality gradually disappears, leaving the wisdom consciousness and the thoroughly established nature that is its object totally non-dual, like fresh water poured into fresh water. The state is non-dualistic in five senses:

1. There is no conceptual appearance.
2. There is no sense of subject and object, which are like fresh water poured into fresh water.
3. There is no appearance of duality.
4. There is no appearance of conventional phenomena; only the thoroughly established nature appears.
5. There is no appearance of difference—although the emptinesses of all phenomena in all world systems appear, they do not appear to be different.[a]

The practitioner re-enters direct perception of emptiness again and again. Much like washing dirty clothing, the grosser levels of dirt are cleansed first, and then gradually the more subtle. In time, all of the afflictive obstructions and obstructions to omniscience are removed.

The wisdom consciousness can counteract the obstructions to omniscience only when it is sufficiently empowered and enhanced through the Bodhisattva practices of the altruistic deeds of giving, ethics, and patience in limitless ways over a limitless period of time, this being at least three periods of countless eons. Attitudes of altruism and the concordant deeds which such motivation induces empower the wisdom consciousness so that it can remove the last traces of the basic systemic distortion of the false appearance of phenomena as if they are established in accordance with the imputational nature.

Types of Paths. In all four schools, paths are presented for Hearers,[b] Solitary Realizers,[c] and Bodhisattvas. It might seem surprising that even the Lesser Vehicle schools—the Great Exposition School and Sūtra Schools—should have paths for Bodhisattvas, since Bodhisattvas are associated primarily with the Great Vehicle. However, a distinction is made between philosophical schools, which are divided into Lesser Vehicle and Great Vehicle, and practitioners of paths, which also are divided into Lesser Vehicle and Great Vehicle. The philosophical schools are divided in this way according to whether they present a selflessness of phenomena (Great Vehicle) or not (Lesser Vehicle). Since the Great Vehicle tenets systems—the Mind-Only and Middle Way Schools—present a selflessness of phenomena in addition to a selflessness of persons, they

[a] The source for the list is Ken-sur Ye-s̄hay-tup-d̄en, late abbot of the L̄o-sel-l̄ing College of Dre-b̄ung Monastic University, presently resettled in Mundgod, Karnataka State, south India. The contents of the list are common knowledge among Ge-luk-b̄a scholars.

[b] *nyan thos, śrāvaka.*

[c] *rang rgyal, pratyekabuddha.*

also speak of "obstructions to omniscience,"[a] these being what prevent simultaneous and direct cognition of all phenomena as well as their final nature. The Lesser Vehicle schools, on the other hand, present Buddhahood as having an omniscience which can *serially* know anything, but not simultaneously.[b]

Even though the Lesser Vehicle schools—the Great Exposition School and Sūtra Schools—do not present a path leading to simultaneous and direct knowledge of all phenomena, they do speak of the path of a Bodhisattva proceeding to Buddhahood when they relate how Shākyamuni Buddha, for instance, became enlightened. Similarly, the Great Vehicle schools—Mind-Only and Middle Way Schools—speak not just about how Bodhisattvas proceed on the path but also about how Hearers and Solitary Realizers, who are Lesser Vehicle practitioners, proceed on the path. In the latter case, the Great Vehicle schools are not reporting how the Lesser Vehicle schools present the path but how the Great Vehicle schools themselves present the path for Hearers and Solitary Realizers whose prime motivation, unlike that of Bodhisattvas, is, for the time being, not the welfare of others but their own liberation from cyclic existence. Therefore, it is said to be possible for someone who is doctrinally a Proponent of Mind-Only to be a Lesser Vehicle practitioner by motivation, in that the person has decided for the time being to pursue his or her own liberation first before becoming primarily dedicated to the welfare of others. Also, it is possible for someone who is, for instance, a Proponent of the Great Exposition to be a Great Vehicle practitioner in terms of motivation, having become dedicated to achieving the enlightenment of a Buddha in order to be of service to all beings.

In the Mind-Only School Following Scripture there are five lineages of practitioners—Hearer, Solitary Realizer, Bodhisattva, the indefinite who switch from one of those three types to another, and those who either temporarily or forever do not have a causal lineage for liberation.[43] The term "lineage"[c] has the sense of a source from which good qualities arise. It is an internal capacity naturally in the mind-basis-of-all, suggested by the fact that even beings who are not presently involved in a spiritual path manifest differing capacities and interests.

Even when such a natural predisposition to spiritual progress is present, it is possible for it not to be manifest due to several types of interference:

---

a *shes sgrib, jñeyāvaraṇa.*

b As is reported in Jam-ȳang-shay-b̄a's *Great Exposition of Tenets* (*kha,* 7b.2), one of the eighteen Sub-schools of the Great Exposition School, the One Convention School (*tha snyad gcig pa, ekavyavahārika*), uses the convention of one instant of a Buddha's wisdom realizing all phenomena. Attempting to explain away this discrepancy to the classificatory scheme, Jam-ȳang-shay-b̄a avers that they employ this convention for a Buddha's one mind realizing all phenomena.

c *rigs, gotra.* Jam-ȳang-shay-b̄a (*Great Exposition of Tenets, nga,* 18b.6) distinguishes between three usages of *rigs* in Tibetan, since it translates three Sanskrit terms: *dhātu, kula,* and *gotra;* here it is the last.

- being without the leisure to practice
- being too attached to objects of desire
- not having the conscientiousness of viewing the faults of afflictive emotions
- having wrong views such as moral nihilism
- having obstructions—these being (1) fruitions of actions in other lifetimes that result in dumbness, stupidity, and so forth; (2) karmic obstructions due to having committed heinous crimes in this lifetime, such as killing one's parents, creating dissent in the spiritual community, and so forth; and (3) having too many afflictive emotions.

Other suppressive influences are to have bad friends, to be destitute, and to be under others' domination.[44]

Conversely, activities and circumstances that can activate this internal capacity are to:

- listen to teachings
- take the teachings to mind properly
- be endowed with inner and outer circumstances that provide the opportunity to practice
- have aspiration for virtuous qualities
- leave the household and take vows
- have the restraint of ethics
- restrain the senses
- know the measure of food (leaving one-third of the stomach empty)
- make an effort not to sleep in the first and third of the three parts of the night
- act within introspection
- stay in an isolated place
- purify obstructions
- dwell in meditative stabilization.[45]

Hearers. Persons show signs of having a particular lineage. The signs that someone is of the Hearer lineage are:

- slight attachment for the body and so forth
- great revulsion for cyclic existence
- avoidance of ill-deeds due to shame, embarrassment, compassion, conscientiousness, and so forth, and having contrition and so forth for ill-deeds that have been committed
- when hearing about and contemplating the forward and reverse processes (how one gets into suffering and how one gets out of suffering) according to the doctrine of the four noble truths, the hairs of the body stand on end and tears well up in the eyes
- assumption of ethics out of wanting protection from fright and out of wishing for good in the future

- taking precepts for the sake of only one's own liberation and not giving them up even for political duties or even if it costs one's life
- dedicating all roots of virtue for the sake of release from cyclic existence.

Hearers, motivated by a wish for their liberation in which all sufferings of cyclic existence are abandoned, train in the three learnings—higher ethics, meditative stabilization, and wisdom. They meditate on the four noble truths, the main path of release being the wisdom realizing the selflessness of persons.

Solitary Realizers. The signs that someone is of the Solitary Realizer lineage are:

- few afflictive emotions and hence disliking commotion and liking to live alone
- low level of compassion and hence little activity of the heart, such as bringing about others' aims through teaching doctrine, and so forth
- great pride and naturally being of middling faculties and hence (1) keeping quiet about having teachers, (2) not having a teacher, and (3) wanting an incomparable form of enlightenment.

These qualities of Solitary Realizers indicate a deep-seated sense of difference from others that leads to living in solitude—the loner.

Etymologically, they are called Solitary Realizers (*pratyekabuddha*) because of becoming buddhafied alone (*eka*), that is to say, they "realize (*buddha*) suchness" without scripture; this is the case with some but not all Solitary Realizers as is explained below. In another way, they realize (*buddha*) conditionality (*prati,* that is, *pratyaya*) through understanding the forward and reverse processes of the twelve links of dependent-arising. (Thus the term "buddha" does not mean that they are Buddhas.)

Those who are definite in the Solitary Realizer lineage are called the Rhinoceros-like,[a] whereas the indefinite are called Congregating.[b] While on the path of preparation, the Rhinoceros-like, for the sake of accumulating unusual collections of merit, please Buddhas for a hundred eons. Then, in their last lifetime, without depending on a teacher, they become skilled in the six topics of scholarship—the aggregates, sense-spheres, constituents, dependent-arising, the suitable and unsuitable, and the four noble truths—and thereby generate the paths of preparation, seeing, meditation, and no more learning in that very lifetime, though not necessarily in one meditative sitting. Like the solitariness of a rhinoceros's horn, in their last lifetime they do not mix with householders, those who have left the household, or other Solitary Realizers. From their long accumulation of merit, they achieve a similitude of a Buddha's physical body having such features as a crown protrusion. The Congregating, as per their name, associate with a teacher but require an extra lifetime to finish the path;

---

a *bse ru lta bu.*

b *tshogs spyod pa.*

they do not necessarily accumulate merit over a hundred eons. Even when Solitary Realizers dwell in villages or towns, they control their bodies and senses tightly, and thus, when they teach those whom they pity, they do so with physical signs and not by speech. Also, they use physical displays of magic to cause the unfaithful to achieve faith.

Like Hearers, both types of Solitary Realizers overcome only the afflictive obstructions preventing liberation from cyclic existence; they do not overcome the obstructions to omniscience. Thus, their scriptures are the same as the Hearers'.

The achievement of liberation from cyclic existence takes a Hearer or Solitary Realizer through five paths. The development of a motivation to achieve liberation for one's own sake marks the beginning of the **path of accumulation**,[a] whereas the other four paths reflect increasing development of wisdom. Specifically, the achievement of a meditative stabilization that is a union of calm abiding and special insight realizing the thoroughly established nature that is the selflessness of persons marks the beginning of the **path of preparation**.[b] The initial direct realization of the selflessness of persons marks the beginning of the **path of seeing**.[c] That same wisdom consciousness when it develops to the point where it can overcome the grossest form of the innate obstructions to liberation from cyclic existence, called the afflictive obstructions,[d] marks the beginning of the **path of meditation**.[e] When the wisdom consciousness has removed the subtlest level of these obstructions, it is called the **path of no more learning**.[f]

Bodhisattvas. The Great Vehicle lineage of Bodhisattvas is superior to the Lesser Vehicle of Hearers and Solitary Realizers because persons endowed with this lineage have very sharp faculties, are involved in helping others, become skilled in all branches of learning, and attain the fruit of the great enlightenment of Buddhahood. The signs that someone has the Great Vehicle lineage are:

- naturally very great compassion
- enthusiasm for the Great Vehicle
- great forbearance in the difficult deeds for gaining the doctrine
- thorough practice of the virtues of the six perfections—giving, ethics, patience, effort, concentration, and wisdom.

The list of qualities communicates that Bodhisattvas have deeper empathy,

---

[a] *tshogs lam, saṃbhāramārga.*

[b] *sbyor lam, prayogamārga.* More literally, this is translated as "path of connection" or "path of linking," since it connects or links to the path of seeing.

[c] *mthong lam, darśanamārga.*

[d] *nyon sgrib, kleśāvaraṇa.*

[e] *sgom lam, bhāvanāmārga.*

[f] *mi slob lam, aśaikṣamārga.*

greater intelligence, and a greater capacity for the hardships of spiritual training.

Advantages of the favored Bodhisattva lineage are that, due to its presence, it is hard to fall into a bad transmigration, and even if one does, one does not experience great pain and is quickly freed. Also, due to it, one is moved by the sufferings of others in bad transmigrations and thus is especially compassionate and makes exertion to assist them in their development.

What distinguishes someone as a Bodhisattva is the engendering of an altruistic intention to become enlightened, which, through training, has become so spontaneous that it is as strong outside of meditation as it is within meditation. It is a mind directed toward enlightenment as a means to bring about others' welfare. As Maitreya's *Ornament for Clear Realization*[a] says, mind generation, that is, this altruistic attitude, is asserted as a wish for complete perfect enlightenment for the sake of others. Jam-ȳang-shay-b̄a formulates a definition of *bodhicitta* (mind of enlightenment, or more freely "mind of altruistic intention to become enlightened") as:[b]

> a main mental consciousness induced by an aspiration for bringing about others' welfare and accompanied by an aspiration to one's own enlightenment.

It is an attitude endowed with two aspirations. The first is an aspiration for others' welfare, and the second is an aspiration for one's own highest enlightenment as a Buddha, the latter being seen as a means for accomplishing the former. Even though one's own enlightenment must be accomplished first in order to bring about others' welfare in the most effective way, service to

---

[a] *mngon rtogs rgyan, abhisamayālaṃkāra,* I.18ab. The Sanskrit is:

> *cittotpādaḥ parārthāya samyaksaṃbodhikāmatā.*

See Th. Stcherbatsky and E. Obermiller, *Abhisamayālaṃkāra-Prajñāpāramitā-Updeśa-Śāstra,* Bibliotheca Buddhica 23 (Osnabrück, Germany: Biblio Verlag, 1970), 4.

[b] Defined more technically within the context of Chandrakīrti's *Supplement to (Nāgārjuna's) "Treatise on the Middle"* (*dbu ma la 'jug pa, madhyamakāvatāra*), an altruistic intention to become enlightened is:

> a main mental consciousness, taking cognizance of others' welfare and [one's own] great enlightenment, that, having the aspect of wanting to attain those, is induced by non-dualistic understanding and great compassion.

In Tibetan:

> *dmigs pa gzhan don dang byang chub chen po la dmigs nas ched du bya ba sems can thams cad kyi don du rnam pa de thob par 'dod pa ngo bo gnyis med kyi blo dang snying rje chen pos drangs pa'i yid kyi rnam shes.*

See Jam-ȳang-s̄hay-b̄a, *Great Exposition of the Middle / Analysis of (Chandrakīrti's) "Supplement to (Nāgārjuna's) 'Treatise on the Middle'": Treasury of Scripture and Reasoning, Thoroughly Illuminating the Profound Meaning [of Emptiness], Entrance for the Fortunate* (*dbu ma chen mo / dbu ma 'jug pa'i mtha' dpyod lung rigs gter mdzod zab don kun gsal skal bzang 'jug ngogs*) (Buxaduor, India: Gomang, 1967), 32b.6.

others—and not one's own enlightenment—is primary in terms of motivation. Enlightenment is seen as a means to bring about others' welfare because a Buddha, being omniscient, knows all possible techniques for advancement and knows the predispositions and interests of other beings.

Some Bodhisattvas' motivation is described as like that of a monarch. They see themselves as first becoming enlightened and then helping others. Other Bodhisattvas' motivation is described as like that of a boatperson; they want to arrive at the freedom of Buddhahood in the company of everyone else just as a boatperson arrives at the other shore with everyone else. Still others' motivation is described as like that of a shepherd; they want to see others safely enlightened before they become enlightened, like a shepherd following the flock home.

It is frequently said that the only realistic mode is the first. Just as the high position of a monarch enables a person to help on a vaster scale, there is no state superior to Buddhahood for accomplishing others' welfare. The descriptions in some sūtras of Bodhisattvas as putting off final enlightenment in order to be of greater service to sentient beings are considered to be exaggerated statements expressing the greatness of their altruistic, shepherd-like motivation. No one, from the viewpoint of this tradition, ever postpones enlightenment; this is simply because one can serve others more effectively with the full enlightenment of Buddhahood.

The achievement of such a state takes a Great Vehicle practitioner through five paths and ten grounds. The development of the altruistic motivation to achieve highest enlightenment marks the beginning of the **path of accumulation.** The achievement of a meditative stabilization that is a union of calm abiding and special insight realizing the thoroughly established nature which is the selflessness of phenomena marks the beginning of the **path of preparation.** The initial direct realization of that thoroughly established nature marks the beginning of the **path of seeing** and the first Bodhisattva ground. That same wisdom consciousness, when it develops to the point where it can overcome the grossest form of innate obstructions both to liberation from cyclic existence and to omniscience, marks the beginning of the **path of meditation**,[a] spanning the second through tenth Bodhisattva grounds. When the wisdom consciousness has removed even the subtlest of both obstructions, it is called the **path of no more learning**, Buddhahood. In this way, the distortions of desire and hatred—as well as the ignorance that is their source—are removed, but love, compassion, faith, and so forth are not thereby extricated. For they do not depend for their existence on ignorance. No matter to what degree love and so forth may at times become involved with ignorance and afflictive emotions such as desire, they have valid cognition as their support and thus are not undermined when systemic distortions are extricated.

Those of indefinite lineage. In this way, there are three lineages of persons

---

[a] *sgom lam, bhāvanāmārga.*

who are definite to be either Hearers, Solitary Realizers, or Bodhisattvas. There is also a lineage of persons whose vehicle is indefinite, that is to say, whose entry into a path depends on outside influences and who, even when they have entered a path, can switch to another due to the influence of a teacher, a friend, and so forth.

Those whose lineage is severed. The Mind-Only School Following Scripture also holds that there are persons who are without a lineage of liberation—this being a temporary condition for some and a basic unalterable condition for others.[a] Although the latter might try to enter the teaching through hearing, thinking, and meditating, such persons are so involved in seeking just the enticing artifacts of cyclic existence that they utterly fail to become discouraged about cyclic existence and cannot generate an attitude of renunciation, great compassion, and so forth. They manifest opposites of the signs of the Hearer lineage and thus have:

---

[a] Shay-rap-gyel-tsen does not accept such a depiction for the followers of Maitreya's *Ornament for the Great Vehicle Sūtras* and so forth; he explains that the reference is only to those whose **developmental lineage** is severed, since there is no one without the naturally abiding lineage of Buddhahood:

> *Objection:* It is established that [Maitreya's *Ornament for the Great Vehicle Sūtras*] is a proprietary text of Mind-Only because it (III.11) speaks of those whose lineage is severed:
>
> Some single-mindedly definitely have bad behavior.
> Some completely destroy white practices.
> Some do have the virtue of concordance with a portion of liberation.
> [Some] are devoid of the causes of having lowly white [virtues].
>
> *Answer:* There is no entailment here either, for there is no one whose naturally abiding lineage is severed, and there are many whose developmental lineage is severed, and, while such is the case in fact, it also is mentioned well in textual systems of the Middle Way—the *Mahāparinirvāṇa Sūtra,* the *Aṅgulimāla Sūtra,* Maitreya's *Sublime Continuum of the Great Vehicle,* and so forth. Moreover, this is to be understood from the fact that, although all sentient beings have the Buddha-matrix, there are many who have not planted seeds of liberation and who have not generated virtues.
>
> That there is no one whose naturally abiding lineage is severed is extensively set forth in this very text [Maitreya's *Ornament for the Great Vehicle Sūtras*]:
>
> Although thusness does not differ in all,
> When it is purified
> They are just Ones Gone Thus.
> Hence all transmigrators have its matrix.
>
> and so forth.

Whereas Dzong-ka-ba sees Maitreya's *Ornament for the Great Vehicle Sūtras* as evincing the view of the Mind-Only School and his *Sublime Continuum of the Great Vehicle* as evincing the view of the Consequence School, Shay-rap-gyel-tsen sees them as harmoniously teaching the Great Middle Way, in which all sentient beings have the Buddha matrix.

- great attachment for the body and so forth
- no revulsion for cyclic existence
- non-avoidance of ill-deeds due to shame, embarrassment, compassion, conscientiousness, and so forth and not feeling contrition and so forth for ill-deeds committed
- when hearing about and contemplating the forward and reverse processes of the four noble truths, the hairs of the body do not stand on end, and tears do not well up in the eyes
- they do not assume ethics even out of wanting protection from fright and out of wishing for good in the future
- they do not take the precepts even for the sake of their own liberation
- they do not dedicate roots of virtue for the sake of release from cyclic existence.

By identifying these qualities with the eternally depraved, the list communicates to practitioners that they must, at all costs, avoid these attitudes—it is a scare tactic.

In this way, according to Ge-luk-b̄a exegesis, the Mind-Only School Following Scripture holds that some beings have no lineage allowing for liberation. Also, they assert that, even among those with the capacity for liberation, some achieve only the path of no more learning of a Hearer or Solitary Realizer and do not attain Buddhahood; others, however, proceed on to Buddhahood. From this perspective, they assert that there are three final vehicles and five lineages—those definite in the three vehicles, those indefinite, and those without a capacity for liberation. That some persons are held to be unalterably doomed to revolving in states of suffering with no chance for liberation and that others are unalterably limited to a lower level of liberation suggests the re-emergence of the Vedic paradigm of outcastes deprived of the privileges of four rigid castes—Brahmins, warriors, merchants, and servants.

The Mind-Only School Following Reasoning, however, argues that everyone eventually achieves Buddhahood. They present the case that even those whose spiritual lineage is temporarily severed eventually achieve highest enlightenment. They hold that:

1. The defilements in the continuum of even those whose lineage is severed can be removed due to the clear light nature of the mind; hence, the defilements are impermanent.
2. Means for abandoning those defilements exist.
3. There are those who know those techniques.
4. Having come to know them, they teach them.
5. When these techniques are taught at an appropriate time such as when persons are bothered by suffering, interest in liberation is generated.

Thereby it is established that even those whose lineage is temporarily severed are able eventually to abandon their defilements. Through this argument the Mind-Only School Following Reasoning establishes that there is only one final vehicle; the other Great Vehicle schools—the Middle Way Autonomy School and the Middle Way Consequence School—hold the same opinion.

Fruits Of The Paths

The three types of paths—Hearer, Solitary Realizer, and Bodhisattva—have different results or fruits. The first two lead to liberation from cyclic existence, whereas the last leads to Buddhahood, a state free both from the obstructions to liberation from cyclic existence and from the obstructions to the omniscience of a Buddha. The most basic systemic distortion impeding full development is removed when altruism and compassionate deeds so enhance wisdom that no trace of assent to the false appearance of the imputational nature or that false appearance itself remains. In this sense, altruism is in the service of wisdom. Also, wisdom is in the service of altruism in that, concordant with Bodhisattvas' fundamental motivation, the full enlightenment gained through this more advanced type of wisdom allows spontaneous altruistic display in forms more numerous than the sands of the Ganges to help sentient beings in accordance with their interests and dispositions. Buddhahood is final in that it is the ultimate path of no more learning—no further development is possible or needed. However, it also is a beginning in the sense that, for the first time, one can serve others to one's full capacity, spontaneously and unceasingly as long as there are beings who need to be helped.

Toward Transformation

Though one of the purposes of such a presentation of tenets undoubtedly is to create a hierarchical structure that puts one's own system at the top with consequent advantages for group cohesion, receipt of donations, and so forth, this genre of religious discourse functions primarily to provide a comprehensive worldview. Its presentations, ranging from the phenomena of the world through to and including the types of enlightenment, give students a framework for study and practice as well as a perspective for relating with other beings. The hierarchical presentation, fortified with reasoned explanation, itself inculcates the basic posture that the power of reason can penetrate the false veils of appearance and lead to perception of a liberative reality. Presentations of tenets are founded on confidence in the mind's ability to overcome tremendous obstacles to the point where love, compassion, and altruism can be expressed in effective, continuous activity, and, therefore, they do more than just structure Indian Buddhist systems; they structure practitioners' perception of their place in a dynamic worldview.

The perspective that emerges is of individuals bound by misconception in a round of suffering and mired in afflictive emotions counterproductive to their own welfare, but also poised on a threshold of transformation. The uncontrolled course of cyclic existence lacks a solid underpinning; it is ready to be transformed into a patterned advance toward liberation. The starkness of the harrowing appraisal of the current situation of multi-layered pain stands in marked contrast to the optimistic view of the salvific development that is possible. Such optimism stems from conviction that the afflictive emotions and obstructions, the causes of misery and finite intelligence, are not endemic to the mind but are peripheral to its nature and thus subject to antidotal influences that can remove them.

This normative vision serves as a powerful force orienting and ordering lives. It stimulates the metaphysical imagination, beckoning, pushing against, and resonating with inner potentials such that persons are drawn into the transformative process. As the context within which six centuries of Tibetan scholars have probed the intricacies of D̄zong-ka-b̄a's *The Essence of Eloquence,* we need to apprehend it with a playful attitude—allowing exploration of this grand perspective without the pressure of commitment. The play does indeed affect and change us, but a playful attitude is markedly different from prejudiced precommitment, built on the premature identification with a tradition sometimes found among new adherents to a religion. Allegiance in the form of exclusivistic adherence often arises through identification with an aggressor and thus evolves out of wanting a power-base to attack others as substitutes for oneself. Commitment to a tradition then becomes self-defeating, since it closes off rather than opens avenues of imaginative exploration for being profoundly affected by the journey.

With a playful attitude, let us turn to D̄zong-ka-b̄a's text.

5. Supernatural Guidance, Exclusivity, and Analytical Investigation

Thrust Of Ḏzong-ka-ḇa's Text

According to Gung-tang,[46] the title of Ḏzong-ka-ḇa's work—*Treatise Differentiating Interpretable and Definitive Meanings: The Essence of Eloquence*—is based on its subject matter. The word "essence" refers to emptiness, and "eloquence" is Buddha's teachings, both Sūtra and Mantra (or Tantra).[a] Their "essence" is emptiness because in order to abandon the obstructions to liberation from cyclic existence and the obstructions to omniscience, it is necessary, as a direct antidote to them, to meditate within taking emptiness as one's object.[b]

A common strategy of interpretation in Tibetan scholarship, which is based on an earlier Indian tradition, is to identify at the beginning of a commentary four factors of a text—the subject matter, the temporary purpose, the essential purpose, and the relationship of these three. As Gung-tang says:

- The **subject matter** of Ḏzong-ka-ḇa's *The Essence of Eloquence* is suchness or emptiness.
- The **temporary purpose** is readers' generation of the wisdom differentiating the meaning of suchness, emptiness.
- Its **final essential purpose** is the attainment of Buddhahood in which, having brought familiarization with the meaning of suchness to completion, one overwhelms all proponents of bad tenets and sets trainees in a state of purification of defilements and release from obstructions.
- The **relationship** between the subject matter of the text and its temporary purpose is that of dependent-arising in that its explanation of the meaning of emptiness (the subject matter) serves as a cause producing realization of emptiness by trainees (the purpose).
- Similarly, the **relationship** between the final essential purpose on the one hand and the subject matter and the purpose on the other may be taken as the factor of realizing that the perfect abandonment of obstructions and realization of selflessness that are attained in Buddhahood arise in dependence upon the explanation of emptiness in this treatise (the subject matter) and realization of such (the purpose).

The relationship among the subject matter, purpose, and essential purpose is, therefore, that of method and what arises from the method, the latter

[a] For more discussion of the title, see *Absorption*, #1-3.

[b] Technically, the object is specified as "object of the mode of apprehension" (*'dzin stangs kyi yul*).

depending on the former. First, the treatise explains suchness; then it must be practiced in the stages of hearing, thinking, and meditation, through which suchness is realized and Buddhahood is eventually attained.

Gung-tang finds sources for his delineation of the four factors at the beginning of Ḏzong-ka-ḇa's work in lines of poetry identified as "the promise of composition" and "the exhortation to listen," just after the obeisances to Buddha, Mañjushrī, and Maitreya as well as to eleven prominent Indian scholars. In his declaration of intent to compose the text, Ḏzong-ka-ḇa speaks of the historical context of his composition, specifically that he considers that he has understood a profound topic that others failed to penetrate. He (*Emptiness in Mind-Only,* 68) says:

> Many who had much hearing of the great texts,
> Who worked with much weariness also at the path of reasoning,
> And who were not low in accumulation of the good qualities of clear realization
> Worked hard at but did not realize this topic[a] which,
>
> Having perceived it well through the kindness of the smooth protector and guru [Mañjushrī],
> I will explain with an attitude of great mercy.
> Listen intently, O you who wish to be unmatched proponents [of doctrine]
> With discriminating analysis realizing the suchness of the teaching.[b]

According to Gung-tang,[47] the **subject matter** is indicated by the "topic" that others had not realized but Ḏzong-ka-ḇa did—the suchness of phenomena, emptiness. The **temporary purpose** is indicated by "Discriminating analysis realizing the suchness of the teaching," this being generation of the wisdom differentiating the meaning of suchness. The **final essential purpose** is indicated by "Unequalled propounders [of doctrine]"—this being the state of Buddhahood in which, having brought familiarization with the meaning of suchness to completion, one overwhelms all proponents of bad tenets and sets trainees in purification and release. The **relationship** of the dependence of each of the latter upon the former is indicated implicitly—the attainment of Buddhahood depends upon generation of the wisdom realizing emptiness, which, in turn, depends upon an explanation of the meaning of emptiness.

Gung-tang[48] explains that the reason for Ḏzong-ka-ḇa's announcing the subject matter and so forth at the beginning of this text is to generate "factually concordant doubt"[c] about emptiness—to cause readers to wonder about emptiness in a proper way, thinking that emptiness *might* be the nature of things—

---

[a] See *Absorption,* #4.

[b] See ibid., #5.

[c] *don 'gyur the tshom.*

whereby, in order to learn more about the topic, they will be led into becoming involved with the text. He points out that it is hard even for such doubt to be generated in those of little merit—those without much virtuous karma acquired through salutary deeds over lifetimes—but that when doubt is generated, it is very beneficial. Even factually concordant doubt, which is the suspicion that emptiness *might* be the mode of subsistence of phenomena (not the suspicion that it probably is not), wreaks havoc with the very seeds of cyclic existence. He cites Āryadeva's *Four Hundred Stanzas on the Yogic Deeds of Bodhisattvas*[a] which says:

> Those of little merit would not even generate
> Mere doubt about this doctrine.
> Even through merely coming to doubt it
> Cyclic existence is torn to tatters.

Through citing this passage on the importance of meritorious karma, Gung-tang communicates the message early in his commentary that penetration of the meaning of emptiness is not confined to philosophy. Rather, defilements of mind must be mitigated by the practice of virtue—which includes generosity, ethics, and patience as well as obeisance, worship, making salutary wishes for development of oneself and others, disclosing ill-deeds, developing an intention not to engage in ill-deeds in the future, asking for the teaching, seeking for it to remain, dedicating the value of one's virtuous practices to all beings, and so forth. A basic theme of the religious culture that he represents is that, even though reasoning is essential to penetrating reality and thereby to undermining the false ideational support of the afflictive emotions that impel cyclic existence, it is not sufficient—many other types of practices are needed in order to prepare the mind and enhance its powers. Reasoning is not a faculty isolated from the rest of the mind but an integral part of mental health, the force of which is determined by the condition of the mind. The liberative directionality of the enterprise is clear—this is not speculative philosophy but a view of reality to be incorporated into one's being for the sake of freeing oneself and others from suffering.

D̄zong-ka-b̄a's explanation of emptiness is intended toward realization, which, in turn, is intended toward attainment of Buddhahood in which service

[a] Stanza 180 (VIII.5). The Tibetan (*sde dge* 3846, 9a.7) is:

bsod nams chung ngu chos 'di la
the tshom za bar yang mi 'gyur
the tshom za ba tsam zhig gis
srid pa hrul por byas par 'gyur//

See Karen Lang, *Āryadeva's Catuḥśataka: On the Bodhisattva's Cultivation of Merit and Knowledge,* Indiste Studier 7 (Copenhagen: Akademisk Forlag, 1986), 81; and *Yogic Deeds of Bodhisattvas: Gyel-tsap on Āryadeva's Four Hundred,* commentary by Geshe Sonam Rinchen, translated and edited by Ruth Sonam (Ithaca, N.Y.: Snow Lion, 1994), 188.

to others is brought to fulfillment. The beginning is an altruistic motivation; the end is altruistic service; the means to accomplish the capacity to do this is the wisdom realizing emptiness. The enlightenment of a Buddha is seen as the means to bring about others' welfare because a Buddha, being omniscient, knows all possible techniques for advancement and knows in detail the predispositions of other beings and thus can match trainees and techniques. As the present Dalai Lama says about the altruistic intention to become enlightened:[49]

> Since Bodhisattvas are seeking to help all sentient beings, they take as their main object of abandonment the obstructions to omniscience and work at the antidote to these obstructions. For, without knowing all, it is possible to help a small number of beings but impossible fully and effectively to help a vast number. This is why it is necessary to achieve Buddhahood in order to be of effective service to sentient beings.

Between the two bodies of a Buddha, Truth Body and Form Body[a] (the latter including the Complete Enjoyment Body and Emanation Bodies), Bodhisattvas primarily seek Form Bodies, since it is through physical form that the welfare of others can be accomplished, this being mainly through teaching what is to be adopted and what is to be discarded in terms of behavior, meditation, and view. Though Truth and Form Bodies necessarily accompany each other and thus are achieved together, Bodhisattvas' emphasis is on achieving Form Bodies in order to appear in myriad forms suitable to the interests and dispositions of trainees and to teach them accordingly. The aspiration to one's own full enlightenment is, therefore, viewed as the means to bring about one's primary aspiration—the accomplishment of altruistic service. In sum, the directionality is toward realization, which, in turn, is directed toward purification, itself directed toward helping others.

The goal is to be of service to others, and to accomplish this it is necessary to purify the mind of the obstructions to liberation from cyclic existence and of the obstructions to omniscience—both of these being accomplished by the wisdom realizing emptiness, the thoroughly established nature. For the wisdom consciousness to destroy the obstructions to omniscience, it must be enhanced by compassion and the deeds motivated by it.

Whether Ḍzong-ka-b̄a intended all of this to be communicated by the title, promise of composition, and exhortation to listen could be questioned. However, at minimum, the exposition of these that his followers have provided reflects the basic cultural context of the corpus of his works as well as those of his followers.

---

[a] *chos sku, dharmakāya; gzugs sku, rūpakāya.*

Divine Guidance

Ḏzong-ka-ḇa begins *The Essence of Eloquence* with a short homage to Mañjushrī and then expressions of worship to Buddha, Mañjushrī, Maitreya, Nāgārjuna, and Asaṅga, as well as to nine other great upholders of the views of the Middle Way and Mind-Only Schools in India. The short homage to Mañjushrī, or Mañjughoṣha, is given in Sanskrit:[50]

Namo gurumañjughoṣāya (Homage to guru Mañjughoṣha).

Namo means homage or obeisance, which is an antidote to pride and is performed by way of body, speech, and mind.[51] *Guru* means "heavy"[a] and in this context refers to the mental continuum weighty with the good qualities of scripture and realization.[b] In the name "Mañjughoṣha,"[52] *mañju* means "smooth" in the sense that the mental continuum of this deity, who is the physical manifestation of the wisdom of all Buddhas, is devoid of the roughness of obstructions to liberation from cyclic existence and the obstructions to omniscience.[53] Also, *ghoṣha* means "melodious," here taken as indicating that this deity of wisdom possesses the sixty branches, or qualities, of the melodious speech of a Buddha. In another interpretation, the softness indicated by the first part of his name is taken as referring to his melodious speech itself, and in still another interpretation his melodious speech softens the continuums of trainees.[54]

As Jay-ḏzün Chö-ḡyi-gyel-tsen[55] and Gung-tang[56] say, the initial homage to Mañjughoṣha is similar to a translator's homage in that translators of scriptures from Sanskrit to Tibetan were instructed to use different homages in order to indicate to which of the three scriptural collections a particular text belongs. Since Ḏzong-ka-ḇa's treatise delineates the suchness of phenomena within differentiating what is interpretable and what is definitive in accordance with the respective systems of the Mind-Only School and the Middle Way School, it is included within the scriptural collection[c] of ultimate Manifest Knowledge[d] of the Great Vehicle. Ken-sur Nga-w̄ang-lek-den,[57] abbot of the Tantric College of Lower Hla-s̄a during the 1950s, reported that, if a text belonged to the scriptural collection of discipline—the training in ethics being the principal topic—homage was paid to the Omniscient One, Buddha himself, the connection being that only an omniscient being knows the subtle relations of actions and their effects, and thus, while alive, only he settled issues of ethics. (The tradition reports that Buddha suggested that, after his death, his followers, upon encountering new situations, should make inferences of what to do based on similar situations among those for which he had already given his opinion.) If the text

[a] See David White, "Why Gurus Are Heavy," *Numen* 33 (1984):40-73.

[b] *rgyud lung rtogs kyi yon tan gyis lci ba;* Jik-may-dam-chö-gya-tso's *Port of Entry,* 17.6.

[c] *sde snod, piṭaka.*

[d] *don dam pa'i chos mngon pa, paramārthābhidharma.*

belonged to the scriptural collection of sets of discourses—the training in meditative stabilization being the principal topic—homage was paid to Buddhas and Bodhisattvas, the connection being that these texts mainly set forth the deeds of Buddhas and Bodhisattvas as well as the stages of yoga to be practiced. If the text belonged to the scriptural collection of Manifest Knowledge—the training in wisdom being the principal topic—homage was paid to Mañjushrī who is the god of wisdom, because the wisdom differentiating the specific and general characteristics of phenomena depends upon him. In this case, D̄zong-ka-b̄a pays homage to Mañjushrī partly in order to indicate that his text is included within the scriptures on ultimate Manifest Knowledge in the Great Vehicle.

As Jay-d̄zün Chö-ḡyi-gyel-tsen[58] and Gung-tang add,[59] even more so, D̄zong-ka-b̄a's obeisance to Mañjushrī is to express worship by way of being mindful of the kindness of his special deity, who also was his lama—the uncommon tutor in dependence upon whom he comprehended this good path, that is to say, realized how to differentiate between what requires interpretation and what is definitive. D̄zong-ka-b̄a mentions this relationship with Mañjushrī in the "promise of composition," immediately following the homages, when in speaking about the difficulty of realizing emptiness, he says that he "perceived it well through the kindness of the smooth protector and guru [Mañjushrī]." D̄zong-ka-b̄a wants his readers to understand that he received divine guidance in his quest for understanding emptiness. He is making a claim for the elevated quality of his text.[a]

In most of D̄zong-ka-b̄a's works there are similar expressions of worship to Mañjushrī, irrespective of whether the topic is included within the category of Manifest Knowledge. In the obeisance to his *Great Exposition of Secret Mantra,* which was written before *The Essence,* he is more explicit about his reliance on Mañjushrī:[60]

> O Mañjughoṣha, sole father of all the Conquerors,
> You are a treasure of wisdom such that having heard
> That you bestow the superior gift of discrimination with a glance
> Of pleasure, granting realisation of the profound thought of the Conquerors,
> I have relied on you continually for a long time
> As my special god and will not forsake your lotus feet.
> For me there is never another refuge.

[a] To undermine this claim of divine guidance, Go-ram-b̄a S̄ö-nam-s̄eng-ge refers in his *Discrimination of Views* (*lta ba'i shan byed theg mchog gnad kyi 'od zer, Sa skya pa'i bka 'bum,* vol. 13, *sde dge* ed., compiled by Bsod nams rgya mtsho [Tokyo: Tokyo Bunko, 1969], 18.3.4), which was finished in 1478, not to D̄zong-ka-b̄a's tutelary deity but to his "tutelary demon" (*bdud yi dam*). See Leonard W. J. van der Kuijp, "Apropos of a Recent Contribution to the History of Central Way Philosophy in Tibet: *Tsong Khapa's Speech of Gold,*" *Berliner Indologische Studien* 1 (1985):71-72 n. 17.

> O Mañjughoṣha, grant the fruit of my wishes.

The present Dalai Lama's commentary on these stanzas brings them to life:[61]

> Then Ḏzong-ka-ḇa takes Mañjushrī, who is the mother, father, and son of all Conquerors, as a special object of worship. He is the mother of all Conquerors in that he is the essence of all wisdoms; the father of all Conquerors in that he takes the form of spiritual guides and causes beings to generate an altruistic aspiration to highest enlightenment; and the son of all Conquerors in that he assumes the form of Bodhisattvas as he did within Shākyamuni Buddha's retinue.
>
> When a trainee pleases him, Mañjushrī can, with merely a glance, bestow the wisdom discriminating the truth in the sense of quickly increasing realisation, like lighting a flame. Ḏzong-ka-ḇa says that having heard such a marvellous account, he has relied on Mañjushrī as his special deity over a long time and will not forsake him in the future, there not being another refuge for him. Ḏzong-ka-ḇa pays homage to Mañjushrī as a treasure of wisdom, arousing his compassion through praise and asking him to bestow the fruition of his wishes.

According to Ḏzong-ka-ḇa's biography, he first made contact with Mañjushrī through one of his teachers, the lama U-ma-ḇa Ḇa-wo-dor-jay,[a] who met manifestly with Mañjushrī and thus could act as a mediator for Ḏzong-ka-ḇa, who at that time could not meet with the deity directly. Later, Ḏzong-ka-ḇa actually met with Mañjushrī and, from that time on, could consult with his divine teacher whenever he wished. It is clear that "meeting with Mañjushrī" is not taken figuratively. As the Dalai Lama says:[62]

> Because Mañjushrī is the natural form of the wisdom of all Conquerors, one relies on him as one's special deity in order to increase the wisdom discriminating the truth. Discriminating wisdom thereby increases as it otherwise would not. Ḏzong-ka-ḇa and Mañjushrī met directly like two people. Originally, Ḏzong-ka-ḇa meditated at Ga-wa-dong (*dga' ba gdong*) in central Tibet in order to achieve a meeting with Mañjushrī. At Ga-wa-dong there was a Kam-ḇa (*khams pa*) lama named Ū-ma-ḇa Ḇa-wo-dor-jay (*dbu ma pa dpa' bo rdo rje*) who had been under Mañjushrī's care for many lifetimes and who had repeated Mañjushrī's mantra, *oṃ a ra pa ca na dhiḥ*, even in his mother's womb. He had been born into a poor shepherd family, and one day when he was out herding sheep he encountered a black Mañjushrī, after which his intelligence increased. When Ḏzong-ka-ḇa met Lama Ū-ma-ḇa at Ga-wa-dong, he was able to ask Mañjushrī questions about the profound emptiness and the vast deeds of compassion of sūtra and tantra through Lama Ū-ma-ḇa.

[a] *dbu ma pa dpa' bo rdo rje.*

> There was a painting of Mañjushrī on the wall of Ḏzong-ka-ḇa's Ga-wa-dong retreat, and upon improvement of his meditation a great light emitted from Mañjushrī's heart. That was the first time Ḏzong-ka-ḇa saw Mañjushrī, and thereafter at his wish he met with Mañjushrī, who taught him the difficult points of the stage of the path. Therefore, Ḏzong-ka-ḇa pays homage to the lowest part of Mañjushrī's body, his feet.

Ḏzong-ka-ḇa's relationship with Mañjushrī is obviously not taken either symbolically as an external description of an internal psychological development or superficially as merely an obligatory repetition of a story to glorify an exalted leader. The meeting is considered to be actual, and the results for Ḏzong-ka-ḇa's development were highly significant. The Dalai Lama's evocative depiction represents the very "stuff" of transmission of the teaching that accompanies the reading of texts, which are treated more like notes on which a teacher expands.

A-ku Ḻo-drö-gya-tso[a] explains that Ḏzong-ka-ḇa's **open** reliance on Mañjushrī is an indication to his followers that they also must depend on Mañjushrī. The commentator's well-taken point recalls Ke-drup's first encounter with Ḏzong-ka-ḇa and demonstrates the importance of Mañjushrī for the Ge-luk-ḇa sect:[63]

> When Ke-drup first met the foremost Ḏzong-ka-ḇa, like the Bodhisattva Always-Crying (*rtag tu ngu, sadprarudita)* when he saw Dharmodgata, from merely seeing Ḏzong-ka-ḇa's glorious form the hairs of his body powerlessly rose, tears of faith streamed from his eyes, and he spontaneously uttered words of praise. Due to former connection, as soon as they met, unparalleled, firm faith was engendered.
>
> That night while dreaming, he became sunk and confused in an omnipresent thick darkness for a long time; then from the east appeared a great wheel with hundreds of swords standing on end and with their handles turned to the center. At the tips of the swords were many hundred of suns, and in the center of the wheel in the midst of a rainbow was the venerable Mañjushrī, with orange body, holding a sword and a book, adorned with jewelled adornments, so youthful that looking knew no satisfaction. Happily, Mañjushrī came to Ke-drup and dissolved into him, whereupon a great sun dawned, immediately clearing away all darkness. The lattice-work of its radiance filled the entire world. That was his dream.
>
> The next day when he met Ḏzong-ka-ḇa, he reported his dream and asked what it meant. The foremost Ḏzong-ka-ḇa answered, "You saw your lama and tutelary deity as undifferentiable. You are a jewel-like person who is a special, intended trainee of Mantra. Just as you saw me as the venerable Mañjushrī, so I am in fact, but persons of low

[a] *a khu blo gros rgya mtsho,* 1851-1930. *Precious Lamp,* 4.2-4.4.

intelligence see me as ordinary. You will bring great help to many trainees."

Then, the foremost Ḏzong-ka-ḇa asked, "Who is your tutelary deity?" Ke-drup replied, "Orange Mañjushrī and Raktayamāri."

Ḏzong-ka-ḇa continued, "In general whether you take Raktayamāri, Kṛṣhṇayamāri, or Bhairava as your tutelary deity, Mañjushrī looks after you since these three are increasing degrees of ferocity of Mañjushrī; however, since my transmission is looked after and blessed by Mañjushrī, you should take Bhairava as your tutelary deity [since the fiercest form is most efficacious]....There are many special purposes; others do not understand the importance of these." Then, without having to be asked, Ḏzong-ka-ḇa immediately conferred the initiation of Vajrabhairava. From that point on, Ke-drup performed the daily rite without break.

Indeed, Mañjushrī became so important for the Ge-luk-ḇa sect that his fiercest manifestation—as Vajrabhairava—became their special protector deity.

Mañjushrī's influence is pervasive; my first teacher of Tibetan Buddhism, the scholar and adept Geshe Wangyal, from a Kalmuck Mongolian area in Astrakhan at the northern tip of the Caspian Sea, praised Mongolians' intensely devoted repetition of Mañjushrī's mantra *oṃ a ra pa ca na dhīḥ*[a] as the reason that so many Mongolians became great scholars of Buddhism. (*Arapacana* is a name of Mañjushrī, and *dhīḥ* is his root syllable.) In 1964, at a Tibeto-Mongolian monastery in New Jersey,[b] I overheard Geshe Wangyal telling a young Kalmuck boy, who was having difficulty with his memorization of prayers, to repeat the mantra either seven, twenty-one, or a hundred times and then to recite *dhīḥ* endlessly—he emphasized **endlessly**. In the daily meditation ritual that those who have taken a Vajrabhairava are committed to perform, the mantra is recited first in a whisper and then, when that has become firm, mentally within a visualization that is like Ke-drup's dream.

Ḏzong-ka-ḇa's mention of his intimate connection with a divine figure endows his text with an exalted, external authority having special powers of cognition, even though, throughout the work, he calls on his readers to examine his points with reasoning. In Tibetan culture, there is a dual relationship with authority—on the one hand, using it to inculcate respect and obedience and, on the other hand, putting what seems to be full confidence in reasoning. Faced with such seeming discrepancy, the culture has opted not for one or the other, or a bland mixture of the two, but for a plenitude of both.

Little is done in Tibet in half measures—from drinking tea (many taking forty to sixty cups a day), to marathon debates in the freezing cold of January (such that the hands crack open and bleed from slapping them together when

[a] Pronounced *oṃ a ra ḇa ḏza na dhīḥ* by Tibetans and Mongolians.

[b] I lived there for five years, from 1963 to 1968.

making a point), to populating a single temple with literally hundreds of images, to claiming an uncountable number of supernatural happenings (many, many statues speaking, images appearing spontaneously out of rock, and so forth), finding not just a few but scores of reincarnated special beings throughout the country, and so on. One of the keys to approaching Tibetan culture is its fascination with **extreme** forms of religious expression, whether in devotion, solitary yoga, philosophical debate, art, social organization around exalted figures, and so forth. Moderation, though seemingly central to Buddhist dictums about the middle way in behavior, view, and meditation, is not the dominant theme. A visit to a Tibetan temple with its hundreds of images or a reliquary with literally tons of gold speaks to the unmoderated vibrancy of the culture.

Great scholastic figures are almost always identified as incarnations of deities or great personages in Indian history. D̄zong-ka-b̄a himself came to be identified as an incarnation of Mañjushrī, not just someone who met with the deity. A double perspective—uncommon and common—is employed; as W̄el-mang Ḡön-chok-gyel-tsen says:[64]

> In accordance with the uncommon [perspective], the Foremost Omniscient [D̄zong-ka-b̄a] was the actual foremost, venerable Mañjughoṣha. However, even in the common perspective, that there is no one among the earlier or later scholars of Tibet who is fit to be the equal of this Foremost One is to be known from the doctrines that he composed.

It is from the "uncommon" perspective that A-ku L̄o-drö-gya-tso[65] similarly says that D̄zong-ka-b̄a was merely putting on a show[a] of meeting with Mañjushrī—that this is merely how the situation appeared in common perception, for he was Mañjushrī himself.

This extra level of hyperbole undermines the impact of D̄zong-ka-b̄a's life-story of hard effort over decades of devotion, study, and meditation. The immediate ascription of divinity to almost anyone who makes a mark on the culture, ranging from political figures, such as the religious kings, to spiritual geniuses, such as founders of sects and authors of college textbooks, separates the gifted from human endeavor. This produces the strange result of denying the efficacy of effort in a religion that by its own description is oriented toward self-development based on inner potential. Descent of the divine seems to have become a predominant means of attracting attention and gaining the sociological, economic, and political benefits that can come with it. By separating off the truly holy, it also excuses usual beings from making an effort—the culture thereby protecting itself from high expectations from practice.

The obvious exaggeration of many of these claims of divine descent has led to the development of a counter-force—evidenced in monks, nuns, and laypersons—which puts little stock in the so-called recognized reincarnations, no

[a] *tshul mdzad pa.*

matter who or what monastic or political institution has put forth the claim. The excessive inflation into divinity conflicts—since it cannot bear reasoned analysis[a]—with the internal demands of the religion (1) to assess accurately one's position in an uncontrolled process of cyclic rebirth into pain and (2) to examine carefully the psychological processes that produce one's entrapment. The disparity between inflation and the need for realistic appraisal yields tension, which, in turn, may feed energy either into that with which one has become involved out of uncontrolled identification with the hated or into what one has chosen, from straightforward analysis, as a sensible alternative.

Acting within the inflated framework provided by the culture, one finds it difficult (but not completely impossible) to appreciate the significance of what someone such as Dzong-ka-ba did through his scholarship and training. After all, he is an incarnation of Mañjushrī! Would you expect less? Particularly damaging is the claim that his works are utterly accurate to and thus repetitious of his Indian sources; this perspective prevents noticing the unusual developments that his insights and efforts wrought for generations of his followers throughout the vast realm of the Tibetan cultural region.

Also, the claim that the Buddhism of one's own sect is the final word, when put together with the hosts of controversy within the sect on what the founder meant, would seem to warrant having been drowned out in ridiculous laughter. However, again, both sides of the matter are preserved; on the one hand, the claims to divinity are so elevated and so manifold that the divine seems to be omnipresently manifest, and, on the other hand, intellectual controversies are encouraged to the point where they are almost without limit. Such disavowal of consistency, however disconcerting and exasperating to both insiders and outsiders, has allowed for the flowering of a multitude of aspects in the culture. It also may represent a wise assessment—not explicitly but through its own dynamics—that life is not so straightforward and simple as to allow for a coherent perspective, that richness is lost when one insists on the drabness of consistency.

In this particular case, Dzong-ka-ba's mention of his reliance on Mañjushrī is not a mere recitation of divine inspiration; Mañjushrī's instructions to him figure prominently in the direction of his scholarship. As Dzong-ka-ba's student Ke-drup reports in his biography of his teacher,[66] when Dzong-ka-ba asked Mañjushrī various questions about the nature of the Sūtra and Mantra paths, the order and precise enumeration of the paths, and points of practice in the development of the meditative state of calm abiding[b] and the wisdom of special

[a] I say this not out of an assumption that encounters with divine personages are impossible but to point out that the culture has incorporated such meetings as a standard way to make exaggerated claims of divine origin much like the fanciful descriptions of products in current advertisements in American culture. It is noteworthy that the current Dalai Lama has pointedly asked his biographer to omit all such exaggerations.

[b] *zhi gnas, śamatha.*

insight,[a] the deity answered that on these matters he need not ask him but should consult the great Indian texts. The significance of this posture—reliance on the great literature of India—for the development of Ḏzong-ka-ḇa's focus of scholarship as well as that of the Ge-luk-ḇa sect (that was to become so influential in Inner Asia) cannot be underestimated. His school places tremendous emphasis on the great texts of Buddhist India as opposed to transmissions of quintessential instructions from teacher to student outside of the structure of these great texts. The high esteem that Ḏzong-ka-ḇa had for the great Indian texts as immensely rich avenues for spiritual progress is the very rationale for his composition of *The Essence of Eloquence.*

However one takes the account of Ḏzong-ka-ḇa's meetings with Mañjushrī—as ex post facto fabrications to authenticate what his own reflections had determined or as actual encounters with the divine that molded his thought—Mañjushrī figures dramatically in the foundation of what came to be the main focus of Ḏzong-ka-ḇa's sect, a devotion to the study of the great texts of Indian Buddhism. These texts are viewed as containing within them the important essentials of the practice of the path and thus provide the unsubstitutable context for the quintessential instructions of the various Indian gurus and Tibetan lamas. This perspective yields the oft-repeated Ge-luk-ḇa criticism of those who seek after quintessential instructions without the background of the great texts and provides the justification for long, scholastic study of these texts (that sometimes also becomes an excuse for not making an effort at meditation).

The several commentaries that I have consulted on this short homage to Mañjushrī afford a picture of a religious culture that balances reliance on supernatural beings with analytical investigation of profound texts. Again, such balance does not mean that Tibetan culture advocates moderate amounts of devotion and philosophical inquiry; both are pursued with vigor. In my estimation, the commentators have, in this case, not overlain an extra level of meaning; rather, they reveal the background of a visionary and meditative environment, fraught with significance, both personally for Ḏzong-ka-ḇa and for the culture that followed him.

Homage To The God Of Gods

Ḏzong-ka-ḇa next pays homage to Buddha from the viewpoint of Shākyamuni's unparalleled teaching of dependent-arising and the emptiness of inherent existence.[67] As Gung-tang's commentator A-ku Ḻo-drö-gya-tso[68] says, this expression of worship itself accords with the principal subject matter of *The Essence of Eloquence*—emptiness. Ḏzong-ka-ḇa (*Emptiness in Mind-Only,* 65) pays homage to Shākyamuni Buddha by way of indicating that the great deities of the Hindu pantheon were overwhelmed by Shākyamuni's magnificence:

---

[a] *lhag mthong, vipaśyanā.*

Homage to the Lord of Subduers, god of gods,
As soon as whose body was seen by those
High-and-mighty with presumptions proclaiming
In the mundane world a great roar of arrogance—

[The gods known as] Bliss-Arising, Cloud Mount, Golden Womb,
Bodiless Lord, Garlanded Belly, and so on—
Even they became like fireflies [overwhelmed] by the sun and thereupon
Paid respect with their beautiful crowns to his lotus feet.

In explaining why Dzong-ka-ba chose to mention explicitly these five gods, Gung-tang[69] says that Brahmā ("Golden Womb"), Viṣhṇu ("Garlanded Belly"), and Shakra ("Cloud Mount") are widely known to be teachers of non-Buddhist systems. Also, Shakra (that is, Indra) is widely held to be the final authority on grammar, due to which those who adhere to the Vedas hold Shakra to be a valid being, and Dzong-ka-ba wanted to refute this. The Sinful Demon ("Bodiless Lord"), through various means, affects the minds of beings, thereby turning them away from Shākyamuni Buddha's teaching. Dzong-ka-ba explicitly mentions these five gods in order to emphasize Shākyamuni conquest over non-Buddhist systems and evil forces that seek to undermine Buddhism.

In an etymology of Bodiless Lord, Gung-tang[70] reports that the word "bodiless" refers to desire, since, despite being bodiless, it abides in the hearts of sentient beings, bringing about the various entanglements of cyclic existence. For the same reason, desire is called a "mental dormancy."[a] As Shāntideva's *Engaging in the Bodhisattva Deeds* says:[71]

The sole cause increasing the hosts of harm
Definitely dwells in my heart...

In this sense, attachment to desire is "bodiless," and thus the being who is that Lord of Love is called the "Lord of the Bodiless," since through various techniques he generates attachment to desire in sentient beings, whereby they are bound in cyclic existence. (The parallels with Cupid are obvious—a god of love who shoots arrows. In the Buddhist version, "Cupid" is a demon; in the culture of romantic love, Cupid is hardly a demon.)

This etymology of "Lord of the Bodiless"—with Gung-tang's grounding it in the Buddhist Shāntideva's text—not only serves to emphasize the crucial role that desire plays as the underpinning of the process of suffering in cyclic existence but also puts part of the blame for desire on an outside force, a demon who incites desire. Had I not heard about this demon from several of my Tibetan teachers, I would have thought that he was to be taken symbolically, but it is clear that he is considered to be an actual being who, along with many perpetrators of harm in the world, is to be thwarted. Two teachers warned that

[a] *yid la nyal.*

meditation should not be tried at sunrise (as opposed to dawn), since it is then that this troublesome demon shoots his five arrows.

I call this a projection of inner forces onto the environment, a phenomenon that we certainly see in plenitude in Tibetan culture.[72] Such dissociability also applies to Euro-American culture's penchant for ridiculously psychologizing uncontrolled contents of mind—to the point where we think of them of as **my** neuroses, **my** unconscious contents, and so forth.[73] Also, from the same point of view, the ascription of autonomy to social and economic forces and viewing ourselves as beings buffeted primarily by these powers such that the focus of improvement is on the level of personal income and the gross national product is just as projective.

In Buddhist and, in this case, Tibetan culture, by projecting unconscious, psychic forces onto the environment, persons absolve themselves of responsibility for important psychic events, thereby seemingly denying basic Buddhist perspectives on karma and its attendant assumption of responsibility as well as the basic Buddhist posture of seeking health through internal, mental transformation. Such projection relieves persons of the crushing weight of full responsibility for their situation and gives them external means—fighting demons—to try to affect these forces. This may be the culture's way of recognizing that control is by no means an easy matter; it also provides a means of not falling under the sway of the hubris of assuming that deep psychic events are somehow owned by oneself or under one's control.

Ascriptions of externality also are signs that Buddhist structural psychology does not have terminology to deal with such impulses on a psychic level. We shall briefly return to this point later[a] when discussing a rather surprising description of mental images as permanent and its unfortunate domination of Ge-luk-b̄a presentations of the imagination (but not the practical usage of it) such that the development of a rich **theory** of imagination was prevented. The practical usage of the imagination found in tantric systems that attained high development in Tibet has to be considered among the richest of the world, but the development of a complex psychological theory of imagination and its uses was stultified by an ascription of permanence to mental images rather than considering them functioning phenomena produced by the mind.

Rejecting a specious etymology. Gung-tang[74] dismisses as senseless another etymology of "Bodiless Lord" that takes the term as referring to gods of the Desire Realm. In that etymology, the gods of the Desire Realm are called bodiless because they are as if bodiless relative to the huge bodies of those in levels above the Desire Realm. He rejects this explanation on the basis that, since there is an increase in size within the Four Concentrations, relative to the third and highest level of the Fourth Concentration, called Great Fruit,[b] those below it also would absurdly have to be considered to be "bodiless."

a See p. 222, footnote c.

b *'bras bu che ba, vṛhatphala.*

To explain: Cyclic existence is composed of an infinite number of world-systems that each have three levels—a Desire Realm with a Form Realm above it, and a Formless Realm. The Form Realm is composed of four levels called the Four Concentrations, and to be reborn there a being has to succeed at cultivating the corresponding meditative state, called a concentration, in a previous lifetime. In the Form Realm, each of the four levels has itself three levels; those on all three levels of the First Concentration are said to have bodies that are a half *yojana* in height, whereas those on the first level of the Second Concentration, called Little Light,[a] on up through the third level of the Fourth Concentration are said to have bodies double the size of those on the previous level. As Vasubandhu's *Treasury of Manifest Knowledge* says:[75]

Those on the first physical level are a half *yojana*.
The bodies of those on Little Light
And above are each doubled.

This being the case, if the above faulty etymology of "Bodiless Lord" were accepted—that is, if we were to accept the principle that a level is called "bodiless" if the body size on that level is smaller relative to the one above it—we would be forced to accept that beings on the first eleven levels of the Four Concentrations would be "bodiless" relative to the twelfth level, Great Fruit. Since this is ridiculous, Gung-tang rejects this etymology of "Bodiless Lord."

These levels of cyclic existence are taken literally; they are basic to the cosmological myth that places beings in a continuum of time and space much as the big bang does in contemporary scientific culture.[b] The frequent mention of cosmological issues, such as this one by Gung-tang, reminds practitioners of their place in a dynamic world-system that is shaped by their own former actions and the predispositions that those actions have established in their minds—these being the two aspects of karma, actions and the potencies established by actions. We ourselves are presently in the Desire Realm, which is divided into the six levels of (proceeding from bottom to top) hell-beings, hungry ghosts, humans, demi-gods, and gods.[c] Above the Desire Realm are two realms of gods—the Form Realm and the Formless Realm. The Form Realm is divided into the Four Concentrations, and each of these, in turn, is divided into three levels:

---

[a] *'od chung ba, parīttābhā.*

[b] The scientific cosmological myth, which is built, like the Buddhist one, on what is currently accepted to be evidence, places humans in a world-system of ever-expanding size until an ultimate collapse and destruction in a black hole. The stark purposelessness that this image conveys has led some contemporaries to see God as behind the process, whereas in Buddhist terms it would be the karma of the beings inhabiting the world-system.

[c] Not all mundane gods are included in the Desire Realm; the beings of the Four Concentrations and Four Formless Absorptions are also gods.

First Concentration
- Brahmā Type
- In Front of Brahmā
- Great Brahmā

Second Concentration
- Little Light
- Limitless Light
- Bright Light

Third Concentration
- Little Bliss
- Limitless Bliss
- Vast Bliss

Fourth Concentration
- Cloudless
- Born from Merit
- Great Fruit

Above the Form Realm, not in terms of physical position—since it is formless—but in terms of rank within cyclic existence, is the Formless Realm, again with four levels:

- Limitless Space
- Limitless Consciousness
- Nothingness
- Peak of Cyclic Existence

Despite the higher **ranking** of demi-gods and gods (the latter including types in the Desire Realm and all those in the Form and Formless Realms), human life is valued for its mixture of pleasure and pain, neither of which is, in general, so predominant that spiritual practice becomes either unthinkable or impossible. Also, the human will, or intentionality,[a] that is the main factor involved in karma, is said to be especially powerful.

Since such a hierarchical structure produced by karma is the general view of cyclic existence and humans' place within it, Gung-tang's commentary—by indirectly bringing up these issues—reminds readers of the power of their own previous actions in shaping their present situation and, by extension, reminds them of the power of present actions to shape the future. A message of the cosmological myth is that through re-directing mental, verbal, and physical actions, improvement of one's situation—and finally a state of freedom—can be gained. His readers are to place themselves in the Buddhist cosmological structure with its implications that:

- They are trapped in a repeated round of suffering.

---

[a] *sems pa, cetanā.*

- Uncontrolled cyclic existence is brought on by their own actions driven by afflictive emotions.
- Advancement within this process of rebirth is achieved by becoming committed to virtuous actions.
- Relief comes through understanding the nature of phenomena.

Superiority

Gung-tang and his commentator A-ku Lo-drö-gya-tso summarize the import of Dzong-ka-ba's homage as a praise of Shākyamuni Buddha from the viewpoint of his being the god of gods—a god superior to all other gods:[76]

> When these great gods of the world were residing in their own places, they became inflated thinking that their intelligence, power, magical activities, and so forth were unmatched, but when they arrived in the presence of the Supramundane Victor [Shākyamuni Buddha], they were overwhelmed with the magnificence of the light rays of his speech, like fireflies by the light of the sun. Their pride and arrogance wilted, and they bowed down, touching their crowns to [Shākyamuni's] lotus feet.

Dzong-ka-ba begins his book with an image of Shākyamuni Buddha's superiority—his power and magnificence due to the profundity of this speech, his teaching.

Many (all?) Indian systems of religion attempt to demonstrate their exclusive hold on the truth by subsuming rival systems. In the case of Sāṃkhya, this is done by claiming temporal priority; Kapila, their founder, is said to be the original teacher, from whose teachings all the other schools split off. The Jainas' account of their founder Arhat's parceling out to the other systems their root texts is particularly pointed; the Jainas, like the Buddhists, do not accept the Vedas as authoritative, and thus in order to put down the Vedas in no uncertain terms, they say that, when Brahmā arrived late after Arhat had already distributed the fundamental texts of the schools, Arhat was at a loss to provide anything worthwhile and, in desperation, gave Brahmā the Vedas, saying, "Great Brahmā, you have come leisurely; you have come very late. Because I have given away all the treatises, use these Vedas."[77] In the text that we are considering, a Buddhist version of the same is to have great Hindu gods wilt in Shākyamuni Buddha's presence, paying homage to him for his profound teaching of dependent-arising.

This fabulous story not only reinforces Buddhist claims to superiority but also establishes a model of proud persons' becoming deflated upon contact with Shākyamuni's teaching—a model presented for the scholars for whom Dzong-ka-ba wrote *The Essence of Eloquence.* The suggestion is that there is something to be found in D̄zong-ka-b̄a's account of Buddha's teaching of emptiness and dependent-arising that will undermine one's self-perception.

Still, in order to undercut any sense of authenticity of the biographies of the Hindu gods and the implicit non-Buddhist cosmology that D̄zong-ka-b̄a's mere mention of these gods might generate, Gung-tang[78] points out that D̄zong-ka-b̄a and others are merely stating stories renowned in the Vedas that are not in fact reliable. For there is a plethora of conflicting stories about Brahmā's birth, such as his arising from a sphere of fire, or being emanated from the seed of the Great Lord, or being engendered from a lotus in the navel of the Pervasive One, or being born from an egg, or that he himself created all the world.[a] Similarly, even though the etymology of "Viṣṇu" is that he pervades and enters all of the stable and the moving—environments and beings—it is said that he once became afraid and ran away, and it is explained that the Great Lord was self-produced (something that, from a Buddhist point of view, is utterly impossible, since, if there was a need for something to be produced even though it already existed, such re-production would have to go on endlessly).

Gung-tang says that these conflicting stories are not fit to be accepted, since the actual fact is that when this world formed, those who do not depend on the ground but live in space form beginning from the higher levels on down to the lower, whereas those who depend on the ground form from the lower to the higher. This means that, from among those levels of worldly beings who live in space, the land of the Third Concentration forms first (beings of the Fourth Concentration are born complete with their own individual lands), then that of the Second Concentration, and then that of the First Concentration, followed by four levels of Desire Realm gods who live in the sky, these being (from top down) the Land of Controlling Others' Emanations, the Land of Enjoying Emanation, the Joyous Land, and the Land Without Combat. Among those that depend on earth, the lands of the hells form first, then those of hungry ghosts, then those of humans, and finally the two levels of gods of the Desire Realm that reside on the earth, these being (from bottom up) the Land of the Four Great Royal Lineages and the Land of the Thirty-Three.[79] Gung-tang avers that here in these non-Buddhist stories the modes of formation are confused.

Gung-tang feels it necessary to undermine the respect that accrues to these non-Buddhist gods when D̄zong-ka-b̄a uses their respect for Shākyamuni Buddha as a means of praising him. However, I would add that his demeaning these gods diminishes the value of their respecting Shākyamuni, if the reference to them is not recognized as a literary motif.

---

[a]   See *Absorption,* #6, 7.

Exclusivity

Gung-tang[80] explains that Dzong-ka-ba's expression of worship to Shākyamuni Buddha—in which these great gods pay homage to him—is not similar in meaning to the many positively oriented statements about Shākyamuni Buddha's having become the crown ornament of all beings, such as when he is called "The teacher of gods and humans." Here in Dzong-ka-ba's expression of worship, Buddha is not being praised from the positive viewpoint of his having become the refuge of all beings from the frights of cyclic existence and solitary peace; rather, he is praised from the viewpoint of having become the unmatched proponent of doctrine upon "having destroyed into total disorder"[a]—with the light rays of his speech—the facsimiles of paths taught by these great gods. The former type of praise, such as when Shākyamuni Buddha is called "the Unequaled Leader, the Teacher, the Supramundane Victor,"[81] is by way of his qualities of vast method, such as great mercy, rather than by way of profundity of view. The latter type of praise, such as when Shākyamuni Buddha is called "the Unmatched Propounder [of doctrine], Supreme Leader, Crown Jewel of the Shākyas," is by way of his profound view of emptiness, and this is the type of praise that Dzong-ka-ba mainly employs here.

Gung-tang[82] stresses that, due to this view of emptiness, the mere fact that the teaching of the insiders—the Buddhists—was revealed by the Supramundane Victor Shākyamuni whereas the fact that the teaching of the outsiders follows after great worldly gods, such as those mentioned in Dzong-ka-ba's expression of worship—Brahmā, Viṣhṇu, and Maheshvara—makes the outsiders' teachings inferior. He adds that the barbarians[b] are said to be followers of demi-gods on whom they depend for refuge and with whom they are in collusion, even though there is no view or meditation to be delineated from texts written by demi-gods; the barbarians, therefore, are in a position inferior to the outsiders who follow the great gods of the world.

Gung-tang[83] identifies the basis for Shākyamuni's greatness as the fact that he taught, under his own power, the profound suchness of dependent-arising (this being a code word for the compatibility of emptiness and dependent-arising). This is the final reason for Shākyamuni Buddha's (1) becoming the unmatched proponent[c] of doctrine upon suppressing with his magnificence all bad proponents of doctrine—the teachers of others' systems, and so forth—and (2) becoming the unsurpassed proponent[d] of doctrine, since his own teaching affords no opportunity for censure by others. He traces this identification back to Dzong-ka-ba's *Praise of the Supramundane Victor Buddha from the Approach of His Teaching the Profound Dependent-Arising,* which is also entitled *The*

---

a *rmeg med du bcom.*

b *kla klo, mlecca.*

c *smra ba zla med.*

d *smra ba bla na med pa.*

Essence of Eloquence (sometimes referred to as "the short *Essence of Eloquence*"), in which he says:[84]

> The reason for viewing you
> As the unmatched proponent [of doctrine]
> Is just this path of dependent-arising.

Also, in the same text, Ḏzong-ka-ḇa repeats that the teaching of dependent-arising is "the cause of your being the unsurpassed proponent."

Gung-tang[85] extends the identification back to sūtra as well as to Nāgārjuna and Chandrakīrti. In the *Condensed Perfection of Wisdom Sūtra,* Buddha speaks of himself as frightening non-Buddhists with his great lion's roar of the wisdom of emptiness:

> The lion of humans, in dependence upon the perfection of wisdom,
> Proclaimed in the world sounds terrifying to many [non-Buddhist]
> Forders.[a]

Nāgārjuna, in his expression of worship to Shākyamuni Buddha at the beginning of his *Treatise on the Middle,* specifically praises him from the viewpoint of his teaching dependent-arisings as being empty of inherent existence:[86]

> I bow down to the perfect Buddha—
> The best of proponents—who propounded
> That what dependently arises
> Has no cessation, no production,
> No annihilation, no permanence, no coming,
> No going, no difference, no sameness,
> Is free of the proliferations [of inherent
> Existence and of duality] and is at peace.

In commenting on this, Chandrakīrti says in his *Clear Words:*[87]

> Because [Nāgārjuna] comprehended dependent-arising just as it was taught, he saw just the One Gone Thus as solely having taught non-erroneously, and he understood all opposing proponents [of doctrine] as like children spouting forth whatever comes to their mind. Thereupon, the master [Nāgārjuna] came to be endowed with great faith, due to which he treated the Supramundane Victor in an elevated way, calling him "the best of proponents."

Shākyamuni Buddha's teaching of dependent-arising is a lion's roar terrifying to non-Buddhists. This teaching is so profound that others' words are reduced to disjointed discourse, aimless spouting.

It could seem that the aim is to become merely an unassailable proponent of a system, a champion debater. However, when Gung-tang identifies

[a] *mu stegs can, tīrthika.*

Dzong-ka-ba's meaning in both its negative and its positive aspects as a state in which one "overwhelms all proponents of bad tenets and sets trainees in purification and release," he has ferreted out Dzong-ka-ba's actual meaning (the interpretation here is not apologetic) as referring to a state of full capability to assist others, which indeed includes having the confidence of unassailability. I find such freedom from authentic challenge to be the prime import of four qualities of Buddhahood called "fearlessnesses." The four fearlessnesses, as explained in a commentary on the coming Buddha Maitreya's ***Sublime Continuum of the Great Vehicle***[88] by Dzong-ka-ba's student Gyel-tsap Dar-ma-rin-chen,[a] are:[89]

1. Fearlessness with respect to the assertion "I am completely and perfectly enlightened with respect to all phenomena." For one will not encounter even the name of an opponent who could correctly say that one does not know such and such a phenomenon. It is achieved through lacking any stinginess with respect to the doctrine.
2. Fearlessness with respect to teaching that the afflictive obstructions are obstacles to liberation and that the obstructions to omniscience are obstacles to simultaneous cognition of all phenomena, and that, therefore, these are to be ceased. For one will not encounter even the name of an opponent who could correctly say that reliance on desire and so forth would not obstruct a being from liberation. It is achieved through not falling under the influence of an obstructive doctrine.
3. Fearlessness with respect to teaching the paths of deliverance. For there is no opponent who could say correctly that these paths are not paths leading to liberation. It is achieved through practicing the paths to liberation.
4. Fearlessness with respect to asserting that the contaminations have been extinguished. For one will not see even the name of an opponent who could correctly dispute the assertion that one has attained the cessation of all afflictions and their potencies. It is achieved through formerly abandoning pride.

Such freedom from anxiety over whether one is right or not and thus whether one could be correctly challenged is, most likely, the context of Dzong-ka-ba's reference here to a Buddha as an "unmatched proponent [of doctrine]." Dzong-ka-ba exhorts those who want such a state, altruistically powerful due to the safety of its valid foundation, to pay close attention to his text.

Still, from the imagery used, it is clear that the perspective is one of dominance and submission—superiority and inferiority, confidence and fright. This is no ecumenical meeting of alternative systems but a clash of opposing ideologies struggling for supremacy—one system bows to the other. The concern with self-identification as distinct from other groups frames the approach such that, even though reasoning is required for overcoming internal tendencies to assent

[a] *rgyal tshab dar ma rin chen,* 1364-1432.

to the false appearance of phenomena, the discussion of this reasoning is framed around external confrontation with other systems.

Ḏzong-ka-ḇa begins his text by lauding Shākyamuni Buddha for his overwhelming non-Buddhist systems in this way and, indeed, the two main thematic structures of his *The Essence of Eloquence* through which he presents the focal topic of emptiness are to **distinguish** the interpretations of emptiness of the various Buddhist systems and to **distinguish** his presentation from that of a contemporary, rival group, the Jo-nang-ḇas, who put forth a synthetic system combining the Great Vehicle schools of thought into one, the Great Middle Way. The raison d'etre of Ḏzong-ka-ḇa's text lies in assuming the task of making these distinctions.

The paradigm of hierarchical dualism in which one system is shown to dominate another with the trappings of martial metaphors is not appealing to many in our present age when unnecessary conflict of systems seems to be bringing the world to its own demise. This model of dominance has had considerable influence in much of Indo-Tibetan Buddhist culture (and in other cultures) and has laid the ideological foundation for the parochial exclusivism between even the divisions within a single Tibetan monastic university, never mind between universities within one sect, between sects, and between religions. When Gung-tang summarizes the import of his explanation of Ḏzong-ka-ḇa's expression of worship to Shākyamuni Buddha, it is clear that such an exclusivistic message is conveyed:[90]

> The import of these points should be understood also in terms of the practice of us followers. When our own teacher is seen as a reliable, authoritative being,[a] except for entering into only his teaching, it is unsuitable to follow after any other, the great gods of the world. Once this is the case, it need not be mentioned that it is unsuitable to enter into teachings by minor non-humans such as the religious system of the goatherd *skar rgyal*[b] or what are renowned as profound quintessential instructions that are based on visions in piddling spiritual experiences.[c]

To indicate that this message of exclusivity has its source in Indian Buddhist writings and is not his own fabrication, Gung-tang cites two commentaries on texts praising Shākyamuni Buddha. First he cites Prajñāvarman's *Commentary*

---

[a] *tshad ma'i skyes bu, pramāṇabhuta.*

[b] The term is obscure; the equivalent Sanskrit may be *tiṣya,* which is the eighth of the twenty-seven constellations; see Vaman Shivaram Apte, *Sanskrit-English Dictionary* (Poona, India: Prasad Prakashan, 1957), 476. The *bod rgya tshig mdzod chen mo* says that *skar rgyal* is one of the twenty-eight constellations and the name of a Buddha; the latter is obviously not appropriate here.

[c] Gung-tang's *Difficult Points,* 13.6: *nyams myong ban bun gyi snang ba la brten pa'i man ngag.*

on (Shaṃkarapati's) "Praise of the Supra-Divine"[a] to substantiate the above description of finding ascertainment with respect to Shākyamuni's teaching and entering into it, and then he cites the same author's *Commentary on (Udbhaṭasiddhasvāmin's) "Exalted Praise"*:[b]

> Then, one who has understood that the doctrines of the scriptures of the One Gone Thus are without unseemliness should cast away the words of the Vedas like hay.

This is certainly not an injunction of someone intent upon dialogue. Exclusivism, moreover, knows no limits; for Gung-tang's citation of this demeaning depiction of the Vedas as like hay undoubtedly was part of the cultural influence that led to my kind, old Tibetan teacher's spitting on the floor when he mentioned the rival college in his own monastic university. In a similar fashion, one of Ḏzong-ka-ḇa's two chief students, Gyel-tsap, concluding his refutation of Jo-nang-ḇa S̄hay-rap-gyel-tsen's presentation of ultimate truth, says:[91]

> Since asserting permanent [functioning] things[c] sets up the system of the [non-Buddhist] Forder Aishvaras, Sāṃkhyas, and Guhya-Vedāntins, it should be forsaken like drops of spit.

The imagery is, to say the least, not conducive to sharing perspectives or even making civil conversation. Quite to the contrary, it incites bitterness and inflames rivalries.

Gung-tang's detailed contextualization of Ḏzong-ka-ḇa's expression of worship to Shākyamuni makes clear the exclusivistic message of the opening of *The Essence of Eloquence,* but the harshness of the images contradicts Ḏzong-ka-ḇa's own depiction of how the process of coming to have faith in Shākyamuni Buddha's teaching is to be effected. With respect to taking refuge in the Three Jewels—Buddha, his doctrine, and the spiritual community—he says in the *Great Exposition of Secret Mantra:*[92]

> You must gain unmoving conviction in the source of refuge. Thereby you will realise that only the Subduer's teaching is the entrance for those wishing liberation. Those with little force of mind will determine this merely through an assumption, but those with strong minds should seek firm conviction induced by valid cognition. Otherwise it will only be an assertion.

---

[a] *lha las phul byung gi bstod pa'i 'grel pa, devātiśayastotra;* Peking 2005, vol. 46.

[b] *khyad par du 'phags pa'i bstod pa'i rgya cher bshad pa, viśeṣastavanāmaṭīkā;* Peking 2002, vol. 46.

[c] See also p. 322 and Cyrus R. Stearns, *The Buddha from Dol po: A Study of the Life and Thought of the Tibetan Master Dolpopa Sherab Gyaltsen* (Albany, N.Y.: State University of New York Press, 1999), 67 and 210 n. 91.

Further, Shamkarapati's *Praise of the Supra-Divine* (*Devātishaya-stotra*) says:

> I am not a partisan of Buddha,
> I do not hate Kapila and the others,
> I hold as a teacher only
> Him whose word possesses reason.

> You should forsake partisanship and hatred for the systems of your own and others' teachers and analyse which of them provide good or bad explanations. Then, you should adopt only that which shows the means of attaining the two aims of trainees [high status within cyclic existence and the definite goodness of liberation and omniscience] and provides correct proofs. The scriptures of the two systems are what are to be analysed to find which does or does not bear the truth; thus, it would not be suitable to cite them as a proof [of their own truth]. Only reasoning distinguishes what is or is not true.

D̄zong-ka-b̄a goes on to show that through reasoning one can determine how the process of cyclic existence is driven by ignorance and how it can be overcome through the wisdom realizing emptiness. He concludes:[93]

> As explained above, the Three Refuges—our Teacher and so forth—are for those wishing liberation, and teachers and so forth who do not accord with them are never [final] refuges. If you have not induced conviction in this, you cannot have a firm mind, single-pointed with respect to your own source of refuge. The arising of such a firm mind relies on seeing, through reasoning, the faults and advantages of the two systems.
>
> Therefore, whether or not a [non-Buddhist] Forder (*Tīrthika*) is actually present [to refute in debate] is inconsequential; if the intelligent wish to generate the special mind of refuge, they must do as was explained above [ascertaining through reasoning that the Three Jewels are the only refuges]. Thus, it should be known that the treatises of logic such as Dharmakīrti's Seven Treatises are a superior means of generating great respect, not merely verbal, for our own teacher Buddha, for his teaching—both verbal doctrine and that of realisation—and for proper practice.

D̄zong-ka-b̄a's concern is with raising adherence to a system above mere repetition of claims of superiority in order to provide focus and energy for practice. This is to be accomplished through reasoned investigation, for which the study of logic and epistemology is needed.

The repetition—throughout his writings—of this theme of the value of reasoned analysis is testimony to his having experienced significant progress in his own spiritual journey through such reflection. He must have found many Buddhists of his time to be mired in mere incantation of the greatness of their system such that he sought to rectify this weakness through calling his followers to exercise their faculties of reason. Indeed, his immense confidence in reasoning to reveal the way set the tone for much of the vast corpus of scholarship that his followers produced. The conviction in reasoning is such that it would seem that, for him, it could reveal the beauty and elegance of a system so finely crafted that, upon gaining this superior perspective, other systems could be abandoned as incomplete, insufficient, and riddled with contradiction.

D̄zong-ka-b̄a claims not only that Buddhism in general has an exclusive hold on the truth but also, as we saw in the last chapter, that his own interpretation of the teaching of the compatibility of emptiness and dependent-arising is unique in Tibet in terms of its accuracy to Indian teachings. He, like Gung-tang, uses a double approach to establishing Shākyamuni Buddha's superiority—strong declaration of a claim and calling for reasoned justification. The only difference that I perceive between his and Gung-tang's approaches is that Gung-tang's contextualization involves harsher metaphors. Both are calling their readers to make seemingly incompatible moves—they compellingly declare Shākyamuni Buddha to be superior and appealingly call for calm, unbiased examination.

These two stances are understandable in the context (1) of the sociological requirements of forming and maintaining a movement and (2) of the spiritual requirements of a system that posits liberation from suffering as emerging from penetrating a veil of appearances that are like illusions. Reasoned investigation that has gained force through reflective meditation is a requirement of a religious system that aims at gaining liberation through overcoming ingrained tendencies to accept appearances as givens. The continued use of hierarchical metaphors and the employment of techniques of unreasoned persuasion—separating the world into right and wrong groups and asking which group you would choose as yours (you would not want to be on the wrong side, would you?)—arises from the knowledge that reasoned investigation is not easy—it is not a matter of an effortless dawning of understanding in full form from stringing words together in logical sequences. Other observers of Buddhist and Tibetan culture might, quite understandably, hold that the real message is just partisan clinging to a system for sociological, economic, and political advantages. I would suggest, however, that, although these systems are *used* this way and are even *built* to incorporate these advantages, they also speak to other concerns.

Furthermore, it would be arrogantly facile to suggest that there is an easily adoptable ecumenical outlook that would solve our current situation of counterproductive conflict among systems. Must adherents to religious systems, for the sake of dialogue, concede beforehand that other systems yield liberation from all suffering? Such strikes me as trivializing the importance of, for instance, this Tibetan Buddhist system's emphasis on a certain type of ignorance as being at the root of suffering and thereby would denude it of the source of its **contribution** to an understanding of bondage and freedom. I would suggest that, once it is understood that liberation is not a matter of merely holding onto the words of a system, help in understanding can come from any quarter, since one system does not contain all insights. For those for whom even this perspective is impossible, dialogue on the contributions by religious systems to social betterment may be possible. For those for whom this also is impossible, dialogue just to get to know the other party better can be fruitful, since it allows feelings of friendship to be established.

That a particular system does not have all the answers, since another system may be more helpful in a particular circumstance, is not new to Buddhism, despite the implications of the paradigm of dominance frequently used by Buddhists. The present Dalai Lama puts forth this perspective in his commentary to the passages from Ḏzong-ka-ḇa's *Great Exposition of Secret Mantra* cited above:[94]

> The path of liberation removes the adventitious defilements from the expanse of suchness which itself is intrinsically pure, and liberation is the state in which these adventitious defilements have been removed. It seems that some teachers did not know this liberation or the path to it and set forth systems in ignorance. The *Kālachakra Tantra*, after setting forth the various systems of Buddhist and non-Buddhist tenets and presenting with reasoning their relative superiority and inferiority, says, "It is not suitable to despise another system." The reason given is that often non-Buddhist systems have been taught through the empowering blessings of Buddhas.
>
> There are cases of teachers' explaining paths in ignorance, but other teachers were emanations of Buddhas, free from all defects and endowed with all attainments. They knew the difference between the mistaken and non-mistaken paths, but because at that point there was no purpose in teaching the non-mistaken path, they set forth a non-final path, pretending not to know another.
>
> One who has the ability should proceed on the non-mistaken path; however, in relation to one for whom another path is suitable, that path is right. For instance, for a person who can practise the view of the Mind-Only School but not the view of the Middle Way School, the Mind-Only view is unmistaken. The same is also true with regard to non-Buddhist teachings. Therefore, other teachers, their doctrines, and practitioners can be refuges, but not final refuges.

In this passage the Dalai Lama, based on traditional sources, frankly admits that the Buddhist teaching does not contain within it everything needed in order to benefit all practitioners; he shows an avenue for appreciating other systems. A particular system, although not final, may be right relative to a particular individual, and, by extension, even the final system, although right in the abstract, may not be right for many persons. Thus, the claims to superior logic in the abstract are overwhelmed by the need to examine the diverse possibilities in relation to particular practitioners. Given the difficulty of penetrating the truth, it is by no means to be presumed that one is a fit receptacle for the highest system.

Still, the Dalai Lama subsumes other worthwhile systems under Buddhism by citing a passage indicating that they were taught by Buddhas under other guises; these teachings are not granted the philosophical finality reserved for certain types of Buddhism. In a later work, however, he seems to move beyond this posture to an appreciation of the world's religions by putting philosophical differences on a secondary level as instruments for another goal. In the chapter "Religious Harmony" in his *Kindness, Clarity, and Insight* he says:[95]

> Although in every religion there is an emphasis on compassion and love, from the viewpoint of philosophy, of course there are differences, and that is all right. Philosophical teachings are not the end, not the aim, not what you serve. The aim is to help and benefit others, and philosophical teachings to support those ideas are valuable. If we go into the differences in philosophy and argue with and criticize each other, it is useless. There will be endless argument; the result will mainly be that we irritate each other—accomplishing nothing. Better to look at the purpose of the philosophies and to see what is shared—an emphasis on love, compassion, and respect for a higher force.

His statement that "philosophical teachings are not the end, not the aim, not what you serve" calls for allegiance not to a system but to the aim of helping others. He advocates that we view our era as a time not of allegiance to systems but of gaining mutual benefit through study of a plurality of systems, dialogue.

This attitude appears to be at variance with the message of Ḏzong-ka-ḇa's initial expression of worship to Shākyamuni Buddha as dominating over other founders of religion. Gung-tang summarizes the essential message of this homage as a call for exclusive attention to Shākyamuni Buddha's teaching:[96]

> That one should train in such [a system of the harmony of emptiness and dependent-arising which are the] tracks of passage of all Conquerors, as clearly revealed by the lama Mañjunātha [Ḏzong-ka-ḇa], without getting involved with facsimiles of religious systems is the essence of the meaning of this first expression of worship.

The exclusivity of "without getting involved with facsimiles of religious systems" contrasts strongly with the attitude advocated in the above passages by the Dalai Lama; the latter's approach to the study of Buddhist philosophy emphasizes the results produced in a practitioner, not the system itself. Still, his outlook is not foreign to either Ḏzong-ka-ḇa or Gung-tang but is a development of the all-embracive altruistic concern that they both frequently call for in their works. Buddhism, in general, and certainly the Buddhism of the Tibetan cultural region are so multifaceted that new perspectives are not so much a matter of formulating an entirely new direction as they are re-constitutions of the tradition by emphasizing another facet already found within the tradition and by carrying out its consequences. It would take, however, considerable persistence for this more open perspective to overwhelm the influence of the parochial partisanship that structures much of Buddhist culture (in the United States, too).

6. Need for Analysis

It is held that Buddha spoke in many different ways according to the capacities of his listeners, and thus Ḏzong-ka-ḇa explains that it is necessary to determine (1) what teachings are definitive in the sense of actually depicting the true fact and (2) what teachings require interpretation. For some teachings were merely contingent on particular trainees' situations that made them temporarily unable to realize the truth, and without identifying these teachings, one might take literally teachings that are not validly founded and are intended only as temporary means to advance certain trainees. Ḏzong-ka-ḇa (*Emptiness in Mind-Only,* 69-71) highlights the role of reasoning in making this differentiation between teachings:

> ...the Compassionate Teacher—perceiving that the thusness of phenomena is very difficult to realize and that, if it is not realized, one [can] not be released from cyclic existence—brings about the thorough understanding of that [suchness] through many modes of skillful means and many approaches of reasoning.[a] Therefore, those having discrimination must work at a technique for thoroughly understanding how suchness is.
>
> Moreover, this depends upon differentiating those meanings that require interpretation and those that are definitive within the scriptures of the Conqueror. Furthermore, the differentiation of those two cannot be done merely through scriptures that state, "This is a meaning to be interpreted; that is a meaning that is definitive." For, [Buddha spoke variously in relation to the thoughts of trainees and] (1) otherwise the composition of commentaries on [Buddha's] thought differentiating the interpretable and definitive by the great openers of the chariot-ways [Nāgārjuna and Asaṅga] would have been senseless; (2) also, scriptures [such as the *Sūtra Unraveling the Thought* and the *Teachings of Akṣhayamati Sūtra*] set forth many conflicting modes of positing the interpretable and the definitive; and (3) through scriptural passages merely saying [about a topic], "This is so," such cannot be posited, and if, then, **in general** it is not necessarily [suitable to accept whatever is indicated on the literal level in sūtras], mere statements [in sūtra] of, "This is [interpretable, and that is definitive]," also cannot establish **about specifics**, the interpretable and the definitive, [that such is necessarily so].
>
> Therefore, one must seek [Buddha's] thought, following the [two]

---

[a] In his *Difficult Points* (35.11), Gung-tang makes an important distinction between *thabs* (*upāya*) as compassion and *thabs* (*upāya*) as skillful means used to lead trainees by way of various techniques; see p. 142.

great openers of the chariot-ways [Nāgārjuna and Asaṅga], who were prophesied as differentiating the interpretable and the definitive in [Buddha's] scriptures and who commented on the thought of the interpretable and the definitive and, moreover, settled it well through reasoning that damages the interpretation of the meaning of definitive scriptures as anything else and establishes that, within their being unfit to be interpreted otherwise, [the final mode of subsistence explained in them] is definite as [just] that meaning. Therefore, in the end, the differentiation [between the interpretable and the definitive] must be made just by stainless reasoning, because if a proponent asserts a tenet contradicting reason, [that person] is not suitable to be a valid being [with respect to that topic] and because the suchness of things also has reasoned proofs which are establishments by way of [logical] correctness.

It is from perceiving the import of this meaning [that differentiation of the interpretable and the definitive cannot be made by scripture alone and that reasoning is required, that Buddha] says:

> Like gold [that is acquired] upon being scorched, cut, and
> rubbed,
> My word is to be adopted by monastics and scholars
> Upon analyzing it well,
> Not out of respect [for me].

Gung-tang lays out the steps of Ḏzong-ka-ḇa's argument:[97]

1. In order to be released from cyclic existence it is necessary to realize suchness—emptiness, the thoroughly established nature.
2. To realize suchness, it is not sufficient to train only in scriptures that require interpretation; rather, one must engage properly in hearing and thinking on definitive scriptures.
3. The determination that a sūtra is definitive cannot be made by the mere fact that there is a scripture saying that it is definitive. For, just as in general it is not necessarily suitable to assert what is indicated on the literal level of a sūtra since Buddha spoke variously in accordance with the needs of trainees—for instance, sometimes he said that there are no external objects and sometimes he said that there are—so, more specifically, it is not suitable to accept a scriptural statement that a certain sūtra is definitive and that another requires interpretation, since Buddha said, for instance, in the *Teachings of Akṣhayamati Sūtra* that the middle wheel of his teaching is definitive but in the *Sūtra Unraveling the Thought* said that it requires interpretation. Therefore, through scriptural citation alone, one cannot differentiate which sūtras require interpretation and which are definitive.
4. Also, persons such as us cannot make the differentiation through our own

powers of mind, nor can we make it following just any of the many schools and great adepts. Hence, the differentiation must be made following either Nāgārjuna or Asaṅga, the two great "chariots" (that is, great leaders) prophesied by the Conqueror Buddha himself as differentiating the interpretable and the definitive.

5. To follow Nāgārjuna or Asaṅga does not mean just to read texts written by them; rather, it means analytically to delineate what is definitive and what requires interpretation within Buddha's scriptures in dependence upon the stainless reasonings through which Nāgārjuna and Asaṅga opened up their respective traditions—the Middle Way School and Mind-Only School. These are reasonings through the power of the fact (and not through citation of scripture) that refute all ambiguities which might allow interpreting the Conqueror's thought otherwise and that establish just what his thought is.
6. Thus, the process meets back just to pure analysis (a) of emptiness—the mode of subsistence of phenomena that is the uttermost meaning to be delineated—and (b) of the paths of reasonings—the uttermost means of delineation—set forth by the two great chariots.

The progression, despite being detailed, is not clear. The problem, as Gung-tang later reveals,[98] is that in order to differentiate with valid cognition between what requires interpretation and what is definitive with respect to Buddha's scriptures, one must delineate emptiness, the thoroughly established nature, but, as Dzong-ka-ba says, to do this it is necessary first to differentiate between the two classes of scriptures. This circularity makes Dzong-ka-ba's presentation difficult to comprehend.

To resolve the issue, Gung-tang distinguishes:

- differentiating between the interpretable and the definitive on the level of the **meaning** expressed by the scriptures, for which realization of emptiness by inferential valid cognition is needed
- differentiating between the interpretable and the definitive on the level of the **words** for which realization of emptiness is not needed—a correct assumption[a] that merely identifies the two classes is sufficient for this.

Gung-tang holds that here Dzong-ka-ba is calling for the latter.

To rephrase with more detail: Gung-tang makes a critical difference between "differentiating the interpretable and definitive **among** scriptures" and "differentiating the interpretable and definitive **with respect to** scriptures."[b] He holds that "differentiating the interpretable and definitive **among** scriptures" means to identify what are interpretable and what are definitive scriptures from

[a] For a discussion of correct assumption, see p. 52.

[b] *gsung rab **kyi** drang nges 'byed pa* and *gsung rab **la** drang nges 'byed pa.* The distinction is as forced in Tibetan as it is in English.

among the scriptures,[a] whereas "differentiating the interpretable and the definitive **with respect to** scriptures" means to differentiate the interpretable and the definitive with respect to the *meaning* of the scriptures, thus requiring extensive delineation of the presentation of the two truths, which itself requires realization of emptiness through inferential valid cognition. The latter is called "differentiating the interpretable and the definitive on the level of the meaning expressed (in the scriptures)"[b] and cannot be required prior to realizing emptiness. The former is called "differentiating the interpretable and the definitive on the level of the words that are the means of expression,"[c] and can be done merely through correct assumption, and thus Gung-tang identifies this as what Ḏzong-ka-ḇa says is required before realizing emptiness.

It is intriguing to note that despite Ḏzong-ka-ḇa's emphasis on reasoning, the identification of the two classes of scripture is based not on one's own reasoning but on tradition. For one must rely on a differentiation of the interpretable and definitive done by someone else, and this he says is limited to two persons prophesied by Buddha, either Nāgārjuna or Asaṅga. In this way, scripture—here being prophecies made by Buddha—which Ḏzong-ka-ḇa earlier said is not sufficient, re-emerges as crucially important. Thus, when he says:

> Therefore, in the end, the differentiation [between the interpretable and the definitive] must be made just by stainless reasoning

it is difficult to hold that this refers to one's own reasoning. Indeed, some Tibetan scholars hold that it is the reasoning used by Nāgārjuna and Asaṅga.

Again, if we take Gung-tang's explanation a step further, how does one choose between the presentations by Nāgārjuna and Asaṅga, which Ḏzong-ka-ḇa and his followers see as not only different but contradictory? Is it by one's own reasoning? It cannot be, on the same grounds as given above—one would have to realize the truth, emptiness, first in order to affirm which one of them was correct about it. Rather, the choice between Nāgārjuna and Asaṅga is done on a verbal level through a correct assumption derived from consulting the tradition, in this case statements by the teachers of one's own sect that Nāgārjuna is right and Asaṅga wrong, or vice versa. In dependence upon such a tradition, a practitioner employs the reasonings put forth by one of these two Indian scholar-adepts and, if successful, confirms that that one is the final authority. The tradition dictates the direction in which the reasoned analysis will take place. Although subsequent internalization of the reasoning in felt experience is crucially important, the process is not as thoroughly reason-based as Ḏzong-ka-ḇa seems to suggest.

Thus, in the Great Vehicle, there are basically two modes of differentiating

[a] *gsung rab kyi nang nas drang don gyi gsung rab dang nges don gyi gsung rab gang yin so sor ngos bzung ba la byed.*

[b] Gung-tang's *Difficult Points,* 37.7: *brjod bya don gyi drang nges 'byed pa.*

[c] Gung-tang's *Difficult Points,* 38.5: *rjod byed tshig gi drang nges 'byed pa.*

what is definitive and what requires interpretation—Asaṅga's mode, which follows the *Sūtra Unraveling the Thought,* and Nāgārjuna's mode, which follows the *Teachings of Akṣhayamati Sūtra.* Based on scripture, Asaṅga and Nāgārjuna made reasoned expositions showing that particular scripture to be definitive. In this book we are considering the first of these.

PART THREE: *EXAMINING THE* SŪTRA UNRAVELING THE THOUGHT

7. Questioning Contradiction

The *Sūtra Unraveling The Thought*

The tradition is that the *Sūtra Unraveling the Thought* was set forth in Vaishāli, India, by the Supramundane Victor, Shākyamuni Buddha.[a] It has ten chapters of questions by nine Bodhisattvas and one Hearer (Subhūti) and replies by Buddha, except in the first chapter, where another Bodhisattva replies. Among these, four chapters—the sixth through ninth—have teachings about the three natures, also called the three characters, but the chapter that differentiates the three natures in detail is the seventh. It has two names, the "Questions of Paramārthasamudgata," since Paramārthasamudgata is the questioner, and the "Chapter of Naturelessness,"[b] since the three non-natures are the topic. The section on the Mind-Only School in Ḏzong-ka-ḇa's *The Essence of Eloquence* is mainly concerned with the seventh chapter's differentiation of what requires interpretation and what is definitive.

The *Sūtra Unraveling the Thought* is central to Asaṅga's presentation of the three natures. As Ḏzong-ka-ḇa (*Emptiness in Mind-Only,* 137-138) says:

> ...in the "Chapter on Suchness" in the *Grounds of Bodhisattvas,* its *Ascertainment,* and the *Summary of the Great Vehicle,* Asaṅga settles through many various explanations just the statement in the *Sūtra Unraveling the Thought* that other-powered natures' emptiness of factors imputed in the manner of entities and attributes is the thoroughly established nature.

The "Questions of Paramārthasamudgata Chapter" of the *Sūtra Unraveling the Thought* explains that:

---

[a] For a discussion of the possible origins of the sūtra, see John C. Powers, *Hermeneutics and Tradition in the Saṃdhinirmocana-sūtra* (Leiden, Netherlands: E. J. Brill, 1993), 4-15.

[b] Another possible translation equivalent for *ngo bo nyid med pa* (*niḥsvabhāva*) is "non-entityness." Despite being admittedly awkward, it closely reflects in both its etymology and its meaning the Sanskrit term *niḥsvabhāva* which is derived from the verbal root *bhū* "to be." For "entity" is derived in its basic form (*es*) from the Latin *esse* "to be" and is derived in its suffixed form from the Sanskrit *as,* which, like *bhū,* means "being." In addition, "entity" means "something that exists as a particular and discrete unit" or "the fact of existence; being" (*The American Heritage Dictionary—Deluxe Edition,* 1993). Non-entityness would be a suitable translation for the negative term *niḥsvabhāva,* if it were not so awkward; other possible translations are "non-thingness," "non-natureness," and "unreality." Since all of these choices are awkward and since *trisvabhāva* is translated as "three natures," I have chosen "non-nature" for *niḥsvabhāva;* it has the additional virtue of reflecting the play between *svabhāva* and *niḥsvabhāva*—(three) natures and (three) non-natures.

- the establishment of other-powered natures such as mind, body, and persons by way of their own character as the referents of conceptual consciousnesses apprehending them in terms of entities and attributes is the chief imputational nature
- other-powered natures' emptiness of such a superimposed nature is their thoroughly established nature.

In his presentation, Ḏzong-ka-ḇa cites several passages from the seventh chapter of the sūtra. Let us cite all of these here as a prelude to detailed consideration of them by Tibetan commentators:

> Then, the Bodhisattva Paramārthasamudgata asked the Supramundane Victor:
>
> > Supramundane Victor, when I was here alone in a solitary place, my mind generated the following qualm. The Supramundane Victor spoke, in many ways, of the own-character of the aggregates. He also spoke of [their] character of production, character of disintegration, abandonment, and thorough knowledge. Just as he did with respect to the aggregates, so he also spoke with respect to the sense spheres, dependent-arising, and the foods. The Supramundane Victor also spoke, in many ways, of the own-character of the truths as well as speaking of thorough knowledge, abandonment, actualization, and meditation. The Supramundane Victor also spoke, in many ways, of the own-character of the constituents, as well as speaking of the various constituents, manifold constituents, [their] abandonment, and thorough knowledge. The Supramundane Victor also spoke, in many ways, of the own-character of the four mindful establishments, as well as speaking of [their] classes of discordances, antidotes, meditation, production of that which has not been produced, the abiding of that which has been produced, non-loss, [their] arising again, and increasing and extending. Just as he did with respect to the mindful establishments, so he spoke with respect to the thorough abandonings, the legs of magical manifestation, the faculties, the powers, and the branches of enlightenment. The Supramundane Victor also spoke, in many ways, of the own-character of the eightfold path of Superiors, as well as speaking of [their] discordances, antidotes, production of that which has not been produced, the abiding of that which has been produced, recollection, [their] arising again, and increasing and extending.
> >
> > Also, the Supramundane Victor said [in the middle wheel

of the teaching], "All phenomena are natureless; all phenomena are unproduced, unceasing, quiescent from the start, and naturally thoroughly passed beyond sorrow."

Therefore, I am wondering of what the Supramundane Victor was thinking when he said, "All phenomena are natureless; all phenomena are unproduced, unceasing, quiescent from the start, and naturally thoroughly passed beyond sorrow." I ask the Supramundane Victor about the meaning of his saying, "All phenomena are natureless; all phenomena are unproduced, unceasing, quiescent from the start, and naturally thoroughly passed beyond sorrow."

Having been asked that, the Supramundane Victor said to the Bodhisattva Paramārthasamudgata:

Paramārthasamudgata, the thought in your mind, properly generated virtue, is good, good. Paramārthasamudgata, you are involved in [asking] this in order to help many beings, to [bring] happiness to many beings, out of compassionate kindness toward the world, and for the sake of the aims, help, and happiness of all beings, including gods and humans. You are good to think to ask the One Gone Thus about this meaning. Therefore, Paramārthasamudgata, listen, and I will explain that in consideration of which I said, "All phenomena are natureless; all phenomena are unproduced, unceasing, quiescent from the start, and naturally thoroughly passed beyond sorrow."

Paramārthasamudgata, thinking of three non-natures of phenomena—character-non-nature, production-non-nature, and ultimate-non-nature—I taught [in the middle wheel of the teaching], "All phenomena are natureless."

Paramārthasamudgata, concerning that, what are character-non-natures of phenomena? Those which are imputational characters.

Why? It is thus: Those [imputational characters] are characters posited by names and terminology[a] and do not subsist by way of their own character. Therefore, they are said to be "character-non-natures."

What are production-non-natures of phenomena?[b] Those which are the other-powered characters of phenomena.

Why? It is thus: Those [other-powered characters] arise

---

[a] See *Absorption,* #104.

[b] See ibid., #76, 77. About "phenomena," see ibid., #71.

through the force of other conditions and not by themselves.[a] Therefore, they are said to be "production-non-natures."

What are ultimate-non-natures? Those dependently arisen phenomena—which are natureless due to being natureless in terms of production—are also natureless due to being natureless in terms of the ultimate.

Why? Paramārthasamudgata, that which is an object of observation of purification in phenomena I teach to be the ultimate, and other-powered characters are not the object of observation of purification. Therefore, they are said to be "ultimate-non-natures."

Moreover, that which is the thoroughly established character of phenomena is also called "the ultimate-non-nature." Why? Paramārthasamudgata, that which in phenomena is the selflessness of phenomena is called their "non-nature." It is the ultimate, and the ultimate is distinguished by just the naturelessness of all phenomena; therefore, it is called the "ultimate-non-nature."

Paramārthasamudgata, it is thus: for example, character-non-natures [that is, imputational natures] are to be viewed as like a flower in the sky.

Paramārthasamudgata, it is thus: for example, production-non-natures [that is, other-powered natures] are to be viewed as like magical creations. From between the [two] ultimate-non-natures, one [that is, other-powered natures] is also to be viewed that way.

Paramārthasamudgata, it is thus: just as, for example, space is distinguished by the mere naturelessness of form [that is, as a mere absence of forms] and pervades everywhere, so from between those [two] ultimate-non-natures, one [that is, the thoroughly established nature] is to be viewed as distinguished by the selflessness of phenomena and as pervading everything.

Paramārthasamudgata, thinking of those three types of naturelessness, I taught, "All phenomena are natureless."

Paramārthasamudgata, concerning that, thinking of just character-non-natures [that is, thinking of just imputational natures which are not established by way of their own character], I taught that all phenomena are unproduced, unceasing, quiescent from the start, naturally thoroughly passed beyond sorrow. Why? Paramārthasamudgata, it is thus: That which does not exist by way of its own character is not produced.

[a] See ibid., #67.

That which is not produced does not cease. That which is not produced and does not cease is from the start quiescent. That which is quiescent from the start is naturally thoroughly passed beyond sorrow [that is, naturally devoid of the afflictive emotions without depending on an antidote]. That which is naturally thoroughly passed beyond sorrow does not have the least thing to pass beyond sorrow.

Moreover, thinking of just the ultimate-non-nature, which is distinguished by the selflessness of phenomena, I taught, "All phenomena are unproduced, unceasing, from the start quiescent, and naturally thoroughly passed beyond sorrow." Why? It is thus: Just the ultimate-non-nature which is distinguished by the selflessness of phenomena only subsists in permanent, permanent time and everlasting, everlasting time. It is the uncompounded final reality of phenomena, devoid of all afflictive emotions. Because that uncompounded [nature] which subsists for permanent, permanent time and everlasting, everlasting time in the aspect of just that reality is uncompounded, it is unproduced and unceasing. Because it is devoid of all afflictive emotions, it is quiescent from the start and naturally thoroughly passed beyond sorrow....

Even though they have interest in that doctrine [of the profound thoroughly established nature], they do not understand, just as it is, the profound reality that I have set forth with a thought behind it. With respect to the meaning of these doctrines, they adhere to the terms as only literal: "All these phenomena are only natureless. All these phenomena are only unproduced, only unceasing, only quiescent from the start, only naturally thoroughly passed beyond sorrow." Due to that, they acquire the view that all phenomena do not exist and the view that [establishment of objects by way of their own] character does not exist. Moreover, having acquired the view of nihilism and the view of the non-existence of [establishment of objects by way of their own] character, they deprecate all phenomena in terms of all of the characters—deprecating the imputational character of phenomena and also deprecating the other-powered character and thoroughly established character of phenomena.

Why? Paramārthasamudgata, it is thus: If the other-powered character and the thoroughly established character exist [by way of their own character], the imputational character is known [that is, is possible]. However, those who perceive the other-powered character and the thoroughly established character as without character [that is to say, as not being established by way of their own character] also deprecate the imputational character. Therefore, those [persons] are said to deprecate even all three aspects of characters....

Then, at that time the Bodhisattva Paramārthasamudgata offered this to the Supramundane Victor:

Supramundane Victor, what the Buddha, the Supramundane Victor, said thinking [of something else]—subtle, supremely subtle, profound, supremely profound, difficult to realize, supremely difficult to realize—is amazing and fantastic. Supramundane Victor, I understand the meaning of what the Supramundane Victor has said as follows: That which is posited by names and terminology—with respect to [other-powered natures which are] (1) the objects of activity of conceptuality, (2) the foundations of imputational characters, and (3) those which have the signs of compositional phenomena—in the character of entities or particulars [such as, "This is] a form aggregate," and that which is posited by names and terminology in the character of entities or the character of particulars [that is, attributes, such as] "the production of the form aggregate," "the cessation of the form aggregate," "the abandonment and thorough knowledge of the form aggregate" are imputational characters. In dependence upon that, the Supramundane Victor designated the character-non-nature of phenomena.

Those which are the objects of activity of conceptuality, the foundations of imputational characters, and have the signs of compositional phenomena are other-powered characters. In dependence on that, the Supramundane Victor, in addition, designated the production-non-nature of phenomena and the ultimate-non-nature.

Supramundane Victor, I understand the meaning of what the Supramundane Victor has said as follows: the thoroughly established character is that which is:

- the thorough non-establishment—of just those [other-powered natures which are] the objects of activity of conceptuality, the foundations of imputational characters, and those which have the signs of compositional phenomena—as that imputational character
- just the naturelessness of only that [imputational] nature
- the absence of self in phenomena

- thusness, and
- the object of observation of purification....

Then, at that time the Bodhisattva also offered this to the Supramundane Victor:

> Initially, in the area of Varaṇāsi in the Deer Park called "Sage's Propounding," the Supramundane Victor thoroughly turned a wheel of doctrine for those engaged in the Hearer Vehicle, fantastic and marvelous which none—god or human—had previously turned in a similar fashion in the world, through teaching the aspects of the four noble truths.[a] Furthermore, that wheel of doctrine thoroughly turned by the Supramundane Victor is surpassable, affords an occasion [for refutation], requires interpretation, and serves as a basis for controversy.
>
> Based on just the naturelessness of all phenomena and based on just the absence of production, the absence of cessation, quiescence from the start, and naturally passed beyond sorrow, the Supramundane Victor turned a second wheel of doctrine, for those engaged in the Great Vehicle, very fantastic and marvelous, through the aspect of speaking on emptiness. Furthermore, that wheel of doctrine turned by the Supramundane Victor is surpassable, affords an occasion [for refutation], requires interpretation, and serves as a basis for controversy.
>
> However, based on just the naturelessness of phenomena and based on just the absence of production, the absence of cessation, quiescence from the start, and naturally passed beyond sorrow, the Supramundane Victor turned a third wheel of doctrine for those engaged in all vehicles, possessed of good differentiation, fantastic and marvelous. This wheel of doctrine turned by the Supramundane Victor is unsurpassable, does not afford an occasion [for refutation], is of definitive meaning, and does not serve as a basis for controversy.

Dzong-ka-ba analyzes these passages in the *Sūtra Unraveling the Thought* within the fourfold context of:

- presenting Indian Mind-Only scholarship on not just the emptiness of apprehended-object and apprehending-subject but also the emptiness of imputation in the manner of entity and attribute so that the architecture of the system can be engaged
- distinguishing the Mind-Only School from the Consequence School and

[a] See ibid., #19, 20.

thus setting the stage for his later exposition of Chandrakīrti's criticism of the Mind-Only School and the Autonomy School

- refining the Korean scholar Wonch'uk's seventh-century presentation
- criticizing the eclecticism of the thirteenth- and fourteenth-century Tibetan scholar-adept Jo-nang-b̄a S̄hay-rap-gyel-tsen (1292-1361), who died four years after D̄zong-ka-b̄a's birth.

Question About Contradiction

Ge-luk-b̄a scholars examine Paramārthasamudgata's question[a] to Buddha about apparent contradictions in his teachings from four viewpoints:

- the structure of the question
- the motivation of the questioner
- the scope of the question—just the second wheel of doctrine, or both the first and the second?
- two important terms—"all phenomena" and "own-character."

Structure Of The Question

The Korean scholar Wonch'uk[b] was born in 612 or 613 in Hsin-lo and ordained as a novice at the age of three; at fifteen he traveled to Ch'ang-an,[c] China, capital of the T'ang dynasty (618-908), where he remained for the rest of his life, dying at Fo-shou-chi Monastery on August 25, 696. He wrote a ten-fascicle commentary on the *Sūtra Unraveling the Thought* that was eventually translated into Tibetan sometime between 815 and 824[d] and thus became part of the cultural milieu in Tibet when D̄zong-ka-b̄a wrote *The Essence of Eloquence* at the turn of the fifteenth century (1407-1408).[e]

In dependence[99] on Wonch'uk's exposition,[100] D̄ra-d̄i Ge-s̄hay Rin-chen-dön-drup,[101] an eighteenth-century follower of Jay-d̄zün Chö-ḡyi-gyel-tsen, divides Paramārthasamudgata's question to Buddha about apparent contradictions in his teaching into four parts:

1. Paramārthasamudgata describes the mode of Buddha's pronouncement of doctrine in the first turning of the wheel of doctrine:

The Supramundane Victor spoke, in many ways, of the own-character

---

[a] For an extensive discussion of the question, see *Absorption*, #10-56.

[b] For a more detailed presentation of Wonch'uk's biography, see *Emptiness in Mind-Only*, 39ff.

[c] Presently called Xian.

[d] For a discussion of how the text came to be translated by Fa-ch'eng, see *Emptiness in Mind-Only*, 44.

[e] For a discussion of Wonch'uk's commentary, see *Absorption*, #8, 9, 13, 14, 16, 18, 39, 43, 48, 49, 60, chap. 13, and the separate section on it.

of the aggregates. He also spoke of [their] character of production, character of disintegration, abandonment, and thorough knowledge. Just as he did with respect to the aggregates, so he also spoke with respect to the sense spheres, dependent-arising, and the foods. The Supramundane Victor also spoke, in many ways, of the own-character of the truths as well as speaking of thorough knowledge, abandonment, actualization, and meditation. The Supramundane Victor also spoke, in many ways, of the own-character of the constituents, as well as speaking of the various constituents, manifold constituents, [their] abandonment, and thorough knowledge. The Supramundane Victor also spoke, in many ways, of the own-character of the four mindful establishments, as well as speaking of [their] classes of discordances, antidotes, meditation, production of that which has not been produced, the abiding of that which has been produced, non-loss, [their] arising again, and increasing and extending. Just as he did with respect to the mindful establishments, so he spoke with respect to the thorough abandonings, the legs of magical manifestation, the faculties, the powers, and the branches of enlightenment. The Supramundane Victor also spoke, in many ways, of the own-character of the eightfold path of Superiors, as well as speaking of [their] discordances, antidotes, production of that which has not been produced, the abiding of that which has been produced, recollection, [their] arising again, and increasing and extending.

2. Paramārthasamudgata describes the mode of Buddha's pronouncement of doctrine in the second turning of the wheel of doctrine:

> Also, the Supramundane Victor said [in the middle wheel of the teaching], "All phenomena are natureless; all phenomena are unproduced, unceasing, quiescent from the start, and naturally thoroughly passed beyond sorrow."

3. Paramārthasamudgata speaks of a qualm he has generated (or pretends to generate for the sake of others):

> Therefore, I am wondering of what the Supramundane Victor was thinking when he said, "All phenomena are natureless; all phenomena are unproduced, unceasing, quiescent from the start, and naturally thoroughly passed beyond sorrow."

4. Paramārthasamudgata asks the question:

> I ask the Supramundane Victor about the meaning of his saying, "All phenomena are natureless; all phenomena are unproduced, unceasing, quiescent from the start, and naturally thoroughly passed beyond sorrow."

Ge-luk-b̄a scholars subject Paramārthasamudgata's question and D̄zong-ka-b̄a's short commentary on it to extensive analysis, sometimes drawing attention to facets of the sūtra that otherwise could easily be missed and at other times endowing the sūtra with retroactive meanings created by analyzing it in the light of subsequent scholastic developments.

Motivation Of The Questioner: Why Does A Tenth-Ground Bodhisattva Need To Ask A Question?

Gung-tang Ḡön-chok-d̄en-b̄ay-drön-may (1762-1823) is one of the most widely respected scholars who took up D̄zong-ka-b̄a's steel bow and arrow, as should be clear from the many fine analytical points that have been cited above. Born in 1762 in Am-do Dzö-ge,[a] south of D̄ra-s̄hi-kyil, 1,050 years after Wonch'uk's birth in Korea, Gung-tang became the chief student of Ḡön-chok-jik-may-w̄ang-b̄o, who himself was the incarnation of Jam-ȳang-shay-b̄a and the chief student of J̄ang-ḡya Röl-b̄ay-dor-jay. His monastery was D̄ra-s̄hi-kyil, and thus he was of the Go-mang tradition, but his appeal in other Ge-luk-b̄a traditions is that, although in his two commentaries he largely explains Jam-ȳang-shay-b̄a's viewpoint, he indicates independence of thought such as when he prefers interpretations of Gung-ru Chö-jung, who preceded Jam-ȳang-shay-b̄a as textbook author of the Go-mang tradition.

Gung-tang reports that, since Paramārthasamudgata is a tenth-ground Bodhisattva (the last level before Buddhahood) who has attained the initiation of great light rays,[b] there is nothing new for him to learn that he did not know before. Paramārthasamudgata himself has no qualms wondering about contradictions in the literal rendering of the sūtras of the first and middle wheels of doctrine.[c] Thus, why does he ask a question?

The Second Dalai Lama[102] explains that Paramārthasamudgata only pretends to have qualms about Buddha's teachings in order to be of assistance to those of the Great Vehicle lineage who will benefit from being taught cognition-only, that is to say, mind-only. Gung-tang adds that the question is out of altruism in order to clear away qualms that other trainees have generated or will generate and thus, when Buddha answers Paramārthasamudgata's question, he begins by saying:[103]

---

a *mdzod dge.*

b Gung-tang's *Difficult Points,* 95.1-95.8. The *Sūtra Unraveling the Thought* itself does not say that Paramārthasamudgata is on the tenth ground.

c As Jam-ȳang-shay-b̄a (*Brief Decisive Analysis,* 487.3-488.1) says, such a qualm could not possibly be generated in Paramārthasamudgata's continuum because he is a person who has experienced attainment of a Great Vehicle path of release of the path of seeing and hence has abandoned what is to be abandoned by the path of seeing on the first Bodhisattva ground, which includes doubt. Jam-ȳang-shay-b̄a also cites the Second Dalai Lama's *Lamp Illuminating the Meaning;* see the next backnote.

> Paramārthasamudgata, the thought in your mind, properly generated virtue, is good, good. Paramārthasamudgata, you are involved in [asking] this in order to help many beings, to [bring] happiness to many beings, out of compassionate kindness toward the world, and for the sake of the aims, help, and happiness of all beings, including gods and humans. You are good to think to ask the One Gone Thus about this meaning.

Gung-tang's refinement is clearly based in the sūtra itself.

Scope Of The Question: Is It Limited To The Second Wheel?

When Paramārthasamudgata questions Buddha, he lays out what the first and second wheels of doctrine teach and then asks Buddha what he was thinking when he taught the second wheel. The apparent limiting of his question to the second wheel might lead one to think that his concern is only with that wheel and its contradiction with the first wheel, and thus it might appear that Paramārthasamudgata is taking the first wheel as definitively acceptable. However, Dzong-ka-ba (*Emptiness in Mind-Only,* 78) cogently explains that, although Paramārthasamudgata does not explicitly ask Buddha what he had in mind when he taught the first wheel, this is done implicitly:

> This asks the following question:
>
> > If the statements in some sūtras [that is, in the middle wheel of the teaching] that all phenomena are natureless, and so forth, and the statements in some sūtras [in the first wheel of the teaching] that the aggregates and so forth have an own-character, and so forth, were left as they are verbally, they would be contradictory. However, since [the Supramundane Victor] must be without contradiction, of what were you [Buddha] thinking when [in the middle wheel of the teaching] you spoke of non-nature, and so forth?
>
> Through that, [Paramārthasamudgata] implicitly[a] asks of what [Buddha] was thinking when [in the first wheel of the teaching] he spoke of the existence of own-character and so forth.[b]

Indeed, later in Paramārthasamudgata's reframing of Buddha's answer, he states that ***both*** wheels require interpretation, and thus it is clear that a question about the first wheel is implicit. Paramārthasamudgata is concerned with Buddha's thought behind the teachings in both wheels of doctrine.

---

[a] See *Absorption,* #56.

[b] See ibid., #21-24.

What Are "Aggregates And So Forth"?

The general context in which the *Sūtra Unraveling the Thought* is read is that of the Great Vehicle even though the sūtra speaks on several occasions about the paths of Hearers and Solitary Realizers. Thus, when D̄zong-ka-b̄a, cited just above, paraphrases Paramārthasamudgata's description of the middle- and first-wheel teachings by saying:

> If the statements in some sūtras [that is, in the middle wheel of the teaching] that all phenomena are natureless, and so forth, and the statements in some sūtras [in the first wheel of the teaching] that the aggregates and so forth have an own-character, and so forth...

it could be thought that "aggregates and so forth," which he mentions with regard to the first wheel, refers to the entire range of phenomena that are set out in the Great Vehicle. This is just how B̄el-jor-hlün-drup of the S̄e-ra Jay tradition takes D̄zong-ka-b̄a's reference:[104]

> In the first wheel, the Supramundane Victor pronounced that phenomena **ranging from forms through to omniscient consciousnesses** are established by way of their own character...

However, the original textbook author of the Go-mang tradition, Gung-ru Chö-jung,[105] and his successor, Jam-ȳang-shay-b̄a,[106] cogently point out that here in the first wheel and thus the Lesser Vehicle, "all phenomena" cannot refer to "phenomena ranging from forms through to omniscient consciousnesses," a standard list of 108 phenomena drawn from Great Vehicle sūtras—such as the Perfection of Wisdom Sūtras—that begins with forms and ends with omniscient consciousnesses.[107] Rather, "aggregates and so forth" refers to the mental and physical aggregates, the sense-spheres, dependent-arising, the foods, the four noble truths, the constituents, and the harmonies with enlightenment—called the seven pronouncements.[a] Thus, in the first wheel of the teaching, the bases of Buddha's teaching are the "seven pronouncements." Also, since the prime of these are the four noble truths, the first wheel is later described in the *Sūtra Unraveling the Thought* as "teaching the aspects of the four noble truths."

Even though all of the first wheel similarly teaches that phenomena are established by way of their own character as the referents of conceptual consciousnesses, the topics that form the floor of this teaching are many and various—the seven pronouncements. On the other hand, when Paramārthasamudgata speaks of the middle wheel, he condenses the teachings into one description, since they all equally speak of all phenomena—ranging from forms through to exalted knowers of all aspects (omniscient consciousnesses)—as natureless.

---

[a] *bka' stsal bdun.*

What Is "Own-Character"?

In all Ge-luk-b̄a systems of interpretation, the three wheels of doctrine as they are described in the *Sūtra Unraveling the Thought* are not general classes into which all of Buddha's teaching can be placed; rather, they are three sets of specific teachings on the nature of objects. About the first wheel, Paramārthasamudgata describes the teachings on the aggregates, sense-spheres,[a] dependent-arising, and foods as having five features:

1. Own-character
2. Production
3. Disintegration
4. Abandonment
5. Thorough knowledge.

The teachings on the four truths are described as having two features:

1. Own-character
2. Thorough knowledge (of true sufferings), abandonment (of true sources of suffering), actualization (of true cessations), and meditation (cultivating true paths).

The teachings on the constituents are described as having three features:

1. Own-character
2. Abandonment
3. Thorough knowledge.

The teachings of the thirty-seven harmonies with enlightenment are described as having eight features:

1. Own-character
2. Discordances
3. Antidotes
4. Production
5. Abiding
6. Non-loss
7. Arising again
8. Increasing.

In each of the seven pronouncements, the first feature—the teaching of "own-character"[b]—is a topic of controversy with respect to its interpretation. Wonch'uk,[108] in his *Great Commentary on the "Sūtra Unraveling the Thought,"*

---

a Lo-sang-w̄ang-chuk (*Notes,* 111.5) draws attention to the fact that the *Sūtra Unraveling the Thought* strangely posits production and disintegration as an attribute of the sense spheres, which include permanent phenomena.

b *rang gi mtshan nyid, svalakṣaṇa.*

takes the term as referring to the unique character or definition of a phenomenon. In the case of form, for instance, this would be obstructiveness. Wonch'uk is referring to the style of teaching in which Buddha speaks of a phenomenon and then describes its specific, or unique, character that distinguishes it from other phenomena. His *Great Commentary on the "Sūtra Unraveling the Thought"* says about the five aggregates:[109]

> "Own-character" is the specific character as in, for instance, the explanation, "Form is that which is obstructive....Consciousness is that which knows."

Wonch'uk similarly refers to teachings in which Buddha says about the first of the twelve sense-spheres, the eye, that it is what has the capacity to see form and says about the first of the twelve links of dependent-arising, ignorance, that it is an obscurative mental factor that is the opposite of knowledge.[110] For him, "own-character" is the nature, or entity, of a phenomenon.

Wonch'uk's interpretation of "own-character" is particularly attractive, since everyone agrees that the first feature, "own-character," refers to the **entity** of the object and the others refer to **attributes** of the object, a frequent theme of the *Sūtra Unraveling the Thought.* However, Dzong-ka-ba and his followers reject Wonch'uk's interpretation that the teaching concerning the "own-character" of phenomena is of their respective definitions, since they hold that this is inconsistent with the usage of the term "character" in "character-non-natures"[a] in Buddha's answer to Paramārthasamudgata's question:

> Paramārthasamudgata, concerning that, what are character-non-natures of phenomena? Those which are imputational characters.
>
> Why? It is thus: Those [imputational characters] are characters posited by names and terminology and **do not subsist by way of their own character**. Therefore, they are said to be "**character-non-natures.**"

Some of Dzong-ka-ba's followers take the "own-character" of Paramārthasamudgata's question as referring to a phenomenon's being established by way of its own character, and some, even more specifically, take it as referring to a phenomenon's being established by way of its own character as the referent of a conceptual consciousness. It is a crucial step in interpreting the seventh chapter of the *Sūtra Unraveling the Thought.* Let us consider this controversy step by step.

Refuting Wonch'uk

In rejecting Wonch'uk's interpretation of "own-character" as the unique

[a] *mtshan nyid ngo bo nyid med pa, lakṣaṇaniḥsvabhāvatā* (Étienne Lamotte, *Saṃdhinirmocanasūtra: L'Explication des mystères* [Louvain: Université de Louvain, 1935], 67 [3], n. 3).

character, or definition, of an object as inadequate, Ḏzong-ka-ḇa (*Emptiness in Mind-Only,* 78-79) himself says:

> In the Chinese *Great Commentary*[a] [on the *Sūtra Unraveling the Thought* by the Korean scholar Wonch'uk], and so forth, "own-character"[b] here [in this passage in the *Sūtra Unraveling the Thought*] is explained as the unique character [of the aggregates and so forth], but this is not right.[c] For the sūtra itself at the point of [speaking about] imputational factors[d] clearly speaks of establishment by way of [the object's] own character [and does not speak of the unique character], and since even imputational factors have a unique characterization, there would be the fallacy that the character-non-nature could not be explained with respect to imputational factors.[e]

Ḏzong-ka-ḇa is referring to the *Sūtra Unraveling the Thought,* which, as cited above, does indeed say:

> Those [imputational characters] are characters posited by names and terminology and **do not subsist by way of their own character.** Therefore, they are said to be **"character-non-natures."**

Ḏzong-ka-ḇa's well-taken point is that, when describing how imputational natures are natureless in terms of character, the sūtra itself says that they "do not subsist by way of their own character,"[f] that is to say, they are not established by way of their own character; the sūtra does not speak about the defining character of an object. Also, imputational natures have the unique characteristic or definition of being *something that is imputed by conceptuality.*[g] Therefore, if the absence of "character" that is mentioned in Buddha's answer when discussing imputational natures merely referred to the non-existence of a unique characterization, such an absence could not be posited with respect to imputational natures, since they do indeed have a unique characterization. Since one of the main points of Buddha's answer is that imputational natures are without the nature of "character," "character" in the answer cannot refer to a unique or uncommon character.

Ḏzong-ka-ḇa's point is cogent, but we need to notice that he makes the extension that the "own-character" of the question also cannot refer to the unique characteristic of an object; he sees a necessary equivalence between the

---

a See *Absorption,* #8.

b See ibid., #27-55, 94.

c See ibid., #48, 39.

d See ibid., #50.

e See ibid., #48.

f *rang gi mtshan nyid kyis rnam par gnas pa ni ma yin pa, svalakṣaṇena avyavasthitaṃ:* Lamotte, *Saṃdhinirmocana,* 68 [4], n. 1.

g *rtog pas btags tsam:* Gung-ru Chö-jung's *Garland of White Lotuses,* 20a.4.

"own-character" mentioned in the question and the "character" mentioned in the answer. According to Dzong-ka-ba, the meaning of Paramārthasamudgata's usage of the term "own-character" in the question indicates that:

- In the first wheel of doctrine, Buddha taught that all phenomena are equally established by way of their own character, whereas
- in the middle wheel he taught that these phenomena are equally not established by way of their own character, and
- these appear to be contradictory.

His interpretation of Paramārthasamudgata's question creates a particularly vexing problem for his followers; namely, if the first-wheel sūtras as described in the *Sūtra Unraveling the Thought* did explicitly teach that phenomena ranging from forms through the thirty-seven harmonies with enlightenment are established by way of their own character, then, since this list of phenomena includes both compounded (impermanent) phenomena and uncompounded (permanent) phenomena, the first-wheel sūtras would explicitly teach that compounded phenomena ranging from forms through the thirty-seven harmonies with enlightenment are established by way of their own character.

For instance, Paramārthasamudgata says, "The Supramundane Victor spoke, in many ways, of the own-character of the aggregates." The problem is that all Ge-luk-ba interpreters agree that the Mind-Only School maintains that compounded phenomena are indeed established by way of their own character; they cogently point to a clear statement of this in the *Sūtra Unraveling the Thought* (*Emptiness in Mind-Only,* 97) itself:[111]

> Paramārthasamudgata, concerning that, thinking of just character-non-natures [that is, thinking of just imputational factors which are not established by way of their own character], I taught that all phenomena are unproduced, unceasing, quiescent from the start, naturally thoroughly passed beyond sorrow.
>
> Why? Paramārthasamudgata, it is thus: **That which does not exist by way of its own character is not produced.** That which is not produced does not cease. That which is not produced and does not cease is from the start quiescent. That which is quiescent from the start is naturally thoroughly passed beyond sorrow [that is, naturally devoid of the afflictive emotions without depending on an antidote]. That which is naturally thoroughly passed beyond sorrow does not have the least thing to pass beyond sorrow.

Since the *Sūtra Unraveling the Thought* itself says, "That which does not exist by way of its own character is not produced," it is clear that in the Mind-Only School, for which the *Sūtra Unraveling the Thought* is foundational, phenomena that are compounded by causes and conditions must be established by way of their own character.

If we consider the topics of the seven pronouncements, almost all of them are compounded phenomena—all five mental and physical aggregates, all twelve links of dependent-arising, all four foods, all six constituents, and all thirty-seven harmonies with enlightenment. From among the others, of the twelve sense-spheres eleven are compounded phenomena; the twelfth, called "phenomena," includes all permanent phenomena as well as compounded phenomena not included in the others. Of the four noble truths, only true cessations are uncompounded—the chief of these being nirvāṇa; the other three are compounded phenomena. Of the eighteen constituents, only one includes uncompounded phenomena, as above with the twelve sense-spheres. In fact, from among the topics of the seven pronouncements, little attention is paid to permanent, uncompounded phenomena, and thus *most* of what the first-wheel sūtras teach, that is, that these seven groups of phenomena are established by way of their own character, would have to be asserted as literally acceptable in the Mind-Only School.

Looking again at Paramārthasamudgata's question, we are faced with the absurdity that almost all of what he describes about first-wheel teachings would have to be accepted literally in the Mind-Only School (the literally acceptable are in bold type):

> **The Supramundane Victor spoke, in many ways, of the own-character of the aggregates. He also spoke of [their] character of production, character of disintegration, abandonment, and thorough knowledge. Just as he did with respect to the aggregates, so he also spoke with respect to the sense-spheres, dependent-arising, and the foods.** The Supramundane Victor also spoke, in many ways, of the own-character of the truths **as well as speaking of thorough knowledge, abandonment, actualization, and meditation.** The Supramundane Victor also spoke, in many ways, of the own-character of the constituents, as well as speaking of the various constituents, **manifold constituents, [their] abandonment, and thorough knowledge. The Supramundane Victor also spoke, in many ways, of the own-character of the four mindful establishments, as well as speaking of [their] classes of discordances, antidotes, meditation, production of that which has not been produced, the abiding of that which has been produced, non-loss, [their] arising again, and increasing and extending. Just as he did with respect to the mindful establishments, so he spoke with respect to the thorough abandonings, the legs of magical manifestation, the faculties, the powers, and the branches of enlightenment.**

All of the phenomena mentioned in bold type are impermanent and thus, in the Mind-Only system, are established by way of their own character. Consequently, if the teaching in question is merely that phenomena are established by way of their own character, the teachings represented by these parts of Paramārthasamudgata's question would be literally acceptable and, hence, definitive. Even among what cannot be accepted literally, the only problems are that *one* of the twelve sense-spheres, *one* of the four truths, and *one* of the eighteen constituents are not established by way of their own character; the other eleven sense-spheres, the other three truths, the other five constituents, and the other seventeen constituents are established by way of their own character.

The devastating situation is that, when first-wheel sūtras explicitly teach that compounded phenomena are established by way of their own character, their explicit teaching (in this regard) would be of definitive meaning, free of any contradiction by reasoning. As Gung-tang says,[112] Paramārthasamudgata's question would be unnecessary. However, this is not feasible, since first-wheel sūtras are clearly described later in the seventh chapter of the *Sūtra Unraveling the Thought* as requiring interpretation. When Paramārthasamudgata (*Emptiness in Mind-Only,* 115-116) summarizes the meaning of Buddha's answers, he says:

> Initially, in the area of Varaṇāsi in the Deer Park called "Sage's Propounding," the Supramundane Victor thoroughly turned a wheel of doctrine for those engaged in the Hearer Vehicle, fantastic and marvelous which none—god or human—had previously turned in a similar fashion in the world, through teaching the aspects of the four noble truths.[a] Furthermore, that wheel of doctrine thoroughly turned by the Supramundane Victor is **surpassable, affords an occasion [for refutation], requires interpretation, and serves as a basis for controversy.**

Paramārthasamudgata characterizes first-wheel sūtras as not being literally acceptable; thus, the mere teaching that compounded phenomena are established by way of their own character could not be his referent.

Gung-ru Chö-jung and Jam-ȳang-shay-b̄a resolve the problem by holding that what D̄zong-ka-b̄a meant is that in the first wheel Buddha taught that all phenomena are **established by way of their own character as the referents of their respective conceptual consciousnesses**. Despite the attractiveness of their explanation, many of D̄zong-ka-b̄a's followers stick with their founder's own words. It seems to me that the reason for the variance in opinion (beyond the culturally approved penchant for disagreement) is that there are two markedly different ways of *describing* the teaching of the first wheel despite the fact that these two roughly come down to meaning the same thing:

1. The first-wheel sūtras teach that each and every phenomenon, whether compounded or uncompounded, is established by way of its own character as the referent of its respective conceptual consciousness.

[a] See *Absorption,* #19, 20.

2. The first-wheel sūtras teach, without discrimination, that all phenomena are established by way of their own character.

The specific problem at which the second mode of description is pointing is that factors imputed in the manner of entity and attribute are uncompounded phenomena and hence are not established by way of their own character but are said to be so established in the first-wheel sūtras when Buddha says that everything is so established. When Buddha teaches that such imputational natures, **which are associated with all phenomena**, are established by way of their own character, this is merely another way of saying that each and every phenomenon is established by way of its own character as the referent of its respective conceptual consciousness—the first mode of description.

Thus, another way of teaching that all phenomena are established by way of their own character as the referents of their respective conceptual consciousnesses is to propound that all phenomena (including factors imputed in the manner of entity and attribute) are established by way of their own character. In accordance with the latter mode of description, it is feasible to speak of the first wheel as not being literally acceptable because it does not discriminate between what is and what is not established by way of its own character and thereby teaches that all phenomena (including such imputational natures) are established by way of their own character.

When this same teaching is described in the first manner, its shortcoming is not with a failure to discriminate between two classes of phenomena in terms of whether they are established by way of their own character or not, but with its teaching that each and every phenomenon is established by way of its own character as the referent of its respective conceptual consciousness, for according to the Mind-Only School no phenomenon, whether compounded or uncompounded, is established by way of its own character **as the referent of its respective conceptual consciousness**. This mode accords more with the style of Paramārthasamudgata's description in the *Sūtra Unraveling the Thought* in which the suggestion is that there is something wrong with how each and every one of the seven categories of phenomena are taught in the first wheel, not with just a few among their sub-divisions.

It seems to me that D̄zong-ka-b̄a passes back and forth between these two modes of description without clearly delineating which one he is using, and Ge-luk-b̄a scholars have differed in how they treat all of his statements one way.

- Jay-d̄zün Chö-ḡyi-gyel-tsen leaves as is D̄zong-ka-b̄a's identification of "own-character" as "established by way of its own character" and only cryptically suggests that the first wheel **also** teaches that phenomena are established by way of their own character as the referents of their respective conceptual consciousnesses.
- Paṇ-chen S̄ö-nam-drak-b̄a[113] likewise leaves D̄zong-ka-b̄a's identification as

is but adds that a difference of entity between subject and object is **also** taught, and some of his contemporary followers (for example, the late Ken-sur Ye-s̄hay-tup-d̄en[a] and Ge-s̄hay Ḡön-chok-tsay-ring[b]) add that the establishment of objects by way of their own character as the referents of conceptual consciousnesses is **also** communicated. Thus, in Jay-d̄zün Chö-ḡyi-gyel-tsen and Paṇ-chen S̄ö-nam-drak-b̄a's traditions any passage that teaches that forms, for instance, are established by way of their own character **also** teaches that forms are established by way of their own character as the referents of their respective conceptual consciousnesses or are external objects. Hence, even though such a passage is factually correct in teaching that forms are established by way of their own character, it is not entailed that the passage is literally acceptable and thus of definitive meaning, since it **also** teaches a false status of objects—that forms are established by way of their own character as the referents of their respective conceptual consciousnesses or are external objects.

Gung-ru Chö-jung and Jam-ȳang-shay-b̄a, however, strictly limit the meaning of "own-character" to the establishment of objects by way of their own character as the referents of conceptual consciousnesses and hold that this is what D̄zong-ka-b̄a meant by "established by way of its own character." Thus, they conclude that what D̄zong-ka-b̄a means is that first-wheel sūtras teach, relative to certain trainees, that each and every phenomenon, whether compounded or uncompounded, is established by way of its own character **as the referent of its respective conceptual consciousness.** They thereby draw attention to the fact that Paramārthasamudgata does not use the second mode of description when he presents his question to Buddha. Indeed, Paramārthasamudgata's presentation of the first-wheel teaching does not in any way suggest that the problem is with the indiscriminate inclusion of such imputational natures (which are never listed in his description!) among what is established by way of its own character. Rather, the style of Paramārthasamudgata's description (especially when taken together with his later summation that first-wheel teachings require interpretation) suggests that there is something unacceptable about each and every first-wheel teaching. Gung-ru Chö-jung (with Jam-ȳang-shay-b̄a following him), basing himself on the style of the sūtra itself and not on D̄zong-ka-b̄a's condensed way of referring to it through the second mode of description, makes the point, cogent within D̄zong-ka-b̄a's general system, that, when Paramārthasamudgata uses the term "own-character" to describe what Buddha teaches in the first wheel, he cannot mean just establishment of objects by way of their own character; rather, he must intend

[a] *mkhan zur ye shes thub bstan,* died 1988.

[b] *dge bshes dkon mchog tshe ring.*

> establishment of by way of their own character as the referents of conceptual consciousnesses. Otherwise, most of what Buddha taught in the first wheel would be literally acceptable.

Despite considerable differences in how these scholars understand certain phrases in the *Sūtra Unraveling the Thought* and in D̄zong-ka-b̄a's text, there is agreement on just what sort of teaching in the first wheel causes it not to be definitive—the teaching that forms and so forth are established by way of their own character as the referents of their respective terms and conceptual consciousnesses and the teaching that forms and so forth are external objects.

My own view accords with Wonch'uk's explanation that "own-character" refers to the specific character, or entity, of an object, but I add that this is within the context of its being established by way of its own character as the referent of a conceptual consciousness. Thus, it seems to me that the "own-character" mentioned in the question could indeed refer to the entity, the unique character, of an object, since such a meaning appears frequently in Buddhist texts and since the format of an *entity* (such as a form) and its *attributes* (such as production and disintegration) is so important in this sūtra. (For more detail, see *Absorption,* chap. 6.)

8. First Two Wheels of Doctrine

What Does The Literal Reading Of The First Wheel Contain?

Gung-tang[114] tackles the basic issue of the meaning of the term "own-character" in Paramārthasamudgata's question through analyzing the teaching in the first wheel of doctrine about forms, which are the first among the five mental and physical aggregates (forms, feelings, discriminations, compositional factors, and consciousnesses), the first of the seven pronouncements. He identifies the *Sūtra of Advice to King Bimbisāra* as a first-wheel sūtra, but, far from containing phrases even distantly resembling the vocabulary of the "establishment of forms by way of their own character as the referents of conceptual consciousnesses," the *Sūtra of Advice to King Bimbisāra* contains only the words "Great King, form has production; it also has disintegration."[a] Since form does indeed have production and disintegration, the literal rendering of the sūtra seems to be acceptable and not subject to the type of qualm that Paramārthasamudgata displays, for he is concerned with teachings the literal rendering of which is not borne out by the facts. The problem is that, even though it is clear that, according to the Mind-Only School, objects are not established by way of their own character as the referents of conceptual consciousnesses, nowhere can the vocabulary of the opposite of this be found in first-wheel teachings.

In an intricately framed presentation, Gung-tang explains away this seemingly devastating situation by showing that the sūtra words, such as "Great King, form has production; it also has disintegration," come to teach **even on the literal level** that production and disintegration are established by way of their own character as the referents of conceptual consciousnesses. His claim is amazing given that the concern is with the **literal** level and given that these words or anything resembling them are obviously lacking.[b]

---

[a] Gung-tang (*Difficult Points,* 80.12-80.16) points out that, although this passage is not found in a sūtra entitled *rgyal po la gdams pa'i mdo,* it is found in *gzugs can snying pos bsu ba,* which is composed of advice to King Bimbisāra (see also Jik-may-dam-chö-gya-tso's *Port of Entry,* 154.3-154.5). In addition, he identifies what is either a mis-translation into Tibetan or corrupt Indian text (80.16-81.5).

Gung-tang (*Annotations,* 14.2) identifies *dmag ldan gzugs can snying po, bzo sbyangs gzugs can snying po,* and *rgyal po gzugs can snying po* as names of Bimbisāra during various stages of his life; as sources for this he cites *'dul ba lung* and *gleng 'bum.*

[b] As A-ku Lo-drö-gya-tso (*Precious Lamp,* 55.5) says about the first-wheel teachings:

> That [objects] are established by way of their own character as the referents of conceptual consciousnesses does not emerge in the words of the first wheel [sūtras] explicitly indicated here [in the *Sūtra Unraveling the Thought*], but it comes to be indicated on the literal level (*'dir dngos su bstan pa'i 'khor lo dang po rnams kyi tshig la rang 'dzin rtog pa'i zhen gzhir rang mtshan gyis grub pa ma thon kyang sgras zin la*

Gung-tang's position is that, although all whatsoever teachings of production and disintegration to trainees of the Low Vehicle schools do not have to teach that objects are established by way of their own character as the referents of their respective terms and conceptual consciousnesses, these words in the *Sūtra of Advice to King Bimbisāra*[a] ("Great King, form has production; it also has disintegration") do because of the mental set of its intended trainees and because of the fact that on this occasion Buddha intends to play into that set. Gung-tang explains that, for the minds of these trainees, the person is a self-instituting controller that does not depend on the mental and physical aggregates, and the aggregates are what are controlled by that person; aside from such a context, these trainees do not know how to posit a person and mental and physical aggregates. Due to this, although Buddha would not teach them that the person and the aggregates are independently individual like a shepherd and his or her herd, he teaches them something that is not true, namely, that there is an I that is established by way of its own character as a referent of terms and conceptual consciousnesses and that there are mental and physical aggregates appropriated by that I that are established this way, too. Buddha also teaches that, since these exist, the production (which is the appropriation of those aggregates) and the disintegration (which is the discarding of them) are established from their own, the object's, side by way of their own character as referents of terms and conceptual consciousnesses and are not just conceptual superimpositions.

The minds of these trainees are so conditioned to conceiving a self of phenomena—that is, to conceiving that objects are established by way of their own character as the referents of conceptual consciousnesses—that, if such were not taught, things would become for them mere figments of the imagination, losing all status and efficacy whatsoever, and there are no trainees to whom Buddha would want to communicate that phenomena are mere figments of the imagination. Thus, for the time being, Buddha cannot teach them the truth—that phenomena are **not** established by way of their own character as the referents of their respective terms and conceptual consciousnesses. Hence, even if the mere words in the *Sūtra of Advice to King Bimbisāra* are "production" and "disintegration," it comes to be that, in terms of what is expressed even on the literal level, Buddha speaks of entities (such as forms) and attributes (such as the production of form or the beauty of a form) as established by way of their own character as the referents of their respective terms and conceptual consciousnesses, a status that neither form nor anything else actually has. In this fashion, the *Sūtra Unraveling the Thought* says:[115]

> ...that which is posited by names and terminology in the character of

---

de bstan par 'gro ba).

See also A-ku Lo-drö-gya-tso's *Precious Lamp*, 296.1.

[a] See *Absorption*, #10.

> entities or the character of particulars [that is, attributes, such as] "the production of the form aggregate," "the cessation of the form aggregate," "the abandonment and thorough knowledge of the form aggregate" are imputational characters.

As Gung-tang says, all observations and apprehensions of production and disintegration by these trainees in accordance with the literal rendering of the *Sūtra of Advice to King Bimbisāra* come to be polluted with the pride of conceit of the opposite of the meaning of selflessness —the opposite of objects' ***not*** being established by way of their own character as the referents of conceptual consciousnesses.

Gung-tang also cites, in abbreviated form, the "Questions of Subhūti Chapter" of the *Sūtra Unraveling the Thought,* in which Subhūti, using the format of the seven pronouncements, speaks of some monks as dealing with these seven under the influence of the pride of conceit. Let us cite the passage in its entirety:[116]

> Supramundane Victor, at one time there was a hermitage in a great forest, and with me there were many monks together in that hermitage in a great forest. These monks, having come together, mutually assembled in the morning. They expounded their understandings by teaching what they had manifestly realized through observing phenomena in various ways. From among them, one expounded his understanding based on observation of the aggregates, observation of the signs of the aggregates, observation of the production of the aggregates, observation of the disintegration of the aggregates, observation of the cessation of the aggregates, and observation of actualization of the cessation of the aggregates.
>
> Just as that one observed the aggregates, so another, based on observation of the sense-spheres, expounded his understanding in the same way. One, based on observation of dependent-arising, expounded his understanding. Another, based on observation of the foods, the signs of the foods, the production of the foods, the disintegration of the foods, the cessation of the foods, and based on observation of the actualization of the cessation of the foods, expounded his understanding. One, based on observation of the [four noble] truths, observation of the signs of the truths, observation of thorough knowledge of the truth [of suffering], observation of the abandonment of the truth [of origin], observation of actualization of the truth [of cessation], and observation of meditative cultivation of the truth [of the path], expounded his understanding. Another, based on observation of constituents, observation of the signs of constituents, observation of the various constituents, observation of the manifold constituents, observation of the cessation of constituents, and observation of the

actualization of the cessation of constituents, expounded his understanding.

One, based on observation of the [four] mindful establishments, observation of the signs of the mindful establishments, observation of the antidotes to the discordances of the mindful establishments, observation of meditative cultivation of the mindful establishments that have not yet been produced, observation of the abiding, non-forgetfulness, arising again, and increasing of the mindful establishments which have been produced, expounded his understanding.

Just as that one [observed] the mindful establishments, in the same way others [observed the four] thorough abandonings, the [four] bases of magical emanations, [five] faculties, the [five] powers, and the [seven] branches of enlightenment. One observed the eight branches of the path of Superiors, observed the signs of the eight branches of the path of Superiors, observed the meditative cultivation of the eight branches of the path of Superiors, observed the production of the eight branches of the path of Superiors that have not yet been produced as well as the abiding, non-deterioration, continued arising, and increase of the eight branches of the path of Superiors which have been produced.

Having seen them expound their understandings based on such observations, I thought thus, "These venerable ones expound their understandings by teaching their realization through observing various phenomena. In that way, even all these prideful venerable ones, not seeking the ultimate which is everywhere of one taste, think in this way within being overcome by the pride of conceit."

Here also, the vocabulary of these objects being "established by way of their own character as the referents of terms and of conceptual consciousnesses" is totally lacking. Rather, what are contrasted are a multiplicity of phenomena (the objects that constitute the seven pronouncements) and "the ultimate which is everywhere of one taste."

In chapter 9 of the sūtra Buddha explains that such a multiplicity of phenomena is taught in both the Lesser Vehicle and the Great Vehicle, but in the latter the vast array of phenomena is taught within the context of the "one mode of the element of attributes,"[a] that is to say, the thoroughly established nature which, when contemplated, gives rise to the attributes of a Superior. Buddha says:[117]

Avalokiteshvara, those having natures of various phenomena that I set forth in the Hearer vehicle—teachings concerning the five aggregates, the six internal sense-spheres, the six external sense-spheres, and so

[a] *chos dbyings, dharmadhātu.*

> forth—are also definitely explained in the Great Vehicle by way of teaching them in terms of the one mode of the element of attributes.

Thus, it is evident that the monks mentioned above misconceive the multiplicity—the five aggregates and so forth—in an overly reified way such that perception of "the ultimate which is everywhere of one taste" is blocked.

The seventh chapter of the *Sūtra Unraveling the Thought* speaks of this reification as an "imputational nature" and, more specifically, as "factors imputed in the manner of entity and attribute" and also says, as quoted above, that imputational natures "do not subsist by way of their own character." Putting together these statements, the various scholastic colleges of the Ge-luk-b̄a tradition cogently identify that the imputational nature being refuted is the establishment of objects by way of their own character as the referents of conceptual consciousnesses or as the referents of words. Their commentary is illuminating.

Gung-tang makes it clear that his point is not **merely** that the intended trainees of the *Sūtra of Advice to King Bimbisāra* are those of the Great Exposition and Sūtra Schools—Lesser Vehicle schools—and that in their systems production and disintegration are necessarily established this way. According to the Proponents of Mind-Only, it is true that these Lesser Vehicle schools hold that anything and everything is established by way of its own character as the referent of conceptual consciousnesses and of terms, and it is true that, if asked, they would hold that anything they were taught is so established, but Gung-tang makes the distinction that Buddha intended that they understand such not with respect to everything he taught them but only with respect to **certain** teachings under **certain** conditions.

Also, even though Proponents of the Great Exposition School and the Sūtra School hold such a **tenet**, this does not entail that all their thoughts are conjoined with qualifying the objects of those thoughts as being established by way of their own character as the referents of conceptual consciousnesses. Otherwise, Proponents of Mind-Only would have to hold the absurd position that Proponents of the Great Exposition and Proponents of Sūtra would never have any correct conceptuality such as in inferentially realizing that products are impermanent, for even such a realization would wrongly involve apprehending that impermanence is established by way of its own character as the referent of a conceptual consciousness.[a]

---

[a] Conceptual consciousnesses are described in D̄zong-ka-b̄a's *Illumination of the Thought* (chap. 6) in the context of the Consequence School as of three types: those conceiving true existence, those conceiving an absence of true existence, and those that conceive neither of these.

> Although, without eradicating the object of the conception of self, you merely withdraw the mind here from going there to objects, through this it cannot be posited that you are engaged in selflessness. The reason is this: When the mind operates on an object, there are three [modes of conception]:

Gung-tang considers absurd consequences of holding the opposite view: If it were simply that these two schools **assert** that production and disintegration are necessarily established by way of their own character as the referents of conceptual consciousnesses, then Buddha's saying in the *Renunciation Sūtra,*[118] "Kāshyapa, I am your teacher; you are my Hearer," would absurdly teach that these phenomena are established this way. It would also absurdly follow that Buddha's teaching points of discipline during the period of the first wheel would communicate that these phenomena are so established. For—in the systems of the Great Exposition School and the Sūtra School—the Teacher, Hearers, and so forth are necessarily established this way. As the early twentieth-century Am-do scholar Jik-may-dam-chö-gya-tso[119] points out, the upshot of these points is that, although such teachings about discipline and so forth were given for trainees having the Hearer lineage, they are not sūtra passages about which Paramārthasamudgata needed to question Buddha, since they do not teach that those phenomena are established by way of their own character as the referents of their respective conceptual consciousnesses.

To repeat but with more detail: The criterion for determining that a passage with the words "Form has production" comes to teach **on the literal level** that form has production that is established in this false way cannot, therefore, be that this was taught to persons who merely hold the tenet that all phenomena are established this way. That this is Ḏzong-ka-ḇa's opinion is clear from his statement (*Emptiness in Mind-Only,* 128) that the type of qualm that Paramārthasamudgata has does not need to be eliminated with respect to Buddha's statements about points of training:

> Therefore, the first wheel in which—stemming from the four truths—[Buddha] said, during the first period [of his teaching], that [phenomena] exist by way of their own character and so forth is indicated as requiring interpretation. Such is not indicated with respect to all scriptures spoken during the first period; for example, there is no need here [in the *Sūtra Unraveling the Thought*] to eliminate qualms with respect

---

> 1 conceiving that the object of observation is truly established
> 2 conceiving that it is not truly established
> 3 conceiving it without qualifying it as either of these two.
>
> Hence, although [the object] is not conceived to be without true establishment, it is not necessarily conceived to be truly established. Similarly, although [when merely withdrawing the mind in meditation] you are not engaged in [conceiving] the two selves, you are not necessarily engaged in the two selflessnesses. For there are limitless [ways of] abiding in a third category of awareness.

Similarly, everything a Proponent of the Great Exposition or a Proponent of the Sūtra School thinks about is not necessarily conceived to be established by way of its own character as the referent of a conceptual consciousness. Nevertheless, it is a **tenet** of those schools that everything is so established.

> to [Buddha's] setting forth points of training such as in his statement to the five [ascetics] at Varaṇāsi during the first period, "The lower robe should be worn in a circular fashion."

This is the reason why the first wheel of the teaching, as described in the *Sūtra Unraveling the Thought,* does not include all sūtras spoken during the first period of Buddha's teaching and, instead, includes only those that teach that objects are established in this particular way. Rather, according to Gung-tang, the trainees for whom Buddha set forth the first wheel of doctrine must be taught, for the time being, that objects are established by way of their own character as the referents of terms and of conceptual consciousnesses because, without such an exaggerated reification of the status of phenomena, they would not know how to posit the existence of a person who experiences fruitions of actions and would not know how to posit the mental and physical aggregates that are fruitions of those actions, due to which they would not come to believe in the effects of actions—karma. From that, they would not develop discouragement concerning cyclic existence and thus would not be able to achieve the path of the middle way even in terms of the selflessness of persons, not to mention the deeper realization of the selflessness of phenomena (which is the realization that phenomena are **not** established this way).

This is because, if trainees of such low lineage are not specifically caused temporarily to conceive that phenomena have such an exaggerated status, they cannot posit phenomena at all. They require solidity; otherwise, they fall to an extreme of nihilism, due to which they deviate from the middle way even in terms of the selflessness of persons. Out of his skill in means, Buddha first teaches to such trainees something that is entirely untrue in order to keep them from the extreme of nihilism. He teaches an exaggerated status of things as an efficacious means[a] to cause them to engage in the mere adoption of virtuous causes and effects and the discarding of non-virtuous causes and effects.

The reason for this teaching is that, in order to realize the selflessness of persons, it is necessary that the substratum—the person—and the mere mental and physical aggregates not be refuted, since selflessness is a quality of an existent object. However, for these trainees of low lineage who are extremely accustomed to the view of a self of phenomena—that is, that phenomena are established in such a solid way—if the concreteness of these phenomena is not taught to them, the person and the aggregates are misunderstood to be like falling hairs misperceived by those with eye disease or like the water in a mirage. Also, they are not content with phenomena as mere factors of appearance of the mind, this not being sufficiently substantial, and, even though this is the truth, if they were taught this, they would be driven to an extreme of deprecation of what does indeed exist, unable thereby to avoid the extreme of deprecation, nihilism. Hence, they are taught that the person and the mental and physical

---

[a] *thabs, upāya.*

aggregates are established concretely by way of their own character as the referents of words and conceptual consciousnesses even though such is not validly founded—since their subscribing to this wrong view prevents them from a nihilistic view.

The mind realizing the selflessness of the person itself will clear away the extreme of exaggerated reification in which persons are viewed to be substantially existent, but, before these trainees can arrive at that point, they are thwarted by their own conditioning to perceive phenomena in an overly concrete way such that, without Buddha's playing into that mind-set, they would fall to an extreme of deprecation. This would make realization of the selflessness of persons impossible. Thus, in such a context, statements such as "Suffering is to be known" come to teach that suffering is established by way of its own character as the referent of words and conceptual consciousnesses, this being due to the combined force of two factors: (1) the trainees' level of understanding and (2) Buddha's intention. Buddha plans to teach the selflessness of persons right after this teaching, and in order to eliminate the danger of those trainees' falling to an extreme of nihilism due to the weakness of their intelligence and in order to give them a basis for achieving the middle way relative to the selflessness of persons, he has the distinct **thought**, or **intention**, to teach that phenomena are established by way of their own character as the referents of words and conceptual consciousnesses even if he does not use those terms.

Due to this combination of factors from the trainees' side and Buddha's side, these statements come to teach such **even on the literal level**. As Jik-may-dam-chö-gya-tso[120] says, literality[a] here is not a matter of what is held within the words[b] but what is held within the listeners' wish to know and the speaker's wish to communicate.[c] Because of Buddha's intentionality, these teachings are posited as examples of a teaching having the indirect intention of causing entry[d] into the doctrine and as having the selflessness of persons as the basis in Buddha's thought. Since Buddha has no such intention when he teaches that robes should be worn in a circular fashion, and so forth, such teachings do not come to indicate that robes and so forth are established by way of their own character as the referents of their respective terms and conceptual consciousnesses.[121]

The trainees' assumption of this wrong view that is the very root of suffering keeps them from the nihilism of being unable to posit persons and the cause and effect of karma. In a somewhat similar fashion, the "Questions of Paramārthasamudgata Chapter" of the *Sūtra Unraveling the Thought* says:[122]

To those sentient beings who from the start do not generate roots of

---

[a] *sgras zin.*

[b] *tshig gis zin pa.*

[c] *shes 'dod dang ston 'dod kyis zin pa.* Jik-may-dam-chö-gya-tso indicates that it still needs to be examined whether this distinction is well founded.

[d] *gzhug pa ldem dgongs.*

> virtue, whose interests are not great, and who have not thoroughly accomplished collections of merit and wisdom, I teach doctrine stemming from production-non-natures [that is, other-powered natures]. From hearing that doctrine, they ascertain dependently arisen compositional phenomena as just impermanent and know them as just unstable, as just unreliable, and as just subject to change, whereupon their minds rise from and become discouraged about compositional phenomena. Their minds having risen and become discouraged, they turn away from ill deeds, [whereby] they do not perform ill deeds and rely on virtue.

This perspective is reflected in current traditions in numerous ways. For instance, the present Dalai Lama speaks of choosing the practice of karma over that of emptiness if the two seem to contradict each other. He[123] says:

> The final reason proving that things are empty of inherent existence is just this dependence on causes and conditions. When people do not understand this doctrine well, they mistakenly think that because phenomena are empty, there is no good and bad, no cause and effect. This is complete misunderstanding.
>
> It is so important to be able to posit and have conviction in cause and effect that it is said that between giving up belief in the cause and effect of actions and giving up belief in emptiness, it is better to give up the doctrine of emptiness.

As Āryadeva says in his *Four Hundred Stanzas on the Yogic Deeds of Bodhisattvas,*[a] "Non-meritorious [activities] are to be overcome first."[b]

Still, this level of teaching is not sufficient because such doctrines do not refute the self of phenomena. Thus, they do not serve as a means of releasing trainees from all coarse and subtle levels of cyclic existence. In this vein, the *Sūtra Unraveling the Thought* continues:

> However, since they do not know, as they are, the aspect of character-non-nature and the aspect of ultimate-non-nature in those [phenomena] that are production-non-natures [that is, since they do not know that the other-powered phenomena of causes and effects are not established in such exaggerated ways], they do not become thoroughly discouraged with respect to all compositional phenomena, do not become

[a] Stanza 190a (VIII.15a). The Tibetan (*sde dge* 3846, 9a.7) is:

bsod nams min pa dang por bzlog/

See Karen Lang, *Āryadeva's Catuḥśataka: On the Bodhisattva's Cultivation of Merit and Knowledge,* Indiste Studier 7 (Copenhagen: Akademisk Forlag, 1986), 82; and *Yogic Deeds of Bodhisattvas: Gyel-tsap on Āryadeva's Four Hundred,* commentary by Geshe Sonam Rinchen, translated and edited by Ruth Sonam (Ithaca, N.Y.: Snow Lion, 1994), 193.

[b] For more discussion on the impact of dependent-arising, see pp. 160-178.

thoroughly devoid of desire, and do not become thoroughly released.[a]

The ultimate-non-nature has to be taught for thorough removal of obstructions.

Does The Middle Wheel Teach That All Phenomena Are *Not* Established By Way Of Their Own Character?

According to Gung-ru Chö-jung, Jam-ȳang-shay-b̄a, Gung-tang, and so forth, when D̄zong-ka-b̄a seems to be saying that Buddha equally taught in the first wheel that phenomena ranging from forms through the thirty-seven harmonies with enlightenment **are established by way of their own character**, he means that on the literal level of the first wheel Buddha taught, relative to certain trainees, these phenomena **are established by way of their own character as the referents of conceptual consciousnesses**. One would therefore expect that, when D̄zong-ka-b̄a says that on the literal level of the middle wheel Buddha equally taught that phenomena ranging from forms through to omniscient consciousnesses **are not established by way of their own character**, this tradition of exegesis would hold that this means that these phenomena **are not established by way of their own character as the referents of conceptual consciousnesses**. However, no Ge-luk-b̄a scholar[124] holds that such is the case. For, if in the middle wheel Buddha taught on the literal level that all phenomena are **not** established by way of their own character as the referents of their respective conceptual consciousnesses, since such is indeed asserted in the Mind-Only School, the literal rendering of the middle-wheel sūtras would be acceptable and hence of definitive meaning.

If the second-wheel teachings were acceptable in their literal rendering, it would be senseless for Paramārthasamudgata (*Emptiness in Mind-Only,* 77-78) to ask Buddha about that in consideration of which he taught the second wheel:

> Therefore, I am wondering of what the Supramundane Victor was thinking when he said, "All phenomena are natureless; all phenomena are unproduced, unceasing, quiescent from the start, and naturally thoroughly passed beyond sorrow." I ask the Supramundane Victor about the meaning of his saying, "All phenomena are natureless; all phenomena are unproduced, unceasing, quiescent from the start, and naturally thoroughly passed beyond sorrow."

The question about what was behind the literal rendering of the second-wheel teachings is artfully framed to be of service to others, providing a dramatic

[a] This passage seems to suggest that to be liberated from cyclic existence it is necessary to realize the selflessness of phenomena; however, Ge-luk-b̄a scholars take the reference as being to the three non-natures *in terms of the selflessness of persons.*

opportunity for Buddha to expound his most profound doctrine in a clear way. Furthermore, Paramārthasamudgata (*Emptiness in Mind-Only,* 116), when summarizing the meaning of Buddha's answer to his question, says that the middle wheel is not definitive and requires interpretation:

> Based on just the naturelessness of all phenomena and based on just the absence of production, the absence of cessation, quiescence from the start, and naturally passed beyond sorrow, the Supramundane Victor turned a second wheel of doctrine, for those engaged in the Great Vehicle, very fantastic and marvelous, through the aspect of speaking on emptiness. Furthermore, **that wheel of doctrine turned by the Supramundane Victor is surpassable, affords an occasion [for refutation], requires interpretation, and serves as a basis for controversy.**

Also, from the earlier discussion, it can be extrapolated that, for Gung-ru Chö-jung, Jam-ȳang-shay-b̄a, and so forth of the Go-mang tradition, if the literal reading of the Perfection of Wisdom Sūtras was merely (as D̄zong-ka-b̄a seems to say it is) that all objects from forms through omniscient consciousnesses are not established by way of their own character, then its indicating that imputational phenomena such as uncompounded space are not established by way of their own character would be literally acceptable.[a] For, in the Mind-Only School, imputational phenomena such as uncompounded space are understood as not established by way of their own character, whereas, according to the Mind-Only School, the Perfection of Wisdom Sūtras are not literally acceptable.

Therefore, although D̄zong-ka-b̄a describes the literal reading of the middle wheel as being that all phenomena are not established by way of their own character, this cannot be what he is getting at. Also, although Gung-ru Chö-jung and Jam-ȳang-shay-b̄a hold that in the first wheel "established by way of their own character" means "established by way of their own character as the referents of their respective conceptual consciousnesses," they hold that here in the middle wheel "not established by way of their own character" cannot mean "not established by way of their own character as the referents of their respective conceptual consciousnesses," since in the Mind-Only School nothing is established this way. If the Perfection of Wisdom Sūtras were saying this, they

[a] Jay-d̄zün Chö-ḡyi-gyel-tsen (*General-Meaning Commentary,* 10a.5-10a.7) mentions this objection to his own position and merely says that there is no entailment that this would make such a sūtra literally acceptable; he does not explain **how** this is so. His point must be that the mere fact that a passage teaches **something** that can be asserted in accordance with how it is taught does not make the passage literally acceptable and thus definitive. However, he still needs to explain what it teaches that is non-factual when it teaches that existent imputational natures are not established by way of their own character, since he holds that in the Mind-Only School imputational natures are not established by way of their own character.

would be definitive, and Paramārthasamudgata would not need to ask a question about them.

Jam-ȳang-shay-b̄a[125] concludes that, because of these reasons, in the context of these middle-wheel sūtras, Buddha's teaching that objects are not established by way of their own character also means, on the literal level, that all phenomena are not established from their own side[a] and are not inherently established,[b] since, according to the Mind-Only School, all phenomena—even existent imputational natures—possess the status of establishment from their own side and inherent establishment. According to Jam-ȳang-shay-b̄a,[126] this is the import of D̄zong-ka-b̄a's (*Emptiness in Mind-Only,* 85) saying:

> ...in the Mother Sūtras [that is, the Perfection of Wisdom Sūtras] and so forth, all phenomena—the five aggregates, the eighteen constituents, and the twelve sense-spheres—are described as without thingness,[c] without an inherent nature,[d] and natureless.[e]

From the fact that D̄zong-ka-b̄a speaks here not just of establishment of objects by way of their own character but also of "inherent existence" and "nature," this wider range of meanings must be extended to his frequent depictions of the middle wheel as teaching on the literal level that all phenomena are not established by way of their own character.

To repeat: Since, according to the Mind-Only School, imputational phenomena are not established by way of their own character, if the Perfection of Wisdom Sūtras taught on the literal level that such phenomena are not established by way of their own character, those sūtras would, in those particular sections, be literally acceptable. Thus, for Gung-ru Chö-jung and Jam-ȳang-shay-b̄a as well as followers like Gung-tang, even though D̄zong-ka-b̄a's depiction of the first wheel as teaching "establishment of objects by way of their own character" means establishment of objects by way of their own character **as the referents of conceptual consciousnesses**, in the middle wheel it means just establishment of objects by way of their own character and also establishment of objects from their own side or inherent establishment. According to standard Ge-luk-b̄a exegesis, the Mind-Only School asserts that uncompounded space and so forth, despite not being established by way of their own character, are established from their own side and are inherently established, and thus, when the Perfection of Wisdom Sūtras say that uncompounded phenomena (or any other permanent or impermanent phenomena) are not established from their own side, such statements cannot be accepted literally.

Ge-luk-b̄a scholars hold that, in the Mind-Only School, imputational

---

a *rang ngos nas grub pa, *svarūpasiddha.*

b *rang bzhin gyis grub pa, svabhāvasiddha.*

c *dngos po med pa.*

d *rang bzhin med pa.*

e *ngo bo nyid med pa.*

phenomena such as uncompounded space are not truly established, are not established by way of their own character, and are not ultimately established, whereas other-powered natures—such as minds and bodies—and thoroughly established natures (emptinesses) **are** truly established, established by way of their own character, and ultimately established. However, **all** phenomena, compounded and uncompounded, inherently exist and are established from their own side. Thus, two levels of existence are to be distinguished, one more substantial and the other less so.

For Jay-d̄zün Chö-ḡyi-gyel-tsen and Paṇ-chen S̄ö-nam-drak-b̄a, the "establishment of objects by way of their own character" that is affirmed in the first wheel of doctrine and that is denied in the second can, in some sense, be said to be the same. However, their followers, feeling the bite of Gung-ru Chö-jung and Jam-ȳang-shay-b̄a's criticism of their explanation of the first wheel, have had to claim that the first wheel **also** teaches that phenomena are established by way of their own character as the referents of their respective conceptual consciousnesses or that subject and object are different entities. They are caught in the same bind as Gung-ru Chö-jung and Jam-ȳang-shay-b̄a, for they cannot hold that the teaching on the literal level of the middle wheel that all phenomena are **not** established by way of their own character also teaches that all phenomena are **not** established by way of their own character as the referents of their respective conceptual consciousnesses or also teaches that subject and object are not different entities, since this would make the middle wheel definitive.

Who Needs To Hear The Literal Level Of The Perfection Of Wisdom Sūtras?

Let us consider a related problem. On the literal level of the middle wheel, Buddha speaks of objects as not being established from their own side—to use Gung-ru Chö-jung and Jam-ȳang-shay-b̄a's depiction—but his teaching this must be for someone's sake, and it obviously is not for Proponents of Mind-Only, since they assert that all phenomena **are** established from their own side. This teaching is typically said, therefore, to be for Consequentialists.[a] However, the issue is not simple. For the assertion that Consequentialists are the trainees of the literal level of the Perfection of Wisdom Sūtras is complicated by the fact that the *Sūtra Unraveling the Thought* says that, if the middle wheel is taken in accordance with its literal reading, one falls to an extreme of nihilism; thus the question of whether Buddha would want Consequentialists to fall to an extreme of nihilism arises. First, the sūtra statement (*Emptiness in Mind-Only,* 95-96):

> Even though they have interest in that doctrine [of the profound thoroughly established nature], they do not understand, just as it is, the

[a] *thal 'gyur pa, prāsaṅgika.*

> profound reality that I have set forth with a thought behind it. With respect to the meaning of these doctrines, they adhere to the terms as only literal: "All these phenomena are only natureless. All these phenomena are only unproduced, only unceasing, only quiescent from the start, only naturally thoroughly passed beyond sorrow." Due to that, they acquire the view that all phenomena do not exist and the view that [establishment of objects by way of their own] character does not exist. Moreover, having acquired the view of nihilism and the view of the non-existence of [establishment of objects by way of their own] character, they deprecate all phenomena in terms of all of the characters—deprecating the imputational character of phenomena and also deprecating the other-powered character and thoroughly established character of phenomena.

It is said that whatever Buddha teaches, he teaches with a purpose, and yet, if the special trainees of the literal level of the middle wheel are Consequentialists, why, according to Proponents of Mind-Only, would Buddha want Consequentialists to fall to an extreme of nihilism?

This issue is not explicitly treated by any of these Tibetan authors, and thus I have questioned numerous Tibetan scholars in India, Tibet, and the United States. The best answer that I have found is that according to the Mind-Only system, far from wanting Consequentialists to fall to an extreme of nihilism, Buddha teaches them that all phenomena do not inherently exist because it is only within such a context that Consequentialists can posit the cause and effect of karma. Consequentialists strongly hold that phenomena cannot be found under analysis such that the only way that they can posit cause and effect is within analytical unfindability. Therefore, from the viewpoint of the Mind-Only School, this teaching in the middle wheel of doctrine is a temporary measure to establish Consequentialists in the adoption of virtue and the discarding of non-virtue, since this provides, for them, a comfortable basis within which the existence of phenomena can be posited. From this viewpoint, Jik-may-dam-chö-gya-tso[127] says that the Mind-Only School does not claim that Consequentialists hold that the effects of actions do not exist, and hence it does not hold that the middle wheel of doctrine teaches or says that the effects of actions do not exist, even though the statement on the literal level that forms and so forth are not established by way of their own character **comes to say**[a] that forms and so forth do not exist at all. Still, since the Mind-Only School asserts that holding, in accordance with the literal reading of the middle-wheel sūtras, that the effects of actions do not exist by way of their own character is a view of deprecation, this school has to say that, even though the Consequentialists **come to deprecate** the effects of actions, they do not hold that the effects of actions do not exist.

---

[a] *gtan med du gsungs par song yang.*

This is how the problem—of how Proponents of Mind-Only, who accept the Perfection of Wisdom Sūtras as the foremost of all of Buddha's word and yet do not assert the literal reading of those sūtras, could identify the Consequentialists as those to whom he wanted to communicate the literal reading—can be handled. The solution is elegant because within Ge-luk-b̄a scholarship it is universally held that (1) the bottom line of theoretical correctness requires that the cause and effect of karma be validly posited and (2) the Consequentialists can do this only within the context of denying that objects are established from their own side. However, the solution is also fishy, in the sense that it is not reflected in the *Sūtra Unraveling the Thought.* For, if that were the case, when in the *Sūtra Unraveling the Thought* Buddha speaks about the second wheel of doctrine, he should have spoken not just of those who form a nihilistic view from taking the Perfection of Wisdom Sūtras literally but also those who posit cause and effect and engage in virtue but with a distorted view of reality that denies the proper status of phenomena. However, nothing even resembling the latter appears in the sūtra or in the Indian literature of the Proponents of Mind-Only. Still, the "solution" is esthetically pleasing even if not convincing in terms of the source texts. It can be seen that the game of exegesis implicitly recognizes that it is necessary to go beyond Indian Buddhist literature, even if for a Ge-luk-b̄a scholar to declare such a posture would be considered tactless.

It strikes me that positing Consequentialists as trainees of the literal level of the Perfection of Wisdom Sūtras can serve another function within the overall Ge-luk-b̄a approach to the *Sūtra Unraveling the Thought* as seen from the viewpoint of the Mind-Only School. For it relieves any pressure to treat the middle wheel like the first wheel which is seen as both **literally** and **explicitly** teaching that objects are established by way of their own character as the referents of conceptual consciousnesses,[a] this being based on Buddha's intention and the mind-set of the trainees. For, in the middle wheel, the main special trainees (not of the literal level but of the explicit teaching of the sūtras) are sharp Bodhisattvas, so sharp that they can understand the words "All phenomena are natureless," as referring to three types of non-nature of three different classes of phenomena, the three natures, respectively. This is just what is said in the seventh chapter of the *Sūtra Unraveling the Thought,* when Buddha (*Emptiness in Mind-Only,* 116-117, footnote m) speaks about the various types of sentient beings to whom he teaches doctrine, among whom the supreme are these sharp Bodhisattvas:

Paramārthasamudgata with respect to this, thinking of just these three

[a] It seems that in the tradition following Gung-ru Chö-jung and Jam-ȳang-shay-b̄a, the explicit teaching and the literal rendering even of the first wheel are to be distinguished—the literal reading requires interpretation because it is unacceptable, but the explicit teaching of the four truths and so forth is acceptable if considered without the qualification that these are established by way of their own character as the referents of their respective conceptual consciousnesses.

> types of non-nature, the One Gone Thus, by way of the aspect of setting forth sūtras of interpretable meaning, taught the doctrine [of the middle wheel] in this way, "All phenomena are natureless; all phenomena are unproduced, unceasing, quiescent from the start, and naturally thoroughly passed beyond sorrow." Regarding that, [when] sentient beings who have generated roots of virtue, have purified the obstructions, have ripened their continuums, have great faith, and have accumulated great collections of merit and wisdom hear this doctrine, they understand—**just as it is**—this which I explained with a thought behind it, and they develop faith in that doctrine. They also realize, by means of their exalted wisdom, **the meaning just as it is**. Also, through cultivating their realization they very quickly attain the very final state.

Due to former practice of virtue, these sharp Bodhisattvas have a mind-set such that they can understand properly, without further commentary such as in the *Sūtra Unraveling the Thought,* that the statements in the Perfection of Wisdom Sūtras, and so forth, that all phenomena are natureless refer to the three types of naturelessness. Also, Buddha **intended** to teach them such, his abbreviated expression being due to his knowing that they would understand it properly. Hence it is commonly accepted that the explicit teaching[a] of the middle wheel is not the literal rendering but what these gifted trainees understand. Thus, why not treat the middle wheel like the first, concluding that **even the literal rendering** comes to be what these sharp Bodhisattvas understand?

The answer has to take into account the fact that the *Sūtra Unraveling the Thought* identifies that the middle wheel is not literally acceptable and requires interpretation. Thus, one advantage of taking the literal rendering of the middle wheel as being that all objects are not established from their own side is that then the literal rendering of the middle wheel clearly requires interpretation—since the notion that all phenomena are not established from their own side is unacceptable in the Mind-Only School—even if its sharpest trainees understand the middle-wheel sūtras in a way that is acceptable.

To repeat with more detail: in the middle wheel the explicit teaching, being what these sharp Bodhisattvas understand, is acceptable, but the literal reading of the middle wheel is unacceptable in terms of fact since in the Mind-Only School all objects—even imputational phenomena—far from **not** being established from their own side, **are** established from their own side. The explicit teaching is what sharp Bodhisattvas understand and thus is acceptable. They realize that the three natures have their own respective type of naturelessness—that imputational natures are empty of being established by way of their own character, that other-powered natures are empty of self-production, and that thoroughly established natures (emptinesses) are the ultimate-non-nature of all

[a] Or, object of expression (*brjod bya*).

phenomena. Even though Buddha intends to teach them this doctrine (which is validated by right cognition) and even though the main listeners' mind-set is such that they understand such a doctrine (despite the words only being that all phenomena are natureless), the buffer preventing this doctrine from becoming the literal rendering of the middle wheel is the insistence that there are trainees of the literal rendering of the middle wheel, these being the Consequentialists who, in order to posit the existence of phenomena, require that objects not be established by way of their own character and not be established from their own side. Once there are trainees for this literal rendering that is other than what sharp Bodhisattvas understand, the mere facts of:

- Buddha's intending that sharp Bodhisattvas understand the three non-natures
- their mind-set that allows them to understand these

are not sufficient to cause the literal rendering of the middle wheel to be what sharp Bodhisattvas understand. This is my speculation on how to keep Gung-tang's artful presentation of the literal level of the first wheel from undoing his own presentation of the middle wheel.

As the reader can see, I, too, have been drawn into the task of discovering (or creating) the coherence of D̄zong-ka-b̄a's and Gung-tang's systems. Still, I would find it difficult to pretend that such a point is of concern to the *Sūtra Unraveling the Thought* or to Indian scholars such as Asaṅga, thus raising the question of what is being explicated—the thought of the *Sūtra Unraveling the Thought* or Gung-tang's comprehension of D̄zong-ka-b̄a's interpretation of it. The answer is that it is the latter and to point out that, since the perspectives of religions are in dynamic development, investigation of later developments can be as rewarding (and sometimes even more so) as investigation of the founder's thought, since the ideas have had time to develop with more fullness.

Still, I would not want to commit myself to an extreme position that D̄zong-ka-b̄a's and Gung-tang's perceptions are utterly unrelated to those of the *Sūtra Unraveling the Thought.* Also, I cannot claim to be coldly dealing in a somehow totally objective fashion with a system out there in a world divorced from myself; the structure, the architecture, of D̄zong-ka-b̄a's and Gung-tang's system comes to life in the mind such that its dynamics open horizons of fascinating connections. This is how interactions between texts and readers work, the renowned hermeneutic circle—the reader not only interprets the text, but the text also affects the reader, changing the interpretation. I want such embeddedness in a dynamic worldview, albeit without the gullibility of swallowing all of its claims.[a] To pretend otherwise—to think that there is a privileged, objective viewpoint not bound by contextuality—is to strangle texts and systems and to want to be dead oneself.

[a] I am not suggesting that Tibetan scholars accept all the claims of the systems they explain.

9. Can a Wrong View Relieve Pain?

As we have seen with respect to first-wheel teachings, Buddha uses the bad predispositions of trainees to their benefit. The practice of a wrong view—by those for whom it is temporarily appropriate—brings progress on the path. But can a misconception that is at the root of all pain—namely, that all phenomena are established by way of their own character as the referents of their respective terms and conceptual consciousnesses—serve to alleviate pain? If it does, what does it mean that perception of the truth liberates? If both the right and the wrong are effective in the process of removing wrong views, can a difference be made between valid cognition and wrong view? Are right and wrong equal?

First, it might seem that, since the ultimate is inexpressible, distinctions between right and wrong—at least with respect to the final truth—could not be made. Dzong-ka-ba[128] cites a passage from the *Sūtra on the Ten Grounds:*[129]

> Just as the wise cannot express or see
> The trail of a bird across the sky,
> So none of the grounds of Conqueror Children [Bodhisattvas]
> Can be expressed. Then how can one listen?

He comments:

> Though a bird crosses the sky, the wise of the world cannot describe its trail in words or see it in their minds. In the same way, though the ultimate grounds—like birds—progress through the sky of the nature of phenomena, even commentators who are Superiors cannot describe the mode of progress in the way that Superiors themselves experience it. Thus, listeners cannot hear about the grounds the way they are perceived.

However, Dzong-ka-ba and his followers emphasize that the inexpressiblity of the ultimate is in the context of the totally non-dualistic experience of those who perceive emptiness directly.[a] They hold that, since the inexpressiblity of the ultimate refers to how it is experienced in such a state, the ultimate in general is indeed expressible. That expressiblity, in turn, is not just theoretical but is grounded in and leads toward experience. They firmly hold that there is discourse that accords with the fact and discourse that does not, but they also hold that the latter can be beneficial for certain trainees at the appropriate time. The question is: If the right and the wrong are effective in the process of removing wrong views, can a difference be made between valid cognitions and wrong views? The issue is a continuation of the famous debate at Sam-yay Monastery in the late eighth century about which it is said that the Chinese monk

---

[a] For a list of the five senses of non-dualism that are present in such an experience, see p. 57.

Hva-shang—the loser in the debate—held that just as dark clouds obstruct the sky, so do light clouds, or whether one is bitten by a white or black dog makes no difference.[130]

In order to maintain the basic tenet of the purifying power of realizing the truth, Gung-tang and A-ku Lo-drö-gya-tso tackle these issues head-on, though they have to resort to carefully framed refinements that self-humorously finish with unconvincing splitting of hairs. They thereby implicitly open up other possibilities.

Central to this topic is the notion of *upāya*[a] (efficacious means). Gung-tang[131] makes a distinction that is fundamental to Ge-luk-ba exegesis. He points out that one meaning of *upāya* is found in the numerous references to a Buddha's "skill in means" (*upāyakauśalya*),[b] and the other is found in the division of Buddhist paths into method (*upāya*)—also translated as "efficacious means"—and wisdom (*prajñā*). In the Great Vehicle the latter primarily refers to great compassion and the altruistic intention to attain highest enlightenment. Gung-tang's opinion that these two are not to be conflated is clearly conveyed by his refuting a scholar who mistakenly takes the term *upāya* as referring to great compassion and the altruistic intention to become enlightened when it should be taken as referring to skill in means. The passage, cited in *The Essence of Eloquence* (*Emptiness in Mind-Only,* 69), is from the *Superior Sūtra of the Questions of Rāṣhṭapāla:*[c]

> Due to being endowed with compassion,
> Through hundreds of skillful means (*upāya, thabs*) and reasonings
> You cause transmigrating beings who wander due to not knowing
> The modes of emptiness, quiescence, and no production
> To enter [into understanding these three doors of liberation].

Dzong-ka-ba comments:

> Thus, it is said that the Compassionate Teacher—perceiving that the thusness of phenomena is very difficult to realize and that, if it is not realized, one [can] not be released from cyclic existence—brings about the thorough understanding of that [suchness] through many modes of skillful means (*upāya, thabs*) and many approaches of reasoning.

Based on this brief commentary, Gung-tang[132] identifies the "many modes of

---

a *thabs.*

b *thabs mkhas / thabs la mkhas pa.*

c *'phags pa yul 'khor skyong gis zhus pa, rāṣṭapālaparipṛcchā;* II.310; contained in the eighteenth chapter of the *Pile of Jewels Sūtra* (*ratnakūṭa, dkon mchog brtsegs pa*). The Sanskrit is found in P. L. Vaidya, *Mahāyānasūtrasaṃgraha,* Buddhist Sanskrit Texts 17 (Darbhanga, India: Mithila Institute, 1961), vol. 1, 154:

> *śūnyāśca śānta anutpādanaya avijānādeva jagadudbhramati/*
> *teṣāmupāyanayayuktiśatairavatārayasyapi kṛpālutayā//*

upāya" as Buddha's skill in means and, specifically, as Buddha's temporarily teaching merely a coarse form of selflessness rather than the most subtle one. Gung-tang[133] explains that *upāya* here refers to leading trainees by way of various techniques and does not refer to *upāya* in the division of Buddhist paths into method and wisdom.

From his example—teaching merely a coarse form of selflessness —we can see that some of these techniques involve teaching what is not final but true, such as a coarse form of selflessness, as if it were final (which is not true). This is a partial truth which is also a partial falsehood.[a] In addition, it is clear that in this tradition other techniques included within a Buddha's skill in means involve teaching what is not at all true, such as a permanent self, but are appropriate and helpful for trainees on certain levels.

In the pair of *upāya* and wisdom, *upāya* refers to the motivating factor that determines what type of enlightenment is achieved. The *upāya* of the Great Vehicle is primarily great compassion, in which one takes upon oneself the burden of freeing all sentient beings from suffering and joining them to happiness; when combined with wisdom, it yields the highest enlightenment, Buddhahood. *Upāya* in the Lesser Vehicle is the intention mainly for oneself to get out of the round of suffering, which, when combined with wisdom, yields the lower enlightenment of a Hearer or Solitary Realizer. In this sense, *upāya* refers to "method" or "efficacious means," since it is the factor determining which type of enlightenment is achieved. Wisdom is indeed a method (that is, efficacious means) for overcoming obstructions, but, because it is not the factor determining which type of enlightenment is achieved, it is not called "method" (*upāya*) in the division of Buddhist paths into *upāya* and wisdom.

Thus, the term *upāya* has two distinct meanings that need to be distinguished. As Gung-tang says, *upāya* as skill in means refers to a high being's ability to teach temporary or provisional techniques that are beneficial but at most are partially false. From this viewpoint it would be wrong to consider compassion (*upāya* in the division of paths into *upāya* and wisdom) to be an instance of *upāya* as skill in means, since then compassion would be mistaken as merely a temporary device for the sake of leading trainees, whereas it actually is fundamental to the achievement of enlightenment and to enlightenment itself. Indeed, compassion is the motivating force behind a Buddha's skill in means, but this does not entail that a Buddha's compassion is an instance of skill in means or of something taught out of skill in means. The practice of compassion prior to Buddhahood and the state of compassion in Buddhahood are not temporary, deceptively restful islands which are used to lure practitioners to their own betterment. The fact that the single term *upāya* is used to refer to compassion and

[a] Many of the notions in this chapter achieved clarity when I responded to John Hick's stimulating paper "Religion as 'Skilful Means': A Hint from Buddhism" at the Sixth Buddhist-Christian Theological Encounter, Boston University (August 1992).

to the ability to make use of provisional techniques easily leads to the misperception that the final state is beyond compassion, whereas it is not.

Therefore, the notion of skill in means does not indicate that anything and everything that a Buddha teaches is merely from skill in means and that there is no truth, only what is used in a specific situation to lead specific trainees. Rather, the notion of skill in means itself suggests that there is truth but that a Buddha often must deviate from teaching the truth in order to be of benefit to others. Still, can falsity remove misconception?

As was detailed in the previous chapter, Gung-tang[134] explains that, although the words of a first-wheel sūtra such as the *Sūtra of Advice to King Bimbisāra* contain only the words "Great King, form has production; it also has disintegration," the sūtra comes to teach **even on the literal level** an untrue status of phenomena, namely, that production and disintegration are established by way of their own character as the referents of words and of conceptual consciousnesses. Fundamental to his discussion is the basic point that according to the Mind-Only School the root of all suffering is the conception that phenomena are established by way of their own character as the referents of their respective terms and conceptual consciousnesses, and thus the first wheel propounds something that not only is untrue but also belief in which constitutes the very source of suffering. Thus, it is clear that, given that whatever Shākyamuni Buddha taught, he taught for a purpose, even the most pernicious misconception somehow can be used to advance progress on the path, in this case by preventing a trainee from falling to the extreme of nihilism. However, if this misconception could effectively remove a wrong view such as nihilism, it would undermine the exaltation of the perception of fact as the panacea removing suffering. There would be no way of determining what reality is.[a] This is just what Gung-tang wants to avoid.

To re-state: There is a hierarchy of views as well as a hierarchy of practitioners, some being considered to be under the influence of low predispositions. Still, since both wrong views and right views bring about progress, do both perform what is properly the function of valid cognition—the elimination of false superimpositions? Are they equally efficacious, in which case the very possibility of a hierarchy of views is overturned? This is the nitty-gritty problem that Gung-tang and A-ku Lo-drö-gya-tso attempt to handle by making hair-splitting distinctions in order to maintain that wrong views can help but do not actually clear away misconceptions. Let us pursue the detail of their argument. It is my conviction that the more detail one analyzes in a system, the broader one's views become, since the pursuit yields insight into the weaknesses in any system and thereby creates openness to other perspectives.

Gung-tang makes the distinction that, when the intended trainees of the first wheel hear the first-wheel teaching that objects are established by way of

[a] As John Hick (143) says, "We are left with nothing but means which are not means to anything, and the whole system collapses into incoherence."

their own character as the referents of their respective terms and conceptual consciousnesses:

1. Their consciousnesses apprehending objects in accordance with the literal level of that teaching **serve as efficacious means of clearing away**[a] the wrong conception of viewing persons, the mental and physical aggregates, and so forth as non-existent. ("*Upāya*" here certainly does not refer to compassion, and it also does not refer to the skill in means of a high being; rather, it has the sense of a means, or technique, taught by someone who has skill in means.)
2. However, this does not make those consciousnesses into valid cognitions[b] that newly eliminate false superimpositions with respect to their objects because they are not **eliminators**[c] of such wrong conceptions.

Frankly, the claim that wrong views can serve as means for clearing away wrong conceptions and yet are not eliminators of wrong conceptions looks like trying to have your cake and eat it, too. Indeed, Gung-tang carefully says "**serve as** efficacious means" (or, more literally, "**go as** efficacious means")[d] which is a standard Tibetan way of avoiding saying that it **is** such, but that looks like double-talk.

Gung-tang gives a helpful example: When someone is afraid upon mistaking a speckled rope for a snake, if the person is told that it is a vine, her or his consciousness thinking that it is a vine serves as an efficacious means of clearing away the fear, but it cannot be said that it eliminates the superimposition of apprehending it as a snake, since, upon examination, the person could find that it is not a vine whereupon the fear could return. His point has to be that, since a consciousness holding a rope to be a vine is simply not valid, the deception can serve to remove the fear of a snake, but it cannot remove the false superimposition of apprehending the rope as a snake—actual elimination of the false superimposition can be done only by valid cognition.

He gives an evocative example: The altruistic intention to become enlightened in the continuum of someone on, for instance, the Great Vehicle path of accumulation[e] is an efficacious means of attaining[f] a Nature Truth Body[g] of a Buddha and thus an efficacious means of abandoning[h] the conception of a self of phenomena, as well as its seeds, which block such attainment. Fundamental to the usage of this example is the cardinal doctrine that the altruistic intention

[a] *de sel ba'i thabs su 'gro ba.*
[b] *tshad ma, pramāṇa.*
[c] *gcod byed.*
[d] *thabs su 'gro ba.*
[e] The first of the five paths; see p. 63.
[f] *ngo bo nyid sku thob pa'i thabs.*
[g] *svabhāvikakāya.*
[h] *spong ba'i thabs.*

to become enlightened cannot eliminate the conception of a self of phenomena, or its seeds, this being done by the wisdom directly realizing emptiness; for it is standard that whatever eliminates the conception of a self of phenomena must ascertain the selflessness of phenomena. However, the altruistic intention to become enlightened is said to empower the wisdom consciousness such that the latter can overcome the conception of a self of phenomena, with the result that the Nature Truth Body of a Buddha—identified as the emptiness of the mind in the continuum of someone who has abandoned all obstructions—is attained. Thus, once the altruistic intention to become enlightened is crucial to enhancing the wisdom consciousness, it must be an efficacious means of attaining a Nature Truth Body and hence an efficacious means of abandoning the conception of a self of phenomena.

To review: Gung-tang is seeking a way to allow for a wrong view to be efficacious and yet not to surrender the fundamental position that only valid cognitions can remove false superimpositions. In a similar way, an altruistic intention to become enlightened (which is not a wrong view) fills just this purpose, since:

- it admittedly is an efficacious means of attaining Buddhahood and thus of a Nature Truth Body, due to which it has to be an efficacious means of abandoning the conception of a self of phenomena that blocks attainment of a Nature Truth Body; however,
- it is commonly held that only the wisdom of selflessness can eliminate the false superimposition of self ("self" here meaning the establishment of objects by way of their own character as the referents of their respective terms and conceptual consciousnesses); and thus
- an altruistic intention to become enlightened does not eliminate the conception of a self of phenomena even if it is an efficacious means of abandoning the conception of a self of phenomena.

The conclusion Gung-tang draws, in brief, is that in a similar way the wrong view that Buddha promotes in the first wheel of the teaching can serve as an efficacious means of clearing away the view of nihilism and yet not eliminate the view of nihilism.

In more detail: In the first wheel of his teaching Buddha taught that all phenomena are established by way of their own character as the referents of their respective terms and conceptual consciousnesses in order that those trainees could avoid the extreme of nihilism that would be generated in them if he taught the truth that phenomena are indeed **not** established this way, since—due to their predispositions—they would think that phenomena are only figments of the imagination. However, if only the truth heals, then one would absurdly have to say that, when the minds of first-wheel trainees apprehending phenomena in accordance with the literal rendering did eliminate the superimposition of viewing persons, the mental and physical aggregates, and so forth as non-existent, those minds would **validly ascertain** that persons and so forth are established by way of their own character as the referents of words and conceptual consciousnesses. However, such could never be so, since persons and so forth simply are not established this way. The premise that Gung-tang is trying to maintain is that the elimination of superimpositions can be done only by valid cognition, but, since he must admit that wrong views can be efficacious under the right circumstances, he must make hair-splitting distinctions. Thus, he concludes that these consciousnesses can serve as efficacious means of clearing away a nihilistic view and can be efficacious means of abandoning a nihilistic view, but they cannot themselves eliminate the false superimpositions of a nihilistic view.

We can see that this explanation forged with intricate distinctions (1) gives latitude to what can be used as efficacious mean for helping trainees such that even non-valid perceptions can serve as efficacious means and (2) restricts what can actually eliminate false superimpositions to valid perceptions. That such distinctions are used to defend this position indicates that Gung-tang adamantly wants to maintain that, although Buddhas use whatever is at hand to help trainees, this does not mean that, among the perceptions they foster in others, some are not right and some are not wrong or that a Buddha has no viewpoint. Rather, certain views are right, and a Buddha has true realization. The status of valid cognition is upheld, even if the route to accomplish it is potentially slippery.

Gung-tang's commentator, A-ku Lo-drö-gya-tso,[135] no doubt sensing the fragility of these distinctions, takes the issue a step further. Basically, he asks, "Is an efficacious means of abandoning an abandoner[a] or not?" He considers Gung-tang's second example, the altruistic intention to become enlightened in the continuum of someone on the Great Vehicle path of accumulation. He says that, once it is an efficacious means of abandoning[b] the conception of a self of phenomena, it must be an abandoner of the conception of a self of phenomena. Nevertheless, he has to draw the line somewhere; so he holds that it is not a clearer away[c] of that misconception. From this splitting of a hair difficult to find even under a powerful microscope, it can be seen that A-ku Lo-drö-gya-tso feels uncomfortable with this tack in the attempt to preserve the uniqueness of valid cognition, even if he is committed to the same agenda.

We have moved from one slippery path to another, for the question remains, "Is an abandoner not a clearer away?" Recognizing that this question must be answered in order to avoid the accusation of double-talk, A-ku Lo-drö-gya-tso says that an awareness apprehending persons, the aggregates, and so forth as established by way of their own character as the referents of conceptual

---

a *spong byed.*

b *spong ba'i thabs.*

c *sel byed.* I recognize that the English translation is awkward, but it is important here to be as literal as possible.

consciousnesses in accordance with the literal rendering of the first wheel is a **temporary** clearer away[a] of the wrong conception viewing the aggregates as non-existent, but it cannot be said to be a clearer away of such. For a mind apprehending persons, the aggregates, and so forth as established this way is a conception of a self of phenomena, and the two conceptions of self (of persons and of phenomena) are the roots **producing** the wrong conception of viewing the aggregates as non-existent in that they are what generate all unsalutary states—not only desire and hatred but also wrong conceptions. A-ku Lo-drö-gya-tso's unstated conclusion is that, since this misconception is the root of all problems, it is not a complete cure even of a tendency to nihilism despite the fact that it can skillfully be used under certain circumstances as a temporary efficacious means of clearing away a tendency to nihilism.

Let us see how this plays out in the example of misperceiving a rope as a snake. On the surface, it seems that, since thinking a rope is a vine does indeed abandon, clear away, and eliminate the fear that it is a snake, it must abandon, clear away, and eliminate the false superimposition that it is a snake. However, has it really eliminated the false superimposition that it is a snake? It cannot be a final cure because, when one notices—upon further investigation—that it is not a vine, there is room for the original fear of a snake to return. Thus, to think that the rope is a vine may temporarily clear away the fear of a snake, but the final cure is to see with incontrovertible valid cognition that it is a rope. It does not seem far-fetched to claim that, by extension, for the trainees of the first wheel the wrong view that phenomena are established by way of their own character as the referents of their respective terms and conceptual consciousnesses serves only as a **temporary** efficacious means to clear away the view of nihilism, since it is subject to contradiction simply because it is **wrong** and thus this source of relief from a nihilistic view is itself shaky. In this way, despite the temporary efficacy of a wrong view, right and wrong are not conflated, nor is the validity of right views undermined. This is an essential point in a system that does not equate all thought as equally blocking perception of the truth.

Still, when this reasoning is applied to the second example, we are left with the inexplicable position that the altruistic intention to become enlightened is a **temporary** efficacious means of attaining the Nature Truth Body of a Buddha and thus a **temporary** efficacious means of abandoning the conception of a self of phenomena. I would prefer to say that it is an **indirect** efficacious means of such, but then I would be forced to hold that thinking a rope is a vine serves as an **indirect** efficacious means of clearing away the fear of a snake, and so forth. I cannot see my way clear of these problems.

I enjoy the resultant conundrum because, through following a particular conceptual road in more than a casual manner, I see that other roads are possible. The more the detail of the issues surrounding Paramārthasamudgata's

---

a *gnas skabs kyi sel byed.*

question to the Buddha is pursued, the more it is clear that this Tibetan tradition of scholar-practitioners makes a valiant attempt to uphold the difference between wrong views and valid cognition. Perception of the difficulties in maintaining a hierarchy of right and wrong conceptions in the face of their efficacy in advancing spiritual progress opens the mind to the viability of other systems. (This attitude could put more emphasis on the *results* of systems of thought.)

Now let us turn to Buddha's answer.

10. Structuring Buddha's Answer

Buddha Replies To Paramārthasamudgata

Buddha begins his reply by praising Paramārthasamudgata's question; then he indicates that he will give an answer, whereupon he proceeds to give the answer itself.[a] Based on Wonch'uk's exposition,[136] scholars such as Jik-may-dam-chö-gya-tso divide the first part of his reply into a brief indication,[b] an extensive explanation,[c] a giving of examples, and a summary sentence. Let us cite this entire section of the sūtra:

> Having been asked that, the Supramundane Victor said to the Bodhisattva Paramārthasamudgata:
>
> > **Praising the question and indicating that he will explain:**[137] "Paramārthasamudgata, the thought in your mind, properly generated virtue, is good, good. Paramārthasamudgata, you are involved in [asking] this in order to help many beings, to [bring] happiness to many beings, out of compassionate kindness toward the world, and for the sake of the aims, help, and happiness of all beings, including gods and humans. You are good to think to ask the One Gone Thus about this meaning. Therefore, Paramārthasamudgata, listen, and I will explain that in consideration of which I said, 'All phenomena are natureless; all phenomena are unproduced, unceasing, quiescent from the start, and naturally thoroughly passed beyond sorrow.'"
> >
> > **The Answer**
> >
> > **Brief indication:** "Paramārthasamudgata, thinking of three non-natures of phenomena—character-non-nature, production-non-nature, and ultimate-non-nature—I taught [in the middle wheel of the teaching], 'All phenomena are natureless.'"
> >
> > **Extensive explanation:** "Paramārthasamudgata, concerning that, what are character-non-natures of phenomena? Those which are imputational characters.
> >
> > "Why? It is thus: Those [imputational characters] are

---

[a] For extensive discussion of the answer, see *Absorption*, #57-167.

[b] *mdor bstan.*

[c] *rgyas bshad.*

characters posited by names and terminology[a] and do not subsist by way of their own character. Therefore, they are said to be 'character-non-natures.'

"What are production-non-natures of phenomena?[b] Those which are the other-powered characters of phenomena.

"Why? It is thus: Those [other-powered characters] arise through the force of other conditions and not by themselves.[c] Therefore, they are said to be 'production-non-natures.'

"What are ultimate-non-natures? Those dependently arisen phenomena—which are natureless due to being natureless in terms of production—are also natureless due to being natureless in terms of the ultimate.

"Why? Paramārthasamudgata, that which is an object of observation of purification in phenomena I teach to be the ultimate, and other-powered characters are not the object of observation of purification. Therefore, they are said to be 'ultimate-non-natures.'

"Moreover, that which is the thoroughly established character of phenomena is also called 'the ultimate-non-nature.' Why? Paramārthasamudgata, that which in phenomena is the selflessness of phenomena is called their 'non-nature.' It is the ultimate, and the ultimate is distinguished by just the naturelessness of all phenomena; therefore, it is called the 'ultimate-non-nature.'"

Examples: "Paramārthasamudgata, it is thus: for example, character-non-natures [that is, imputational natures] are to be viewed as like a flower in the sky. Paramārthasamudgata, it is thus: for example, production-non-natures [that is, other-powered natures] are to be viewed as like magical creations. From between the [two] ultimate-non-natures, one [that is, other-powered natures] is also to be viewed that way. Paramārthasamudgata, it is thus: just as, for example, space is distinguished by the mere naturelessness of form [that is, as a mere absence of forms] and pervades everywhere, so from between those [two] ultimate-non-natures, one [that is, the thoroughly established nature] is to be viewed as distinguished by the selflessness of phenomena and as pervading everything."

Summary: "Paramārthasamudgata, thinking of those

---

[a] See *Absorption,* #104.

[b] See ibid., #76, 77. About "phenomena," see ibid., #71.

[c] See ibid., #67.

> three types of naturelessness, I taught, "All phenomena are natureless."

Buddha explains that when, in the Perfection of Wisdom Sūtras, he said that all phenomena are natureless, he was thinking of three types of phenomena called the three natures (or three characters) and three types of naturelessness. Roughly speaking:

1. **Imputational natures**—or, more specifically, the establishment of objects as the referents of conceptual consciousnesses and the appearance of such—are not established by way of their own character and thus are without the nature of being established by way of their own character; rather, they are posited by names and terminology. Thus, imputational natures are **character-non-natures.**
2. **Other-powered natures**—that is to say, impermanent phenomena—are without the nature of being produced in and of themselves; rather, they are produced in dependence upon an aggregation of causes and conditions. Thus, other-powered natures are **production-non-natures**. Other-powered natures also are not the ultimate that is the final object of observation for purifying obstructions and hence are **ultimate-non-natures.**
3. **Thoroughly established natures**—that is to say, emptinesses—are the ultimate and are the very absence of objects' being established by way of their own character as the referents of conceptual consciousnesses. Thus, they are **ultimate-non-natures.**

Even though in the Perfection of Wisdom Sūtras Buddha repeatedly uttered the words "All phenomena are natureless" and did not—in spoken words—make any other specification, he makes it clear here in the *Sūtra Unraveling the Thought* that he was thinking of three different classes of phenomena and different types of naturelessness with respect to each of them.

The three classes of phenomena are the three natures: imputational, other-powered, and thoroughly established natures. The type of nature that imputational natures do not have is establishment by way of their own character. The type of nature that other-powered natures do not have is self-production. Another type of nature that other-powered natures do not have is that they are not the ultimate through meditation upon which obstructions are removed. Thoroughly established natures are the very non-establishment of objects in accordance with the imputational nature and thus are ultimate-non-natures. (Thoroughly established natures, emptinesses, **are** such absences and also themselves lack such establishment.) Therefore, the first naturelessness is said to be in terms of "character"—that is, imputational natures are without establishment by way of their own character; the second naturelessness is said to be in terms of "production"—that is, other-powered natures are without self-production; and the third naturelessness, which is twofold, is said to be in terms of the ultimate—that is, other-powered natures are not the ultimate, whereas thoroughly established natures are ultimate-non-natures themselves. Dzong-ka-ba (*Emptiness in Mind-Only*, 83) cites Asaṅga's *Compendium of Ascertainments*:[138]

> *Question:* Thinking of what did the Supramundane Victor say [in the middle wheel] that all phenomena are natureless?
>
> *Answer:* Here and there he said such through the force of taming [trainees], thinking of three types of non-nature.

He then cites Vasubandhu's *The Thirty*:[139]

> Thinking of three types of non-nature
> Of the three types of natures [respectively],
> He taught [in the Perfection of Wisdom Sūtras]
> That all phenomena are natureless.

In this way, **all** phenomena are indeed natureless but not in the same way; rather, there are three classes of phenomena that are natureless in three different ways (or four when counting the two types of ultimate-non-nature).

Hence, the literal reading of the Perfection of Wisdom Sūtras that all phenomena are natureless, that is to say, that all phenomena are not established from their own side, should not be taken as literally acceptable. Rather, one should consider the basis in Buddha's thought—what Buddha had in mind when he spoke such words—and interpret the literal reading otherwise. According to Paṇ-chen Sö-nam-drak-ba's tradition:[140]

- In the first wheel of the teaching, the explicit teaching and what Buddha had in mind behind the teaching are contradictory
- In the middle wheel of the teaching, the determination of what is behind the literal rendering allows one even to get at what Buddha was teaching **explicitly**, to get at the meaning that he was **explicitly** expressing, given the mind-set of the chief trainees hearing this teaching.

In the middle wheel, sharp trainees understand the Perfection of Wisdom Sūtras in terms of the three natures and the three non-natures. The *Sūtra Unraveling the Thought* itself says:[141]

> In this way, Paramārthasamudgata, various types of faith of sentient beings are seen with regard to my disciplinary doctrine, which was explained well, which was taught well, my doctrine which was explained with a very pure thought, which was well propounded. Paramārthasamudgata, with respect to this, thinking of just these three types of non-natures, the One Gone Thus, by way of the aspect of setting forth sūtras of interpretable meaning, taught the doctrine in this way, "All phenomena are natureless; all phenomena are not produced, not ceasing, quiescent from the start, and naturally thoroughly passed beyond

> sorrow." Regarding that, when sentient beings who have generated great roots of virtue, have purified the obstructions, have ripened their continuums, who have great faith and have accumulated great collections of merit and wisdom—hear this doctrine, they understand, **just as it is**, this which I explained with a thought behind it, and they develop belief in that doctrine. They also realize, by means of their exalted wisdom, **the meaning just as it is**. Also, through cultivating their realization, they very quickly attain the very final state. Furthermore, they thoroughly experience faith in me, and say, "Ah! The Supramundane Victor has become completely enlightened; he has become completely enlightened with respect to all phenomena."

Thus, Paṇ-chen S̄ö-nam-drak-b̄a makes a distinction between the literal reading and the explicit teaching (or meaning communicated) with respect to the middle wheel of the teaching but not with respect to the first wheel. The literal reading of the middle wheel is not literally acceptable, whereas the explicit teaching, which is other than the literal reading, is literally acceptable, for the explicit teaching is the three non-natures in terms of the three natures.

It is not claimed that, in the *Sūtra Unraveling the Thought,* the brief indication—which is the first sentence of Buddha's answer to Paramārthasamudgata's question—openly says all this. Rather, the immediately following extensive explanation addresses explicitly and separately the three types of phenomena and their respective non-natures.

Structure Of The Extensive Explanation

Gung-ru Chö-jung[142] and Jam-ȳang-shay-b̄a[143] present the structure of Buddha's extensive reply in three sections corresponding to the three non-natures, each of which, following Wonch'uk's *Extensive Commentary,*[144] is in five parts. With respect to character-non-natures, the five parts are:

1. An explicit, rhetorical[a] question asking for illustrations of the character-non-nature: "Paramārthasamudgata, concerning that, what are character-non-natures of phenomena?"
2. An explicit explanation that factors imputed in the manner of entity and attribute are character-non-natures: "Those which are imputational characters."
3. A rhetorical inquiry into the reasons for that: "Why?"
4. A reply to that inquiry: "It is thus: Those [imputational characters] are characters posited by names and terminology and do not subsist by way of their own character."

[a] I have added the word "rhetorical" in items 1 and 3, since Buddha speaks all the lines.

5. Summation: "Therefore, they are said to be 'character-non-natures.'"

Like Wonch'uk, Jam-ȳang-shay-b̄a[a] applies the same five-part structure to the discussion of the other two non-natures. With respect to (self-)production-non-natures, the five parts are:

1. An explicit, rhetorical question asking for illustrations of the production-non-nature: "What are production-non-natures of phenomena?"
2. An explicit explanation that other-powered natures are production-non-natures: "Those which are the other-powered natures of phenomena."
3. A rhetorical inquiry into the reasons for that: "Why?"
4. A reply to that inquiry: "It is thus: Those [other-powered natures] arise through the force of other conditions and not by themselves."
5. Summation: "Therefore, they are said to be 'production-non-natures.'"

The same five parts are to be found in Buddha's extensive reply about ultimate-non-natures:[b]

1. An explicit, rhetorical question asking for illustrations of the ultimate-non-nature: "What are ultimate-non-natures of phenomena?"
2. An explicit explanation that other-powered natures are also non-natures in terms of ultimate, in the sense that they are not the ultimate: "Those dependently arisen phenomena—which are natureless due to being natureless in terms of production—are also natureless due to being natureless in terms of the ultimate."
3. A rhetorical inquiry into the reasons for that: "Why?"
4. A reply to that inquiry: "Paramārthasamudgata, that which is an object of observation of purification in phenomena I teach to be the ultimate, and other-powered characters are not the object of observation of purification."
5. Summation: "Therefore, they are said to be 'ultimate-non-natures.'"

Buddha goes on to give a second answer to the inquiry for illustrations of ultimate-non-natures, which can be structured the same way:

2. An explicit explanation that thoroughly established natures, emptinesses, are ultimate-non-natures in that they are the very naturelessness of phenomena—in the sense of being their absence of being established by way of their own character as the referents of conceptual consciousnesses—and thus are the ultimate: "Moreover, that which is the thoroughly established

[a] Gung-ru Chö-jung does not explicitly extend these five to the ultimate naturelessness.

[b] Though Jam-ȳang-shay-b̄a indicates that the five are to be applied to the ultimate-non-nature, he does not spell them out, undoubtedly because the structure is by now clear.

character of phenomena is also called 'the ultimate-non-nature.'"

3. A rhetorical inquiry into the reasons for that: "Why?"
4. "A reply" to that inquiry: "Paramārthasamudgata, that which in phenomena is the selflessness of phenomena is called their 'non-nature.' It is the ultimate, and the ultimate is distinguished by just the naturelessness of all phenomena."
5. Summation: "Therefore, it is called the 'ultimate-non-nature.'"

Through such clear delineation, Buddha teaches that:

- imputational natures are character-non-natures, in the sense that they are not established by way of their own character
- other-powered natures are production-non-natures, since they are not produced by themselves
- other-powered natures are also ultimate-non-natures, since they are not the ultimate
- thoroughly established natures, emptinesses, are ultimate-non-natures.

In this way, the three classes of phenomena—imputational, other-powered, and thoroughly established natures—are called not just the three natures and the three characters but also the three non-natures. Though this teaching is not given on the **literal** level of the Perfection of Wisdom Sūtras, it is held to be the **explicit** teaching of those sūtras, given the mind-set of very sharp listeners.

This terminology comes to life only when, upon perceiving a phenomenon such as a table, for instance, one reflects that it is a production-non-nature, and so forth. Left on the abstract level, the teaching merely seems to be a superficially intellectual exercise, but it is not. The terminology itself, once applied to and incorporated into perception of everyday objects, is evocative.

A table, a body, a mind, or a person is an other-powered nature as well as a production-non-nature. An absence of self-production, fraught with implications that run counter to ordinary perception, is present with each of these objects. Similarly, with each object is a falsely imputed status—an imputational nature—that seems to subsist in the nature of the object but does not, and thus with each object is a seeming status that is qualified by a crucial character-non-nature. Furthermore, each object has with it a profound nature, a thoroughly established nature, that is constituted by the object's non-establishment in accordance with its false appearance, and when this ultimate-non-nature is noticed, one is gradually relieved of the afflictive emotions and blockages promoted by unwitting assent to the false appearance.

Examples

Buddha compares character-non-natures, that is, imputational natures, to a flower of the sky. Due to an eye disease,[a] the figure of a flower appears in the sky, but in fact there is no flower in the sky; just so, imputational natures are merely imputed by conceptuality.[145] Still, this does not mean that all imputational natures do not exist, for uncompounded space, for instance, is an **existent** imputational nature, as is an object's being the referent of a term and of a conceptual consciousness (with the qualification that it is not established so **by way of its own character**).

Buddha compares production-non-natures, these being other-powered natures which are necessarily without self-production, to magical creations. As Jik-may-dam-chö-gya-tso[146] says, the main other-powered nature is unreal ideation, which itself is used as a code word for other-powered natures. Jik-may-dam-chö-gya-tso aligns factors of the example and of the exemplified this way:

The pebbles and sticks that are the bases of illusion	Unreal ideation[b] (that is, other-powered natures)
The pebbles and sticks being affected by the mantra and substance, that is, salve, that the magician uses	Unreal ideation (other-powered natures) being affected by predispositions for mistaken dualistic appearance
The appearance—to the audience—of the sticks and pebbles as horses, elephants, and so forth due to being affected by the magician's mantra and salve	The appearance of unreal ideation (other-powered natures) as distant and cut off due to being affected by predispositions for mistaken dualistic appearance

The example of a magical illusion does not indicate that other-powered natures do not exist; rather, it indicates that, due to predispositions deposited by former misperceptions, other-powered natures are made to appear to exist in a false aspect—with subject and object distant and cut off as different entities and as established by way of their own character as the referents of their respective conceptual consciousnesses.

Buddha says that from between the two ultimate-non-natures, other-powered natures—which are posited as ultimate-non-natures, since they are not the ultimate—are again to be viewed as like a magician's illusions. Then addressing the other ultimate-non-nature, he says that the thoroughly established nature which is both the ultimate and the absence of the nature that is the (falsely imputed) self of phenomena—the absence of a difference of entity of subject and object or the absence of an object's being established by way of its own character as the referent of a conceptual consciousness—is like space. As Jik-may-dam-chö-gya-tso[147] puts it, just as space is distinguished, or posited, by way of a mere negation of obstructive contact and pervades all physical phenomena in the sense of existing with them, so the thoroughly established nature

a *rab rib.*

b For a discussion of this term, see *Emptiness in Mind-Only,* 307.

is distinguished by way of a mere elimination of a self of phenomena and pervades all phenomena as their mode of subsistence.

What Was Behind The Teaching Of No Production And So Forth?

Buddha continues his explanation, pointing out that from two perspectives—imputational natures and thoroughly established natures—he taught in the Perfection of Wisdom Sūtras that all phenomena are unproduced, unceasing, quiescent from the start, and naturally thoroughly passed beyond sorrow. With respect to the first, the perspective of imputational natures (*Emptiness in Mind-Only,* 97), Jik-may-dam-chö-gya-tso, based on Wonch'uk's exposition,[148] divides Buddha's exposition into four parts—a brief indication,[a] an inquiry,[b] an explanation,[c] and final summary.[d]

1. Brief indication: "Concerning that, thinking of just character-non-natures [that is, thinking of imputational natures], I taught that all phenomena are unproduced, unceasing, quiescent from the start, naturally thoroughly passed beyond sorrow."
2. Rhetorical inquiry: "Why?"
3. Explanation: "Paramārthasamudgata, it is thus: That which does not exist by way of its own character is not produced. That which is not produced does not cease. That which is not produced and does not cease is from the start quiescent. That which is quiescent from the start is naturally thoroughly passed beyond sorrow [that is, naturally devoid of the afflictive emotions without depending on an antidote]. That which is naturally thoroughly passed beyond sorrow does not have the least thing to pass beyond sorrow."
4. Final summary: "Therefore, thinking of character-non-natures, I taught, 'All phenomena are unproduced, unceasing, quiescent from the start, and naturally thoroughly passed beyond sorrow.'"

Jik-may-dam-chö-gya-tso[149] rephrases the explanation so that the progression of reasons is obvious:

> Imputational natures do not have the least thing to pass beyond sorrow because they are naturally thoroughly passed beyond sorrow (naturally devoid of the afflictive emotions without depending on an antidote), since they are quiescent from the start, since they are not suitable to be phenomena of the afflictive emotions, since they are

---

a *mdor bstan.*
b *brtag pa.*
c *rnam par bshad pa.*
d *mjug bsdu ba.*

> uncompounded phenomena, since they are devoid of production and cessation, since they do not exist by way of their own character.

The final and hence root reason is that imputational natures are not established by way of their own character. Thus it is implied that all products are established by way of their own character.

Buddha's exposition (*Emptiness in Mind-Only,* 98) of why, in consideration of thoroughly established natures, he taught in the Perfection of Wisdom Sūtras that all phenomena are unproduced, unceasing, quiescent from the start, and naturally thoroughly passed beyond sorrow is similarly divided into four parts but with two parts to the third:[150]

1. Brief indication: "Moreover, thinking of just the ultimate-non-nature, which is distinguished by the selflessness of phenomena, I taught, 'All phenomena are unproduced, unceasing, from the start quiescent, and naturally thoroughly passed beyond sorrow.'"
2. Rhetorical inquiry: "Why?"
3. Brief indication: "It is thus: Just the ultimate-non-nature which is distinguished by the selflessness of phenomena only subsists in permanent, permanent time and everlasting, everlasting time. It is the uncompounded final reality of phenomena, devoid of all afflictive emotions."

   Extensive explanation: "Because that uncompounded [nature] which subsists for permanent, permanent time and everlasting, everlasting time in the aspect of just that reality is uncompounded, it is unproduced and unceasing. Because it is devoid of all afflictive emotions, it is quiescent from the start and naturally thoroughly passed beyond sorrow."
4. Final summary: "Therefore, thinking of the ultimate-non-nature which is distinguished by the selflessness of phenomena, I taught, 'All phenomena are unproduced, unceasing, quiescent from the start, and naturally thoroughly passed beyond sorrow.'"

Jik-may-dam-chö-gya-tso[151] rephrases the explanation so that the progression of reasons is obvious:

> The selflessness of phenomena is quiescent from the start and naturally thoroughly passed beyond sorrow because of being devoid of all afflictive emotions, since it is unproduced and unceasing, since it is uncompounded, since it is distinguished by the selflessness of phenomena.

The above has provided a rudimentary structuring of Buddha's answer to Paramārthasamudgata's question. In the next five chapters, we will consider in detail the individual three natures and their respective non-natures.

11. Other-Powered Natures: Impact of Dependent-Arising

To recapitulate: In the middle wheel of the doctrine, such as in the Perfection of Wisdom Sūtras, Buddha uttered the words of sūtra, "All phenomena are natureless." In the third wheel of doctrine, Buddha explains what, in his own thought, was behind that teaching. Specifically, in the seventh chapter of the *Sūtra Unraveling the Thought,* he explains that he had been speaking from within a perspective of dividing phenomena into three types, each of which has its respective naturelessness. He says that:

- imputational natures are natureless in terms of character
- other-powered natures are natureless in terms of (self-)production and are natureless in terms of the ultimate (since they are not the ultimate)
- thoroughly established natures are the ultimate-non-nature itself.

Although Buddha sets forth the three non-natures in that order, he explains (as will be detailed below, p. 161) that he **initially** teaches the second of these—that is, that other-powered natures are production-non-natures. Since this is the order in which he leads trainees, let us turn to it first.[a]

In brief, other-powered natures[b] are things produced under the power, or influence, of causes and conditions that are other than them. The type of nature that they lack is self-production; they are not produced without depending upon specific causes and conditions—they are not produced of themselves. Thus, each and every other-powered nature is a production-non-nature, something that does not have the nature of self-production. As Buddha (*Emptiness in Mind-Only,* 87) says in the seventh chapter of the *Sūtra Unraveling the Thought:*

> What are production-non-natures of phenomena? Those which are the other-powered characters of phenomena.
>
> Why? It is thus: Those [other-powered characters] arise through the force of other conditions and not by themselves. Therefore, they are said to be "production-non-natures."

A-ku Lo-drö-gya-tso[152] renders the meaning of the passage in syllogistic form:

> With respect to the subjects, other-powered natures, they are called production-non-natures because, from a positive point of view, they

---

[a] All of the Tibetan sources teach the three in their order of presentation of the three non-natures. However, the order of practice is an important facet of this doctrine, allowing much easier comprehension of its import, and thus I am presenting the three non-natures this way.

[b] For an extensive discussion of other-powered natures, see *Absorption,* #66-77, 127-128.

> arise from other conditions and, from a negative point of view, they are not produced through their own essences.

He points out that the reason from the positive point of view indicates itself the meaning of "other-powered nature"—namely, something that is a dependent-arising, something that arises from other conditions.

Another passage from the same chapter of the *Sūtra Unraveling the Thought* (that is not cited by these commentators) gives a vivid sense of **why** Buddha first teaches about production-non-natures, that is to say, why he first teaches about other-powered natures. In explaining various levels of his teaching, Buddha says about the initial level:[153]

> Paramārthasamudgata, regarding that, I teach doctrines concerning production-non-natures to those beings who from the start have not generated roots of virtue, who have not purified the obstructions, who have not ripened their continuums, who do not have much belief, and who have not achieved the collections of merit and wisdom. These beings, having heard these doctrines, discriminate compositional phenomena which are dependent-arisings as impermanent and discriminate them as just unstable, unworthy of confidence, and as having a nature of change, whereupon they develop fear and discouragement with respect to all compositional phenomena.
>
> Having developed fear and discouragement, they turn away from ill deeds. They do not commit any ill deeds, and they resort to virtue. Due to resorting to virtue, they generate roots of virtue that were not [previously] generated, purify obstructions that were not purified, and also ripen their continuums which were not ripened. On that basis, they have much belief, and they achieve the collections of merit and wisdom.

When untrained persons understand that phenomena are not produced of themselves but depend upon causes and conditions, they realize that their own wishes are not supreme, that they are bound in a web of causes and conditions, and that their actions mold their own future. That phenomena are not under their own power means here that they are under the "other-power" of causes and conditions, specifically of karma—actions. Realizing this, practitioners reform their behavior, turning away from ill-deeds and toward virtuous behavior so that they can influence their own future.

Buddha goes on to say that, even though practitioners make great progress through understanding that other-powered natures are (self-)production-non-natures, they still cannot become released from cyclic existence, and thus in the next level of his teaching he explains the character-non-nature and the ultimate-non-nature. This results in a three-staged teaching:

- Initially his trainees learn that things are produced from causes and conditions and hence are unstable, due to which they turn away from excessive involvement in and attachment to temporary, non-independent events
- Then, it is possible for them to reflect on the fact that a phenomenon's being a referent of conceptual thought and a referent of terminology is not established by way of its own character
- Thereby, it is possible for them to reflect on the ultimate—that is, other-powered natures' emptiness of being established in this false way.

The sūtra itself makes clear that this is the mode of progression of practice. Although—in terms of his explanation of the three non-natures which we have been considering—Buddha speaks of the character-non-nature first, in terms of practice the production-non-nature is first.

A Typology Of Religious Experience

The gradation of teachings that the *Sūtra Unraveling the Thought* presents under the format of the three non-natures resonates with a basic typology of religious persons offered by the Bengali scholar Atisha (982-1054) in his *Lamp for the Path to Enlightenment.*[154] Although Atisha does not cite the *Sūtra Unraveling the Thought* in his own commentary, his presentation of religious motivation provides the context from which Ge-luk-ba scholars view gradations of teachings and thus is important, at minimum, for locating the import of the sūtra for these scholars.

Atisha wrote the *Lamp for the Path to Enlightenment* in 1042-1043 in Tibet at To-ling[a] Monastery in the central Himalayas near Mount Kailash; he is said to have originally composed the text in Sanskrit while "simultaneously" dictating a Tibetan translation.[155] Although only three folios in length, it came to have great influence in most Tibetan orders, and Dzong-ka-ba considered it to be even the root text for his 523-folio *Great Exposition of the Stages of the Path,* a work of paramount importance throughout much of the vast region of Inner Asia. Let us consider at length this presentation of levels of religious persons, since it highlights the importance of Buddha's first teaching about production-non-natures (that is, other-powered natures).

In the third through fifth stanzas of the *Lamp for the Path to Enlightenment,* Atisha speaks of persons as being of three types:

> Persons who seek for their own sake
> The mere pleasures of cyclic existence
> By whatsoever techniques
> Are to be known as low.
>
> Persons who seek merely their own peace—

[a] *mtho gling.*

Having turned their backs on the pleasures of cyclic existence
And having a turning away from sinful deeds—
Are to be called "middling."

Persons who thoroughly wish
To extinguish thoroughly all sufferings of others
[Through inference of such] by way of the suffering
Included in their own continuum are supreme.[a]

This typology of three levels of beings—those of small, middling, and great capacity—served as the framework for Ḏzong-ka-ḇa's *Great Exposition of the Stages of the Path* and has formed much of the perspective out of which his followers both wrote texts and viewed the world, through to the present day.[156] Among Ḏzong-ka-ḇa's followers, Jam-ȳang-shay-ḇa formulated definitions for the three types of beings, basing his exposition on Atisha's stanzas but, typical to his style, drawing on a wide range of Indian texts, sūtras and treatises, the latter including the works of Maitreya and Asaṅga.[157]

Beings of small capacity. Jam-ȳang-shay-ḇa formulates the definition of a being of small capacity as:

a person who seeks mere high status[b] in cyclic existence.[c]

He draws this definition from Atisha's third stanza:

Persons who seek for their own sake
The mere pleasures of cyclic existence
By whatsoever techniques
Are to be known as low.

Jam-ȳang-shay-ḇa takes Atisha's word "mere" in the phrase "The mere pleasures of cyclic existence" as eliminating that persons on this level seek anything beyond high status within cyclic existence—the pleasures of this or future

---

[a] For another translation, see Richard Sherbourne, S.J., *A Lamp for the Path and Commentary* (London: George Allen and Unwin, 1983), 5. My only substantial difference is with respect to the fifth stanza, which he translates as:

One who wholly seeks a complete end
To the entire suffering of others because
Their suffering belongs to his own [conscious] stream,
That person is a Superior.

Sherbourne sees this level of person as understanding that others' suffering is included within one's own mental continuum; such both is unlikely and differs from Jam-ȳang-shay-ḇa's more cogent interpretation of this stanza, which will be given later.

[b] *mngon mtho, abhyudaya.* The term refers to the elevated (*ud*) states of happiness as humans, demi-gods, or gods relative to animals, hungry ghosts, and hell-beings.

[c] *'khor ba, saṃsāra.* Jam-ȳang-shay-ḇa's *Decisive Analysis of (Maitreya's) "Ornament for Clear Realization,"* 25.15: *'khor ba'i mngon mtho tsam don du gnyer ba'i gang zag de.*

lifetimes as a human, demi-god, or god within the round of birth, aging, sickness, and death—and he takes the mention of "for their own sake" as eliminating that such persons seek to bring about others' welfare.

Drawing on Asaṅga's *Compendium of Ascertainments,* Jam-ȳang-shay-b̄a divides this first class of beings—those of small capacity—into three levels: low of the small, middling of the small, and supreme of the small. As the definition of a being of the low level of small capacity, he gives:

> a person who seeks the mere happiness of this lifetime through non-religious[a] means.[b]

This description of the lowest level of those of small capacity is based on Asaṅga's speaking of "the first of those partaking of desires" as "the lowest beings." Jam-ȳang-shay-b̄a's saying that they use "non-religious means" is based on Asaṅga's identification of them as "rash,"[c] or lacking consideration of their own circumstances.

The definition of a being of the middling level of small capacity is:

> a person who achieves [the mere happiness of] this lifetime through religious and non-religious means.

As is clear in Asaṅga's *Compendium of Ascertainments,* the distinctiveness of persons on this level is that they **also** use religious means to bring about happiness in this lifetime. Asaṅga identifies them as both "rash" and "non-rash." Though the middling of the small use "religious" means in their pursuit of pleasure in this lifetime, Ken-sur Nga-w̄ang-lek-den,[d] abbot of the Tantric College of Lower Hla-s̄a just before the escape in 1959, speaks of both the low and the middling among those having small capacity as beneath the count of religious practitioners due to their short-term motivation. In his *Meditations of a Tibetan Tantric Abbot,* which I translated and edited from lectures that he gave in Wisconsin in 1965, he says:[158]

> The small of the small are those who strive after the happiness of this life, and except for that, they do not think about anything. They do not engage in the practice of Buddhism, Christianity, Islam, or the like. As an example of such a being there are cows, or even if they are humans, they only destroy religious practice; they do not achieve any virtue at all. They are like animals.
>
> The middling of the small engage in both religious and non-religious practices. The intent of their practice is to achieve merely the

a *chos min.*

b Jam-ȳang-shay-b̄a's *Decisive Analysis of (Maitreya's) "Ornament for Clear Realization,"* 25.20: *chos min gyis tshe 'di'i bde ba tsam don du gnyer ba'i gang zag de.*

c *bab col.*

d *mkhan zur ngag dbang legs ldan,* 1900-1971.

> happiness of this life. Even though they do engage in religious practice, it is not for the sake of their parents or of their future lives, but just for the sake of happiness in this lifetime itself. The way in which a being whose capacity is middling of the small engages in so-called religious practice is not suitable; therefore, it actually cannot function as religious practice.

Ken-sur Nga-w̄ang-lek-den was fond of relating stories from oral traditions with great vividness such that it almost seemed that he was present at these events—the vivid detail and sense of presence at once enlivening the account and suggesting that a great deal of it was fabrication (historical accounts did not take on the guise of objective reporting). On one occasion he told of a question put to Atisha about the effects of using religious means with a motivation limited to improvement of the present lifetime. He reported that Atisha's answer was that the effect was rebirth in a hell, this being because good karma was being consumed through directing its effects to the superficial affairs of this lifetime, thereby leaving bad karmas to manifest in the next lifetime. Whether his story relates an actual encounter with Atisha or not, since it is widely renowned in this tradition, it provides a boundary line between religious and nonreligious experience—and also between what can and cannot be included within the scope of Buddhist soteriology[a]—as seen by this tradition. The crucial

[a] The term "soteriology" at first seems out of place when considering the "self-help" presentations of Buddhism that predominate in the Tibetan cultural region. "Soteriology," which is built from the Greek *sōter* ("savior") and means a "doctrine of salvation" or "way of salvation" (see Ninian Smart, "Soteriology," in *Encyclopedia of Religion,* ed. Mircea Eliade [New York: Macmillan, 1986], vol. 13, 418), seems to require an external agency that saves and rescues beings, whereas the Buddhism of this area **for the most part** (exceptions to be discussed) emphasizes that the preconditions necessary for liberation from suffering are within each individual and also that the techniques of rescue are to be implemented by practitioners themselves, not by an external savior. Exalted beings may help by teaching the path and by providing booster-blessings, but the path can be put into practice only by individuals. Thus, in translating these systems' terminology for release from undesirable states, I prefer such terms as "liberation" over "salvation" and "liberative" over "soteriological."

There are indeed external rescuers who assume considerable importance in Tibet, such as the female deity Tārā, whose very name means "Rescuer" or "Savioress"; also, the purpose of a majority of mantras is to call on deities such as Mañjushrī for help. However, the main brunt of the normative tradition, as it is explained in the lecture halls and debating courtyards of Tibetan religious orders, does not view the process of gaining freedom as being from an external agency. Even though many cultural practices in the Tibetan-Mongolian cultural region turn this orientation on its head through almost countless forms of "other-help" remedies ranging from attending cleansing rituals, to purchasing charms, to drinking holy water, to merely seeing people purported to be holy, to propitiating mundane deities—the extreme extent of which flies in the face of the basic call to make effort at internal practice—the normative tradition as well as much informed practice of the path is founded on "self-help," albeit with boosts from the outside. Thus, "soteriology" seems, from many viewpoints, to be out of place in discussing the Buddhism of this region.

issue is motivation: the scope of the non-soteriological is limited to the affairs of this lifetime, whereas the scope of the soteriological is more long-term, taking into account other lifetimes.

This perspective is seen in the definition of a being of the supreme level of small capacity:[a]

Still, I shrink from using neologisms such as "lysiology" or even the simpler but awkward "liberatology." Also, there are a number of uses of the terminology of "saving" in English in a reflexive context—saving oneself from trouble, and so forth, and the basic Sanskrit word that can be taken as meaning "religion," *dharma*, which is built from the verbal root *dhṛ* meaning "to hold," is etymologized as referring to doctrines (or practices) that hold a practitioner back from fright—specifically from the frights of:

1. being reborn in a bad transmigration
2. being trapped in the round of suffering whether in a good or a bad transmigration
3. all sentient beings' being limited by obstructions preventing full development
4. ordinary appearances and the conception of ordinariness, that is, the conception of being ordinary.

The practices of self-help hold practitioners back, rescue, and save them from unwanted states. Hence, with the proviso that "self-help" is accepted as an integral part of "soteriology" and that an external savior is not the primary concern, I will use the term here.

Ninian Smart makes just such an allowance for self-help when he says about soteriology:

> The implication of the idea is that human beings are in some kind of unfortunate condition and may achieve an ultimately good state either by their own efforts or through the intervention of some divine power.

He does not limit the scope of "soteriology," despite its etymology, to other-help but also includes self-help.

However, I take issue with his limiting the scope of soteriology to the achievement of "an ultimately good state," for an important distinction needs to made with respect to Buddhist traditions: The "good states" that are being sought are not necessarily ultimate, since they are of two types, one provisional and the other ultimate—respectively, (1) release from low levels of transmigration into higher levels as humans, demi-gods, or gods and (2) release from the entire round of suffering. The latter is also envisioned as having two levels, the first being attainment of a lower enlightenment that is mere liberation from the round of suffering and the second being attainment of the supreme enlightenment of altruistically effective Buddhahood. Because the levels of concern, or "unfortunate conditions" from which Buddhists are trying to free themselves, are both provisional and ultimate, soteriology in this context cannot be limited to leading practitioners to ultimate states. The lower limit of soteriology in many Buddhist traditions is rescue from certain unfavorable conditions in a future lifetime, the goal being a more favorable state which, however, is still trapped within the round of suffering. Such saving is an important part of this tradition (as will be discussed later), and thus it would be an unwarranted superimposition to limit its soteriology, its doctrine of salvation, to more profound levels.

[a] Jam-ȳang-shay-b̄a's *Decisive Analysis of (Maitreya's) "Ornament for Clear Realization,"* 26.10: *tshe 'di la ched cher mi byed par chos kho nas phyi ma'i 'khor ba'i bde ba tsam don du gnyer ba'i gang zag de.*

> a person who seeks the mere happiness of a future cyclic existence [that is, a future lifetime] by only religious means, not emphasizing this lifetime.

Again, Jam-ȳang-shay-b̄a's source is Asaṅga's *Compendium of Ascertainments,* where Asaṅga refers to this third level as "supreme" within the low and describes it "as partaking of desire without rashness due to solely [making use of] religious means." Ḏzong-ka-b̄a's *Great Exposition of the Stages of the Path* says:[159]

> A special being of small capacity, not working greatly for this life, seeks the wonderful features of high states[a] in future lifetimes and engages in achieving their causes.

Ken-sur Nga-w̄ang-lek-den's description of the supreme of the small is more vivid:[160]

> The great of the small, or the best of the small, mainly engage in religious practice for the sake of their future lives. They do indeed seek happiness, comfort, food, drink, resources, and so forth for this lifetime, but this is not their main activity. They are mainly seeking happiness in future lives. The religious practice done by these persons is not for the sake of others; it is for their own welfare. Such seekers are called beings whose capacity is the best of the small, but, among actual religious practitioners, those who are engaged in religious practice for the sake of achieving happiness within cyclic existence in a future lifetime are the lowest of the low.
>
> Why are they seeking happiness in future lives? They have identified the cause and effect of actions, and they know their ill-deeds and virtues. They know that after death they will experience pleasures in their future lives from virtuous causes and that they will experience sufferings due to non-virtuous causes. They know that this life will finish and that when it does finish, if in their future lives they are born in bad transmigrations as hell beings, hungry ghosts, or animals, they will have great suffering. They know that if they are born as gods or humans, it will be a little better. Therefore they seek a good transmigration in the future. They know that no matter how long this lifetime is, it will not last many years and that there are innumerable births in future lives until cyclic existence is finished. Therefore, rather than seek their own welfare in this lifetime, which is so short, and suffer for it in the future in a bad transmigration, they begin to practice.

The shift to a longer range perspective—from concentrating on the pleasures of this lifetime to those of future lifetimes—constitutes the first step in becoming a religious person.

---

a *mtho ris kyi phun tshogs.*

From this description, we can identify that in this tradition the initial soteriological experience is of a change of motivation, in the sense not of turning away from happiness but of recognizing that happiness needs to be achieved beyond the present lifetime and thus appropriate means must be implemented in order to gain it. This requires turning away from sole involvement with the temporary pleasures of the present in order to ensure pleasure in the future. Instead of seeking pleasure through the direct activities of accumulating wealth, power, and friends, they view the ten virtues (abstaining from killing, stealing, sexual misconduct, lying, divisive talk, harsh speech, senseless chatter, covetousness, harmful intent, and wrong views) as a better means for gaining a high position in the long run. Still, those same virtues, without the motivation of improvement of future lives, are not included within the practice of religion and cannot constitute initial soteriological experience. With such a motivation, the virtues rescue, save, and hold one back from the frights of lower transmigrations as hell-beings, hungry ghosts, and animals.

Ḡön-chok-jik-may-w̄ang-b̄o, recognized as Jam-ȳang-shay-b̄a's reincarnation, reformulates his predecessor's definition of a **person** of supreme small capacity in terms of the **path** of such a person.[a] In his *Presentation of the Grounds and Paths: Beautiful Ornament of the Three Vehicles,*[161] he says:

> The definition of a path of a special being of small capacity is a thought posited from the viewpoint of mainly seeking mere high status within a future cyclic existence for one's own sake alone. Illustrations of this are, for instance:
>
> - an awareness in the continuum of a being of small capacity that realizes the imminence of death
> - an awareness of ethics in the continuum of a being of small capacity that is an abandoning of the ten non-virtues.
>
> These are called paths of a being of small capacity because—in dependence upon them—persons who possess [such awarenesses] in their continuum are caused to proceed to a state of high status [that is, as a human or god].

Ḡön-chok-jik-may-w̄ang-b̄o refines Jam-ȳang-shay-b̄a's definition by adding the word "mainly," thus suggesting that a person on this level is principally involved in seeking happiness in a future lifetime but could also seek liberation from cyclic existence or even altruistic Buddhahood but in a minor way. He gives, as illustrations of a path of such a being, an awareness realizing the imminence of death and an ethical awareness involved in renouncing the ten

[a] At the end of his presentation of the three types of persons, Jam-ȳang-shay-b̄a (*Decisive Analysis of "Ornament for Clear Realization,"* 29.9) says, "The paths of the three persons are easily understood from those three definitions." Ḡön-chok-jik-may-w̄ang-b̄o may have taken his cue from this suggestion.

non-virtues, but he qualifies these illustrations as being "in the continuum of a being of small capacity." These awarenesses themselves are not necessarily limited to those of supreme small capacity; rather, they are suitable illustrations only if accompanied by the particular motivation of such a person, that is, seeking high status within cyclic existence.

The attitudes developed by a being of supreme small capacity constitute the initial stages toward fulfilling the import of Buddha's statement in the *Sūtra Unraveling the Thought,* cited above, that through teaching character-non-natures:

> ...those beings who from the start have not generated roots of virtue, who have not purified the obstructions, who have not ripened their continuums, who do not have much belief, and who have not achieved the collections of merit and wisdom...discriminate compositional phenomena which are dependent-arisings as impermanent and discriminate them as just unstable, unworthy of confidence, and as having a nature of change, whereupon they develop fear and discouragement with respect to all compositional phenomena.

Though on this level beings have not turned away from all of the phenomena of cyclic existence, they have recognized the process of causes and conditions that construct cyclic existence and are seeking to mold their futures more intelligently.

Beings of middling capacity. Just as persons become of supreme small capacity by extending the perspective that forms the basis of their behavior to include seeking relief from suffering in future lifetimes, persons advance to middling capacity by extending their concern for the plight of suffering to the entirety of cyclic existence. Jam-ȳang-shay-b̄a's definition of a being of middling capacity is:[a]

> a person who is posited from the viewpoint of mainly seeking liberation for his or her own sake by way of turning the mind away from the marvels of cyclic existence.[b]

---

[a] Jam-ȳang-shay-b̄a's *Decisive Analysis of (Maitreya's) "Ornament for Clear Realization,"* 26.18: *'khor ba'i phun tshogs la blo log pa'i sgo nas rang kho na'i don du thar pa gtso bor don gnyer gyi cha nas bzhag pa'i gang zag de.*

[b] As before, Ḡön-chok-jik-may-w̄ang-b̄o reformulates Jam-ȳang-shay-b̄a's definition of a *person* of middling capacity in terms of a *path* of a being of middling capacity. His *Presentation of the Grounds and Paths* (423.1) says:

> The definition of a path of a being of middling capacity is a thought posited from the viewpoint of mainly seeking liberation for the sake of oneself alone, from the viewpoint of having turned the mind away from the marvels of cyclic existence. An illustration of a path of a being of middling capacity is, for instance, an awareness in the continuum of a being of middling capacity that realizes the sixteen [attributes of the four noble truths], impermanence and so forth. These are called paths

Jam-ȳang-shay-b̄a draws this definition from Atisha's *Lamp for the Path to Enlightenment* (stanza 4):

> Persons who seek merely their own peace—
> Having turned their backs on the pleasures of cyclic existence
> And having a nature of turning away from sinful deeds—
> Are to be called "middling."

He takes Atisha's phrase "merely their own peace" as indicating that persons on this level (mainly)[162] seek only their own welfare; he takes the mention of their "having turned their backs on the pleasures of cyclic existence" as indicating that they have overcome their attachment to the marvels of cyclic existence; and he takes "having a nature of turning away from sinful deeds" as indicating a nature of avoiding sinful activities at all times.

Jam-ȳang-shay-b̄a points out that such a strict description does not hold true for all persons of middling capacity, since some beings on this level still engage in sinful deeds. He says:[163]

> There are beings of middling capacity of indefinite lineage who—although they have an intention to leave cyclic existence like a blazing fire—engage in sinful deeds through the force of afflictive emotions or [bad] friends. Not only that, but also there are beings of great capacity who do such.

As sources for such waywardness, he cites Maitreya's *Ornament for the Great Vehicle Sūtras,* "Through the afflictive emotions oneself is destroyed, sentient beings are destroyed, and ethics are destroyed," and the *Nirvāṇa Sūtra,* "Bodhisattvas are not as concerned with crazy elephants and so forth as they are with bad friends." He also cites the *Compilations of Indicative Verse:*[164]

> Do not company with sinful friends.
> When those not committing sins
> Acquaint with those committing sins,
> The qualm is generated that they will commit sins.

The indefiniteness that is the result of not having reached an irreversible level of the path may be the reason for Jam-ȳang-shay-b̄a's using, in the definition of a being of middling capacity, the phrase "posited from the viewpoint of," which is usually stipulated in order to indicate that there are exceptions.

About this level, D̄zong-ka-b̄a's *Great Exposition of the Stages of the Path* says:[165]

> A being of middling capacity, having generated discouragement with respect to all of cyclic existence, takes as the object of attainment

---

of a being of middling capacity because in dependence on them persons who possess them in their continuum are caused to progress to the state of liberation.

> liberation—release from cyclic existence—for one's own sake and thereupon engages in the three trainings, the technique and path for [achieving liberation].

Again, Ken-sur Nga-w̄ang-lek-den's description is more vivid:[166]

> If you are among the best of the small who have great intelligence, you have much to consider about at this point. You think, "For the sake of not being born in a bad transmigration in my future life—as a hell being or hungry ghost or an animal—and for the sake of being born in a good transmigration—as a god or a human—I am going for refuge to the Three Jewels." But then you wonder, "Is that sufficient?" When you examine this, you see that even if you ask the Three Jewels for help in attaining the rank of a god or a human in your next lifetime, and even if you attain the rank of a god or a human in your next lifetime, you will be born, grow old, become sick, and die. Therefore, merely gaining happiness in the next lifetime is not sufficient. You have arrived at great understanding. Whether a life is good or bad, unless you do not have to take rebirth at all through the force of contaminated actions, it is not at all suitable.
>
> When such understanding forms, you have exceeded the qualities of thought of beings of small capacity. But still you have not arrived at the state of the middling or of the great but you are superior to the small. Progressing in your thought, you gradually decide that you must obtain liberation from all types of cyclic existence and no longer be subject to birth by the force of contaminated actions and afflictive emotions; you must have the bliss of the extinguishment of suffering. You realize that the causes of contaminated actions are the afflictive emotions themselves and that these enemies cause the trouble.
>
> Thus you think, "Overcoming these enemies which are the afflictive emotions, I must attain freedom from bondage. I must attain happiness which is the extinguishment of all suffering for myself." This intention to gain liberation from cyclic existence is the attitude of being of middling capacity.

The shift in perspective that takes place with this second level of soteriological experience is more long range in that it takes account not just of the next lifetime (or a few future lifetimes) but of the whole series of lifetimes and the precariousness of one's situation. Through practice of the path, one is seeking to be rescued, saved, and held back from the entire uncontrolled round of birth, aging, sickness, and death in all of its forms.

The difference in the scope of the soteriological perspective—the range of that from which one is seeking to be rescued—comes from more accurately penetrating the nature of appearances. This is done by understanding the pervasiveness of the suffering of being under the uncontrolled influence of karma and afflictive emotions and by understanding that any state within cyclic existence, no matter how pleasurable, will eventually lead to lower states, given the undeniable presence of negative karma.

Den-ma Lo-chö Rin-bo-chay, commenting on Gön-chok-jik-may-wang-bo's text, states the development of increasing scope clearly:[167]

> Beings of small capacity have concern for the sufferings that would take place in their own future lifetime; this is the limit of their thought, and thus it is not vast. Beings of middling capacity know that it will not help at all merely not to undergo the suffering of a bad transmigration in the next lifetime. They realize that even if they live at the peak of cyclic existence[a] it is like living in a hell in a pot of molten copper because they are about to fall into that. There is no difference between the peak of cyclic existence and a hell with respect to the suffering of pervasive conditioning.[b] Even if, at the peak of cyclic existence, there is no suffering of mental or physical pain or suffering of change, when the actual meditative absorption that a person has in that state degenerates, then the person will fall from that state and be reborn in a state of the manifest suffering of physical and mental pain and the suffering of change. Thus, they understand that even in the best of rebirths within cyclic existence one has not passed beyond a state having the nature of the three sufferings. Hence, in order to attain a liberation in which none of these three sufferings will have to be experienced, persons of middling capacity cultivate paths such as realization of the sixteen aspects of the four noble truths and so forth. Their thought is vaster than that of beings of small capacity. More accurate realization of the situation of cyclic existence leads to a reformation of motivation.

This is just the point that Buddha communicates through teaching the production-non-nature. As the *Sūtra Unraveling the Thought* says:

> These beings, having heard these doctrines, discriminate compositional phenomena which are dependent-arisings as impermanent and discriminate them as just unstable, unworthy of confidence, and as having a nature of change, whereupon they develop fear and discouragement with respect to all compositional phenomena.

On this level, soteriological experience is comprised predominantly by generating disgust for the entire round of uncontrolled rebirth. This experience lays the groundwork for realization of the emptiness and selflessness that Buddha subsequently communicates—in the language of the *Sūtra Unraveling the*

---

[a] *srid rtse, bhavāgra.*

[b] *khyab pa 'du byed kyi sdug bsngal.*

Thought—through teaching the character-non-nature and the ultimate-non-nature. As before, the advance comes not from turning away from happiness but from recognizing a greater happiness and the means to achieve it. This greater perspective impels meditation on the thoroughly established nature in terms of the selflessness of persons in order to undermine the afflictive emotions that are built on misperception. Such meditation, in turn, leads to direct cognition of the true status of persons such that, gradually, various levels of afflictive emotions are removed from the mental continuum forever.

Beings of great capacity. Just as persons become of middling capacity by extending their motivational outlook to include seeking relief from all of cyclic existence, persons advance to great capacity by extending their understanding of their own plight in cyclic existence to a realization that others are in a similar plight. Jam-ȳang-shay-b̄a's definition of a being of great capacity is:[a]

> a person who—by way of having come under the influence of great compassion—is posited from the viewpoint of seeking an exalted knower of all aspects[b] [that is, the omniscience of Buddhahood] in order that Buddhahood might be attained in the continuums of other sentient beings.

Ḡön-chok-jik-may-w̄ang-b̄o's reformulation of Jam-ȳang-shay-b̄a's definition of a **person** of great capacity in terms of the **path** of a being of great capacity brings clarity to this level:[168]

> The definition of a path of a being of great capacity is a thought that is posited by way of seeking [to attain] an exalted knower of all aspects [that is, omniscience] for the sake of other sentient beings' attaining Buddhahood from the viewpoint of having come under the influence of great compassion. Illustrations of a path of a being of great capacity are the great compassion or the pure unusual altruistic attitude in the continuum of a being of great capacity. These are called paths of a being of great capacity because, in dependence upon them, persons who possesses them in their continuum are caused to progress to unsurpassed enlightenment.

Jam-ȳang-shay-b̄a draws his definition from Atisha's *Lamp for the Path to Enlightenment* (stanza 5):

> Persons who thoroughly wish
> To extinguish thoroughly all sufferings of others

---

[a] Jam-ȳang-shay-b̄a's *Decisive Analysis of (Maitreya's) "Ornament for Clear Realization,"* 27.17: *snying rje chen po'i gzhan dbang du gyur pa'i sgo nas sems can gzhan rgyud la sangs rgyas thob phyir du rnam mkhyen don du gnyer ba'i cha nas bzhag pa'i gang zag de.*

[b] *rnam mkhyen, sarvākārajñāna.*

> [Through inference of such] by way of the suffering
> Included in their own continuum are supreme.

Jam-ȳang-shay-b̄a takes the phrase "by way of the suffering included in their own continuum" as indicating how these persons infer others' suffering based on experience of their own. He takes Atisha's mention of "others" as indicating their being intent on others' welfare and his mention of "all sufferings" as referring to all levels of suffering in cyclic existence, both gross and subtle. He takes "extinguish thoroughly" as indicating the extinguishment of obstructions together with their predisposing latencies,[a] and he takes "thoroughly wish" as indicating that these persons wish to relieve other beings of sufferings through a **variety** of techniques.

About this level, D̄zong-ka-b̄a says:[169]

> A being of great capacity, due to being under the other-influence of great compassion, has taken Buddhahood as [his or her] object of attainment for the sake of extinguishing all the sufferings of sentient beings and thereupon trains in the six perfections, the two stages [of Highest Yoga Tantra, that is, generation and completion stages], and so forth.

On this level, practitioners are said[170] to be concerned about four defective conditions in **all** sentient beings:

1. cyclic existence
2. seeking a solitary peace which is mere liberation for their own sake
3. obstructions to liberation
4. obstructions to omniscience.

The shift in perspective that takes place with this third and last level of religious experience is of far wider scope in that others' suffering has become the primary concern. Den-ma L̄o-chö Rin-b̄o-chay speaks movingly of this universal responsibility:[171]

> Sentient beings' births are limitless, without beginning. Hence, there is not a single being who has not been one's mother. At the time when they were our mother, they protected us with kindness just as our mothers of this lifetime did. It would be very bad if one had no thought to help these beings who have been one's mother and been very kind to oneself since beginningless time, but rather discarded them. For instance, take the case of a mother who was blind and crazy and who went walking along the edge of an abyss into which she could easily fall. If her only child, seeing this, remained playing and enjoying him/herself, this would be considered vulgar even in the world. In just this way, sentient beings, our aged mothers, are as if blind, not

[a] *bag chags, vāsanā.*

> knowing the discarding of non-virtues and the adoption of virtues, how to practice the path. Although they want happiness, they do not know how to achieve the causes of happiness; although they do not want suffering, they powerlessly achieve its causes. Thus, they are as if crazed. Moreover, because they have accumulated many non-virtues and continue to do so, they are walking alongside the abyss of bad transmigrations. Just as the child should try to stop her or his blind, crazed mother from wandering along the edge of an abyss, so we should develop the compassion that seeks to free sentient beings from this state in which, though wanting happiness, they do not know how to achieve its causes and hence are bereft of happiness, and though not wanting suffering, powerlessly achieve its causes again and again. It is not sufficient just to think "How nice it would be if these beings were free from suffering"; rather one must assume the burden of doing this oneself.
>
> When one considers whether one has the capacity to free all sentient beings from suffering, one understands that at present one does not. Who has such a capacity? When one investigates, one sees that it is a Buddha, a Supramundane Victor, one who has removed all faults and perfected all attributes. Thus, beings of great capacity are those who generate an altruistic intention to become enlightened, thinking, "I will attain Buddhahood in order to establish all sentient beings in the great liberation of the non-abiding nirvāṇa."[a]

Den-ma Lo-chö Rin-bo-chay's usage of the image of an only child's relationship to her or his helpless mother is typical of the teachings for inculcating this altruistic attitude. An ordinary attitude of filial concern is made extraordinary by extending its scope beyond its usual range, to all beings. Just as, on the level of the practices of a being of low and middling capacity, the quest for happiness is not forsaken but is reaffirmed with a higher goal, so here ordinary concern and compassion are not replaced by other-worldly attitudes but are extended far beyond their usual scope and are thereby transformed.

In the earlier phase, the scope of a practitioner's soteriological concern (and hence of spiritual experience) advanced from concern with suffering in a future life to concern with one's own cyclic existence in general; now it advances to concern with the plight of all sentient beings. All beings are to be rescued, saved, and held back from all levels of suffering.

In terms of **how** such progress in an ever-widening perspective is made, one passes from the level of ordinary low capacity to that of special low capacity by reversing the emphasis on the appearances of the present lifetime; this is done by realizing that:

---

[a] *mi gnas pa'i myang 'das, apratiṣṭhitanirvāṇa.*

- the present situation endowed with pleasurable features is valuable
- one will not stay long in this life
- lifetimes as animals, hungry ghosts, and hell-beings are bereft of such fortunate circumstances.[172]

Then one passes from this level to that of a being of middling capacity by reversing the emphasis on the appearances of future lives, thereby developing an intention definitely to leave cyclic existence. This is done by reflecting on the inevitable effects of karma and the many varieties of suffering certain to be induced by one's own bad karma. It is necessary to meditate on:

- suffering so that a wish to separate from cyclic existence will be generated
- impermanence so that attachment to the mental and physical aggregates of this life will be eliminated
- the thoroughly established nature in terms of the selflessness of persons so that attachment to what belongs to oneself (including one's own body) will be overcome.[173]

Through this process, an attitude seeking liberation can be generated in full form. Then one advances to the level of a being of great capacity by developing the unusual compassion of being willing oneself to take on the burden of freeing other beings from suffering and joining them with happiness. This is done by meditatively cultivating a sense of closeness with all beings and by becoming aware of their suffering, as inferred from one's own situation which was realized earlier on the paths of beings of small and middling capacity.

The paths of the three levels thereby serve as an integrated gradation of practices; it is not that they are mutually contradictory. Ḏzong-ka-ḇa's *Great Exposition of the Stages of the Path* makes this point clearly:[174]

> Since the paths of the other two types of beings are included in complete form within the stages of the path of a being of great capacity, those two [that is, the paths of beings of small and middling capacity] are parts, or branches, of the Great Vehicle path....Here, one is not being led on the path of a being of small capacity who takes as the object of attainment **merely** the happiness of cyclic existence nor on the path of a being of middling capacity who takes as the object of attainment **mere** liberation from cyclic existence for one's own sake alone. Rather, some of the paths shared with those two are treated as prerequisites for being led on the path of a being of great capacity, and thus they are to be treated as branches of the deeds of the path by a being of great capacity.

Later, Ḏzong-ka-ḇa explains what these shared paths are:[175]

> On the occasion of [the practices of] a being of small capacity, one contemplates how the harms of the pain of the bad transmigrations

> befall oneself, and on the occasion of [the practices of] a being of middling capacity one contemplates the way in which even in [a lifetime of] high status there is suffering and no peaceful happiness. Then through meditation within inferentially extending one's own experience also to other sentient beings who are [seen to be] close to oneself, [these earlier contemplations] serve as causes for generating love and compassion, and, from that, one generates the attitude of an altruistic intention to become enlightened. Therefore, training in the attitudes shared with beings of small and middling capacity is a technique for generating the non-artificial attitude of an altruistic intention to become enlightened; it is not the case that one is being led on some separate path.

By not cultivating the merely self-directed aspects of the paths of the lower levels, the paths of the three levels come to form a coherent, integrated whole.[a] The higher levels do not cancel the lower ones but are built on the lower and continue to be reinforced by them. This is because beings of middling and great capacity need a continuum of favorable lives in order to complete their respective paths and thus still need the practices of a being of small capacity in order to ensure good rebirths. Also, the great compassion that is so central to the motivation of a being of great capacity is founded on realistic appraisal of one's own plight in cyclic existence as is understood through the practices of a being of small and middling capacity. Even more so, realization of emptiness (the thoroughly established nature in terms of the selflessness of persons)—detailed on the level of practice for a being of middling capacity for gaining liberation from cyclic existence—is preliminary to realizing the thoroughly established nature in terms of the selflessness of phenomena through concentration on which one is liberated from the obstructions to omniscience, the primary intent of a being of great capacity. Thus, for a being of great capacity, the practices of all three beings are intertwined; the lower ones both form the foundation for the higher and remain important aspects of continual practice. It can be seen that the lower levels of soteriological concern cannot be dismissed as merely preliminary, in favor of more ultimate concerns; they remain an important aspect of a practitioner's intentionality throughout the entire scope of practice. The picture that emerges from considering such a broad range of practices is far richer than what is gained from considering only ultimate concerns.[b]

---

[a] The presentation of this ordered system itself induces advancement in soteriological perspective and spiritual experience, although ultimately it is accomplished in meditation and a complete transformation of attitude.

[b] The doctrine of three types of beings forms an integrated series of practices for one individual and also constitutes a typology supposedly applicable to all beings; anyone and everyone can be classified within this rubric. Most ordinary beings, including animals, are the low of the low capacity since the scope of their concern is mainly limited to the temporary affairs of this lifetime; those who also employ religious means to achieve happiness in

To summarize: The process of self-education, self-help, and self-rescue is a **withdrawal** from lower involvements—first from seeking pleasures only within the scope of the present lifetime, then from seeking the pleasures of cyclic existence in general, and then from self-centeredness. At the same time, it requires an **extension** to higher involvements—first to concern with future lifetimes, then to liberation from all of cyclic existence, and then to others' welfare. Buddha announces in the *Sūtra Unraveling the Thought* that he begins his teaching of the three natures and the three non-natures with that of other-powered natures and their production-non-nature in order to initiate this transformation of perspective.[a]

Nature Of Production

As cited at the beginning of this chapter, the *Sūtra Unraveling the Thought* says:

---

this lifetime are middling of the low; those who are about to generate a non-artificial form of an intention to leave cyclic existence in all its aspects are of middling capacity, as are all Low Vehicle practitioners right through to those who have attained the state of a Foe Destroyer. Those who have generated the unusual compassion described above are, in turn, classified as beings of great capacity.

As a typology for humanity in general, this system has obvious faults. It cannot classify the most compassionate Christians, for instance, as any of these, since they are not mainly seeking either (1) "an exalted knower of all aspects so that Buddhahood might be attained in the continuums of other sentient beings" as a being of great capacity would, or (2) "liberation for one's own sake" as a being of middling capacity would, or (3) "the mere happiness of a future lifetime" as a being of supreme low capacity would, or (4) "the mere happiness of this lifetime through religious and non-religious means" as a being of middling low capacity would, or (5) "the mere happiness of this lifetime through non-religious means" as a being of low low capacity would. The typology has similar, severe difficulties with Hindu systems, adherents to which, because of being considered not to recognize properly the process of cyclic existence, would probably be classified as beings of the middling low variety, outside the realm of religious practitioners.

Though the typology is aimed at including all beings, its failure to recognize other traditions as even within the count of religions suggests that a hidden agenda is to exclude practitioners of other religions from the count of religious beings. This is not surprising in a parochial culture, but such harsh exclusivity does run counter to the advocacy of universal compassion. Followers quickly learn to bifurcate their minds such that they are deeply moved by calls to unbiased compassion and yet participate with vigor in exaggerated discrimination against other groups. At times, when confronted with such exclusivity, I have wondered whether it is just that a message of universal compassion is being wrapped in a package of parochialism or whether a message of parochial prejudice is being wrapped in the package of universal compassion. Nevertheless, the typology says much about the direction of Indo-Tibetan Buddhist religious experience and can be used within such a framework.

[a] It is crucial to recognize this point, for otherwise one would wrongly assume from the order of Buddha's presentation of three non-natures—when he responds to Paramārthasamudgata's question about what was behind his teaching in the Perfection of Wisdom Sūtras that all phenomena are natureless—that he initially teaches the character-non-nature.

> What are production-non-natures of phenomena? Those which are the other-powered characters of phenomena.
>
> Why? It is thus: Those [other-powered characters] arise through the force of other conditions and not by themselves. Therefore, they are said to be "production-non-natures."

What is the nature in terms of production that other-powered natures lack? It cannot be mere production, simply because other-powered natures are indeed produced from causes and conditions. As the *Sūtra Unraveling the Thought* itself says, "Those [other-powered natures] **arise** through the force of other conditions." In this vein, Jam-ȳang-shay-b̄a[176] points out that the fact that other-powered natures are production-non-natures cannot mean that other-powered natures are not produced from other-powered natures, that is, from compounded phenomena. Rather, when the sūtra says that other-powered natures are production-non-natures, the production that other-powered natures lack is self-powered production.[a] This has the same import as production through their own power,[b] causeless production,[c] production by way of its own entity,[d] and arbitrary, or capricious, production.[e] Such self-powered production is not relative to the existence of its causes—it is production without reliance on the production of its causes.

What Does "Phenomena" Mean?

When Buddha starts to speak of the production-non-nature, he speaks of "phenomena" saying, "What are production-non-natures of phenomena?" Is he suggesting that a production-non-nature—about which he himself subsequently says, "Those arise through the force of other conditions and not by themselves"—can be posited with respect to each and every phenomenon, including permanent phenomena which are **not** arisen from causes and conditions? Or is he using the word "phenomena" loosely within having divided all phenomena into three classes—imputational, other-powered, and thoroughly established

[a] *bdag nyid kyi dbang gis skye ba:* Jam-ȳang-shay-b̄a's *Great Exposition of the Interpretable and the Definitive,* 69.3. In the next line, Jam-ȳang-shay-b̄a says that this means to be "produced from causes that are just the entity itself without depending on causes and conditions" (*rgyu rkyen la ma ltos par* ***bdag nyid gcig bu'i*** [or, as in the Hla-s̄a Go-mang edition, *pu'i*] *rgyu las skye ba*). Jik-may-dam-chö-gya-tso (*Port of Entry,* 181.5) says that Jam-ȳang-shay-b̄a appears here to be self-contradictory, but his edition of Jam-ȳang-shay-b̄a's text misreads ***bdag nyid gcig pa'i*** ("which are the same entity"). Even the correct reading could be misinterpreted to refer to production from causes that are the same entity as the effect, but Jam-ȳang-shay-b̄a's intent is clearly not this.

[b] *rang dbang gis skye ba.*

[c] *rgyu med las skye ba.*

[d] *ngo bo nyid kyis skye ba.*

[e] *'dod rgyal du skye ba,* literally "production in the manner of wish being dominant."

natures—and thus means, "**From among** phenomena what are production-non-natures"?

Jik-may-dam-chö-gya-tso[177] decisively points out that both the *Sūtra Unraveling the Thought* and Dzong-ka-ba's *The Essence of Eloquence* are clear that a production-non-nature must be a **composite** of (1) being produced from causes and (2) not being produced causelessly, and hence only other-powered natures, and not all phenomena, are production-non-natures. This is because imputational natures and thoroughly established natures, not being produced, do not fulfill the first criterion.

The point is crucial; let us cite the *Sūtra Unraveling the Thought* again:

> What are production-non-natures of phenomena? Those which are the other-powered characters of phenomena.
>
> Why? It is thus: Those [other-powered characters] **arise through the force of other conditions and not by themselves**. Therefore, they are said to be "production-non-natures."

The sūtra clearly says that it is because other-powered natures have the **two** qualities of arising through the force of other conditions and of not arising by themselves that they are called production-non-natures. This combination constitutes the very meaning of a production-non-nature, and thus permanent phenomena cannot be production-non-natures.

A-ku Lo-drö-gya-tso[178] similarly explains that the *Sūtra Unraveling the Thought* here is speaking within the context of having divided all phenomena into the three classes of the three natures and thus is explicitly referring only to compounded phenomena, actual other-powered natures, as being production-non-natures. Still, in a brilliant extrapolation[179] he shows that, even though the sūtra does not **explicitly** indicate that a production-non-nature is to be applied to permanent, uncompounded phenomena, such can be done based on taking the meaning of "other-powered nature" in a broader sense.[a] He does this

[a] Gung-tang (*Difficult Points*, 126.8; *Annotations*, 25.2) makes a brief suggestion that one should seek out the thought behind Jam-yang-shay-ba's inconsistency on whether the character-non-nature can be extended to permanent phenomena. He is referring to a later section where Jam-yang-shay-ba makes the hair-splitting distinction that:

- uncompounded phenomena **are** included in what is merely explicitly indicated by the word "phenomena" in the *Sūtra Unraveling the Thought* when it says, "What are production-non-natures of phenomena?" but
- uncompounded phenomena do not have the full meaning that the sūtra thereupon explicitly indicates about production-non-natures.

Jam-yang-shay-ba makes the distinction that **mainly** the passage explicitly teaches the production-non-nature in the context of compounded phenomena and even if it **mainly** does not explicitly teach the production-non-nature with respect to uncompounded phenomena, it nevertheless **explicitly** does so. However, in a seeming about-face, he goes on to say that, although one can posit an other-powered nature with respect to uncompounded phenomena, this is a case of merely designating the convention "other-powered nature" with respect to

through creatively adapting an etymology of "other-powered nature" found in Asaṅga's *Summary of the Great Vehicle*. Asaṅga says:[180]

> Why are they called "other-powered natures"? Since they are produced from their respective seeds that are predisposing latencies, they are under the other-influence of conditions.[181] Having been produced, their

---

them, since they are not **actual** other-powered natures. He concludes by saying that it should be examined whether one should make the logical extension that the production-non-nature is posited with respect to uncompounded phenomena in a similar, merely imputed manner.

Jam-ȳang-shay-b̄a clearly has not come to a decision on the matter, and Gung-tang suggests that Jam-ȳang-shay-b̄a's "thought"—this being a polite way of referring to unresolved ramifications of the issue—should be pursued. However, Gung-tang himself pursues the topic only briefly in his *Annotations* (16.1-16.4).

A-ku L̄o-drö-gya-tso (*Precious Lamp,* 87.4-93.3), taking his lead from Gung-tang's short exposition, treats the issue in considerable detail, which I find to be particularly interesting and revealing. A good deal of my interest comes from the fact that while in Hla-s̄a in October 1986, I debated this issue with a monk from the Jay College of S̄e-ra Monastic University. A group of monks had gathered, and after debating and talking back and forth with them on a few issues, I jokingly announced that I would hold Jam-ȳang-shay-b̄a's positions—since the Jay College uses the textbooks of Jay-d̄zün Chö-ḡyi-gyel-tsen and not Jam-ȳang-shay-b̄a—if they cared to debate against them. I was immediately pressed with this very issue and, not remembering Jam-ȳang-shay-b̄a's presentation on the point, was roundly trounced. Had I remembered his stance, I would have had to hold that the *Sūtra Unraveling the Thought* explicitly applies the production-non-nature to all phenomena including uncompounded phenomena but that the full meaning of the production-non-nature that the sūtra (*Emptiness in Mind-Only,* 87) explicitly thereupon indicates in the passage, "Those [other-powered characters] arise through the force of other conditions and not by themselves. Therefore, they are said to be 'production-non-natures,'" does not apply to uncompounded phenomena. Thus, even if I had remembered his position, it would have been double-talk, as Gung-tang suggests when he says that Jam-ȳang-shay-b̄a's thought needs to be pursued but then does not himself pursue it. In short, A-ku L̄o-drö-gya-tso removes the double-talk simply by refusing to allow, unlike Jam-ȳang-shay-b̄a, that the sūtra explicitly applies, in either a main or a secondary way, the production-non-nature to uncompounded phenomena.

A-ku L̄o-drö-gya-tso (*Precious Lamp,* 93.2), after giving the explanation that will follow, politely praises it as a unique, good explanation by Jam-ȳang-shay-b̄a and Gung-tang. More realistically, with Gung-tang's help, he found sense in Jam-ȳang-shay-b̄a's statement that all phenomena—even uncompounded phenomena—are included within the term "phenomena" of the question in the *Sūtra Unraveling the Thought,* "What are production-non-natures of phenomena?" but that uncompounded phenomena do not have the full meaning of the answer to that question, "Those [other-powered characters] arise through the force of other conditions and not by themselves. Therefore, they are said to be 'production-non-natures.'" Still, having figured out why Jam-ȳang-shay-b̄a was struggling with the issue, A-ku L̄o-drö-gya-tso did not accept Jam-ȳang-shay-b̄a's claim that the passage **explicitly** teaches a production-non-nature with respect to uncompounded phenomena. Only compounded phenomena, dependent-arisings, are **actual** production-non-natures. The praise should go to A-ku L̄o-drö-gya-tso for unraveling this point with such clarity.

entities cannot remain more than an instant. Hence, they are called "other-powered."

Asaṅga indicates that other-powered natures are not self-powered or autonomous for two reasons:

1. because they are produced under the influence of causes and conditions—specifically the seeds of perception that give rise to them—these being other than themselves
2. because they do not have the power to remain even for a second instant.

A-ku Lo-drö-gya-tso adapts these two points to permanent phenomena by drawing a parallel between the impermanent and the permanent:

1. Even though uncompounded phenomena are not **produced** from causes, they are factors of appearance that **dawn** to the mind through the force of the maturation of internal, predisposing latencies.
2. Even though uncompounded phenomena do not **depend on conditions** that produce them, they must **abide in dependence** upon their respective final reality[a] just as clouds depend upon the sky. The thoroughly established nature of uncompounded phenomena is their final reality that immutably serves as their **basis**, and those uncompounded phenomena themselves are posited as their own other-powered natures.

In a sense, therefore, uncompounded space is the "other-powered nature" of uncompounded space, for as Gung-tang[182] notes, the other-powered nature of sound has to be just sound[b] even if the impermanence of sound does not have to be just sound. In the same way, the other-powered nature of an uncompounded phenomenon can be said to be that very uncompounded phenomenon itself.

A-ku Lo-drö-gya-tso analyzes the opposite of the etymology of "other-powered" so that he can posit a production-non-nature for uncompounded phenomena as well. Once, from a positive viewpoint, the etymology of "other-powered" has been understood, then something's non-existence as an entity that is the opposite of this etymology is the meaning of that phenomenon's production-non-nature. Hence, something similar can also be applied to uncompounded phenomena with respect to their being production-non-natures. Specifically:

- A compounded phenomenon's **non-existence** as an entity that is not produced from its respective seed, which is a predisposing latency, and hence is not under the other-influence of conditions and can abide for more than an instant is the meaning of its production-non-nature.
- Similarly, an uncompounded phenomenon's production-non-nature can

[a] *chos nyid, dharmatā;* I translate this also as noumenon.

[b] That is, sound is the other-powered nature of sound.

> be posited as (1) the **non-existence** of its dawning without depending on the maturation of a predisposing latency and (2) its **not having** the power to remain under its own power without depending on its own final mode of subsistence—that is, without depending on its emptiness of being established by way of its own character as the referent of a conceptual consciousness.

In this way, the meaning of the production-non-nature comes down to the selflessness of phenomena.

Though in the *Sūtra Unraveling the Thought* such an extension of the etymological meanings of "other-powered nature" and "production-non-nature" is not explicitly applied to uncompounded phenomena, A-ku Lo-drö-gya-tso cogently finds its application to uncompounded phenomena to be profoundly meaningful. I would add that this extension to uncompounded phenomena can be applied back to compounded phenomena, for they, too, depend on their final reality.

Still, it needs to be remembered that Buddha's purpose in teaching the production-non-nature at this point is mainly to draw his listeners into recognizing that the experiences they are undergoing are under the influence of causes and conditions and are not produced in and of themselves. He is seeking to draw them into basic religious practice, and thus the main impact of "other-powered nature" at this point does not involve the profound aspects of the dawning of phenomena in dependence on internal latencies and of their dependence on their final nature and hence does not involve realization of the selflessness of phenomena. Rather, Buddha is seeking to draw "those beings who from the start have not generated roots of virtue, who have not purified the obstructions, who have not ripened their continuums, who do not have much belief, and who have not achieved the collections of merit and wisdom" into discriminating "compositional phenomena which are dependent-arisings as impermanent and discriminating them as just unstable, unworthy of confidence, and as having a nature of change, whereupon they develop fear and discouragement with respect to all compositional phenomena." He does this so that:

> Having developed fear and discouragement, they turn away from ill deeds. They do not commit any ill deeds, and they resort to virtue. Due to resorting to virtue, they generate roots of virtue that were not [previously] generated, purify obstructions that were not purified, and also ripen their continuums which were not ripened. On that basis, they have much belief, and they achieve the collections of merit and wisdom.

The teaching of the other-powered nature is to awaken liberative concern through suggesting the tenuousness, the contingency, of everything subject to causes and conditions as well as the malleability of caused phenomena. (A-ku Lo-drö-gya-tso's ingenious explanation takes the message even further to the profound topic of the thoroughly established nature—the non-establishment of the imputational nature in other-powered natures—glimpses of which strengthen the quest for liberation by revealing that the pain of cyclic existence and the confinement of mind are not endemic to our situation but are removable.)

Thus, the doctrine of other-powered natures has the dual function of:

1. stimulating practitioners to reformation of behavior through understanding the impact of causality, and
2. providing a framework for understanding emptiness by teaching that other-powered natures are bases of the mis-imagination of the imputational nature and thus are bases of the thoroughly established nature which is the absence of that imputational nature.

For the first purpose, other-powered natures are necessarily limited to impermanent phenomena, whereas for the latter purpose, the term can, in some fashion, include all phenomena, including existent imputational natures and emptinesses, since they serve as bases of their own emptiness—their own thoroughly established nature. The tension between the two modes has led to creative ways of accommodating the dual role.

12. Imputational Natures I: The Illusion

From among the three natures and the three non-natures, the imputational nature[a] and the character-non-nature receive the most analysis by Ge-luk-b̄a scholars, largely because some of D̄zong-ka-b̄a's statements on the topic seem to be at odds with each other. They have attempted in radically different ways to make consistent sense out of his often cryptic exposition, creating a plethora of distinctions that at times open up insight into issues of great import and at other times almost close down the mind's ability to stay with the topic due to their convoluted, hair-splitting character. Complicating the difficulty is the format of pretending not to criticize D̄zong-ka-b̄a but to find what his real thought is.

As we have seen, Buddha explains in the *Sūtra Unraveling the Thought* that he first teaches the production-non-nature—that is to say, he teaches about other-powered natures—in order to instill in his listeners a sense of impermanence and a sense of the dependence of compounded phenomena upon causes and conditions, thereby fostering a strong wish to practice virtue. Then Buddha explains that this teaching is not sufficient:[183]

> Indeed, they have achieved [beneficial forces] ranging from generation of roots of virtue to collections of merit and wisdom, but because they do not understand, as they really are, the two aspects—the character-non-nature and the ultimate-non-nature—with respect to those production-non-natures [that is, other-powered natures], they do not develop discouragement toward all compositional phenomena, they do not become thoroughly separated from desire, and they do not become completely released. They do not become completely released from the thorough afflictions that are the afflictive emotions; they do not become completely released from the thorough afflictions that are actions; and they also do not become completely released from the thorough afflictions that are births.
>
> Therefore, the One Gone Thus also teaches them doctrines concerning the character-non-nature and the ultimate-non-nature in order that [those beings] become thoroughly discouraged with respect to all compositional phenomena, become thoroughly separated from desire, become thoroughly released, thoroughly pass beyond the thorough afflictions that are the afflictive emotions, thoroughly pass beyond the thorough afflictions that are actions, and thoroughly pass beyond the thorough afflictions that are births. Because, hearing these doctrines, they do not conceive other-powered natures to have the character of

---

[a] For an extensive discussion of imputational natures, see *Absorption,* #78-93, 104-126, 129-146.

> the imputational nature, they believe and distinguish production-non-natures [that is, other-powered natures] to be without the nature of character and without the nature of the ultimate, whereupon they realize them just as they are.

Buddha explains that after teaching about the production-non-nature, he teaches about the character-non-nature and the ultimate-non-nature in order to bring about complete liberation.

The clearly stated aim of these teachings is to cause his listeners not to "conceive other-powered natures to have the character of the imputational nature," due to which they will understand other-powered natures "to be without the nature of character and without the nature of the ultimate." That the aim is to cease believing in a status superimposed on other-powered natures is mirrored in Ge-luk-ba scholars' repeated emphasis on realizing that other-powered natures are not established by way of their own character as the referents of terms and of conceptual consciousnesses.

That in the above citation the *Sūtra Unraveling the Thought* says that the cure is to view **other-powered natures** as character-non-natures and as ultimate-non-natures seems, on the surface, to contradict Buddha's statements earlier in chapter 7 of the *Sūtra:*

- that it is imputational natures (and implicitly **not** other-powered natures) that are character-non-natures
- that, although other-powered natures are ultimate-non-natures, in the sense that they **are not** the ultimate, it is thoroughly established natures (and **not** other-powered natures) that are ultimate-non-natures, in the sense that they **are** the ultimate.

The apparent contradiction is that Buddha in the above citation says that his teaching culminates in the realization that **other-powered natures** (which are by now understood to be production-non-natures) are **character**-non-natures and ultimate-non-natures. Still, it is not difficult to determine that here Buddha is speaking in a looser sense, for although it is indeed the case that imputational natures are character-non-natures, one is to understand that other-powered natures are not established **in accordance with** the imputational nature and in this sense are character-non-natures. Also, although it is the case that thoroughly established natures are ultimate-non-natures, one is to understand that other-powered natures are empty of the imputational nature and in this sense are ultimate-non-natures.

What emerges from this passage is the importance of taking other-powered natures as the bases of meditation, despite the fact that the part of the chapter that we are considering speaks of three subjects (imputational natures, other-powered natures, and thoroughly established natures) and associates three predicates (character-non-nature, production-non-nature, and ultimate-non-nature) with them. Since the main meditation is that other-powered natures are empty of being established in accordance with the imputational nature, it is important to keep this perspective—and its consequent call for flexibility—in mind when, in this chapter and the next, we take imputational natures as the main subject and explore how they are character-non-natures.

Identifying Imputational Natures

As was pointed out in the previous chapter, the *Sūtra Unraveling the Thought* (*Emptiness in Mind-Only,* 86) gives two reasons why imputational natures are not established by way of their own character, one positive and one negative:[184]

> It is thus: Those [imputational characters] are characters posited by names and terminology and do not subsist by way of their own character. Therefore, they are said to be "character-non-natures."

In order to appreciate both the profundity of thought and the intellectual machinations involved in Tibetan scholars' re-formulation of Ḏzong-ka-ḇa's thought, we will carefully consider in this chapter the subject ("imputational natures") and in the next chapter the predicate ("are character-non-natures") as well as the twofold reason ("because they are posited by names and terminology and do not subsist by way of their own character").

What are the imputational natures that do not subsist, that is, are not established, by way of their own character? Among the more renowned imputational natures are uncompounded space, analytical cessations, and non-analytical cessations. However, according to Gung-ru Chö-jung,[185] Jam-ȳang-shay-ḇa,[186] and others, even Proponents of Sūtra—rated below Proponents of Mind-Only—realize with valid cognition that such imputational phenomena are not established by way of their own character, for they understand that these are generally characterized phenomena[a]—objects that do not have specific characteristics that can serve as appearing objects in direct perception. This is because Proponents of Sūtra understand that these exist but are not functioning things producing effects. Uncompounded space cannot produce an effect since it is a mere absence of obstructive contact, and cessations (or, more properly, states of having ceased) cannot produce effects since they are mere absences of afflictive emotions, and so forth.[b]

---

[a] *spyi mtshan, sāmānyalakṣaṇa.*

[b] In this vein, later in the text Ḏzong-ka-ḇa (*Emptiness in Mind-Only,* 198) says in a passage replete with technical terminology (the passage is taken from an opponent's objection, but this part is a commonly held assertion):

> Also, even if it were being refuted that the self-isolate of the conceived object [of a conceptual consciousness] is established by way of its own character, since it is confirmed even for Proponents of Sūtra that the objects of comprehension of an

Because even the Proponents of Sūtra realize that generally characterized phenomena are not established by way of their own character, the Mind-Only School cannot merely be refuting that imputational phenomena—that is to say, any and all generally characterized phenomena—are established by way of their own character. Otherwise, there would be no way to rank the Mind-Only School as superior to the Sūtra School, and it is clear that the *Sūtra Unraveling the Thought,* as well as the founder of the Mind-Only School, Asaṅga, sees this view as superior to any found in the Lesser Vehicle schools.

Thus, here in the *Sūtra Unraveling the Thought* the term "imputational nature" (or "imputational character") has a more restricted meaning than it does in more general usage, where it means any imputational factor—these being all permanent phenomena except emptinesses as well as non-existents. Tibetan scholars make the cogent point that a more restricted meaning must be identified in order to illuminate the meaning of the sūtra. Thus, when the *Sūtra Unraveling the Thought* says:

> Those [imputational characters] are characters posited by names and terminology and do not subsist by way of their own character. Therefore, they are said to be "character-non-natures"

it is not suitable to restate its meaning syllogistically as:

> With respect to the subject, **imputational factors**, there are reasons for calling them "character-non-natures" because they are called such since (1) from the positive side they are only posited by names and terminology and (2) from the negative side they are not established by way of their own character.

For this syllogistic reformulation merely mirrors the words of the sūtra. Indeed, the Second Dalai Lama[187] makes just such a faux pas when he restructures the sūtra statement in syllogistic form as:

> With respect to the subject, **imputational factors**, they are called "character-non-natures" because they are only posited by names and terminology and are not established by way of their own character.

> inferential valid cognition are generally characterized phenomena [and] do not exist as [functioning] things, this is not feasible.

In general, the object of comprehension of an inferential cognition can be any phenomenon, impermanent or permanent, but here the reference is to the appearing objects of inferential cognition, these being generally characterized phenomena. This identification is based on Gung-ru Chö-jung's (*Garland of White Lotuses,* 19b.3) specifying that the objects of comprehension of a conceptual consciousness are sound-generalities (*sgra spyi, śabdasāmānya*) and meaning-generalities (*don spyi, arthasāmānya*). However, A-ku Ḷo-drö-gya-tso (*Precious Lamp,* 238.4), pursuing a different agenda, identifies this as the factor, for instance, of forms and so forth being objects of names and terminology (*gzugs sogs ming brda'i yul yin pa'i cha lta bu*). For more discussion of this passage, see *Absorption,* #125.

Nevertheless, Gung-tang[188] excuses the Second Dalai Lama's taking "imputational factors" as the subject by saying that he intends it to refer to the imputational factors **relevant at this point**[189] and thus not imputational nature in general[190] either in the sense of the mere general category or in the sense of all that are included within the category, such as uncompounded space and so forth. Gung-tang's positing of the Second Dalai Lama's thought is actually polite criticism.

Indeed, commentary should flesh out what the term "imputational natures"[a] means if it is to offer anything more than the bare reading of the sūtra. In this fashion Ƀel-jor-hlün-drup,[191] after framing the point the same way:

> It follows with respect to the subject, **imputational natures**, that there is a reason for saying they are "character-non-natures" because they are only posited by names and terminology and are not established by way of their own character

immediately identifies the imputational natures referred to here:

> Here, "posited by names and terminology" is in reference to **imputational natures that are factors imputed in the manner of entities and attributes**, whereby it only indicates [some imputational natures]; it is not in reference to all imputational natures. For below, Ḏzong-ka-ḇa explains that, even though generally characterized phenomena and space cannot be posited by merely names and terminology, they are imputational natures that are merely imputed by conceptuality.

Paṇ-chen Sö-nam-drak-ḇa,[192] author of the textbook literature of the Lo-sel-ling College of Dre-ḇung Monastic University, gives more detail. Despite using the vague term "imputational factors" when framing the basic statement,[b] he, like Ƀel-jor-hlün-drup, explains that the imputational factors explicitly indicated on this occasion in the *Sūtra Unraveling the Thought* must be just **imputational factors imputed in the manner of entity and attribute.**[c] As support for his position he cites a clear statement by Ḏzong-ka-ḇa (*Emptiness in Mind-Only,* 110):

> With respect to the imputational factor of which [other-powered natures] are empty, on both occasions of identifying the imputational

---

[a] *kun btags.*

[b] Like the Second Dalai Lama, Paṇ-chen Sö-nam-drak-ḇa (*Garland of Blue Lotuses,* 27b.5) says:

> Imputational factors are posited as character-non-natures because they are posited by only names and terminology and are not established by way of their own character.

[c] Paṇ-chen Sö-nam-drak-ḇa's *Garland of Blue Lotuses,* 28a.5: *ngo bo dang khyad par la kun btags pa'i kun btags.*

> factor in the sūtra it does not speak of any other imputational factor than just factors imputed in the manner of entities and attributes. I will explain the reason for this later.

Paṇ-chen S̄ö-nam-drak-b̄a then supplies D̄zong-ka-b̄a's later explanation (*Emptiness in Mind-Only,* 217):

> Although among imputational factors in general there are many, such as all generally characterized phenomena, space, and so forth, the reason why these are not [explicitly] mentioned in the *Sūtra Unraveling the Thought* is that they are not relevant on the occasion of the imputational factor, the emptiness of which is posited as the thoroughly established nature.

D̄zong-ka-b̄a cogently explains that the *Sūtra Unraveling the Thought* is concerned only with the imputational nature relevant to positing the thoroughly established nature, this being why the sūtra is not concerned with other imputational natures such as uncompounded space, and so forth.

Paṇ-chen S̄ö-nam-drak-b̄a does not leave the topic there; he identifies both an existent and a non-existent imputational nature that are relevant.[193]

- The existent is, for instance, a form's being the referent of a conceptual consciousness apprehending a form.[a]
- The non-existent is, for instance, a form's **establishment by way of its own character** as the referent of a conceptual consciousness apprehending a form.[b]

Both of these are imputational factors in the imputation of an entity.

As support for his identification of existent and non-existent imputational factors, Paṇ-chen S̄ö-nam-drak-b̄a cites D̄zong-ka-b̄a (*Emptiness in Mind-Only,* 210):

> Thus, form and so forth being the referents of conceptual consciousnesses[c] is an imputational factor posited by name and terminology, but, since it is established by valid cognition, it cannot be refuted.[d] However, that it is established **by way of the thing's own character** is an imputational factor posited only nominally that does not occur among objects of knowledge [that is, does not exist]. Hence, among what are posited by names and terminology there are two [types], those established by valid cognition and those not established by valid cognition.[e]

a *gzugs gzugs 'dzin rtog pa'i zhen gzhi yin pa.*

b *gzugs gzugs 'dzin rtog pa'i zhen gzhir rang gi mtshan nyid kyis grub pa.*

c See *Absorption,* #78-82.

d See ibid., #108.

e See ibid., #88.

The quotation establishes that Paṇ-chen S̄ö-nam-drak-b̄a's identification of the imputational nature is indeed well-founded in D̄zong-ka-b̄a's own words. But then he mysteriously proceeds to identify a further existent imputational nature in the imputation of an entity:

- the **superimposed factor** that a form is established by way of its own character as the referent of a conceptual consciousness apprehending a form.[a]

He does not explain what this "superimposed factor" is, but Gung-tang, a follower of Gung-ru Chö-jung and Jam-ȳang-shay-b̄a, identifies it as:

- the **appearance** that a form is established by way of its own character as the referent of a conceptual consciousness apprehending a form.[b]

The late Ken-sur Ye-s̄hay-tup-d̄en from L̄o-s̄el-l̄ing College,[194] a follower of Paṇ-chen S̄ö-nam-drak-b̄a, indicated his consternation with Paṇ-chen S̄ö-nam-drak-b̄a for introducing this element, wondering aloud what it could possibly mean. His unspoken anxiety was that this is just what the rival Go-mang tradition in Dre-b̄ung Monastic University identifies as the existent imputational nature relevant here.[c]

Jay-d̄zün Chö-ḡyi-gyel-tsen,[d] textbook author of the Jay College S̄e-ra Monastic University, structures the sūtra passage in syllogistic form similarly as:

> With respect to the subject, **imputational factors imputed in the manner of entity and attribute**, there are reasons for calling them "character-non-natures" because they are called such since (1) from the positive side they are only posited by names and terminology and (2) from the negative side they are not established by way of their own character.

Indeed, the topic of entities and attributes is an underlying theme of the *Sūtra Unraveling the Thought* that surfaces in the first, sixth, and seventh chapters,

---

a *gzugs gzugs 'dzin rtog pa'i zhen gzhir rang gi mtshan nyid kyis grub par sgro btags pa'i cha.*

b *gzugs gzugs 'dzin rtog pa'i zhen gzhir rang gi mtshan nyid kyis grub par snang ba.*

c See *Absorption*, #79, 96-98.

d Jay-d̄zün Chö-ḡyi-gyel-tsen's *General-Meaning Commentary,* 11b.1, 13a.5. Without mentioning B̄el-jor-hlün-drup by name, he criticizes his using "imputational natures" as the subject (11a.3-11b.2).

D̄ra-d̄i Ge-s̄hay Rin-chen-dön-drup, a follower of Jay-d̄zün Chö-ḡyi-gyel-tsen, gives a similar formulation in his *Ornament for the Thought* (21.4):

> With respect to the subject, **imputational factors imputed in the manner of entity and attribute with regard to forms and so forth**, there are reasons for calling them "character-non-natures" because they are called such since (1) from an exclusionary viewpoint establishment by way of their own character is eliminated and (2) from an inclusionary viewpoint they are established as only entities posited by names and terminology.

and thus let us take a temporary diversion to trace its development in the sūtra.

The notion is introduced in the first chapter when the Bodhisattva Gambhīrārthasaṃdhinirmochana explains to the Bodhisattva Vidhivatparipṛcchaka the difference between how persons who are obscured and persons who are not obscured view phenomena and their attributes.[195]

> When those sentient beings—who have childish natures, obscured natures, and natures of disordered wisdom, who do not realize that these are grasses, leaves, twigs, pebbles, and stones—see and hear those, they think this, "This herd of elephants which is an appearance exists; the herd of horses which is an appearance, and cavalry, chariots, infantry, wealth, pearls, gems, conch-shells, crystal, coral, grain, treasuries, and granaries exist."
>
> Having thought this, they emphatically apprehend and emphatically conceive in accordance with how they see and hear. They also subsequently impute conventional designations, "This is true; the other is false." Later, these must be closely examined by them.
>
> When other sentient beings—who do not have childish or obscured natures, and who have natures endowed with wisdom, who realize that these are grasses, twigs, pebbles, and stones—see and hear these, they think, "These which appear in this way are not herds of elephants, and these which appear in this way are not herds of horses, cavalry, chariots, infantry, wealth, pearls, gems, conch-shells, crystals, coral, grain, treasuries, granaries, and storehouses, and that with respect to which there arises a discrimination of a herd of elephants and a discrimination of the **attributes** of a herd of elephants and those with respect to which there arises discrimination of the **attributes** of collections of wealth, grain, treasuries, and storehouses are creations of magic."
>
> Having thought: "These deceive the eye," they do not emphatically apprehend or emphatically conceive in accordance with how they see and hear, and thereupon they do not subsequently impute conventional designations: "This is true; the other is false." It is like this: They subsequently impute conventional designations in accordance with objects. Later it is not necessary that these beings closely examine those conventional designations.
>
> Similarly, when those sentient beings—who have childish natures, who are ordinary beings, who have not attained the supramundane wisdom of Superiors, who do not manifestly cognize the inexpressible reality of all phenomena—see and hear these compounded and uncompounded things, they think: "These compounded and uncompounded things which appear exist."

> Having thought this, they emphatically apprehend and emphatically conceive these in accordance with how they are seen and heard. They also subsequently impute conventional designations: "This is true; the other is false." Later these must be closely examined by them.
>
> Regarding that, when those sentient beings—who do not have childish natures, who see the truth, who have attained the supramundane wisdom of Superiors, who manifestly cognize the inexpressible reality of all phenomena—see and hear these compounded and uncompounded things, they think, "These compounded and uncompounded things which appear are non-existent. Those with regard to which the discrimination of compounded and uncompounded and the discrimination of **attributes** of compounded and uncompounded operate are compositional signs that arise from mental construction, like a magician's illusions. These obscure the mind."
>
> Having thought thus, with respect to these [compounded and uncompounded things], they do not emphatically apprehend or emphatically conceive in accordance with how they see and hear, and thereupon they do not subsequently impute conventional designations—"This is true; the other is false." It is like this: due to thoroughly understanding objects just as they are they impute conventional designations [based on their understanding], and later it is not necessary that these beings closely examine those conventional designations.
>
> Son of good lineage, in that way, by way of a Superior's exalted wisdom and a Superior's vision, Superiors completely realize things to be inexpressible, and because they completely realize the ineffable reality, they nominally designate "compounded" and "uncompounded."

In the sixth chapter the theme emerges embedded within central vocabulary of the system of the sūtra. Buddha, in replying to a question by the Bodhisattva Guṇākara, asks a rhetorical question and answers it:

> Guṇākara, what is the imputational character of phenomena? It is that which is posited by nominal terminology as the **entities and attributes** of phenomena due to imputing whatsoever conventions.

Again, in the seventh chapter the terminology of entities and attributes is employed three times when the Bodhisattva Paramārthasamudgata explains back to the Buddha the import of what Buddha has taught him:

> Those which are posited by nominal terminology—to the objects of activity of conceptuality, that is to say, the foundations of imputational characters and those which have the signs of compounded phenomena—as the character of **entities** [such as] "form aggregate" or **attributes** [such as "the production of form"] and that which is posited

> through nominal terminology as the character of entities or the character of **attributes** [such as] "the production of the form aggregate," "the cessation [of the form aggregate]," "the abandonment and thorough knowledge [of the form aggregate]" are imputational characters. In dependence upon those, the Bhagavan designated the character-non-nature of phenomena....
>
> Supramundane Victor, I offer, in this way, the meaning pronounced by the Bhagavan: Those which are posited by nominal terminology—to the objects of activity of conceptuality, that is to say, the foundations of imputational characters and those which have the signs of compounded phenomena—as the character of **entities** [such as] "the truth of suffering" or the character of **attributes** [such as] "knowledge of the truth of suffering" are imputational characters. In dependence upon those, the Bhagavan designated the character-non-nature of phenomena....
>
> Supramundane Victor, I offer in this way the meaning pronounced by the Supramundane Victor: Those which are posited by nominal terminology—to the objects of activity of conceptuality, that is to say, the foundations of imputational characters and those which have the signs of compounded phenomena—as the characters of **entities**, [such as] "pure meditative stabilizations," or as the characters of **attributes**, [such as] "discordances and antidotes of meditative stabilizations," "cultivation of meditative stabilizations," "production of [meditative stabilizations] that have not yet been produced," "production and abiding, non-forgetfulness, further arising, and increasing and extending [of meditative stabilizations]" are imputational characters. In dependence upon those, the Bhagavan designated the character-non-nature of phenomena.

In these three chapters the *Sūtra Unraveling the Thought* expresses a concern with an exaggeration of the status of phenomena through the approach of the designation of an object's basic entity and of its attributes. Paṇ-chen Sö-nam-drak-b̄a's and Jay-d̄zün Chö-ḡyi-gyel-tsen's identification of imputational natures in this context as factors imputed in the manner of entities and attributes is clearly justified in the sūtra.

Not only is the theme of entities and attributes mentioned in the sūtra in connection with imputational natures but also D̄zong-ka-b̄a at least indirectly identifies—a great many times—that imputational natures in this context are factors imputed in the manner of entities and attributes. I will cite these passages mainly to draw attention to this important theme and also to show that Paṇ-chen Sö-nam-drak-b̄a's and Jay-d̄zün Chö-ḡyi-gyel-tsen's identification is clearly based in their founder's words. D̄zong-ka-b̄a (*Emptiness in Mind-Only*, 110) says:

> With respect to the imputational factor of which [other-powered natures] are empty, on both occasions of identifying the imputational factor in the sūtra it does not speak of any other imputational factor than just **factors imputed in the manner of entities and attributes.**

And (*Emptiness in Mind-Only,* 112):

> ...the imputational factors are **factors imputed in the manner of entity** [such as] "right meditative stabilization" **and of attributes** [such as] their respective discordances, antidotes, and so forth mentioned earlier.

And (*Emptiness in Mind-Only,* 104-105):

> The three phrases [that is, "the objects of activity of conceptuality," "the foundations of imputational characters," and "those which have the signs of compositional phenomena"] indicate the bases of the imputation of imputational factors[—these being other-powered natures].
>
> The rest of it indicates the mode of imputation. The imputation as "This is a form aggregate," is the mode of **imputation of an entity,** and the imputation as "[This] is the production of a form aggregate," and so forth is the mode of **imputation of particulars, or attributes.**

And (*Emptiness in Mind-Only,* 137):

> ...in the "Chapter on Suchness" in the *Grounds of Bodhisattvas,* its *Ascertainment,* and the *Summary of the Great Vehicle,* Asaṅga settles through many various explanations just the statement in the *Sūtra Unraveling the Thought* that other-powered natures' emptiness **of factors imputed in the manner of entities and attributes** is the thoroughly established nature.

And (*Emptiness in Mind-Only,* 142):

> The foundations of imputational characters, those which have the signs of a compositional phenomenon, and the bases of **imputation in the manner of entities and attributes** [explicitly mentioned] in the *Sūtra Unraveling the Thought* refer [mainly] to other-powered natures.

And (*Emptiness in Mind-Only,* 143):

> Concerning this, the extreme of superimposition is refuted by the teaching that phenomena are ultimately empty of **factors imputed in the manner of entity and attribute.**

And (*Emptiness in Mind-Only,* 194-195):

> However, the *Sūtra Unraveling the Thought* explains that other-powered natures are not established by way of their own character as **factors imputed in the manner of entity and of attribute** and that, therefore, the absence of [such] a nature of character is the selflessness of phenomena.[a] Thus, implicitly it teaches that a consciousness conceiving that **factors imputed in the manner of entity and attribute** are established by way of their own character in other-powered natures is a consciousness conceiving a self of phenomena.

And (*Emptiness in Mind-Only,* 195-196):

> Those imputational factors—which are such that a consciousness conceiving imputational factors to be established by way of their own character is asserted to be a consciousness conceiving a self of phenomena—are the **nominally and terminologically imputed factors** [in the imputation of] the aggregates and so forth **as entities**, "This is form," and **as attributes**, "This is the production of form," and so forth.[b] Since the aggregates and so forth do exist as just those [entities of such nominal and terminological imputation], the [mere] conception that they exist as those [entities of nominal and terminological imputation] is not a superimposition; rather, the conception that the aggregates and so forth exist by way of their own character as those entities [of nominal and terminological imputation] is a superimposition.

And (*Emptiness in Mind-Only,* 201):

> For this reason, even the Hearer schools have assertions of tenets that are superimpositions opposite to this—that is, holding that forms and so forth are established by way of their own character as **imputed by names as entities and attributes.**

And (*Emptiness in Mind-Only,* 212):

> The aforementioned conception **that factors imputed in the manner of entity and attribute** exist by way of their own character or exist ultimately is the main obstruction to omniscience.

And (*Emptiness in Mind-Only,* 212-213):

> In dependence upon a verbalizing name [such as "pot"], the verbalized meaning [such as that which is bulbous, flat-bottomed, and capable of holding fluid], and the relationship between the name and the meaning, [the phenomena ranging from forms through to omniscient consciousnesses] appear to a mental conceptual consciousness [to be established by way of their own subsistence] **as the entities and the**

---

[a] See *Absorption,* #95, 98, 99, 102, and 103.

[b] See ibid., #79, 96-98, 100, and 93.

> **attributes** of the objects verbalized. Objects conceived in accordance with such appearance [to be separate entities from their respective conceptual consciousnesses] do not exist, and hence unmistaken [consciousnesses] apprehending such also do not exist.

And (*Emptiness in Mind-Only,* 213):

> Moreover, they thoroughly understand that those names are only exhausted as **factors imputed in the manner of entities and in the manner of attributes.**

And (*Emptiness in Mind-Only,* 214):

> Therefore, when they apprehend these as just exhausted as only mental verbalization and when they do not apprehend meanings as well as names involving **factors imputed in the manner of entities and attributes** nor [anything] involving [factors imputed] in the manner of entity and attribute [as other than only being imputed by conceptuality, that is to say, when they do not apprehend these] as having the factual character [of subsisting as external objects, they attain] the four thorough examinations [which are entities of the path of preparation] and the four thorough knowledges [which are entities of the path of seeing], just as they are in reality.

And (*Emptiness in Mind-Only,* 217):

> Therefore, it is also not that a negation of an otherness of substantial entity between apprehended-object and apprehending-subject is absent in the statements in the *Sūtra Unraveling the Thought* that the emptiness of **imputational factors imputed in the manner of entities and attributes** is the thoroughly established nature.

And (*Emptiness in Mind-Only,* 221-223):

> Conceptualization [that factors imputed] **in the manner of entity and attribute** [are established by way of their own character] and conceptualization apprehending amorphous wholes generate the foundations of [fictional] proliferations—the things that are the objects observed by conceptuality.

And (*Emptiness in Mind-Only,* 223):

> In that way, [Asaṅga] asserts that a consciousness conceiving a self of phenomena—which conceives **that factors imputed in the manner of entities and attributes** are established by way of their own character in phenomena—acts as the root of the view of the transitory [as substantially established I and mine].

And (*Emptiness in Mind-Only,* 226):

> [According to you, Ḏzong-ka-ḇa,] on all occasions of the emptiness of **factors imputed in the manner of entity and attribute** and factors imputed in the manner of other substantial entities of apprehended-object and apprehending-subject—(1) just other-powered natures must be taken as the bases of emptiness [that is, the things that are empty] and (2) their emptiness in terms of the two above-mentioned [imputational natures] must be taken as the thoroughly established nature.

And (*Emptiness in Mind-Only,* 235):

> Since an **imputational factor imputed to phenomena in the manner of entity and attribute** is a phenomenon-constituent and a phenomenon-sense-sphere, statements that those two [that is, phenomenon-constituent and phenomenon-sense-sphere] are established by way of their own character without differentiating [from among phenomena what does and does not exist by way of its own character] also[a] require interpretation.

In the face of these clear statements, it can be concluded that Paṇ-chen Sȫ-nam-drak-ḇa's and Jay-ḏzün Chö-ḡyi-gyel-tsen's identification of the relevant imputational nature as **imputational factors imputed in the manner of entity and attribute** indeed reflects their founder's thought.

Imputation in the manner of an entity is illustrated by a factor imputed in the manner of the entity of form as in "This is a form," but specifically refers to the superimposed factor that a thing appropriate to be called form is established by way of its own character as the referent of the term "form." A factor imputed in the manner of an attribute is often described as a factor imputed in the manner of an attribute of form, for instance, as in "This is the production of form," but specifically refers to the superimposed factor that a thing appropriate to be called form is established by way of its own character as the referent of the term "production of form." According to these scholars, in the *Sūtra Unraveling the Thought* the explicitly indicated non-existent imputational nature includes this twofold misapprehended status of the establishment of an object, such as a bulbous-bellied, flat-bottomed thing able to hold water, by way of its own character as the referent of the term "pot" and as the referent of the term "beautiful."

Also, just as these have been explained with respect to **terms** for entities and attributes, so such is to be applied to conceptual consciousnesses thinking about entities and attributes. Hence, the imputational nature being refuted here is not either the act of imputation or the means of imputing—words and conceptual consciousnesses, since these are impermanent phenomena and hence other-powered natures—but a status of objects that is falsely imputed.

[a] About the word "also," see ibid., #52, 53.

The issue revolves around whether, for instance, that which is bulbous, flat-based, and able to hold fluid is **established by way of its own character** as an entity that is the referent of the term "pot" and **established by way of its own character** as an entity that is the referent of the attributional term "production of pot" (or "beaútiful"). Thus, the illusion is not that objects are referents of terms and thoughts; rather, it is that objects are **established by way of their own character** as the referents of conceptual consciousnesses and of words.

For this reason, "factors imputed in the manner of entity and attribute" (which might also be translated as "imputation of entity and attribute") does not refer to the **act** of imputing or the **words** through which imputation is accomplished, since both of these, being produced phenomena, are other-powered natures and hence necessarily established by way of their own character. Rather, the (non-existent) imputational nature that is refuted is an over-reified status of objects as references of terms and thoughts.

As was mentioned above, Paṇ-chen S̄ö-nam-drak-b̄a briefly identifies the imputed factor as, for instance, a form's being the referent of a conceptual consciousness apprehending a form.[a] Indeed, in *The Essence* D̄zong-ka-b̄a repeatedly makes the focus of discussion the status of forms and so forth as **being the foundations of thoughts and words.** I will cite all these passages because of the importance of the notion. In chapter 10 D̄zong-ka-b̄a (*Emptiness in Mind-Only,* 210) says:

> Thus, form and so forth **being the referents of conceptual consciousnesses**[b] is an imputational factor posited by name and terminology, but, since it is established by valid cognition, it cannot be refuted.[c] However, that it is **established by way of the thing's own character** is an imputational factor posited only nominally that does not occur among objects of knowledge [that is, does not exist]. Hence, among what are posited by names and terminology there are two [types], those established by valid cognition and those not established by valid cognition.[d] Still, this system[e] asserts that once something is only posited by names and terminology, cause and effect are not suitable to occur in it.

Just before that passage, he (*Emptiness in Mind-Only,* 209) says:

> Also, even when one conceives that form and so forth **being the referents of conceptual consciousnesses** is established ultimately or by

---

[a] *gzugs gzugs 'dzin rtog pa'i zhen gzhi yin pa.*

[b] See *Absorption,* #78-82.

[c] See ibid., #108.

[d] See ibid., #88.

[e] The Consequence School asserts the opposite—that causes and effect are possible and, in fact, only occur in what are merely posited by names and terminology. See ibid., #74.

way of its own character, this is similar to conceiving that form and so forth are established by their own character as the foundations of imputation with a name.

And (*Emptiness in Mind-Only,* 209-210):

> If the explicit object of the imputation of terminology [that is, a term-generality or meaning-generality] were established by way of its own character in the entity of that object, then there would be faults such as that without depending upon making the association of the terminology [with the object through being taught the name of the object], an awareness of the name would be generated, and so forth. However, such fallacies do not accrue to the establishment, by way of its own character, of form and so forth **being the foundations of the imputation of terminology and the referents of conceptual consciousnesses.**[a]

Earlier in the same chapter, he (*Emptiness in Mind-Only,* 196) says:

> If the refutation that forms and so forth **being objects of names and terminology** is established by way of their own character were a refutation of their being explicit objects of [terms that are] means of verbalization, then there would be no need to prove—that other-powered natures are empty of that—to the Proponents of [Truly Existent External] Objects.

And (*Emptiness in Mind-Only,* 204):

> Therefore, when the convention "form" is imputed, if one examines how [for instance] **blue's being a basis of the imputation of the convention** for form appears, it does not appear [to childish beings] to be posited by names and terminology but appears as if established through the force of [blue's] own mode of subsistence.

And (*Emptiness in Mind-Only,* 208):

> If a bulbous **thing's being a referent or foundation of the convention "pot"** were established by way of the bulbous thing's own mode of subsistence or its own character, it would not be posited through the force of terminology [that is, language], in which case even an awareness that has the terminology ["pot"] as its object would not depend upon [making the connection of] the terminology [to the object through being taught language].

And (*Emptiness in Mind-Only,* 209):

> Also, even when one conceives that form and so forth **being the**

[a] See ibid., #126.

> **referents of conceptual consciousnesses** is established ultimately or by way of its own character, this is similar to conceiving that form and so forth are established by their own character as the foundations of imputation with a name.

And (*Emptiness in Mind-Only,* 210):

> However, such fallacies do not accrue to the establishment, by way of its own character, of form and so forth **being the foundations of the imputation of terminology and the referents of conceptual consciousnesses.**[a]

And (*Emptiness in Mind-Only,* 211):

> Just so, it is also not contradictory that:
>
> - a consciousness's **being a referent of conceptual consciousnesses** is an imputational factor that is not ultimately established, but
> - a consciousness is ultimately established.

And (*Emptiness in Mind-Only,* 214-215):

> ...there is no fault, for when it is refuted through reasoning that blue's **being the referent of a conceptual consciousness**—conceiving the apprehended-object as a factuality other [than the consciousness apprehending it]—exists by way of its own character, it will be established that [a consciousness] apprehending blue to which **blue's being the referent of a conceptual consciousness** appears is mistaken with respect to its appearing object.

And (*Emptiness in Mind-Only,* 215):

> *Objection:* Then, when it is refuted with reasoning that a consciousness's **being a referent of a conceptual consciousness** is ultimately established, it would be proven that the self-cognizing consciousness—perceiving [the consciousness]—is mistaken with respect to its appearing object because when [that consciousness] appears, [its being a referent of a conceptual consciousness] appears to be established by way of its own character. Since, when that has been proven, this consciousness would not exist as established by way of its own character as an experiencing entity, a tenet of the Yogic Practitioners would be discarded.
>
> *Answer:* That fault does not exist because a **consciousness's being the referent of a conceptual consciousness** does not appear to a self-cognizing consciousness, whereas **blue's being a referent of a conceptual consciousness** for conception as an external object does appear to

[a] See ibid., #126.

[a consciousness] apprehending blue. This is because there is no contradiction in the fact that **being the referent** [of a conceptual consciousness] is not suitable to appear to a self-cognizing consciousness and so forth, for which dualistic appearance has vanished, but appears to [a consciousness] apprehending blue that is endowed with dualistic appearance.

And (*Emptiness in Mind-Only,* 217):

> *Objection:* Because blue's **being the referent of a conceptual consciousness** is just posited through the force of conceptuality, it does not appear to [an eye consciousness, for instance,] which is devoid of conceptuality.
>
> *Answer:* Then, because a magician's illusion is just posited by conceptuality, a magical illusion **being** a horse or elephant also would [absurdly] not appear to [the sense consciousnesses of an audience whose eyes have been affected by the force of the mantra repeated by the magician, those sense consciousnesses being] devoid of conceptuality.

These nineteen instances naturally lead us to identify that a phenomenon's **being the referent of a conceptual consciousness** is the existent imputational nature that is relevant here—the relevance being that its emptiness of being established by way of its own character constitutes the selflessness of phenomena explicitly indicated at this point in the *Sūtra Unraveling the Thought.* Indeed, this identification illuminates the meaning of the sūtra considerably and backs up Paṇ-chen Sö-nam-drak-b̄a's identification of the existent and non-existent imputational natures relevant here given above:[a]

- The existent is, for instance, a form's being the referent of a conceptual consciousness apprehending a form.[b]
- The non-existent is, for instance, a form's being **established by way of its own character** as the referent of a conceptual consciousness apprehending a form.[c]

In this vein, Tsay-d̄en-hla-ram-b̄a,[d] a Mongolian who was requested by the Jay

[a] Jay-d̄zün Chö-ḡyi-gyel-tsen (*General-Meaning Commentary,* 12.1.2) also speaks of "form's being the referent of the term 'form'" (*gzugs gzugs zhes pa'i sgra 'jug pa'i 'jug zhi yin pa*) as being an existent imputational nature and as being an imputational nature explicitly indicated on this occasion.

[b] *gzugs gzugs 'dzin rtog pa'i zhen gzhi yin pa.*

[c] *gzugs gzugs 'dzin rtog pa'i zhen gzhir rang gi mtshan nyid kyis grub pa.*

[d] *tshe brtan lha rams pa;* his position on this topic is found in A-ku L̄o-drö-gya-tso's *Precious Lamp,* 75.6-77.4. Ge-s̄hay Ye-s̄hay-tap-kay (*shar tsong kha pa blo bzang grags pas mdzad pa'i drang ba dang nges pa'i don rnam par phye ba'i bstan bcos legs bshad snying po,* Tā la'i bla ma'i 'phags bod, vol. 22 [Varanasi, India: vāṇa dbus bod kyi ches mtho'i gtsug lag slob gnyer khang, 1997], 327-332), in a list of fifty-eight commentaries on D̄zong-ka-b̄a's *The Essence*

College of Se-ra Monastic University to respond to Gung-tang's refutation of several points in Jay-dzün Chö-gyi-gyel-tsen's commentary,[a] cogently views Buddha as saying:

> With respect to the subject, forms and so forth **being the referents of conceptual consciousnesses**, there are reasons for calling this a "character-non-nature" because the reasons are that (1) from the positive side such is only posited by names and terminology and (2) from the negative side such is not established by way of its own character.

Forms' being the referents of conceptual consciousnesses does exist, since forms are indeed the referents of conceptual consciousnesses, but being such does not subsist in objects by way of its own character as we perceive it to do. Rather, it is only posited by names and terminology. This explanation is elegantly straightforward and reflects Dzong-ka-ba's own presentation of the topic. Furthermore, instead of merely repeating the sūtra's mention of imputational factors, it performs the commentarial function by identifying just what the relevant imputational nature is.

Thus, the imputational natures relevant here are:

- forms and so forth being the referent of conceptual consciousnesses apprehending entities and of terms expressing entities
- forms and so forth being the referent of conceptual consciousnesses apprehending attributes and of terms expressing attributes.

Correspondingly, the non-existent imputational natures relevant here are:

- forms and so forth being established by way of their own character as the referent of conceptual consciousnesses apprehending entities and of terms expressing entities
- forms and so forth being established by way of their own character as the referent of conceptual consciousnesses apprehending attributes and of terms expressing attributes.

I find this formulation to be particularly evocative and to reflect Dzong-ka-ba's opinion.

---

of Eloquence, reports (331) that three of these are listed under the title of *dri lan blo gsal mgul rgyan* by *tshe brtan lha rams pa* in *bod kyi bstan bcos khag gcig gi mtshan byang dri med shel dkar 'phreng ba* (mtsho sngon dpe skrun khang, 1985), 614. The three are:

- *rgyal ba dge 'dun rgya mtsho dang 'jam dbyangs dga' blo 'jam dbyangs 'dbyangs chos bshes sogs kyi drang nges gsung rgyun dri med lung rigs gter mdzod*
- *drang nges legs bshad snying po'i spyi don legs pa drang nges rnam 'byed kyi dga' gnad cung zad btus pa*
- *legs bshad snying po'i mtha' dpyod mkhas pa'i dbang po 'jam dbyangs chos dpal kyi gsung rgyun.*

[a] This was reported by the late Ge-shay Ye-shay-wang-chuk of Hla-sa.

13. Imputational Natures II: Linguistic Dependence

Reviewing The Subject: "Imputational Characters"

Let us review Ge-luk-b̄a scholars' various identifications of imputational natures in Buddha's statement discussed in the previous chapter. First, the *Sūtra Unraveling the Thought* (*Emptiness in Mind-Only,* 86) says:

> Those [imputational characters] are characters posited by names and terminology and do not subsist by way of their own character. Therefore, they are said to be "character-non-natures."

It seems that this could be rendered syllogistically as:

> With respect to the subject, **imputational factors,**[a] there are reasons for calling them "character-non-natures," because they are called such since (1) from the positive side they are only posited by names and terminology and (2) from the negative side they are not established by way of their own character.

Problem: Several Ge-luk-b̄a scholars[196] point out that the reference of the subject "imputational factors" cannot be just any imputational natures because even Proponents of Sūtra, a school lower than the Mind-Only School, realize that an imputational nature such as uncompounded space is not established by way of its own character, and thus absurdly they would realize emptiness as it is defined in the Mind-Only School. Therefore, what are the imputational natures explicitly indicated here in the *Sūtra Unraveling the Thought*?

Solutions: Paṇ-chen S̄ö-nam-drak-b̄a[b] and Jay-d̄zün Chö-ḡyi-gyel-tsen,[197] reflecting D̄zong-ka-b̄a's exegesis, reformulate the sūtra passage as:

> With respect to the subject, **imputational factors in the imputation of entity and attribute**, there are reasons for calling them "character-non-natures," because they are called such since (1) from the positive

---

[a] *kun btags.*

[b] Paṇ-chen S̄ö-nam-drak-b̄a's *Garland of Blue Lotuses,* 27b.5. Paṇ-chen S̄ö-nam-drak-b̄a, despite using the vague term "imputational natures" when he says:

> Imputational natures are posited as character-non-natures, because they are posited by only names and terminology and are not established by way of their own character.

explains later (28a.5) that the imputational natures explicitly indicated on this occasion in the *Sūtra Unraveling the Thought* must be just imputational factors in the imputation of entities and attributes.

> side they are only posited by names and terminology and (2) from the negative side they are not established by way of their own character.

Both scholars further refine the subject, with the result that it reads, as Tsay-d̄en-hla-ram-b̄a explicitly refines it:[198]

> With respect to the subject, **forms and so forth being the referents of conceptual consciousnesses**, there are reasons for calling this a "character-non-nature," because the reasons are that (1) from the positive side such is only posited by names and terminology and (2) from the negative side such is not established by way of its own character.

Now that the subject has been identified, let us turn to the predicate.

The Predicate: "Are Character-Non-Natures"

In the sentence (*Emptiness in Mind-Only*, 86):

> Imputational natures are called "character-non-natures" because (1) from the positive side they are only posited by names and terminology and (2) from the negative side they are not established by way of their own character

most of the textbook traditions hold that "character-non-nature" means "something lacking the nature of being established by way of its own character." Their reasons are simply that:

- the *Sūtra Unraveling the Thought* says that they are called "character-non-natures" because they are "posited by names and terminology and **do not subsist by way of their own character,**" and
- Ge-luk-b̄a scholars agree that "do not subsist by way of their own character" means "are not established by way of their own character" and that in the Mind-Only School this is equivalent to "not truly established" and "not ultimately established."

Thus, once it is said in the sūtra that imputational natures are called "character-non-natures" because they are not established by way of their own character, the nature of character that imputational natures lack must mean establishment by way of their own character.[a]

It is important to remember that even though, in explaining the character-non-nature, it is emphasized that this imputational nature itself is not established by way of its own character, the central meditation is that **other-powered natures** are not established by way of their own character as the referents of conceptual consciousnesses or as the referents of words. The two:

---

[a] For the different opinion of the Go-mang tradition, see *Absorption*, #27.

1. that forms and so forth being the referents of conceptual consciousnesses is not established by way of its own character
2. that other-powered natures are not established by way of their own character as the referents of conceptual consciousnesses or as the referents of words

amount to the same thing, but the latter reflects more closely the mode of procedure in meditation.

Now let us turn to the reasons.

The First Reason: Posited By Names And Terminology

When Buddha answers his rhetorical question about why imputational natures are character-non-natures, he gives two reasons, one positive and one negative. He (*Emptiness in Mind-Only,* 86) says:

> Those [imputational characters] are characters posited by names and terminology and do not subsist by way of their own character.

The positive reason is that imputational natures are "posited by names and terminology," and the negative reason is that they "do not subsist by way of their own character." To comprehend why imputational natures are character-non-natures, it is necessary to draw out the implications of these two reasons.

For me, the starting point is an intuitive reading of the passage. The suggestion is that there are two distinct classes of objects:[a]

1. Those that are established by way of their own character and are not posited by names and terminology.

   Illustrations: other-powered natures and thoroughly established natures.

2. Those that are posited by names and terminology and are not established by way of their own character.

   Illustrations: uncompounded space, being the referent of words and conceptual consciousnesses, establishment of objects by way of their own character as the referents of conceptual consciousnesses, and the horns of a rabbit. (The first two are existent, and the latter two are not.)

These can be rephrased as:

1. Whatever is established by way of its own character is not posited by names and terminology.

---

[a] I am using the term "objects" loosely, since some in the second class do not exist, and it is standardly considered that objects (*yul, viṣaya*) exist.

> Illustrations: other-powered natures and thoroughly established natures.

2. Whatever is posited by names and terminology is not established by way of its own character.

> Illustrations: uncompounded space, being the referent of words and conceptual consciousnesses, establishment of objects by way of their own character as the referents of conceptual consciousnesses, and the horns of a rabbit.

Their negative correlates are:

1. Whatever is not established by way of its own character is necessarily posited by names and terminology.

> Illustrations: uncompounded space, being the referent of words and conceptual consciousnesses, establishment of objects by way of their own character as the referents of conceptual consciousnesses, and the horns of a rabbit.

2. Whatever is not posited by names and terminology is necessarily established by way of its own character.

> Illustrations: other-powered natures and thoroughly established natures.

The two classes are both all-inclusive of what exists and mutually exclusive—nothing is both of them.

Also, non-existents such as an object's being established by way of its own character as the referent of a conceptual consciousness are included in the second category—posited by names and terminology and not established by way of their own character. Ḏzong-ka-ḇa (*Emptiness in Mind-Only,* 86) suggests that whatever is not established by way of its own character is necessarily posited by names and terminology when he says:

> The nature of character that imputational factors[a] do not have is to be taken as establishment, or subsisting, by way of their own character.[b] Here, the measure indicated[c] with respect to existing or not existing by way of [an object's] own character is: not to be posited or to be posited in dependence upon names and terminology.[d]
>
> Furthermore, that which is posited [in dependence upon names and terminology] is not necessarily existent [since, for instance, the

[a] See *Absorption,* #83.

[b] See ibid., #29, 94.

[c] *bstan tshod;* see ibid., #96.

[d] See ibid., #105-109.

> horns of a rabbit or a difference of entity between subject and object are posited in dependence upon names and terminology but do not exist].

He indicates that even non-existents, never mind all existent imputational natures, are among what are "posited in dependence upon names and terminology." As B̄el-jor-hlün-drup says:[199]

> That which is posited by names and terminology does not necessarily exist, for, although a sky-flower is posited by names and terminology, it does not exist.

Thus, since we know that, for D̄zong-ka-b̄a, other-powered natures and thoroughly established natures are established by way of their own character, there are only two classes of objects—those that are posited by names and terminology and those that are established by way of their own character. In confirmation of this, in the section on the Consequence School much later in *The Essence of Eloquence* he says:

> [Yogic Practitioners] propound that, since [imputational natures] can be posited by names and terminology, [imputational natures] are not established by way of their own character.

The reason he cites for why the Proponents of Mind-Only propound that imputational natures are not established by way of their own character is that they can be posited by names and terminology. He does not say that some imputational natures can and some cannot.

However, in startling contradiction, late in the section on the Mind-Only School (*Emptiness in Mind-Only,* 217-218) he posits three classes of objects:

> Although among imputational factors in general there are many, such as all generally characterized phenomena and space, and so forth, the reason why these are not [explicitly] mentioned in the *Sūtra Unraveling the Thought*[a] is that they are not relevant on the occasion of the imputational factor, the emptiness of which is posited as the thoroughly established nature.[b] Although many of those are existents that cannot be posited by names and terminology, they are not established by way of their own character because of being only imputed by conceptuality.[c]

Here D̄zong-ka-b̄a strangely says that "many" existent imputational natures

---

[a] See ibid., #139, for six mentions of space in the *Sūtra Unraveling the Thought* as an example for the thoroughly established nature. The point here is that space is not relevant on the occasion of identifying the thoroughly established nature.

[b] See ibid., #85, 89-92.

[c] See ibid., #105-109.

cannot (and thus **are not**) posited by names and terminology; nevertheless, he says that these same imputational natures are only imputed by conceptuality and hence are not established by way of their own character. In this passage he clearly holds that there are many existent imputational natures that are only imputed by conceptuality but are not posited by names and terminology.

(We need to notice that he admits that the phenomena that are imputed by conceptuality but are not posited by names and terminology are not even mentioned in the *Sūtra Unraveling the Thought,* and thus when we turn our attention to this class of phenomena, we become involved in issues that are not treated in the sūtra. Still, a reason for considering them is that the *Sūtra Unraveling the Thought* presents a theory of three natures that include **all** phenomena, and Indian, Chinese, and Tibetan scholars became interested in considering marginal phenomena to see where and how these might fit into the schema. Subjecting the thought of the sūtra to tangential concerns can be highly illuminating because it creates a jarring dissonance in the midst of which insight can be gained; the danger, however, is that these analyses might turn into diversions that distract from the meaning and insights of the sūtra in favor of extrinsic entanglements. We will need to keep the latter in mind as we pursue how Dzong-ka-ba's successors try to unravel the problem of his seeming self-contradiction.)

According to this statement, it is not the case that whatever is not established by way of its own character is necessarily posited by names and terminology, for uncompounded space is not established by way of its own character and yet is not posited by names and terminology; rather, it is only imputed by conceptuality. Thus, according to this schema, there are three classes of objects:

1. Those that are established by way of their own character.

   Illustrations: other-powered natures and thoroughly established natures.

2. Those that both are posited by names and terminology and are imputed by conceptuality.

   Illustrations: being the referent of words and conceptual consciousnesses and establishment of objects by way of their own character as the referents of conceptual consciousnesses.

3. Those that are only imputed by conceptuality and are not posited by names and terminology.

   Illustration: uncompounded space.[a]

Here whatever is not established by way of its own character is necessarily

[a] Whether non-existents such as the horns of a rabbit are included in the second or third categories or both is unclear to me.

imputed by conceptuality but is not necessarily posited by names and terminology. Ḍzong-ka-ḅa cryptically suggests but does not elucidate a distinction between being posited by names and terminology and being imputed by conceptuality.

Handling Inconsistency

By the rules of the game, Ḍzong-ka-ḅa's followers cannot just say that their leader made two contradictory statements on this issue and that one of them is right and the other is wrong. Rather, they must explain his statements so as to make them non-contradictory, even if this is done within only a guise of non-criticism. This is how allegiance and rational inquiry are wedded. It is still rational inquiry because the guise is self-conscious though very seldom openly admitted in print. I seek here to point out their tactics.

In positing Ḍzong-ka-ḅa's thought, Gung-ru Chö-jung[200] and Jam-ȳang-shay-ḅa[201] find (that is, create) a consistency between these two radically different presentations by making ingenious refinements. They cite examples—found in the Second Dalai Lama's commentary[a]—of objects that are only imputed by conceptuality but are not posited by names and terminology. The first is sound's emptiness of being permanent, which is not posited by the mere words "Sound is empty of permanence." The other one is the selflessness of the aggregates, which is not posited by the mere words "The aggregates are selfless." Hence, these imputational phenomena are not posited by only names and terminology. From this, we can see that to be posited by names and terminology is taken to mean "language-dependent."[b]

Both Gung-ru Chö-jung and Jam-ȳang-shay-ḅa make a distinction that the Second Dalai Lama does not. They distinguish between "only posited by names and terminology"[c] and "posited by only names and terminology"[d] (notice that

---

[a] Second Dalai Lama's *Lamp Illuminating the Meaning of (Ḍzong-ka-ḅa's) Thought,* 16.4. They cite the Second Dalai Lama's examples without pointing out that they differ greatly from the Second Dalai Lama on the issue. The Second Dalai Lama holds that Ḍzong-ka-ḅa's statement that imputational natures are posited by names and terminology is restricted to imputational natures in the imputation of entity and attribute and concludes that all imputational natures are not necessarily able to be posited by names and terminology; however, Gung-ru Chö-jung and Jam-ȳang-shay-ḅa apply the statement to all imputational natures. The Second Dalai Lama views the two examples as imputational natures that are **not** posited by names and terminology.

[b] In all Ge-luk-ḅa systems, existent imputational natures are uncompounded phenomena and thus are not created. They may come into being and go out of being, existing at some time but not all times, but they are not produced by causes and conditions. Hence, I use the term "language-dependent" rather than "language-created."

[c] *ming brdas bzhag tsam.*

[d] *ming brda tsam gyis bzhag pa.*

the word "only" appears before "posited" in the first phrase and after "posited by" in the latter). Whereas the Second Dalai Lama merely holds that sound's emptiness of being permanent and the selflessness of the aggregates are not posited by names and terminology, they contend that, although these are not posited by only names and terminology, they are only posited by names and terminology because of being only imputed by conceptuality.

By moving the word "only," Gung-ru Chö-jung and Jam-ȳang-shay-b̄a make a distinction that cogently provides a key to understanding D̄zong-ka-b̄a's cryptic statements, although, at first reading, the maneuver appears to be fishy. As an example, they cite the great difference between saying that the Sūtra School only holds Buddha's teaching and that only the Sūtra School holds Buddha's teaching. The first "only" eliminates that the Sūtra School ever does not hold Buddha's teaching, and this is true, whereas the second "only" eliminates that any school other than the Sūtra School holds Buddha's teaching. The second statement is false, since the Mind-Only School and so forth also hold Buddha's teaching.[a]

Jam-ȳang-shay-b̄a takes the Second Dalai Lama's first example of an object that is merely imputed by conceptuality but is not posited by names and terminology—sound's emptiness of being permanent—as meaning that it is not established by way of its own character and, instead of that, is only posited by names and terminology. (Although sound's impermanence is established by way of its own character, its emptiness of permanence is only conceptually imputed and thus cannot be established by way of its own character, since it is a mere absence of something other than a self of phenomena or a self of persons.) Still, what does it mean that sound's emptiness of permanence is only posited by names and terminology? Jam-ȳang-shay-b̄a holds that "name" in this context means a term expressing that object,[b] and although "terminology"[c] usually has

---

[a] Gung-ru Chö-jung (*Garland of White Lotuses,* 26a.2-2bb.1) and Jam-ȳang-shay-b̄a (*Great Exposition of the Interpretable and the Definitive,* 60.6-61.6) give further examples. Something that is said to be only imputed by the Sūtra School is not necessarily imputed only by the Sūtra School. For instance, (from the viewpoint of the Mind-Only School) even though external objects are only factors superimposed by the Sūtra School, external objects are not factors superimposed by only the Sūtra School, since the Consequence School also has such a superimposition. Something that the Sūtra School asserts is only an assertion by them but is not necessarily an assertion by only them.

Another example they give seems more questionable: D̄zong-ka-b̄a's student Gyel-tsap says that the severance of the continuum of matter (or body) and consciousness at the time of a remainderless nirvāṇa (*lhag med myang 'das, nirupadhiśeṣanirvāṇa*) is asserted to be only imputed by the Hearer Schools (the Great Exposition and Sūtra Schools); however, Gung-ru Chö-jung and Jam-ȳang-shay-b̄a claim that Gyel-tsap does not intend to eliminate that most Proponents of Mind-Only Following Scripture (that is, those following Asaṅga) also assert the same. Perhaps they are indicating Gyel-tsap **should** not have meant to eliminate such.

[b] *ming: rang zhes rjod pa'i sgra.*

[c] *brda.*

the same meaning as "name," in order to avoid redundancy he takes it to mean a conceptual consciousness apprehending that object.[a] (This explanation of "terminology" is well-founded in the tradition, since a common dictum is that names and conceptual consciousnesses engage their objects similarly.)

Now, since it is taken for granted that sound's emptiness of permanence is only imputed by conceptuality, it also is only posited by the conceptual consciousness apprehending it and thus is posited by terminology. However, it is not posited by only a name (a term expressing it) and terminology (a conceptual consciousness apprehending it) simply because it is not so easy to realize sound's emptiness of permanence. One cannot just say or think, "Sound is empty of permanence," and thereby realize it. Rather, an inference based on a correct reasoning proving sound to be empty of permanence, such as by way of the fact that it is a product, is needed. The words themselves or the mere conceptual consciousness repeating the words is not sufficient to posit sound's emptiness of permanence.[202] As Ḏzong-ka-ḇa's student Ke-drup says:[203]

> Concerning this, a sound's emptiness of permanence, for instance, does not become an object of awareness merely through the force of predispositions of being accustomed to the verbalization, "There is no permanent sound," and so forth. It also cannot be posited by the mere convention of the verbalization, "Permanence does not exist among sounds." However, since it is a generally characterized phenomenon that is imputed by conceptuality, it must be taken as an illustration of an imputational nature. [Ḏzong-ka-ḇa's statement is in reference to] these.

Also, the selflessness of the aggregates is not posited by the mere words "The aggregates are empty of a self," or by the mere wish that this be so, and thus to realize the selflessness of the aggregates, one has to realize that a self of persons is not observed by valid cognition.[204]

Gung-ru Chö-jung and Jam-ȳang-shay-ḇa solve the mystery of Ḏzong-ka-ḇa's superficially contradictory statements by adjusting the word "only." They explain that, in the first two passages cited above, Ḏzong-ka-ḇa means "only posited by names and terminology":

> The nature of character that imputational natures do not have is to be taken as establishment or subsisting by way of their own character. Here, the measure indicated with respect to existing or not existing by way of [an object's] own character is: not to be posited or to be posited in dependence upon names and terminology [**that is, only posited by names and terminology**].
>
> Furthermore, that which is posited [in dependence upon names and terminology] is not necessarily existent.

---

[a] *rang 'dzin rtog pa.*

Gung-ru Chö-jung and Jam-ȳang-shay-b̄a hold that the second passage should similarly read:

> [Yogic Practitioners] propound that, since [imputational natures] can be posited by names and terminology [**that is, are only posited by names and terminology**, imputational natures] are not established by way of their own character.

In the third passage, however, they say that D̄zong-ka-b̄a is referring to "posited by only names and terminology":

> Although among imputational natures in general there are many, such as all generally characterized phenomena and space, and so forth, the reason why these are not [explicitly] mentioned in the *Sūtra Unraveling the Thought* is that they are not relevant on the occasion of the imputational factor, the emptiness of which is posited as the thoroughly established nature. Although many of those are existents that cannot be posited by names and terminology [**that is, are not posited by only name and terminology**], they are not established by way of their own character because of being only imputed by conceptuality.

The cogent principle behind Gung-ru Chö-jung and Jam-ȳang-shay-b̄a's attempt to resolve the problem is that, since names and conceptual consciousnesses (here called "terminology") engage their objects similarly, if an object is only imputed by conceptuality, it must be only posited by names and terminology. Thus, for them, D̄zong-ka-b̄a's meaning in this passage must be that many existent imputational natures, such as sound's emptiness of permanence, are not posited by only names and terminology but are only posited by names and terminology. They thereby forge consistency in what appears to be inconsistent.

Is Gung-ru Chö-jung and Jam-ȳang-shay-b̄a's interpretation far-fetched? Although at first blush the manipulation of "only" smells of rank apologetic, I think they are right on the mark. For it is obvious that D̄zong-ka-b̄a, at different times, had in mind but did not explain two different meanings for the same term, and they have ferreted them out. It would, however, be far-fetched to claim that D̄zong-ka-b̄a intended the discrepancy. Indeed, when Gung-ru Chö-jung and Jam-ȳang-shay-b̄a claim that they are merely positing D̄zong-ka-b̄a's thought, they are pointing out that they have resolved an issue that the founder left hanging.

One expects Gung-ru Chö-jung and Jam-ȳang-shay-b̄a to return to the agenda of the *Sūtra Unraveling the Thought* and proceed to explain that factors imputed in the manner of entity and attribute (which are existent imputational natures) are indeed posited by only names and terminology and to elaborate on how this is done, but they drop the topic without ever returning to this crucial point. However, the eighteenth-century scholar D̄ra-d̄i Ge-s̄hay (a follower of Jay-d̄zün Chö-ḡyi-gyel-tsen) explains that factors imputed in the manner of entity and attribute are indeed posited by names and terminology. He says:[a]

> Since forms and so forth as referents of names and conventions must be understood in dependence upon name and terminology appearing as objects of awareness, forms and so forth are only posited as such by name and terminology.

D̄ra-d̄i Ge-s̄hay explains that some existent imputational natures—namely, forms and so forth as referents of names and conventions—are posited by names and terminology in addition to being only imputed by conceptuality. This makes good sense out of D̄zong-ka-b̄a's statement given above that **many** imputational natures cannot be posited by names and terminology but are only imputed by conceptuality, since it conversely suggests that there **are** some imputational natures that are both. Also, due to the fact that the imputational natures listed in this passage (see the citation just before the one from D̄ra-d̄i Ge-s̄hay) solely are existent imputational natures, it is likely that D̄zong-ka-b̄a means that there are some **existent** imputational natures that are both posited by names and terminology and only imputed by conceptuality. D̄ra-d̄i Ge-s̄hay provides us with at least one, forms and so forth as referents of names and conventions—one that is especially relevant to the discussion in the *Sūtra Unraveling the Thought.* He keeps the discussion grounded in the agenda of the sūtra.

What does it mean for the imputational natures relevant on this occasion in the *Sūtra Unraveling the Thought* to be posited by names and terminology or, in Gung-ru Chö-jung and Jam-ȳang-shay-b̄a's vocabulary, to be posited by only names and terminology? What does it mean that the **appearance** of objects as established by way of their own character as the referents of their respective conceptual consciousnesses is posited by only names and terminology? The immediate intuition that this appearance is due to the usage of language seems to me to be the best explanation.

Once Buddha says that imputational natures are posited by names and terminology, we can see that there are some objects whose character is linguistically dependent in this sense whereas others are not. Thus, within existents, there are two categories, those that are linguistically dependent and those that are not. When Buddha says that imputational natures "do not subsist by way of their own character," it can be seen that they do not have their own, non-subjectively dependent character. They have a character that has come to exist through names and terminology.

The false appearance of objects as innately the referents of thoughts and words is due to the beginningless usage of verbalization such that this untrue aspect occurs in all perceptions even to an animal or to a baby that does not

---

[a] As reported by A-ku L̄o-drö-gya-tso (*Precious Lamp,* 81.4): *ming dang tha snyad kyi gzhir gzugs sogs 'di dag ming brda blo yul du shar ba la ltos nas go dgos pas na/ der ming brdas bzhag pa tsam yin gyi.* Notice that by using the awkward construction *ming dang tha snyad kyi* ***gzhir*** *gzugs sogs 'di dag* he avoids saying *gzugs sogs 'di dag ming dang tha snyad kyi gzhi* ***yin pa.***

know language. Past usage of vocabulary for entities and attributes leads to the impression that objects, by their very nature, are fit as referents of terms and thought. Thus, that objects are referents of terms and thoughts is merely posited or "created" by usage of language over countless lifetimes; objects are not established by way of their own character as such, even though they appear to be established this way.

As Ser-shül Lo-sang-pün-tsok[205] says, a bulbous, flat-bottomed thing's being a basis of language for pot means that, through the force of predispositions established by prior verbalization, it appears to be a basis of terminology for pot and is held to be such by conceptual consciousnesses. Due to this, a bulbous thing is posited as a basis of terminology for pot, and except for that, it is not established as a basis for language by way of its being so with a status of externality. I think that this is what Dzong-ka-ba, Gung-ru Chö-jung, and Jam-yang-shay-ba mean.

Jay-dzün Chö-gyi-gyel-tsen similarly holds that the meaning of something's being posited by names and terminology refers to the fact that its appearance to the mind depends upon language. As long as we take language as including **past** usage of language, we can avoid the fault that this false appearance of externality would absurdly not occur to newborn babies and animals who do not know language. This is just what Ser-shül Lo-sang-pün-tsok emphasizes—the deceptive display is due to repeated association of language with objects. For him,[206] that the appearance of something to the mind depends on language means that its appearance is contingent upon the activation of predispositions established through repeated conditioning to language-dependent conceptuality, not just at present but over lifetimes.

Are Only Non-Existents Posited By Only Names And Terminology?

The nineteenth-century Mongolian scholar Nga-wang-bel-den,[a] in carrying out what he believes (and I do not believe) to be the implications of Jam-yang-shay-ba's exposition,[207] draws the conclusion that only non-existents are posited by only names and terminology. When Dzong-ka-ba (*Emptiness in Mind-Only,* 218) says that "many of those are **existents** that cannot be posited by names and terminology," Nga-wang-bel-den takes this as meaning that there are no existent imputational natures that can be posited by only names and terminology and that just non-existents can be posited by only names and terminology.

This means that, according to Nga-wang-bel-den's interpretation of Jam-yang-shay-ba's position, only something that does not exist at all—such as the establishment of objects by way of their own character as the referents of conceptual consciousnesses—both is only posited by names and terminology and is posited by only names and terminology. Since that objects are the referents of conceptual consciousnesses (without the qualification that this is

[a] *ngag dbang dpal ldan,* b. 1797.

by way of the objects' own character) does exist, a consequence of this interpretation is that such is **not** posited by only names and terminology simply because it exists. Similarly, the **appearance** to an eye consciousness, for instance, that a shape or color is established by way of its own character as the referent of a conceptual consciousness cannot be posited by only names and terminology simply because it exists, although, being an imputational phenomenon, it is only imputed by conceptuality and hence only posited by names and terminology.

Still, Jam-ȳang-shay-b̄a, as per Nga-w̄ang-b̄el-den, does not hold that something that is posited by only names and terminology is posited just through saying or thinking words; rather, to be posited by only names and terminology means that an object is found when it is sought among or separate from its bases of imputation. Thus, according to him, since Ge-luk-b̄a scholars unanimously agree that only the Consequentialists hold that all existents are posited upon being found when sought among or separate from its bases of imputation, none of the other schools, including the Mind-Only School, could assert that **any** existent is posited by only names and terminology. By holding that the Consequentialists' meaning of being posited by only names and terminology is the one Jam-ȳang-shay-b̄a has in mind in this discussion of the Mind-Only School, Nga-w̄ang-b̄el-den highlights the radical nature of the Consequentialists' assertion.

However, as revealing as that is, I think that Nga-w̄ang-b̄el-den has missed the point. For I take D̄zong-ka-b̄a's statement that "many of those are existents that cannot be posited by names and terminology" as referring just to existent imputational natures **other than those relevant on this occasion** and, among them, not even all of them, just "many of those." He is saying that many existent imputational natures cannot be posited by only names and terminology but that existent imputational natures such as a form's being the referent of names and conceptual consciousnesses or the appearance of objects as established by way of their own character as the referents of their respective names and conceptual consciousnesses are indeed posited by only names and terminology. Many of those other imputational natures, such as uncompounded space, cannot be posited by only names and terminology, even if they are only posited by names and terminology.

In the debating courtyard, I immediately would be asked to give at least one other existent imputational nature, not relevant on this occasion, that also is posited by only names and terminology. I would point to other linguistically dependent phenomena such as its being suitable to call any object by any name[a] (which is explained briefly in the next section).

It seems to me that Ge-luk-b̄a scholars' over-concern with the status of existent imputational natures, such as uncompounded space, that are not openly addressed in the *Sūtra Unraveling the Thought*—a topic of some interest

[a] *sgra byung grags pa.*

also to their earlier Indian and Chinese counterparts—has led them away from tackling the more pressing issue of just what, in a positive sense, it means for factors imputed in the manner of entity and attribute to be posited by only names and terminology. Instead of concentrating on this, they proceed on the negative route, trying to tackle what it means for all imputational natures to be only imputed by conceptuality and only posited by names and terminology.

A Theory Of Perception

Still, an elaborate theory of sense perception without external objects impinging on consciousness is presented within this material, largely as a result of determining what parts of perception are dependent upon previous verbalization and conceptualization. As Ḏzong-ka-ḇa's student Ke-drup explains it, this influence comes from sentient beings having been accustomed—over a beginningless continuum of lives—to applying names to objects. In Gung-ru Chö-jung and Jam-ȳang-shay-ḇa's terms:

- Objects' being the referents of terms is **only posited** by names and terminology; that is to say, it comes to be through the repeated association of names with objects and does not subsist in objects themselves.
- This conditioning also makes objects appear as if established by way of their own character as the referents of terms and thought. Such establishment is also **only posited** by names and terminology and, in addition, does not—nor ever will—exist.

Ke-drup's explication, written sometime between 1424 and 1428, involves a complex description of different aspects in the appearance of a patch of blue to an eye consciousness and thus reveals a theory of perception. Ke-drup uses Asaṅga's presentation[a] of categories of objects and the respective seeds generating their appearance but in a different way—that is, to account for the veridical and non-veridical layers of appearance that occur without intervention by any current conceptuality:[208]

> When a languaged[b] person's mind turns to [an object such as a patch of] blue and the blue appears to [that person's] eye consciousness seeing blue,
>
> - not only does blue appear as blue, and
> - not only does blue appear as an external object, but also
> - there is a mode of appearance in which just that blue appears to be the blue that is the referent or foundation of the conventions,

[a] This is in the second chapter of his *Summary of the Great Vehicle;* see p. 436ff.

[b] *brda la byang ba'i skyes bu.* This refers to someone who knows language, as opposed to the very young, and so forth.

> "This is blue," "This blue is an entity of form," "This is blue's production," and so forth.

How is it known that such [an appearance] exists? [That is, how is it known that blue appears to a non-conceptual eye consciousness to be the referent of the conventions, "This is blue," "This blue is an entity of form," "This is blue's production," and so forth?] It is through the fact that this eye consciousness, by its own force,[a] induces a conceptual consciousness that takes just the appearance of blue—in accordance with how it appears to the eye consciousness—as an object of attention or memory and thereupon adheres to it within using the convention, "This is blue."

Also, that such exists is known through the following fact:

> When [a person is] asked, "What is the nature of the object in the expression 'blue'?" the force of this eye consciousness also[209] can induce a conceptual consciousness that—adhering just to the appearance of blue in accordance with how it appears to the eye consciousness—motivates the answer, "Its nature is form."

For these very reasons, it also is established that, when blue appears to be the blue that is the referent of the convention "blue,"[b] there exists a mode of appearance in which blue appears as a referent of the convention "blue" **from the side of the mode of subsistence of its own factuality.**[c] This is the meaning of blue's appearing to be **established by way of its own character** as the blue that is the referent of the convention "blue." Likewise, the meaning of blue's appearing to be **established by way of its own character** as the form and so forth that are the referents of the conventions, "This is an entity of form," "This is the production of such and such," and so forth, is also similar to this.

Such an appearance to an eye consciousness [that is, the appearance of blue as the blue that is the referent or foundation of the conventions, "This is blue," "This blue is an entity of form," "This is blue's production," and so forth] is not one that dawns through the power of blue's mode of subsistence. It is also not produced through seeds that are predispositions of [the object's] own concordant type, as is the case with the blue that appears to that eye consciousness. Rather, it is merely an appearance that dawns from the force of predispositions

---

[a] The phrase "by its own force" means that nothing else beyond the appearance of blue is required to induce a conceptual consciousness thinking, "This is blue."

[b] *sngon po'i tha snyad kyi gzhir gyur pa'i sngon po.*

[c] *rang gi dngos po'i gnas tshul gyi ngos nas.*

> infused through being accustomed to the frequent association—by conceptual consciousnesses from beginningless time—of conventions for entity and attribute, "This is blue," and "This is form," "This is the production of a form," and so forth. Those predispositions are called "predispositions of verbalization."[a]
>
> This is only an appearance that dawns through the force of predispositions infused due to being accustomed to the usage of conventions by conceptual consciousnesses. Hence, this appearance is called an "appearance only posited by names and terminology" and an "appearance posited through the force of conceptuality."

Before unpacking this highly informative but also dense explanation, let us add several crucial details (while repeating others) from an exposition written in 1928 by A-ku Lo-drö-gya-tso. On the topic of how one enters into cognition-only, he gives a condensed version of Dzong-ka-ba's argument about the relationship between the two types of emptiness (see Part 5) but expansively applies this topic of seeds, also called potencies, predispositions, or latencies—discussed by Asaṅga in the second chapter of his *Summary of the Great Vehicle* (see p. 436ff.)—to the layers of perception.

According to A-ku Lo-drö-gya-tso and other Ge-luk-ba scholars, Asaṅga in his *Summary of the Great Vehicle* does not accept either that a sense consciousness nakedly apprehends an external object or that it actually knows a likeness, or representation, of the object cast by the object. Rather, they see Asaṅga as presenting—in a discussion of the seed aspect of the mind-basis-of-all[210]—a system in which different types of internal potencies, residing with the mind-basis-of-all, are behind the appearance not only of the object but also of the subject perceiving that object, much like a dream. A-ku Lo-drö-gya-tso relates four types of appearances to four types of seeds:[b]

---

[a] That is, predispositions infused by previous verbalization.

[b] A-ku Lo-drö-gya-tso's *Precious Lamp,* 260.4-261.2. To account for the two aspects of the appearance of the self of phenomena—that is, the appearance of object and subject as different entities and the appearance of objects as established by way of their own character as the referents of their respective terms and conceptual consciousnesses—he expands on a threefold presentation by Ke-drup (*Opening the Eyes of the Fortunate,* 231-232; see also the excellent translation by José Ignacio Cabezón, *A Dose of Emptiness* [Albany, N.Y.: State University of New York Press, 1992], 62) who draws out the significance of this description of perception:

> In that way, even among the appearances to one sense consciousness arisen from a stable predisposition [that is, a factually concordant sense consciousness, not an erroneous consciousness] three factors are to be differentiated:
>
> 1. An other-powered nature which is an object that accords with its mode of appearance
> 2. An existent imputational nature which is such that an object that accords with its mode of appearance is only posited by names and terminology

> When, through initially making examination by way of the four examinations (*Emptiness in Mind-Only*, 213-214), one refutes that phenomena are established by way of their own character as the referents of names and terminology, one ascertains that the conceptual consciousnesses to which such appears are mistaken. Thereupon, one enters into cognition-only, in which [it is understood that] apprehended-object and apprehending-subject related with a conceptual mental consciousness do not exist in accordance with their dualistic appearance. In dependence upon this, one realizes that a sense consciousness is mistaken with respect to appearance, since an eye consciousness apprehending blue, for instance, has four appearances:
>
> 1. Appearance of blue as blue through the force of predispositions of [perceptions of] similar type[a]
> 2. Appearance of blue as the referent of a conceptual consciousness through the force of predispositions of verbalization[b]
> 3. Appearance [of blue] as established by way of its own character as the referent of verbal conventions through the force of predispositions of the view of self[c]

> 3. A mere factor imputed by a conceptual consciousness which is such that an object that accords with its mode of appearance cannot be posited as existing even by way of names and terminology.

The first is the actual object, such as a chair. The second is its being the referent of the thought "chair" or the object verbalized by the name "chair." The third is its being established by way of its own character as the referent of the thought "chair" or the object verbalized by the name "chair." The first exists by way of its own character; the second exists but is only posited by names and terminology, that is, it comes to be only by way of names and terminology; the third does not exist at all.

In order to preserve the possibility of correct conceptuality, Ke-drup then stresses that there are three types of conceptual consciousnesses that adhere to these three types of appearance, the first two being correct and the third being wrong:

> The modes of adherence by conceptual consciousnesses—that adhere to the objects appearing to that [sense consciousness]—also are threefold. Those, furthermore, are individual conceptual consciousnesses, and are not cases of the modes of adherence of one conceptual consciousness being differentiated into three types.

This crucial point allows for the existence of factually concordant conceptual consciousnesses, since, if only one conceptual consciousness had these three types of adherence as parts of its mode of apprehension, there would not be any factually concordant conceptual consciousnesses. Still, it needs to be investigated whether these three are being split for the sake of a formal concern with maintaining validity among conceptual consciousnesses, for it seems extremely difficult, in experience, to separate out these three. They certainly **seem** to be inextricably bound up with each other.

[a] *rigs mthun gyi bag chags.*

[b] *mngon brjod kyi bag chags, abhilāpavāsanā.*

[c] *bdag lta'i bag chags, ātmadṛṣṭivāsanā.*

4. Appearance [of blue] as an external object, distant and cut off, through the force of predispositions of the branches of cyclic existence.[a]

And therefore:

1. The appearance in accordance with the first is a specifically characterized phenomenon[b]
2. The appearance in accordance with the second is permanent [that is, non-disintegrating]

3-4. Those appearances in accordance with the latter two do not occur among objects of knowledge [that is, do not exist].

Realizing that a sense consciousness is mistaken with respect to appearance, one enters into cognition-only related with non-conceptual sense consciousnesses.

Now, let us begin to unpack these notions by discussing the four types of seeds that yield four types of appearances.[211]

1. Perceptions infuse the mind-basis-of-all with predispositions for similar perceptions in the future,[c] and it is due to these predispositions of similar

---

a *srid pa'i yan lag gi bag chags, bhavāṅgavāsanā.*

b *rang mtshan, svalakṣaṇa.*

c Concerning predispositions of similar type, Ke-drup (*Opening the Eyes of the Fortunate,* 230.6; see also Cabezón, *A Dose of Emptiness,* 61) cites Asaṅga's *Summary of the Great Vehicle,* which says:

> *Question:* If the foundations of appearances as [external] objects, which are [actually] cognition-only, are other-powered natures, how are they other-powered? Why are they called "other-powered"?
>
> *Answer:* Since they are produced from their respective predisposing seeds, they are under the control of other conditions. Also, having been produced, their entities cannot remain more than a moment. Hence, they are called "other-powered."

Ke-drup is sensitive to the fact that Asaṅga never uses the vocabulary of "predispositions of similar type," and thus he proceeds to claim that nevertheless this is Asaṅga's meaning:

> "Their respective predisposing [seeds]" refers to predispositions of similar type. Moreover, what are "predispositions of similar type"? They are potencies producing later consciousnesses similar to the former consciousnesses that infuse these potencies in the mind-basis-of-all when [those former consciousnesses] cease. Therefore, an appearance of blue to a later eye consciousness is an imprint of a predisposition infused by a former eye consciousness; it is not an imprint of a predisposition infused by a conceptual consciousness.

Ke-drup emphasizes that the appearance of a patch of blue is not "an imprint of a predisposition infused by a conceptual consciousness" because then blue and so forth would be linguistically and conceptually dependent, and this would exclude blue and so forth from being

type that a patch of blue, which is the "appearing object"[a] of an eye consciousness apprehending it, appears. The blue is an existent phenomenon that is impermanent and hence is an other-powered nature. This mode of appearance has its own specific characteristics that can serve as an appearing object of a directly perceiving eye consciousness, and hence the patch of blue is called a specifically characterized phenomenon.

2. The beginningless usage of verbalizations for entity and attribute with regard to objects infuses the mind-basis-of-all with predispositions of verbalization, due to which the appearance of objects as being the referents of conceptual consciousnesses occurs. Since objects are indeed established as and come to exist as referents of conceptual consciousnesses in dependence on language and conceptuality, their being such referents exists but does not exist in the nature of the objects themselves. Thus, their being referents is said to be permanent,[b] not in the sense of existing forever but in the sense of not being a disintegrative phenomenon.[c] This mode of appearance exists imputedly in that it is only posited by names and terminology. That such an appearance occurs along with the object is confirmed by the fact that an eye consciousness that apprehends blue can—**through its own power, that is, without intervention by any other consciousness**—call forth, in a person who knows language, a conceptual consciousness that thinks, "This is blue." For, if a patch of blue did not appear to be a basis of language, it would not call forth a conceptual consciousness apprehending blue, just as it does not call forth a conceptual consciousness apprehending red.
3. Due to predispositions of the view of self,[d] the appearance that objects are

established by way of their own character and hence absurdly could not be other-powered natures. He is indicating that the apparent meaning of Asaṅga's statement (p. 437) that the first nine of the fifteen "cognitions"—which includes many, if not all, impermanent objects—arise from predispositions of verbalization needs to be discounted and the statement put into another context, but he does not say what that context is. To twist Asaṅga's statement to fit Ke-drup's more developed presentation, perhaps we could say that what Asaṅga means is that the factor of an object's being the referents of words and conceptuality is due to predispositions of verbalization, but we would have to admit that there would be no reason for him to single out the first nine cognitions.

[a] *snang yul, *pratibhāsaviṣaya.*

[b] It might be more evocative to call this an abstraction.

[c] Based on Dharmakīrti's epistemology, Ge-luk-ba̠ scholars are unable to admit to the existence of mental images as mentally dependent **impermanent** phenomena. This leads to a consequent poverty of a developed theory of mental imagery, despite the obvious presence of a complicated hidden theory of the usage of the imagination in the practice of meditation in both sūtra and tantra.

[d] As will be cited later (p. 437), the predispositions of the view of self cause generation of an awareness in which the afflicted intellect views the mind-basis-of-all and thinks, "I," this being the view of a self of persons; thus, the relationship of this type of predisposition with

established by way of their own character as the referents of a conceptual consciousness occurs. Since objects are not established this way, such establishment does not occur among objects of knowledge, that is to say, does not exist. Such a status is solely imputed by conceptuality and thus cannot be posited as **existing** through names and terminology, since it does not exist at all, even though the appearance of such false establishment exists. That such an appearance occurs along with the object is confirmed by the fact that:

- When asked what the nature of the meaning of the expression "blue" is, one answers, "Its nature is form," by way of the mind's adhering to how blue appears to that eye consciousness as established from its own side as the foundation of names and terminology.
- The conceptual consciousness that motivates such an answer is induced by that eye consciousness through its own power, that is, without intervention by any other consciousness.

This is because, to an innate awareness, a form does not appear in the aspect of just being imputed as "form" on top of form by term and conceptuality but appears as a basis of such through its own mode of subsistence, without such depending on being posited by names and terminology.

4. Due to predispositions of the branches of cyclic existence[a]—birth, aging, and so forth—the appearance of subject and object as separate entities, distant and cut off,[b] occurs. Since subjects and objects do not exist this way, their establishment as such is only imputed by conceptuality and does not exist.

---

the view of a self of phenomena is unclear. It appears that, in order to account for generation of this aspect of misapprehension of a self of phenomena, the "view of self" is here being extended to include the apprehension that objects are established by way of their own character as the referents of a conceptual consciousness; this infuses the mind-basis-of-all with predispositions that generate future, similar misapprehensions. Tibetan scholars creatively seek here to round out Asaṅga's system.

[a] The connection between the predispositions of the branches of cyclic existence and the appearance of subject and object as separate entities is difficult to posit, except to note that A-ku Lo-drö-gya-tso, committed to Jam-yang-shay-ba's notion (pp. 421-429) that the appearance of subject and object as separate entities and the appearance of objects established by way of their own character as the referents of words and conceptual consciousnesses are different imputational natures—needs a fourth type of predisposition, and this is the only one left. Jik-may-dam-chö-gya-tso (*Port of Entry*, 553.4) does not put this fourth appearance in his list of coordinated appearances and predispositions and later (*Port of Entry*, 563.5) calls for analysis as to whether the two types of appearances of the object of negation in the selflessness of phenomena are imputational natures that are different entities, or only differentiated by way of conceptually isolatable factors (*ldog chas phye ba*).

[b] *rgyang chad*

This exposition, built on Ke-drup's, identifies the layers of appearance, actual and false, that four types of predispositions manifest. Since these four types of latencies give rise to their respective portions of appearance, even to veridical sense consciousnesses, and some of the layers are false even if the main one is not, sense consciousnesses are mistaken in terms of appearance[a]—since, once consciousnesses are polluted by predispositions of externality, for instance, their objects appear within being qualified by a false sense of externality—even if not mistaken in what they apprehend.[b] Thoroughly understanding the way that sense consciousnesses are mistaken, one enters into realization of cognition-only, the absence of external objects, even regarding sense consciousnesses.

This presentation is an inventive extension by Tibetan scholars who seek to explain the full complexity of the appearance of objects just from internal seeds. Whereas Asaṅga (p. 436ff.) speaks only of three types of predisposing latencies and only relates them with the appearance of specific groups of objects,[c] this tradition also utilizes a fourth, predispositions of similar type—to explain the various layers or aspects of appearance of a single sense object. Jik-may-dam-chö-gya-tso[212] mentions a fifth to account for special appearances at Buddhahood—uncontaminated predispositions causing the production of the signs and beauties of a Buddha's body and so forth. He also suggests that there are more types of predispositions but does not specify what they are,[d] although later he speaks of a Buddha's cognizing all phenomena through the force of having completed the two collections of merit and wisdom.[213]

The upshot of this presentation is, as Jik-may-dam-chö-gya-tso[214] says, that forms and so forth **in accordance with how they appear to ordinary consciousnesses of confined beings**—who are constricted due to not having turned the mind toward a study of emptiness—are imputational,[e] that is, fake, made up, false. This is because, when the eye consciousnesses, for instance, of confined beings look at a patch of blue, the appearance of blue from over there to here, from the object's side to the subject's side, is not the actual patch of blue but rather a merely imputed factor of appearance that dawns due to the power of predispositions of ignorance from beginningless conditioning. If it were the case that this was not a mere factor of mistaken appearance but a non-mistaken appearance, then it would be veridical, whereupon forms and so forth would be established as other-factualities, distant and cut off from the perceiving mind; however, such is refuted by reasoning.[f]

---

a *snang ba.*

b *'dzin pa.*

c See the footnotes to his explanation (p. 436ff.).

d Jik-may-dam-chö-gya-tso's *Port of Entry,* 553.1: *mtshan dpe sogs skyed byed zag med kyi bag chags* ***sogs*** *du ma.*

e Jik-may-dam-chö-gya-tso's *Port of Entry,* 551.1: *tshur mthong gi shes pa rang dga' ba la snang tshod ltar gyi gzugs sogs kun btags yin.*

f For the reasonings, see chapter 22, p. 465ff.

What, then, is the actual patch of blue? Jik-may-dam-chö-gya-tso describes how the actual patch of blue is not what appears to be a different entity from the consciousness but also is not the consciousness itself, the concern being that, if it were a consciousness, it would have to apprehend an object. The conclusion is that it is an appearance-factor of the consciousness:[215]

> [The actual patch of blue] is not this which appears from there to here as if it were a factuality different other than the consciousness apprehending blue, and it also is not the consciousness apprehending blue, and it also is not non-existent. Rather, just as, with regard to a dream-elephant, it is not posited that there is a factually established elephant in that situation of appearance and also the dream-consciousness itself is not posited as the dream-elephant but an appearance-factor of that consciousness which is produced from the same predisposition as that consciousness is posited as the dream-elephant, so the actual patch of blue is a mere appearance produced from a predisposition similar in type to that consciousness apprehending blue.

This raises the problem that, since it must be said that (1) confined beings associate language with forms and so forth in accordance with how objects mis-appear to them and (2) what they see is this mis-appearance, their naming and seeing would seem to be non-veridical. However, Jik-may-dam-chö-gya-tso says that it is not so, since naming and seeing such can **be posited as**[a] naming and seeing the actual, inexpressible object:[216]

> Through associating language with that, it serves as associating language with the actual inexpressible blue, and through seeing that, it can be posited that the inexpressible blue is seen. It is like, for example, the fact that in the system of the Sūtra School:
>
> - Although the basis of the explicit association of the language "pot" and the appearing object [of a conceptual consciousness apprehending a pot] is an appearance as opposite from not being pot,
> - through explicitly associating language with this [appearance as opposite from not being pot], it is posited that pot is explicitly verbalized, and
> - through the explicit appearance of this [appearance as opposite from not being pot], it is posited that pot actually appears.

In one way, these moves preserve connection with the world of objects, and in another way they seem to back away from the impact of the above analysis of the infected, non-veridical aspects of appearance. So that the impact is not lost, Jik-may-dam-chö-gya-tso concludes:[217]

> The inexpressible patch of blue does not explicitly appear to a

[a] Jik-may-dam-chö-gya-tso's *Port of Entry*, 557.1: *'jog thub pa.*

> confined being without depending on the appearance of the imputational blue because whenever a patch of blue appears to a confined being, only an aspect of appearing from there to here occurs. This is because when a subsequent conceptual consciousness induced by that sense consciousness applies a linguistic convention, it associates language within conceiving of a "blue that exists over there."

The impact of imputational natures' being posited by names and terminology is no less than that objects do not exist "over there," despite the seeming evidence of sense perception. Believing that they do is the ultimate source of pain and confinement.

The Second Reason: Established By Way Of Its Own Character

The *Sūtra Unraveling the Thought* says that imputational natures are without a nature of character, and it identifies "character" as subsisting, or establishment, by way of its own character. Taking their cue from this section of the sūtra, Ḏzong-ka-ḇa and his followers make a focal point of their exegesis the point that Proponents of Mind-Only assert that imputational natures are not established by way of their own character, but other-powered natures and thoroughly established natures are. It is likely that their emphasis on this point is due to the fact that their favored system, the Consequence School, does not assert that anything is established by way of its own character. Complex and intriguing, this topic of what "established by way of its own character" means is vital to the Ge-luk-ḇas' presentation of the positions of the Mind-Only and Middle Way Schools on the final nature of phenomena—emptiness—and, thereby, on the meaning of the existence of an object.

Ḏzong-ka-ḇa (*Emptiness in Mind-Only,* 86-87) points out that "established by way of its own character" has different meanings in the Mind-Only and Consequence Schools:

> Moreover, the mode of positing [something in dependence upon names and terminology in this Mind-Only system] is very different from the Consequence School's positing existents through the force of nominal conventions [even if the terminology is similar]. Therefore, the meaning of existing and not existing by way of [the object's] own character[a] [here in the Mind-Only School] also does not agree [with the interpretation of the Consequence School].

Ḇel-jor-hlün-drup's[218] short commentary adds considerable clarity:

> Furthermore, this system of positing [phenomena] by terminology is very different from that of the Consequence School. For, in the system of the Proponents of Cognition, there is a common locus of that

[a] See *Absorption,* #113-116.

which is posited by terminology and that which is found when one searches for the imputed object in the imputation of conventions; [in contrast] the Consequentialists assert that the term "only" in "posited by only terminology" eliminates that the imputed object in the imputation of conventions is found when sought. Therefore, the two, Consequentialists and Proponents of Cognition, also do not agree on the meaning of [something's] existing or not existing by way of its own character. This is because:

- the Consequentialists assert that, if something existed [that is found] when the imputed object in the imputation of conventions was sought, then it would exist by way of its own character
- the Proponents of Cognition assert that that which exists by way of its own entity without being posited by the force of conventions exists by way of its own character.

Even though both the Mind-Only School and the Consequence School, hold that imputational natures are "only posited by names and terminology," they do not mean the same thing by the term. The meanings of "only posited by names and terminology" and "established by way of its own character," as embedded in their respective systems, differ greatly. For, as Jam-ȳang-shay-b̄a[219] explains, the Proponents of Mind-Only are seen as holding that the term "only" in "only posited by names and terminology" eliminates merely that the object is established by way of its own character and does not eliminate that the object is established from its own side, whereas the Consequentialists assert that it eliminates both. As D̄ra-d̄i Ge-s̄hay Rin-chen-dön-drup says,[220] this means that for the Proponents of Mind-Only it is possible for something—such as existent imputational natures—to be established from their own side and not to be established by way of their own character.

The implications of this crucial point are that D̄zong-ka-b̄a and his followers hold that in the Mind-Only School, existent imputational natures are:

- only imputed by conceptuality,[a]
- established from their own side,[b]
- inherently established,[c] and
- established by the force of their own measure of subsistence,[d] but
- not established by way of their own character.[e]

For Ge-luk-b̄a scholars, the Mind-Only tenet that imputational natures are only posited by names and terminology could not possibly eliminate that

---

[a] *rtog pas btags tsam.*

[b] *rang ngos nas grub pa.*

[c] *rang bzhin gyis grub pa.*

[d] *rang gi gnas tshod kyi dbang gis grub pa.*

[e] *rang gi mtshan nyid kyis ma grub pa.*

imputational natures are established from their own side, as it does in the Consequence School. Otherwise, those who generate realization of the Mind-Only view would realize emptiness, as it is described in the Consequence School, with respect to some phenomena; namely, they would realize that existent imputational natures are empty of establishment from their own side.

Still, why would it not be appropriate to hold that Proponents of Mind-Only realize emptiness—as it is presented in the Consequence School—just with respect to imputational natures but not with respect to other phenomena? Could we say that they have not yet arrived at the point where they can realize that other-powered and thoroughly established natures do not inherently exist but do indeed realize such with respect to more insubstantial phenomena, namely, imputational natures such as uncompounded space and an object's being the referent of a conceptual consciousness? The negative answer to this lies in Āryadeva's famous dictum for the Middle Way School that a consciousness viewing the emptiness of one thing views the emptiness of all things. His *Four Hundred* says:[221]

> That which is the viewer of one thing
> Is explained to be the viewer of all.
> That which is the emptiness of one
> Is the emptiness of all.

This stanza is taken as establishing the dictum that upon inferentially realizing the emptiness of one thing, one can—through the functioning of that reasoning—realize the emptiness of any other object just by turning one's mind to it, without using any further reasoning. This being the case, there is no way that a Proponent of Mind-Only could realize emptiness, as it is presented in the Consequence School, with respect to one phenomenon and not realize it with respect to other phenomena. Hence, in order to posit that Proponents of Mind-Only have indeed realized something with respect to imputational natures when they claim realization that imputational natures are not established by way of their own character, it is necessary to posit a different meaning of "establishment by way of its own character" for the Mind-Only School than what this means in the Consequence School.

If Proponents of Mind-Only could realize emptiness as it is described in the Consequence School without respect to even one phenomenon, they could realize it with respect to all phenomena, and consequently they would not hold that other-powered natures are established by way of their own character. However, their source sūtra, the *Sūtra Unraveling the Thought,* clearly says,[222] "That which does not exist by way of its own character is not produced," and thus other-powered natures, being produced, must be established by way of their own character. In sum, Ge-luk-b̄a scholars—in order to accommodate the differentiation between the Mind-Only School and the Consequence School—hold that, in the Mind-Only School,

- that something is not established by way of its own character does not entail that it does not inherently exist or is not established from its own side or is not established by the force of its own measure of subsistence
- instead, it means that it does not truly exist[a] or ultimately exist.[b]

It is crucial to note that the Indian Proponents of Mind-Only do not openly make most of these distinctions; specifically, they do not employ the vocabulary that imputational natures are established from their own side and inherently exist. Indeed, it strikes me as absurd even to imagine that a Proponent of Mind-Only would say that objects are established from their own side as the referents of words and conceptual consciousness! Once they assert that objects are not established by way of their own character as the referents of their respective names and conceptual consciousnesses, they would not turn around and assert that they are established from their own side this way or inherently established this way, since this would vitiate the impact of their original statement. However, most Ge-luk-b̄a scholars,[c] upon examining the implications of the controversies between the Mind-Only School and the Middle Way School, hold that in fact the Mind-Only School does come to assert this; they all say that in the Mind-Only School itself, whatever exists is necessarily established from its own side and necessarily is inherently established, and thus being the referent of words and conceptual consciousnesses, since it exists, is itself inherently established. These Ge-luk-b̄a scholars come to this conclusion based on the evidence of extensive controversy between the Mind-Only and the Consequence Schools and based on the fact that the Mind-Only School does assert that other-powered natures are established by way of their own character. The latter is cogently seen as a sign that the Mind-Only School does not assert that even imputational natures are not established from their own side, for if they did, they could easily carry this over to all other phenomena. The point is subtle and intriguing; nevertheless, to claim that the school holds that objects are established from their own side as the referents of their respective names and conceptual consciousnesses undermines the force of the prime Mind-Only tenet. Let us trace how these scholars get themselves into this spot.

Levels Of Existence

According to standard Ge-luk-b̄a positions, there are two levels of existence in the Mind-Only School:

1. Mere existence, which entails existence from the object's own side, inherent existence, and existence by the force of its own measure of subsistence[d]

---

a *bden par yod pa.*

b *don dam par yod pa.*

c For Gung-tang's disagreement with this, see *Absorption,* #122.

d "Existence" and "establishment" are equivalent in this context.

2. A more substantial level of existence, which is called existence by way of the object's own character, true existence, and ultimate existence.

Thus, in the Mind-Only School, whatever exists (including existent imputational natures) necessarily also exists from its own side. As D̄ra-d̄i Ge-s̄hay Rin-chen-dön-drup[223] says, to be existent, or established, from its own side means that the thing in question can be found upon searching for it from the side of its basis of imputation. The bases of imputation of a chair are its parts, the collection of its parts, and so forth, and the various Ge-luk-b̄a traditions claim that, in the Mind-Only School and all other non-Consequentialist systems, something from within those bases of imputation—in this case, the collection of its parts—is asserted to be the chair. Similarly, it is claimed that, according to the Mind-Only School following Asaṅga, when persons are sought analytically among their bases of imputation, the mind-basis-of-all is found, and that, according to the Mind-Only School following Dignāga and Dharmakīrti, when persons are sought analytically among their bases of imputation, a subtle neutral type of mental consciousness is found. This is because the mind-basis-of-all and the mental consciousness, respectively, are what goes from lifetime to lifetime, carrying the predispositions accumulated from actions.

Ge-luk-b̄a scholars uniformly hold that the Mind-Only School's assertion that the mind-basis-of-all or the mental consciousness is the person that is found upon analyzing what is behind the imputation "person" is a clear sign that they assert that objects are established from their own side, since this constitutes the very meaning of being established from its own side, being inherently established, and being established by the force of its own measure of subsistence. These terms mean nothing more nor less than that something is found when the object imputed is sought. Thus, even though on the surface it would appear that to be established from its own side would have just the same meaning as established by way of its own character, it does not—it merely means that the object exists, since, if it were not analytically findable, it would be as good as a complete fiction. This is why the Proponents of Mind-Only quarrel so much with the Consequentialists—the latter hold that nothing is findable among or separate from its bases of imputation.

Ge-luk-b̄a scholars' delineation of the radical nature of the Consequentialists' position is evocative, but it is important to notice that there is not a single line of Indian Mind-Only literature that openly identifies the mind-basis-of-all as what is found when a person is sought among his or her bases of imputation. Rather, such is gleaned from contextual analysis of the school's philosophical positions, its debates with the Consequence School, and Chandrakīrti's presentation of the uniqueness of the Consequentialist tenet that phenomena do not inherently exist and that a mind-basis-of-all does not exist.[a] Indeed, this

[a] See Daniel Cozort, *Unique Tenets of the Middle Way Consequence School* (Ithaca, N.Y.: Snow Lion, 1998).

position that in the non-Consequentialist schools something must be found when an object imputed is sought is the pivot of Ge-luk-b̄a presentations of the four schools of tenets and thus of the superiority of the Consequence School.

As Jam-ȳang-shay-b̄a[224] puts it, in the Mind-Only School imputational natures are not established by way of their own character, but they inherently exist and exist from their own side. Thus, two classes of existents are distinguished, those that are substantially existent in the sense of being truly established or, in other words, established by way of their own character, and those that are imputedly existent in the sense of being nominally imputed. Hence, the non-establishment of imputational natures by way of their own character cannot mean that they do not exist from their own side or do not inherently exist; rather, "inherent existence" and "existence from its own side" merely mean that when an object, such as uncompounded space (or even something's being the referent of a conceptual consciousness), is sought among its bases of imputation, it is found. Mere existence entails, in the Mind-Only School but not in the Consequence School, that an object can be found under such analysis; thus, if imputational natures did not inherently exist, they would not exist at all, and if imputational natures did not exist at all, there absurdly would not be two classes of existents. This point is made clearly by D̄zong-ka-b̄a's student Ke-drup in his *Opening the Eyes of the Fortunate:*[225]

> Concerning that, the meaning of the statement that "Imputational natures do not exist by way of their own character" is that they do not truly exist. If that were not so, it would have to be explained as meaning that they do not exist at all, in which case imputational natures would not occur among objects of knowledge, whereby whatever is an established base [that is, an existent] would necessarily be substantially established.

Consequentialists, on the other hand, assert that if, with respect to existents, one is not satisfied with the mere imputation of nominal conventions from the subject's side and, instead of that, analyzes whether something is established as that object or not, at the end of such analysis it is not found. Therefore, Consequentialists do not differentiate between something's being established by way of its own character and its being inherently existent.

Proponents of Mind-Only assert that at the end of such analysis, something is found that is the object, whereby they hold that all phenomena are undifferentiatedly inherently established and established from their side; otherwise, objects would be mere figments of the imagination. In addition, the meaning of an object's being established by way of its own character is not constituted merely by this level of existence but is more substantial. It can be concluded, therefore, that the Mind-Only School and the Middle Way School posit different measures of what it means for something to be established by way of its own character. As Ḏzong-ka-ḇa (*Emptiness in Mind-Only,* 86-87) says:

> Moreover, the mode of positing [something in dependence upon names and terminology in this Mind-Only system] is very different from the Consequence School's positing existents through the force of nominal conventions [even if the terminology is similar].

According to A-ku Ḻo-drö-gya-tso's distillation of the issue,[226] in the Autonomy and Consequence Schools, the meaning of something's being established by way of its own character is that it is findable when the object imputed is sought—the Consequence School refuting this in each and every phenomenon and the Autonomy School (as well as all other schools) affirming such a status in all phenomena. He says that in the Mind-Only School, the term means that the object is established without being only posited by names and terminology.

Summary

As Gung-tang says,[227] though both Proponents of Mind-Only and Consequentialists say that imputational phenomena are only imputed by conceptuality and are not established by way of their own character, in their respective systems what the term "only" eliminates and what it means to be established by way of their own character differ greatly. Both the Proponents of Sūtra and the Proponents of Mind-Only assert that imputational phenomena are not established by way of their own character in accordance with what that means in their own system. However, both the Proponents of Sūtra and the Proponents of Mind-Only come to assert that imputational phenomena are established by way of their own character in accordance with the meaning described in the Consequence School, that is, that when the object imputed is sought, it is found. For the Mind-Only School, the illusion is that, although objects' being the referent of thoughts and terms does indeed exist, it is misperceived as subsisting naturally in objects by way of their own character. The falsity of this linguistically dependent illusion must be seen in order to undo the basic distortion of the mind. Emptiness—the thoroughly established nature, the absence of such a status in objects—must be seen.

14. Other-Powered Natures Are Not the Ultimate

The *Sūtra Unraveling the Thought* treats the ultimate-non-nature in two ways, one with respect to other-powered natures[a] and another with respect to thoroughly established natures. Other-powered natures are ultimate-non-natures in that they are **not** the ultimate, whereas thoroughly established natures are ultimate-non-natures in that they **are** both the ultimate and the non-nature that is the very absence, or non-existence, of the object of negation in selflessness. This dual treatment of the ultimate-naturelessness offers much information about other-powered natures and thoroughly established natures.

Other-Powered Natures As Ultimate-Non-Natures

The *Sūtra Unraveling the Thought* (*Emptiness in Mind-Only,* 88) initially discusses the ultimate-naturelessness with respect to other-powered natures, also called "other-powered characters":

> What are ultimate-non-natures? Those dependently arisen phenomena—which are natureless due to being natureless in terms of production—are also natureless due to being natureless in terms of the ultimate.
>
> Why? Paramārthasamudgata, that which is an object of observation of purification in phenomena I teach to be the ultimate, and other-powered characters are not the object of observation of purification. Therefore, they are said to be "ultimate-non-natures."

Since other-powered natures are not what is observed and cognized in order to become purified of the obstructions to enlightenment, they are not the ultimate; only the thoroughly established nature—emptiness—is the ultimate. Therefore, other-powered natures are said to be without the nature of the ultimate; they are ultimate-non-natures.

The suggestion is that beings usually take phenomena that arise in dependence upon causes and conditions to be final, as if there were nothing beyond them. By pointing out that these are not ultimates, Buddha is calling attention to a more profound reality, as well as a conflict between appearance and reality.

Other-powered natures not only are natureless in terms of self-production but also are natureless in terms of the ultimate. The reason for the latter is that only a final object of observation of an exalted wisdom purifying obstructions is the ultimate, and other-powered natures are not such. For, as Jam-ȳang-shay-b̄a says,[228] only through observing thoroughly established natures and meditating upon them are obstructions removed, this being because, when taking

---

[a] For an extensive discussion of how other-powered natures are not the ultimate, see *Absorption,* #127-138.

emptiness to mind, the mind is engaged in a mode of apprehension explicitly contradictory to conceiving self. For example, since one form of the conception of a self of phenomena is to conceive that objects are established by way of their own character as the referents of conceptual consciousnesses, a practitioner needs to meditate on objects' **non**-establishment this way.

One must meditate on the emptiness of such establishment; it is not sufficient merely to concentrate on other-powered natures, for, through observing and thereupon meditating on other-powered natures, one cannot remove obstructions by way of engaging in a mode of apprehension that is explicitly contradictory to conceiving self. This is simply because one is not paying attention to the opposite of what ignorance misconceives in objects—one must realize the **absence** of objects' being established by way of their own character as the referents of words and conceptual consciousnesses. The sūtra's clear statement that other-powered natures are not the object of observation for purifying obstructions and hence not the ultimate is contrary to a notion currently prevalent among certain Japanese,[a] American,[b] and other scholars that the thoroughly established nature is just a purified version of the other-powered nature.

Still, one might (mistakenly) think that other-powered natures are the ultimate because both they and thoroughly established natures are called "ultimate-non-natures," and thoroughly established natures are the ultimate. However, as Gung-tang[229] cogently points outs, other-powered natures' ultimate-non-nature is not the **actual** ultimate-non-nature, this being found only in the second mode of positing the ultimate-non-nature—that is, thoroughly established natures' ultimate-non-nature, in the sense that the latter are both the ultimate and the non-existence of the nature of what is negated in selflessness. The reason for saying that other-powered natures are also "ultimate-non-natures" is only to clear away the qualm that they might be the ultimate.

Why Single Out Other-Powered Natures As Ultimate-Non-Natures?

But why does the *Sūtra Unraveling the Thought* single out and thus limit the qualm to other-powered natures? Why not mention that existent imputational natures such as uncompounded space also are not the ultimate and thus ultimate-non-natures? About this, Dzong-ka-ba (*Emptiness in Mind-Only,* 89-90) says:

---

[a] See Appendix 2, as well as Gadjin Nagao, "The Logic of Convertibility," in *Mādhyamika and Yogācāra* (Albany, N.Y.: State University of New York Press, 1991), 123-153; and "The Buddhist Worldview as Elucidated in the Three-Nature Theory and Its Similes," *The Eastern Buddhist* 16 (1983):1-18.

[b] See Appendices 1 and 3, as well as Alan Sponberg, "The Trisvabhāva Doctrine in India and China: A Study of Three Exegetical Models," *Bukkyō Bunka Kenkyū-jo Kiyō* 21 (1982):97-119.

Question: Why are imputational factors not also posited [at this point in the *Sūtra Unraveling the Thought*] as ultimate-non-natures?

Answer: If [something] were posited as [an ultimate-non-nature] merely through not being an object of observation of purification, that would be true [that is, imputational natures also would have to be posited as ultimate-non-natures]. However, in the context of refuting a misconception, other-powered natures are posited as ultimate-non-natures due to not being objects of observation of purification, whereas imputational factors are not posited [as ultimate-non-natures].

Question: How is that?

Answer: When one understands that obstructions are purified through meditation observing other-powered natures' emptiness of the imputational factor[—for example, through meditating on other-powered natures' emptiness of being established by way of their own character as the referents of words and of conceptual consciousnesses—], there arises the qualm that, since, in that case, [the pure exalted wisdom] must also observe the other-powered natures that are the substrata [of the quality of emptiness, those other-powered natures] also would be objects of observation of purification, due to which they would be ultimates. [Thus, such a qualm needs to be alleviated with respect to other-powered natures.] However, such a qualm does not occur with respect to imputational factors.[a]

The fault of that qualm does not exist.[b] It is like the fact that just as although the conception that sound is permanent is overcome by ascertaining sound as impermanent, it is not contradictory that the conception of permanence is not overcome through [merely] observing sound.

D̄zong-ka-b̄a says that just because something is not an "object of observation" of a path of purification of obstructions, this does not warrant its being called an "ultimate-non-nature" in this passage in the sūtra.

To unpack his reasoning, let us first consider the term "object of observation by a path of purification."[c] Here it refers to the object being cognized in order to overcome an obstruction. For instance, a consciousness of meditative equipoise of the path of seeing of the Great Vehicle directly perceives the selflessness of phenomena—the non-establishment of objects by way of their own character as the referents of conceptual consciousnesses; hence, this selflessness is its "object of observation," as the term is used here in the sūtra. The more usual meaning of "object of observation," as it has come to be employed in technical vocabulary in Ge-luk-b̄a scholarship, is different. With respect to an

---

[a] See *Absorption,* #129-138, 140, 141.

[b] See ibid., #131.

[c] *rnam dag lam gyi dmigs pa,* or *rnam dag lam gyi dmigs yul.*

eye consciousness apprehending blue, blue itself is its object of observation, but in the context of a path consciousness realizing selflessness—the thoroughly established nature—the "object of observation" refers to the object or objects **with respect to which** selflessness is being realized. Since a path of seeing of the Great Vehicle realizes selflessness—emptiness—with respect to all phenomena, all phenomena are its objects of observation, or bases with respect to which emptiness is being realized. Those substrata, in fact, are not apprehended when the thoroughly established nature is directly realized by anyone but a Buddha; thus, in such a context the term "object of observation" does not even mean that the object is observed or apprehended; rather, the term merely indicates that all phenomena are bases with respect to which the thoroughly established nature is realized.

That is how the term "object of observation" has come to be used with respect to a path-consciousness directly realizing emptiness in meditative equipoise. Here, however, in the *Sūtra Unraveling the Thought* the term "object of observation" clearly does not refer to those bases but to the thoroughly established nature—emptiness or selflessness itself. This is why Jam-ȳang-shay-b̄a,[230] for instance, in discussing this passage, always uses the term "**final** object of observation by a path of purification"[a] and not just "object of observation." In a similar fashion, the Second Dalai Lama uses both "**final** object of observation of purification" and "**main** object of observation of purification."[b]

Thus, if other-powered natures were posited as "ultimate-non-natures" merely because they are not final objects of observation by a path of purification, there would indeed be the fault that existent imputational natures such as uncompounded space also should be posited as "ultimate-non-natures," since they also are not final objects of observation by a path of purification. However,

---

a *rnam dag lam gyi dmigs pa mthar thug.*

b *rnam dag gi dmigs pa'i gtso bo:* the Second Dalai Lama's *Lamp Illuminating the Meaning,* 19.5. *rnam dag dmigs pa'i gtso bo:* L̄o-sang-trin-lay-ye-s̄hay's *Summarized Meaning,* 156.15.

The thoroughly established nature is the **final** object of observation by a path of purification, and indeed such a path observes, or apprehends, it; however, despite the fact that phenomena such as chairs are objects of **observation** by a path of purification, they are not observed or apprehended by it—they are only bases with respect to which emptiness is realized. Hence, the term "object of observation" in this context, as it has come to be used in Ge-luk-b̄a scholarship, is somewhat misleading. The usage of the term "objects of observation" even for objects that are not being observed may have come from systems that hold that even during direction perception of emptiness the phenomena qualified by emptiness still appear; this is called "meditative equipoise with appearance" (*mnyam bzhag snang bcas*). D̄zong-ka-b̄a held this notion earlier in his life but then switched to the opinion that the objects qualified by emptiness do not appear during meditative equipoise (*mnyam bzhag snang med*). His own commentary (*legs bshad gser 'phreng*) on Maitreya's *Ornament for Clear Realization* reflects his earlier notion, whereas his student Gyel-tsap's commentary (*rnam bshad snying po rgyan*) reflects his later view.

the reason why other-powered natures are posited as such is not merely this but is relative to a misconception about them.

So far, Dzong-ka-ba is clear, but what is the misconception? A long history of scholarship has yielded several interpretations of the issue, two of which seem to me to be the most plausible:[a]

Jik-may-dam-chö-gya-tso: Relative to the sūtra's style of teaching that other-powered natures are bases of emptiness, it is more difficult to generate the qualm that imputational natures might be final objects of observation by a path of purification.

Ge-u-tsang:[231] Those who are practicing the Mind-Only view might have the qualm that mind-only is a final object of observation by a path of purification.

Jik-may-dam-chö-gya-tso[232] stresses the focal point that the qualm arises around how the *Sūtra Unraveling the Thought* explains the process of meditating on emptiness. The sūtra repeatedly explains that one must take other-powered natures as substrata of emptiness and must realize that they are empty of being established in accordance with exaggerated factors imputed in the manner of entity and attribute. Because, in the process of meditating, one must take cognizance of other-powered natures as objects of observation with respect to which emptiness is realized, the qualm arises that, since these are objects of observation of an exalted wisdom, they might be ultimates. Since the style of the sūtra is to explain the process of meditating on emptiness in terms of realizing that other-powered natures are empty of the imputational nature and never speaks of realizing that imputational natures are empty of the imputational nature, it is more difficult **relative to the sūtra's style of teaching** to generate the qualm that imputational natures might be ultimates.

The interpretation by Ge-u-tsang, an early nineteenth-century follower of Jay-dzün Chö-gyi-gyel-tsen, innovatively attributes the qualm—that other-powered natures might be a final object of observation by a path of purification—to those who are practicing the Mind-Only view. He says that just as when light reflected in water suddenly appears on a wall, one has the sense that it is shining forth from the wall but in fact is just the radiance of the water itself, so when a practitioner ascertains the ultimate according to the Mind-Only School, there is a time when all coarse appearances of external objects vanish, since one has understood that all objects are not different entities from the mind. Because there is nothing other to be seen separate from the mind, there is a strong possibility that one would have the qualm that the mind is a final object found by a consciousness analyzing the ultimate, that is, a final object of observation by a path of purification.

Ge-u-tsang points to the fact that the qualm that the *Sūtra Unraveling the Thought* is countering—when it identifies that other-powered natures are not

---

[a] For others, see *Absorption*, #129-138.

the ultimate—is concerned with other-powered natures, the **chief** of which is the mind.[a] In many texts of the Mind-Only School, the identification of other-powered natures is done mainly in terms of the mind, such as when Maitreya's *Differentiation of the Middle and the Extremes* says,[b] "Unreal ideation exists," in which "ideation" (here meaning any dualistic consciousness) is intended to stand for other-powered natures in general.[c] Also, when one understands that a difference of entity between subject and object does not exist, one sees the appearance of objects as the self-effulgence of the mind, and hence one might think that the mind is a final object of observation by a path of purification. Thus, because the mind is the principal other-powered nature, when the *Sūtra Unraveling the Thought* explains that other-powered natures are natureless in terms of the ultimate, it is clearing up a qualm that arises from having practiced the Mind-Only view, namely, that the mind is the ultimate. Ḡe-u-tsang's explanation, based on practical application of doctrine in meditation, makes a great deal of sense.

As the late Ḏa-drin-rap-ḏen[233] says in his expansion of Ḡe-u-tsang's position, the qualm that the mind is a final object of observation by a path of purification arises when, upon taking cognizance of the mind, one ascertains that it is not established by way of its own character as the referent of the convention "mind." Due to realization of this, the phenomena—such as forms—that serve as objects of the mind can be ascertained as of the entity of the mind, and through the force of cultivating this ascertainment its impact is experienced, due to which one comes to generate belief in the statements—as found in Maitreya's *Ornament for the Great Vehicle Sūtras* and so forth—that the nature of the mind is clear light. When yogis one-pointedly sustain the continuum of this ascertainment, the inexpressible, luminous, and cognitive nature of mind dawns, whereby a qualm wondering whether obstructions are purified through meditation observing the mind is generated.[d] He emphasizes that in this process of meditation not only is the mind identified in vivid experience but also realization of its emptiness of the imputational nature is sustained; merely concentrating on the mind without sustaining the view of emptiness cannot overcome wrong conceptions. He thereby draws out the significance of Ḏzong-ka-ḇa's

---

a This is how Ge-luk-ḇa scholars get around having to say that, according to the Mind-Only School, only mind exists.

b I.2a. For a discussion of this quotation, see *Emptiness in Mind-Only,* 182ff. and 305ff.

c Again, this is how Ge-luk-ḇa scholars get around having to say that, according to the Mind-Only School, only mind exists.

d In a provocatively brief aside, Ḏa-drin-rap-ḏen (*Annotations,* 19.3-21.2) says that it is an unparalleled quintessential instruction of the Mind-Only School to "mix" that mind—the continuum of which is being sustained in meditation—with the mind-basis-of-all as much as one can. One wishes that he would have said more on this point, since little is mentioned in Indo-Tibetan Mind-Only literature about the relation of the mind-basis-of-all to the luminous and cognitive nature of all consciousnesses.

speaking of observing "other-powered natures," the chief of which is the mind, and meditating on its "emptiness of the imputational nature." Ge-u-tsang and Da-drin-rap-den evocatively place the qualm in the context of practice.

Gung-tang[234] and A-ku Lo-drö-gya-tso[235] make a detailed and intriguing refutation of Ge-u-tsang's position in the course of which they make interesting points but, in my opinion, over-extend the general Ge-luk-ba dictum that in the Great Vehicle the ultimate is a mere negative.[a] Their over-stated case is an extension of solid evidence both in the sūtra and in Indian treatises. First, they point to the fact that the *Sūtra Unraveling the Thought* clearly identifies, as the final object of observation by a path of purification, only a real nature[b] that is a **mere elimination** of an object of negation, and thus a qualm that the mind is the ultimate would occur only for those who are not familiar with the tenets of the sūtra. For the sūtra speaks of the ultimate as just the emptiness of the imputational nature in other-powered natures; it never speaks of the mind as the ultimate—it never speaks of other-powered natures as the ultimate. Gung-tang and A-ku Lo-drö-gya-tso cite the seventh chapter of the *Sūtra Unraveling the Thought* (*Emptiness in Mind-Only,* 108):[c]

> The thoroughly established character is that which is...:
>
> - just the naturelessness of only that [imputational] nature,
> - the absence of self in phenomena,
> - thusness,[d] and
> - the object of observation of purification.

Using a list of equivalents, the sūtra speaks of the thoroughly established nature as being just an absence, that is to say, just an elimination, just the

---

[a] For a discussion of negatives, see p. 242ff.

[b] *chos nyid, dharmatā.* I also translate this as noumenon.

[c] Paramārthasamudgata is offering back to Buddha what he has understood. With more context, the quote is:

> Supramundane Victor, I offer the meaning of what the Supramundane Victor has said as follows: The thoroughly established character is that which is:
>
> - the thorough non-establishment—of just those [other-powered natures which are] the objects of activity of conceptuality, the foundations of imputational characters, and those which have the signs of compositional phenomena—as that imputational character,
> - just the naturelessness of only that [imputational] nature,
> - the absence of self in phenomena,
> - thusness, and
> - the object of observation of purification.
>
> In dependence on that, the Supramundane Victor, in addition, designated the ultimate-non-nature of phenomena.

[d] *de bzhin nyid, tathatā* (Étienne Lamotte, *Saṃdhinirmocanasūtra: L'Explication des mystères* [Louvain: Université de Louvain, 1935], 82 [25], n. 32).

non-existence of a self of phenomena; it says that only this is the object of observation by a path of purification. The thoroughly established nature is a specific absence, namely, the non-existence of the imputational nature, the self of phenomena, "self" being another name for the imputational nature the non-existence of which constitutes selflessness, emptiness. In Ge-luk-b̄a vocabulary, the self of phenomena is establishment of objects by way of their own character as the referents of conceptual consciousnesses, as well as establishment of subject and object as different entities.

Then Gung-tang[236] demonstrates that not only is the *Sūtra Unraveling the Thought* clear on the fact that the ultimate is a mere absence (see the next chapter for many citations from the sūtra that make this same point, pp. 261-265), but also Asaṅga explains that only a mere emptiness of the object of negation appears to a wisdom consciousness of a Superior's meditative equipoise. His *Summary of the Great Vehicle*[a] says, "A non-conceptual consciousness is like a person whose eyes are closed." Since nothing but an absence—which is other-powered natures' emptiness of the imputational nature—appears, such a non-conceptual consciousness of meditative equipoise is said to be "without appearance."[b] No conventional phenomenon, such as the luminous and cognitive nature of the mind, appears, and thus non-conceptual realization is compared to closed eyes. From this evidence, Gung-tang draws the conclusion that **for those who know these tenets** there could be no qualm that the luminous and cognitive nature of the mind is the final object of observation by a path of purification.

He gives more evidence: Asaṅga's *Grounds of Hearers* says about the path of preparation, "At that time, appearance of the mind has as if ceased." Gung-tang says[237] that, if this is what Asaṅga says about the path of preparation (from among the five paths of accumulation, preparation, seeing, meditation, and no more learning), what need is there to mention that the mind would not appear to a wisdom-consciousness of the path of seeing! Also, he points to the fact that Asaṅga's *Summary of the Great Vehicle*[238] speaks of three different modes of understanding over the path of preparation and the path of seeing. The three levels of understanding reality occur on (1) the first two levels of the path of preparation, called heat and peak, (2) the last two levels of the path of preparation, called forbearance and supreme mundane qualities, and (3) the path of seeing:[239]

---

[a] See Étienne Lamotte, *La Somme du grand véhicule d'Asaṅga,* reprint, 2 vols., Publications de l'Institute Orientaliste de Louvain 8 (Louvain: Université de Louvain, 1973), vol. 1, 78 (VIII.16), and vol. 2, 244-245; and John P. Keenan, *The Summary of the Great Vehicle by Bodhisattva Asaṅga: Translated from the Chinese of Paramārtha* (Berkeley, Calif.: Numata Center for Buddhist Translation and Research, 1992), 96-97. For S̄hay-rap-gyel-tsen's opinion that such passages indicate that Asaṅga's *Summary of the Great Vehicle* denies that mind truly exists, see p. 303ff.

[b] *snang med.*

Heat and peak levels of the path of preparation: One can ascertain through the force of one's own experience that the wisdom of meditative equipoise in one's own continuum is involved in an imputational appearance of phenomena as external objects; hence the levels of heat and peak are called "grounds of realizing the emptiness of objects, understanding the imputational nature."

Forbearance and supreme mundane qualities levels of the path of preparation: Through the force of experience one cannot ascertain that an imputational appearance of objects—thoroughly afflicted phenomena and purified phenomena—as external objects exists for the wisdom of meditative equipoise in one's own continuum, but one can ascertain through the force of one's own experience the mere appearance of apprehending-subjects—which are singled out as "other-powered natures" because they are the principal other-powered natures—as if they are external objects. Hence, these two levels are called "grounds of the yoga of mind-only, understanding other-powered natures."

Path of seeing: For an exalted wisdom of meditative equipoise on the path of seeing, however, not only have appearances of object and subject vanished but also all dualistic appearances—the appearances of conventionalities and so forth—have vanished. Hence, the path of seeing is called the "ground of the yoga of non-appearance, understanding the thoroughly established nature."

Through this presentation, one can understand that Asaṅga clearly does not assert that mind-only appears during uncontaminated meditative equipoise.[a] (The apparent assumption is that, since mind is a conventionality and Asaṅga says that conventionalities do not appear on the path of seeing, mind could not appear and thus could not be a final object of observation by a path of purification and hence could not be a thoroughly established nature.)

Since both the *Sūtra Unraveling the Thought* and Asaṅga clearly describe the thoroughly established nature as **just** the non-existence of the imputational nature in other-powered natures, A-ku L̄o-drö-gya-tso[240] draws the more measured conclusion that, although the qualm that the luminous and cognitive nature of the mind is the thoroughly established nature **can** indeed arise, it **mostly** would not arise for those who are well acquainted with the tenets of the Mind-Only School. He, like Gung-tang, is making the point that another explanation of the qualm must be given. This is where I think that they are over-extending the above-mentioned cogent points of doctrine concerning the object of meditation as a mere absence.

[a] Janice D. Willis, in her *On Knowing Reality: The Tattvārtha Chapter of Asaṅga's Bodhisattvabhūmi* (New York: Columbia University Press, 1979; reprint, Delhi: Motilal Banarsidass, 1982), rightly emphasizes this point; however, she draws the conclusion that these texts by Asaṅga do not evince a view of mind-only. Ge-luk-b̄a scholars, on the other hand, see a harmony between holding a view of mind-only and holding that emptiness is the object realized by a path of purification; see Appendix 3, p. 506ff., and *Emptiness in Mind-Only,* 37-38.

Specifically, it seems to me that the qualm that the sūtra answers does not have to be from those who are well acquainted with Mind-Only tenets, and thus I find their rejection of Ḡe-u-tsang's evocative contextualization of the qualm to be unwarranted. Their rejection stems from over-emphasizing the Ge-luk-b̄a tenet that in the Great Vehicle the ultimate is a mere negative such that they adopt the pose that only those ignorant of Mind-Only tenets would even think that mind-only is the ultimate. What better way to disenfranchise those who hold the opposite opinion of the Mind-Only School than to claim that only those ignorant of the tenets of the school could hold the opinion that mind-only is the object of a wisdom consciousness!

However, there is a history of Ge-luk-b̄a scholars' strained attempts to explain away statements by authoritative Indian scholars to the contrary that reveals this posture to be a polarized claim aimed at disenfranchising other opinions. The fact that exaggeration is used as a tool to ostracize the opposition exposes the tension involved in holding the assertion that in Mind-Only tenets the ultimate is clearly depicted as a mere negative. It would be more to the point to admit that, although such is clear in the *Sūtra Unraveling the Thought,* the opposite notion—that mind is the ultimate—also occurs in other texts.

One might think that given such hyperbole suggesting that only the untutored would opine that the mind is ultimate, a reasoned case presenting the notion that would not be made by a bona fide Ge-luk-b̄a scholar, but Jang-ḡya, for instance, makes just such a proposal. Also, rather than resorting to hyperbole, A-ku Lo-drö-gya-tso and Jik-may-dam-chö-gya-tso offer straightforward, detailed refutations of his opinion that the mind is the ultimate. Again, Tibetan culture opts for a plenitude of approaches—absurd calls to partisanship on the one hand and thorough examination of sources on the other. Before turning to this crucial controversy, however, we need first to consider the general topic of positive and negative phenomena.

Kinds Of Negatives

Aspiring Tibetan scholars learn about positive and negative phenomena in the first phase of their scholastic education in a study of epistemology, called The Collected Topics of Prime Cognition.[a] After learning basic divisions of objects such as the permanent and the impermanent, the manifest and the hidden, the specifically characterized and the generally characterized, and cause and effect as well as abstract topics such as conceptually isolatable factors and phenomena that are not themselves (such as definition which itself is not a definition but a definiendum), they approach the subject of positive and negative phenomena— a topic given particular attention due to D̄zong-ka-b̄a's emphasis on its importance. The main purpose of this intense attention is to inculcate an appreciation

---

[a]   For a translation of the Go-mang version, see Anne Carolyn Klein, *Knowing, Naming, and Negation* (Ithaca, N.Y.: Snow Lion, 1988), 93-113.

of the fact that an emptiness is neither a positive phenomenon nor even a negation that implies something positive, but is a mere negative.

The division of phenomena into positive objects and negative objects is mostly word-bound in the sense of usually (but not always) being determined by the absence or presence of a negative term, such as "non-" in the terms that express them. Still, positives and negatives are not terms themselves or acts of affirmation or negation but are phenomena, objects. A positive phenomenon[a] is defined as:[241]

> a phenomenon that is not an object realized—by the conceptual consciousness apprehending it—in the manner of an explicit elimination of its object of negation.

First, a positive thing is a phenomenon, an existent; a non-existent such as the horns of a rabbit could never be a positive phenomenon. Second, the division into positive and negative phenomena is made by way of how objects appear to conceptual consciousnesses; if a conceptual consciousness must realize the object by way of explicitly eliminating an object of negation, the object is not positive but negative. For instance, to realize non-cow, cow must be explicitly eliminated, but to realize cow, non-cow does not have to be **explicitly** eliminated though indeed it is **implicitly** eliminated. Thus, non-cow is a negative phenomenon, and cow is a positive phenomenon.

The definition of a negative phenomenon is:

> an object realized—by the conceptual consciousness apprehending it—in the manner of an explicit elimination of its object of negation.

Again, a negative must be an object, an existent, a phenomenon. It is also something that must be conceptually realized through the explicit negation of an object of negation. Illustrations of negative phenomena are non-pot,[b] non-non-pot,[c] opposite from non-pot,[d] and non-existence of pot.[e] Although non-non-pot means pot, it must be realized by way of explicitly eliminating non-pot and thus is a negative phenomenon. Although it does not exist as a different entity from pot, which is a positive phenomenon, it is merely different from pot and is a negative.

Some negatives imply a positive phenomenon in their place, such as when we say about a corpulent person called Devadatta, "Fat Devadatta does not eat during the day." The meaning implied is that Devadatta eats, even a great deal, at night. Fat Devadatta's not eating during the day is a negative phenomenon but one that implies something in place of its object of negation. Devadatta is

---

[a] *sgrub pa, vidhi.*

[b] *bum pa ma yin pa.*

[c] *bum pa may in pa ma yin pa.*

[d] *bum pa my yin pa las log pa.*

[e] *bum pa med pa.*

the basis of the negation; eating during the day is the object of negation; and eating at night is a positive phenomenon implied in place of the object of negation. Such a negation is called an affirming negative.[a] Thus, the fact of fat Devadatta's not eating during the day is an affirming negative, for phenomena are the objects of inquiry even if the determination is made by way of how conceptuality approaches those phenomena. Within affirming negatives, it is one that implicitly suggests a positive phenomenon in place of its object of negation.

A mountainless plain, on the other hand, is an affirming negative that **explicitly** suggests or indicates a positive phenomenon (a plain) in place of its object of negation (mountains). Another type of affirming negative is one that **by context** suggests a positive phenomenon in place of its object of negation; for instance, being told that Shākyamuni was either a brahmin or a *kṣatriya* (member of the royal or warrior class) and was not a brahmin suggests, by context, that he was of the royal caste. A positive phenomenon (being a *kṣatriya*) is suggested in place of the object of negation (being a brahmin) in this context.

An emptiness, despite being a negative phenomenon, is none of these, for all of them suggest something positive in place of the negation of the objection of negation, whereas an emptiness does not suggest anything positive. An emptiness is a non-affirming negative, defined as:

> a negative that is such that the term expressing it does not suggest in place of the negation of its own object of negation another, positive phenomenon that is its own object suggested.

For example, the non-existence of the horns of a rabbit is expressed by the sentence "The horns of a rabbit do not exist," and this does not suggest anything positive in place of the horns of a rabbit. Though it can suggest another non-affirming negative such as the non-existence of the beauty of the horns of a rabbit, it does not suggest any positive phenomenon in place of its object of negation.

In the same way, an emptiness merely eliminates the establishment of objects by way of their own character as the referents of conceptual consciousnesses. It does not imply anything positive in its place. The basis of negation is any phenomenon. The object of negation is its establishment by way of its own character as the referent of a conceptual consciousness, and nothing is implied in place of the object of negation. For instance, in the case of the emptiness of the body, the body—the basis of negation—is a positive phenomenon, but it is not implied in place of the object of negation; rather, it is that which is empty

[a] *ma yin dgag, paryudāsapratiṣedha.* The division of negatives, or negations, into affirming and non-affirming, or implicative and non-implicative, is traced to Mimāṃsā injunctions to refrain from activities that either imply another activity in its place or not; see J. F. Staal, "Negation and the Law of Contradiction in Indian Thought," *Bulletin of the School of Oriental and African Studies* 25, no. 1 (1962):56-57.

of such establishment. An emptiness is the mere elimination of such establishment; thus, it is a mere negative, a non-affirming negative, a mere absence of its object of negation.

Non-affirming negatives are divided into two classes—those whose object of negation does occur among objects of knowledge and those whose object of negation does not occur among objects of knowledge. For example, the non-existence of the horns of a rabbit negates the horns of a rabbit which do not exist anywhere; and similarly, the absence of objects' being established by way of their own character as the referents of conceptual consciousnesses eliminates such establishment which never has nor will occur anywhere. Thus, these two are non-affirming negatives whose object of negation does not occur among objects of knowledge—that is to say, among existents. On the other hand, the non-existence of a pot, such as on a certain table, eliminates the existence of a pot there and does not suggest that anything else is on that table. Therefore, the non-existence of a pot is a non-affirming negative whose object of negation, pot, does occur among objects of knowledge.

Through making this division in terms of whether the object negated is, in general, an existent or not, it is being stressed that an emptiness is a lack of something that never did nor will exist. Though an emptiness exists, its object of negation never does. Realization of an emptiness, therefore, is not a case of destroying something that once existed nor a case of realizing the passing away of something that did exist. Rather, it means to realize a quality of objects, a negative attribute, that is the mere absence of something that never existed but nevertheless was imagined to occur. The consequence of such false imagination is tremendous suffering in the round of cyclic existence.

Even though nothing is more negative than a non-affirming negative and even though emptiness—the final nature and ultimate reality of all phenomena—is such a non-affirming negative not implying anything positive in its place, it is central to the realization of emptiness that it is compatible with existence. Though in the perspective of a consciousness realizing emptiness, nothing is implied in place of the object of negation, the understanding of emptiness is said to assist in understanding how phenomena exist.

Even though in this way emptiness and existence are vitally compatible, it is repeatedly emphasized in Ge-luk-b̄a scholarship that emptiness is a non-affirming negative because in direct realization of emptiness, except at Buddhahood, all that appears is emptiness. A mere vacuity that is the elimination—the negative—of such exaggerated existence dawns, and the meditator remains in space-like meditative equipoise contemplating and comprehending the absence of such existence in a totally non-dualistic manner.

As we have seen, it is repeatedly said that to develop an antidote to habitual assent to the seeming existence of objects as separate entities from the consciousnesses apprehending them or as established by way of their own character as the referents of conceptual consciousnesses, it is necessary to cultivate a wisdom consciousness capable of paying attention to just the absence of such establishment. The emphasis on the fact that emptiness is a non-affirming negative indicates the degree to which practitioners must understand the absence of a wrongly imputed status of phenomena on which the emotions of desire, hatred, bewilderment, enmity, jealousy, and so forth are built. A consciousness conceiving phenomena to be established by way of their own character as the referents of words and of conceptual consciousnesses serves as the underpinning of these afflictive emotions binding beings in cyclic existence; a wisdom consciousness perceiving the same phenomena in an opposite way is needed.

The existence of an object established by way of its own character as the referent of a term or of a conceptual consciousness never did nor could occur, but beings conceive the opposite and thus have been drawn beginninglessly into cyclic existence. Extrication from that misconception can happen only through realizing the statuslessness of such reified existence, becoming accustomed to it in intense meditation, and realizing it directly in meditative equipoise, in which nothing but emptiness appears and the mind is merged with it like fresh water poured into fresh water. Such direct cognition must be re-entered over and over again. Meditation on emptiness is the medicine that, when accompanied with compassionate method, can clear away all obstructions such that unimpeded altruistic activity is manifested. Thus, though emptiness is a mere negative, it is a doctrine neither of nihilism nor of agnosticism, but a confident affirmation of a basic nature, the realization of which yields powerful, beneficial results.

Understood this way, realization of emptiness—the non-affirming negative that is the ultimate truth (not in the sense of being all that exists but in the sense of being something that exists the way it appears in direct perception)—not only indicates compatibility with knowledge of phenomena and activity but also is the key, when accompanied by practice of great compassion, to transformation into a supremely effective altruistic state.

With this exposition of negative phenomena as background, let us return to the controversy over whether Proponents of Mind-Only are proving a mere absence of a difference of entity between subject and object or are also proving that subject and object are one entity.

Do Practitioners Of Mind-Only Meditate On Mind-Only?

Jang-ḡya challenges the common Ge-luk-b̄a notion that the view of mind-only is just of a non-affirming negative. His argument that the view being realized also includes the oneness of entity of apprehended-object and apprehending-subject begins with establishing that one and many, or singular and plural, are a dichotomy. He does this so as to suggest that, upon proving that subject and object are not different, they are necessarily realized to be one entity. He[242] says:

> When it is refuted that a patch of blue and the eye consciousness apprehending it are different substantial entities, they must be

> established as one substantial entity because those two are substantially established, and one and different are a dichotomy. If one and different were not a dichotomy such that—within the context of existent phenomena—the elimination of oneness affirms difference and the elimination of difference affirms oneness, all of the reasonings of the lack of being either one or plural [or one and many, or one and different] such as the proof that a person is selfless through the reason of being devoid of true oneness or true plurality would absurdly be indecisive.

Jang-gya posits a hypothetical objection that is based on the assumption that a mere negative must be what is being proven:

> *Objection:* That is true, but a mere negation of a difference of substantial entity is taken as the predicate of the probandum,[a] whereas a oneness of substantial entity is not taken as the predicate of the probandum, because a non-affirming negative that is a mere elimination of an object of negation must be the predicate of the probandum, since that is the procedure of proofs delineating the ultimate.

In response, Jang-gya affirms that in the texts of Nāgārjuna and his spiritual sons and in Dzong-ka-ba's commentaries on Nāgārjuna's *Treatise on the Middle* and Chandrakīrti's *Supplement to (Nāgārjuna's) "Treatise on the Middle"* as well as Gyel-tsap's commentary on Maitreya's *Ornament for Clear Realization* and Ke-drup's *Opening the Eyes of the Fortunate,* and so forth, it is repeatedly said that in the Middle Way School a non-affirming negative must be the predicate of the probandum (such as in proving that a body is empty of true existence) and that this is a fundamental tenet of that school.[b] However, he says that such should not be extended to the Mind-Only School. He offers these reasons:

- Neither Indian texts of the Mind-Only School nor texts by Dzong-ka-ba and his two spiritual sons, Gyel-tsap and Ke-drup, say that only a non-affirming negative is to be taken as the predicate of the probandum in proofs of selflessness in the Mind-Only School system. Even though Gyel-tsap[243] in his commentary on Dharmakīrti's *Ascertainment of Prime Cognition* says that, in the case of the reasoning of the simultaneity of the

[a] The probandum is what is being proven; it consists of a subject and predicate, as in "The subject, a patch of blue and eye consciousness apprehending it, are not different entities." In this example, "a patch of blue and eye consciousness apprehending it" is the subject, and "not different entities" is the predicate.

[b] Jang-gya (*Presentation of Tenets,* 251.18) points out that this can be understood also from Bhāvaviveka's criticizing Buddhapālita for contradicting the tenet of the Middle Way School that a non-affirming negative is to be taken as the predicate of the probandum. For an extended discussion of this topic, see Jeffrey Hopkins, *Meditation on Emptiness* (London: Wisdom, 1983; rev. ed., Boston: Wisdom, 1996), 455-468.

certification of subject and object, a non-affirming negative must be what is proven, Gyel-tsap never says this with regard to the Mind-Only system in general.

- Most of the reasonings put forward to prove cognition-only in Asaṅga's *Summary of the Great Vehicle, Grounds of Bodhisattvas,* and *Compendium of Ascertainments* as well as in Vasubandhu's *The Twenty* and *The Thirty* take just cognition-only (which is an affirming negative) as the predicate of the probandum.
- Many reasonings described in Dignāga's *Compilation of Prime Cognition* and Dharmakīrti's *Commentary on (Dignāga's) "Compilation of Prime Cognition"* and *Ascertainment of Prime Cognition* as well as their commentaries—such as the reasoning proving that forms and so forth are of the substantial entity of the consciousness apprehending them, the reasoning proving the feasibility of the presentation of two modes among awarenesses, and the reasoning proving the feasibility of the observed-object-condition[a] of a sense consciousness according to Mind-Only system—mostly take affirming negatives or positive phenomena as the predicate of the probandum, and these are said to prove selflessness.

Concluding this part of his presentation, J̄ang-ḡya self-consciously announces that he is sticking his neck out, proclaiming the opinion[b] that in the Mind-Only system the reasonings proving selflessness do not have to prove a non-affirming negative. As Jik-may-dam-chö-gya-tso[244] summarizes J̄ang-ḡya's position (before rejecting it), cognition-only is both what is found by a reasoning consciousness analyzing the ultimate and the predicate of the probandum in a syllogism proving the ultimate.

J̄ang-ḡya does not leave the matter there; through citing another hypothetical objection he reveals what is behind the opponent's position that just a non-affirming negative is proven in the reasonings establishing the selflessness of phenomena is an over-anxious attempt to maintain that in the Middle Way School just a non-affirming negative is being proven:

> *Objection:* Your proposition is that, due to the fact that oneness of substantial entity and difference of substantial entity are a dichotomy, when difference is refuted, oneness must be established, whereby it is suitable for the reasonings proving selflessness also to prove oneness of substantial entity. However, this is not feasible. For, if that were the case, then in the system of the Middle Way School when it is proven

a *dmigs rkyen, alambanapratyaya.*

b J̄ang-ḡya's *Presentation of Tenets,* 252.13: *kho bo cag mgrin pa bsal nas 'chad do.* It could be speculated that J̄ang-ḡya's openness to this reinterpretation within Ge-luk-ba scholarship arose from his presence in Beijing and knowledge of Mind-Only Buddhism in China. Indeed, he chose to begin writing this book on all four Indian Buddhist schools with an exposition of the Mind-Only School.

> that a sprout, for instance, does not truly exist, that it conventionally exists would also become what is proven, since—in the context of existent phenomena—if something is not truly existent, it necessarily is conventionally existent.

Jang-ḡya agrees that in the Middle Way School just a non-affirming negative is what is being proven, and thus he responds that the two cases are not parallel because:

- in the system of the Middle Way School a reasoning consciousness analyzing the ultimate is examining whether a sprout truly exists or not and is not examining whether or not it conventionally exists, and hence a mere elimination of true existence is what is being proven—not that it conventionally exists or that an absence of true existence exists
- many texts of the Middle Way School, such as Nāgārjuna's *Refutation of Objections,* explain that, since truly existing and not truly existing are explicit contradictories, when one is eliminated the other must be established.

However, the hypothetical opponent persists:

> *Objection:* Even in the Mind-Only system a reasoning consciousness analyzing the ultimate is examining whether, for instance, a patch of blue and the eye consciousness apprehending it are or are not different substantial entities and is not examining whether they are or are not one substantial entity.

Jang-ḡya responds by way of multiple reasons that this is a wrong notion:

1. It contradicts the tenets of the Mind-Only School for four reasons:

- The Mind-Only tenet system is distinguished by its propounding that these appearances of visible forms, sounds, and so forth as if they were external objects are actually of the nature of internal consciousness or the substantial entity of consciousness.
- The reasonings proving that imputational factors are not established by way of their own character and that forms are empty of being external objects are said to be techniques for entering into the suchness of cognition-only.
- The suchness of cognition-only is asserted to be the final suchness to be meditated upon by Bodhisattvas.
- The suchness of cognition-only is asserted to be just the oneness of entity of forms, and so forth, and consciousness.

2. It contradicts reason:

- If—through the reasoning examining whether or not forms, and so forth, exist as different substantial entities from consciousness—Proponents of

Mind-Only did not realize that forms, and so forth, are of the entity of consciousness, then through this procedure they could not feasibly enter into, that is to say, understand, cognition-only.

- If—through the reasoning examining whether or not forms, and so forth, exist as different substantial entities from consciousness—Proponents of Mind-Only realize that forms, and so forth, are of the entity of consciousness, then, if they realize cognition-only through that reasoning, this would contradict the position that the reasoning analyzing the ultimate does not find that forms, and so forth, are of the entity of consciousness.
- If another reasoning is needed to realize that forms, and so forth, are of the entity of consciousness, then a consciousness realizing that forms, and so forth, are the same substantial entity as consciousness would not be a consciousness that analyzes the ultimate, whereby it would absurdly have to be a consciousness analyzing the conventional. In that case, Proponents of Mind-Only would hold the amazing position that a valid cognition analyzing the ultimate does not find suchness, whereas a valid cognition analyzing the conventional realizes the suchness of cognition-only.
- Furthermore, if this reasoning—that analyzes whether or not forms are different substantial entities from consciousness but, according to the opponent, does not analyze whether or not they are one entity—is a decisive reasoning with respect to the mode of being of forms, then demonstrate what harm there would be to the (obviously unacceptable) position that the reasoning analyzing the mode of being of persons analyzes whether a self-sufficient person exists or does not exist as truly different from the mental and physical aggregates but does not analyze whether or not a self-sufficient person exists or does not exist as truly one with the mental and physical aggregates is a decisive reasoning with respect to the mode of being of the person!
- If the opponent claims that it is not a decisive reasoning but is the supreme of reasonings analyzing the mode of being, then J̄ang-ḡya complains that he could not bear to debate with someone who puts forth a proposition the mere utterance of which exposes its own weakness.[a]

J̄ang-ḡya's detailed presentation that the reasonings proving emptiness in the Mind-Only system also prove cognition-only, an affirming negative, reveal the importance he attaches to the point.

Response To J̄ang-ḡya

Most Ge-luk-b̄a scholars find it particularly irksome that this respected scholar holds that the reasonings proving emptiness also prove mind-only, since

[a] See J̄ang-ḡya (*Presentation of Tenets,* 254.15ff.) for a third set of reasonings that revolve around the topic of prime cognition and its fruit.

mind-only would become a final object of observation by a path of purification and thus an ultimate and a thoroughly established nature. Gung-tang,[a] perhaps for political reasons, refrains from open criticism. Also, his call to his readers to examine whether Jang-gya is just saying this to accord with earlier assertions is uncharacteristically limp, given that Jang-gya explicitly says he is sticking out his neck and lays out such a careful argument. However, A-ku Lo-drö-gya-tso[245] feels no such restraint, pointedly remarking that Jang-gya's assertion "contradicts the entire systems of the Proponents of Mind-Only Following Scripture and Proponents of Mind-Only Following Reasoning."

A-ku Lo-drö-gya-tso treats the issue at length,[246] but Jik-may-dam-chö-gya-tso[247] breaks Jang-gya's argument down into thirteen propositions and methodically, if at times laconically, refutes them. Therefore, let us turn to his exposition.

1. **Jang-gya:** Neither Indian texts of the Mind-Only School nor texts by Dzong-ka-ba and his two spiritual sons, Gyel-tsap and Ke-drup, say that only a non-affirming negative is to be taken as the predicate of the probandum in proofs of selflessness in the Mind-Only School system.

   Jik-may-dam-chö-gya-tso: This is not right because, aside from the numerous citations—in Dzong-ka-ba's *The Essence of Eloquence,* Ke-drup's *Opening the Eyes of the Fortunate,* and so forth—of the *Sūtra Unraveling the Thought* as well as Asaṅga's and Vasubandhu's own texts that even in the Mind-Only system a non-affirming negative is posited as the thoroughly established nature explicitly proven by the reasoning proving selflessness, nothing clearer is needed. Also, *The Essence* says that in both the Mind-Only School and the Middle Way School the entity of the ultimate truth is a non-affirming negative:[248]

   > Therefore, except for differences in the object of negation, the two openers of the chariot-ways agree in positing as the ultimate truth just the elimination of self—the respective object

[a] Gung-tang's *Annotations,* 26.2. Gung-tang (*Annotations,* 26.1) and A-ku Lo-drö-gya-tso (*Precious Lamp,* 97.6) call attention to evidence, presumably cited by others, that the thoroughly established nature is **not** just a mere absence—specifically, the statement in Asaṅga's *Summary of Manifest Knowledge* that the four subsequent forbearances and four subsequent knowledges of the path of seeing (see *Absorption,* #144) have an apprehender, that is, a consciousness, as their object. They explain away Asaṅga's statement by maintaining that:

- He is referring to an ascertaining consciousness that arises **after** those subsequent forbearances and subsequent knowledges and is induced by them.
- He is not referring to the objects comprehended by the actual subsequent forbearances and subsequent knowledges.

In order to square Asaṅga's statement here with his statements described above (p. 240), such a tack does indeed have to be taken, and thus I do not think that Gung-tang and A-ku Lo-drö-gya-tso are merely explaining away a contrary statement.

> of negation—in dependent-arisings that are the bases of negation. Hence, it is not feasible to posit an ultimate other than that.

Also, Ke-drup's *Great Exposition of Instructions on the View*[a] says that in the face of a reasoning consciousness analyzing the ultimate (that is, a consciousness realizing the ultimate) there is nothing other than just a non-affirming negative:

> Concerning the selflessness of phenomena in the Mind-Only system...it is definite that, except for only a non-affirming negative that is the elimination of such an imputational nature, appearances of other-powered natures have vanished [in the face of the realization of suchness].

Comment:[b] I agree with Jik-may-dam-chö-gya-tso that the *Sūtra Unraveling the Thought* makes many statements indicating that the ultimate is a mere negative (see pp. 261-265) and that D̄zong-ka-b̄a emphasizes this point. However, on three occasions[249] Jik-may-dam-chö-gya-tso himself makes reference to several places in the writings of D̄zong-ka-b̄a's student Ke-drup that the clear light nature of the mind is a thoroughly established nature. Similarly, it is necessary for most Ge-luk-b̄a scholars to write off the fact that an exalted wisdom itself is called a non-perverse, or non-erroneous, thoroughly established nature by claiming that this is an extension of the category of the object, emptiness, to the subject, the wisdom consciousness.[c] As Ḡön-chok-jik-may-w̄ang-b̄o says:[250]

> When divided, there are two types of thoroughly established natures, non-perverse and immutable. An example of the first is a Superior's wisdom during meditative equipoise. An example of the second is the real nature of phenomena. Although non-perverse thoroughly established natures are stated as a division of thoroughly established natures, they [actually] are not thoroughly established natures. This is because they are not final objects of observation by a path of purification through observation of which obstructions are extinguished.

2. **J̄ang-ḡya:** Most of the reasonings put forward to prove cognition-only in Asaṅga's *Summary of the Great Vehicle, Grounds of Bodhisattvas,* and *Compendium of Ascertainments* as well as in Vasubandhu's *The Twenty* and *The Thirty* take just cognition-only (which is an affirming negative) as the predicate of the probandum.

---

[a] *lta khrid chen mo.*

[b] In order not to leave the debate with Jik-may-dam-chö-gya-tso's response, as if he has the last word, I add open-ended comments to suggest that these issues are difficult to settle.

[c] See also three instances of D̄zong-ka-b̄a's explaining away statements that a wisdom consciousness itself is an ultimate (*Emptiness in Mind-Only,* 163-165, 166-167).

Jik-may-dam-chö-gya-tso: This is wrong because, although—among the theses being proven by reasonings explicitly proving selflessness in Asaṅga's *Summary of the Great Vehicle* and so forth—some are non-affirming negatives and some are not, only a non-affirming negative is held to be the **fundamental** explicit predicate of the probandum.

Comment: Jik-may-dam-chö-gya-tso seems to be trying to wiggle out of the spot J̄ang-ḡya has put him in; his position needs to be documented if it is to be anything more than a claim.

3. **J̄ang-ḡya:** Many reasonings described in Dignāga's *Compilation of Prime Cognition* and Dharmakīrti's *Commentary on (Dignāga's) "Compilation of Prime Cognition"* and *Ascertainment of Prime Cognition* as well as their commentaries—such as the reasoning proving that forms and so forth are of the substantial entity of the consciousness apprehending them, the reasoning proving the feasibility of the presentation of two modes among awarenesses, and the reasoning proving the feasibility of the observed-object-condition of a sense consciousness according to the Mind-Only system—mostly take affirming negatives or positive phenomena as the predicate of the probandum, and these are said to prove selflessness.

   Jik-may-dam-chö-gya-tso: This is wrong because those three reasonings, aside from proving selflessness indirectly, do not explicitly do so.

Comment: Again, Jik-may-dam-chö-gya-tso gives the distinct impression—by claiming that these reasonings prove selflessness only indirectly—that he is attempting to wriggle out of a tight spot. More elaboration is needed to make his position convincing.

4. **J̄ang-ḡya:** The Mind-Only tenet system is distinguished by its propounding that these appearances of visible forms, sounds, and so forth as if they are external objects are actually of the nature of internal consciousness; they are the substantial entity of consciousness. Hence, a reasoning consciousness analyzing the ultimate must be examining whether or not forms, and so forth, are the same substantial entity as consciousness.

   Jik-may-dam-chö-gya-tso: Such is not entailed, for then it would absurdly follow that, even in the Consequence School, a reasoning consciousness analyzing the ultimate would be examining whether objects are merely imputed, because the tenet system of the Consequence School is distinguished by its propounding that objects are merely imputed by conceptuality. The entailment is parallel.

Comment: It does not seem to me that the two cases are exactly parallel, since the single most fundamental tenet of the Mind-Only School is that objects are of the same entity as the consciousness apprehending them, whereas in the

Consequence School the tenet that objects are merely imputed by conceptuality, despite being crucial, is not the single most fundamental tenet of the school, which is that objects are empty of inherent existence.

5. **J̄ang-ḡya:** The reasonings proving that imputational factors are not established by way of their own character and that forms are empty of being external objects are said to be techniques for entering into the suchness of cognition-only, and hence an affirming negative is being established.

   Jik-may-dam-chö-gya-tso: Such is not entailed because the suchness of cognition-only is the non-affirming negative that is the emptiness of a difference of substantial entity between apprehended-object and apprehending-subject.

Comment: Jik-may-dam-chö-gya-tso, here and in his responses to items 6 through 7, 9, and 10, insists that the suchness of cognition-only is a mere non-affirming negative—the elimination of a difference of substantial entity between a form and the consciousness apprehending it, for example—and is not a oneness of substantial entity of apprehended-object and apprehending-subject. However, it strikes me as odd that, if Asaṅga and so forth merely meant that realization of the emptiness of external objects is a technique for (that is, toward) understanding a mere negative of a difference of entity between subject and object, they would incur the fault of redundancy, since the two realizations would be exactly the same. It strikes me as counter-intuitive to use the term "cognition-only" for a mere negative. I find it similarly unsatisfying to claim, as most Ge-luk-ḡba scholars do, that, when Nāgārjuna uses the term "clear light" in the sūtra system he is referring to a mere negative of inherent existence.

6. & 7. **J̄ang-ḡya:** The suchness of cognition-only is asserted to be the final suchness to be meditated upon by Bodhisattvas, and the suchness of cognition-only is asserted to be just the oneness of substantial entity of forms, and so forth, and consciousness; hence an affirming negative is being established.

   Jik-may-dam-chö-gya-tso: There is no entailment because the suchness of consciousness cognition-only is taken to be the non-affirming negative that is the emptiness of a difference of substantial entity between apprehended-object and apprehending-subject and because that non-affirming negative is what is meant by the oneness of essence of forms, and so forth, and consciousness.

Comment: See the comment to item 5.

8. **J̄ang-ḡya:** If—through the reasoning examining whether or not forms, and so forth, exist as different substantial entities from consciousness—Proponents of Mind-Only did not realize that forms, and so forth, are of

the essence of consciousness, then through this procedure they could not feasibly enter into, that is to say, understand, cognition-only.

Jik-may-dam-chö-gya-tso: This is wrong because otherwise there would be the absurd consequence that in the system of the Consequence School the reasoning explicitly proving selflessness would not be able to bring about (subsequent) understanding that objects are merely nominal and are merely imputed. This is because it does not explicitly find anything other than a mere negative of true existence.

Comment: Here and in his response to item 11, Jik-may-dam-chö-gya-tso employs the negative reasoning that, if a tenet of the Middle Way School would not be feasible, a parallel tenet could not be allowed in the Mind-Only School. While I find the challenge provocative, it again indicates that the assertion that in the Middle Way School just a non-affirming negative is being proven is so central (and perhaps so sensitive) that it is used to determine the tenets of other schools.

9. **J̄ang-ḡya:** If—through the reasoning examining whether or not forms, and so forth, exist as different substantial entities from consciousness—Proponents of Mind-Only realize that forms, and so forth, are of the essence of consciousness, then, if they realize cognition-only through that reasoning, this would contradict the position that the reasoning analyzing the ultimate does not find the suchness of cognition-only.

   Jik-may-dam-chö-gya-tso: There is no such fallacy because we do not assert that—through the reasoning examining whether or not forms, and so forth, exist as different substantial entities from consciousness—it is realized that forms, and so forth, are of the essence of consciousness.

Comment: See the comment to item 5.

10. **J̄ang-ḡya:** If cognition-only is found through another reasoning, then a consciousness analyzing the ultimate would not find the suchness of cognition-only.

    Jik-may-dam-chö-gya-tso: This is wrong because:

    - It is permissible that a oneness of substantial entity of apprehended-object and apprehending-subject is found through a reasoning such as "A form and the consciousness apprehending it are one substantial entity because of being phenomena produced within not being separate in terms of substantial entity," but such an inference, aside from analyzing a conventionality, does not analyze the ultimate.
    - A oneness of substantial entity of a form and the consciousness apprehending it is not the suchness of cognition-only.

Comment: See the comment to item 5.

11. **J̄ang-ḡya:** The reasoning that analyzes whether or not forms are different substantial entities from consciousness but, according to the opponent, does not analyze whether or not they are one entity would not be a decisive reasoning with respect to the mode of being of forms.

    Jik-may-dam-chö-gya-tso: In analyzing whether something in question exists or does not exist as different substantial entities, it is not being analyzed whether they are one substantial entity, but such a reasoning does not thereby become indecisive with respect to the mode of being. This is because to analyze whether something in question exists or does not exist as a substantial entity it is necessary to analyze whether it exists as one substantial entity or different substantial entities, but to analyze whether something exists or does not exist as different substantial entities it is not necessary to analyze whether it exists or does not exist as one substantial entity. This is because it is like the fact that to analyze whether something does or does not truly exist, it is necessary to analyze whether it exists as a truly existent one or a truly existent plurality, but to analyze whether something does not exist as a truly existent one, it is not necessary to analyze whether it exists as a truly existent plurality.

Comment: See the comment to item 8.

12. **J̄ang-ḡya:** This reasoning—that analyzes whether or not forms are different substantial entities from the consciousness apprehending them—establishes that a form and the consciousness apprehending it are one entity and thus is a decisive reasoning with respect to the mode of being of forms.

    Jik-may-dam-chö-gya-tso: If it were the case that the reason (that is, the denial that a patch of blue and the consciousness apprehending it are different substantial entities) proves that those two are one substantial entity, then there would have to be cases of having ascertained the reason (that is, that those two are not different substantial entities) but not having ascertained the thesis (that is, that those two are one substantial entity). Hence, this fact, rather than aiding your position, harms it.

Comment: Jik-may-dam-chö-gya-tso's point is that, if the reason proves the thesis, then there must be someone who has realized the reason but has not yet realized the thesis. In Buddhist logic, a reason is valid only if there is someone who has realized the reason but not yet the thesis that it proves; reasoning is not abstract but bound to a situation of creating new understanding. If that is so, then knowledge that a form and the consciousness apprehending it are not different substantial entities does not imply knowledge that they are one substantial entity. The point is well-taken, but I presume that J̄ang-ḡya would respond that he is referring to just such a process.

13. **J̄ang-ḡya:** Even though Gyel-tsap in his commentary on Dharmakīrti's *Ascertainment of Prime Cognition* says that, in the case of the reasoning of the simultaneity of the certification of subject and object, a non-affirming negative must be what is proven, Gyel-tsap never says this with regard to the Mind-Only system in general.

Jik-may-dam-chö-gya-tso: If Gyel-tsap's statement is not in reference to the Mind-Only system in general, then J̄ang-ḡya ought to say whose system it is!

Comment: It seems to me that J̄ang-ḡya could answer that this is the system of Dharmakīrti's *Ascertainment of Prime Cognition* and that it is unwarranted to extend every position of that text to the Mind-Only system in general. As Jik-may-dam-chö-gya-tso[251] himself says after explaining the reasoning of the certainty of simultaneous certification of subject and object, it needs to be analyzed why, whereas the reasoning of the certainty of simultaneous certification is the main reasoning delineating the emptiness of difference of entity of subject and object, D̄zong-ka-b̄a (*Emptiness in Mind-Only,* 218) does not even put it in his list of reasonings proving the emptiness of difference of entity of subject and object. He says no more, but the obvious motive behind D̄zong-ka-b̄a's not even listing it is that he did not view the reasoning of certainty of simultaneous certification—which is given in both Dharmakīrti's *Commentary on (Dignāga's) "Compilation of Prime Cognition"* and his *Ascertainment of Prime Cognition*—as a **main** reasoning settling the emptiness of difference of entity of subject and object in the Mind-Only School simply because it is never mentioned by Maitreya, Asaṅga, Vasubandhu, and Dignāga.[a] I will stick my neck out and say that the statement renowned and repeated among Ge-luk-b̄a scholars that the emptiness of apprehended-object and apprehending-subject as different entities cannot be demonstrated without the reasoning of the certainty of simultaneous certification is a deprecation of the Mind-Only works of Maitreya, Asaṅga, Vasubandhu, and Dignāga and does not take into account the fact that, as J̄ang-ḡya[252] says, it is unclear in the writings of Asaṅga whether he asserts self-cognizing consciousness or not and the reasoning revolves around such an assertion.

a It might seem that D̄zong-ka-b̄a is willing to mention a reasoning mentioned by none of these authors when he (*Emptiness in Mind-Only,* 218) lists Dharmakīrti's "reasoning refuting that the character of an apprehending-subject is produced from the apprehended-object and is similar to the apprehended-object," but this reasoning is an enlargement of Dignāga's "reasoning refuting that an aggregation of particles or an [individual] minute particle."

Other-Powered Natures Are Not The Ultimate But Are Ultimately Established

Other-powered natures such as chairs, tables, and minds are not ultimates, but does this fact also mean that other-powered natures do not ultimately exist and do not exist by way of their own character? At the end of this section on the fact that other-powered natures are ultimate-non-natures because they are not final objects of observation by a path of purification, Ḏzong-ka-ḇa refers to a later explanation in connection with Asaṅga's *Compendium of Ascertainments*[a] that, even though other-powered natures are not ultimates, they are ultimately established. He (*Emptiness in Mind-Only,* 90) says:

> Although other-powered natures are not established as the ultimate when [the term] ultimate is taken as [referring to] the object of observation of purification, it will be explained later whether or not they are established as another [type of] ultimate.

As Jam-ȳang-shay-ḇa[253] frames his meaning, other-powered natures are not ultimates in the sense of being final objects of observation by a path of purification simply because they are not ultimate truths, but they are ultimately established because they are not merely imputed by conceptuality.

Jik-may-dam-chö-gya-tso[254] adds a further reason why other-powered natures are ultimately established—this being that viewing them not to be ultimately established is considered a view of deprecation in the Mind-Only system. In commenting on Asaṅga's *Grounds of Bodhisattvas,* Ḏzong-ka-ḇa (*Emptiness in Mind-Only,* 142-143) says:

> The mode of deprecating other-powered things is not [constituted by considering them] "not to exist conventionally" or "not to exist in general" [as the extreme of deprecation is described in the Consequence School]; rather, it is in accordance with the earlier explanation [by Asaṅga] that [conceiving] the **ultimately** existent not to exist [ultimately] is a deprecation.

The "earlier explanation" (*Emptiness in Mind-Only,* 141) is Asaṅga's clear statement in the *Grounds of Bodhisattvas:*

> ...there are those who ruin [the doctrine of the Great Vehicle and the correct delineation of suchness by] making deprecation—of [other-powered natures, that is to say,] real things ultimately existing with an inexpressible essence, which serve as the bases of the signs of imputed words, the supports of the signs of imputed words—as "not existing in each and every way."

Once it is a deprecation to view other-powered natures as not ultimately

[a] See *Emptiness in Mind-Only,* 144, and mainly 158 through the end of the chapter.

existing, it is clear that in this system impermanent phenomena, despite not being ultimate truths, do ultimately exist.

Basic Message Of The First Ultimate-Non-Nature

The passage in the *Sūtra Unraveling the Thought* that posits other-powered natures and not imputational natures as ultimate-non-natures emphasizes the frequently reiterated point that other-powered natures are not the thoroughly established nature—they are not their own final mode of subsistence. Also, since beings usually conceive not just the mind but any other-powered nature to be its own real nature, it is relevant to emphasize, at least for beginners, that each and every other-powered nature is not its own ultimate.

Gung-tang[255] explains that Buddha's teaching the first mode of positing the ultimate-non-nature—that is, that other-powered natures are without the nature of being the ultimate—is for the sake of trainees' understanding the fact they must delineate the second mode of positing the ultimate-non-nature—the thoroughly established nature. Brilliantly synthesizing the basic thrust of the Great Vehicle tenets systems, he explains that the beginningless wandering of sentient beings in cyclic existence is due to adhering to the mode of appearance of phenomena as if it were true and thereupon being drawn into desire and hatred. These afflictive emotions, in turn, motivate contaminated actions that establish potencies in the mind, refueling the process of cyclic existence. Therefore, in order to cut the root of cyclic existence, it is necessary to stop assenting to exaggerated appearances, and since this cannot be accomplished by making them not appear as by closing one's eyes, it is necessary to desist from adhering to the present mode of appearance as if it were the mode of subsistence of things—it is necessary to examine the meaning of emptiness, the actual mode of being. If this were not the case and there were no hidden mode of subsistence beyond how other-powered natures are seen, heard, and known at present by ordinary beings, it would absurdly follow that all common beings would have already seen the truth and that yogis' analytical search for the ultimate mode of subsistence of phenomena would be senseless. As the third chapter of the *Sūtra Unraveling the Thought* says:[256]

> If the character of compositional phenomena and the character of the ultimate were not different, then even all childish ordinary beings would see the truth, and, while ordinary beings, they would attain the highest achievement and would attain blissful nirvāṇa. Moreover, they would have manifestly and completely realized unsurpassed, perfect enlightenment.

And:[257]

> Yogis also would not search for an ultimate beyond all compositional

> things as they are seen, as they are heard, as they are differentiated, and as they are thoroughly known.

By citing these passages, Gung-tang embeds this spiritual appeal in the context of the *Sūtra Unraveling the Thought,* which makes these points in a discussion of the relation between the ultimate and phenomena—the primary message being that though the ultimate is not separate from phenomena, it is not constituted by those phenomena themselves.

Gung-tang adds that no matter how much the Mind-Only and the Middle Way Schools differ with respect to the boundaries of what constitutes the ultimate, they agree in asserting that if one adheres to the mere way things presently appear, one is bound in cyclic existence. In order to proceed on the path releasing one from cyclic existence it is necessary to cease adhering to how things appear as if this were their mode of being.

Gung-tang describes the plight of cyclic existence as being based on untrained assent to the false appearance of phenomena. He offers a straightforwardly simple and penetratingly profound exposition that Buddha taught the first mode of positing the ultimate-non-nature so that his listeners would realize that other-powered natures do not constitute the ultimate and thereby would be stimulated to seek the actual ultimate which Buddha is about to describe in the second mode of positing the ultimate-non-nature.

15. Thoroughly Established Natures

Actual Ultimate-Non-Natures

Thoroughly established natures[a] are called ultimate-non-natures because they are the ultimate and are the non-existence of the nature of the object negated in selflessness. As we have seen in the previous chapter, the *Sūtra Unraveling the Thought* (*Emptiness in Mind-Only,* 88) calls other-powered natures ultimate-non-natures because they are **not** objects of observation by a path of purification; it then (*Emptiness in Mind-Only,* 90) goes on to explain how thoroughly established natures are ultimate-non-natures:

> What are ultimate-non-natures? Those dependently arisen phenomena—which are natureless due to being natureless in terms of production—are also natureless due to being natureless in terms of the ultimate.
>
> Why? Paramārthasamudgata, that which is an object of observation of purification in phenomena I teach to be the ultimate, and other-powered characters are not the object of observation of purification. Therefore, they are said to be "ultimate-non-natures."
>
> Moreover, that which is the thoroughly established character of phenomena is also called "the ultimate-non-nature." Why? Paramārthasamudgata, that which in phenomena is the selflessness of phenomena is called their "non-nature." It is the ultimate, and the ultimate is distinguished by just the naturelessness of all phenomena; therefore, it is called the "ultimate-non-nature."

The thoroughly established nature is **just** the absence of "nature" or "self," which, in terms of the selflessness of phenomena explicitly indicated in this part of the *Sūtra Unraveling the Thought,* refers to objects' being established by way of their own character as the referents of conceptual consciousnesses.

At this juncture, Ge-luk-b̄a scholars cite only the passage in the *Sūtra Unraveling the Thought* given above as an illustration of the sūtra's position on the ultimate; however, there are many more such passages that are particularly telling to cite, given the proclivity of some American, European, and Japanese scholars to interpret the thoroughly established nature as a purified version of other-powered natures. Since these passages lend considerable credence to the notion that the ultimate, according to the *Sūtra Unraveling the Thought,* is a mere absence of self—this view being at variance with more positive identifications of the ultimate—let us cite all of them.

In the third chapter of the *Sūtra Unraveling the Thought,* called the

---

[a] For an extensive discussion of thoroughly established natures, see *Absorption,* #147-167.

"Questions of the Bodhisattva Suvishuddhamati," Buddha explains how the character of the ultimate (the thoroughly established nature) and the character of compositional phenomena (other-powered natures) are neither different nor non-different; he does this by indicating four fallacies that would result from each position. In indicating the fallacies in holding that the character of the ultimate and the character of compounded phenomena are different, Buddha (*Emptiness in Mind-Only,* 91) says:[258]

> If the character [that is, entity] of compositional things[a] and the character of the ultimate were different [entities],[259] then just the **mere** selflessness and the **mere** naturelessness [of the self of phenomena] of compositional things would not be [their] ultimate character.

Buddha indicates that, if the character, or entity, of the ultimate, were isolatedly different from compounded entities, then it could not be said that the selflessness of compounded phenomena is their own ultimate character, for it would be totally separate.

In saying this, Buddha refers to the ultimate character as "just the mere absence of self and just the mere absence of inherent nature of compounded phenomena."[b] He clearly says that the ultimate, the thoroughly established nature, is constituted by a mere absence. It is crucial to note that in making the point that the ultimate and compounded phenomena are neither different nor non-different, Buddha does not draw the conclusion that compounded phenomena—other-powered natures—are the ultimate; he clearly describes the ultimate as a mere absence. From this, we see the cogency of A-ku Lo-drö-gya-tso's assertion that, since the tenets of the Mind-Only School are primarily based on the *Sūtra Unraveling the Thought,* anyone familiar with its tenets mostly would not suspect that other-powered natures such as the mind are the final object of observation of an exalted wisdom purifying obstructions, that is to say, the thoroughly established nature. Those not so familiar, however, could easily have such a qualm.

Buddha goes on to say that compounded phenomena have different characters and then draws the following conclusion:

> And so yogis also search for an ultimate beyond all compounded things as they are seen, as they are heard, as they are differentiated, and

---

[a] *'du byed, saṃskāra.* In this context, the term may have a wide meaning that also includes permanent phenomena such as uncompounded space; in that case, it would mean "all phenomena," rather than just compositional things, which are necessarily impermanent. However, Wel-mang Gön-chok-gyel-tsen's *Notes on (Gön-chok-jik-may-wang-bo's) Lectures* (402.1) glosses "compositional things" (*'du byed*) with "compounded things" (*'dus byas*), which excludes permanent phenomena.

[b] *'du byed rnams kyi bdag med pa tsam dang rang bzhin med pa tsam nyid* (*Sūtra Unraveling the Thought,* 24.1).

> as they are thoroughly known, and the ultimate is thoroughly distinguished by the **selflessness** of compounded things.

Here Buddha indicates that the ultimate is beyond compounded things (even if it is neither different nor non-different from them), and then he describes the ultimate as the selflessness of compounded things. He goes on to give examples of the ultimate and the compounded as being neither nor non-different—a conch and its whiteness; gold and its yellowness; a vina (a stringed instrument) and its melodiousness; the black *agaru* tree and its fragrant smell; pepper and its heat; the Indian almond[a] and its astringency; cotton and its softness; butter and clarified butter; compounded phenomena and their impermanence; contaminated things and suffering; phenomena and the selflessness of persons; desire and its unpeacefulness. All of these qualities are part and parcel of the things they characterize, but they are not those things themselves. Buddha concludes:

> Similarly, Suvishuddhamati, it is not easy to designate the character of the compounded and the character of the ultimate as being either different characters or non-different characters.

It is in such a context that Buddha, as quoted above, says that the ultimate—the thoroughly established nature—is just the mere absence of self.

Elaborating on this point, in the fourth chapter, the "Questions of Subhūti," Buddha speaks of the ultimate as being of one taste with all phenomena:

> Therefore, Subhūti, I thoroughly teach that the "ultimate" is that which is the object of observation for purification of the aggregates....That object of observation for purification is of one taste with all of the aggregates and is of a character which is not different [from the aggregates].

The ultimate is that through observation of which the mental and physical aggregates become purified. Though of one taste with the mental and physical aggregates and not of a different character from them, we know from the third chapter that it is not non-different from them also.

As in the passage from the seventh chapter, cited above, Buddha speaks, in the fourth chapter, of "thusness, the ultimate, the selflessness of phenomena" synonymously:

> Moreover, Subhūti, monastics who practice yoga, having completely realized thusness, the ultimate, the selflessness of phenomena of one aggregate do not [have to] seek individually for thusness, the ultimate, the selflessness of phenomena in those [phenomena] that are other than that...

The ultimate is just the selflessness of phenomena.

---

[a] *myrobalan arjuna; Terminalia catappa.*

That the ultimate is not compounded phenomena themselves, even if it is of one taste with them, is clear from Buddha's saying in the same chapter:

> If it were compounded, it would also not be the ultimate because of not being ultimate. It would be necessary to search for another ultimate.

The ultimate is not compounded phenomena themselves; it is a mere absence of self associated with compounded phenomena.

That the ultimate is something within compounded phenomena that, when seen and meditated upon, purifies the mind is clear in the sixth chapter, the "Questions of the Bodhisattva Guṇākara," which lays out the three natures. There, Buddha describes the imputational nature as "that which is posited by nominal terminology in the manner of entities and attributes of phenomena due to imputing whatsoever conventions." He describes the other-powered nature as "just the dependent-arising of phenomena." He describes the thoroughly established nature as "that which is the suchness of phenomena, that which Bodhisattvas realize through the cause of effort and through the cause of proper mental application" and says that "through thoroughly accomplishing familiarization with that, one thoroughly accomplishes [all of the stages] up to unsurpassed complete perfect enlightenment." That the thoroughly established nature is not the other-powered nature itself is clear again when Buddha says:

> Other-powered [natures] are permanently and forever thoroughly not established as [having] the imputational character, and are without that inherent nature; **just** that non-establishment or lack of inherent nature is to be viewed as the thoroughly established character.

Again, the thoroughly established nature is restricted by the term "just" to other-powered natures' non-establishment as having the imputational nature. The thoroughly established nature is a mere absence of that imputational nature in other-powered natures. Through contemplating it, one becomes purified.

Similarly, in the seventh chapter, the "Questions of the Bodhisattva Paramārthasamudgata," which is the focus of the Mind-Only section of Ḏzong-ka-ḇa's *The Essence of Eloquence,* Buddha speaks of the thoroughly established nature as just selflessness (*Emptiness in Mind-Only,* 90). This occurs right after his discussion of other-powered natures as being natureless in terms of the ultimate:

> Moreover, that which is the thoroughly established character of phenomena is also called "the ultimate-non-nature." Why? Paramārthasamudgata, that which in phenomena is the selflessness of phenomena is called their "non-nature." It is the ultimate, and the ultimate is

> distinguished by **just** the naturelessness of all phenomena; therefore, it is called the "ultimate-non-nature."

The ultimate is defined as selflessness and as being just the absence of the relevant nature—which here is objects' establishment by way of their own character as the referents of thought and language—in all phenomena.

Giving examples of the three non-natures, Buddha (*Emptiness in Mind-Only,* 94-95) compares the ultimate-non-nature to space, which is a mere absence of forms:

> Paramārthasamudgata, it is thus: just as, for example, space is distinguished by the **mere** naturelessness of form [that is, as a mere absence of forms] and pervades everywhere, so from between those [two] ultimate-non-natures, one [that is, the thoroughly established nature] is to be viewed as distinguished by the selflessness of phenomena and as pervading everything.

Just as uncompounded space is a mere absence of form, so the ultimate-non-nature is a mere absence of a self of phenomena. In these passages there is not even a hint that the ultimate is the mind or any other other-powered nature.

As Jam-ȳang-shay-b̄a[260] says, there is no way to assert that the thoroughly established nature is a positive entity, because the sūtra (*Emptiness in Mind-Only,* 90) clearly speaks of the thoroughly established nature as a non-affirming negative that is a mere negation of the self that is the object of negation:

> ...that which in phenomena is the selflessness of phenomena is called their "non-nature." It is the ultimate, and the ultimate is distinguished by **just** the naturelessness of all phenomena; therefore, it is called the "ultimate-non-nature."

The "naturelessness of all phenomena" to which the sūtra refers is the absence of the self that is the object of negation in relation to all phenomena, and "just the naturelessness" refers to **just** the non-existence of that object of negation or the **mere** non-existence of that object of negation. D̄zong-ka-b̄a (*Emptiness in Mind-Only,* 90-91) makes this point clearly:

> Since the thoroughly established nature of phenomena—the selflessness of phenomena[a]—is the object of observation of purification, it is the ultimate. Also, since it is distinguished by, that is to say, is posited by way of the mere naturelessness of a self in phenomena, it is also called "the non-nature of phenomena," whereby it is called "the ultimate-non-nature."

---

[a] Here, D̄zong-ka-b̄a specifies the thoroughly established nature as being the selflessness of **phenomena**, seeming to exclude the selflessness of persons; however, in other places he seems to include both. See *Absorption,* #153-167.

That the thoroughly established nature is "distinguished by just the naturelessness of all phenomena" means that it is posited by way of the mere nonexistence, or mere negation, of that object of negation. For the word "just"[a] is a negative term[b] meaning "only,"[c] and "distinguished"[d] means "posited."[e] For such reasons, Jam-ȳang-shay-b̄a[261] concludes that the thoroughly established nature cannot be said to be positive and independent; rather, it is a "non-affirming negative."[f] He emphasizes this point in contrast to S̄hay-rap-gyel-tsen's presentation that the ultimate is not a mere negative; see 273ff. and 316ff.

Realization Of The Ultimate Truth Is Not The Final Goal

Despite the Ge-luk-b̄a emphasis on the tenet that the thoroughly established nature is a mere emptiness, or absence, this does not mean that the goal of practice is either a mere negative or cognition of a mere absence.[262] Similarly, that the "ultimate truth" is a mere absence does not mean that the goal is a mere absence or realization of a mere absence; rather, the ultimate truth is the final nature of what exists. Because the terms "ultimate truth" and "thoroughly established nature" seem to suggest that only it finally exists and because the term "conventional truth" seems to suggest that objects such as tables exist only for an ignorant, or at least highly provisional, consciousness, it is understandable that many have mistakenly drawn the conclusion that the doctrine of the Great Vehicle Buddhism is excessively negative, unable to affirm the existence of anything except emptiness, which they take to be nothingness.

Much misinterpretation of Buddhism has come from suppositions that (1) since emptiness is the ultimate truth and the thoroughly established nature, realization of it must be the final state, and (2) since direct realization of emptiness requires withdrawing from phenomena, Buddhists are ultimately seeking an isolated state at best and obliteration at worst. The procedure of the spiritual path, however, indicates that these opinions are wrong. Direct realization of emptiness takes place at the beginning of the path of seeing, at which point the

a *nyid,* which in Sanskrit is, most likely, *eva.*

b Jik-may-dam-chö-gya-tso (*Port of Entry,* 196.2) objects to Jam-ȳang-shay-b̄a's calling *nyid* here a negative term, because it is not a negative term when it is used with the first two non-natures; Jik-may-dam-chö-gya-tso maintains that it is used for emphasis (*nges bzung*). However, Jam-ȳang-shay-b̄a's point must be that the (second) term *nyid* in *don dam pa ni chos thams cad kyi ngo bo nyid med pa* ***nyid*** *kyis rab tu phye ba yin pas* is used in the context of **limiting** that by which the ultimate is posited and thus is a negative term meaning "only" (*tsam*), which negates anything else. That the (second) *nyid* is used for emphasis and that it is a negative term do not strike me as mutually exclusive.

c *tsam, mātra.*

d *rab tu phye ba.*

e *rab tu bzhag pa.*

f *med dgag, prasajyapratiṣedha.*

first of the ten Bodhisattva grounds (called "grounds" because they are the basis on which other great mental qualities grow) is attained; thus it is clear that direct realization of the ultimate truth—the thoroughly established nature, emptiness—is not the final goal. Neither the thoroughly established nature nor the ultimate consciousness realizing it is the final goal; that goal is Buddhahood—a state of fully empowered capacity effectively to help others.

A thoroughly established nature—an ultimate truth—is a **specific** negative; in the Mind-Only School, this is, for instance, an absence of objects' being established by way of their own character as the referents of terms and conceptual consciousnesses. It is not everything that exists but the final mode of subsistence, the mode of being, of what exists, and thus it does not deny or cancel the existence of phenomena. That such is so and that the final state is not a mere absence are obvious from the *Sūtra Unraveling the Thought*'s long presentation (in its eighth chapter) of the stages of the path and (in the tenth chapter) of the Truth and Form Bodies of a Buddha. The thoroughly established nature, emptiness, is not the final state but a status of phenomena that must be taken as an object of observation and meditation in order to bring about purification.

With respect to the term "ultimate truth," a truth is something that exists the way it appears in direct perception. It does not deceive; there is no conflict between appearance and fact. An emptiness is an ultimate truth in that it is a **truth**,[a] existing the way it appears in direct perception, for an **ultimate**[b] consciousness.[c] In this context, an ultimate consciousness refers not to the final consciousness attained through practice of the path, that is to say, a Buddha's

---

a *bden pa, satya.*

b *don dam, paramārtha.*

c The Sanskrit for "ultimate truth," *paramārthasatya,* is etymologized three ways within identifying *parama* as "highest" or "ultimate," *artha* as "object," and *satya* as "truth." In the first way, *parama* (highest, ultimate) refers to a consciousness of meditative equipoise directly realizing emptiness; *artha* (object) refers to the object of that consciousness, emptiness; and *satya* (truth) also refers to emptiness in that in direct perception emptiness appears the way it exists; that is, there is no discrepancy between the mode of appearance and the mode of being. In this interpretation, a *paramārthasatya* is a "truth-that-is-an-object-of-the-highest-consciousness."

In the second way, both *parama* (highest, ultimate) and *artha* (object) refer to a consciousness of meditative equipoise directly realizing emptiness in that, in the broadest meaning of "object," both objects and subjects are objects, and a consciousness of meditative equipoise directly realizing emptiness is the highest consciousness and thus highest object; *satya* (truth), as before, refers to emptiness. In this second interpretation, a *paramārthasatya* is an emptiness that exists the way it appears to a highest consciousness, a "truth-of-a-highest-object."

In the third etymology, all three parts refer to emptiness in that an emptiness is the highest (the ultimate) and is also an object and a truth, a "truth-that-is-the-highest-object." See Donald S. Lopez Jr., *A Study of Svātantrika* (Ithaca, N.Y.: Snow Lion, 1986), 314-315. Chandrakīrti, the chief Consequentialist, favors the third etymology in his *Clear Words;* see Jang-gya's *Presentation of Tenets,* 467.18.

omniscient consciousness, but to a reasoning consciousness realizing emptiness. Such ultimate consciousnesses are of two varieties, non-conceptual and conceptual. A non-conceptual ultimate consciousness is one of meditative equipoise in which a yogi directly realizes emptiness, whereas a conceptual ultimate consciousness is one that realizes emptiness through the medium of a conceptual image. Both are called "reasoning consciousnesses,"[a] most likely because they are generated from having **analyzed with reasoning** to determine whether an object exists in accordance with the superimposition of the imputational nature.

Hence, even though an emptiness is an ultimate truth and a thoroughly established nature, it is not all that exists, and it does not negate other phenomena. For conventional truths also exist, and an emptiness is merely an absence of a falsely conceived status of a phenomenon, not the non-existence of that phenomenon. Thus, emptiness is the ultimate truth and the thoroughly established nature but not in the sense that finally, when you get right down it, it and only it exists and everything else only exists for ignorance and not in the sense that realization of it constitutes the ultimate state. Rather, it is the mode of subsistence of things that appears non-delusively to a consciousness of meditative equipoise and thus is a truth-for-an-ultimate-consciousness.

Everything else appears delusively, even in direct perception, except to a Buddha. Aside from the context of the direct perception of emptiness, everything appears to be established by way of its own character as the referent of terms and conceptual consciousness; also, everything appears to be a different entity from the consciousness apprehending it, but is actually not so. Thus, all phenomena except emptinesses are things that **seem**—to an ignorant consciousness that conceals the truth—to exist the way they appear. These objects are taken by ignorance to exist the way they appear.

This does not mean that objects other than emptiness exist only for ignorance and therefore do not actually exist. Rather, the **truthness** of such objects—their existing the way they appear—is posited only by ignorance, a consciousness concealing the way things actually exist; and this truthness does not exist at all. The basis of division into the two truths is objects of knowledge, existents; hence, both ultimate truths and conventional truths exist, although only ultimate truths are **actual** truths in that only they exist the way they appear in direct realization.

Therefore, that emptiness is called the ultimate truth[b] does not in any way imply (although it admittedly seems so from the words) that the final state is mere cognition of emptiness. The final state is a union of pure body and pure speech unendingly and spontaneously bringing about the advancement of other beings. Emptiness, the thoroughly established nature, is called the ultimate object because of being the object of a consciousness of meditative equipoise on reality and because of being the ultimate nature of objects, but it is not

[a] *rigs shes.*

[b] *don dam bden pa, paramārthasatya.*

ultimate, in the sense that mere realization of it is the final state. Rather, the ultimate goal is to have a combination of direct realization of emptiness and direct comprehension of all conventional objects in order to be of service to others. Thus, emptiness is the essence of Buddha's teachings, in the sense that through realization of it altruistic aims can be achieved as they could not otherwise be.

Syllogistic Summation

We have been considering the statement in the *Sūtra Unraveling the Thought* (*Emptiness in Mind-Only,* 90) identifying the ultimate-non-nature:

> Moreover, that which is the thoroughly established character of phenomena is also called "the ultimate-non-nature." Why? Paramārthasamudgata, that which in phenomena is the selflessness of phenomena is called their "non-nature." It is the ultimate, and the ultimate is distinguished by just the naturelessness of all phenomena; therefore, it is called the "ultimate-non-nature."

A-ku Lo-drö-gya-tso[263] renders the meaning of this passage in syllogistic form:

> With respect to the subject, the thoroughly established nature, there is a reason for calling it the "ultimate-non-nature," for it is called such (1) since it is the final object of observation by a path of purification and hence is the **ultimate** and (2) since it is distinguished by a mere negation of the self of phenomena [and thus is the **non-nature** of such a superimposed status].

PART FOUR: *THOROUGHLY ESTABLISHED NATURE ENDOWED WITH BUDDHA QUALITIES*

16. A Different Perspective: The Jo-nang-b̄a Synthesis

A prime point that D̄zong-ka-b̄a makes in *The Essence of Eloquence* is that those who take the *Sūtra Unraveling the Thought* to be definitive and yet hold that the thoroughly established nature is something other than a mere elimination of an object of negation are mistaken. He points to the fact that the sūtra itself is clear that the thoroughly established nature is a mere absence of the imputational nature in other-powered natures. The fundamental principle is that, because beings misapprehend the status of phenomena, attention must be paid to the **lack** of such a status in order to overcome the tendency to this basic error and all the ills that are built on it.[a]

His emphasis on this point stems from a wish to counter the then popular opinion of the Jo-nang-b̄as, a syncretic sect that reached its ascendency in fourteenth-century Tibet around the works of the brilliant scholar-yogi Döl-b̄o-b̄a S̄hay-rap-gyel-tsen.[b] The primary source for Jo-nang-b̄a opinions is his *The Mountain Doctrine: Ocean of Definitive Meaning*,[c] which he finished writing

---

[a] For S̄hay-rap-gyel-tsen's possible rebuttal that his system does include this type of meditation, see p. 331ff.

[b] For a short biography, see *Emptiness in Mind-Only*, 47ff. For an excellent, detailed biography, see Cyrus R. Stearns, *The Buddha from Dol po: A Study of the Life and Thought of the Tibetan Master Dolpopa Sherab Gyaltsen* (Albany, N.Y.: State University of New York Press, 1999), 11-39.

[c] *ri chos nges don rgya mtsho;* I have primarily used two editions:

- Gangtok, Sikkim: Dodrup Sangyey Lama, 1976. All references are to this edition.
- Amdo, Tibet: 'dzam thang bsam 'grub nor bu'i gling, n.d. This edition has few textual errors and includes most of S̄hay-rap-gyel-tsen's outline to the text, embedded within it.

I also made infrequent use of:

- Matthew Kapstein, *The 'Dzam-thang Edition of the Collected Works of Kun-mkhyen Dol-po-pa Shes-rab-rgyal-mtshan: Introduction and Catalogue,* vol. 2, 25-707 (Delhi: Shedrup Books, 1992). This edition is in cursive print, with the unfortunate oddity that it does not differentiate between the very frequently used letters *pa* and *sa.* However, Kapstein is to be lauded for making this edition of the Collected Works available.
- Beijing: mi rigs dpe skrun khang, 1998. I have heard that this edition has a considerable number of errors.

In the colophon to the *Ocean of Definitive Meaning* (491.2), S̄hay-rap-gyel-tsen explains the meaning of "mountain doctrine":

> The mountain doctrine of those practicing profound yoga in isolated mountain retreats (*ri khrod dben par zab mo rnal 'byor spyod pa rnams kyi ri **chos***).

I am preparing an abridged translation of the text that includes all of S̄hay-rap-gyel-tsen's own statements, a large number of the scriptural citations sufficient to convey his points, and the complicated outline of the text that appears just before it in the author's Collected Works

before the consecration on October 30, 1333, of a great monument (*stūpa*) that he constructed. The *Ocean of Definitive Meaning*—a long text of 247 folios that would run at least 500 pages in translation—is a sustained argument about the matrix of One Gone Thus, built around objections and answers and replete with citations of sūtras, tantras, and Indian treatises. It thereby follows the format, inherited from India, of a presentation by way of both reasoning and scripture—the latter being so rich that the book also can be considered an anthology, a veritable treasure trove of literature about the matrix of One Gone Thus.

The *Ocean of Definitive Meaning* is divided into three extensive sections—basis, path, and fruit, preceded by a brief explanation of all three. The **basis** is the ground on which the **path** acts to rid it of obstructions, thereby yielding the **fruit** of practice. Here I will draw from all three sections in order both to give a palpable sense of Shay-rap-gyel-tsen's system and to contrast it to Dzong-ka-ba's.

The Matrix Of One Gone Thus Endowed With Buddha Qualities

The basis is the matrix of One Gone Thus which itself is the thoroughly established nature. Shay-rap-gyel-tsen asserts that the matrix of One Gone Thus is:

- the uncontaminated primordial wisdom empty of all the phenomena of cyclic existence
- permanent, stable, eternal, everlasting, uncompounded by causes and conditions, and intrinsically possessing the ultimate qualities of a Buddha such as the ten powers.[264]

The Jo-nang-bas assert that, despite being a special wisdom, the ultimate—the matrix of One Gone Thus—is not compounded by causes and conditions. Shay-rap-gyel-tsen cites a sūtra source:[265]

> Although all Buddhas earnestly examined it in all ways, they would not find that the matrix of One Gone Thus is produced [from causes and conditions]. In all sentient beings there exists an unproduced basic constituent of a Buddha, a basic constituent adorned with the infinite, auspicious marks and beauties of a Buddha.

Since the matrix of One Gone Thus is intrinsically endowed from beginningless time with the ultimate qualities of a Buddha's Body of Attributes,[a] it is not something that did not exist before and is newly produced.

From this point of view, Shay-rap-gyel-tsen repeatedly speaks of the basis

---

and greatly facilitates access to his arguments.

[a] *chos sku, dharmakāya.* I often have translated this term as "truth body," but "Body of Attributes" seems more to fit the meaning in this context, since Shay-rap-gyel-tsen emphasizes that ultimate Buddha qualities already exist in the matrix of One Gone Thus.

(the actual way things are even in an ordinary state) and the fruit as undifferentiable:

> These, as well as the *Compendium of Precious Qualities,*...say that this which is the Body of Attributes, matrix of One Gone to Bliss, noumenal element, is the very perfection of wisdom, which is the undifferentiable entity of basis and fruit, the Buddha lineage, and say that it exists at all time as the basis of all phenomena.[266]

> Since the Vajrasattva that is the undifferentiable entity of basis and fruit is endowed with all aspects, it is endowed with all colors. Therefore, since it just abides as the ultimate undifferentiable entity of basis and fruit, this very chapter of the vajra lineage [in the *Hevajra Tantra*] is also the fruit.[267]

> The *Mahāparinirvāṇa Sūtra*...also has statements that basis and fruit are undifferentiable since it says that just this noumenal element that is the basis of all also is the great fruit, final exalted wisdom, great teacher, and so forth. Similarly, the *Ultimate Golden Light Sūtra*...also says that just this Body of Attributes is the cause, foundation, fruit, basis, Great Vehicle, the entity of One Gone Thus, the matrix of One Gone Thus, and so forth.[268]

He quotes the *Descent into Laṅkā Sūtra:*

> Mahāmati, what is the thoroughly established nature? It is thus: Since the thusness devoid of signs, names, characteristics of things, and conceptuality is an attainment of realization by a Superior's exalted wisdom, it is an object of activity by a Superior's exalted wisdom of individual knowledge. Mahāmati, this thoroughly established nature is the matrix, the mind, of One Gone Thus.

He comments:[269]

> In this way, it says that this which is the noumenon—the thoroughly established nature—is the matrix and mind of Ones Gone Thus. This also is in consideration of the thoroughly established nature that is the undifferentiable entity of basis and fruit since just it also is the five self-arisen exalted wisdoms.

Although Shay-rap-gyel-tsen holds that the basis and the fruit are undifferentiable, he makes the distinction that, while a person is still a sentient being, the basis is obstructed by defilements, and, when a person has become a Buddha, the basis has separated from defilements:[270]

> That all sentient beings nevertheless do not perceive [the ultimate qualities] is due to being obstructed by adventitious defilements, since

> those [ultimate qualities] are not objects of consciousness and since they are objects of activity just of self-cognizing exalted wisdom, as is said in the *Mahāparinirvāṇa Sūtra*...and in the *Great Drum Sūtra*....Thereby, many very profound sūtras set forth a plenitude of examples for and reasons why, although the pure nature—the matrix of One Gone to Bliss—dwells in all sentient beings, it is not seen and is not attained if it is not separated from adventitious defilements.

Among these examples, Shay-rap-gyel-tsen[271] cites one found in many sūtras and treatises that most aptly makes the point that the basis and fruit are the same. An unknown treasure (basis) exists under the home of a poor person that must be uncovered (path) through removing obstructive dirt (defilements), yielding the treasure (fruit) that always was there. Just as the treasure already exists and thus requires no further fashioning, so the matrix of One Gone Thus, endowed with Buddha qualities, already dwells within each sentient being and needs only to be freed from defilements.

> Here those who wish to bring about the welfare of all sentient beings with the Form Bodies [of a Buddha]—upon attaining the supreme liberation, the Body of Attributes of natural clear light, self-arisen exalted wisdom, the finality of purity, self, bliss, and permanence—should initially understand that just as a great treasure of jewels exists under the ground of a poor person's home but, being obscured by earth and rock to a depth of seven humans, is neither seen, realized, or attained and as a consequence the person remains just in suffering, so the great treasure of the qualities of the clear light Body of Attributes [of a Buddha] exists at all times in all beings—oneself and others—but, being obscured by adventitious defilements, is neither seen, realized, or attained and as a consequence all beings remain just in suffering. It is to be comprehended well that [the great treasure of the qualities of the clear light Body of Attributes] is just attained and just perceived from stainless scriptures and reasonings that are endowed with the special quintessential instructions of a holy lama. This is similar to the knowledge—from those with the divine eye revealing that treasure well—that a great treasure is just to be gained and the earth and rocks covering it are just to be removed. It is also similar to the knowledge that if the earth and rocks are not cleared away, the treasure will not be gained and that through merely removing those, it will be gained. That which is to be practiced upon comprehending such is to make effort at achieving the collections of pure exalted wisdom, together with its accompanying factors, for the sake of clearing away all adventitious defilements. This is similar to removing the earth and rocks to a depth of seven humans. That which is attained through having practiced such is the effect of having separated [from these defilements]—the

uncontaminated Body of Attributes—and the great treasure of qualities from which there is no separation. This is similar to attaining well just that treasure of jewels.

Through this scripture-based example, Šhay-rap-gyel-tsen emphasizes that:

- The Body of Attributes of a Buddha pre-exists within sentient beings.
- There are scriptures, reasonings, and also special quintessential instructions revealing the presence of this internal treasure called the matrix of One Gone Thus, or the matrix of One Gone to Bliss.
- The practice of wisdom, along with its accompanying factors of merit, is required to remove the defilements preventing realization of this resource.

In order to avoid having to hold that ordinary sentient beings are already Buddhas because they possess Buddha qualities, he makes a distinction between ultimate and conventional Buddha and makes a distinction between ultimate and conventional qualities. Ultimate Buddha and Buddha qualities are already present in the noumenon, whereas conventional Buddha and conventional Buddha qualities must be attained. First he cites scripture, Maitreya's ***Sublime Continuum of the Great Vehicle*** (II.5) and the ***Lion's Roar of Shrīmālādevī Sūtra,*** to demonstrate that Buddha qualities are indeed present, after which he resolves the apparent contradiction that sentient beings are not already Buddhas:[272]

> Moreover, the holy Ajita [that is, Maitreya] says that this very matrix of One Gone Thus, clear light nature, and uncreated noumenon is endowed undifferentiably with the inseparable Buddha qualities passed beyond the count of the grains of sands of the banks of the Ganges:
>
> Because [the uncontaminated expanse,] the clear light [of the pure nature] is not [newly] made from causes and conditions,
> And its manifestations are indivisible [from it] and [the number of qualities] is beyond the number of sands of the Ganges,
> It just possesses all of the Buddha qualities
> [The powers and so forth, form the start, spontaneously].
>
> Also, the ***Lion's Roar of Shrīmālādevī Sūtra...,***[273] rare as an ***udumbara*** flower, extensively says that faulty factors such as production and cessation do not exist by way of their own nature[a] and that the Buddha element or elemental Buddha[b]—endowed with multitudes of qualities established by way of their own nature, the endless noumenal signs and beauties [of a Buddha]—exists in all sentient beings.
>
> Here also with regard to the signs and beauties [of a Buddha], if

---

a *rang bzhin gyis med pa.*

b *sangs rgyas kyi dbyings sam dbyings kyis sangs rgyas.*

> one knows the distinction of the two truths [that is, conventional and ultimate], one will not be bewildered with respect to Buddha's word. Moreover, the signs and beauties that are said to be naturally complete in the very matrix of One Gone Thus, the noumenal element, are qualities of the **ultimate** Body of Attributes, not of the **conventional** Form Bodies. Since it is said that "The thirty-two marks are complete...," the final marks and beauties set forth in the profound tantra sets are to be understood—exactly as they are—from the quintessential instructions of an excellent lama and hence are not objects of logical argumentation.

He makes a distinction between noumenal qualities and qualities of conventional Form Bodies:[274]

> Similarly, since the marks and beauties that are complete in the matrix of One Gone to Bliss are endowed with all aspects, all capacities, all faculties, and all good qualities of the noumenon, they are not the same as the marks and beauties of conventional Form Bodies.

From this, it can be seen that, even though ultimate Buddha marks, beauties, and so forth exist intrinsically in the continuums of all sentient beings, they are obscured by ignorance and thus cannot perform the activities of a Buddha, which can be done only when conventional Buddha qualities are attained. As he says at the beginning of the section on the path in the *Ocean of Definitive Meaning*:[275]

> Although in that way all the inseparable good qualities of the ultimate Buddha, the Body of Attributes, abide integrally[a] in all sentient beings, it is not that the path—the two collections [of merit and wisdom] are not needed. This is because adventitious defilements must be removed and because the aims of all sentient beings must be brought about upon producing the conventional Form Bodies. Concerning that, here in order for it to become a complete good path, it is necessary to fulfill pure and developed view, meditation, and behavior.

Then, through an elaborate, reasoned argument he directly addresses the issue of whether endowment with Buddha qualities would absurdly make ordinary sentient beings Buddhas, concluding that it does not. In this case, he speaks about Buddha qualities in terms of negative and positive aspects, called qualities of abandonment of defilements and qualities of realization, by using here the vocabulary of:

- primordial abandonment and realization that are contained within the noumenon
- abandonment and realization that are attained through practicing the path.

---

[a] *rang chas su;* literally, on their own part.

He speaks of abandonment and realization separately using these two formats of primordial endowment and attainment through practicing antidotes to defilements:[276]

> *Objection:* If the ultimate Buddha intrinsically exists in all sentient beings, then they intrinsically would have final abandonment [of defilements] and have final realization.
>
> *Answer:* This must be taught upon making a distinction. Hence, there are two types of abandonment—the abandonment of all defilements which is their primordial absence of inherent establishment and the extinguishment of adventitious defilements upon being overcome by antidotes. Concerning those, the first is complete within the noumenon:
>
> - because of containing the entire meaning of:
>
>   Extinguishment is not extinguishment by antidotes.
>   Because of being extinguished from before, it is taught as extinguishment.[a]
>
>   and [Maitreya's *Sublime Continuum of the Great Vehicle* (I.15)]:
>
>   Due to realizing the quiescent nature of goings [that is, all persons and phenomena]
>   They [perceive] the very mode [of being of phenomena],
>   Because of natural thorough purity
>   And because the afflictive emotions are extinguished from the start.
>
>   and:
>
>   The afflictive emotions forever do not exist—
>   Voidness of defilements in the beginning, middle, and end.
>
>   and, "At all times devoid of all obstructions," and so forth
>
> - because it is beyond the phenomena of consciousness
> - because it is definitely released from all obstructions
> - because of completely having abandoned afflictive emotions,

---

[a] *Questions of King Dhāraṇīshvara Sūtra* (Peking 814, vol. 32). Dzong-ka-ba cites this in his *Extensive Explanation of (Chandrakīrti's) "Supplement to (Nāgārjuna's) 'Treatise on the Middle'": Illumination of the Thought* (*dbu ma la 'jug pa'i rgya cher bshad pa dgongs pa rab gsal*; Peking 6143, vol. 154) as:

> Extinction [in this case] is not [caused] by means of an antidote.
> It is so called because of primordial extinction.

secondary afflictive emotions, and thorough afflictions as well as their predispositions

because of the absence of dust,[a] dustlessness, absence of defilements, abandonment of faults, and flawlessness.

Hence, natural abandonment is primordially complete in the ultimate noumenal Buddha because that noumenon is the One Gone Thus primordially released and because of being the Buddha prior to all Buddhas.

Although the second abandonment [that is, the extinguishment of adventitious defilements upon being overcome by antidotes] does not exist in sentient beings who have not cultivated the path, this does not involve a fault in our tenets because it is not asserted that all sentient beings are Buddhas or have attained Buddhahood and because it is not asserted that conventional Buddhahood exists in all sentient beings.

Similarly, there are also two types of Buddha-realization, the self-arisen exalted wisdom which is the primordial realization of the noumenon—knowing itself by itself[b]—and the other-arisen exalted wisdom which is realization produced from having cultivated the profound path. The first is complete within the noumenon:

- because that factuality contains all self-knowledge and other-knowledge
- because of being the sacred ultimate,[c] all-conscious and all-knowing
- because of being unfluctuating individual self-knowledge
- because of being the pervasive lord that is the essence of the five self-arisen exalted wisdoms
- because of holding the mode of non-dualistic exalted wisdom
- because of having the essence of the ten pure exalted wisdoms
- because of being the container of the ten pure exalted wisdoms.

Hence, natural fundamental abandonment and realization are complete in the ultimate noumenon because these have the same import as the statements [in Maitreya's *Sublime Continuum of the Great Vehicle* (I.155)]:

> The essential constituent is empty of the adventitious [defilements]
> Which have the character of being separable [from its entity].
> It is not empty of the unsurpassed [qualities of the powers and so forth]

[a] *rdul.*

[b] *rang gis rang rig pa.*

[c] *dam pa po.* The translation is doubtful; perhaps it could mean "ultimate being."

> Which have the character of not being separable [from it].
>
> And (I.154ab):
>
> > This [basic constituent of the pure nature] has no [previously existent faults of afflictive emotions] to be removed,
> > And not the least [factor of ultimate good qualities] to be [newly] established.
>
> Therefore, since the first type of realization [self-arisen exalted wisdom that is the primordial realization of the noumenon] is indivisibly complete in the noumenon, it is the case that where that noumenon exists, that realization also exists. Although the second type of realization [realization produced from having cultivated the profound path] is not complete in sentient beings who have not entered the path and although they have not directly realized selflessness, this does not involve a fault in our tenets; the reasons are as before.

In this way, S̄hay-rap-gyel-tsen maintains primordial endowment of the Body of Attributes and yet the need for defiled beings to attain their conventional manifestation.[a]

In order to show how the matrix of One Gone Thus yields Buddhahood, he briefly addresses the topics of its two divisions, called the two causal lineages.

---

[a] Tāranātha (*The Essence of Other-Emptiness*, 508.6), second in the Jo-nang-b̄a school only to S̄hay-rap-gyel-tsen, gives a brief summary of which Buddha qualities are ultimate and which are conventional:

> Therefore, the exalted wisdom of the basic element of attributes necessarily is only the ultimate truth, but, although the other four exalted wisdoms are mainly the primordially abiding ultimate, each in a minor way has conventional parts that are newly attained through having cultivated the path. The ten powers, four fearlessnesses, and so forth also are similar to those [four exalted wisdoms in mainly being the primordially abiding ultimate but in a minor way having conventional parts that are newly attained]. The qualities of exalted body—the marks, the beauties, and so forth—and the qualities of exalted speech—the sixty branches and so forth—each equally have conventional and ultimate portions. Likewise, the Nature Body is only ultimate; the Body of Attributes is mostly ultimate; the two, the Complete Enjoyment Body and Emanation Bodies, have equal portions when a division of actual and imputed types is not made; moreover, the appearances of exalted activities in others' perspectives are conventional, whereas the exalted wisdom of power is ultimate. Therefore, all exalted body, exalted wisdom, qualities, and activities that are included within the ultimate abide primordially in the matrix of One Gone Thus. When one person is buddhafied, those are not newly attained and are merely separated from defilements that obscure them, but those that are conventional are newly attained. Those that are ultimate in past Buddhas and in future Buddhas are one entity, and even those that are conventional are indivisible in nature upon attaining Buddhahood and thereafter but at the point of attainment are different; hence, they are unpredicable as either the same or different.

The first is the noumenal clear light itself, the natural lineage,[a] and the other consists of the spiritual activities of accumulating wisdom and merit, the developmental lineage.[b] From those two, respectively, arise the two Buddha Bodies—the Body of Attributes and Form Bodies, the latter consisting of a Complete Enjoyment Body and Emanation Bodies.

Basis	*Path*	*Fruit*
Natural lineage	Collection of wisdom	Body of Attributes
Developmental lineage	Collection of merit	Form Bodies

As he says:[277]

> The expanse that is the non-conceptual, clear light noumenon is the natural lineage. The developmental lineage dependent on it is a special virtue aroused from planting and furthering seeds of liberation; it produces the Form Bodies of a One Gone Thus. In this way, it is said that two types of lineage having the natures of the two truths—the one existing as the basic disposition and the other not—serve as the basis. In this [double] context, the paths of the collection of wisdom and the collection of merit are practiced, [from which] the two types of effect Bodies—Body of Attributes and Form Bodies—are attained. Maitreya's *Sublime Continuum of the Great Vehicle* (I.149-150) says:
>
> > Like a treasure [that naturally remains under the ground] and a fruit tree [that gradually grows with exertion]
> > The lineage is to be known as having two aspects—
> > [The pure expanse] that naturally abides since beginningless [time]
> > And [the developmental lineage of] supreme virtue [newly] aroused [through the exertion of hearing and so forth].
> >
> > It is asserted that the Three Bodies of a Buddha
> > Are attained through these two causal lineages.
> > Through the first, the first body [the Body of Attributes, is attained];
> > Through the second, the latter two [Bodies of Complete Enjoyment and Emanation are attained].
>
> Also, Maitreya's *Ornament for the Great Vehicle Sūtras,* a text of the Great Middle Way,[c] says:

[a] *rang bzhin gnas rigs.*

[b] *rgyas 'gyur gyi rigs.*

[c] *dbu ma chen po.* It may be the case that the reason why Shay-rap-gyel-tsen mentions the Great Middle Way for the first time at this point in the *Ocean of Definitive Meaning* is that some scholars, such as Lo-den-shay-rap (*blo ldan shes rab,* 1059-1109), hold that Maitreya's

> Natural and developmental,
> Support and what is supported,
> Just existent and not existent.

Also:[278]

> These are the natural lineage—the ultimate Buddha permanently abiding primordially in the ordinary state—the basis of purifying defilements. The expansive lineage dependent upon it gives rise to special roots of virtue from planting and developing seeds of liberation.

A central point is that the doctrine of pre-existent Buddha qualities does not eliminate the need for practice of the path. Consequently, when describing the final Buddha qualities, he even uses the vocabulary of "**effects** of separation"[a] and "**effects** that are produced"[b] and titles the section on the path "Explaining How Effects of Separation and of Production Are Attained through the Path."[c] Given the nuances of S̄hay-rap-gyel-tsen's position, it seems to me that, when A-ku L̄o-drö-gya-tso ignores these and spells out supposed, absurd consequences of the position that Buddha qualities exist within ordinary sentient beings, they do not hit the mark. The absurd consequences he draws are:[279]

- If a Buddha exists intrinsically in the continuums of all sentient beings, then the matrix of One Gone Thus in the continuum of a donkey absurdly would be a person who has abandoned the obstructions, since it is a Buddha and, in fact, is the Buddhas of the five lineages [Akṣhobhya, Ratnasambhava, Amitābha, Amoghasiddhi, and Vairochana].

Ornament for the Great Vehicle Sūtras is a text of the Mind-Only School.

[a] *bral ba'i 'bras bu.* For these two, see also Cyrus R. Stearns, *The Buddha from Dol po: A Study of the Life and Thought of the Tibetan Master Dolpopa Sherab Gyaltsen* (Albany, N.Y.: State University of New York Press, 1999), 84.

[b] *bskyed pa'i 'bras bu.* By viewing Buddha qualities as being present from the start and yet as being "effects," the Jo-nang-b̄as, like all systems, try to have their cake and eat it too. The move is similar to the Ge-luk-b̄a assertion that in the Middle Way School the matrix of One Gone Thus is the emptiness of a defiled mind and thus not compounded by causes and conditions but still is a "cause" of enlightenment though not an **actual** cause.

[c] As Tāranātha says immediately after the citation above (p. 280, footnote a):

> Therefore, newly attained effects that are to be produced through cultivating the path are produced effects, due to which they do not truly exist, whereas the primordially abiding Buddha is merely separated from the covering over that Buddha through cultivating the path, due to which it is called an "effect of separation" and the path also is called a "cause of its separation." These are merely imputed cause and effect, not actual cause and effect. This effect of separation also is not an analytical separation described in *Manifest Knowledge,* "Separation is a mental extinguishment." Rather, it is an ultimate effect of separation and an ultimate true cessation in accordance with the statement in the *Questions of King Dhāraṇīṣhvara Sūtra,* "Since it is primordially extinguished, it is called 'extinguishment.'"

- If that is accepted, it absurdly follows that it cognizes all phenomena, since it is a Buddha Superior.[a]
- If that is accepted, it absurdly follows that the objects of that matrix of One Gone Thus are not limited to just this other-emptiness. (If this is accepted, the Jo-nang-b̄as contradict their assertion that just this other-emptiness is its object.)
- If, however, the Jo-nang-b̄as say that being a Buddha Superior does not entail cognizing all phenomena, then it absurdly follows that there is a Buddha Superior who does not know how to bring about the welfare of sentient beings.

As can be seen from the above description of S̄hay-rap-gyel-tsen's complex position, he explicitly attempts to avoid these problems by holding that Buddha qualities are of two types—ultimate and conventional. He asserts that, although ultimate, noumenal Buddha qualities are present in each sentient being, conventional Buddha qualities are yet to be attained, and thus he does not assert that sentient beings are Buddhas, or Buddha Superiors as A-ku L̄o-drö-gya-tso puts it. That A-ku L̄o-drö-gya-tso avoids addressing this distinction, central to S̄hay-rap-gyel-tsen's system, weakens his argument. As S̄hay-rap-gyel-tsen[280] bitingly says:

> Therefore, the very many perverse challenges such as, "If Buddha existed in sentient beings, all actions, afflictive emotions, and sufferings would not exist," and so forth, and "Sentient beings would realize all knowables," and so forth are spoutings forth by those who do not know the difference between the existence [that is, presence] of such and such and being such and such.[b] This is because the existence [that is, presence] of such and such does not establish being such and such.[c] If it did, then, since explanations exist in humans, are humans explanations?![d]

---

[a] *sangs rgyas 'phags pa;* the term is used to refer to a **person** who is enlightened. The Nature Body of a Buddha Superior is buddha but not a Buddha Superior, because of not being a person.

[b] *yod pa dang yin pa'i khyad par.*

[c] *yod pas yin par mi 'grub.*

[d] Tāranātha (*The Essence of Other-Emptiness,* 513.1) similarly says:

> *Objection:* It is not feasible for Buddha qualities to exist in sentient beings' continuums; for example, if the power of knowing sources and non-sources [that is, direct knowledge of cause and effect]* existed in sentient beings' continuums, sentient beings absurdly would understand all sources and non-sources.
>
> *Answer:* This also is not correct, because we do not assert that whatever is [in] the continuums of sentient beings is a Buddha. And, if such necessarily follows due to the fact that a Buddha and Buddha qualities dwell in the continuums of sentient beings, then would it necessarily follow that, when a Buddha resides on a throne, even the throne would know all objects of knowledge? Therefore, how

That A-ku L̄o-drö-gya-tso simply ignores this challenge by S̄hay-rap-gyel-tsen and the distinctions made in his elaborate explanations leaves them unscathed, still ringing with their impact.

The Ultimate Is Other-Empty, Not Self-Empty

In this way, since the matrix of One Gone Thus is empty of all the phenomena of cyclic existence but replete with the phenomena, or qualities, of enlightenment, it is not empty of itself. S̄hay-rap-gyel-tsen cites:[281]

> The basis-of-all which is the pure, primordial wisdom is empty of all phenomena of cyclic existence; therefore, it is an emptiness of the other—permanent, stable, eternal, and everlasting.[a]

If it were self-empty, it would not exist at all:[282]

> Moreover, if everything were self-empty, then the Body of Attributes of release also would be self-empty, and if that is accepted, it also would be totally non-existent, whereby this would accord with the systems of the Forder Nirgranthas, and so forth, as is extensively explained in the *Mahāparinirvāṇa Sūtra*....[283] Also, that same sūtra, using the non-existence of a horse in a cow and the non-existence of a cow in a horse, pronounces that the ultimate noumenon, the great nirvāṇa, is other-empty in the sense of not being empty of itself. It extensively says:
>
> > Child of good lineage, it is thus: nirvāṇa is not formerly non-existent, like the non-existence of earthenware in clay. It is not non-existent upon ceasing, like earthenware's non-existence upon being destroyed. It is also not utterly non-existent, like the hairs of a turtle or the horns of a rabbit. Rather, it accords with the non-existence of the one in the other. Child of good lineage, as you propound, a horse does not exist in a cow, but it is not suitable to say that a cow does not exist [in a cow], and a cow does not exist in a horse, but it is not suitable to say that even a horse does not exist [in a horse]. Nirvāṇa also is like that; nirvāṇa does not exist in afflictive emotions, and afflictive emotions do not exist in

could the eight collections of consciousness in the continuums of sentient beings be a Buddha! Even the Buddha who resides there does not reside in the manner of conventional support and that which is supported but abides there in the manner of [being] the ultimate noumenon.

*See Jeffrey Hopkins, *Meditation on Emptiness* (London: Wisdom, 1983; rev. ed., Boston: Wisdom, 1996), 208.

[a] *gzhan stong rtag brtan g.yung drung ther zug.*

> nirvāṇa. Hence, it is said to be the non-existence of the one in the other.

Therefore, he speaks of the thoroughly established nature not as empty of merely a non-existent object of negation, as Ḏzong-ka-ḇa does, but as empty of the other two natures—imputational natures and other-powered natures:

> Of what is it devoid? It is devoid of whatever is an imputational or an other-powered nature, conventional forms and so forth.

Shay-rap-gyel-tsen gives a careful analysis of a sūtra passage that indicates that the ultimate is of a different order of being, beyond the temporary nature of other-powered natures, which, like hail-stones, may appear solid but quickly disappear. In a passage from the *Aṅgulimāla Sūtra,* Mañjushrī—the god of wisdom—pretends not to understand emptiness properly, holding that everything, even Buddha qualities, is empty. Aṅgulimāla, a sinner famed for having killed 999 persons and cut off a single finger (*aṅguli*) from each to make a rosary (*māla*) but who then became a follower of Buddha, scathingly corrects the god of wisdom in what can be seen is a genre of comedy:

> Aṅgulimāla said to Mañjushrī:
>
> > Mañjushrī, if you are the supreme of those seeing the great emptiness, then what is it to see emptiness? What is the meaning of "empty, empty"? O, one endowed with great mind, speak quickly; cut off my doubts.
>
> Then, the youthful Mañjushrī spoke in verse to Aṅgulimāla:
>
> > The Buddha is like space;
> > Space is signless.
> > The Buddha is like space;
> > Space is produced signlessly.
> > The Buddha is like space;
> > Space is formless.
> > Attributes[a] are like space;
> > The One Gone Thus is the Body of Attributes.
> > Exalted wisdom is like space;
> > The One Gone Thus is the Body of Attributes.
> > Exalted wisdom unapprehendable, unfathomable,
> > Desireless is the One Gone Thus.
> > Liberation is like space;
> > Space also is signless.
> > Liberation is the Buddha, One Gone Thus.

---

[a] *chos, dharma.*

> How could you, Aṅgulimāla, understand
> Empty nothingness!

Then, Aṅgulimāla further said this to the youthful Mañjushrī:

> It is like this: For example, a rain-storm falls from a great cloud, and a person with a childish nature picks up a piece of hail. Thinking that it is a precious vaiḍūrya jewel, the person carries it home and, not daring to hold it due to its great coldness, thinks to treat it as a treasure and carefully puts it into a vase. Seeing that round piece of hail melt, the person thinks, "[It has become] empty," and turns speechless. Similarly, venerable Mañjushrī, one who meditates on extreme emptiness and considers emptiness to be profound uncomfortably sees all phenomena to be destroyed. Even the non-empty liberation is seen and considered to be emptiness. It is like this: For example, having thought that a piece of hail is a jewel, the person meditates even on jewels as empty. Likewise, you also consider non-empty phenomena to be empty. Seeing phenomena as empty, you also destroy non-empty phenomena as empty. [However] empty phenomena are other; non-empty phenomena are other. The tens of millions of afflictive emotions like hail-stones are empty. The phenomena in the class of non-virtues, like hail-stones, quickly disintegrate. Buddha, like a vaiḍūrya jewel, is permanent. The scope of liberation also is like a vaiḍūrya jewel.
>
> Space also is Buddha-form; there is no form of any Hearers and Solitary Realizers. The liberation of a Buddha also is form. Even if the liberations of Hearers and Solitary Realizers are formless, do not make the discrimination of non-division, saying, "The character of liberation is empty."
>
> Mañjushrī, an empty home in a built-up city is called empty due to the absence of humans. A pot is empty due to the absence of water. A river is empty due to water not flowing. Is a village that is without householders called "empty, empty"? Or are the households empty in all respects? They are not empty in all respects; they are called empty due to the absence of humans. Is a pot empty in all respects? It is not empty in all respects; it is called "empty" due to the absence of water. Is a river empty in all respects? It is not empty in all respects; it is called "empty" because water is not flowing. Similarly, liberation is not empty in all respects; it is called "empty" because of being devoid of all defects. A Buddha, a Supramundane Victor, is not empty but is called "empty"

> because of being devoid of defects and due to the absence of humanness and godhood that have tens of millions of afflictive emotions.
>
> Alas, venerable Mañjushrī, acting out the behavior of an ant, you do not know the real meaning of empty and non-empty. The Naked Ones[a] also meditate on all as empty; do not say anything, you ant of the Naked Ones!

Shay-rap-gyel-tsen explains the meaning of the quotation as being that the mere finding that some phenomena are empty does not make all phenomena, such as the great liberation, also empty:

> The passage from "The Buddha is like space" through "How could you, Aṅgulimāla, understand / Empty nothingness!" which indicates, in accordance with the assertions of some—that everything is a self-emptiness of nothingness is an introduction by Mañjushrī. [It leads] to [Aṅgulimāla's] delineating the difference between self-emptiness and other-emptiness, despite the fact that [Mañjushrī actually] knows [the difference].
>
> Then, using the example of a hail-stone becoming non-existent upon melting, Aṅgulimāla teaches that all afflicted and non-virtuous phenomena are empty; this teaches that all that are included among mundane conventional truths are empty of themselves and of [their own] entities. Using the example of a vaiḍūrya jewel which does not become non-existent upon melting, he teaches that the final liberation, Buddhahood, is not empty; this teaches that the ultimate supramundane truth, the Body of Attributes, is not empty by way of its own entity. Using the example of an empty home, an empty vase, and an empty river, he teaches an emptiness of all defects; this teaches that the final liberation is an other-emptiness. All descriptions of non-emptiness—"liberation is not empty in all respects," "a Supramundane Victor is not empty," "non-empty phenomena are other," and so forth—mean that the ultimate noumenon is not itself empty of itself. The very many statements in other sūtras and tantras of "is not empty" and "non-empty" also are similar.
>
> The Superior Mañjushrī knows well both self-emptiness and other-emptiness, but for the sake of teaching that those unskillful persons who assert that everything is only self-empty are like the Naked Ones and in order to indicate that the proposition that everything is self-emptiness is just ant[-like], relative to propositions made within good differentiation of what is and is not self-empty, [Aṅgulimāla] says, "Venerable Mañjushrī, acting out the behavior of an ant, you do not know the real meaning of empty and non-empty. The Naked

[a] *gcer bu pa, nirgrantha;* the Jainas.

> Ones also meditate on all as empty; do not say anything, you ant of the Naked Ones!" and "you also consider non-empty qualities to be empty. Seeing phenomena as empty, you also destroy non-empty qualities as empty," and so forth. These are advice and teachings for those who one-pointedly have decided that self-emptiness—which is that subjects that cannot bear analysis[a] and finally disintegrate are empty by way of their own entities—is the final profundity.

S̄hay-rap-gyel-tsen's point is that just as a home is empty of humans, so the great liberation is empty of defects—which are other than itself and do not exist in reality—but it itself is not empty of itself. The great liberation does not melt under examination; it can bear analysis.

In this way, the thoroughly established nature itself ultimately exists. As the *Ocean of Definitive Meaning* says:[284]

> The imputational nature is empty in the sense of always not existing. Other-powered natures, although tentatively existent, are empty in the sense of not existing in reality; those two are fabricated and adventitious. It is said that the noumenal thoroughly established nature exists because the emptiness that is the [ultimate] nature of non-entities [that is, emptiness that is the ultimate nature which is the opposite of non-entities][b]—due to being just the fundamental nature—is not empty of its own entity, and it is also said that it does not exist because of being empty even of other-powered natures.

Thus that the thoroughly established nature inherently exists means simply that it is the ultimate nature. Conversely, since other-powered natures are not the ultimate nature, they are empty of their own entities; they are self-empty. He says:[285]

> Respectively the forms and so forth of adventitious defilements are empty of their own entities—an emptiness of non-entities[c]—and the forms and so forth of the matrix of One Gone to Bliss are the ultimate, other-empty—emptiness that is the [ultimate] nature of non-entities.[d]

---

[a] This is a source indicating that S̄hay-rap-gyel-tsen asserts that the thoroughly established nature is truly established in the sense of being able to sustain reasoned analysis. In D̄zong-ka-b̄a's presentation of the system of the Middle Way School, nothing—not even emptiness—can bear ultimate analysis; otherwise, it would be truly established. In D̄zong-ka-b̄a's presentation of the system of the Mind-Only School, everything that exists is able to bear ultimate analysis as that is defined in the Consequence School, and thus even existent imputational natures inherently exist, even though, according to the Mind-Only School's own vocabulary, they are not truly established; see *Absorption,* #121.

[b] See two footnotes below.

[c] *dngos po med pa stong pa nyid.*

[d] *dngos po med pa'i ngo bo nyid stong pa nyid.* S̄hay-rap-gyel-tsen (*Ocean of Definitive*

Šhay-rap-gyel-tsen depicts the middle wheel of doctrine and Nāgārjuna's Collections of Reasonings as presenting the view that phenomena are, **in the face of their final nature**, as unfounded as a flower of the sky, the horns of a rabbit, and the child of a barren woman:[286]

> In order to realize well the correct view that is commonly renowned, it is necessary to conclude that all phenomena are like a flower of the sky since—in their mode of abiding—they are not anything and are not established as anything, like the horns of a rabbit and the child of a barren woman. Since sources for this are well renowned in the middle wheel of Buddha's word and in Nāgārjuna's Collections of Reasonings, and so forth, and since here an exposition on this topic would be too much, I will not write on it.

The second wheel of doctrine is seen as providing a means for entry into meditative equipoise beyond conceptuality:[287]

> Since, when yogically working on the perfection of wisdom, it is necessary to be devoid of all conceptuality, all objects are refuted for the sake of stopping all apprehending-subjects, [in the second wheel of doctrine Buddha] was intent on teaching everything as emptiness through many aspects such as everything's non-existence, non-establishment, voidness, and so forth but was not intent on differentiating existence, non-existence, and so forth, due to which the second wheel of doctrine is said to be "through the aspect of speaking on emptiness."

However, its blanket teaching of emptiness and non-existence does not take into account that the ultimate truly exists:[288]

> About the second wheel—for certain reasons such as that, out of purposeful intent, it teaches that even what are not self-empty are self-empty, and so forth, and is not possessed of good differentiation, that is to say, is not without internal contradictions—[the *Sūtra Unraveling the Thought*] says that it "is surpassable, affords an occasion [for refutation], requires interpretation, and serves as a basis for controversy." About the third wheel—by reason that, opposite from those, it differentiates meanings well just as they are, and so forth—it says that it "is unsurpassable, does not afford an occasion [for refutation], is of definitive meaning, and does not serve as a basis for controversy."

Meaning, 304.6) explains that this means the emptiness that is the ultimate nature which is the opposite of non-entities, that is, conventionalities (*kun rdzob las bzlog pa don dam pa'i ngo bo nyid*). Non-entities here are imputational natures, which include other-powered natures and thus are all conventionalities.

In Ge-luk-b̄a explanations, this emptiness is emptiness of the nature of non-entities, that is to say, the emptiness of the inherent existence of non-things, or non-products.

The third wheel, however, clearly differentiates what does and does not truly exist:[289]

> The first wheel of doctrine accords with a precursor to meditating on the profound definitive meaning of the Great Vehicle; the second wheel of doctrine accords with practicing a special meditative stabilization of equipoise on the profound meaning; and the third wheel accords with [the system of] profound secret mantra identifying—within good differentiation—existence, non-existence, and so forth.

Within seeing an underlying harmony to the three wheels of doctrine, he indicates that the third wheel of doctrine makes clear that the ultimate truly exists and thus is distinctively superior.

S̄hay-rap-gyel-tsen sees—as the meaning of a great many pronouncements in Great Vehicle scriptures about non-existence and existence—that the non-existent are conventionalities and the existent is the noumenon:

> Here, in accordance with the statement, in that way, of the meaning of not existing and not not existing, Maitreya's *Differentiation of the Middle and the Extremes* says, "Not existent, and also not non-existent,"[a] and moreover the thought of all the statements—in a great many stainless texts of the Middle Way—of being devoid of the extremes of existence and non-existence is that:
>
> - Since all dependently arisen conventionalities do not really exist, when one realizes such, one does not fall to an extreme of existence and is released from the extreme of superimposition.
> - Since the ultimate noumenon that is beyond dependent-arising[b]

[a] For D̄zong-ka-b̄a's objection to a similar passage, see *Emptiness in Mind-Only,* 188, "The meaning is not to explain [as the Jo-nang-b̄as do] that the non-empty is the thoroughly established nature and the non-non-empty are the other two natures [that is, other-powered natures and imputational natures]."

[b] *don dam rten 'brel las 'das pa'i chos nyid;* S̄hay-rap-gyel-tsen's *Ocean of Definitive Meaning,* 196.2. Although S̄hay-rap-gyel-tsen (see p. 333, footnote b) indicates that the noumenon is included among *dharmas,* he is clear that all dependent-arisings are impermanent and deceptive, and thus the noumenon is not a dependent-arising. These positions would seem to contradict the frequently cited dictum from Nāgārjuna's *Treatise on the Middle* (XXIV.19; Peking 5224, vol. 95, 9.3.5):

> Because there are no *dharmas*
> That are not dependent-arisings,
> There are no *dharmas*
> That are not empty.

However, S̄hay-rap-gyel-tsen (*Ocean of Definitive Meaning,* 378.1) explains that this is not Nāgārjuna's meaning:

> That passage says that whatever are dependent-arisings are emptinesses, but it does not say that whatever are emptinesses are dependent-arisings. If it is asserted that

> never is non-existent, when one realizes such, one does not fall to an extreme of non-existence and is released from the extreme of deprecation.

Otherwise, those who, in accordance with the assertions of some, assert that just one phenomenon which is not existent and also non-existent is the definitive meaning devoid of extremes, "Just the ultimate does not ultimately exist and also does not not ultimately exist," do not accord with the meaning of the mode of subsistence and contradict the thought of the Buddhas and the great Bodhisattvas.

The Ultimate Is An Affirming Negative, Not A Non-Affirming Negative

Since the ultimate, although absent the phenomena of cyclic existence, is replete with beneficial qualities, it is not a mere absence. In the *Ocean of Definitive Meaning,* Shay-rap-gyel-tsen identifies the ultimate as an affirming negative (nine times), something that implies a positive in place of the negation. For instance:[290]

> The earlier statements due to the perspective of trainees that all—liberation and so forth—do not exist, are empty, selfless, and so forth are in consideration of the non-existence of whatsoever [object of negation] in something, whereas the later statements of non-emptiness, the existence of self, and so forth are in consideration of the remainder after the negation.[a] Therefore, the fact that, although earlier and later scriptures seem to be contradictory but are, when analyzed well, non-contradictory is because an affirming negative exists as the basis of a non-affirming negative and because an exalted wisdom in which all fundamental good qualities are contained abides—in the manner of thorough establishment pervading space—in the basis which from the start is naturally pure and devoid of all defects.

And:[291]

> When, through having yogically made endeavor at the perfection of wisdom, a meditative stabilization that is a union of calm abiding and

---

> all whatsoever emptinesses are dependent-arisings, then since all the synonyms of the basis of emptiness—the ultimate, noumenon, limit of reality, and so forth—are emptinesses, they would be dependent-arisings, and it would have to be asserted that they are also compounded, impermanent, false, deceptive, and so forth.

It seems to me that Shay-rap-gyel-tsen holds that when Nāgārjuna speaks of *dharmas* in this passage, he is using a narrower usage of *dharmas* to refer to all dependent-arisings, and thus the statement does not indicate that all emptinesses are dependent-arisings.

[a] Literally, "the remainder of the non-existence."

special insight has been generated, one needs to be taught within differentiating existence and non-existence, emptiness and non-emptiness, and so forth, and needs to identify these in accordance with how they abide and how they are:

- because all do not abide as non-existent and non-established, and so forth, and there exists an affirming negative as the basis of non-affirming negatives—such as non-existence and emptiness and the basis of them
- because an inclusionary elimination abides as the basis of an exclusionary elimination
- because realization that contains all final good qualities spontaneously abides in the basis that naturally has abandoned all defects.

Therefore, the third wheel of doctrine is said to be "possessed of good differentiation."

The ultimate, that is, the matrix of One Gone Thus, is the basis of the mere elimination of the self of persons and the self of phenomena, whereby it itself is an inclusionary negative, indicating something positive, not a mere negation. That ultimate truth is by nature endowed with realization of all good qualities and abandonment of all defects.

Great Middle Way

It is clear that S̄hay-rap-gyel-tsen considered his lengthy presentation of the matrix of One Gone Thus and attendant topics such as other-emptiness to be unique in Tibet. He even named one of his texts *The Fourth Council*,[a] seemingly because he considered that in Tibet only he understood and thoroughly propounded a doctrine that is so profound as to be like a further council beyond the three in India during which Buddha's doctrines were collected. In it, he calls this system the Great Middle Way:[292]

The entire profundity spoken in the third wheel of doctrine
Is not a conventionality but the ultimate truth—
Not impermanent but permanent, stable, and everlasting,
Not imputational but the thoroughly established primordial wisdom.
It is not of the Proponents of True Existence but of the Great Middle
Way.

In his *Ocean of Definitive Meaning*, S̄hay-rap-gyel-tsen frequently indicates his indebtedness to the *Kālachakra Tantra* and the "three cycles of Bodhisattva commentaries,"[b] these being:

---

[a] *bka' bsdu bzhi pa.*

[b] *sems 'grel skor gsum.* S̄hay-rap-gyel-tsen refers to these three as the quintessential

1. Kalkī Puṇḍarīka's[a] *Great Commentary on the "Kālachakra Tantra": Stainless Light*[b]
2. Vajragarbha's[c] *Extensive Commentary on the "Condensed Meaning of the Hevajra Tantra"*[d]
3. Vajrapāṇi's[e] *Meaning Commentary on the "Chakrasaṃvara Tantra."*[f]

The latter two commentaries are done in the manner of the *Kālachakra Tantra,* that is to say, using the grid of the *Kālachakra* system.

A prime project of the *Ocean of Definitive Meaning* is to show that the Great Middle Way is the final system of both the tantras and the Great Vehicle sūtras, as well as the thought of the texts by many Great Vehicle scholars usually considered to be either Proponents of Mind-Only or Proponents of the Middle. Shay-rap-gyel-tsen cites sūtra after sūtra to show that the Great Middle Way, or Ultimate Mind-Only,[g] Final Mind-Only,[h] and Supramundane Mind-Only[i] which is beyond consciousness,[j] is their final thought. For instance, he cites the *Descent into Laṅkā Sūtra:*[293]

> Similarly, the *Descent into Laṅkā Sūtra* says that, for the time being, one is taught mind-only, but finally having thoroughly passed beyond that, one is taught the middle without appearance, and that, having also passed beyond this, one is taught the middle with appearance and that, if one does not arrive at that, one has not seen the profound meaning of the Great Vehicle. It says:
>
> Relying on mind-only,
> One does not imagine external objects.
> Relying on non-appearance,
> One passes beyond mind-only.

instructions of tenth grounders.

[a] *rigs ldan pad ma dkar po.* Shay-rap-gyel-tsen also refers to him as *spyan ras gzigs dbang phyug* (Avalokiteshvara) or *'jig rten dbang phyug* (Lokeshvara).

[b] *bsdus pa'i rgyud kyi rgyal po dus kyi 'khor lo'i 'grel bshad rtsa ba'i rgyud kyi rjes su 'jug pa stong phrag bcu gnyis pa dri ma med pa'i 'od ces bya ba, vimālaprabhānāmamūlatantrānusāriṇīdvādaśasāhasrikālaghukālacakratantrarājaṭīkā;* Peking 2064, vol. 46.

[c] *rdo rje snying po.*

[d] *kye'i rdo rje bsdus pa'i don gyi rgya cher 'grel pa, hevajrapiṇḍārthaṭīkā;* Peking 2310, vol. 53.

[e] *phyag na rdo rje.*

[f] *mngon par brjod pa 'bum pa las phyung ba nyung ngu'i rgyud kyi bsdus pa'i don rnam par bshad pa, lakṣābhidhanāduddhṛtalaghutantrapiṇḍārthavivaraṇa;* Peking 2117, vol. 48.

[g] *don dam pa'i sems tsam;* Shay-rap-gyel-tsen's *Ocean of Definitive Meaning,* 213.1.

[h] *mthar thug gi sems tsam;* ibid., 213.4.

[i] *'jig rten las 'das pa'i sems tsam;* ibid., 213.6.

[j] *rnam shes las 'das pa;* ibid., 213.2.

Relying on observing reality,
One passes beyond non-appearance.
If yogis dwell in non-appearance,
They do not perceive the Great Vehicle.

and so forth.

Similarly, [the *Descent into Laṅkā Sūtra*] speaks of the ground, the ultimate mind—which is devoid of compounded objects and subjects as well as causation and is without conventional mind—the natural expanse, the vajra body, the supreme Brahmā as mind-only:

When one who is devoid of compounded
Objects apprehended and apprehenders
And sees the mindless mind-only,
I speak of this as mind-only.

And similarly, it speaks of the basis devoid of conventional mind, thusness, limit of reality, natural nirvāṇa, noumenal element, variegated body of the all-good, clear light basis devoid of all extremes such as existence and non-existence and so forth as mind-only.

Also, that very [*Descent into Laṅkā Sūtra*] speaks of the basis—which is without the appearance of external adventitious defilements and which is matrix of One Gone to Bliss, noumenal element, ultimate mind appearing in the aspects of bodies, enjoyments, abodes, and so forth—as mind-only:[a]

I describe as mind-only
The non-existence of external appearances,
The mind appearing variously
As like bodies, enjoyments, and abodes.

The meaning of such statements again and again of ultimate mind-only beyond conventional mind-only should be understood in reliance upon the profound quintessential instructions of the three cycles of Bodhisattva commentaries. Therefore, you should not propound that

---

[a] Peking 775, vol. 29, 53.4.2, chap. 3; Daisetz Teitaro Suzuki, trans., *The Lankavatara Sutra* (London: Routledge and Kegan Paul, 1932), 133 (33). See Jñānashrībhadra's commentary, Peking 5519, vol. 107, 138.1.8. Translated with bracketed material from Nga-w̄ang-b̄el-den's *Annotations, dngos,* 104a.8ff., the passage reads:

[Objects] do not exist as external objects as perceived
The mind appears as various [objects through the power of predispositions].
[Because the mind is generated] in the likeness of bodies [senses], enjoyments [objects of senses], and abodes [physical sense organs and environments],
I have explained [that all phenomena are] mind-only.

For a citation of this by Jam-ȳang-shay-b̄a, see Jeffrey Hopkins, *Meditation on Emptiness* (London: Wisdom, 1983; rev. ed., Boston: Wisdom, 1996), 613.

the *Descent into Laṅkā Sūtra* and so forth are proprietary texts of mind-only that is not beyond consciousness, upon mistaking statements in them about ultimate mind-only.

Also, statements in those texts of worldly mind-only are doors to and methods for entering suchness; they are not taking [worldly mind-only] to be final. Concerning this, that very sūtra [the *Descent into Laṅkā*] says:

> External appearances to humans,
> Related with predispositions of conceptuality
> And involving various mental factors,
> Are mundane mind-only.

This is the same as the mind-only renowned to logicians.[a] It is not suitable to be final mind-only because that very *Descent into Laṅkā Sūtra* speaks at length of the difference between the forms of mind-only, mundane and supramundane with:

> As long as the mind operates,
> So long is one a worldly nihilist.

and:

> If the mind operates
> In the aspects of apprehended-object and apprehending-subject,
> That is a mundane mind,
> It also is not fit as mind-only.

and:

> Like clouds in space,
> The mind also does not appear.
> The mind accumulates karma.
> Exalted wisdom clears it away.
> Wisdom thoroughly attains
> Non-appearance and also power.

Then he faces, straight on, the objection that Nāgārjuna does not assert a matrix of One Gone Thus endowed with Buddha qualities:[294]

> *Objection:* Although others assert the matrix of One Gone to Bliss as of definitive meaning, it is not so asserted in the Middle Way School.
>
> *Answer:* The honorable Superior Nāgārjuna asserts it. His *Praise of the Noumenal Element* says:

---

[a] *rtog ge pa dag;* Shay-rap-gyel-tsen's *Ocean of Definitive Meaning,* 213.4

Homage and obeisance to the noumenal element
Definitely dwelling in all sentient beings,
Which if one does not thoroughly know
One wanders in the three existences.

From having purified just that
Which serves as the cause of cyclic existence,
That very purification is nirvāṇa.
The Body of Attributes also is just that.

Just as due to being mixed with milk,
The essence of butter is not seen,
So due to being mixed with afflictive emotions
The noumenal element also is not seen.

Just as through having purified milk
The essence of butter becomes undefiled,
So through having purified the afflictive emotions
The noumenal element becomes very undefiled.

Just as a butter lamp dwelling inside a pot
Is not in the least perceived,
So inside the pot of afflictive emotions
The noumenal element also is not perceived.

From whatsoever directions
Holes in a pot arise,
From those very directions
A nature of light arises.

When by the vajra meditative stabilization
The pot has been broken,
It illuminates throughout
The limits of space.

The noumenal element is unproduced.
It never comes to cease.
At all times it is without afflictive emotions,
In the beginning, middle, and end free from defilement.

Just as a cat's eye gem
At all times is luminous
But dwelling inside a stone
Its light is not manifest,

So the noumenal element obscured
By afflictive emotions is very undefiled

But its light is not manifest in cyclic existence,
Becoming manifest light in nirvāṇa.

and:

Even undefiled sun and moon
Are obscured by the five obscurations—
Clouds, mist, smoke,
The face of Rāhu, dust, and so forth.

Just so the mind of clear light
Is obscured by the five obscurations—
Desire, harmful intent, laziness,
Excitement,[295] and doubt.

When an [asbestos] garment stained
With various contaminations and to be cleansed by fire
Is put in fire, its stains
Are burned but it is not.

So with regard to the mind of clear light
Which has the stains of desire and so forth
Its stains are burned by wisdom's fire
But not clear light, its thusness.

All the sūtras spoken by the Conqueror
That teach emptiness
Overcome afflictive emotions
But the essential constituent does not deteriorate.

Just as water existing on the sphere of earth
Resides without defilement,
So the exalted wisdom inside afflictive emotions
Abides without defilement.

and:

Just as a child exists
In the belly of the womb but is not seen,
So the noumenal element covered with afflictive emotions
Also is not seen.

and:

Just as a river in summer
Is said to be "warm"
But in cold season
Is said to be "cold,"

> So when covered with the nets of afflictive emotions
> It is called "sentient being"
> But when separated from afflictive emotions,
> Just it is called "Buddha."

Thus Nāgārjuna speaks at length—by way of many examples—of the matrix of One Gone to Bliss that is equivalent to the noumenal element, Body of Attributes, mind of natural clear light, self-arisen exalted wisdom, and so forth. Also, this master says that just this is the source of all Buddhas:

> This is the ultimate truth.
> Without appearing and without signs,
> It is called ultimate truth,
> The source of all Ones Gone Thus.[a]

S̄hay-rap-gyel-tsen then turns to others renowned as Proponents of the Middle—Āryadeva, Bhāvaviveka, and Chandrakīrti:[296]

Also, Āryadeva asserts it. In his *Lamp Compendium for Practice* he says that the ultimate truth is bodiless, unexampled, devoid of all endeavor, known by oneself individually, and hence it is not to be understood without teaching from the mouth of a guru. His words are:

> Just as a butter lamp dwelling in a pot
> Does not illuminate outside
> But if that pot is broken
> Then the light of the butter lamp illuminates,
>
> So the pot is one's own body
> And thusness is like the butter lamp.
> When broken well by the words of the guru,
> The Buddha wisdom becomes manifest.
>
> The yoga is well taught
> From the mouth of the guru
> Such that from space space arises
> And space sees space.

Turning to Bhāvaviveka, S̄hay-rap-gyel-tsen explains away his usage of "consciousness" rather than "exalted wisdom":

---

[a] D̄zong-ka-b̄a's tradition takes Nāgārjuna's referent to be the emptiness of a mind that is together with defilement and that is like an element in that meditation on it yields the qualities of Buddhahood, but it does not itself contain Buddha qualities. S̄hay-rap-gyel-tsen's tradition takes it to be an element endowed with ultimate Buddha qualities. Again, the issue is not whether there is a matrix of One Gone Thus, but whether Buddha qualities are contained within it.

Also other synonyms for this are cited in the master Bhavya's *Lamp for (Nāgārjuna's) "Wisdom" of the Middle Way:*

> It is called consciousness,[a]
> Clear light, nirvāṇa,
> All-emptiness, and Body of Attributes.

[The term] consciousness on this occasion is in consideration of consciousness of the noumenon and pure consciousness because it is used as a synonym for the clear light Body of Attributes.

Chandrakīrti, however, is a problem because he explicitly refutes a matrix of One Gone Thus endowed with Buddha qualities in his *Supplement to (Nāgārjuna's) "Treatise on the Middle,"* but Shay-rap-gyel-tsen explains away Chandrakīrti's objections as confined to opinions earlier in his life:

> *Objection:* Is it not that the matrix of One Gone Thus is refuted by the master Chandrakīrti in the *Supplement to (Nāgārjuna's) "Treatise on the Middle"*?
>
> *Answer:* He clearly teaches it in his *Clear Lamp Commentary on the Guhyasamāja* because he says:
>
> > The syllable *oṃ* is the matrix of One Gone Thus. Since it gives rise to the unbreakable body of the yogi, it causes attainment of the vajra body.
>
> and:
>
> > The source of all Buddhas is all sentient beings because of being the matrix of One Gone Thus.
>
> and so forth. Even in the *Supplement to (Nāgārjuna's) "Treatise on the Middle"* Chandrakīrti says:[b]

---

[a] *rnam shes.*

[b] VI.222a-223b. Chandrakīrti gives a triple explanation—as supreme, other, and transcendent; see Louis de la Vallée Poussin, *Madhyamakāvatāra par Candrakīrti,* Bibliotheca Buddhica 9 (Osnabrück, Germany: Biblio Verlag, 1970), 339-340. Shay-rap-gyel-tsen reads this as referring to three qualities of other-emptiness, whereas Dzong-ka-ba (*Illumination of the Thought* [Sarnath, India: Pleasure of Elegant Sayings Press, 1973], 439.13) sees it as explaining that "other-factuality" itself has three meanings:

- The emptiness of inherent existence (*rang bzhin stong pa nyid*) is **supreme** in the sense that it exists without ever deviating from the character of suchness.
- The non-conceptual exalted wisdom, the excellent supramundane exalted wisdom is **other,** and the emptiness of inherent existence is the object realized by that exalted wisdom.
- The emptiness of inherent existence is **transcendent** in that "transcendent" refers to the limit of reality which here is the nirvāṇa that is the extinction of cyclic existence.

Thus, for Dzong-ka-ba, the passage is not about other-emptiness. He then is forced to

> Whether Buddhas arise or not,
> In actuality the emptiness
> Of all entities is proclaimed
> As other-factuality.
>
> Limit of reality and thusness
> Are the emptiness of other-factuality.
>
> [and Chandrakīrti's own commentary says,] "Other-factuality is the supreme suchness. Its supremacy is just its permanent existence." Since such also appears, it is suitable to analyze whether he speaks in self-contradiction. I wonder if earlier during his period of philosophical studies, he generated qualms [about the matrix of One Gone Thus], but later through entering into profound Secret Mantra his mental development emerged and his tenets changed.

Having shown that famous Proponents of the Middle[a] are actually Proponents of the **Great** Middle Way, Shay-rap-gyel-tsen proceeds to show the same for those usually categorized as Proponents of Mind-Only—Maitreya, Asaṅga, Vasubandhu, and so forth. In order to demonstrate this, he breaks down artificial boundaries:[297]

> Similarly mistaken are those who assert that Maitreya's *Differentiation of the Middle and the Extremes* and so forth are proprietary texts of Mind-Only by reason of the fact that they teach the three natures, eight collections of consciousness, and so forth, because these are also taught in sūtras and tantras of the final Middle Way. Furthermore, the meaning of the statement in Maitreya's *Differentiation of the Middle and the Extremes,* "All are just name-only," contradicts the view of the Mind-Only School.

He shows how other-emptiness is taught by Maitreya:[298]

> On the occasion of teaching suchness in Maitreya's *Ornament for the Great Vehicle Sūtras,* the ultimate is said to be other-empty; it renders a definition of the ultimate in verse as follows:[299]
>
> Not existent and not non-existent, not the same and not another,
> Not produced or disintegrating, not diminished or increasing,

explain defensively that the purpose of this emptiness, despite repeating the emptiness of inherent existence, is for the sake of eliminating the qualm that suchness would truly exist if one asserts that it is the fundamental disposition of things, that it exists forever, and that it is the object of comprehension of non-conceptual exalted wisdom. Since all three of these reflect Shay-rap-gyel-tsen's opinion, it is clear that Dzong-ka-ba's intent is to eliminate Shay-rap-gyel-tsen's reading that Chandrakīrti himself allows for other-emptiness.

[a] At other places he cites Buddhapālita, Shāntideva, and Kamalashīla.

Also not purified and yet becoming purified—
These are characteristics of the ultimate.

With respect to the meaning of this, the thought is:

- "Not existent": imputational natures and other-powered natures do not really exist.
- "Not non-existent": the noumenal thoroughly established nature is not not really existent.
- "Not the same": the three natures are not the same entity.
- "Not other": the three natures are also not different entities—the reason for this and the previous point being that entities are not really established in imputational natures and other-powered natures.
- Since the noumenal thoroughly established nature that is the basis empty of imputational natures and other-powered natures is uncompounded, it is "not produced or disintegrating, not diminished or increasing".
- Since the thoroughly established nature is naturally pure, its entity does not have anything that requires being purified.
- To attain the thoroughly established nature it must "become purified" of adventitious defilements.

That which has all five characteristics of non-duality is the definition of the ultimate. This has been explained in accordance with [Vasubandhu's] commentary. Consequently, since here also the noumenal thoroughly established nature which is empty of imputational natures and other-powered natures is said to exist as the ultimate, the ultimate is well confirmed as an other-emptiness.[a]

Shay-rap-gyel-tsen quotes widely from Maitreya's *Sublime Continuum of the Great Vehicle* (see p. 277ff. passim) and defends[300] its explanation that the teaching of a matrix of One Gone Thus endowed with Buddha qualities has a purpose. He does this under the heading:

Abandoning The Sinful View Of Mistaking [The Teaching Of The Matrix Of One Gone Thus] As Requiring Interpretation From The Fact That In The *Sublime Continuum Of The Great Vehicle* A Purpose [For Teaching It] Is Indicated.

Turning to Asaṅga's *Summary of Manifest Knowledge,* which some take to be common to the Lesser Vehicle and Great Vehicle, he shows that even it evinces the view of Great Middle Way:[301]

Moreover, this text [Asaṅga's *Summary of Manifest Knowledge*]:

---

[a] For Dzong-ka-ba's explanation of this stanza, see *Emptiness in Mind-Only,* 159.

- quotes a sūtra beyond mind-only:

  Bodhisattvas in meditative equipoise,
  Perceive a mental image, and hence
  Upon reversing the discrimination of objects,
  Definitely apprehend a discrimination of [the mind] itself.
  In that way they abide within internal mind
  And realize the absence of an apprehended-object.
  After that, they know the absence of an apprehender
  And then they know the unapprehendable.

- quotes scriptural passages beyond mind-only:

  Where eye and ear and
  Likewise, nose, tongue, body,
  And mind as well as name and form
  All entirely cease.

  Those in whom eyes cease and discriminations of colors become non-existent, up to and including, phenomena cease and discriminations of phenomena become non-existent know the source.

- and moreover refutes that dependent-arisings are produced from the four extremes
- speaks of the production-non-nature, and
- says that all phenomena are unproduced, unceasing, quiescent from the start, naturally thoroughly passed beyond sorrow and empty of the two selves, and so forth.

Consequently, [Asaṅga's *Summary of Manifest Knowledge*] is endowed with the profound quintessential instructions of the three cycles of Bodhisattva commentaries. Hence, if, upon forsaking the hosts of asserters and the [bad] predispositions [accrued] from creating dissension, one considers it well, it is clear that in the end it is a text beyond mind-only although it temporarily teaches mind-only.

S̄hay-rap-gyel-tsen stresses that Asaṅga's *Summary of the Great Vehicle* also speaks of a reality beyond mind:[302]

> On the occasion of the Bodhisattva's concordance with definite differentiation [that is, the path of preparation], they abide in mind-only, and, just after that, they directly see the mind also as non-existent. From that point, they have thoroughly passed beyond mind-only. In [Vasubandhu's] *Commentary on (Maitreya's) "Differentiation of the Middle and the Extremes"* this mode is called the "technique for entering into the character of non-existence." Asaṅga's *Summary of the*

Great Vehicle says that this is the technique and door for entering into suchness, "Entry there." This is not confined just to mind-only; the *Summary of the Great Vehicle* says:[303]

> How does one enter into the thoroughly established nature? One enters upon having overcome even the discrimination of cognition-only. At that time, for Bodhisattvas who have destroyed the discrimination of objects, there is no opportunity for the arising of mental verbalizations—which have arisen from the cause that are predispositions of the doctrines of hearing—to appear as objects. Therefore, even the perception of cognition-only does not arise.

and [the *Summary of the Great Vehicle* also says]:

> Moreover since, when non-conceptual exalted wisdom
> Is active, there is no appearance of any objects,
> It should be understood that objects do not exist.
> Since they do not exist, cognition does not exist.

These and other statements that cognition does not exist are extremely contradictory with the assertion that Proponents of Mind-Only ultimately assert that consciousness is true.[a]

Shay-rap-gyel-tsen sees Vasubandhu as presenting a final view beyond mind-only:[304]

> Likewise, Vasubandhu's statement in commentary on "That is the middle path":
>
> > Thus, this is taken as concordant with what appears in the Perfection of Wisdom [Sūtras], and so forth, "All these are not empty and are also not non-empty.
>
> contradicts the Mind-Only School. And in his commentary on:
>
> > Consciousnesses to which cognitions

[a] For Gung-tang's explanation, see p. 240ff.; for Nga-w̄ang-b̄el-den's, see p. 475. Shay-rap-gyel-tsen (*Ocean of Definitive Meaning*, 155.4) also refers to Asaṅga's *Grounds of Bodhisattvas* and so forth. Unlike Shay-rap-gyel-tsen, Dzong-ka-b̄a takes the tack that the references to a reality beyond mind are in reference to emptiness itself. In the Mind-Only School, this is the emptiness of factors imputed in the manner of entity and attribute and the emptiness of subject and object as different entities, both of which are concordant with mind-only, that is, no external objects. In the Middle Way School, the reality beyond mind is the emptiness of true existence, which refers to a canceling of not phenomena but an exaggerated status and thus leaves the dependent-arising of phenomena compatible with emptiness. For Dzong-ka-b̄a, appearance is compatible with emptiness, and hence the doctrine of emptiness, if understood properly, does not require rescuing through resorting to another category.

Of objects, sentient beings, and self appear
Are thoroughly produced. Their factuality does not exist.
Since those do not exist, these also do not exist.

his teaching that mind [that is, the mind-basis-of-all, afflicted] intellect, and [six operative] consciousnesses exist conventionally but do not ultimately exist also contradicts the Mind-Only School:

> "Their factuality does not exist" [means that] appearances as objects and sentient beings are aspectless and that appearances as self and as cognitions are wrong appearances. Since objects do not exist, apprehending consciousnesses also do not exist.

In this way, S̄hay-rap-gyel-tsen boldly draws the great tantras and sūtras as well as the prominent early Great Vehicle scholars into the sphere of the Great Middle Way. Since he breaks boundaries between set systems, it is no wonder that his grand, over-arching, iconoclastic perspective shocked Tibetan scholars from his own day to the present. It offers so much food for thought that it is no wonder that D̄zong-ka-b̄a's teacher, the S̄a-ḡya scholar Ren-da-wa Shön-nu-l̄o-drö[a]—over three readings—first found it unappealing, then appealing, and then unappealing. So provocative, it has to be taken into account.

Synonyms

Through inspired, long lists of synonyms of the ultimate, the style itself of much of S̄hay-rap-gyel-tsen's *Ocean of Definitive Meaning* communicates the richness of the other-emptiness matrix of One Gone Thus:

> Consequently, the fundamental noumenon that is empty of all phenomena, the sole expanse of the ultimate is taught with a great many synonyms in the profound sūtras and tantras—emptiness, signlessness, and so forth as well as natural nirvāṇa, expanse of selfhood, Buddha-nature, and so forth as well as Heruka, Vajrasattva, the syllable *evaṃ, ahaṃ,* Great Seal, source of phenomena, *bhaga* [vagina], vajra, the syllable *a,* and so forth.[305]
>
> One should perceive the meaning of great import in the statements in a great many profound tantras through many forms of syllables, words, and phrases that just that fundamental nature—from the start without the entities of the two selves—the ultimate, emptiness, natural clear light, endowed with all aspects, the natural innate exalted wisdom transcending the momentary abides as the self that is thusness, the pure self, forever without interruption. This completely depends on the profound quintessential instructions for experiencing the meaning

[a] *red mda' ba gzhon nu blo gros,* 1349-1412.

of the eloquent statements by tenth-ground Bodhisattvas, such as the three Bodhisattva commentaries [see p. 293].[306]

> ...all those that are stated in many forms—Vajrasattva, Vajradhara, great seal, Vishvamātā, Vajranairātmya, Vajravarahī, *evaṃ, ahaṃ,* source of phenomena, *bhaga, vajra,* great secrecy, water-born [that is, lotus], realm of space, and so forth as well as matrix of One Gone to Bliss, expanse of nirvāṇa, Buddha-nature, pure self, mind of natural clear light, naturally pure mind, ultimate mind of enlightenment, suchness, emptiness, limit of reality, thusness, Body of Attributes, expanse of reality, Nature Body, naturally pure lineage, and so forth—are just the same as the naturally pure expanse, the ultimate truth itself, the exalted wisdom knowing itself by itself.[307]

> Just the expanse of the five self-arisen exalted wisdoms that dwells pervasively in all the stable and the moving and has the nature of Heruka, the mandala wheel, the lord of the mandala, the syllable *a,* and so forth is the great life of all living beings.[308]

> Here just the expanse of reality in which the ultimate grounds are complete is taught as the basis-of-all, the matrix of One Gone to Bliss, and also the ultimate virtue.[309]

> Similarly, just this which is the entity of the basis, or lineage, thusness, the Body of Attributes, is said, like space, to pervade all phenomena. The *Sky-Traveler Vajra Tent Tantra* says:
>
> > The Buddha, the great seal
> > The wondrous great bliss resides like space
> > Wherever the realms of space are
> > And in the thousands of realms of the world.
>
> And so forth. Thus it is taught that just this vajra lineage, or naturally thoroughly pure lineage is the Buddha, the great seal, and the wondrous great bliss and also that it pervades all and serves as the basis of all, like space.[310]

> The permanent, uncompounded primordial wisdom,
> The permanent, uncompounded five Victors,
> The permanent, stable, everlasting, constant five Knowledge
> Women...[311]

There is nothing pedestrian about these many image-provoking excursions through the religious vocabulary of Great Vehicle philosophy. They are inspired and inspiring, evocative to the point of being thrilling—much of the message of the *Ocean of Definitive Meaning* being right here. As elaborate as Shay-rap-gyel-tsen's argument is, one cannot be distracted by it from noticing the heights to which the style of large portions of the text draws the mind and spirit.

Mixing Sūtra And Mantra

Ḡön-chok-jik-may-w̄ang-b̄o[312] reports that S̄hay-rap-gyel-tsen skillfully expounds his views within associating the *One Hundred Thousand Stanza Perfection of Wisdom Sūtra* and the *Kālachakra Tantra* and also within associating the *Matrix of One Gone Thus Sūtra* with the *Kālachakra Tantra,* doing this so well that many of Bu-d̄ön's students chose to study with him, and also some latter-day Ge-luk-b̄a scholars became enamored of his *Ocean of Definitive Meaning.* He chillingly adds that it is renowned that these Ge-luk-b̄a scholars, due to this, suffered interferences.[313] Ḡön-chok-jik-may-w̄ang-b̄o's student Gung-tang[a] similarly reports a criticism that the Jo-nang-b̄as mixed the vocabulary of the Kālachakra system into a discussion of sūtra positions; he complains that their explanation is something that never appeared before S̄hay-rap-gyel-tsen.

Indeed, S̄hay-rap-gyel-tsen holds that when conventionalities are ceased in the primordial wisdom, not only does the primordial wisdom, which is called the pure self, manifest but also bodies of empty form (a topic of the *Kālachakra Tantra*) adorned with the major and minor marks of a Buddha do. From this viewpoint, he asserts that the primordial wisdom—the Buddha nature—has an essence of the Form Bodies of the five Conqueror lineages.[b] Since the vocabulary of five Conqueror lineages comes from the Mantra Vehicle, Gung-tang criticizes him for applying the unique vocabulary of Mantra to the Definition Vehicle, that is, the Sūtra Great Vehicle, also called the Perfection Vehicle.

The basic criticism is that S̄hay-rap-gyel-tsen mixes Sūtra and Mantra systems, but this is not new information, since this indeed is just what he says he is doing:[314]

> Tantras should be understood by means of other tantras.
> Sūtras should be understood by means of other sūtras.

---

[a] Gung-tang's *Difficult Points,* 137.14. He attributes this opinion to *rin chen tog gi dbang po rdo rje;* Geshe Thupten Gyatso (oral discussion) identified *rin chen tog* as the author and *dbang po rdo rje* as the title of his text. W̄el-mang Ḡön-chok-gyel-tsen's *Notes on (Ḡön-chok-jik-may-w̄ang-b̄o's) Lectures* (399.5) reports that Yar-drok-b̄a (*yar 'brog pa*) initially wrote *rdo rje'i thog tog* to refute S̄hay-rap-gyel-tsen, an answer to which was composed by the latter's student Nya-b̄ön (*nya dpon*) and that, in response to it, Yar-drok-b̄a wrote a text entitled *dbang po'i rdo rje,* which is filled with slurs against S̄hay-rap-gyel-tsen such as "messenger of an evil devil" (*ngan bdud kyi pho nya*) but has few effective refutations of his views.

[b] These are the so-called *dhyāni* Buddhas, a fiction that never appears in the literature. Many thanks to Professor Karen Lang for this point.

Sūtras should also be understood by means of the tantras.
Tantras should also be understood by means of the sūtras.
Both should be understood by means of both.

It seems to me that, since Shay-rap-gyel-tsen himself announces that he draws on sūtra to explain tantra, and vice versa, the mere repetition of this by his critics falls flat.

In reaction to Shay-rap-gyel-tsen's eclectic syncretism, Dzong-ka-ba stresses the distinction of systems—this perspective so orienting his followers that even Ge-luk-ba sub-groups stress their distinctive presentations to the exclusion of other sub-groups within their own sect. Thus, in contrast to Shay-rap-gyel-tsen's stimulating usage of a great variety of texts from purportedly divergent systems to disclose the single meaning of the matrix of One Gone Thus, Ge-luk-ba scholars point to explicit arguments between systems that these very texts contain. This is the raison d'être of chapters 6 through 9 of the Mind-Only section of *The Essence of Eloquence* and has led to an emphasis within Ge-luk-ba scholarship on separating out a plurality of systems in Indian Buddhism and the creation of a plurality of systems among the followers of Dzong-ka-ba with the result that Ge-luk-ba scholars often treat expositions as mere systems rather than as probing a topic. Still, both approaches can be productive—on the one hand using the two forms of Buddha's teaching to explain each other and on the other hand recognizing the different systems within each.[a]

Comparison Of Jo-nang-ba And Ge-luk-ba On The Buddha Nature

According to Ge-luk-ba explanations, the matrix of One Gone Thus is not endowed with Buddha qualities, conventional or ultimate, simply because Buddha qualities could not be obscured by obstructions and defilements. Therefore, it might seem that much of the Jo-nang-bas' long list of attributes of the matrix of One Gone Thus could never apply to the matrix of One Gone Thus as it is conceived in Ge-luk-ba texts. Nevertheless, interesting results come from juxtaposing the vocabularies of different Buddhist systems such as when the current Dalai Lama[315] says that the fundamental innate mind of clear light—a topic only of Highest Yoga Mantra—is what Maitreya is finally getting at in his *Sublime Continuum of the Great Vehicle.*

Indeed, a comparison of their assertions on the Buddha nature shows that this is not a case of never-the-twain-shall-meet.[b] According to standard

[a] I also find both approaches to be frustrating, when carried to their extreme. One reason for my compatibility with the present Dalai Lama is that he often draws on a multitude of presentations and systems to probe an issue—the issue being put to the forefront—while doing this within awareness that he is drawing from a plenitude of sources.

[b] The history of rivalry between Ge-luk-ba and Jo-nang-ba and the continuation of the

Ge-luk-b̄a presentations of their own final system, the Middle Way Consequence School, the matrix of One Gone Thus is not a positive phenomenon but a negative phenomenon, and, among negatives, it is a mere absence, a mere elimination of inherent existence. This absence is called a non-affirming negative because it does not imply anything positive in place of the negation of inherent existence. It is simply a lack of inherent existence of a mind that is defiled—a mere absence of a status that would, if it existed, make enlightenment impossible, and thus it makes enlightenment possible.

However, in Ge-luk-b̄a presentations of the Mind-Only School following Asaṅga,[a] the matrix of One Gone Thus is not an emptiness but an impermanent phenomenon, a naturally present seed in the mind-basis-of-all, that upon activation can develop into Buddhahood. Because it is impermanent, it is **truly established** and **established by way of its own character**, and this seed of enlightenment itself is a **positive phenomenon,** not a mere absence or even an affirming negative. Although it is not an **autonomous** entity since it is impermanent and hence an other-powered nature, it resides in the mind naturally—intrinsic to the mind and not newly deposited by actions of body, speech, or mind, as most seeds or potencies are.

Also, according to Ge-luk-b̄a presentations of Highest Yoga Tantra, the fundamental innate mind of clear light can be considered an **other-emptiness** in that it is empty of being any of the coarser levels of consciousness.[316] Even though a chair is not a table and a table is not a chair and hence they are empty of each other and thus other-empty in this respect, this fact is not significant in terms of practicing the path in either the Ge-luk-b̄a or the Jo-nang-b̄a systems, and thus this does not warrant being called the emptiness of the chair or the emptiness of the table in either system. Still, in Ge-luk-b̄a, the fundamental innate mind of clear light is empty of being the coarser levels of consciousness, and those coarser levels of consciousness are empty of being the fundamental innate mind of clear light, and a significant feature of the Highest Yoga Tantra path is to stop the coarser levels of consciousness in order to manifest this most subtle mind. Thus, that the fundamental innate mind of clear light is empty of being the coarser levels of consciousness is important, and this other-emptiness warrants being called an emptiness even if it is not an emptiness of inherent existence (though in Ge-luk-b̄a it does not rule out an emptiness of inherent existence, as it does in S̄hay-rap-gyel-tsen's system). Thus, even in Ge-luk-b̄a presentations, there is an acceptable way of using the term "other-emptiness"

---

rivalry in Ge-luk-b̄a debating courtyards despite the repression of the Jo-nang-b̄a school during the reign of the Fifth Dalai Lama make Ge-luk-b̄a scholars present their tenets in public as if there was no common ground. However, their devotion to debate and the consequent demand that individual scholars take the side of the heretic opponent (and win) have resulted in some of their scholars looking into the Jo-nang-b̄a position with a kinder eye.

[a] See Gareth Sparham, *Ocean of Eloquence: Tsong kha pa's Commentary on the Yogācāra Doctrine of Mind* (Albany, N.Y.: State University of New York Press, 1993), 87-94.

with regard to the fundamental innate mind of clear light despite the long history of disputation against the Jo-nang-b̄as' particular presentation of it.

In Ge-luk-b̄a, this other-emptiness does not contradict "self-emptiness" for the entity of the fundamental innate mind of clear light is itself empty of inherent existence and thus is also "self-empty," but not in the Jo-nang-b̄a sense of self-canceling as the ultimate would be if it were self-empty. For the Jo-nang-b̄as, the final reality, which includes the most profound wisdom, could never lack inherent existence since that would mean it is non-existent (see p. 285ff.).

According to Highest Yoga Tantra as presented in Ge-luk-b̄a texts, every sentient being has a fundamental innate mind of clear light that is a **positive phenomenon** or an affirming negative, but not **autonomous** since it is produced by causes and conditions. In the ordinary state, it is not active, and hence there is a question of whether, despite being a consciousness, it does not engage any objects. As the nineteenth-century Inner Mongolian scholar Nga-w̄ang-b̄el-den says in his *Presentation of the Grounds and Paths of the Four Great Secret Tantra Sets: Illumination of the Texts of Tantra:*[317]

> Sentient beings have gross temporary bodies and minds and subtle fundamental bodies and minds. As long as the gross body performs the activities of moving and so forth, the fundamental body does not rise in the aspect of the face and arms [and so forth of a deity]. When the activity of moving, etc., of the gross body is severed by the power of all the coarse winds dissolving into the indestructible drop at the heart, the fundamental body rises in the aspect of face and arms and performs the activities of going and coming and so forth. In the continuums of sentient beings there exist simultaneously two mental consciousnesses, the subtle and the coarse, but there is no fallacy of contradiction with sūtra and there is no fallacy that it follows that there are two continuums [in one person]. This is because:
>
> - As long as a gross mind performs the activity of apprehending the aspect of an object of observation, a subtle mind does not apprehend the aspect of an object of observation.
> - When a subtle mind apprehends the aspect of an object of observation, a coarse mind, having stopped, does not exist.
>
> Such a meaning is stated in the *Notes on Kay-drup-jay's Words.* [Nevertheless] when debating, it is difficult to posit a consciousness without an object of comprehension [as would be the case with a subtle mind when a coarse mind is apprehending an object]; therefore, this must be analyzed.

In Ge-luk-b̄a scholasticism, it is uncomfortable to posit a consciousness, no matter how subtle, that does not have an object, and indeed the difficulties with asserting that the fundamental innate mind of clear light has no object when coarse winds are operating suggest why the Jo-nang-b̄as hold that the matrix of One Gone Thus has itself as the object of its mode of apprehension, or, to put it more simply, is aware of itself. As S̄hay-rap-gyel-tsen[a] says:

> ...there are also two types of Buddha-realization, the self-arisen exalted wisdom that is the primordial realization of the noumenon—knowing itself by itself[b]—and the other-arisen exalted wisdom that is realization produced from having cultivated the profound path. The first is complete within the noumenon...

It may be that when a practitioner gets down to the subtle level of the matrix of One Gone Thus, this deep level of mind is effortlessly experienced in a way that can be described only as the mind's knowing itself, and thus there is special value in teaching that beings already have internally an exalted wisdom consciousness that is cognizant of itself.

Still, as Gung-tang[318] emphasizes, the Jo-nang-b̄as' positing of a positive self-powered final nature contradicts the clear explanations in their own source sūtras that the final nature—the thoroughly established nature—is a non-affirming negative, a mere elimination of an object of negation, as when the *Sūtra Unraveling the Thought* (*Emptiness in Mind-Only,* 91) says:

> If the character [that is, entity] of compositional things and the character of the ultimate were different [entities], then just the **mere** selflessness and the **mere** naturelessness [of the self of phenomena] of compositional things would not be [their] ultimate character.

and (*Emptiness in Mind-Only,* 90):

> ...the ultimate is distinguished by just the naturelessness of all phenomena

and so forth.

Gung-tang's teacher, Ḡön-chok-jik-may-w̄ang-b̄o, in lectures written down by W̄el-mang Ḡön-chok-gyel-tsen, calls attention to D̄zong-ka-b̄a's emphasis on the fact that the thoroughly established nature is a mere negative and the innovation that this brought to the world of Tibetan Buddhism:[319]

> Many earlier great Tibetan scholars, not knowing that emptiness is a non-affirming negative, asserted that emptiness is an affirming negative or asserted that it is a positive entity. Many such assertions arose in the past. That nowadays when anyone does not take emptiness to be a non-affirming negative, everyone breaks into laughter is due to the compassion of the Foremost Lama [D̄zong-ka-b̄a].

The stress that he put on the delineation of the thoroughly established nature as

---

a For more context, see p. 280ff.

b *rang gis rang rig pa.*

a mere negative distanced his system from many other Tibetan explanations to the point where his followers find those to be ridiculous.

Gung-tang avers that Shay-rap-gyel-tsen mistook the mention—in Maitreya's *Sublime Continuum of the Great Vehicle*—of an uncontaminated **consciousness** that exists in all beings for an actual uncontaminated primordial **wisdom**. In the first chapter of Maitreya's text, nine examples are given to illustrate how the matrix of One Gone Thus—a Buddha nature—exists in the continuums of all beings as a great, hidden, unused treasure:[320]

> That [such an essential constituent now] dwells inside the covering of afflictive emotions [of sentient beings]
> Is to be known by way of examples [as its entity cannot now be known].
>
> Like a Buddha [dwelling inside] an ugly lotus, honey in [the middle of many] bees,
> A kernel inside a husk, gold within filth,
> A treasury [of jewels] in the earth [under the house of the destitute, the capacity of growing] stalks and so forth [existing] in a small seed,
> The image of a Conqueror [made from a precious substance] inside a tattered garment,
>
> A lord of humans [who is a Universal Monarch] inside the womb of a lowly woman,
> And a precious [golden] image in an earthen [mold],
> This [naturally pure] essential constituent dwells in sentient beings
> Obscured with the adventitious defilements of afflictive emotions.
>
> The [obscuring] defilements are similar to a lotus, living [bees], husk, filth, earth,
> Fruit, tattered garment, woman pained by burning suffering, and earth constituent.
> The precious essential constituent [naturally] undefiled [from the start, which is what is obscured] is similar
> To the Buddha, honey, kernel, gold, treasure [of jewels],
> Nyagrodha tree, precious image, supreme lord of the continents, and precious statue.

Expanding on the example of honey in the midst of bees, Maitreya's text says:[321]

> Just as a person, skilled [in analyzing honey] upon seeking it,
> Sees honey [of excellent taste and potency] surrounded [and protected] by a swarm of bees,
> And thoroughly removes it from the swarm of bees
> Through [various] methods [such as using smoke and thereby gets the honey],

So the great sage [Buddha], having perceived with the all-knowing eye
The essential constituent of [individual] knowledge like honey,
Works at totally removing the obstructions, like bees,
To that [basic constituent].

Just as a person seeking honey, [having seen] honey obstructed by many thousands of ten millions of bees
Removes those and makes use of the honey [for medicine, food, and so forth] according to his or her wish,
So the Conqueror—skilled in destroying the afflictive emotions, like bees, [which obstruct] the **uncontaminated consciousness**, like honey,
Existing in [all] embodied beings—is like a person skilled [in taking honey].

Maitreya's mention of an "uncontaminated consciousness" is taken by Ge-luk-b̄a scholars to be the pure, naturally undefiled nature of consciousness present in all beings, but it is taken by the Jo-nang-b̄as to refer to a primordial wisdom endowed with Buddha qualities and present in all beings. Indeed, Maitreya's example of honey is more like the Jo-nang-b̄a presentation, for honey itself is present in a honeycomb surrounded by bees; it is not a substance that needs further refinement.

The Jo-nang-b̄a view of the presence of a permanent matrix endowed with Buddha qualities within all sentient beings accords with seven of the nine metaphors—a Buddha inside an ugly lotus, honey in the midst of bees, a kernel inside a husk, gold within filth, a treasury of jewels under the house of the destitute, a statue of a Buddha inside a tattered garment, and a precious image in a clay mold. The Ge-luk-b̄a presentation of a naturally uncontaminated consciousness that can **develop** into Buddhahood accords with two of the examples—the capacity of growth existing in a small seed and the fetus of a Universal Monarch dwelling inside the womb of a lowly woman.

In Ge-luk-b̄a, the basic position that all minds are impermanent phenomena compounded by causes and conditions makes a permanent mind utterly unthinkable, but it needs to be seen that these two approaches may be using the term "permanent" in different ways.[a] In Ge-luk-b̄a, the emphasis of the word

[a] I say this despite the fact that S̄hay-rap-gyel-tsen (*Ocean of Definitive Meaning,* 127.1) clearly indicates that he does not take the permanent and uncompounded features of the matrix of One Gone Thus to be merely permanent in the sense that a continuum of moments goes on forever and to be merely that the matrix of One Gone Thus is not compounded by afflicted causes and conditions:

> Furthermore, the holy Superior Lokeshvara [that is, Kalki Puṇḍarīka] says that the exalted wisdom of thusness transcends momentariness:
>
> > The exalted wisdom that is devoid of single or plural moments is the thusness of Conquerors.

"permanent" is on not being produced by any sort of causation, impure or pure, whereas in other schools "permanent" sometimes signifies a higher order of entity beyond just not being subject to causation. Even Ge-luk-b̄a scholars, despite maintaining a strict theoretical incompatibility between consciousness and permanence, resort to the realm of analog when speaking about the fusion of object and subject that occurs in direct realization of emptiness, comparing the relationship between emptiness and the mind directly realizing it to water poured into water which become so undifferentiably mixed that they cannot be identified separately. To convey a sense of this level of the path, they resort to an analog, while maintaining a presentation of the separateness of wisdom and emptiness in their theoretical discussions.

Other schools, however, make the equivalence of emptiness and the mind realizing it a foundation of their theoretical explanations, thereby endowing those descriptions with the psychological impact of the most profound state. Ge-luk-b̄a scholarship stems, to a large extent, from opting in favor of a position that is more philosophically defensible in terms of early stages of the path, though difficult in later stages, and consequently Ge-luk-b̄a scholarship can sometimes offer more "food for thought" for beginners. The other style offers immediately evocative insights even for some beginners but, unless one can stay with such a profound level, sometimes seems to lack steps of progress that stimulate development. This latter point perhaps is one of the reasons why S̄hay-rap-gyel-tsen is critical of N̄ying-ma approaches to the spiritual path.[a]

The Jo-nang-b̄a and the Ge-luk-b̄a insistence on a seamless system (despite great seams that they themselves try to bridge) results in magnificent enterprises

---

> Moreover, the statements by the holy Conqueror Maitreya that the noumenon, the Nature Body, is a permanent nature, "The exalted wisdom devoid of single and plural moments is the suchness of the Conquerors," and that the final buddha is uncompounded with "It is uncompounded and spontaneous" [*Sublime Continuum,* I.5], and so forth, are in consideration that it is devoid of momentariness. Hence, those who assert that:
>
> - all statements that the Body of Attributes or exalted wisdom are permanent are in consideration that their **continuum** is permanent and [the Body of Attributes or exalted wisdom] are [actually] impermanent due to being momentary
> - all statements that the Buddha or exalted wisdom are uncompounded are in consideration that they are not compounded by actions and afflictive emotions
>
> are reduced to merely not realizing these meanings of great import because of just not seeing these profound scriptures.

Since D̄zong-ka-b̄a's opinions about the matrix of One Gone Thus as presented in the Middle Way School are included in these two positions that S̄hay-rap-gyel-tsen explicitly rejects, there is no way to claim that somehow the two systems are saying the same thing.

[a] See *Emptiness in Mind-Only,* 52-53.

that are often evocative but at other times breed conceptual complexities that can close down insight, when they are not released from the context of their one-sidedness. However, when one-sided conceptualization is placed in the context of the "other side of the coin," a sense of wholeness—unbridgeable by words but stimulated by words from seemingly diametrically opposed systems—may emerge. The Jo-nang-b̄a position draws attention to the **mind** of reality—its constancy, its fundamental nature, its being both under and beyond the realm of compounded phenomena. Because of the immediate sense of a relation between that fundamental mind with ordinary mind, one is beckoned to a state in which mind is already grounded. The immanence of reality—its accessibility to manifest experience—is thereby highlighted. (Still, it cannot be said that the same is not true for those who have trained in the complexities of the view of reality as a non-affirming negative.)

17a. Analysis of Ge-luk-b̄a Criticisms of the Jo-nang-b̄a View: I

D̄zong-ka-b̄a's presentation of the Mind-Only section of *The Essence of Eloquence* has five major agendas (*Emptiness in Mind-Only,* 54) that stand in relationship to S̄hay-rap-gyel-tsen's views:

- To show that the *Sūtra Unraveling the Thought* presents the ultimate as a mere absence and thus to undermine S̄hay-rap-gyel-tsen's view that the ultimate is positive;
- To demonstrate how the founder of the Mind-Only system, the fourth-century north Indian sage Asaṅga, relied primarily on the *Sūtra Unraveling the Thought* and thus to undercut S̄hay-rap-gyel-tsen's notions that Asaṅga's texts could differ from the presentations in this sūtra;
- To detail the objections—found in chief works by Asaṅga—to doctrines of the Middle Way School and thereby to refute S̄hay-rap-gyel-tsen's attempt to amalgamate parts of the classical texts by Asaṅga—that are usually recognized as of the Mind-Only School—with classical texts of the Middle Way School to form a Great Middle Way;
- To show how texts by Maitreya and Indian scholars, which are prevalently recognized as Mind-Only, accord with presentations in the *Sūtra Unraveling the Thought* and in the above-mentioned works by Asaṅga and thereby further to undercut S̄hay-rap-gyel-tsen's finding multiple systems in their texts; and
- To present how the truth behind false superimpositions contrary to the nature of phenomena is realized through opposing misconceptions about the status of phenomena and thereby to counter S̄hay-rap-gyel-tsen's supposed depiction of manifesting a positive ultimate.

There are eleven major refutations that, while incorporating the above points, fall into three categories and one additional criticism. Let us consider these in detail in this and the next three chapters.

1. "Self-Contradiction": Claiming To Follow The *Sūtra Unraveling The Thought* But Asserting That The Thoroughly Established Nature Is Positive

D̄zong-ka-b̄a (*Emptiness in Mind-Only,* 92) berates S̄hay-rap-gyel-tsen for, on the one hand, asserting that the *Sūtra Unraveling the Thought* is definitive and, on the other hand, not following its clear teaching that the thoroughly established nature is a mere negative. He says that, instead, S̄hay-rap-gyel-tsen opts for the view that the final reality is positive:

> It is contradictory [for the Jo-nang-b̄as], while asserting the teaching of the meaning of suchness in this sūtra to be definitive, not to posit the immutable thoroughly established nature by way of an elimination-isolate[a]—which is the mere elimination of an object of negation—but rather to assert it as a positive, self-powered [uncontaminated wisdom], whose appearance as an object of awareness does not depend on the elimination of an object of negation.[b]

D̄zong-ka-b̄a's cogent position that the *Sūtra Unraveling the Thought* speaks of the ultimate only as a mere negative was discussed above,[c] and he accuses S̄hay-rap-gyel-tsen of holding that the thoroughly established nature is positive.

S̄hay-rap-gyel-tsen's opinion, however, is more nuanced. Although in the *Fourth Council* he does not use the term "positive"[d] for the thoroughly established nature, he speaks of it as an **affirming negative**. This means that, opposite to D̄zong-ka-b̄a's depiction of his opponent's position here, the thoroughly established nature appears to the mind through the route of eliminating an object of negation, albeit within implying a positive phenomenon. Also, in the *Ocean of Definitive Meaning* (see sample quotations, p. 292ff.) S̄hay-rap-gyel-tsen emphasizes that it is necessary to delineate the difference between non-affirming negatives and affirming negatives, the thoroughly established nature being the latter (he uses the term "affirming negative" nine times and "inclusionary elimination" five times). Still, in the *Ocean of Definitive Meaning* he uses the term "positive" three times about the ultimate:[322]

> Similarly, those who assert that in the mode of subsistence, except for exclusions and non-affirming negatives, there are not at all any inclusions, positives, or affirming negatives are extremely mistaken because I have repeatedly explained and will explain that:
>
> - Natural exclusion, negation, and abandonment are complete in the mode of subsistence since all faults are naturally non-existent and non-established in the mode of subsistence.
> - Natural realizations of the inclusionary, the positive, and affirming negatives are primordially complete [in the mode of subsistence] since all noumenal qualities are naturally complete in their basis.

---

a For a discussion of isolates (or conceptually isolatable phenomena), see Daniel E. Perdue, *Debate in Tibetan Buddhism* (Ithaca, N.Y.: Snow Lion, 1992), 695-771; and Georges B. J. Dreyfus, *Recognizing Reality: Dharmakīrti's Philosophy and Its Tibetan Interpretations* (Albany, N.Y.: State University of New York Press, 1997); see the latter's index under "distinguisher."

b See *Absorption*, #62-65.

c For types of negatives, see pp. 242-258; for quotations from the *Sūtra Unraveling the Thought*, see pp. 261-266.

d *sgrub pa, vidhi.*

Thus, Shay-rap-gyel-tsen's opinion is that the ultimate, the matrix of One Gone to Bliss, is a combination of affirming negatives and positives.

That Dzong-ka-ba is exaggerating for the sake of effect—when he reduces Shay-rap-gyel-tsen's opinion to being that the ultimate is just positive—can be seen by the fact that he treats Shay-rap-gyel-tsen's assertion that the ultimate is a negative (with imputational natures and other-powered natures as the objects of negation) later in the section on the Mind-Only School (see p. 328ff. and *Emptiness in Mind-Only,* 226-227). Here, he does not show **how** Shay-rap-gyel-tsen comes to maintain that the matrix of One Gone Thus is realized without eliminating an object of negation, that is, is (just) positive, but he does in the section on the Consequence School through analyzing how the permanence of the matrix of One Gone Thus appears to the mind:[323]

> With respect to how, if [the teaching of a permanent matrix of One Gone Thus endowed with Buddha qualities] was held to be literal, it would be the same as propounding that a self exists: [Buddha] teaches that a matrix of One Gone Thus exists, [but he does this] in the context of considering a meaning in his thought. [Such is] for instance,
>
> - emptiness—the mere elimination of the proliferations of existence by way of [the object's] own character
> - non-production—the mere elimination of the proliferations of production by way of [the object's] own character
> - selflessness—the mere elimination of the proliferations of a self of phenomena.
>
> However, if that was not the case and [the matrix of One Gone Thus endowed with Buddha qualities] were as it is taught in the literal reading, then even its permanence [as in the statement that the matrix is permanent and stable][324] would not be an **absence** of disintegration—a **mere elimination** whose object of negation is disintegration. Due to this, [the permanence of the matrix endowed with Buddha qualities] would not need to be posited from the viewpoint of eliminating an object of negation [namely, disintegration] but would be a permanence appearing as a positive entity just as blue or yellow [appears to and is a cause producing an eye consciousness apprehending blue or yellow]. In that case, [its mode of permanence] would not differ from the mode of permanence in the [non-Buddhist] Forders' propounding a permanent self. Thereby [those who propound a matrix endowed with Buddha qualities] would come to assert a permanent [and yet] functioning thing.
>
> The damages [that is, refutations] to that [permanent and stable matrix][325] are the reasonings refuting the permanent [entities] which are asserted by Others' Schools [that is, non-Buddhist schools]—these

> being set forth by our own upper and lower schools. Hence, even those [upper and lower Buddhist schools] do not assert such a meaning [that is, such a matrix].[326]

To try to unpack this crucial but cryptically brief refutation, let us start with a standard Ge-luk-b̄a definition of the permanent:

> That which is a common locus of [being] a phenomenon and non-momentary.[a]

Momentariness is eliminated, but being a phenomenon is included; hence—for those Ge-luk-b̄a scholars such as Paṇ-chen S̄ö-nam-drak-b̄a who hold that whether a definiendum (such as the permanent) is positive or negative and, within the latter, an affirming negative or non-affirming negative is determined by its definition—the permanent would be an affirming negative.[b] D̄zong-ka-b̄a, however, defines the permanent as "a mere elimination whose object of negation is disintegration" and thus must hold that it is a non-affirming negative.[c] He seeks to show that for S̄hay-rap-gyel-tsen the ultimate is not a non-affirming negative by indicating that the permanence of the matrix of One Gone Thus endowed with Buddha qualities comes to be positive in his system.

Next, let us clear away a common misunderstanding about D̄zong-ka-b̄a's system. It indeed is the case that, in his presentation of the Mind-Only and Middle Way Schools, the ultimate must be a non-affirming negative and thus must be arrived at through the elimination of an object of negation (see chart).

D̄zong-ka-b̄a's Assertions on the Ultimate Truth in Great Vehicle Schools

SCHOOL	OBJECT OF NEGATION	SELFLESSNESS / ULTIMATE TRUTH
Mind-Only School	Establishment by way of objects' own character as the referents of their respective terms and conceptual consciousnesses Establishment of object and subject as separate entities	Mere absence of establishment by way of objects' own character as the referents of their respective terms and conceptual consciousnesses Mere absence of establishment of object and subject as separate entities
Middle Way Autonomy School	True establishment	Mere absence of true establishment
Middle Way Consequence School	Inherent establishment	Mere absence of inherent establishment

Thus it might seem that only a conceptual consciousness could realize the ultimate. However, **prior** reasoned elimination of that object of negation is

[a] *chos dang skad cig ma ma yin pa'i gzhi mthun pa;* see Perdue, *Debate in Tibetan Buddhism,* 279.

[b] Roughly speaking, they hold this with respect to the category; it is obvious that they do not hold that whatever is permanent has to be an affirming negative.

[c] I wonder how he would avoid the fault that the horns of a rabbit are permanent.

sufficient. Both Shay-rap-gyel-tsen and Dzong-ka-ba hold that a wisdom of meditative equipoise on the path of seeing or path of meditation is non-conceptual and that Buddhahood is totally beyond conceptuality. Non-conceptual realization is hallowed as the only means to overcome obstructions from the root.

In Dzong-ka-ba's formulation, it is a distinctive tenet of the Great Vehicle schools that a mere absence—an emptiness which is a permanent phenomenon—can serve as an appearing object[a] of a direct perception, but not in the sense that it produces the consciousness. In the Sūtra School, however, the appearing objects of a wisdom consciousness are the impermanent aggregates of mind and body that are implicitly understood to be selfless.[b] In Dzong-ka-ba's depiction of the Great Vehicle schools a mere absence—an emptiness—appears to a wisdom consciousness of direct perception not through the route of the appearance of a generic image, but explicitly appears within being the appearing object.

Shay-rap-gyel-tsen emphasizes that a mere absence cannot appear to the mind and thus in the Great Middle Way, or Ultimate Mind-Only, the ultimate truth is an affirming negative (see p. 292ff.), not a non-affirming negative:[327]

Since there are innumerable cases of knowing within not appearing,

---

a *snang yul, *pratibhāsaviṣaya.*

b As Gön-chok-jik-may-wang-bo says:

> Because the appearing object of direct perception must be a specifically characterized object, the Proponents of Sūtra do not assert that the subtle selflessness of persons is the object of the mode of apprehension by an uninterrupted path of a Hearer's [or anyone's] path of seeing. This is because they assert that the subtle selflessness of persons is realized *implicitly* by Hearers [and so forth] through *explicit* comprehension of compositional phenomena [the mental and physical aggregates] that are devoid of a self of persons.

Sopa and Hopkins comment:

> The object comprehended by an uninterrupted path belonging to a path of seeing or a path of meditation must be perceived directly. Whatever is perceived directly must be a specifically characterized phenomenon, and such are always compounded phenomena. An emptiness, however, is an uncompounded phenomenon and, therefore, not a specifically characterized phenomenon. Since an emptiness cannot be cognized directly, it is asserted that a yogic direct perception does not *explicitly* cognize selflessness. Rather, it cognizes the mind and body as no longer qualified with such a self. Thus, it is compounded phenomena, the mental and physical aggregates, that are directly cognized, and thereby the emptiness of a self of persons is *implicitly* realized. This fact greatly distinguishes the Proponents of Sūtra from the Great Vehicle schools, which assert direct cognition of emptiness itself.

See Geshe Lhundup Sopa and Jeffrey Hopkins, *Cutting through Appearances: The Practice and Theory of Tibetan Buddhism* (Ithaca, N.Y.: Snow Lion, 1989), 245-246.

> knowing does not entail appearance [of the object], like knowing the past and the future which are separated [from the present] by many eons and knowing selflessness and so forth even though those do not appear.

He takes it for granted that selflessness—an absence of self—could not appear to the mind:[328]

> If in order [for an omniscient mind] to know [conventional phenomena] those phenomena definitely had to appear, then there would be the great absurdity that the great many non-affirming negatives such as no self, no sentient being, no living being, no nourisher,[a] and so forth and all past and future phenomena which are separated [from the present] by long periods would have to appear to an omniscient exalted wisdom because it knows those.

S̄hay-rap-gyel-tsen's epistemology accords with what Ge-luk-b̄a scholars ascribe to Lesser Vehicle schools: permanent phenomena do not appear to a direct perception.

Contrary to mere negatives which cannot appear to a direct perception, the noumenon does appear:[329]

> Therefore, this statement that this exalted wisdom [of omniscience] knows negative phenomena **whereas they do not appear** and knows the basis of negation, the noumenon, **upon its appearance** is so in fact. Hence, this clears away the assertion by some that the noumenon does not appear to that exalted wisdom and also clears away the assertion that its realization of the noumenon is an implicit realization[b] because:
>
> - It is said again and again—that the noumenon explicitly appears to that exalted wisdom—through "The great illumintion, the great clarity," and so forth, and through examples such as magical reflections [in mirrors used for prognostication].
> - The noumenon is the basis of negation [of imputational natures and other-powered natures] and is an affirming negative, not a mere emptiness and a non-affirming negative.
>
> Consequently, those mistakes are perverse views asserting that the noumenon is equivalent to self-emptiness. Also, the mistake that in the mode of subsistence there are no inclusionary attributes is the same. For if all were self-empty, whatever are self-empty are non-affirming negatives and those are aside from only positive attributes.

[a] The list is perhaps drawn from the *Teaching of Akṣhayamati Sūtra;* see Jeffrey Hopkins, *Meditation on Emptiness,* 599.

[b] D̄zong-ka-b̄a does not hold either of these views.

For Shay-rap-gyel-tsen, the objects of negation are imputational natures and other-powered natures, leaving a thoroughly established nature that is not a mere elimination but is endowed with Buddha qualities such as the marks and beauties of a Buddha's body as well as the ten powers and so forth, which he says are also permanent and an inherent endowment.

It seems to me that Dzong-ka-ba makes the extrapolation that these Buddha qualities such as physical marks and wisdom[a] must be impermanent, and thus the ultimate truth, as described by Shay-rap-gyel-tsen, has to be able to impinge on, not just appear to, consciousness, producing awarenesses the way blue or yellow contribute to the engendering of an eye consciousness. In that case, the permanent matrix of One Gone Thus would be a functioning thing[b] that produces effects. The accusation is that such a combination of functionality and permanence is asserted by non-Buddhist schools but is refuted as utterly impossible by all Buddhist schools.[c] Dzong-ka-ba concludes that even lower Buddhist schools do not assert a matrix of One Gone Thus presently endowed with Buddha qualities, and thus the Jo-nang-ba assertion puts it beyond the pale of Buddhist systems.[d]

---

[a] Dzong-ka-ba, given his own identification of the ultimate as a non-affirming negative, makes the separation of wisdom and the ultimate a frequent theme in his writings, despite the fact that he recognizes the fact that, in direct realization of emptiness—the thoroughly established nature—both emptiness and the wisdom consciousness realizing it are undifferentiable in experience, like fresh water poured into fresh water. Dzong-ka-ba's aim is to undermine Shay-rap-gyel-tsen's opinion that the thoroughly established nature is both emptiness and exalted wisdom, but to accomplish this he must explain away statements in authoritative Indian texts that appear to agree with Shay-rap-gyel-tsen's view. For four such occurrences, see *Emptiness in Mind-Only,* 163/296, 164/297, 166/298—the numbers after the slashes refer to the Synopsis.

[b] *dngos po.* See also *Absorption,* #65.

[c] Dzong-ka-ba does not identify here how lower Buddhist schools refute the non-Buddhist assertion of a functioning permanent entity, since it is considered to be common knowledge among scholars. Basically, the refutation is that the permanent cannot act, since either it would always produce the same effect or it would never produce an effect.

[d] See also 381ff. Dzong-ka-ba's student Gyel-tsap (*How to Practice the Two Stages of the Path of the Glorious Kālachakra,* vol. 1, 123.5 (18a.5) similarly excoriates Shay-rap-gyel-tsen for identifying empty forms—permanent forms that inhere in fundamental reality—as ultimates. Gyel-tsap takes these "empty forms and so forth" as positive phenomena in Shay-rap-gyel-tsen's system:

> Asserting that positive phenomena, such as empty forms and so forth, which do not rely on the elimination of an object of negation are permanent [functioning] things as well as being ultimate truths deprecates the entire [*Kālachakra*] *Tantra* as well as the commentaries. Also, since asserting permanent [functioning] things sets up the system of the [non-Buddhist] Forder Aiṣhvaras, Sāṃkhyas, and Guhya-Vedāntins, it should be forsaken like drops of spit.

The invective is typical and is on a par with Shay-rap-gyel-tsen's depiction of doctrines—common to the Nying-ma sect—that call for recognizing conceptuality as the Truth Body of

Still, it seems to me that D̄zong-ka-b̄a's assertion that emptiness is the appearing object of a wisdom of direct perception in meditative equipoise and yet there is no current conceptual elimination of an object of negation may itself suggest that for someone familiar with emptiness it openly impinges on the mental consciousness. Also, Maitreya's *Sublime Continuum of the Great Vehicle* (I.40) contains a suggestion that reality indirectly impinges even on the awareness of ordinary beings, beckoning us toward liberation through its contrast with the situation of pain:

> If the basic Buddha element did not exist,
> Discouragement with the suffering [of cyclic existence] would not occur
> And the desire for nirvāṇa as well as seeking [methods for attaining it]
> And wishing [for it] would also not exist.

---

a Buddha as "the secret work of devils" (see Cyrus R. Stearns, *The Buddha from Dol po: A Study of the Life and Thought of the Tibetan Master Dolpopa Sherab Gyaltsen* [Albany, N.Y.: State University of New York Press, 1999], 101).

Gyel-tsap does not explain his meaning. However, it seems to me that, since the term "empty" in "empty forms" is said to mean devoid of, or beyond, material particles, empty forms also would seem to be affirming negatives. As the Dalai Lama says:

> "Aspected emptiness," on the other hand, refers to empty forms. Hence, whereas the object of negation of unaspected emptiness is inherent existence, the object of negation of aspected emptiness is material phenomena composed of particles. Therefore, "aspected emptiness" refers to various forms, or physical objects, that are beyond materiality.

H.H. the Dalai Lama, Tenzin Gyatso, and Jeffrey Hopkins, *The Kālachakra Tantra: Rite of Initiation* (London: Wisdom, 1985; 2d rev. ed. 1989), 211-212. From the viewpoint of this type of explanation, empty forms would be affirming negatives, not positive phenomena.

17b. Analysis of Ge-luk-b̄a Criticisms of the Jo-nang-b̄a View: II

2. "Self-Contradiction": Claiming To Follow The *Sūtra Unraveling The Thought* But Asserting That The Thoroughly Established Nature Is Empty Of Other-Powered Natures And Imputational Natures

Over the course of the Mind-Only section of *The Essence of Eloquence,* D̄zong-ka-b̄a makes the point that in the *Sūtra Unraveling the Thought* the thoroughly established nature is described as other-powered natures' emptiness of the imputational nature, but, contrary to this, S̄hay-rap-gyel-tsen holds that the thoroughly established nature is empty of other-powered natures and imputational natures. Corollary assertions by S̄hay-rap-gyel-tsen are that other-powered natures and imputational natures are self-empty but the thoroughly established nature is other-empty, and hence all conventional phenomena are only fancied by a mistaken mind and are not established in the slightest, whereas the thoroughly established nature is truly established.

D̄zong-ka-b̄a (*Emptiness in Mind-Only,* 107-108) quotes a clear statement in the *Sūtra Unraveling the Thought* specifying that the thoroughly established nature is the mere absence of the imputational nature in other-powered natures:

> *Question:* If the thoroughly established nature is the ultimate-non-nature, what is it?
>
> *Answer:* About that, in the *Sūtra Unraveling the Thought* [the Bodhisattva Paramārthasamudgata says during his rerendering of the meaning of Buddha's answer]:
>
> The thoroughly established character is that which is:
>
> - the thorough non-establishment—of just those [other-powered natures which are] the objects of activity of conceptuality, the foundations of imputational characters, and those which have the signs of compositional phenomena—as that imputational character,
> - just the naturelessness of only that [imputational] nature,
> - the absence of self in phenomena,
> - thusness, and
> - the object of observation of purification.
>
> "[The absence of self] in phenomena..." identifies as the thoroughly established nature just that selflessness of phenomena called "thusness"

through observation of and meditation on which obstructions are purified.[a] What is the selflessness of phenomena? It is "just the naturelessness [of the imputational nature that is the object of negation in the view of selflessness]." "Just" means "only that."[b]

What sort of nature is non-existent? With "of only that [imputational] nature," it speaks of the imputational nature mentioned before.[c] "Only" eliminates anything else; therefore, it does not refer to the naturelessness [that is, the absence] of the other two natures [that is, other-powered natures and imputational natures as the Jo-nang-bas say] but means that the non-existence of the nature of only the imputational factor is taken as the thoroughly established nature.

With respect to what is explained by the previous "just those," the statement "of **just those** [other-powered natures] which are (1) the objects of activity of conceptuality, (2) the foundations of imputational characters, and (3) those which have the signs of compositional phenomena" indicates that other-powered natures are the bases of emptiness. Then, "non-establishment as the imputational character" very clearly [indicates] that the emptiness of the imputational factor in **just those** [other-powered natures] is the thoroughly established nature.

Dzong-ka-ba thereby cogently establishes that in the system of the *Sūtra Unraveling the Thought:*

- Other-powered natures are the bases of emptiness.
- The imputational nature is that of which other-powered natures are empty, that is to say, the object of negation.
- The mere absence of the second in the first is the thoroughly established nature.

With this as a background, he (*Emptiness in Mind-Only,* 109) attacks Shay-rap-gyel-tsen for holding that the thoroughly established nature is the basis of emptiness and that of which it is empty is other-powered natures and imputational natures:

> Hence, it is contradictory [for the Jo-nang-bas] to assert that this sūtra's teaching on the mode of emptiness is of definitive meaning and to assert that the last nature's emptiness of the first two natures is the thoroughly established nature [that is to say, that the thoroughly established nature's emptiness of the imputational and other-powered natures is the thoroughly established nature]. Also, with respect to the mode of emptiness, it is not [as in the Jo-nang-bas' assertion] the negation of something that exists somewhere else, like a place's being

[a] See *Absorption,* #153-167.

[b] See ibid., #97.

[c] See ibid., #169.

> empty [or devoid] of a pot. Rather, just as a person is without substantial existence, so other-powered natures are empty of being established as the imputational nature. Therefore, the sūtra speaks of "the thorough non-establishment of just those [other-powered natures]...as that imputational character."

Let us examine the three parts of Ḏzong-ka-ḇa's criticism one by one:

a. Does Shay-rap-gyel-tsen hold that the *Sūtra Unraveling the Thought* is definitive with respect to its teaching about the mode, or style, of emptiness?
b. Does Shay-rap-gyel-tsen hold that the thoroughly established nature is the basis of emptiness and that of which the thoroughly established nature is empty is imputational natures and other-powered natures?
c. Does Shay-rap-gyel-tsen compare the style of emptiness to a place's being devoid of a pot?

First Question About The Second "Contradiction": Does Shay-rap-gyel-tsen Hold That The *Sūtra Unraveling The Thought* Is Definitive With Respect To Its Teaching Of The Style Of Emptiness?

Shay-rap-gyel-tsen clearly asserts that the *Sūtra Unraveling the Thought* is definitive with respect to its teaching of the style of emptiness, when, in the *Ocean of Definitive Meaning,* he vigorously presents the position that the *Sūtra Unraveling the Thought* teaches the doctrine of the Great Middle Way. He[330] does this in response to the hypothetical objection by a follower of the Middle Way School who asserts that the middle wheel of doctrine, not the final wheel, is definitive:[a]

> With respect to this, a certain person's assertion that this sūtra [that is, the *Sūtra Unraveling the Thought*] requires interpretation is not right because such is not stated and is also not reasonable, and also there is no damage to its being definitive.
>
> *Objection:* Since the middle wheel of doctrine is Middle Way and the last is Mind-Only, the middle just abides as definitive and the final just abides as requiring interpretation, whereby there is damage [to the *Sūtra Unraveling the Thought's* being definitive].[b]

---

[a] This passage is treated in Matthew Kapstein, "From Kun-mkhyen Dol-po-pa to 'Ba'-mda' Dge-legs: Three Jo-nang-pa Masters on the Interpretation of the *Prajñāpāramitā,*" in *Tibetan Studies: Proceedings of the 7th Seminar of the International Association for Tibetan Studies, Graz 1995,* vol. 1, ed. Helmut Krassser, Michael Torsten Much, Ernst Steinkellner, and Helmut Tauscher (Vienna: Verlag der österreichischen akademie der wissenschaften, 1997), 458.

[b] This is the type of position that Ḏzong-ka-ḇa holds.

Answer: This is extremely, greatly unreasonable because there is not any scripture or reasoning [for the position] that the final wheel of doctrine is a proprietary text of Mind-Only and because [the *Sūtra Unraveling the Thought*] teaches in a manner beyond Mind-Only, teaches the final meaning of the Great Middle Way, and teaches in accordance with the final meaning of the Vajra Vehicle. Also, in this scripture itself—from its saying that in the third wheel the naturelessness, the absence of production, the absence of cessation, quiescence from the start, and naturally passed beyond sorrow of phenomena is taught—it is established that it is not a proprietary text of Mind-Only.

Objection: Whereas it is the case that, because the perfection of wisdom is taught in the second wheel, it is definitive and unsurpassed, this scripture [that is, the *Sūtra Unraveling the Thought*]—since it just teaches the opposite of that—requires interpretation and has a thought behind it.[a]

Answer: These are the words of one who has not analyzed well because [the *Sūtra Unraveling the Thought*] does not indicate that [scriptures] are interpretable, surpassable, and so forth by reason of their teaching the perfection of wisdom but indicates such by other reasons, such as that they teach what is not self-empty as self-empty. The absence of production, the absence of cessation, quiescence from the start, and naturally passed beyond sorrow are taught even in the third wheel and are taught in the Vajra Vehicle. By reason of teaching unclearly, clearly, and very clearly, there are great and also very great differences of being obscured, not obscured, and so forth with respect to the meaning of those. Therefore, even the statements of being surpassable or unsurpassable, affording an opportunity [for refutation] or not affording an opportunity, and so forth are due to differences in those texts with respect to whether the final profound meaning is unclear and incomplete or clear and complete, and so forth, and not from the entity of the meaning.

These statements are unmistakable evidence that S̄hay-rap-gyel-tsen does indeed hold the *Sūtra Unraveling the Thought* itself to be definitive about the mode of emptiness.

Nevertheless, I would add that, when it comes to expounding the view of other-emptiness, S̄hay-rap-gyel-tsen does not cite the *Sūtra Unraveling the Thought;* rather, he cites a great many other sūtra sources, the prime among

[a] D̄zong-ka-b̄a asserts that, according to the Mind-Only School, both the middle wheel and the final wheel teach the actual emptiness; however, the middle wheel lacks the clarity that all but the sharpest Bodhisattvas require for comprehending the doctrine of the three natures and three non-natures as is set forth in the *Sūtra Unraveling the Thought* (see p. 138); thus the objector's opinion here does not prefigure his position.

which are the *Mahāparinirvāṇa Sūtra,* the *Lion's Roar of Shrīmālādevī Sūtra,* and the *Aṅgulimāla Sūtra.* Dzong-ka-ba undoubtedly noticed this omission as well as the different mode of speaking about emptiness that is found in the *Sūtra Unraveling the Thought* and thus made this sūtra the focus of his own presentation. His argument, however, is weakened by the fact that he does not directly address these other scriptures.

Second Question About The Second "Contradiction": Does Shay-rap-gyel-tsen Hold That The Thoroughly Established Nature Is The Basis Of Emptiness And That Of Which The Thoroughly Established Nature Is Empty Is The Other Two Natures?

Dzong-ka-ba (*Emptiness in Mind-Only,* 226-227) makes the cogent case that the innate misconception of the self of phenomena must be countered by taking those very same phenomena—which are misperceived so as to lead beings into suffering and finitude—as the substrata and by seeing that they do not have the falsely superimposed quality of the imputational nature. In this way, he indicts Shay-rap-gyel-tsen for putting forth a system that is inadequate to the task of opposing the basic ignorance that draws beings into suffering and finitude:

> With respect to that, when the thoroughly established nature that is the selflessness of phenomena is delineated in either the Yogic Practice School or the Middle Way School, the bases of emptiness with respect to which [the thoroughly established nature] is delineated are relative to those bases with respect to which a self of phenomena is conceived by a consciousness conceiving a self of phenomena. It is like, for example, the fact that if you wish to remove the suffering of fright from someone upon that person's apprehending a rope as a snake, you must show—upon taking the rope as the basis of emptiness—that it is empty of a snake. However, it is not suitable to take the rope's **emptiness** of a snake as the basis of emptiness and say that it is empty [of being a rope and a snake] because of existing as factually other [than them].
>
> Furthermore, with respect to the conception of a self of phenomena, such conceptions as that directionally partless minute particles exist and that objects of apprehension composed of them exist or that a moment of consciousness that has no earlier and later temporal parts exists or that a consciousness that is a continuum composed of those exists—these being imputed only by those whose awarenesses have been affected by [mistaken] tenets—occur only among those proponents of tenets and do not exist among other sentient beings. Therefore, though an emptiness that is no more than merely an absence of

those [objects of negation] is taught, it does not at all harm the innate conception of self that has resided [in the mental continuum] beginninglessly. Therefore, it must be taught that those bases—that the innate conception of self conceives as self—are empty of self in the way that such is conceived. It must be understood that the refutation of imputational factors that are constructed by tenet systems is a branch [of the process] of refuting that [innate conception of self].

This being the case, since ordinary sentient beings conceive just these other-powered internal and external things—eyes, forms, and so forth which are objects seen, heard, and so forth—as self [that is, as objects and subjects that are different entities or as established by way of their own character as the referents of conceptual consciousnesses and of words], emptiness must be delineated within taking just these as the bases of emptiness. The error does not come through holding that the other two natures [that is, other-powered natures and imputational natures] exist as other factualities in the thoroughly established nature. Therefore, how could selflessness be delineated within thinking [as the Jo-nang-b̄as do] that the thoroughly established nature is empty because of existing as factually other than the other two natures!...

Therefore, without letting it become like the worldly [example] of putting a scapegoat effigy at the western door when a demon is bringing harm at the eastern door, one should meditate on an emptiness that is such that the emptiness of the imputational self as it is conceived in just those other-powered natures—these being the bases apprehended as self—is the thoroughly established nature. If this is done, it will serve as an antidote to the conception of self.[a] If, on the other hand, one meditates on an emptiness the mode of which is other than this style, it will not harm the conception of self at all.[b]

D̄zong-ka-b̄a cites teachings in the *Sūtra Unraveling the Thought* that speak of other-powered natures as the bases of emptiness and, in addition, twice bolsters his opinion that other-powered natures must be taken as the bases of emptiness through paraphrasing statements, found in similar form in several Indian treatises, that clearly posit other-powered natures as the bases of emptiness. On the first occasion, he (*Emptiness in Mind-Only,* 147-148) paraphrases Asaṅga:

Thus, the *Grounds of Bodhisattvas* says that:

---

[a] "Self" here does not mean "person" but (1) the establishment of objects by way of their own character as the referents of conceptual consciousnesses and of words and (2) the establishment of subject and object as different entities.

[b] For a thorough explanation of this quotation, see the Synopsis in *Emptiness in Mind-Only,* 335-341.

- the non-existence of something [that is, the imputational nature] in whatsoever [other-powered nature] is [the thoroughly established nature which is] the emptiness of that [imputational nature],
- the remainder [that is, the other-powered nature] exists [ultimately], and
- one who perceives such is non-erroneously oriented to emptiness.

The emptiness—in the things of forms and so forth—of the entities imputed to them by words is the meaning of the earlier phrase ["the non-existence of something, that is, the imputational nature in whatsoever other-powered natures is the thoroughly established nature which is the emptiness of that imputational nature"].[a] The remaining [ultimate] existence is the [ultimate] existence of the mere things that are the bases of imputation and the mere imputing [words].

That of which [phenomena] are empty is the imputational factor; the bases that are empty are other-powered natures; the emptiness that is the latter's emptiness of the former is the thoroughly established nature. The meaning of the existence and non-existence of those is as explained before [that is, existing **ultimately** and not existing **ultimately**].

And on the second occasion he (*Emptiness in Mind-Only,* 183-185) paraphrases Vasubandhu's commentary on the first stanza of Maitreya's *Differentiation of the Middle and the Extremes:*

> Correct knowledge, just as it is, of existence and non-existence is said [in sūtra] to be non-erroneous orientation toward emptiness:
>
> > In something [that is, other-powered natures] the non-existence of something [that is, the imputational nature] is the emptiness of that [imputational nature], and the remainder [that is, the other-powered nature and thoroughly established natures] exist there.
>
> Since this [passage in Maitreya's *Differentiation of the Middle and the Extremes*] also indicates this, it teaches the real emptiness.
>
> "In something" [indicates] the bases of emptiness, other-powered natures, [the main of which is] unreal ideation. In the phrase "the non-existence of something," that which is non-existent is the imputational factor, the duality of a difference in substantial entity between object

---

[a] It is clear from Ṡhay-rap-gyel-tsen's commentary on a similar quotation, given below (p. 331ff.), that he would accept all of the bracketed interpolations (used to make clear how Ḍzong-ka-ḅa takes this passage) up until this point. The further interpolations of "ultimate" would not be accepted, as they refer to other-powered natures here in this quotation.

and subject. By saying that it does not exist in that, it indicates that the former [other-powered natures] are empty of this latter [imputational nature].

If that [imputational nature] does not exist, what is there that exists left over after that? [The phrase] "Ideation exists" and the third line indicate that [what are left over after the negation] are the two, other-powered natures and thoroughly established natures. The fourth line eliminates another qualm [concerning the reason why common beings do not realize the emptiness of duality that is the mode of subsistence of forms and so forth, this being because they have the mistaken appearance of duality that serves to obstruct it].

D̄zong-ka-b̄a then cites Sthiramati's commentary, which specifies that "unreal ideation"—a code word for other-powered natures—does not just exist but **inherently** exists:

> Just this explanation by Vasubandhu in this way of the meaning of what is empty and of that of which it is empty is indicated clearly by Sthiramati, whose *Explanation of (Vasubandhu's) Commentary* says:
>
> > In order to refute the deprecation of everything by some who think that all phenomena are utterly, utterly without an inherent nature like the horns of a rabbit, [the text] says, "Unreal ideation exists." "Inherently" is an extra word [to be added to "exists"].
>
> The phrase "ideation exists" is not complete just by itself; therefore, a remainder must be added, and it is this: "inherently." Thus, ideation is not just existent but is **inherently** existent or existent in the sense of being **established by way of its own character.**[a] These modes of existence are also similar with respect to thoroughly established natures.

D̄zong-ka-b̄a's evidence is good, as long as one accepts his repeated point that, when Asaṅga and so forth speak of the "existence" of other-powered natures they are referring to "ultimate existence" (or "existence by their own character" or "real existence").[b] However, S̄hay-rap-gyel-tsen's opinion on this topic is more nuanced than D̄zong-ka-b̄a's criticism—as cogent as it is—suggests.

S̄hay-rap-gyel-tsen[331] deals with this type of passage head-on through analyzing—in the format of a debate—a similar statement in Asaṅga's *Summary of Manifest Knowledge.* Rather than giving his usual other-emptiness opinion that the thoroughly established nature is empty of imputational natures and other-powered natures, he admits to a hypothetical opponent that Asaṅga does indeed take other-powered natures as the bases of emptiness:

---

[a] See *Absorption,* #117, 118.

[b] For a detailed discussion of his presentation of this point, see p. 353ff.

This way of delineating emptiness well, upon differentiating self-emptiness and other-emptiness in this manner, is also set forth by the holy Superior Asaṅga, Proponent of the Great Middle Way.[a] His *Summary of Manifest Knowledge* of the final Great Middle Way[b] says:

> What is the character of emptiness? That in which something does not exist is to be seen correctly as empty of it. That which is the remainder here is to be thoroughly known correctly and properly as existing here. This is called correct and proper—non-erroneous—orientation to emptiness.
>
> What does not exist in what? A permanent, stable, everlasting, and immutable subject, self, and mine[c] does not exist in the aggregates, constituents, and sense-spheres.[d] Therefore, those are empty of that.
>
> What is the remainder there? Just that selflessness. In that way, self does not exist, but selflessness is to be understood as existing—emptiness.[e] In consideration of this, the Supramundane Victor said, "I thoroughly, correctly, and properly see the existent as existent and also the non-existent as non-existent."[f]

This means: One is to see the basis of emptiness in which whatsoever empty phenomenon[g] does not exist as empty of that phenomenon. The basis of emptiness that is the remainder of the emptiness of that phenomenon—the noumenal thoroughly established nature—is to be

---

a *dbu ma pa chen po.*

b *mthar thug gi dbu ma'i chos mngon pa.*

c *rtag pa dang brtan pa dang ther zug dang mi 'gyur ba'i chos can dang bdag dang bdag gi med do;* Shay-rap-gyel-tsen's *Ocean of Definitive Meaning,* 191.4. It is important to notice that the subject, self, and mine are said here not to be permanent, stable, and everlasting, but Shay-rap-gyel-tsen (*Ocean of Definitive Meaning,* 68.6) does not shy away from asserting that the noumenon, the matrix of One Gone Thus, is permanent, stable, and everlasting:

> Concerning that, since the matrix of One Gone to Bliss is empty of the two selves, it is not similar to the self of Forders, and because the uncompounded noumenon transcends the momentary, it is permanent, stable, and everlasting.

d Here Asaṅga, consistent with his approach in the *Summary of Manifest Knowledge,* speaks of the three natures in terms of the selflessness of persons.

e It seems to me that Shay-rap-gyel-tsen's point is that the self does not exist as permanent, stable, everlasting, and immutable, but selflessness exists as permanent, stable, everlasting, and immutable.

f Shay-rap-gyel-tsen (*Ocean of Definitive Meaning,* 203.3-205.2) cites similar passages from the *Sūtra of the Great Emptiness* and explains them as teaching other-emptiness.

g *stong pa'i chos;* the term refers to that of which something is empty. Despite using the word "phenomenon" (*chos*), which in other contexts is equivalent to existent (*yod pa*), it is not implied here in this context that the object being negated exists.

thoroughly, correctly, and properly known as always existing here. This realization of the empty phenomenon as self-empty and the basis of emptiness as other-empty is called correct and proper—non-erroneous—orientation to emptiness. Otherwise, if one asserts all as just self-empty or all as just other-empty, this is not non-erroneous.

Some might think: Is it not that [Asaṅga] describes the bases of the emptiness of self and mine here as the aggregates, constituents, and sense-spheres? Why do you assert here that the base of emptiness is the noumenon, the thoroughly established nature?

Answer: Although here, tentatively,[a] it is said that the aggregates, constituents, and sense-spheres which are included in other-powered natures are the bases of emptiness, in the end the basis of emptiness even of the other-powered natures that are bases of emptiness is the noumenon, the thoroughly established nature; consequently, those [that is, the noumenon and the basis of emptiness] are equivalent. Even thusness is said to be among certain constituents and sense-spheres that are included in the uncompounded,[b] and hence from even its being said that thusness is a basis of the emptiness of self and mine, in the end a basis of emptiness is the noumenon, the thoroughly established nature; consequently, there is no fallacy.

Also, the statement:

> What is the remainder there? Just that selflessness. In that way, self does not exist, but selflessness is to be understood as existing—emptiness.

---

[a] *re zhig:* S̄hay-rap-gyel-tsen's *Ocean of Definitive Meaning,* 192.3.

[b] Among the eighteen constituents, the phenomenon-constituent (*chos kyi khams, dharmadhātu*) contains all phenomena not included in the other constituents, and thus all permanent phenomena, including thusness, or emptiness, are contained therein. Since all eighteen constituents are said to be bases of emptiness, thusness itself, or emptiness, must also be a basis of emptiness. The same is so for the phenomenon-sense-sphere (*chos kyi skye mched, dharmāyatana*) among the twelve sense-spheres.

D̄zong-ka-b̄a, however, seems not to recognize S̄hay-rap-gyel-tsen's open acceptance that thusness is included among the constituents and sense-spheres when he (*Emptiness in Mind-Only,* 85) says:

> Also, with respect to the need for [Buddha's] doing thus, in the Mother Sūtras [that is, the Perfection of Wisdom Sūtras] and so forth, all phenomena—the five aggregates, the eighteen constituents, and the twelve sense-spheres—are described as without thingness, without an inherent nature, and natureless. In particular, mentioning all the terminological variants of the ultimate—emptiness, the element of [a Superior's] qualities, thusness, and so forth—he said that these are natureless. Therefore, who with a mind would propound that the ultimate is not among the phenomena about which it is said that phenomena are natureless!

See *Absorption,* #63-64.

[indicates] that selfless other-powered natures, the remainder of the non-existence of the imputational nature, tentatively exist,[a] [whereas] the noumenal, selfless thoroughly established nature—the remainder of the emptiness even of other-powered natures—really exists.[b] Respectively, these are conventionally existent and ultimately existent.

> In consideration of this, the Supramundane Victor said, "I thoroughly, correctly, and properly see the existent as existent and also the non-existent as non-existent."

Thus, the bases of the emptiness of the imputational nature are other-powered natures. The basis of the emptiness of even other-powered natures is the thoroughly established nature. A basis that is empty of the noumenal thoroughly established nature utterly does not occur because it is the suchness that spontaneously abides forever and everywhere.

In that passage, Shay-rap-gyel-tsen demonstrates that:

- There are two types of bases of emptiness—one is other-powered natures and the other is the noumenal thoroughly established nature. (Since Dzong-ka-ba also holds that the thoroughly established nature is empty, he would agree that there are two bases of emptiness.[c] However, his criticism of Shay-rap-gyel-tsen is so unnuanced that one would mistakenly think that Shay-rap-gyel-tsen only asserted that the thoroughly established nature is the basis of emptiness.)
- Both of these bases of emptiness are included in Asaṅga's reference to constituents and sense-spheres because, among the eighteen constituents, the phenomenon-constituent contains all phenomena not included in the other constituents, and thus all permanent phenomena, including thusness, or emptiness, are contained therein. Since Asaṅga says that the constituents (and thus all eighteen) are bases of emptiness, thusness itself, or emptiness, must also be a basis of emptiness. The same is so for the phenomenon-sense-sphere among the twelve sense-spheres. (Dzong-ka-ba agrees the emptiness also is a basis of emptiness, but he does not agree with Shay-rap-gyel-tsen about of which it is empty; see the next point.)
- In terms of the three natures: the aggregates, constituents, and sense-spheres are **other-powered natures**, except for those instances of the constituents and sense-spheres that are permanent phenomena; self and mine are the **non-existent imputational nature**; the emptiness of the

[a] *re zhig yod pa;* Shay-rap-gyel-tsen's *Ocean of Definitive Meaning,* 192.6.

[b] *yang dag par yod pa;* Shay-rap-gyel-tsen's *Ocean of Definitive Meaning,* 193.1.

[c] In addition, Dzong-ka-ba holds that existent imputational natures, such as uncompounded space, also are bases of emptiness. Shay-rap-gyel-tsen does not mention these.

imputational nature in other-powered natures is the **thoroughly established nature.** (D̄zong-ka-b̄a would make the distinction that here Asaṅga speaks of the three natures in terms of the selflessness of persons. In terms of the selflessness of phenomena, the non-existent imputational nature would have to be identified as a difference of entity between apprehended-object and apprehending-subject, or the establishment of object by way of their own character as the referents of conceptual consciousnesses and the objects verbalized by words; S̄hay-rap-gyel-tsen does not present the latter in the *Ocean of Definitive Meaning.*)

- Hence, that of which the two types of bases of emptiness[a] are empty is "self and mine." (D̄zong-ka-b̄a agrees, as long as the reference is to the three natures in terms of the selflessness of persons and as long as "self" means a person substantially established in the sense of being self-sufficient and "mine" means objects of use by such a substantially established person; this means that, for D̄zong-ka-b̄a, self and mine do exist but not in this way.)

- What remains are other-powered natures and the thoroughly established nature. (D̄zong-ka-b̄a agrees, as long as it is understood that existent imputational natures, such as uncompounded space, also exist; S̄hay-rap-gyel-tsen, as will be seen below in the next quotation, says that all imputational natures do not exist.)

- Other-powered natures tentatively exist, or conventionally exist, whereas the thoroughly established nature really exists, or ultimately exists. (D̄zong-ka-b̄a disagrees; according to him, in the Mind-Only School, **both** other-powered natures and the thoroughly established nature really exist, ultimately exist, exist by way of their own character, truly exist, and so forth.[b] Also in the Middle Way Consequence School, **both** other-powered natures and the thoroughly established nature conventionally exist and do not really exist, ultimately exist, exist by way of their own character, truly exist, and so forth. Thus, from D̄zong-ka-b̄a's viewpoint, S̄hay-rap-gyel-tsen represents neither the Mind-Only position which is the opinion of the *Sūtra Unraveling the Thought* nor the Middle Way Consequence position which is the opinion of the Perfection of Wisdom Sūtras.)

- The thoroughly established nature is empty of imputational natures and other-powered natures. (It needs to be understood that, in D̄zong-ka-b̄a's system, a chair is empty of a cup—that is, a chair is not a cup—and a cup is empty of a chair, but this does not constitute the emptiness of either the

---

[a] As quoted above (p. 333), S̄hay-rap-gyel-tsen says:

> Even thusness is said to be among certain constituents and sense-spheres that are included in the uncompounded, and hence from even its being said that thusness is a basis of the emptiness of self and mine…

[b] For D̄zong-ka-b̄a's highly nuanced treatment of this topic, see below, p. 353ff.

cup or the chair. Thus, he would agree that the thoroughly established nature is empty of the other two natures in S̄hay-rap-gyel-tsen's sense that it is not those two, but he does not agree that realization of this constitutes realization of emptiness.)

•   A basis that is empty of the thoroughly established nature does not occur. (Ḏzong-ka-b̄a agrees.)

It is intriguing that, in commenting on this passage in Asaṅga's *Summary of Manifest Knowledge,* S̄hay-rap-gyel-tsen does not force the first part of the passage somehow to yield his usual other-emptiness opinion that the thoroughly established nature is empty of imputational natures and other-powered natures. Rather, he follows Asaṅga in positing that other-powered natures are empty of the imputational nature and thus other-powered natures are the bases of emptiness, and then he extends this same type of emptiness even to the thoroughly established nature in that it also is the basis of the emptiness of self and mine, that is to say, a non-existent imputational nature. Finally, however, he adds the crucial other-emptiness notion that the thoroughly established nature is empty of other-powered natures. His source for this is Asaṅga's singling out selflessness as the remainder of the negation and not other-powered natures.

S̄hay-rap-gyel-tsen bolsters his presentation with an extensive citation from the *Sūtra of the Great Emptiness,* which contains the same teaching on the meaning of emptiness and what remains. He says:[332]

> Moreover, the *Sūtra of the Great Emptiness* speaks at length about the mode of other-emptiness:
>
>> Ānanda, it is thus: for example, although this good building of Mṛgāramata[a] is empty of elephants, horses, bulls, sheep, roosters, and pigs and is empty of jewels, grain, [a type of] shell,[b] and gold and is empty of male and female servants, wage-earners,[c] men, women, boys, and girls, this also has a non-emptiness relative to only the community of monastics, or those other than the ones [listed above]. Ānanda, although that in which something does not exist is to be correctly seen as "empty of it," that which is the remainder here is to be thoroughly known correctly and properly as "existing there." Ānanda, this is correct and proper—non-erroneous— orientation to emptiness.
>
> At the end of saying that, and so forth, [Buddha] pronounces:
>
>> Although they do not have the situation of the afflictive

---

a   *ri dags 'dzin gyi ma.*

b   *mgron bu;* or *'gron bu* (cowries, that is, small shells used as dice).

c   *zho shas 'tsho ba dag;* this may refer to paid soldiers.

> emotions dependent on the contaminations of desire, the contaminations of existence, and the contaminations of ignorance, they have situations of afflictive emotions merely dependent upon only a body of the six sense-fields that serve as a condition of life. Ānanda, therefore, although that in which something does not exist is to be correctly seen as "empty of it," that which is the remainder here is to be thoroughly known correctly and properly as "existing there." Ānanda, that which is the non-existence of contaminations due to the extinguishment of contaminations and is the uncompounded release is unsurpassed orientation to emptiness. Ānanda, those Ones Gone Thus, Foe Destroyers, completely perfect Buddhas, Supramundane Victors who arose in the past accomplished and dwelt [in that state] upon having manifested—through the body—the unsurpassed orientation to emptiness which is the non-existence of contaminations due to the extinguishment of contaminations and is the uncompounded release.

After this, it also applies the same with respect to present and future Buddhas. Thus, after having said much about how the mode of being empty of some phenomena but not being empty of some—using the example that the good building of Mṛgāramata is empty of horses, elephants, and so forth, but is not empty of monastics, and so forth—it says that Buddhas, although empty of all contaminations, are not empty of the uncompounded emptiness that is release. This also clearly teaches the ultimate other-emptiness, the basis of emptiness. The statement that this orientation to emptiness is correct and proper, non-erroneous, implicitly indicates that orientation to an emptiness in which everything is empty of its own entity is not correct.

Although D̄zong-ka-b̄a does not directly treat either the passage in Asaṅga's *Summary of the Great Vehicle* or the extensive passage in the *Sūtra of the Great Emptiness,* he does treat similar passages in two other texts, as cited above. He (see above, p. 330; *Emptiness in Mind-Only,* 148) takes Asaṅga's declaration in the *Grounds of Bodhisattvas* that the remainder exists as referring to other-powered natures:

> The remaining [ultimate] existence is the [ultimate] existence of the mere things that are the bases of imputation and the mere imputing [words].

And, in paraphrasing Vasubandhu's commentary on the first stanza of Maitreya's *Differentiation of the Middle and the Extremes,* he (see above, p. 331; *Emptiness in Mind-Only,* 184) takes Maitreya as indicating that the remainder is both the thoroughly established nature and other-powered natures:[a]

> If that [imputational nature] does not exist, what is there that exists left over after that? [The phrase] "Ideation exists" and the third line indicate that [what are left over after the negation] are the two, other-powered natures and thoroughly established natures.

To eliminate the possibility that "existence" could refer merely to conventional existence, Ḏzong-ka-ḇa (see above, p. 331; *Mind-Only,* 185) cites Sthiramati's *Explanation of (Vasubandhu's) Commentary:*

> In order to refute the deprecation of everything by some who think that all phenomena are utterly, utterly without an inherent nature like the horns of a rabbit, [the text] says, "Unreal ideation exists." "Inherently" is an extra word [to be added to "exists"].

Finally, in his summation on this topic in Maitreya's *Differentiation of the Middle and the Extremes,* Ḏzong-ka-ḇa (*Emptiness in Mind-Only,* 188) concludes:

> In accordance with the explanations by the master Vasubandhu and his student [Sthiramati], the existent is ideation; the non-existent is duality [that is, difference of entity between object and subject]; and the existent [that is, the remainder] is the mutual existence of the two, ideation and emptiness.

Ḏzong-ka-ḇa thereby marshals evidence to support the notion that in the Mind-Only School other-powered natures are considered to remain after the negation of the imputational nature and to be established by way of their own

---

[a] Ḏzong-ka-ḇa's student Ke-drup (*Opening the Eyes of the Fortunate,* 208.3; see also José Ignacio Cabezón, *A Dose of Emptiness* [Albany, N.Y.: State University of New York Press, 1992], 46) speaks only of other-powered natures as being the remainder:

> [Vasubandhu's] commentary says that just this is non-erroneous entry into emptiness by way of understanding, "The non-existence of something in something is [its] emptiness of that, and what is left over in that really exists in it." Therefore, the existent remainder is that indicated in [the first line of Maitreya's stanza], "Unreal ideation[—ideation being the main other-powered nature—]exists [by way of its own character in that it is produced from causes and conditions]." Hence, it means that other-powered natures—the remainder of the emptiness of imputational natures—exist. Moreover, if that were taken as mere existence, then since imputational natures also are merely existent, one would not be able to differentiate [between the mode of existence of other-powered natures and imputational natures]. Therefore, it must be taken as true existence; also, here [in Vasubandhu's commentary] "really exists in it" sets forth [true existence].

My guess is that the failure to mention the thoroughly established nature is merely inadvertent, since Maitreya's text is so clear on this point; however, it does reflect Ke-drup's and subsequent Ge-luk-ḇa scholars' emphasis (or over-emphasis) on the true existence of other-powered natures in the Mind-Only system.

character such that they could not be canceled in a greater reality, even if they do not appear to a non-Buddha's mind realizing emptiness. It is clear that he does this to oppose S̄hay-rap-gyel-tsen's view presented above.

Let us consider D̄zong-ka-b̄a's evidence. Asaṅga's *Grounds of Bodhisattvas* says:[a]

> How is emptiness apprehended well? One thoroughly sees that, because such and such does not exist in something, that thing is empty of it and thoroughly knows just as it is that what remains here exists here. This is called non-erroneous orientation to emptiness just as it is. It is thus: The phenomena that are the entities of the words imputing as "form" and so forth do not exist in the things indicated as "form" and so forth. Consequently, the things called "form" and so forth are empty of the entities of the word imputing "form" and so forth. What is the remainder of the things called "form" and so forth? It is thus: They are these mere bases[b] of imputing "form" and so forth. Thoroughly knowing both of those—the existence of the mere things and the existence of the mere imputing as mere things—one does not superimpose [existence] on what does not exist and also does not deprecate the real. Neither adding on nor diminishing, one is said to thoroughly realize with correct wisdom.

Paraphrasing this, D̄zong-ka-b̄a (*Emptiness in Mind-Only,* 146-147) says (I will give it first without bracketed annotations):

---

[a] Peking 5538, vol. 110, 144.5.6-145.1.5; see also Janice D. Willis, *On Knowing Reality: The Tattvārtha Chapter of Asaṅga's Bodhisattvabhūmi* (New York: Columbia University Press, 1979; reprint, Delhi: Motilal Banarsidass, 1982), 18, 117, and 163; for the Sanskrit of the first three sentences, see *Emptiness in Mind-Only,* 400, footnote a. For a similar discussion in the context of Maitreya's *Differentiation of the Middle and the Extremes,* see *Emptiness in Mind-Only,* 183ff.

S̄hay-rap-gyel-tsen (*Ocean of Definitive Meaning,* 307.4) cites this passage from Asaṅga's *Grounds of Bodhisattvas* after saying:

> Therefore, the proposition that all twenty emptinesses are self-emptinesses is not the meaning of the great thought of the Conquerors because the ultimate truth, the natural lineage, all attributes which are qualities of the Body of Attributes, and the emptinesses of nature, of the nature of non-entities, and of other entities are emptinesses but are not self-emptinesses. Concerning that, because the enjoyer, enjoyed, and so forth are empty of their own respective entities, they are that which is non-existent there; they are not established as anything and do not exist even a little. The basic element of attributes which is the basis empty of those phenomena is what remains; it really exists.

[b] The Peking edition (5538, vol. 110, 145.1.2) misreads *tshig;* the Sanskrit is *āśraya* (Nalinaksha Dutt, *Bodhisattvabhūmi [Being the XVth Section of Asangapada's Yogacarabhumi],* Tibetan Sanskrit Works Series 7 [Patna, India: K. P. Jayaswal Research Institute, 1966], book 1, chap. 4, 32.18).

Thus, the *Grounds of Bodhisattvas* says that:

- the non-existence of something in whatsoever is the emptiness of that,
- the remainder exists, and
- one who perceives such is non-erroneously oriented to emptiness.[a]

The emptiness—in the things of forms and so forth—of the entities imputed to them by words is the meaning of the earlier phrase. The remaining existence is the existence of the mere things that are the bases of imputation and the mere imputing.

That of which [phenomena] are empty is the imputational factor; the bases that are empty are other-powered natures; the emptiness that is the latter's emptiness of the former is the thoroughly established nature. The meaning of the existence and non-existence of those is as explained before.

With bracketed annotations based on what Dzong-ka-ba gradually unfolds in this passage, the passage is clearer:

Thus, the *Grounds of Bodhisattvas* says that:

- the non-existence of something [that is, the imputational nature] in whatsoever [other-powered nature] is [the thoroughly established nature which is] the emptiness of that [imputational nature],
- the remainder [that is, the other-powered nature] exists [ultimately], and
- one who perceives such is non-erroneously oriented to emptiness.

The emptiness—in the things of forms and so forth—of the entities imputed to them by words is the meaning of the earlier phrase ["the non-existence of something, that is, the imputational nature in whatsoever other-powered natures is the thoroughly established nature which is the emptiness of that imputational nature"]. The remaining [ultimate] existence is the [ultimate] existence of the mere things that are the bases of imputation and the mere imputing [words].

That of which [phenomena] are empty is the imputational factor; the bases that are empty are other-powered natures; the emptiness that is the latter's emptiness of the former is the thoroughly established nature. The meaning of the existence and non-existence of those is as

[a] Shay-rap-gyel-tsen (*Ocean of Definitive Meaning*, 203.3-205.2) cites similar passages from the *Sūtra of the Great Emptiness* (see p. 336ff.) and explains them as teaching other-emptiness. He also cites a similar passage from Asaṅga's *Summary of Manifest Knowledge* to establish that Asaṅga sets forth the view of the Great Middle Way. It is safe to assume that Dzong-ka-ba implicitly is seeking to refute his interpretation.

> explained before [that is, existing **ultimately** and not existing **ultimately**].

The late D̄a-drin-rap-d̄en[333] summarizes the meaning of the passage:

> The non-existence of the entity of the imputational nature that is the object of negation—establishment of objects by way of their own character as the referents of conceptual consciousnesses—in other-powered natures which are the bases of imputation is the thoroughly established nature that is the emptiness of that. The remainder—the mere things that are the bases of imputation and the imputing [words]—exist. Those who perceive such are non-erroneously oriented with regard to emptiness because they understand a composite of appearance and emptiness that clears away the two extremes.

Their commentary is borne out by Asaṅga's own explanation given above. He is speaking about a remainder of other-powered phenomena.

A-ku L̄o-drö-gya-tso[334] identifies the remainder as **both** the bases of emptiness (other-powered natures) and emptiness (thoroughly established natures). He explains that meditative equipoise sees emptiness and that the wisdom of subsequent attainment sees the bases of emptiness and emptiness as truly existent. As Jik-may-dam-chö-gya-tso[335] points out, however, this type of double identification of what remains accords with that presented in the first two stanzas of chapter 1 of Maitreya's *Differentiation of the Middle and the Extremes* (*Emptiness in Mind-Only,* 182); he draws the cogent conclusion that it must be said that in the explicit teaching at this point in the *Grounds of Bodhisattvas* nothing other than other-powered natures is identified as what remains, whereas in general this type of passage in Asaṅga's Five Treatises on the Grounds teaches that emptiness, the thoroughly established nature, is also among the remainder.

It is likely that the fact that Asaṅga's *Grounds of Bodhisattvas* explicitly speaks of other-powered natures as the remainder and Maitreya's *Differentiation of the Middle and the Extremes* speaks of both other-powered natures and the thoroughly established nature as the remainder is the reason why S̄hay-rap-gyel-tsen, when unpacking the quote from Asaṅga's *Summary of Manifest Knowledge* which explicitly speaks only of emptiness as the remainder, considers two levels of remainder. He speaks of other-powered natures as tentatively, or conventionally, existing and the thoroughly established nature as really, or ultimately, existing:

> Also, the statement:
>
> > What is the remainder there? Just that selflessness. In that way, self does not exist, but selflessness is to be understood as existing—emptiness.

[indicates] that selfless other-powered natures, the remainder of the non-existence of the imputational nature, tentatively exist,[a] [whereas] the noumenal, selfless thoroughly established nature—the remainder of the emptiness even of other-powered natures—really exists.[b] Respectively, these are conventionally existent and ultimately existent.

This dual reading of the meaning of existence is reflected in the exposition of Maitreya's first two stanzas by Tibet's second great Jo-nang-ba scholar-yogi, Tāranātha (1575-1634), in his *The Essence of Other-Emptiness:*[336]

Maitreya's *Differentiation of the Middle and the Extremes*[c] says:

---

[a] *re zhig yod pa;* Shay-rap-gyel-tsen's *Ocean of Definitive Meaning,* 192.6.

[b] *yang dag par yod pa;* Shay-rap-gyel-tsen's *Ocean of Definitive Meaning,* 193.1.

[c] I.1-1.2; Peking 5522, vol. 108, 19.4.5. The Sanskrit, from Gadjin M. Nagao, *Madhyāntavibhāga-bhāṣya* (Tokyo: Suzuki Research Foundation, 1964), 17, is:

abhūta-parikalpo 'sti dvayan tatra na vidyate/
śūnyatā vidyate tv atra tasyām api sa vidyate//

na śūnyaṃ nāpi cāśūnyaṃ tasmāt sarvvam [Pandeya: sarvaṃ] vidhīyate/
satvād asatvāt satvāc [Pandeya: *sattvādasattvāt sattvāc*] *ca madhyamā pratipac ca sā//*

See also Ramchandra Pandeya, *Madhyānta-vibhāga-śāstra* (Delhi: Motilal Banarsidass, 1971), 9, 13.

With bracketed additions reflecting Tāranātha's commentary in *The Essence of Other-Emptiness* (503.1), the stanzas read:

Unreal ideation exists [conventionally].
Duality [of apprehended-object and apprehending-subject and so forth] does not exist there [in ideation].
[The exalted wisdom of] emptiness [truly] exists [in the manner of the noumenon] here [in unreal ideation].
Also that [unreal ideation] exists [as an entity without true existence] in that [noumenon].

[The noumenal wisdom is] not empty and [conventionalities are] not non-empty,
Thereby all is explained.
Due to the [the noumenal wisdom's true] existence and due to the non-existence [of change within it, it always] exists.
Therefore that is the middle path.

With bracketed additions reflecting Dzong-ka-ba's commentary, the stanzas read:

Unreal ideation[—ideation being the main other-powered nature—]exists [by way of its own character in that it is produced from causes and conditions].
Duality [of subject and object in accordance with their appearance as if distant and cut off] does not exist in that [ideation].
[The thoroughly established nature which is the] emptiness [of being distant and cut off] exists [by way of its own character as the mode of subsistence] in this [ideation].
Also that [ideation] exists [as an obstructor] to [realization of] that [emptiness].

Unreal ideation exists.
Duality does not exist there.
Emptiness exists here.
Also that exists in that.

Not empty and not non-empty,
Thereby all is explained.
Due to existence and due to non-existence, existence.
Therefore that is the middle path.

With respect to delineating conventional truths, mere unreal ideation—that is to say, consciousnesses to which various appearances dawn—exists conventionally. However, the factor of the object-apprehended and the factor of apprehender which appear to that [ideation] do not exist even conventionally, since they are merely imputed by an awareness. Consequently, even conventional truths are released from the two extremes: ideation is released from the extreme of non-existence and the extreme of annihilation through asserting that it conventionally exists, and ideation is released from the extreme of permanence and the extreme of existence through being beyond all superimposed factors of relative phenomena, such as the factors of object-apprehended and apprehender, and so forth.

It is being said that:

- The exalted wisdom of emptiness, that which is beyond proliferation, truly exists—in a noumenal manner—in that unreal ideational consciousness.
- On the occasion of defilement, those consciousnesses exist in that noumenon as entities without true existence—adventitious

---

[Thus, other-powered natures and thoroughly established natures] are not empty [of establishment by way of the object's own character] and are not non-empty [of subject and object being distant and cut off].

Thereby all [of the mode of thought in the teachings in the Perfection of Wisdom Sūtras, and so forth, of not being empty and of not being non-empty] is explained [thoroughly].

Due to the existence [of the other-powered nature that is the erroneous ideation apprehending object and subject as distant and cut off, the extreme of non-existence is avoided] and due to the non-existence [of distant and cut off object and subject—in accordance with how they are apprehended by that ideation—as their mode of subsistence, the extreme of existence is avoided, and ideation and emptiness] exist.

Therefore that [thoroughly established nature which is the emptiness of distant and cut off object and subject and which is the voidness of the two extremes in other-powered natures] is the middle path [that is to say, is established as the meaning of the middle].

defilements suitable to separated, defilements to be abandoned.

Consequently, the ultimate truth also is devoid of the two extremes. Since emptiness is truly established and all phenomena included within the two, apprehended-object and apprehending-subject, such as ideation and so forth, are without true existence, [the ultimate truth] is free from the extremes of existence and non-existence, permanence and annihilation.

Therefore, conventionalities—the two, apprehended-object and apprehending-subject—except for only being the dawning of mistaken appearances, are empty of their own entities, and, because something established as an other-entity from within the division of the pair—self and other—does not occur among objects of knowledge, conventionalities are empty in all respects and hence are not non-empty. The noumenal wisdom is primordially established by way of its own entity and never changes; hence, it is not empty of its own entity and always exists.

Although Maitreya merely says that unreal ideation and emptiness exist, without differentiating types of existence:

- Tāranātha—utilizing S̄hay-rap-gyel-tsen's exposition of other-powered natures as conventionally existing—takes the existence of unreal ideation (a code word for other-powered natures) as meaning conventional existence.
- D̄zong-ka-b̄a, to undermine S̄hay-rap-gyel-tsen's reliance on two levels of existence in order to give the ultimate truth more status, develops an elaborate explanation (see p. 353ff. and especially *Emptiness in Mind-Only,* 158-171) that in Mind-Only texts the usage of the term "conventional existence" for other-powered natures refers to their being conventional truths and not to their conventionally existing and thus is not antithetical to their being established by way of their own character and ultimately existent.

In order to bolster his position, D̄zong-ka-b̄a cites Sthiramati's clear exposition that the existence of unreal ideation refers to its inherent existence:[a]

> Just this explanation by Vasubandhu in this way of the meaning of what is empty and of that of which it is empty is indicated clearly by Sthiramati, whose *Explanation of (Vasubandhu's) Commentary* says:
>
> > In order to refute the deprecation of everything by some who think that all phenomena are utterly, utterly without an inherent nature like the horns of a rabbit, [the text] says,

[a] D̄zong-ka-b̄a takes "inherent existence" here to mean existence by way of its own character and ultimate existence since he holds that even existent imputational natures inherently exist.

"Unreal ideation exists." "Inherently" is an extra word [to be added to "exists"].

The phrase "ideation exists" is not complete just by itself; therefore, a remainder must be added, and it is this: "inherently." Thus, ideation is not just existent but is **inherently** existent or existent in the sense of being **established by way of its own character.**[a] These modes of existence are also similar with respect to thoroughly established natures.

If Ṡhay-rap-gyel-tsen takes Sthiramati to be a proponent of the Great Middle Way, one wonders how he might interpret this statement. Perhaps he could say that "inherently existent" means "substantially existent" as when the Maitreya Chapter of the *Twenty-five Thousand Stanza Perfection of Wisdom Sūtra* (*Emptiness in Mind-Only,* 350) says:

These imputed forms [that is, forms themselves] should be viewed as substantially existing [that is, conventionally existing] because conceptuality substantially exists and not because forms exist under their own power.

Or, perhaps he could say that "inherently existent" means "substantially existent" in the sense of being able to perform the function of creating effects, as it does in other contexts.

In any case, Ṡhay-rap-gyel-tsen finds support from other sources for his treatment of existence and non-existence:

In consideration of these different modes of emptiness of the three natures in this way, Maitreya's *Ornament of the Great Vehicle Sūtras* of the final Middle Way also says:

If one knows the emptiness of the non-existent
And likewise the emptiness of the existent
And the nature-emptiness,
It is said that one knows emptiness.

The imputational nature is empty in the sense of always not existing. Other-powered natures, although tentatively existent, are empty in the sense of not existing in reality; those two are fabricated and adventitious. [Maitreya] says that the noumenal thoroughly established nature exists because the emptiness that is the [ultimate] nature of non-entities [that is, emptiness that is the ultimate nature which is the opposite of non-entities]—due to being just the fundamental nature—is not empty of its own entity, and he also says that it does not exist because of being empty even of other-powered natures. For the

[a] See *Absorption,* #117, 118.

Differentiation of the Middle and the Extremes of the final Middle Way also says:

> The three natures are [respectively] always non-existent,
> Existent but not suchness,
> And the existent and non-existent suchness.

Also, the statement in Asaṅga's *Summary of Manifest Knowledge* of the final Middle Way:

> Emptiness is of three aspects—
> Emptiness of nature,[a]
> Likewise emptiness of not being existent,
> And natural emptiness.[b]

Shay-rap-gyel-tsen's commentary before the quotation from Maitreya's *Differentiation of the Middle and the Extremes* makes it clear that the meaning of the inherent, or ultimate, or real, or true existence of the ultimate is that the thoroughly established nature merely is the ultimate nature. Other-powered natures are not the ultimate nature and thus are empty of their own entities.[c] (Dzong-ka-ba does not treat any of these passages directly.)

Also, it can be seen from how Shay-rap-gyel-tsen treats the passage in Asaṅga's *Summary of Manifest Knowledge* that he posits a three-staged approach to emptiness:

- In the first, other-powered natures are the bases of emptiness, and that of which they are empty is "self" and "mine."
- In the second, the thoroughly established nature is the basis of emptiness, and that of which it is empty is "self" and "mine."
- In the third, the thoroughly established nature is the basis of emptiness, and that of which it is empty is other-powered natures and imputational natures.

This is a far cry from Dzong-ka-ba's claim that Shay-rap-gyel-tsen takes only the thoroughly established nature as the basis of emptiness. Still, it needs to be explored whether Shay-rap-gyel-tsen uses this format of a threefold approach to emptiness anywhere other than in handling this passage.

Dzong-ka-ba treats at length a hypothetical objection by Shay-rap-gyel-tsen's followers that Vasubandhu himself, in his *Conquest over Objections about the Three Mother Scriptures,* takes the thoroughly established nature as the basis of emptiness and speaks of its emptiness of the other two natures. The

---

a *ngo bo nyid kyis stong pa nyid.*

b *rang bzhin gyis stong pa nyid.*

c Ge-luk-ba scholars oppose the opinion that whatever is not the ultimate nature is necessarily empty of its own entity, both for the Mind-Only School and for the Middle Way School; they berate this as a devaluing of conventionalities.

objection is based on S̄hay-rap-gyel-tsen's own citation of the *Conquest over Objections,* but I will forgo describing the controversy here because I have treated it at length in *Emptiness in Mind-Only* (225-233, 335-341). D̄zong-ka-b̄a's basic points are that S̄hay-rap-gyel-tsen mis-read the *Conquest over Objections* and that there is solid evidence that Vasubandhu did not compose the text.

Third Question About The Second "Contradiction": Does S̄hay-rap-gyel-tsen Compare The Style Of Emptiness To A Place's Being Devoid Of A Pot?

D̄zong-ka-b̄a (see the quotation from *The Essence of Eloquence* given at the start of the second basic contradiction, pp. 325-326) next criticizes S̄hay-rap-gyel-tsen for comparing the style of emptiness to a place's being devoid of a pot. He (*Emptiness in Mind-Only,* 227) makes a similar criticism in the section on S̄hay-rap-gyel-tsen's reading of the *Conquest over Objections about the Three Mother Scriptures:*

> Furthermore, the conception that a self of phenomena exists is not a conception that some other thing exists, as in the conception that fire exists on a pass. Rather, one conceives that when there is an appearance—[to] one's own mind—as external object and internal subject in the manner of being separate, distant, and cut off, these are established in the way that they appear. Hence, as an antidote to this, it is taught that appearances as object and subject are [in fact] not established as other substantial entities of apprehended-object and apprehending-subject, but it is not taught that apprehended-object and apprehending-subject do not exist as other factualities with respect to that [thoroughly established nature].[a] Therefore, Sthiramati's *Explanation of*

[a] It seems to me that D̄zong-ka-b̄a wants to keep the framework of the first clause in this sentence, "Hence, as an antidote to this, it is taught that appearances as object and subject are [in fact] not established as other substantial entities of apprehended-object and apprehending-subject" (*de'i gnyen por yul yul can du snang ba de gzung 'dzin rdzas gzhan du ma grub ces stong gyi*) when rendering his refutation of S̄hay-rap-gyel-tsen's position in the second clause, "but it is not taught that apprehended-object and apprehending-subject do not exist as other factualities **with respect to that** [thoroughly established nature]" (*gzung 'dzin don gzhan du de la med do zhes ston pa min no*). In the second clause he uses "apprehended-object and apprehending-subject" rather than "appearances as object and subject" and "other factualities" rather than "other substantial entities of apprehended-object and apprehending-subject." If he had not used these equivalents, the second clause would read, "but it is not taught that appearances as object and subject are [in fact] not established as other factualities **with respect to that** [thoroughly established nature]."

The demonstrative pronoun "that" at the end of the sentence is hard to unpack. I identify the antecedent—due to the similarity of topic—as being "the thoroughly established nature" (*Emptiness in Mind-Only,* 227) found six lines earlier in the Tibetan:

> *(Vasubandhu's) Commentary on (Maitreya's) "Differentiation of the Middle and the Extremes"* also says that it is not like a temple's being empty of monastics and so forth but like a rope's being empty of a snake. The other mode of emptiness of a self of phenomena [that is, objects' emptiness of establishment by way of their own character as the referents of conceptual consciousnesses] is also that way.

Shay-rap-gyel-tsen does indeed make similar comparisons but in a more nuanced way than Dzong-ka-ba's brief criticism would suggest. In explaining the difference between what is self-empty and what is other-empty, he[337] cites the *Aṅgulimāla Sūtra* (for the complete citation, see p. 286ff.), which, while not speaking about a place that is empty of, or without, a pot, does speak of a piece of hail which is empty of a jewel, a home that is empty of humans, a pot that is empty of water, a river that is empty of water, and a village that is empty of humans.

The first of these, a piece of hail that is empty of a jewel, is in fact like Dzong-ka-ba's preferred example drawn from Sthiramati, a rope that is empty of a snake, and the other four are like the example that Dzong-ka-ba criticizes, a

---

> Therefore, how could selflessness be delineated within thinking [as the Jo-nang-bas do] that **the thoroughly established nature** is empty because of existing as factually other than the other two natures!" (***yongs grub*** *ngo bo nyid gzhan gnyis don gzhan du yod pa stong ngo zhes bdag med gtan la 'bebs pa ga la yin; Emptiness in Mind-Only,* 442.22).

However, Jik-may-dam-chö-gya-tso (*Port of Entry,* 683.1) offers a different reading:

> Furthermore, the conception that a self of phenomena exists is not a conception that some other thing exists because:
>
> - when the two—apprehended-object and apprehending-subject—appear as object and subject separately in the manner of being distant and cut off, one conceives that these are established in the way that they appear, and hence
> - as an antidote to the conception that they are established this way, it must be taught that apprehended-object and apprehending-subject are [in fact] not established as other substantial entities, but
> - it is not taught that, with regard to the establishment of apprehended-object and apprehending-subject, the basis of emptiness does not exist **with respect to/in** apprehended-object and apprehending-subject (*gzung 'dzin rdzas gzhan du grub pa ni stong gzhi gzung 'dzin* ***de la*** *med do zhes ston pa ma yin*),* since
> - a consciousness conceiving a self of phenomena conceives that [apprehended-object and apprehending-subject] exist in the way that they appear.

*This difficult clause might also be rendered differently as, "it is not taught that the establishment of apprehended-object and apprehending-subject does not exist **with respect to/in** the basis of emptiness, apprehended-object and apprehending-subject," but one of Dzong-ka-ba's chief points is that the basis of emptiness is not the thoroughly established nature, as Shay-rap-gyel-tsen claims, but the very phenomena themselves. (If Jik-may-dam-chö-gya-tso's text read *gzung 'dzin rdzas gzhan du grub pa ni stong gzhi* ***yongs grub de la*** *med do zhes ston pa ma yin,* it would reflect Shay-rap-gyel-tsen's opinion that Dzong-ka-ba is refuting.)

place that is empty of a pot. A piece of hail never was, is, or will be a jewel, and a rope never was, is, or will be a snake, whereas:

- a home sometimes is and sometimes is not empty of—that is to say, without—humans
- a pot sometimes is and sometimes is not empty of water
- a riverbed sometimes is and sometimes is not empty of water
- a village sometimes is and sometimes is not empty of humans.

Although D̄zong-ka-b̄a uses the example of a rope that is never a snake, and a snake does exist somewhere else, the point of the example is not that a snake exists elsewhere but that a rope is misconceived to be a snake. In the selflessness of phenomena in D̄zong-ka-b̄a's system, that of which other-powered natures are empty is an imputational nature that never did, does, or will exist—which, in the above quotation, is said to be a difference of entity between subject and object, evocatively specified as the sense that external object and internal subject are separate, distant, and cut off.

D̄zong-ka-b̄a's criticism is that, just as a home is empty of humans who exist somewhere else or a place is empty, or without, a pot that exists somewhere else, so, in S̄hay-rap-gyel-tsen's system, the great liberation is empty of defects that exist somewhere else, and thus, the basis of emptiness—the great liberation, or thoroughly established nature—is empty of an existent object of negation. (It needs to be stressed that, in D̄zong-ka-b̄a's own system, the thoroughly established nature is indeed empty of other-powered natures in the sense that it is not other-powered natures; however, he holds that realization of this does not constitute realization of emptiness. In his system, other-powered natures must be taken as the bases of emptiness, and realization of emptiness means to understand that they are empty of a non-existent imputational nature, a non-existent status that is falsely imagined in them, specifically that they are separate, distant, and cut off from the consciousness apprehending them or that they are established by way of their own character as the referents of their respective terms and conceptual consciousnesses. For D̄zong-ka-b̄a, even realization of the emptiness of the thoroughly established nature means to understand that it is empty of a non-existent imputational nature, a non-existent status falsely imagined in it, which is that it is separate, distant, and cut off from the consciousness apprehending it or that it is established by way of its own character as the referent of its terms and conceptual consciousnesses.)

S̄hay-rap-gyel-tsen divides phenomena into those that are self-empty and those that are other-empty, the former being other-powered natures and imputational natures and the latter being the thoroughly established nature and its plenitude of equivalents. When he does this within blatantly using the examples that he does, he would seem to be subject to Sthiramati's criticism, adduced by D̄zong-ka-b̄a, that emptiness is not like a temple's being empty of monastics. However, S̄hay-rap-gyel-tsen[338] deals with this problem head-on, again through the medium of a debate about the meaning of an authoritative passage, in this case what is likely Sthiramati's source, the *Descent into Laṅkā Sūtra*. That sūtra[339] calls one thing's emptiness of another the worst of all emptinesses and to be avoided:

> *Objection:* The *Descent into Laṅkā Sūtra* speaks of seven emptinesses and says that, from among these, the emptiness that is the-one-being-empty-of-the-other[a] is the lowest of all seven and says, "Such an emptiness is to be thoroughly abandoned." Therefore, how does your ultimate other-emptiness differ from this?
>
> *Answer:* That is not so because:
>
> - the emptiness that is the-one-being-empty-of-the-other and the emptiness that the *Descent into Laṅkā Sūtra* says is the lowest are in consideration of the emptiness that is the-one-being-empty-of-the-other **with regard to conventional phenomena**, and furthermore
> - the ultimate nature's emptiness of conventional, adventitious phenomena is more extremely different than just very different.
>
> The *Descent into Laṅkā Sūtra* says:
>
> > Mahāmati, what is the exalted wisdom of Superiors, the great emptiness? It is thus: the exalted wisdom of Superiors realized by oneself individually is empty of all views and faulty predispositions. Therefore, it is called "the ultimate exalted wisdom of Superiors, the great emptiness."
>
> Thus, from among the seven emptinesses, it calls the ultimate exalted wisdom of Superiors, which is an other-emptiness empty of all views and faulty predispositions, the great emptiness.
>
> Therefore, a building's emptiness of horses and elephants and other such emptinesses are set forth as **examples** [or analogs] of the ultimate other-emptiness but are not set forth as the meaning of emptiness. Those are neither the conventional emptiness nor the ultimate emptiness. Consequently, just as self-emptiness does not function as the ultimate emptiness, other-emptiness also does not function as the conventional emptiness. Therefore, **in consideration of the conventional emptiness** [the *Descent into Laṅkā Sūtra*] says that, since the emptiness that is the-one-being-empty-of-the-other is the worst of emptinesses, it is to be abandoned, and we also assert this in just that way. Hence, we do not have any fault of contradicting scripture.

Shay-rap-gyel-tsen's cogently framed opinion is that in the *Descent into Laṅkā*

[a] *gcig gis gcig stong pa'i stong nyid;* Shay-rap-gyel-tsen's *Ocean of Definitive Meaning,* 201.3.

Sūtra the criticism of one thing's emptiness of another is in the context of mistaking this type to be the conventional emptiness, whereas the actual conventional emptiness is a self-emptiness. He explains that nevertheless a building's emptiness of horses and elephants is to be taken as a crude example of the mode of emptiness of the ultimate, even though it itself is not an ultimate emptiness.

His explication might appear to be merely a cleverly crafted attempt to get around a clear criticism of other-emptiness, but he immediately provides a quotation from the *Descent into Laṅkā Sūtra* itself that positively speaks of the exalted wisdom of Superiors as devoid of views and faulty predispositions and thus as the great emptiness. "Emptiness" here clearly means that the exalted wisdom is an other-emptiness, empty of faults that are other than it. Given this nuanced treatment, D̄zong-ka-b̄a's brief mention of Sthiramati's statement that emptiness is not like a rope's being empty of a snake appears weak.[a]

Even though D̄zong-ka-b̄a's case that S̄hay-rap-gyel-tsen's treatment of the thoroughly established nature does not follow the *Sūtra Unraveling the Thought* is strong, D̄zong-ka-b̄a himself introduces other sources when he brings up Sthiramati and, implicitly, the *Descent into Laṅkā Sūtra.* Since it is clear that he is seeking to demonstrate contradiction with more sūtras than just the *Sūtra Unraveling the Thought*—no matter how central it is to the system of Asaṅga and his followers—the absence of a more nuanced and developed critique of S̄hay-rap-gyel-tsen's argument, which cites many sūtras including the *Descent into Laṅkā,* is puzzling.

Further Consideration Of The Second "Contradiction"

We have considered at length one quotation from D̄zong-ka-b̄a's *The Essence of Eloquence* indicting S̄hay-rap-gyel-tsen for claiming to follow the *Sūtra Unraveling The Thought* but asserting that the thoroughly established nature is empty of other-powered natures and imputational natures. Now let us consider together five other indictments of the doctrine of other-emptiness for devaluing conventional phenomena. D̄zong-ka-b̄a (*Emptiness in Mind-Only,* 129) says:

> Also, they make the differentiation that except for the real nature, all substrata [that is, all conventional phenomena]—aside from being fancied by a mistaken awareness—do not have entities that are established in the slightest, whereas the real nature is truly established. They assert this differentiation of no true establishment and true establishment to be the meaning of the good differentiation [by the final wheel of doctrine] mentioned earlier.

[a] Jam-ȳang-shay-b̄a (*Great Exposition of Tenets, ca* 17b.6) also merely cites the statement in the *Descent into Laṅkā Sūtra* that this type of emptiness is the lowest, or worst, without countering S̄hay-rap-gyel-tsen's explanation even though on the previous page he mentions him by name (*kun mkhyen jo nang ba chen po;* 16a.5) as well as the *Ocean of Definitive Meaning* (16a.8).

And (*Emptiness in Mind-Only,* 157-158):

> Furthermore, one later [scholar] explains that it is the thought of Asaṅga and his brother [Vasubandhu] that:
>
> - the first nature [the imputational nature] does not exist even conventionally,
> - although the middle one [the other-powered nature] exists conventionally, it does not exist ultimately, and
> - the latter [the thoroughly established nature] ultimately exists.
>
> This also is outside this system [of Mind-Only as commented upon by Asaṅga and Vasubandhu]. In particular, the [wrong] assertion—that the meaning of other-powered natures' existing conventionally is just that a **mistaken** consciousness conceives that production, cessation, and so forth exist in them, whereas **in fact** production, cessation, and so forth do not exist—is the final deprecation of other-powered natures, due to which the other two natures are also deprecated. Hence, this is the chief of annihilatory views described earlier in Asaṅga's *Grounds of Bodhisattvas* as a deprecation of all three natures. Know this as an undispellable contradiction in the position of those who assert that the *Sūtra Unraveling the Thought* is of definitive meaning [and assert that other-powered natures are empty of inherent existence].

And (*Emptiness in Mind-Only,* 186):

> ...since just this [establishment by way of its own character] also is described as ultimate establishment, the explanation [by the Jo-nang-b̄as and so forth] that in this system other-powered natures are empty of themselves is not at all the case.

And (*Emptiness in Mind-Only,* 188):

> The meaning is not to explain [as the Jo-nang-b̄as do] that the non-empty is the thoroughly established nature and the non-non-empty are the other two natures [that is, other-powered natures and imputational natures].

And (*Emptiness in Mind-Only,* 188):

> This should not be taken in accordance with the [Jo-nang-b̄as'] explanation—which is opposite from that of these [masters, Vasubandhu and Sthiramati]—that they assert that, since, concerning these two [that is, other-powered natures and the thoroughly established nature], the one exists as factually other than the other, they are empty [of each other].

S̄hay-rap-gyel-tsen's explanation of the passage from Asaṅga's *Summary of Manifest Knowledge* cited above (see p. 332-336) confirms that he holds that other-powered natures only conventionally exist. Also, in other places he repeats the point that other-powered natures do not really exist, as in:[340]

> Moreover, the Conqueror Maitreya speaks of the meaning of not really existing and of really existing with respect to phenomena and the noumenon [respectively]. His *Differentiation of Phenomena and Noumenon,*[341] *Ornament for the Great Vehicle Sūtras,*[342] and so forth teach that imputational and other-powered phenomena do not really exist and that the noumenal thoroughly established nature really exists. These also indicate the meaning of self-emptiness and other-emptiness.

He clearly views that other-powered natures conventionally exist and the thoroughly established nature really or ultimately exists, and thus D̄zong-ka-b̄a repeatedly emphasizes evidence to the contrary such that it becomes a major theme of the Mind-Only section of *The Essence of Eloquence.* In a multi-stepped argument he points out that:

- The *Sūtra Unraveling the Thought* itself says that imputational natures (and hence not other-powered natures) are character-non-natures in the sense that they are not established by way of their own character (*Emptiness in Mind-Only,* 79, 86); hence other-powered natures are established by way of their own character.
- The *Sūtra Unraveling the Thought* (*Emptiness in Mind-Only,* 97) indicates that other-powered natures are established by way of their own character when it says, "That which does not exist by way of its own character is not produced." For it (*Emptiness in Mind-Only,* 87) also says, "Those [other-powered characters] **arise** through the force of other conditions and not by themselves," and Asaṅga's *Compendium of Ascertainments* (*Emptiness in Mind-Only,* 88) says, "Because compositional phenomena are dependent-arisings, they are **produced** through the power of conditions and not by themselves," and hence other-powered natures are produced, due to which they must be established by way of their own character (see also *Emptiness in Mind-Only,* 95-97).
- Asaṅga himself indicates that "established by way of its own character" and "ultimately established" have the same meaning when, in his *Grounds of Bodhisattvas* (*Emptiness in Mind-Only,* 140-148), he describes the extreme of superimposition as conceiving "own-character" in imputational natures and describes the extreme of deprecation as denying the ultimate existence of other-powered natures.[a]

[a] For Gung-tang's speculation on why Asaṅga uses these different terms for the two extremes, see *Emptiness in Mind-Only,* 142, footnote a.

- When in the *Grounds of Bodhisattvas* and the *Compendium of Ascertainments* Asaṅga says that other-powered natures exist, he means that they are established by way of their own character and ultimately exist and when he says that an extreme of deprecation is to hold that other-powered natures do not exist, he means that it is an extreme of deprecation to hold that other-powered natures are not established by way of their own character and do not ultimately exist (*Emptiness in Mind-Only,* 144, 151-153); and, similarly, Vasubandhu's and Sthiramati's commentaries on Maitreya's *Differentiation of the Middle and the Extremes* indicate that the existence of other-powered natures means that they are ultimately existent and established by way of their own character, as does Sthiramati's *Commentary on (Vasubandhu's) "The Thirty"* (*Emptiness in Mind-Only,* 182-189).
- When Asaṅga and so forth say that other-powered natures conventionally exist, they have other meanings in mind that do not contradict other-powered natures being established by way of their own character (*Emptiness in Mind-Only,* 158-171).
- That Maitreya's *Ornament for the Great Vehicle Sūtras* posits eight thoughts behind the explanation in the Perfection of Wisdom Sūtras of attaining forbearance with respect to the doctrine of non-production indicates that the system of that text does not assert that other-powered natures are not established by way of their own character (*Emptiness in Mind-Only,* 173-176).
- When the *Sūtra Unraveling the Thought* and Maitreya's *Ornament for the Great Vehicle Sūtras* compare other-powered natures to illusions, this does not contradict their being established by way of their own character (*Emptiness in Mind-Only,* 176-181).
- Asaṅga's brief explanation of the four examinations and four thorough knowledges in his *Summary of Manifest Knowledge* (*Emptiness in Mind-Only,* 213-214) is understood as presenting that other-powered natures are established by way of their own character when the detailed explanation of these in the Chapter on Suchness in Asaṅga's *Grounds of Bodhisattvas* is consulted (Ḏzong-ka-ḇa's student Ke-drup[343] brings out this significance of his teacher's citation of Asaṅga's *Summary of Manifest Knowledge*).
- Asaṅga's *Summary of Manifest Knowledge* and *Summary of the Great Vehicle* explain the thought behind the statements in the Perfection of Wisdom Sūtras that all phenomena are natureless, and Vasubandhu's *Principles of Explanation* explains that the statements of naturelessness in the Perfection of Wisdom Sūtras are not to be taken literally (*Emptiness in Mind-Only,* 236-241).

In this case, Ḏzong-ka-ḇa's presentation is a highly nuanced, thoroughgoing argument that takes account of a wide variety of S̄hay-rap-gyel-tsen's sources. The very twists and turns of his explanation of the usage of conventional and ultimate existence, however, suggest the possibility of other readings, although the creativity of his own explanation is indeed impressive.

However, it does not seem to me that, with regard to the second contradiction—claiming to follow the *Sūtra Unraveling The Thought* but asserting that the thoroughly established nature is empty of other-powered natures and imputational natures—D̄zong-ka-b̄a has striven to give a thoroughgoing treatment of S̄hay-rap-gyel-tsen's sources for taking the thoroughly established nature as the basis of emptiness and for considering it to be empty of other-powered natures and imputational natures. I imagine that, if D̄zong-ka-b̄a were before me now, he would suggest that, based on those that he did treat, I could figure out how to explain away S̄hay-rap-gyel-tsen's other source quotes and that what he had done was sufficient to undermine his predecessor's system, but it does not strike me that such a task would be easy.

17c. Analysis of Ge-luk-b̄a Criticisms of the Jo-nang-b̄a View: III

3. "Self-Contradiction": Claiming To Follow The *Sūtra Unraveling The Thought* But Asserting That All Sūtras Of The Third Period Are Definitive, Not Differentiating Between The Third Wheel And The Third Period Of Buddha's Teaching

To review: Without ever mentioning S̄hay-rap-gyel-tsen by name, D̄zong-ka-b̄a unrelentingly criticizes the eclecticism of his view. Basically, he takes him to task for:

- On the one hand, he uses the *Sūtra Unraveling the Thought* to determine that the third wheel of doctrine is definitive.[a]
- But then for delineating what the thoroughly established nature is, he ignores what the *Sūtra Unraveling the Thought* itself says about the ultimate and cites other sūtras spoken during the third period of Buddha's teaching that speak of a fully developed Buddha nature endowed with the major and minor marks of a Buddha.

D̄zong-ka-b̄a's complaint is that, relying on the *Sūtra Unraveling the Thought*, the Jo-nang-b̄as[b] establish that the third wheel of Buddha's doctrine is definitive but then, in self-contradiction, assert that the thoroughly established nature is a positive, self-powered entity despite the fact that the *Sūtra Unraveling the Thought* describes the ultimate as a mere absence—or, as it is described in more elaborate vocabulary, a mere elimination of an object of negation. As Jam-ȳang-shay-b̄a succinctly says,[344] since even the Jo-nang-b̄as hold that it is suitable to

---

[a] In the seventh chapter of the *Sūtra Unraveling the Thought*, Paramārthasamudgata (*Emptiness in Mind-Only*, 116-117) speaks of the third wheel of doctrine as being definitive:

> Based on just the naturelessness of phenomena and based on just the absence of production, the absence of cessation, quiescence from the start, and naturally passed beyond sorrow, the Supramundane Victor turned a third wheel of doctrine for those engaged in all vehicles, possessed of good differentiation, fantastic and marvelous. This wheel of doctrine turned by the Supramundane Victor is unsurpassable, does not afford an occasion [for refutation], is of definitive meaning, and does not serve as a basis for controversy.

[b] S̄hay-rap-gyel-tsen (*Ocean of Definitive Meaning*, 177.3) cites the *Sūtra Unraveling the Thought* after saying:

> Concerning the differences of the three wheels of doctrine with regard to requiring interpretation or being definitive and with regard to clearly teaching within good differentiation or not, the *Sūtra Unraveling the Thought* says...

Also, he defends taking the *Sūtra Unraveling the Thought* literally (see pp. 326-327).

take the *Sūtra Unraveling the Thought* literally, the thoroughly established nature cannot be held to be positive and self-powered.

D̄zong-ka-b̄a concludes that the Jo-nang-b̄as should have determined, based on Buddha's description of the ultimate in the *Sūtra Unraveling the Thought,* that other teachings that a Buddha nature endowed with the Buddha qualities is present in all beings were given for the sake of certain trainees and are not to be taken literally. His central point is that from the description of third-wheel teachings in the *Sūtra Unraveling the Thought* itself, it has to be concluded that **only** those few teachings that differentiate between establishment and non-establishment by way of its own character are third-wheel teachings. A consequence of this strict delimitation of the third wheel is the (at first blush counter-intuitive) assertion that most of Buddha's teachings during the third and last period of his life are not third-wheel teachings as described in the *Sūtra Unraveling the Thought.*

Thus, a decisive issue for D̄zong-ka-b̄a is that S̄hay-rap-gyel-tsen mistakenly concludes that, when the *Sūtra Unraveling the Thought* says that the third wheel of doctrine is definitive, it means that all sūtras taught during the third period of Buddha's teaching are definitive, including those propounding that Buddha qualities are already present in the continuums of each being. According to D̄zong-ka-b̄a, the Jo-nang-b̄as have failed to distinguish between the **third wheel** of doctrine and the sūtras spoken during the **third period** of Buddha's teaching. The third wheel, as can be seen from a close reading of the *Sūtra Unraveling the Thought,* consists of just those sūtra passages that clearly differentiate between what is and is not established by way of its own character. The sūtras of the third period, however, contain many teachings not concerned with this topic. In this vein, D̄zong-ka-b̄a (*Emptiness in Mind-Only,* 129) says:

> Therefore, some [earlier Tibetan scholars, specifically the Jo-nang-b̄as, wrongly] establish in dependence upon this *Sūtra [Unraveling the Thought]* that all sūtras spoken during the third period are of definitive meaning and then [mistakenly] assert as literal some [sūtras actually] spoken for the sake of leading those having the lineage of Other [Non-Buddhist] Schools who adhere to the propounding of self.[a]

---

[a] D̄zong-ka-b̄a's student Ke-drup (*Opening the Eyes of the Fortunate,* 243.5; see also José Ignacio Cabezón, *A Dose of Emptiness* [Albany, N.Y.: State University of New York Press, 1992], 71-72) describes the ways in which the *Sūtra Unraveling the Thought* and other sūtras that S̄hay-rap-gyel-tsen calls third wheel differ greatly:

> Also, a certain [S̄hay-rap-gyel-tsen] asserts that a meaning in accordance with the measure indicated on the literal level by the words of a sūtra—that is established as such [that is, a literal meaning which exists as described]—is a definitive meaning and that the opposite requires interpretation. Thereupon, he propounds that the final wheel—the *Sūtra Unraveling the Thought* and so forth—are of definitive meaning and that the middle wheel—the Perfection of Wisdom Sūtras and so forth—are of interpretable meaning. That scholar also propounds that the *Matrix*

> *of One Gone to Bliss Sūtra,* the *Ornament Illuminating Exalted Wisdom Sūtra,* the *Great Drum Sūtra,* the *Sūtra for Maudgalyāyana,* the *Superior Sūtra of Questions by King Dhāraṇīshvara,* the *Mahāparinirvāṇa Sūtra,* and so forth are definitive sūtras of the last wheel.
>
> This is uncritical because the mode of teaching in these latter sūtras and that in the *Sūtra Unraveling the Thought* are dissimilar in all respects. How are they dissimilar?
>
> - The *Sūtra Unraveling the Thought* sets forth three final vehicles, as cited above, whereas these latter [sūtras] set forth one final vehicle.
> - The *Lion's Roar of Shrīmālādevī* explains that Hearer Foe Destroyers assume a body of a mental nature due to [two] conditions—the level of the predispositions of ignorance and uncontaminated karma. That, moreover, is not suitable to happen on the occasion of a nirvāṇa with remainder because the body of a Foe Destroyer is an aggregate of suffering impelled by [contaminated] karma and afflictive emotions and, therefore, this must apply to a Foe Destroyer who has actualized a nirvāṇa without remainder. However, the assumption of a body by a Foe Destroyer who has attained a nirvāṇa without remainder greatly contradicts the schema of three final vehicles [set forth in the *Sūtra Unraveling the Thought* because a Foe Destroyer, according to that system, has no body at all].
>
> Therefore, when commenting on the meaning of the *Sūtra Unraveling the Thought,* Asaṅga's *Compendium of Ascertainments* clearly sets forth three final vehicles, and the Foremost Venerable [Maitreya] also sets such forth in his *Ornament of the Great Vehicle Sūtras.* [However,] when commenting on the thought of the sūtras on the matrix [of One Gone Thus], and so forth, Maitreya's *Sublime Continuum of the Great Vehicle* and Asaṅga's commentary on it set forth one final vehicle.

Also (Ke-drup's *Opening the Eyes of the Fortunate,* 241.1; see also Cabezón, *A Dose of Emptiness,* 70-71):

> Moreover, a certain [Shay-rap-gyel-tsen (*Ocean of Definitive Meaning,* 172.3)] cites this passage in the *Questions of King Dhāraṇīshvara Sūtra* [also called the *Sūtra Teaching the Great Compassion of a One Gone Thus* (*de bzhin gshegs pa'i snying rje chen po bstan pa'i mdo, tathāgatamahākaruṇānirdeśasūtra;* Peking 814, vol. 32, 300.5.4ff.)]:
>
>> O child of good lineage, for example, skillful jewelers, who know well how to cleanse a jewel, take a very impure jewel from a jewel-mine. They soak it in a strong solution of soda and thereupon clean it with a black haircloth. However, they do not leave off effort with just that; after that, they soak it in a strong solution of quicksilver and thereupon clean it with wool. However, they also do not leave off effort with just that; after that, they soak it in the juice of a great herb and thereupon clean it with a fine cloth. Having been thoroughly cleaned, the jewel—free from the three types of defilements—is called "the great lineage of *vaiḍūrya*" (cat's-eye gem).
>>
>> Just so, O child of good lineage, the One Gone Thus also, having ascertained the thoroughly impure [Buddha] constituent of sentient

And (*Emptiness in Mind-Only,* 128):

> Furthermore, the explanation that the third wheel is of definitive meaning is [in reference to] those of good differentiation as explained before, and not all [doctrines spoken during that period]. This is very clear in the *Sūtra [Unraveling the Thought]* itself. For example, when [Buddha] was about to pass beyond sorrow [that is, die], he said that it would be suitable [to use his earlier declarations] concerning similar [ethical] situations [as a basis for deciding new issues that he had not addressed, this teaching] being called the "condensed discipline," but [even though that instruction occurred during the final period of his

---

> beings, causes sentient beings who like cyclic existence to be discouraged with it through disquieting discourse on its impermanence, suffering, selflessness, and uncleanliness, introducing them to the disciplinary doctrine of Superiors.
>
> The One Gone Thus does not leave off effort with just that; after that, he causes them to realize the One Gone Thus's own mode through discourse on emptiness, signlessness, and wishlessness. Moreover, the One Gone Thus does not leave off effort with just that; after that, he causes those sentient beings with various causal natures to enter the land of a One Gone Thus through discourse on the irreversible wheel [and] discourse on the complete purity of the three spheres [of agent, action, and object]. When they have entered and realized the noumenon of a One Gone Thus, they are called "the unsurpassed boon."

[S̄hay-rap-gyel-tsen] propounds that this passage teaches that—through the stages of the three wheels of doctrine—coarse, subtle, and very subtle defilements obstructing the matrix of One Gone Thus are purified gradually and that therefore just the last wheel is definitive.

That is uncritical and also contradicts his own assertions. How? When the example and the exemplified are put together in terms of their similarities in terms of qualities, just as only one jewel is gradually cleansed by three means of cleansing, so it has to be asserted that the three levels of coarse and subtle defilements in the continuum of only one trainee are gradually purified by the three wheels that serve as means of purification. In that case, this contradicts the explanation in the *Sūtra Unraveling the Thought* that the lineages of trainees of the three wheels are different. Also, this contradicts even your own proposition and assertion that the lineages of trainees are different. Also, it would [absurdly] follow what whoever is a special trainee for whom the Supramundane Victor turned the wheel of doctrine necessarily enters the three vehicles in series.

Moreover, "discourse on the irreversible wheel" refers to teaching one final vehicle, and, since, as already explained earlier, the teaching that there are three final vehicles is in the last wheel [which teaches three final vehicles, S̄hay-rap-gyel-tsen's position] is senseless. Therefore, that sūtra merely teaches that—for purifying the basic constituent—initially as a path for ripening [the mental continuum] impermanence, suffering, and so forth are taught and then the paths of release of the coarse and subtle selflessnesses of phenomena, are taught in series, whereby defilements are purified.

teaching] this *Sūtra [Unraveling the Thought]* does not indicate that it is of definitive meaning.

Buddha's teaching near the time of his death about how to resolve ethical situations in the future occurred during the third **period** of his life, but it is not a teaching of the third **wheel** of doctrine as described in the *Sūtra Unraveling the Thought.* For the three wheels of doctrine, as posited in the seventh chapter of the *Sūtra Unraveling the Thought,* are solely concerned with Paramārthasamudgata's qualm about Buddha's having initially said that all phenomena are established by way of their own character and later his saying that all phenomena are not established by way of their own character—the former being the first wheel of doctrine and the latter being the middle wheel of doctrine, while the third wheel of doctrine is Buddha's subsequent differentiation into what are and are not established by way of their own character. As described in the *Sūtra Unraveling the Thought,* the three wheels, therefore, do not include all sūtra passages spoken during those periods. That is Dzong-ka-ba's position.

He complains that, because of not having understood what the *Sūtra Unraveling the Thought* actually says about the context of the three wheels of doctrine, Tibetan scholars misidentify all sūtras spoken during those three periods as the respective three wheels of doctrine. Then, like the Jo-nang-bas, they either have to take all those spoken during the third period as definitive, or, like Bu-dön (a prolific fourteenth-century scholar and founder of his own sect), they have to claim that the *Sūtra Unraveling the Thought* is not to be taken literally in its explanation of the differentiation of the definitive and the interpretable with respect to the three wheels of the teaching. According to Dzong-ka-ba, both have not understood that the three wheels as described in the *Sūtra Unraveling the Thought* merely refer to three types of specific passages found in sūtras of those periods. Dzong-ka-ba avers that both the Jo-nang-bas and their critics would have understood this if they had examined the *Sūtra Unraveling the Thought* carefully. He (*Emptiness in Mind-Only,* 130-131) says:

It appears that, without analyzing in detail:

- the way in which the question about dispelling contradictions in the sūtras arose [this being with regard to the seemingly contradictory teachings in the first wheel that all phenomena are established by way of their own character and in the middle wheel that all phenomena are not established by way of their own character],
- the way the Teacher answered it [this being to indicate the bases in his thought and how it would be extremist to hold that those two wheels of doctrine are literal, the first being an extreme of permanence and the second being an extreme of annihilation], and
- the way [teachings] are posited as interpretable and definitive in

> dependence upon this [that is to say, the division not being made by way of time but being made by way of differentiating or not differentiating among the three natures in terms of which are truly established and which is not],
>
> even both of these [that is, the Jo-nang-b̄as and Bu-d̄ön, and so forth] appear to be debating merely [about whether all sūtras that were spoken during the third period are definitive or not, in dependence] upon the [summary] passage [in the *Sūtra Unraveling the Thought*] that makes the division into what requires interpretation and what is definitive.

For D̄zong-ka-b̄a, the root cause of the Jo-nang-b̄as' error is their having missed ascertaining the description of the thoroughly established nature as a mere negative in the *Sūtra Unraveling the Thought.* Had they understood this point, they would have concluded that the sūtras spoken during the third period that teach a matrix of One Gone Thus, an ultimate truth endowed with Buddha qualities, within each being could not possibly be definitive.

From this viewpoint, he concludes that the Jo-nang-b̄as mistakenly consider sūtras—which Buddha set forth for the sake of drawing non-Buddhists toward his teaching of selflessness—to be definitive and based their description of the thoroughly established nature on them. It is in reference to these sūtras that D̄zong-ka-b̄a (*Emptiness in Mind-Only,* 129) says, as cited above:

> Therefore, some [earlier Tibetan scholars, specifically the Jo-nang-b̄as, wrongly] establish in dependence upon this *Sūtra [Unraveling the Thought]* that all sūtras spoken during the third period are of definitive meaning and then [mistakenly] assert as literal some [sūtras actually] spoken for the sake of leading[a] those having the lineage of Other [Non-Buddhist] Schools who adhere to the propounding of self.

His principal (and perhaps only) reference is to a description in the *Descent into Laṅkā Sūtra* of other sūtras that teach such a matrix of One Gone Thus. According to him, Buddha himself says that his teaching of a matrix of One Gone Thus endowed with Buddha qualities requires interpretation. D̄zong-ka-b̄a refers to but does not cite the passage here; let us cite it in its entirety:[b]

---

a *drang ba'i phyir du gsungs pa; Emptiness in Mind-Only,* 390.22.

b Peking 775, vol. 29, 39.5.5ff, chap. 2; Daisetz Teitaro Suzuki, trans., *The Lankavatara Sutra* (London: Routledge and Kegan Paul, 1932), 68-70. The passage up through "How could those with thoughts fallen into incorrect views conceiving of self come to be endowed with thought abiding in the spheres of the three liberations and quickly manifestly and completely purified in unsurpassed complete perfect enlightenment" is quoted in Chandrakīrti's *Commentary on the "Supplement"* (Peking 5263, vol. 98, 136.1.4ff), commenting on VI.95; Louis de la Vallée Poussin, *Madhyamakāvatāra par Candrakīrti,* Bibliotheca Buddhica 9 (Osnabrück, Germany: Biblio Verlag, 1970), 251-252; Jñānavajra's commentary is Peking

Mahāmati said, "The matrix of One Gone Thus taught in other sūtras spoken by the Supramundane Victor was said by the Supramundane Victor to be naturally radiant, pure, and thus from the beginning just pure. The matrix of One Gone Thus is said to possess the thirty-two signs [of a Buddha] and to exist in the bodies of all sentient beings.

"The Supramundane Victor said that, like a precious gem wrapped in a dirty cloth, the matrix of One Gone Thus is wrapped in the cloth of the aggregates, constituents, and sense-spheres, overwhelmed by the force of desire, hatred, and ignorance, and dirtied with the defilements of conceptuality.

"Since this which is dirtied with the defilements of conceptuality was said to be permanent, stable, and everlasting,[a] Supramundane Victor, how is this propounding of a matrix of One Gone Thus not like the [non-Buddhist] Forders' propounding of a self? Supramundane Victor, the Forders teach and propound a self that is permanent, the creator,[b] without qualities, pervasive, and non-perishing."

The Supramundane Victor said, "Mahāmati, my teaching of a matrix of One Gone Thus is not like the Forders' propounding of a self. O Mahāmati, the completely perfect Buddhas, Ones Gone Thus, Foe Destroyers, teach a matrix of One Gone Thus for the meaning of the words emptiness, the limit of reality, nirvāṇa, no production, signlessness, wishlessness, and so forth. So that children might avoid the fear of selflessness, they teach through the means of a matrix of One Gone Thus the state of non-conceptuality, the object [of wisdom] free from appearances.

"Mahāmati, future and present Bodhisattvas—the great beings—should not adhere to this as a self. Mahāmati, for example, potters make a variety of vessels out of one mass of clay particles with their hands, manual skill, a rod, water, string, and mental dexterity. Mahāmati, similarly the One Gone Thus also teach the selflessness of

---

5520, vol. 107, 246.4.4.

[a] *rtag pa, brtan pa, ther zug.*

[b] Chandrakīrti's *Commentary on the "Supplement"* (Peking 5263, vol. 98, 136.1.8) reads "non-creator" (*byed pa po ma yin pa*), in accordance with which Poussin's translation is "non-agent" (Louis de la Vallée Poussin, *Madhyamakāvatāra par Candrakīrti,* Bibliotheca Buddhica 9 [Osnabrück, Germany: Biblio Verlag, 1970], 251), and the Sanskrit, which he cites (251 n. 1), reads *nityo 'kartā;* however, the two commentaries on the *Descent into Laṅkā Sūtra* by Jñānashrībhadra (Peking 5519, vol. 107, 113.2.5) and Jñānavajra (Peking 5520, vol. 107, 246.5.1) read "agent/creator" (*byed pa*), as does Shay-rap-gyel-tsen (*Ocean of Definitive Meaning,* 66.6). It is likely that the ambiguity arises because *nityo 'kartā,* without the virama, is *nityo kartā,* and hence "permanent [and] agent," or as Suzuki translates it, "eternal creator" (Daisetz Teitaro Suzuki, trans., *The Lankavatara Sutra* [London: Routledge and Kegan Paul, 1932], 69). According to Jik-may-dam-chö-gya-tso's *Port of Entry* (454.6), it should be "non-creator [of the manifestations]."

phenomena that is an absence of all conceptual signs. Through various [techniques] endowed with wisdom and skill in means—whether they teach it as the matrix of One Gone Thus or as selflessness—they, like a potter, teach with various formats of words and letters.

"Therefore, Mahāmati, the teaching of the matrix of One Gone Thus is not like the teaching propounding a self for Forders. Mahāmati, in order to lead[a] Forders who are attached to propounding a self, the Ones Gone Thus teach the matrix of One Gone Thus through the teaching of a matrix of One Gone Thus. Thinking, 'How could those with thoughts fallen into incorrect views conceiving of self come to be endowed with thought abiding in the spheres of the three liberations and quickly manifestly and completely purified in unsurpassed complete perfect enlightenment,' for their sake, Mahāmati, the Ones Gone Thus, Foe Destroyers, completely perfect Buddhas, teach the matrix of One Gone Thus. Consequently, that is not the same as propounding the self of Forders. Therefore, Mahāmati, in order to overcome the view of Forders, they cause them to engage the matrix of One Gone Thus, selflessness.[b] It is this way: this teaching of the emptiness of phenomena, non-production, non-dualism, and absence of inherent existence is the unsurpassed tenet of Bodhisattvas; through thoroughly apprehending this teaching of the profound doctrine, one thoroughly apprehends all sūtras of the Great Vehicle."[c]

In the Mind-Only section of *The Essence of Eloquence,* D̄zong-ka-b̄a only obliquely refers to this passage when he (*Emptiness in Mind-Only,* 129) says, "assert as literal some [sūtras actually] spoken for the sake of leading those having the lineage of Other [Non-Buddhist] Schools who adhere to the propounding of self." However, in the section on the Consequence School, he analyzes and contextualizes the passage at considerable length in order to answer S̄hay-rap-gyel-tsen's detailed explanation of the passage.

---

[a] *drang ba'i phyir.* Poussin (*Madhyamakāvatāra,* 251 n. 1) gives the speculated Sanskrit in brackets as *ākarṣaṇārthaṃ.* The same Sanskrit but without brackets is given in P. L. Vaidya, *Saddharmalaṅkāvatārasūtram,* Buddhist Sanskrit Texts 3 (Darbhanga, India: Mithila Institute, 1963), 33.25. Suzuki (*Lankavatara Sutra,* 69.34) translates this word as "in order to awaken" in "Thus, Mahāmati, the doctrine of the Tathāgata-garbha is disclosed in order to awaken the philosophers from their clinging to the idea of the ego." However, "lead" accords with the meanings given in Vaman Shivaram Apte, *Sanskrit-English Dictionary* (Poona, India: Prasad Prakashan, 1957), 199, as an adjective, "attracting, carrying to another place" and as a noun, "pulling, drawing, attracting."

[b] *de bzhin gshegs pa'i snying po bdag med pa, tathāgatanairātmyagarbha.*

[c] This final sentence is not in the Peking edition (775, vol. 29, 40.2.6), nor in Vaidya (33), nor in Suzuki's translation (70).

Shay-rap-gyel-tsen's Treatment Of The Passage From The *Descent Into Laṅkā Sūtra*

In essence, Shay-rap-gyel-tsen makes the case that, although this passage from the *Descent into Laṅkā Sūtra* says that the teaching of such a matrix of One Gone Thus is "spoken for the sake of leading trainees,"[a] it does not say that such a teaching "requires interpretation."[b] He emphasizes that all teachings, including definitive ones, are for the sake of leading trainees, and thus that a teaching is for the sake of leading trainees does not mean that it is not definitive and requires interpretation.

Let us cite Shay-rap-gyel-tsen's detailed, point-by-point explanation. First, he indicates that the matrix of One Gone Thus is indeed not like the self that is propounded by non-Buddhists since it is empty of a self of persons and a self of phenomena. Also, it is not a mere space-like absence but is endowed with the ultimate qualities of Buddhahood. In order to allow that the marks and beauties of a Buddha could exist in the continuums of defiled sentient beings, he makes a distinction between the marks and beauties of a Buddha that inhere in the noumenon and those of conventional Form Bodies. Thus, the presence of ultimate Buddha qualities does not necessitate that sentient beings are already Buddhas, since they have not achieved the **conventional** Form Bodies of a Buddha. He says:[345]

> Concerning that, since the matrix of One Gone to Bliss is empty of the two selves, it is not similar to the self of Forders, and because the uncompounded noumenon transcends the momentary, it is permanent, stable, and everlasting. It is not that it—like space—is without any of the good qualities, powers, and aspects of a Buddha, and it is not like the self of persons that Forders impute to be permanent. Similarly, since the marks and beauties that are complete in the matrix of One Gone to Bliss are endowed with all the aspects, all the capacities, all the faculties, and all the good qualities of the noumenon, they are not the same as the marks and beauties of conventional Form Bodies.

If the passage from the *Descent into Laṅkā Sūtra* did show that the teaching of the matrix of One Gone Thus endowed with Buddha qualities is provisional, this would undermine Shay-rap-gyel-tsen's own central teaching; hence, he proceeds to show that the mere fact that the *Descent into Laṅkā Sūtra* says that this teaching **leads** trainees does not have to indicate that such a teaching is of interpretable meaning (*drang don, neyārtha*), that is to say, has a meaning that is to be **led** elsewhere. His grounds are threefold:

---

a *gdul bya drang ba'i phyir du gsungs pa.*

b *drang don, neyārtha;* more literally this would be translated as "a meaning that must be led."

- Just because a teaching has a purpose, this does not make the scripture non-definitive.
- The term "interpretable meaning" (*drang don, neyārtha*) itself is not used in the *Descent into Laṅkā Sūtra* about this type of teaching.
- To hold that the teaching of a matrix of One Gone Thus requires interpretation would contradict the *Descent into Laṅkā Sūtra* itself.

S̄hay-rap-gyel-tsen says:

> Here, the statement, "in order to lead Tīrthikas who are attached to propounding a self," indicates the purpose [of teaching the matrix of One Gone Thus], but this does not cause it to become a case of speaking in a manner that requires interpretation in that it, like the words of *ma'i la du,*[a] imparts that something non-existent exists. Why? It is because, although there are cases of speaking of the matrix of One Gone Thus in consideration of thusness, emptiness, and so forth and there are cases of speaking by way of many synonyms such as emptiness, thusness, and so forth in consideration of the matrix of One Gone Thus, all those are equivalent.

His point is that the teaching of emptiness and the teaching of a matrix of One Gone Thus amount to the same thing but are given for different trainees depending on their disposition.

He accuses those—who view the teaching of emptiness and the teaching of a matrix of One Gone Thus as not implying each other—of being too literal:

> Although these [teachings] are just equivalent, that which accords in vocabulary for the thought of some persons does not accord with the minds of others, and that which accords with their minds does not accord with the others' minds. Consequently, the fundamental noumenon that is empty of all phenomena, the sole expanse of the ultimate, is taught with a great many synonyms in profound sūtras and tantras—emptiness, signlessness, and so forth as well as natural nirvāṇa, expanse of selfhood, Buddha-nature, and so forth as well as Heruka, Vajrasattva, the syllable *evaṃ, ahaṃ,* great seal, source of phenomena, *bhaga,* vajra, the syllable *a,* and so forth. Due to this, seeing that, if here it were taught with the vocabulary of emptiness and selflessness, it would not be meaningful and that, if it is taught with the vocabulary of the matrix of One Gone to Bliss, it would be very meaningful, [Buddha] spoke this way. This is the meaning [of Buddha's explanation in the *Descent in Laṅka Sūtra* about the teaching of a matrix of One Gone Thus].
>
> Hence, although they are one with respect to how they abide in fact, it is not that the styles of teaching in words and phrases do not

[a] S̄hay-rap-gyel-tsen's *Ocean of Definitive Meaning,* 69.3; meaning unknown.

differ for some with respect to vocabulary. Therefore, the *Mahāparinirvāṇa Sūtra* as translated by Hlay-da-wa[a] also says:

> If he taught, "The matrix of One Gone Thus is empty," childish ones would meditate on a nihilistic, frightful perversion.[b] The intelligent understand that the permanent and everlasting exists in only an illusory-like manner.

and so forth.

His basic point is that the matrix of One Gone Thus is devoid of the self of persons and the self of phenomena (and thus is illusory-like) and, at the same time, is the pure self, whereby it both is unlike the permanent self taught by the non-Buddhist Forders and yet appeals to them. As he says later:

> *Objection:* If the matrix of One Gone to Bliss and the expanse of selfhood[346] are synonyms, then [the matrix of One Gone to Bliss] would not differ from the self of Forders. If they are not synonyms, then although taught with those names, Forders who adhere to a self could not be led [by those teachings].
>
> *Answer:* There is no fault because [the matrix of One Gone to Bliss] is the basis that is empty of the two selves and is the self of thusness, the pure self, and so forth.

Although the matrix of One Gone Thus is empty of a self of persons and a self of phenomena, Shay-rap-gyel-tsen calls it "pure self," a recurrent theme in the *Ocean of Definitive Meaning:*[347]

> It is said that, although this appears to contradict the earlier statements of selflessness, there is no fault because the *Mahāparinirvāṇa Sūtra* extensively says:
>
> > Child of good lineage, in the wheel of doctrine turned earlier at Varaṇāsi, impermanence, suffering, emptiness, and selflessness were taught. When turning the wheel of doctrine here in this Kushīnagarī, I taught permanence, bliss, self, and thorough purity.
>
> and:
>
> > Child of good lineage, that which has permanence, bliss, self, and thorough purity is called the "meaning of pure truth."
>
> and:
>
> > Uncompounded is the great nirvāṇa; permanent is nirvāṇa.

---

a *lha'i zla ba.*

b *yon po.*

> Permanent is the self; the self is thoroughly pure. The thoroughly pure is called "bliss." Permanent, blissful, self, and thoroughly pure is the One Gone Thus.

and:

> Child of good lineage, "self" means the matrix of One Gone Thus. The existence of the Buddha-nature in all sentient beings is the meaning of "self."

and:

> The Buddha-nature cannot be, by its own nature, made non-existent; it is not something that becomes non-existent. Just the inherent nature called "self" is the secret matrix of One Gone Thus; in this way that secret matrix cannot be destroyed and made non-existent by anything.

and:

> The character of the supramundane self is called the "Buddha-nature"; apprehending it as self in that way is called "very supreme."

and:

> One sense power of a One Gone Thus sees form, hears sound, smells odor, experiences taste, feels tangible objects, and knows phenomena; however, the six sense powers of a One Gone Thus do not see form, do not hear sound, do not smell odor, do not experience taste, do not feel tangible objects, and do not know phenomena. Because of being powers, the sense powers exercise power; such powers are called "great self."

Also, in no sense does he shy away from the vocabulary of permanence with respect to the matrix of One Gone Thus. As cited above, he says:

> Concerning that, since the matrix of One Gone to Bliss is empty of the two selves, it is not similar to the self of Forders, and because the uncompounded noumenon transcends the momentary, it is permanent, stable, and everlasting. It is not that it—like space—is without any of the good qualities, powers, and aspects of a Buddha, and it is not like the self of persons that Forders impute to be permanent.

He even says that the matrix of One Gone Thus is partless, reminiscent of the Sāṃkhya teaching that the nature, or general principal, is partless:

> Just that final Buddha, the matrix of One Gone Thus, the ultimate

clear light, expanse of reality, self-arisen exalted wisdom, great bliss, and partless pervader of all is said to be the basis and source of all phenomena and also is said in reality to be the basis that is empty of all phenomena, the void basis, and the basis pure of all defilements. It also is said to be endowed with the qualities of the Body of Attributes—beyond the count of the sands of the Ganges River—within an indivisible nature.[348]

Furthermore, if the matrix of One Gone Thus did require interpretation, thusness—the noumenal element—also would require interpretation. And if that is accepted, the ultimate, uncompounded Buddha—the Body of Attributes—also would require interpretation. If that also is accepted, then all those that abide forever, partless, omnipresent, and pervading all—the ultimate deities, such as Chakrasamvara, Hevajra Kālachakra, and so forth, as well as ultimate mantras, tantras, hand gestures, mandalas, and so forth—would most absurdly require interpretation. However, that is not the case.[349]

If in that way through merely hearing the name of the matrix of One Gone to Bliss one will attain Buddhahood, what need is there to mention faithfully respecting it, meditating upon it upon having actualized it, and so forth! Therefore, the wise who are imbued with compassion should teach it without regard for their life and those who seek liberation should seek it, listen to it, and so forth, even upon being swallowed in a great whirlwind of fire. Since the *Mahāparinirvāṇa Sūtra*..., the *Aṅgulimāla Sūtra*..., the *Great Drum Sūtra*..., the *Great Cloud Sūtra*..., and others again and again eloquently pronounce such at length, be endowed with great effort day and night in faithful and respectful hearing, thinking, and meditating on the alternative internal knowledge, the Buddha-nature, the natural great nirvāṇa, thusness, self, pure self, matrix of One Gone to Bliss, clear light nature, perfection of wisdom, source of phenomena,[a] great seal, syllable *a,* ultimate truth, syllable *evaṃ,* Vajrasattva, androgynous state, partless omnipresent pervader, endowment with the supreme of all aspects, vajra sun and moon, sixteen thusnesses, twelve true meanings, immutable thoroughly established nature, great vajra-sphere mandala, essence of the mantra-sphere, omnipresent element of phenomena, the aspectless endowed with all aspects, that which is passed beyond all worldly exemplification, great wish-granting jewel, and supreme vast great wish-granting tree.[350]

Furthermore, in reliance on the lamp of profound quintessential

[a] *chos 'byung.* This could also be translated as "source of attributes."

instructions, it should be understood that all mentions of the definitive, final emptiness in the profound tantra sets, such as:

- partless, omnipresent pervader
- the great one endowed with the powerful ten aspects[a]
- the vajra-sun of great illumination
- *a,* the supreme of all letters
- the supreme nature of all things
- the formless excellence of beautiful form

and so forth, are in consideration of the ultimate, other-emptiness, the emptiness that is the [ultimate] nature of non-entities [that is, emptiness that is the ultimate nature which is the opposite of non-entities]. Similarly, the emptiness that is set forth in elevated and stainless sūtras, tantras, and treatises as equivalent and synonymous with all the manifold [indications of reality]:

- thusness
- limit of reality
- signless expanse
- ultimate truth
- expanse of reality
- ultimate mind of enlightenment
- the letter *e* [in *evaṃ*]
- the secret
- the great secrecy
- the essential constituent of space
- *bhaga*[b]
- source of attributes
- water-born[c]
- vajra
- triangle
- the letter *a*
- lion-throne
- locus of bliss
- the Blissful[d]
- great seal
- perfection-of-wisdom-goddess

---

a The root mantra of Kālachakra, *haṃ kṣhaḥ ma la va ra ya,* contains ten letters—*h, kṣh, m, l, v, r,* and *y* as well as the *visārga* in *kṣhaḥ,* which appears as a half moon, the *anusvāra* in *haṃ,* and the vowel *a,* which is the "life" of the consonants.

b That is, vagina.

c That is, lotus.

d *bde ba can, sukhāvatī.*

- Vishvamātā[a]
- Vajravarahī
- Vajranairātmya
- Goddess having Variegated Form

and so forth, is not a mere self-empty, emptiness of non-entities, but is in consideration of the basis of emptiness, the ultimate other-emptiness, the emptiness that is the [ultimate] nature of non-entities [that is, emptiness that is the ultimate nature which is the opposite of non-entities].[351]

He explains the purpose of these various forms of teaching what has the same meaning:[352]

> Emptiness, limit of reality, nirvāṇa, non-production, signlessness, basis of selflessness, and matrix of One Gone Thus are indeed one, but, having perceived that if it is taught by way of emptiness, selflessness, and so forth, some generate fright at the mere name, [Buddha] causes them to enter into the non-conceptual sphere of natural clear light—without the appearance of adventitious defilements—that has the meaning of emptiness and selflessness.

He cites the *Descent into Laṅkā Sūtra* itself to buttress the point:[353]

> The Supramundane Victor said, "Mahāmati, my teaching of a matrix of One Gone Thus is not like the Forders' propounding of a self. O Mahāmati, the completely perfect Buddhas, Ones Gone Thus, Foe Destroyers, teach a matrix of One Gone Thus for the meaning of the words emptiness, the limit of reality, nirvāṇa, no production, signlessness, wishlessness, and so forth. So that children might avoid the fear of selflessness, they teach through the means of a matrix of One Gone Thus the state of non-conceptuality, the object [of wisdom] free from appearances.
>
> "Mahāmati, future and present Bodhisattvas—the great beings—should not adhere to this as a self. Mahāmati, for example, potters make a variety of vessels out of one mass of clay particles with their hands, manual skill, a rod, water, string, and mental dexterity. Mahāmati, similarly the Ones Gone Thus also teach the selflessness of phenomena that is an absence of all conceptual signs. Through various [techniques] endowed with wisdom and skill in means—whether they teach it as the matrix of One Gone Thus or as selflessness—they, like a potter, teach with various formats of words and letters.
>
> "Therefore, Mahāmati, the teaching of the matrix of One Gone Thus is not like the teaching propounding a self for Forders.

[a] Kālachakra consort.

> Mahāmati, in order to lead[a] Forders who are attached to propounding a self, the Ones Gone Thus teach the matrix of One Gone Thus through the teaching of a matrix of One Gone Thus. Thinking, 'How could those with thoughts fallen into incorrect views conceiving of self come to be endowed with thought abiding in the spheres of the three liberations and quickly manifestly and completely purified in unsurpassed complete perfect enlightenment,' for their sake, Mahāmati, the Ones Gone Thus, Foe Destroyers, completely perfect Buddhas, teach the matrix of One Gone Thus. Consequently, that is not the same as propounding the self of Forders. Therefore, Mahāmati, in order to overcome the view of Forders, they cause them to engage the matrix of One Gone Thus, selflessness. It is this way: this teaching of the emptiness of phenomena, non-production, non-dualism, and absence of inherent existence is the unsurpassed tenet of Bodhisattvas; through thoroughly apprehending this teaching of the profound doctrine, one thoroughly apprehends all sūtras of the Great Vehicle."

S̄hay-rap-gyel-tsen draws attention to the fact that the *Descent into Laṅkā Sūtra* itself never says that the teaching of a matrix of One Gone Thus requires interpretation:[354]

> Consequently, although there is a great difference between requiring interpretation[b] and being spoken for the sake of leading trainees,[c] some who have not understood this [hold] that the *Descent into Laṅkā Sūtra* says that the matrix of One Gone to Bliss requires interpretation. This is the basis of their error because this text [the *Descent into Laṅkā Sūtra*] does not mention "requiring interpretation."

He strikes the absurdity that if a scripture required interpretation just because it had a purpose, then all of Buddha's scriptures would require interpretation:[355]

> If that were not the case and if due to just this phrase, "in order to lead," [a teaching] would require interpretation, then the statement [in Maitreya's *Ornament for the Great Vehicle Sūtras*], "In order to lead some,"[d] which sets forth the purpose of teaching one final vehicle would also most absurdly be a passage showing [that the teaching of one final vehicle] requires interpretation. Moreover, since all the profound paths of definitive meaning were spoken for the sake of leading trainees from the states of cyclic existence and of solitary peace to the supreme city of the great liberation, all of them most absurdly would just require interpretation.

---

a *drang ba'i phyir;* see p. 363, footnote a.

b *drang don.*

c *gdul bya drang ba'i phyir du gsungs pa.*

d *kha cig dag ni drang phyir dang.*

As a crowning point, he cites passages from the *Descent into Laṅkā Sūtra* itself that affirm the existence of such a matrix of One Gone Thus:[356]

> If the matrix of One Gone to Bliss did not exist in fact, this would incur the irreversible fallacy of contradicting the statements in the *Descent into Laṅkā Sūtra* that the mind beyond argumentation, essence of the ultimate ten grounds, natural clear light, Buddha matrix, natural virtue, basis free from all positions, final source of refuge, and exalted Buddha wisdom is the matrix of One Gone to Bliss. The *Descent into Laṅkā Sūtra*[357] itself says:
>
> > Abiding in equipoise internally on the Buddha ground, the matrix of One Gone Thus, with the Buddha mind he heard sounds from within space, "O Lord of Laṅkā, good, good. Lord of Laṅkā, you are good. In the way that you are training, so yogis should train. In the way that you see, the Ones Gone Thus and phenomena should be viewed. If these are viewed otherwise, one will dwell in annihilation."
>
> and so forth, and:
>
> > The nature of the mind is clear light,
> > The virtuous matrix of One Gone Thus,
> > The substantial cause of sentient beings,
> > Devoid of limitation and non-limitation.
> > Just as—through being cleansed—the color of gold,
> > Pure gold, and bronze are seen, so is
> > The matrix of One Gone Thus afflicted with adventitious defilements.
> > Persons do not exist, and aggregates do not exist.
> > Always meditating on peace
> > In the uncontaminated Buddha-wisdom,
> > I go for refuge to that.
> > The supreme of proponents reveals
> > That the mind, with a nature of clear light,
> > Exists together with the afflictive emotions
> > Of mind and so forth and self.
>
> and:
>
> > The matrix of One Gone Thus
> > Is not in the sphere of logicians.

In this way, Shay-rap-gyel-tsen presents a lengthy argument that contains within it responses to possible indictments against his literal acceptance of a matrix of One Gone Thus endowed with Buddha qualities.

D̄zong-ka-b̄a's Rebuttal

D̄zong-ka-b̄a's initial response (*Emptiness in Mind-Only,* 129) to S̄hay-rap-gyel-tsen is laconic:

> Therefore, some [earlier Tibetan scholars, specifically the Jo-nang-b̄as, wrongly] establish in dependence upon this *Sūtra [Unraveling the Thought]* that all sūtras spoken during the third period are of definitive meaning and then [mistakenly] assert as literal some [sūtras actually] spoken for the sake of leading those having the lineage of Other [Non-Buddhist] Schools who adhere to the propounding of self.

He seems to rely merely on the mention of the word "lead" in the *Descent into Laṅkā Sūtra,* whereas S̄hay-rap-gyel-tsen has already offered a thoroughgoing response to such a position by convincingly:

- showing that even all definitive scriptures lead trainees
- demonstrating that the *Descent into Laṅkā Sūtra* itself equates the teaching of the matrix of One Gone Thus and the teaching of emptiness, and
- suggesting that the *Descent into Laṅkā Sūtra* itself teaches a matrix of One Gone Thus endowed with the Buddha qualities (the issue being not whether a matrix of One Gone Thus exists but whether it is endowed with Buddha powers and qualities).

To repeat: At first blush, it seems that D̄zong-ka-b̄a's argument revolves around the usage of the phrase "for the sake of leading" in the *Descent into Laṅkā Sūtra,* since he, as quoted above, uses those very words "assert as literal some [sūtras actually] spoken **for the sake of leading** those having the lineage of Other [Non-Buddhist] Schools who adhere to propounding a self." However, at the beginning of the section on the Middle Way School in *The Essence of Eloquence* he shows that his argument is not so simple. There, obviously in response to S̄hay-rap-gyel-tsen, he states that scriptures are not called "interpretable" (or "to be led") because they lead trainees; rather, they are called this because their meaning must be led elsewhere—that is, interpreted—in order to disclose the intent of the passage either on a conventional level or in terms of the final nature of phenomena. D̄zong-ka-b̄a says:[358]

> Though it is indeed the case that trainees are to be led by sūtras requiring interpretation, this is not the meaning of *neya.*[a] Rather, it [refers to] whether the meaning of the sūtra does or does not need to be interpreted as other than that.
>
> Among those in which the meaning needs to be interpreted there are two types:

[a] *drang;* literally "to be lead" but translated here as "requiring interpretation" for the sake of clarity.

- One type is, for instance, the need to interpret the [literally unacceptable] statement that father and mother are to be killed in "Having killed father and mother..." This must be interpreted as other than the meaning of the explicit reading; that is to say, father and mother are to be taken as [referring to] "existence" [that is, a fully potentialized karma that will produce the next lifetime, this being the tenth member of dependent-arising of cyclic existence] and attachment [the ninth member].
- In the second type, with respect to the [literally acceptable] statement, for instance, that from wholesome and unwholesome actions effects of pleasure and pain [respectively] arise, [if] someone propounds, for instance, that:

> The production of pleasure and pain by the two actions is the mode of being of those two, and there is no mode of being of those other than this, due to which the suchness of the objects [mentioned] in that sūtra is definite as just this and hence it is not suitable to interpret [the suchness of the objects mentioned in that sūtra] as other than this,

it is to be explained that the suchness of the two objects [taught] in that [sūtra, namely, wholesome and unwholesome actions] must be interpreted as other than the explicit reading.[a]

---

[a] Jam-ȳang-shay-b̄a restates D̄zong-ka-b̄a's meaning:

Here [in the system of the Consequence School] the way that texts requiring interpretation are to be interpreted [or literally, "led"] does not refer to **leading** trainees—as by the indirect teachings [of a real self for the sake of] introducing them [to virtuous endeavor] but to **interpreting** the subject being discussed. In brief, there are two ways of interpretation:

1. The literal meaning of the passage is not even suitable to be what is expressed by the sūtra: For instance, "Father and mother are to be killed," [which actually teaches that "existence" and "attachment" are to be abandoned.
2. The literal meaning of the passage is suitable to be what the sūtra expresses but interpretation is required to determine the mode of existence of the phenomena discussed in the text:] For instance, though the teaching that pleasures are produced from wholesome actions and sufferings from unwholesome actions is literal, it would not be suitable to assert these facts as the mode of existence of the two. One must interpret their mode of existence otherwise, as lacking self [that is, inherent existence].

Thus, there are, in brief, two modes of interpretation: of that which is not literally acceptable in order to discover the subject matter and of the literally acceptable to discover the nature of the phenomena discussed.

Adapted from Jeffrey Hopkins, *Meditation on Emptiness* (London: Wisdom, 1983; rev. ed., Boston: Wisdom, 1996) , 600.

Thus, D̄zong-ka-b̄a clearly denies that *neyārtha* (literally, "a meaning to be led") merely means that trainees are led by that teaching. From this, it is obvious that his argument—that the matrix of One Gone Thus mentioned in this passage in the *Descent into Laṅkā Sūtra* requires interpretation—does not revolve around the mere usage of the word "lead," as it might seem from his brief treatment in the section on the Mind-Only School.

Indeed, D̄zong-ka-b̄a gives a multi-faceted argument in the section on the Consequence School of *The Essence of Eloquence*. There, he essentially makes the case that the *Descent into Laṅkā Sūtra* itself clearly indicates that the teaching of a matrix of One Gone Thus endowed with Buddha qualities is not to be taken literally, since, otherwise, it would be like the Forders' teaching of a self, which they intend to be taken literally. He[359] begins by citing a passage in the *Descent into Laṅkā Sūtra*[360] that immediately precedes Mahāmati's question and Buddha's answer and, according to him, sets the context as a discussion of non-literal teachings:

> Sūtras that teach in conformity with the thoughts of sentient beings have meaning that is mistaken; they are not discourse on suchness. Just as, for example, a deer is deceived by a waterless mirage into conceiving water, so doctrine that is taught [in conformity with the thoughts of sentient beings] pleases children but is not discourse setting out the exalted wisdom of Superiors. Therefore, you should follow the meaning and not be enamored of the expression.

Since Mahāmati's question about a matrix of One Gone Thus endowed with Buddha qualities appears right after this statement about teachings that are not literally acceptable, like the water that a deer sees in a mirage, D̄zong-ka-b̄a uses this platform to analyze how Buddha's response indicates that, indeed, such a teaching is not literal.

Whereas D̄zong-ka-b̄a paraphrases Buddha's answer, Jik-may-dam-chö-gya-tso[361] structures Buddha's response into three basic parts—brief indication, extensive explanation, and summary. The first sentence is the brief indication:

> Mahāmati, my teaching of a matrix of One Gone Thus is not like the Forders' propounding of a self.

The extensive explanation contains five sections:

1. The purpose of teaching such a matrix: "So that children might avoid the fear of selflessness, they teach through the means of a matrix of One Gone Thus."
2. The basis in Buddha's thought, that is, the reality behind this provisional teaching: "O Mahāmati, the completely perfect Buddhas, Ones Gone Thus, Foe Destroyers, teach—as a matrix of One Gone Thus—the meaning of the words emptiness, the limit of

reality, nirvāṇa, no production, signlessness, wishlessness, and so forth." And: "...teach the state of non-conceptuality, the object of activity [of wisdom] free from appearances."

3. An example for such a provisional teaching: "Mahāmati, for example, potters make a variety of vessels out of one mass of clay particles with their hands, manual skill, a rod, water, string, and mental dexterity."
4. How to associate the example with the exemplified: "Mahāmati, similarly the One Gone Thus also teaches the selflessness of phenomena that is an absence of all conceptual signs. Through various [techniques] endowed with wisdom and skill in means—whether they teach it as the matrix of One Gone Thus or as selflessness—they, like a potter, teach with various formats of words and letters."
5. Demonstration of a proof—through the sign that Buddha spoke in such a provisional way—that the teaching of the matrix and the propounding of an existent self are not the same: "Therefore, Mahāmati, the teaching of the matrix of One Gone Thus is not like the teaching propounding a self for Forders. Mahāmati, in order to lead Forders who are attached to propounding a self, the Ones Gone Thus teach the matrix of One Gone Thus through the teaching of a matrix of One Gone Thus." And: "Mahāmati, future and present Bodhisattvas—the great beings—should not adhere to this as a self." And: "Thinking, 'How could those with thoughts fallen into incorrect views conceiving of self come to be endowed with thought abiding in the spheres of the three liberations and quickly manifestly and completely purified in unsurpassed complete perfect enlightenment,' for their sake, Mahāmati, the Ones Gone Thus, Foe Destroyers, completely perfect Buddhas, teach the matrix of One Gone Thus."

The final sentence is the summary:

> Consequently, that is not the same as propounding the self of Forders. Therefore, Mahāmati, in order to overcome the view of Forders, they cause them to engage the matrix of One Gone Thus, selflessness.

In his analysis, Dzong-ka-ba emphasizes that, although when Buddha taught a matrix of One Gone Thus endowed with Buddha qualities, he intended his listeners to apprehend that such a matrix exists, he had it in mind to later teach them about emptiness (during which they would understand that the doctrine of a matrix of One Gone Thus endowed with Buddha qualities requires interpretation). This future-directed intention distinguishes Buddha's teaching of the matrix from the Forders' teaching of self:[362]

> As the **basis in his thought**, [Buddha] was thinking of the emptiness which is the selflessness of phenomena. His **purpose** was to dispel the fear of selflessness and to gradually lead those adhering to propounding a self to selflessness. Through the sign of [Buddha's] setting out [the teaching of a matrix of One Gone Thus with that basis in his thought and with that purpose] it is established that the two, the [Buddha's] propounding that a matrix of One Gone Thus exists and the [non-Buddhists'] propounding that a self exists, are not similar. Consequently:
>
> - what the Proponents of an Existent Self are considering when they propound such is just the measure of what they teach, whereas
> - the meaning of the Teacher's thought—what he was considering [that is, emptiness] when he spoke—and the literal meaning [that is, a matrix of One Gone Thus] are very much in disagreement
>
> and:
>
> - the teaching—by the Proponents of an Existent Self—that the self is permanent and so forth is **at all times** for the sake of making more firm their ascertainment of just that literal meaning, whereas
> - what the Teacher said is a case of **temporarily** indicating that such a literal meaning [that is, a matrix of One Gone Thus endowed with Buddha qualities] exists, this being for the sake of leading [trainees] **later** to the meaning [that is, emptiness] which he was considering when he set forth such [a matrix of a One Gone Thus].
>
> Therefore, those two are not similar.

The bottom line for both S̄hay-rap-gyel-tsen and D̄zong-ka-b̄a is to show how the non-Buddhists' teaching of self and Buddha's teaching of a matrix are not similar, since Buddha clearly says in the *Descent into Laṅkā Sūtra* that the two differ. For S̄hay-rap-gyel-tsen, the two teachings are not similar because the matrix and selflessness are equivalent and are only verbal variants, whereas, for D̄zong-ka-b̄a, the two teachings are not similar because:

- The immediately preceding passage in the *Descent into Laṅkā Sūtra* sets the scene so that it is understood that the teaching of such a matrix is a provisional teaching.
- Buddha intends to teach selflessness **later.**
- The teaching of such a matrix is similar to affirming the type of self that

non-Buddhists teach and thus is non-literal[a] even though it does not resemble the intentionality with which non-Buddhists teach self.

Dzong-ka-ba holds that the teaching of such a matrix is for those who temporarily cannot bear the teaching of selflessness. He thereby suggests that the Jonang-bas are beneath the range of Buddhist systems:[363]

> Once the meaning of permanence is asserted to be a [positive] inclusionary [that has the aspects of the marks and beauties of a Buddha][364] rather than a [negative] exclusionary that is a mere elimination of disintegration, one temporarily is also not suitable as a vessel for explanation of the two selflessnesses which involve teaching—as suchness, selflessness—a mere elimination of the proliferations of the two selves. Hence, those sūtras' setting forth [a matrix of One Gone Thus] as described above [in Mahāmati's question in the *Descent into Laṅkā Sūtra*] is for the sake of abandoning fear with respect to selflessness and leading those who are attached to propounding a self.

For Dzong-ka-ba, the position of the *Descent into Laṅkā Sūtra* is so obvious that he accuses Shay-rap-gyel-tsen of twisting passages to fit his own agenda:[365]

> [The *Descent into Laṅkā Sūtra*] is clearly indicating that this is how similarity should be determined [if the teaching of a matrix of One Gone Thus and the teaching of a permanent self were similar]. Consequently, if the teaching of a matrix of One Gone Thus as [described] before [in Mahāmati's question] were held to be literal, it would be similar to propounding that a self exists. The damage to the explicit [teaching of such a matrix of One Gone Thus] also is just this [mode of similarity].[366] That it is unsuitable to hold [the teaching of a matrix of One Gone Thus] to be literal is very clear from the earlier example of a mirage and its application to the exemplified and then the statement "You should follow the meaning. Do not be enamored of the expression…" Hence, what knowledgeable person would debate about whether or not this sūtra establishes that the setting out of such [a matrix of One Gone Thus] in other sūtras requires interpretation by way of indicating the basis in [Buddha's] thought, the purpose, and the damage to the literal reading! [It certainly does!]
>
> However, if one does not assert [this topic] in accordance with how it is expounded by this [scriptural passage from the *Descent into Laṅkā Sūtra*],[367] then it is a quintessential instruction of Indian scholars [that one should] explain that [the *Descent into Laṅkā Sūtra* at this point][368] requires interpretation upon demonstrating damage by

[a] For Dzong-ka-ba's intriguing explanation of how acceptance of such a permanent, stable matrix of One Gone Thus endowed with Buddha qualities is similar to asserting a permanent self, see 318ff.

reasoning to its literal meaning. Hence, [you, S̄hay-rap-gyel-tsen] should do it that way, but, if you say that even the former sūtra passage [from the *Descent into Laṅkā Sūtra*] does not teach [that the teaching of such a matrix is not literal],[369] you are reduced to only showing your own nature.

Around two hundred years later, S̄hay-rap-gyel-tsen's follower, Tāranātha,[370] responds first with the incisive remark that the *Descent into Laṅkā Sūtra* does not say that the matrix of One Gone Thus is not endowed with Buddha qualities but says that it is empty:

> The [*Descent into Laṅkā*] *Sūtra* itself states—as the reason for non-similarity with the Forders—that the matrix of One Gone to Bliss is empty; it does not state that it is without the marks and beauties [of a Buddha].

Indeed, in the *Descent into Laṅkā Sūtra,* Buddha does not say that the teaching of a One Gone Thus endowed with Buddha qualities requires interpretation because it is not endowed with Buddha qualities. Also, he does not say that he plans to teach emptiness later. Rather, he indicates that the teaching of such a One Gone Thus is imbued with emptiness, even if the term is not explicitly mentioned. Tāranātha's implication is that this endowment with emptiness is what distinguishes it from the non-Buddhists' teaching of a self. Read this way, the passage in the *Descent into Laṅkā Sūtra* shows how the teaching of such a matrix is literally acceptable. Having made this thought-provoking point, Tāranātha finishes with an invective equal to D̄zong-ka-b̄a's:

> Therefore, previous explanations that a matrix of One Gone to Bliss that has the luminous and complete marks and beauties requires interpretation are reduced to mere deception of the world with lies.

D̄zong-ka-b̄a finishes his argument by citing a passage from Nāgārjuna's *Compendium of Sūtra.* In it, Nāgārjuna—whom S̄hay-rap-gyel-tsen asserts is a Proponent of the Great Middle Way and who thus should assert that the teaching of a matrix of One Gone Thus endowed with Buddha qualities is literal—shows that he takes this passage in the *Descent into Laṅkā Sūtra* to indicate that such a teaching requires interpretation. D̄zong-ka-b̄a quotes Nāgārjuna's transitional statement, which occurs after citing passages from the Perfection of Wisdom Sūtras and before citing the passage in question from the *Descent into Laṅkā Sūtra:*

> Furthermore, Nāgārjuna's *Compendium of Sūtra* makes the transitional statement:
>
> > The One Gone Thus teaches various approaches of vehicles

> through the force of taming, whereby he teaches this profound noumenon.
>
> Then, he quotes the sūtra passages [from the *Descent into Laṅkā Sūtra*][371] cited above. That he uses the proximate term "this" in "this profound noumenon" is [in reference to] the statements of the emptiness which is the selflessness of phenomena, it being the case that he cited, just before this, many sūtras such as Perfection of Wisdom Sūtras and so forth. "Through the force of taming" [means that various approaches of vehicles] are set forth through the force of trainees' thought; it has the import of the earlier statement [from the *Descent into Laṅkā Sūtra*], "This is discourse pleasing children, not discourse on suchness."[a]

D̄zong-ka-b̄a cites this evidence of Nāgārjuna's opinion in pointed response to S̄hay-rap-gyel-tsen's claim (see p. 296) that Nāgārjuna asserts that a matrix of One Gone Thus endowed with Buddha qualities is definitive. Still, we have seen enough to know that neither S̄hay-rap-gyel-tsen nor Tāranātha would remain silent.

[a] This is a paraphrase; see p. 375.

17d. Analysis of Ge-luk-b̄a Criticisms of the Jo-nang-b̄a View: IV

4. "Self-Contradiction": Claiming To Follow Buddhist Views And Yet Straying From Any Great Vehicle System

S̄hay-rap-gyel-tsen holds that all conventional phenomena are self-empty in the sense of being empty of their own true establishment but that the ultimate is other-empty in the sense of being empty of conventional phenomena and yet is truly established. D̄zong-ka-b̄a stingingly indicts this position as being heretical, representing neither the system of the Mind-Only School nor the system of the Middle Way School. However, S̄hay-rap-gyel-tsen's intent is not to be either a proponent of Conventional Mind-Only nor a proponent of the Middle Way School as it is widely renowned but to put forward a superior system called the Great Middle Way, or Ultimate Mind-Only. For this reason, he makes the case at length (see p. 294ff.) that authors usually associated with the Mind-Only School and Middle Way School are, in their most profound writings, Proponents of the Great Middle Way, also called Ultimate Mind-Only.

That S̄hay-rap-gyel-tsen holds that **all** of the main Great Vehicle proponents—up to but not including Chandrakīrti except perhaps in tantric works (see p. 300)—uphold this system sets the stage for D̄zong-ka-b̄a's dramatic and inflammatory accusation that his system is outside of **any** Great Vehicle system. D̄zong-ka-b̄a seeks to undermine the credibility of S̄hay-rap-gyel-tsen's reading of these scholars; first, he (*Emptiness in Mind-Only*, 83) states his thesis:

> Hence [it is contradictory for some, namely, Döl-b̄o-b̄a and others] to explain that the statements in the Perfection of Wisdom Sūtras, and so forth, that all phenomena are natureless are in consideration [only] of all conventional phenomena [which, according to them, are self-empty in the sense of being empty of their own true establishment] but do not refer to the ultimate [which, they say, is itself truly established and empty of being any conventional phenomenon]. They thereby contradict the *Sūtra Unraveling the Thought* as well as the texts of Asaṅga and his brother [Vasubandhu] and are also outside the system of the Superior father [Nāgārjuna], his spiritual sons, and so forth.

The pivot of D̄zong-ka-b̄a's indictment is to hold his opponents, identified here as Döl-b̄o-b̄a S̄hay-rap-gyel-tsen and others,[a] to a strict reading of the *Sūtra*

---

[a]   D̄zong-ka-b̄a himself does not identify that he is speaking about S̄hay-rap-gyel-tsen, but his commentators do:

- Gung-ru Chö-jung's *Garland of White Lotuses* (18b.1) and Jam-ȳang-shay-b̄a's *Great Exposition of the Interpretable and the Definitive* (45.6): "the omniscient Jo-nang-b̄a"

Unraveling the Thought and thereby prevent them from their grand synthesis of Great Vehicle doctrines. Namely, the Jo-nang-b̄a system is impossible according to the Mind-Only School due to accepting the *Sūtra Unraveling the Thought* (as well as the works of Asaṅga and Vasubandhu) to be definitive but asserting that emptiness (the thoroughly established nature) is a truly established, positive, and self-powered entity,[a] whereas, according to D̄zong-ka-b̄a's reading of these texts, the ultimate—despite being truly established—is a mere negative, a mere absence. Also, their position contradicts Nāgārjuna as well as Buddhapālita, Bhāvaviveka, and Chandrakīrti in that, according to D̄zong-ka-b̄a, these Proponents of the Middle hold that the ultimate is not truly established.

D̄zong-ka-b̄a (*Emptiness in Mind-Only,* 84-85) goes on to make the point that, in the *Sūtra Unraveling the Thought,* Buddha explains his teaching in the Perfection of Wisdom Sūtras that all phenomena are natureless by explicitly correlating the three natures and three non-natures—the explanation being needed because in the Perfection of Wisdom Sūtras he had, in great detail, spoken of all phenomena as being natureless without, on the literal level, distinguishing which type of phenomena lacked which type of nature:

> It is thus: [When Paramārthasamudgata] asks about that in consideration of which [Buddha] spoke of non-nature, he is asking (1) about what [Buddha] was thinking when he taught non-nature and (2) about the modes of non-nature. Also, the answer indicates those two respectively. From between those two, let us explain the first [that is, what Buddha had as the basis in his thought when in the Perfection of Wisdom Sūtras he taught that all phenomena are natureless. There,

---

(*kun mkhyen jo nang pa*)

- Paṇ-chen S̄ö-nam-drak-b̄a's *Garland of Blue Lotuses* (13b.6): "the omniscient Döl-b̄o-ba" (*kun mkhyen dol po ba*)
- Gung-tang's *Difficult Points* (98.7): "Jo-nang-b̄a" or "Jo-nang-b̄as" (*jo nang pa*)
- A-ku L̄o-drö-gya-tso's *Precious Lamp* (70.3): "Jo-nang-wa S̄her-gyen-b̄a" (*jo nang ba sher rgyan pa*); "S̄her-gyen-b̄a" is a contraction of "S̄hay-rap-gyel-tsen"
- D̄a-drin-rap-d̄en's *Annotations* (12.5): "the omniscient Döl-b̄o-ba and so forth" (*kun mkhyen dol po ba la sogs pa*).

I also have no doubt that D̄zong-ka-b̄a is referring to S̄hay-rap-gyel-tsen.

[a] The discussion at this point is drawn from Gung-tang's *Difficult Points,* 139.11-142.12. D̄zong-ka-b̄a (*Emptiness in Mind-Only,* 186) also indicts S̄hay-rap-gyel-tsen for having strayed from the main Mind-Only commentators when he fails to hold that other-powered natures are established by way of their own character:

> The meaning of the brothers' [that is, Asaṅga's and Vasubandhu's] texts accords with just this, and since just this [establishment by way of its own character] also is described as ultimate establishment, the explanation [by the Jo-nang-b̄as and so forth] that in this system other-powered natures are empty of themselves is not at all the case.

> Buddha] said that the limitless divisions of instances of phenomena ranging from forms through to exalted knowers-of-all-aspects have no nature or inherent nature. These phenomena are included in the three non-natures [that is, three natures[a]—imputational, other-powered, and thoroughly established natures].[b] Thinking that when it is explained how those are natureless, it is easy to understand [the individual modes of thought that were behind his statement in the Perfection of Wisdom Sūtras], he included [all phenomena] into the three non-natures [that is, three natures. For] all ultimate and conventional phenomena are included within those three.

D̄zong-ka-b̄a's point is that in the Perfection of Wisdom Sūtras, Buddha—on the literal level—speaks of the ultimate as being natureless numerous times, and thus the *Sūtra Unraveling the Thought*, with Asaṅga and Vasubandhu following, explain that this teaching was given in consideration of **three** bases in Buddha's thought—namely, that imputational natures are character-non-natures, other-powered natures are production-non-natures, and thoroughly established natures are ultimate-non-natures. S̄hay-rap-gyel-tsen, on the other hand, holds that the statements in the Perfection of Wisdom Sūtras that all phenomena are not truly established are in consideration only of conventional phenomena (and hence only other-powered natures and existent imputational natures), and in this way he contradicts the statement in the *Sūtra Unraveling the Thought* that this teaching was in consideration of **three** bases in the Teacher's thought, one of which is the ultimate, the thoroughly established nature. Just prior to his attack on S̄hay-rap-gyel-tsen, D̄zong-ka-b̄a (*Emptiness in Mind-Only,* 83) quotes Asaṅga's and Vasubandhu's statements of the same:[c]

---

[a] D̄zong-ka-b̄a's usage of "non-natures" suggests that for him the individual three non-natures and the three natures are equivalent (see *Absorption,* #101), as long as the **actual** ultimate-non-nature is restricted to thoroughly established natures (see ibid., #147, 148). For me, they are indeed equivalent.

[b] See ibid., #73, 72, 101.

[c] Jik-may-dam-chö-gya-tso (*Port of Entry,* 169.3) questions the relevance of D̄zong-ka-b̄a's citing these two texts, since the Jo-nang-b̄as hold that they evince the view of the Mind-Only School rather than their own Great Middle Way. However, it seems to me that Jik-may-dam-chö-gya-tso is mistaken because S̄hay-rap-gyel-tsen himself (*Ocean of Definitive Meaning,* 223.2) cites Vasubandhu's *The Thirty* to show that it teaches the Great Middle Way which is beyond mind-only:

> Also, although Vasubandhu's *The Thirty* is renowned to be a text of mind-only, in the end it speaks of what has passed beyond cognition-only. Right after saying:
>
> > When apprehensions of consciousness
> > Are not apprehended, then
> > One abides in cognition-only.
>
> it says:
>
> > Due to the non-existence of the apprehended, the apprehender does not

Moreover, Asaṅga's *Compendium of Ascertainments* says:

> *Question:* Thinking of what did the Supramundane Victor say [in the middle wheel] that all phenomena are natureless?
>
> *Answer:* Here and there he said such through the force of taming [trainees], thinking of three types of non-nature.

Also, Vasubandhu's *The Thirty*[a] (stanza 23) says:

> Thinking of three types of non-nature
> Of the three types of natures [respectively],
> He taught [in the Perfection of Wisdom Sūtras]
> That all phenomena are natureless.

By stressing that the *Sūtra Unraveling the Thought* as well as Asaṅga and Vasubandhu explain the statements of no true establishment in the Perfection of Wisdom Sūtras in consideration of **three** bases in the thought of the Teacher, Dzong-ka-ba seeks to forcefully demonstrate that it is undeniable that the Perfection of Wisdom Sūtras say that the ultimate also is without true establishment even if the Proponents of Mind-Only do not take these statements literally.

Dzong-ka-ba (*Emptiness in Mind-Only,* 83) continues the indictment in the same tenor:

> Also, with respect to the need for [Buddha's] doing thus, in the Mother Sūtras [that is, the Perfection of Wisdom Sūtras] and so forth, all phenomena—the five aggregates, the eighteen constituents, and the twelve sense-spheres—are described as without thingness, without an inherent nature, and natureless. In particular, mentioning all the terminological variants of the ultimate—emptiness, the element of [a

---

> exist.
> That is no-mind, non-apprehension.
> This supramundane exalted wisdom
> Has been transformed
> Through having abandoned the two assumptions of bad states.
> Just that is the uncontaminated element of attributes,
> Inconceivable element of attributes, virtue, and stability.
> This is bliss, the body of release,
> The attributes of a Great Subduer.

Also, although in the *Ocean of Definitive Meaning* Shay-rap-gyel-tsen does not refer to Asaṅga's *Compendium of Ascertainments,* Asaṅga's *Compendium of Ascertainments* (Peking 5539, vol. 111, 83.2.6-107.5.1) cites the *Sūtra Unraveling the Thought* almost in its entirety, and Shay-rap-gyel-tsen holds that this sūtra evinces the view of the Great Middle Way (see p. 326).

[a] See *Absorption,* #61.

> Superior's] qualities, thusness, and so forth—he said that these are natureless. Therefore, who with a mind would propound that the ultimate is not among the phenomena about which it is said that phenomena are natureless![a]

However, the issue is not as simple as D̄zong-ka-b̄a's remarks seem to make it. Let us consider the depiction of the middle and final wheels of doctrine in the *Ocean of Definitive Meaning* in order to determine whether S̄hay-rap-gyel-tsen, as D̄zong-ka-b̄a claims, does not recognize that the Perfection of Wisdom Sūtras say that the ultimate[b] is not truly established.

For S̄hay-rap-gyel-tsen, the final wheel of doctrine **clearly** teaches a truly established "other-emptiness"—that is, a thoroughly established nature that is empty of imputational natures and other-powered natures—and hence is definitive, whereas the middle wheel does **not clearly** teach the actual mode of subsistence of phenomena and hence requires interpretation. He refers to the third wheel as teaching directly and clearly and to the other two wheels as teaching obliquely by way of intentional speech:[372]

> Consequently, the noumenal ultimate truth which is the basis of the emptiness of all phenomena that abide as empty is the final definitive meaning of the profound scriptures, whether those that directly teach clearly or those that teach by way of intentions.[c]

In this way, he is able to frame the three wheels of doctrine as a harmonious whole:[373]

> The first wheel of doctrine accords with a precursor to meditating on the profound definitive meaning of the Great Vehicle; the second wheel of doctrine accords with practicing a special meditative stabilization of equipoise on the profound meaning; and the third wheel

---

[a] See ibid., #63-65.

[b] It needs to be kept in mind that S̄hay-rap-gyel-tsen does not assert the ultimate in the way that D̄zong-ka-b̄a identifies the position either of the Proponents of Mind-Only or of the Proponents of the Middle: that a mere elimination of an object of negation is the actual emptiness. He asserts that this sort of emptiness is an annihilatory emptiness, since it denies the presence of Buddha qualities in ultimate reality.

[c] *ldem po dag gis.* There is a widely renowned list of four intentions (*ldem dgongs bzhi, catvāro 'bhisaṃdhaya*):

1. Intending entry (*gzhug pa la ldem por dgongs pa, avatāranābhisaṃdhi*)
2. Intending the characters (*mtshan nyid la ldem por dgongs pa, lakṣanābhisaṃdhi*)
3. Intending an antidote (*gnyen po la ldem por dgongs pa, pratipakṣābhisaṃdhi*)
4. Intending translation (*sbyor ba la ldem por dgongs pa/ bsgyur ba la ldem por dgongs pa, pariṇāmābhisaṃdhi*).

For discussion of these, see *Absorption,* chap. 19.

> accords with [the system of] profound secret mantra identifying—within good differentiation—existence, non-existence, and so forth.

Still, he does not obliterate any difference between the teachings of the middle and final wheels. For he holds that the middle wheel of doctrine teaches what is non-empty to be empty—that is, that the ultimate is empty of true establishment—and he says that the middle wheel is even internally contradictory:[374]

> Similarly, about the second wheel—for certain reasons such as that, out of purposeful intent, it teaches that even what are not self-empty are self-empty, and so forth, and is not possessed of good differentiation, that is to say, is not without internal contradictions, it is said that it "is surpassable, affords an occasion [for refutation], requires interpretation, and serves as a basis for controversy." The third wheel—by reason that, opposite from those, it differentiates meanings well just as they are, and so forth—it is said that it "is unsurpassable, does not afford an occasion [for refutation], is of definitive meaning, and does not serve as a basis for controversy."

He repeats this point later:[375]

> Similarly, it should be understood that all statements—in these and those texts of the middle wheel of doctrine—of the non-self-empty as self-empty are just of interpretable meaning with a thought behind them; this depends on the lamp of unique quintessential instructions of good differentiation.[a]

The "purposeful intent" of, or "thought behind," the second wheel is to draw practitioners into a state of non-conceptual meditative equipoise:[376]

> Therefore, although the meaning of the last two wheels of doctrine and the Vajra Vehicle are one, when they are practiced, one sets in equipoise in the conclusive profound noumenon devoid of proliferation in accordance with the middle wheel, and then when making distinctions in subsequent attainment [after meditative equipoise], one individually discriminates phenomena in a correct way, at which time one makes identifications upon good differentiation in accordance with what is said in the final wheel and in the Vajra Vehicle. When [this procedure is followed], practice of the meaning of all the scriptures of the Great Vehicle becomes complete, unmistaken, and just thoroughly pure. Hence, here I will teach within making good differentiation of existing and not existing in the mode of subsistence, emptiness and non-emptiness of its own entity, exclusionary elimination and inclusionary elimination, non-affirming negation and affirming

[a] The reference here is to three cycles of Bodhisattva commentaries; see p. 293.

> negation, abandonment and realization, and so forth—in accordance with how these are in the basic disposition of things.

S̄hay-rap-gyel-tsen holds that the middle wheel overstates the doctrine of self-emptiness when it extends this to the ultimate, but he again describes the difference between the middle and final wheels as being whether the actual ultimate is unclear or clear:[377]

> *Objection:* Whereas it is the case that, because the perfection of wisdom is taught in the second wheel, it is definitive and unsurpassed, this scripture [that is, the *Sūtra Unraveling the Thought*]—since it just teaches the opposite of that—requires interpretation and has a thought behind it.
>
> *Answer:* These are the words of one who has not analyzed well because [the *Sūtra Unraveling the Thought*] does not indicate that [scriptures] are interpretable, surpassable, and so forth by reason of their teaching the perfection of wisdom but indicates such by other reasons, such as that they teach what is not self-empty as self-empty. The absence of production, the absence of cessation, quiescence from the start, and naturally passed beyond sorrow are taught even in the third wheel and are taught in the Vajra Vehicle. By reason of teaching unclearly [in the middle wheel], clearly [in the third wheel], and very clearly [in tantra], there are great and also very great differences of being obscured, not obscured, and so forth with respect to the meaning of those. Therefore, even the statements of being surpassable or unsurpassable, affording an opportunity [for refutation] or not affording an opportunity, and so forth are due to differences in those texts with respect to whether the final profound meaning is unclear and incomplete or clear and complete, and so forth, and not from the entity of the meaning.

On the one hand, he holds that the middle wheel of doctrine misrepresents the nature of the ultimate for a purpose, and, on the other hand, he insists that although "the entity of meaning" of the middle and final wheels is the same, the middle wheel is merely unclear. Setting aside how one might try to rescue this apparent contradiction, we can readily see that S̄hay-rap-gyel-tsen recognizes that middle wheel sūtras such as the Perfection of Wisdom Sūtras say that the ultimate is not truly established. Thus, it is difficult to figure out what D̄zong-ka-ba̅ means when he claims that S̄hay-rap-gyel-tsen maintains that the ultimate truth is not among what is taught in the Perfection of Wisdom Sūtras to be natureless, that is to say, without true establishment, and thus denies the obvious.

Furthermore, S̄hay-rap-gyel-tsen faces head-on the issue of why the

Perfection of Wisdom Sūtras require interpretation. He does this through the threefold format of:

- the purpose for teaching the non-factual
- the basis in Buddha's thought, that is, what reality he had in mind behind such non-factual statements
- the damage to such scriptures being definitive.

First, Shay-rap-gyel-tsen states a hypothetical challenge to his position:[378]

> *Objection:* If the basic element of attributes, thusness, limit of reality, and so forth are not self-empty, what is the thought of extensive statements in the Mother of Conquerors [that is, the Perfection of Wisdom Sūtras]:
>
> > The basic element of attributes is empty of the basic element of attributes. Thusness is empty of thusness. The limit of reality is empty of the limit of reality. The inconceivable expanse is empty of the inconceivable expanse.
>
> and:
>
> > The perfection of wisdom is empty of the perfection of wisdom; that which is empty is not the perfection of wisdom; it is without production....An exalted knower of all aspects is empty of an exalted knower of all aspects; that which is empty is not an exalted knower of all aspects; it is without production.
>
> and:
>
> > If even the perfection of wisdom itself is very much nonexistent, how could going or coming exist in it!

The opponent's position is that even the ultimate is self-empty, that is, empty of itself because the Perfection of Wisdom Sūtras say so.[a] Shay-rap-gyel-tsen responds first with an appeal to the *Sūtra Unraveling the Thought* against taking those statements in the Perfection of Wisdom Sūtras literally:

> *Answer:* Those statements were made in consideration of their requiring interpretation because the *Sūtra Unraveling the Thought* says:
>
> > Based on just the naturelessness of all phenomena and based on just the absence of production, the absence of cessation,

---

[a] In Ge-luk these sūtra statements of self-emptiness are explained away as referring not to phenomena being empty of themselves but to being empty of the object of negation in selflessness, whether this be a difference of entity of subject and object as in the Mind-Only School or inherent existence as in the Consequence School.

> quiescence from the start, and naturally passed beyond sorrow, the Supramundane Victor turned a second wheel of doctrine, for those engaged in the Great Vehicle, very fantastic and marvelous, through the aspect of speaking on emptiness. Furthermore, that wheel of doctrine turned by the Supramundane Victor is surpassable, affords an occasion [for refutation], requires interpretation, and serves as a basis for controversy.

> Similarly, it should be understood that all statements—in these and those texts of the middle wheel of doctrine—of the non-self-empty as self-empty are just of interpretable meaning with a thought behind them; [understanding] this depends on the lamp of unique quintessential instructions of good differentiation [found in the three cycles of Bodhisattva commentaries (see p. 293)].

Then, he explains the purpose for such a non-literal teaching:

> Here the **purpose** of speaking in consideration of such is to thoroughly pacify apprehension, discrimination, and conceptualization of the basic element of attributes and so forth as this or that.

In the second wheel Buddha was seeking to provide yogis with a means to enter into non-conceptual wisdom, and thus he spoke in a negative manner about both phenomena and the noumenon in order to cut off conceptualization in such a meditative state (see pp. 290 and 386).

Next, he shows the damage against accepting the Perfection of Wisdom Sūtras literally:

> About the **damage** to their being of definitive meaning, it is because:
>
> - the basic element of attributes, thusness, limit of reality, and so forth are said[a] to be all ultimate deities, mantras, tantras, mandalas, and mudrās—the final Buddha, four bodies, five wisdoms, letter *E*, *bhaga,* source of attributes, water-born [that is, lotus], secrecy, great secrecy, letter *A*, perfection-of-wisdom-goddess, Vishvamātā, Vajravarahī, and so forth; the syllable *VAṂ,* great bliss, drop, vajra, Heruka, suchness, self-arisen Buddha, and so forth; Vajradhara, Vajrasattva, the syllables *EVAṂ,* Kālachakra, Vajrabhairava, Vajraishvara, Chakrasaṃvara, Guhyasamāja, Hevajra, and so forth—and those also are said to be the noumenon, thusness, and so forth, and
> - those are said to be entities of endless attributes such as the powers, fearlessnesses, and so forth that are non-self-empty qualities.

[a] S̄hay-rap-gyel-tsen's appeal here appears to be to scripture rather than to reason, although he has provided copious reasonings elsewhere in the *Ocean of Definitive Meaning.*

The basic thrust is that once the ultimate is replete with Buddha qualities, there is no way that it can be empty of itself.

Lastly, Shay-rap-gyel-tsen shows what Buddha had in mind when he taught that the noumenon, the basic element of attributes, is self-empty. This is not what Buddha intended to communicate at that time but the true fact that he had in his own mind. It is like thinking one thing but saying something that, despite being somewhat related with what one is actually thinking, will be understood differently by a particular audience to their own benefit. The point here is to identify that foundation:

> Here, with regard to the **basis in [Buddha's] thought**, such was said in consideration that all [conceptual] apprehensions as those—that is, as the basic element of attributes and so forth—and all subjects involved with those[a]—are self-empty. This is because all phenomena—forms and so forth—are said to be in three categories and, from among them, those said to be self-empty are in consideration of imputational and other-powered forms and so forth.

He avers that what Buddha had in his own mind must be that **conceptualizations** of the ultimate are self-empty. Why? Because the teachings of self-emptiness are necessarily in consideration of imputational natures and other-powered natures and not in consideration of thoroughly established natures themselves. Shay-rap-gyel-tsen does not cite his sources here for delimiting the range of self-emptiness, but they obviously are the *Extensive Explanation of the One Hundred Thousand Stanza Perfection of Wisdom Sūtra* and the *Commentary on the Extensive Mother, the Twenty-Five Thousand, and Eighteen Thousand Stanza Perfection of Wisdom Sūtras,* which he cites elsewhere in the *Ocean of Definitive Meaning.*[379] This is why Dzong-ka-ba, upon reporting that Shay-rap-gyel-tsen considers these texts to be by Vasubandhu,[b] presents a case that they are by Daṃṣhṭasena and goes to lengths to show that Shay-rap-gyel-tsen has not even understood Daṃṣhṭasena's meaning (see *Emptiness in Mind-Only,* 225-232 and 335-341).[c]

---

[a] *de rnams kyis khyab pa'i chos can;* Shay-rap-gyel-tsen's *Ocean of Definitive Meaning,* 338.5. Here *chos can* likely means "consciousnesses" although it could also mean "phenomena."

[b] I have not found an explicit statement of this by Shay-rap-gyel-tsen in the *Ocean of Definitive Meaning,* but I do not doubt it.

[c] *The Blue Annals* reports that the three monks who escaped Lang-darma's (*glang dar ma*) persecution of Buddhism in Central Tibet in the ninth century and fled to Am-do instructed an Am-do monk Ge-wa-sel (*dge ba gsal*) who became a learned and important figure in the re-introduction of the discipline to Central Tibet. When the monk died, he told his students that he must go to the Joyous Heaven (*dga' ldan, tuṣita*) because Asaṅga and Daṃṣhṭasena, who have interpreted the meaning of the Mother Sūtras differently, are currently there, and he wants an answer to this controversy. This story indicates that the dispute between Daṃṣhṭasena and classical Mind-Only was well known at this early point in Tibet. See dpa'

S̄hay-rap-gyel-tsen concludes the discussion with a clear statement of what not being self-empty means:

> Similarly, the statements:
>
> > Because the basic element of attributes does not exist, Bodhisattvas do not apprehend a prior limit. Because thusness, the limit of reality, and the inconceivable basic element do not exist, Bodhisattvas do not apprehend a prior limit.
>
> are of interpretable meaning, with a thought behind them, as above. Such was stated in consideration that, although the basic element of attributes is not non-existent, **adventitious** attributes undifferentiably [that is, without exception] do not exist in them. These [non-literal teachings] are for the sake of pacifying discriminations and conceptualizations as this and that....In that way, the mode of emptiness of the noumenal thusness is not that it is empty of itself but is that it is the basis empty of other phenomena.
>
> Concerning this—whether form bodies of buddhas come to the world or do not come, whether persons realize it or do not realize it, see it or do not see it—the limit of reality which has many synonyms such as source of attributes and so forth has abided thusly without changing, indestructible and not susceptible to being abandoned, without difference earlier and later, always partless, omnipresent, and all-pervasive. That is the meaning of not being empty of its own entity.

This elaborate explanation that the Perfection of Wisdom Sūtras do indeed state that the ultimate is without true establishment and hence require interpretation makes one wonder what D̄zong-ka-b̄a could have meant when he (*Emptiness in Mind-Only,* 85) says:[a]

> In particular, mentioning all the terminological variants of the ultimate—emptiness, the element of [a Superior's] qualities, thusness, and so forth—he said that these are natureless. Therefore, who with a mind would propound that the ultimate is not among the phenomena about which it is said that phenomena are natureless!

---

bo gtsug lag phreng ba, *mkhas pa'i dga' ston* (Beijing: mi rigs dpe skrun khang), 470.5-470.8; and George N. Roerich, trans., *The Blue Annals* (Delhi: Motilal Banarsidass, 1976), 67. Thanks to Kevin Vose for the reference.

[a] Gung-tang (*Difficult Points,* 140.13ff.) similarly evinces what seems to be a deliberate blindness to S̄hay-rap-gyel-tsen's project when he buttresses D̄zong-ka-b̄a's opinion with an elaborate explanation. For attempts to explain away D̄zong-ka-b̄a's statement, see *Absorption,* #63-64.

PART FIVE:
VIEWS ON THE TWO EMPTINESSES

18. Does the *Sūtra Unraveling the Thought* Teach Mind-Only?

As we have seen, the Ge-luk-b̄a order[a] is deservedly known for its highly developed scholasticism, with competing colleges presenting well-reasoned but often conflicting arguments on major and minor topics. For more than two decades I have been intrigued by presentations in their philosophical literature that the Yogic Practice School, or Mind-Only School as it is frequently called, closely associates two types of emptiness. It is widely thought that in the Yogic Practice School the conception of a difference of substantial entity between apprehended-object and apprehending-subject[b] is the conception of a self of phenomena.[c] However, D̄zong-ka-b̄a emphasizes that:

1. In chapter 7 of the *Sūtra Unraveling the Thought* emptiness is explained differently, and hence the misconception of the opposite of emptiness must also be different.
2. The emptiness explained in this fashion is extremely important for Asaṅga.
3. Consequently, practitioners also must understand it, not just the absence of a difference of entity between apprehended-object and apprehending-subject.

He (*Emptiness in Mind-Only,* 194-195) says:

> In many texts of this system there is no explanation of a consciousness conceiving a self of phenomena aside from saying that a consciousness conceiving apprehended-object and apprehending-subject as other substantial entities is a consciousness conceiving a self of phenomena. However, the *Sūtra Unraveling the Thought* explains that other-powered natures are not established by way of their own character as factors imputed in the manner of entity and of attribute and that, therefore, the absence of [such] a nature of character is the selflessness of phenomena.[d] Thus, implicitly it teaches that a consciousness conceiving that factors imputed in the manner of entity and attribute are established by way of their own character in other-powered natures is a consciousness conceiving a self of phenomena. Also, Asaṅga's *Grounds of Bodhisattvas, Compendium of Ascertainments,* and *Summary of the Great Vehicle* with much striving establish that the emptiness of what

[a] An early version of chapters 18-21 appeared as "A Tibetan Contribution on the Question of Mind-Only in the Early Yogic Practice School," in the *Journal of Indian Philosophy* 20 (1992):275-343.

[b] *gzung 'dzin rdzas tha dad du 'dzin pa, *grāhyagrāhakadravyabhedagrāha.*

[c] *chos kyi bdag tu 'dzin pa, dharmātmagraha.*

[d] See *Absorption,* #95, 98, 99, 102, and 103.

> is conceived by such [a consciousness conceiving a self of phenomena] is the final meaning of the middle and is the thoroughly established nature that is the selflessness of phenomena. Therefore, if you do not know what this imputational factor that is a superimposed factor[a] of a self of phenomena on other-powered natures is, you will not know in a decisive way the conception of a self of phenomena and the selflessness of phenomena in this [Mind-Only] system.

Dzong-ka-ba's presentation of this type of emptiness for the Yogic Practice School appears to have been unique in Tibet. His student Ke-drup says:[380]

> What this system takes to be the superimposition of a self of phenomena and what it asserts to be the selflessness of phenomena that thoroughly negates it are final topics very difficult to realize. Nevertheless, here in the Range of Snow Mountains [Tibet], just our Omniscient Foremost One [Dzong-ka-ba] clarified [these topics]. All others who claim to be scholars, aside from speaking of the sole factor of just the negation of a difference of substantial entity between a sense consciousness and its appearing object, blue and so forth, could not utter even the mere linguistic conventions of how to posit the imputational nature that is the imputation in the manner of entity and attribute and how to posit the selflessness of phenomena that negates such [an imputational nature] as being established by way of its own character. Having confused themselves as being in the class of captains of intelligence grasping hold of the oar of analysis in the ocean of tenets of Cognition-Only, they are only incapable of climbing on the great ship of the great texts of this system.[b]

---

[a] See ibid., #79, 96-98, and 100.

[b] Contrary to this attribution of uniqueness, Ke-drup himself (Ke-drup's *Opening the Eyes of the Fortunate,* 217.4; see also José Ignacio Cabezón, *A Dose of Emptiness* [Albany, N.Y.: State University of New York Press, 1992], 52-53) proceeds to suggest that some Tibetans mistakenly identified Asaṅga as solely putting forth this style of emptiness:

> Concerning that, the two—Dharmakīrti's *Commentary on (Dignāga's) "Compilation of Prime Cognition"* and *Ascertainment of Prime Cognition*—explain that a consciousness conceiving apprehended-object and apprehending-subject related with a sense consciousness as different substantial entities is a consciousness conceiving a self of phenomena, but, except for that, they do not treat a consciousness conceiving the imputation in the manner of entity and attribute as established by way of its own character as a consciousness conceiving a self of phenomena and thereupon clearly explain a mode of refuting that [objects] are established in accordance with how they are apprehended by that [type of consciousness conceiving a self of phenomena]. However, to take seeing merely this as a reason and hold that:
>
> - a selflessness of phenomena that is a negation of imputation in the manner of entity and attribute as established by way of their own character is the system of Asaṅga

By insisting on the importance of not confining one's study of the Yogic Practice School to the emptiness of a difference of entity between subject and object and on the value of expanding it to include the emptiness of objects' being established by way of their own character as the referents of terms and conceptual consciousnesses, Dzong-ka-ba and those in his tradition emphasize the difference between these two types of emptiness, but they also tie the two together intimately.

Over the past two decades, I have read various Ge-luk-ba texts and have discussed with many Ge-luk-ba scholars the issue of **how** these types of emptiness are related, but despite my asking probing questions, it often seemed that these scholars and their textbooks were merely repeating a fixed, but not illuminating explanation. When examined even superficially, their explanations did not seem to hold together. Thus, when I saw the works of contemporary scholars outside the Tibetan community who forcefully argue that these two types of emptiness are not related in the early Yogic Practice School of India and that a doctrine of mind-only (no external objects) was not put forth in the early Yogic Practice School, it seemed that, using their reasoning, I would be able to take apart what little argument Ge-luk-ba scholars could muster for the opposite opinion.

However, it has turned out not to be such a simple matter. For, upon closer examination, some Ge-luk-ba scholars, even though they may not have perceived the historical development of these views, indeed have made carefully documented presentations relating these two types of emptiness, first detailing the Indian sources in the early Yogic Practice School and then building on those in a profoundly creative way.

Two Types Of Emptiness

The gateway to liberation is to realize that phenomena do not exist in accordance with false superimpositions that are the root of suffering. The absence of such a superimposed status is called emptiness, and two different subtle emptinesses are set forth in Mind-Only literature. These are the emptiness of external

---

- a selflessness of phenomena that is a negation of apprehended-object and apprehending-subject related with sense consciousnesses as other substantial entities is the system of Dignāga and Dharmakīrti

is the talk of those who have seen too little.

Ke-drup surely seems to be indicating that there are some who actually held that Asaṅga's presentation of the selflessness of phenomena is of the former type, but Jik-may-dam-chö-gya-tso (*Port of Entry,* 562.2) explains away this suggestion by asserting that Ke-drup is speaking hypothetically and is not referring to actual scholars who take this position. (Shay-rap-gyel-tsen does not mention such a conception of a self of phenomena or such an emptiness in his *Ocean of Definitive Meaning.*)

objects[a] and the emptiness of factors imputed in the manner of entity and attribute.[b] The first, the emptiness of external objects, is also called the emptiness of apprehended-objects and apprehending-subjects existing as different substantial entities.[c] This is explained as meaning that a form—a table, for instance—appears to be a different substantial entity from the eye consciousness apprehending it but is not. In other words, a table appears to be distant and cut off[d] from the apprehending consciousness but is not. Thus, a table is said to be empty of being a different entity from a valid consciousness, such as an eye consciousness, cognizing it; this is the emptiness of the table. Similarly, the eye consciousness apprehending the table is not a different entity from the table that it apprehends, and thus, from this point of view, the consciousness's absence of being a different entity from the table it perceives is the emptiness of the consciousness. Both the table and the consciousness exist, but both lack a certain quality—difference of entity—in relation to each other. That is one type of emptiness.

The other type of emptiness is the emptiness of factors imputed in the manner of entity and attribute. This is described as an object's absence of being established by way of its own character as a referent of terminology or of a conceptual consciousness.[e] This refers to, for instance, a table's not being established by the force of its own measure of subsistence[f] as the basis or referent (1) of the spoken terminology "table" and (2) of thoughts of table. Although a table is indeed the referent of the thought "This is a table" or of the spoken word "This is a table," it is not so established **by way of its own character** or **by way of its own mode of subsistence**. The absence of this status is called the "emptiness of a factor imputed in the manner of an entity." Similarly, although the table is indeed the referent of the thought "This table is beautiful" or of the spoken word "This table is beautiful," it is not so established **by way of its own**

---

[a] *phyi rol don gyis stong pa, bāhyārthaśūnya.*

[b] *ngo bo dang khyad bar du kun btags pas stong pa'i stong pa nyid.* Since factors imputed in the manner of entity and attribute do indeed exist, it is their being established by way of their own character that is refuted. The general term "empty of imputed factors" (*kun btags kyis stong pa, parikalpitaśūnya*) without the qualification "in the manner of entity and attribute" can be used more widely to include the emptiness of any type of fictional imputation, including that of externality.

[c] *bzung 'dzin rdzas tha dad kyis stong pa, *grāhyagrāhakadravyabhedaśūnya.* In Ge-luk-b̄a scholastic literature, the term "different substantial entity" (*rdzas tha dad*) is used for impermanent phenomena, whereas "different entity" (*ngo bo tha dad*) is used for a pair of permanent phenomena, such as uncompounded space and its emptiness, or for a pair of permanent and impermanent phenomena, such as uncompounded space and the valid consciousness apprehending it.

[d] *rgyang chad du snang ba.*

[e] *rang zhes rjod pa'i sgra jug pa'i jug gzhir rang gi mtshan nyid kyis ma grub pa; rang 'dzin rtog pa'i zhen gzhir rang gi mtshan nyid kyis ma grub pa.*

[f] *rang gi gnas tshod kyi dbang gis ma grub pa.*

character or **by way of its own mode of subsistence.** The absence of this status is called the "emptiness of a factor imputed in the manner of an attribute." The negative, the emptiness, of such establishment, in the manner of either entities or attributes, is the second type of emptiness.

That, in brief, is a standard Ge-luk-b̄a explanation of the two types of emptiness, which the scholars of this tradition then proceed to associate by maintaining that through realizing the emptiness of the latter type of imputational nature one enters into realization of the emptiness of subject and object as different entities. For instance, the eighteenth-century Mongolian scholar J̄ang-ḡya Röl-b̄ay-dor-jay says after presenting the emptiness of factors imputed in the manner of entity and attribute:[381]

> Through the mode of emptiness just explained, one enters into [that is, understands] cognition-only[a] which is subject and object's emptiness of being other substantial entities.

D̄zong-ka-b̄a's Presentation

In chapter 10 of *The Essence of Eloquence,* D̄zong-ka-b̄a addresses at length the issue of the relationship between realization of the emptiness of an imputational nature as put forth in the "Chapter on Suchness" in Asaṅga's *Grounds of Bodhisattvas* and realization of cognition-only, which D̄zong-ka-b̄a specifies as meaning no external objects. With extensive reasoning and citation of sources, he proposes that the two are related in the sense that realization that objects are not established by way of their own character as the referents of names and of conceptual consciousnesses is an entrance to realizing the non-difference in entity between subject and object.

This presentation contrasts sharply with recent publications by scholars of Buddhism who—contrary to a long tradition especially of French scholars such as Étienne Lamotte, Sylvain Lévi, and Louis de la Vallée Poussin—attempt to show that the view of Asaṅga's *Grounds of Bodhisattvas* is **not** of mind-only in the idealist sense of denying external objects. Among contemporary scholars holding that an idealist doctrine of mind-only is foreign to the *Grounds of Bodhisattvas* is Lambert Schmithausen of the University of Hamburg,[382] who holds that the text is essentially pre-Asaṅga. His interpretation differs in important respects from that of Janice Dean Willis of Wesleyan University,[383] who attributes the text to Asaṅga. Willis's presentation provides points of contrast with Tibetan views on the topic, whereas D̄zong-ka-b̄a's and Schmithausen's analyses can be seen as contributing harmoniously, but in different ways, to our understanding.

First, to elucidate D̄zong-ka-b̄a's position, I will use, in addition to his *The*

---

[a] *rnam pa rig pa tsam, vijñaptimātra.* For a discussion of various translations of this term, see p. 38, footnote b.

Essence of Eloquence, four commentaries on that text from the fifteenth through early eighteenth centuries, as well as oral commentary from the late Ge-luk-b̄a scholar Ye-s̄hay-tup-d̄en,[a] who served as abbot of the L̄o-s̄el-l̄ing College of Dre-b̄ung Monastic University during the time of its relocation in Mundgod, Karnataka State, India, in the 1970s.

The Issue

D̄zong-ka-b̄a (*Emptiness in Mind-Only,* 200) addresses an objection that the type of emptiness as described in the *Sūtra Unraveling the Thought* does not involve the meaning of mind-only, which means the absence of a difference of entity between subject and object:

> Moreover, this mode of emptiness [that is, other-powered natures' emptiness of the imputational nature as explained in the *Sūtra Unraveling the Thought*] does not involve the meaning of cognition-only that is the negation of apprehended-object and apprehending-subject as different substantial entities. Hence, how could it be feasible [for Asaṅga's *Grounds of Bodhisattvas* and so forth] to describe it as the selflessness of phenomena that is the object observed by [the path] purifying the obstructions to omniscience?
>
> Therefore, explain the reasons why these contradictions do not exist in this system!

It is unclear whether this is a hypothetical objection stated for the sake of developing understanding by drawing out issues that should be considered or whether it represents an opinion held in Tibet or India. The commentaries that I am using do not identify any such tradition of scholarship, but it still would be premature to decide that the objection is not based on a tradition. In any case, it is an important qualm, the answer to which provokes understanding of what constitutes emptiness in the Yogic Practice School.

In response, D̄zong-ka-b̄a indicates that Asaṅga's *Grounds of Bodhisattvas* teaches that this other mode of emptiness—phenomena's lack of being established by way of their own character as the referents of conceptual consciousnesses—must be meditated on in order to overcome the obstructions to omniscience. He thereby establishes that for Asaṅga such an emptiness is a selflessness of phenomena and is an object of meditation for purifying the obstructions to omniscience. He (*Emptiness in Mind-Only,* 200-201) notes that Asaṅga's *Summary of the Great Vehicle* associates this mode of emptiness with cognition-only, which is unambiguously identified even by the objector as meaning an absence of difference of entity between subject and object:

> In Asaṅga's *Grounds of Bodhisattvas,* this mode of emptiness [set forth

[a] *mkhan zur ye shes thub bstan,* d. 1988.

> in the *Sūtra Unraveling the Thought*] is explained as the object observed by the exalted wisdom purifying the obstructions to omniscience and as the middle path abandoning the two extremes of which there is none higher, and his *Summary of the Great Vehicle* says that entry by way of this [mode of emptiness] is entry into cognition-only.

Somehow, by understanding that objects are not established by way of their own character as the referents of conceptual consciousnesses, one comes to understand "cognition-only."

In order to explain how one enters into cognition-only through this route, Dzong-ka-ba sets forth the reasoning proving the emptiness of such an imputational nature as found especially in Asaṅga's *Summary of the Great Vehicle* which, in verse form, is especially cryptic. Dzong-ka-ba (*Emptiness in Mind-Only*, 207-208) says:

> So that one might realize reasonings proving that other-powered natures are empty of the imputational factor—such reasonings not being set forth in the *Sūtra Unraveling the Thought*—three reasonings each are set out in Asaṅga's *Grounds of Bodhisattvas* and *Compendium of Ascertainments*. Moreover, Asaṅga's *Summary of the Great Vehicle* states a question:
>
>> What [reasonings] make it evident that other-powered entities which appear to be imputational natures are not of such a nature?
>
> In answer to that question, it says:
>
>> Because an awareness does not exist prior to name,
>> Because manifold, and because unrestricted,
>> There are the contradictions of being in the essence of that, of many entities,
>> And of the mixture of entities. Therefore, it is proven.

The stanza, fleshed out with rudimentary commentary, becomes clearer:

> [If, for instance, a bulbous, flat-bottomed thing able to hold fluid were established through the force of its own mode of subsistence as the referent of the verbal convention "pot,"
>
> 1. The imputational nature would exist in] the essence of that [bulbous thing], but this is contradicted by the fact that an awareness [of the name of an object] does not exist prior to [learning its] name.
> 2. [One object that has many names would have to be] many entities, but this is contradicted by the fact that many [names are used for one object].

3. The entities [of many objects that have the same name] would be mixed, but this is contradicted by the fact that [a name is] not restricted [to one object].

Therefore, it is proven [that objects are not established by way of their own character as the referents of terms and conceptual consciousnesses].

Dzong-ka-ba (*Emptiness in Mind-Only,* 208-209) expands:

> *Establishing [through the first reasoning] that other-powered natures are empty of the imputational nature due to its being contradictory [for the imputational nature] to be in the essence of that phenomenon:* Let us express—in a way easy to understand—how this is. If a bulbous thing's being a referent or foundation of the convention "pot" were established by way of the bulbous thing's own mode of subsistence or its own character, it would not be posited through the force of terminology [that is, language], in which case even an awareness that has the terminology ["pot"] as its object would not depend upon [making the connection of] the terminology [to the object through being taught language]. Hence, an awareness thinking "pot" with respect to a bulbous thing would [absurdly] be generated [just from seeing the bulbous thing] prior to imputing the name "pot" [that is to say, prior to learning that it is called "pot"].
>
> *Establishing [through the second reasoning that other-powered natures are empty of the imputational nature] by way of the contradiction that just one object would be many entities of objects:* According to the other party [who holds that an object's being a referent of the convention of its name is established by way of the mode of subsistence of the object], the usage of many names such as Shakra, Indra, Grāmaghātaka, and so forth for one object must be by way of the force of the thing itself [since, according to the other party, this god is established by way of his own character as the referent of those names], and [in that case] just as [different meanings dependent upon each of those names] appear [individually] to conceptual consciousnesses, so [the one object, the sole Shakra, would have to] subsist in fact [as individual objects], whereby the [one] object would [absurdly] become many.
>
> *Establishing [through the third reasoning that other-powered natures are empty of the imputational nature] by way of the contradiction that the entities of unmixed objects would be mixed:* According to the other party, when the one name "Upagupta" is used for two beings, there is no difference in [the fact that] an awareness thinking, "This is Upagupta," is generated [with regard to both of them], and [if those

two persons of different continuums are established by way of their own character as referents of the one name "Upagupta"] the names of those [two] and the conceptual consciousnesses [that are aware of such would have to] operate with respect to those two [persons] through the force of the things themselves. Therefore, those two objects[—the two persons of different continuums—absurdly] would be one object [that is, would be one person with one continuum].

That objects are established by way of their own character as the referents of conceptual consciousnesses or as the referents of terms is refuted by way of necessary consequences that common experience shows to be absurd.

It is noteworthy that none of these consequences is that if objects were established by way of their own character as the referents of conceptual consciousnesses, then those objects would be names and thus the possession of names would entail possession of those objects. Hence, not even the reasoning, never mind the conclusion, is aimed at negating the sense that objects are words. Rather, what is being refuted **through the three reasons** is that objects exist by way of their own mode of subsistence as the referents of words and conceptual consciousnesses.[a]

After giving a similar set of reasonings from Asaṅga's *Grounds of Bodhisattvas* and considering related issues (*Emptiness in Mind-Only,* 209ff.), Dzong-ka-ba (*Emptiness in Mind-Only,* 212) raises the question that is at the heart of our present concern:

> *Question:* How does one enter into cognition-only through these reasonings?

As Da-drin-rap-den frames the question:[384]

> In dependence upon this mode of proof that factors imputed in the manner of entity and attribute are empty of being established by way of their own character, how does one enter into cognition-only, that is to say, into truly established consciousness without external objects?

The answer is by no means easy to comprehend, perhaps because of its profundity or perhaps because the connection between the realizations of these two types of emptiness is forced. First I shall give Dzong-ka-ba's response without annotations bracketed in it and then with those annotations.

Dzong-ka-ba's response (*Emptiness in Mind-Only,* 212-213) without annotations:

> *Answer:* When that phenomena ranging from forms through to exalted knowers of all aspects are the foundations of the imputation of

[a] For more on the triple reasoning, see p. 466ff., as well as *Emptiness in Mind-Only,* 206-210, 324-326.

nominal conventions and the referents of conceptual consciousnesses is refuted as ultimately established, one enters into cognition-only which is the non-dualism of apprehended-object and apprehending-subject. In doing this, one thinks:

> In dependence upon a verbalizing name, the verbalized meaning, and the relationship between the name and the meaning, appear to a mental conceptual consciousness as the entities and the attributes of the objects verbalized. Objects conceived in accordance with such appearance do not exist, and hence unmistaken [consciousnesses] apprehending such also do not exist.

With annotations added, the passage reads:

> *Answer:* When that phenomena ranging from forms through to exalted knowers of all aspects [that is, omniscient consciousnesses] are the foundations of the imputation of nominal conventions and the referents of conceptual consciousnesses is refuted as ultimately established, one enters into cognition-only which is the non-dualism of apprehended-object and apprehending-subject. In doing this, one thinks:
>
>> In dependence upon a verbalizing name [such as "pot"], the verbalized meaning [such as that which is bulbous, flat-bottomed, and capable of holding fluid], and the relationship between the name and the meaning, [the phenomena ranging from forms through to omniscient consciousnesses] appear to a mental conceptual consciousness [to be established by way of their own subsistence] as the entities and the attributes of the objects verbalized. Objects conceived in accordance with such appearance [to be separate entities from their respective conceptual consciousnesses] do not exist, and hence unmistaken [consciousnesses] apprehending such also do not exist.

Ḏzong-ka-ḇa supports his commentary with the description of the four thorough examinations[a] and four thorough knowledges[b] in Asaṅga's *Summary of the Great Vehicle,* in which the mode of explanation is in harmony with that in Asaṅga's "Chapter on Suchness" in the *Grounds of Bodhisattvas.* That citation (*Emptiness in Mind-Only,* 213-214), together with bracketed commentary by Ḏa-drin-rap-ḏen, some of which makes explicit the connection with external objects (at best implicit in Asaṅga's text), is:

> It is thus: such Bodhisattvas making effort at entering into cognition-only thoroughly understand—with respect to the mental verbalization

[a] *yongs su tshol ba, paryeṣaṇā.*

[b] *yongs su shes pa, parijñāna.*

[that is, conceptual consciousnesses] to which letters [that is, names] and the meanings [to which those names refer] appear—that those lettered names are exhausted as only [posited by] mental conceptuality [and are not established in accordance with how they appear to refer to the object verbalized. This is the **examination of names.**]

They also thoroughly understand that the meaning depending on letters is just exhausted as only a mental verbalization [that is, as only imputed by conceptuality and not established by way of its own character as the referent of the verbalizing name. This is the **examination of meaning.**]

Moreover, they thoroughly understand that those names are only exhausted as factors imputed in the manner of entities and in the manner of attributes. [That is, they understand that the two imputational natures in the manner of entities and attributes—which are factors imputed individually by the two types of names imputing entities and attributes—are only exhausted as imputed by conceptuality and are not established by way of their own character. These are the **examinations of factors imputed in the manner of entity and in the manner of attribute.**]

Therefore, when they apprehend these as just exhausted as only mental verbalization and when they do not apprehend meanings as well as names involving factors imputed in the manner of entities and attributes nor [anything] involving [factors imputed] in the manner of entity and attribute [as other than only being imputed by conceptuality, that is to say, when they do not apprehend these] as having the factual character [of subsisting as external objects, they attain] the four thorough examinations [which are entities of the path of preparation] and the four thorough knowledges [which are entities of the path of seeing], just as they are in reality. Through these, they enter into cognition-only concerning those mental conceptual consciousnesses to which letters and meanings appear. [By way of establishing that:

- although name, meaning, entity, and attribute **seem** to mental conceptuality to be different entities from the mind,
- the other-powered natures of forms and so forth are the same substantial entity as mind, and
- uncompounded phenomena are the same entity as mind,

they understand that name, meaning, entity, and attribute are of the essence of cognition.]

Since our purpose here is to provide the context of a larger issue, I will merely cite the brief explanation of the four thorough examinations and four thorough knowledges in Jang-ǵya's *Presentations of Tenets:*[385]

Phenomena are not established by way of their own character as the referents of names, and thought which apprehends them so is mistaken. It is undeniable that beings perceive objects as if they were established by way of their own character as the referents of names; this false perception must be destroyed.

One is exhorted to engage in the four examinations and the four knowledges:

1. Examination into whether names are merely adventitious, mere imputation, or whether they are imputed through the force of the object's own mode of being
2. Examination into whether objects by way of their character or adventitiously exist as referents of names
3. Examination into whether in the imputation of entities the relationship between the word and the object exists substantially
4. Examination into whether objects are established by way of their own character as the referents of the imputation of qualities, such as their production, destruction, color, impermanence, and use.

1. Knowledge that names do not exist inherently in the objects they denote
2. Knowledge that objects do not exist inherently as the referents of the imputation of names
3. Knowledge that the imputation of entities based on the relationship of names and objects does not exist inherently
4. Knowledge that the imputation of qualities does not exist inherently.

The latter four are realized conceptually on a Bodhisattva's paths of accumulation and preparation and directly or non-conceptually on the paths of seeing, meditation, and no more learning. They act as a means of entering into a realization of mind-only.

Through establishing that a mental consciousness is mistaken when it apprehends objects as established by way of their own character as the referents of names, it is also established that such an appearance to a sense consciousness is mistaken. It is thereby negated that objects are external entities, unrelated to consciousness, and thus it is established that objects are only appearances to the consciousness that apprehends them. Thereby, it is refuted that a spot of blue, for instance, is a different entity from its perceiving consciousness.

Somehow, through proving that the appearance of objects as established by way of their own character as the referents of names and of conceptual consciousnesses is false, it is negated that "objects are external entities, unrelated to consciousness." Does this mean that since an eye consciousness falsely perceives a white snow mountain as blue, the white snow mountain must be the same entity as an internal consciousness? If so, is a fault with the consciousness merely being transferred to the object? Or, is the relationship between an object's being established by way of its own character as the referent of a conceptual consciousness and its being established as an entity external to the consciousness apprehending it not so tenuous? It seems to me that there is a special, intimate relation between these two, though it has not been explained with evocative clarity in any of the material cited so far.

Ḏzong-ka-ḇa goes on to consider the objection that Asaṅga's discussion has revolved around **conceptual** consciousnesses and how objects falsely appear to them. Implicit is the tenet that the object of negation—the two selves of phenomena negated in the selflessness of phenomena: (1) the establishment of objects by way of their own character as the referents of conceptual consciousnesses and (2) their establishment as different entities from the consciousnesses apprehending them—appears also to **sense** consciousnesses, which, by definition, are non-conceptual. Implicit also is the principle that any full-fledged selflessness of phenomena must apply also to the appearance of objects to non-conceptual consciousnesses. The appearance of what is negated in the selflessness of phenomena cannot be limited to conceptual consciousnesses, and emptiness, therefore, cannot be limited just to conceptual objects.

The objector is attempting to undermine Ḏzong-ka-ḇa's association of the two types of emptiness by showing that Asaṅga's reference is limited to **conceptual** consciousnesses whereas the appearance of subject and object as different entities obviously occurs also to **non-conceptual** consciousnesses. Ḏzong-ka-ḇa (*Emptiness in Mind-Only,* 214-215) states the objector's position and his answer:

> *Objection:* This refutes apprehended-object and apprehending-subject related with conceptual mental consciousnesses, but it does not refute—through reasoning—apprehended-object and apprehending-subject related with non-conceptual consciousnesses that arise from stable predispositions. Therefore, how could this be feasible for entering into cognition-only?
>
> *Answer:* [This reasoning can establish that, since a sense consciousness is mistaken with respect to its appearing object, apprehended-object and apprehending-subject are not other substantial entities. Hence] there is no fault, for when it is refuted through reasoning that blue's being the referent of a conceptual consciousness—conceiving the apprehended-object as a factuality other [than the consciousness apprehending it]—exists by way of its own character, it will be established that [a consciousness] apprehending blue to which blue's being the referent of a conceptual consciousness appears is mistaken with respect to its appearing object. This is because, when it

> [that is, blue's being the referent of a conceptual consciousness] appears, it appears as established by way of its own character. When it has been established [that a consciousness apprehending blue to which blue's being the referent of a conceptual consciousness appears is mistaken with respect to its appearing object], it has been established that blue does not exist as another substantial entity from the consciousness perceiving it [but instead is established as cognition-only].

This cryptic reply lays out a multi-stepped process of understanding that connects the realizations of the two emptinesses.

- First, an object's being established by way of its own character as the referent of a conceptual consciousness **conceiving that it is a different entity from the consciousness apprehending it** is refuted. (He mysteriously adds the bold material here without any explicit justification, loading the argument in his favor.)
- Through that, it will be established that any consciousness (including the non-conceptual) to which blue appears to be established by way of its own character as the referent of a conceptual consciousness is mistaken with respect to its appearing object,[a] in that the object **appears** to be established by way of its own character as the referent of a conceptual consciousness but is not.
- This, perforce, establishes that blue does not exist as a different substantial entity from the consciousness to which it appears.

He has explicitly connected the two realizations, but there is still considerable need for clarity. The relationship seems to be forced.

The next chapter considers how five later Ge-luk-b̄a scholars interpret the relationship between these two kinds of emptiness and their respective objects of negation.

[a] *snang yul, *pratibhāsaviṣaya.*

19. Clarifying the Relationship between the Two Types of Emptiness

Ke-Drup

The commentary by Ke-drup, one of Dzong-ka-ba's two chief students depicted to the right and left of him in paintings—much as Shāriputra and Maudgalyāyana are depicted at the sides of Shākyamuni Buddha—repeats much of Dzong-ka-ba's phraseology on the topic of the entry into mind-only but makes interesting additional comments in order to bring more clarity to his teacher's exposition. With this added material in bold print, his commentary in *Opening the Eyes of the Fortunate* reads:[386]

> **With respect to how one enters into cognition-only through refutation of the extreme of superimposition as explained above, it is as is stated in Asaṅga's *Summary of the Great Vehicle*.** When that phenomena ranging from forms through to exalted knowers of all aspects [that is, omniscient consciousnesses] are the foundations of the imputation of nominal conventions and the referents of conceptual consciousnesses is refuted as ultimately established, one enters into cognition-only which is the non-dualism of apprehended-object and apprehending-subject. In doing this, one thinks:
>
>> In dependence upon a verbalizing name [such as "pot"], the verbalized meaning [such as that which is bulbous, flat-bottomed, and capable of holding fluid], and the relationship between the name and the meaning, [the phenomena ranging from forms through to omniscient consciousnesses] appear to a mental conceptual consciousness **as if established from the side of their own respective mode of subsistence** as the entities and the attributes of the objects verbalized, **whereupon a mental conceptual consciousness adheres** [to such an appearance as being factual]. Objects conceived in accordance with such appearance do not exist, and hence an unmistaken **mode of apprehension** conceiving such also does not exist.
>
> **Just through negating this superimposition it also will effortlessly be refuted that apprehended-object and apprehending-subject related with external objects have an otherness of substantial entity. This is as follows: When it is refuted through reasoning that forms and so forth exist in accordance with the mode of adherence that adheres to them as established by way of their own character as the**

> **referents, or foundations of reference, of the conventions of entity and attribute, their existence in accordance with the mode of appearance of sense consciousnesses to which such appears is also refuted. Thereby, it will be established that sense consciousnesses are mistaken with respect to their appearing objects, and when this has been established, it is refuted that the apprehended-object[a] is produced through the power of an external object. Consequently, it is also refuted that blue and so forth exist as other substantial entities from the sense consciousnesses that perceive them.**

Whereas Dzong-ka-ba cited the appropriate passage from Asaṅga's *Summary of the Great Vehicle* after his explanation, Ke-drup merely refers to it at the beginning, without citing it. This is a tactical move consonant with his wish to get beyond Dzong-ka-ba's overly concise style; the Indian text is even more opaque on the central issue being considered, and thus, by not citing it, Ke-drup gives himself greater freedom to employ his own, more accessible idiom. Still, he announces the general topic in Dzong-ka-ba's own words, repeating his teacher's statement that specifies cognition-only as meaning the non-duality of apprehended-object and apprehending-subject. Thus, for him as for Dzong-ka-ba, the issue is **how** one comes to understand such non-duality of subject and object through understanding the emptiness of the imputation in the manner of entity and attribute. Unlike the American and Japanese scholars considered in the Appendices, neither of them tries to make "cognition-only" mean something else.

Ke-drup proceeds to reframe Dzong-ka-ba's argument in a style that is much clearer than his teacher's, thereby fulfilling his stated intent of bringing clarity to the founder's explanation. Nearly halfway into the Mind-Only section of his *Opening the Eyes of the Fortunate* but before the passage cited above, he speaks of the need for clarification of Dzong-ka-ba's unique contribution:[b]

> Even though our Omniscient Foremost One [Dzong-ka-ba] has already extended the kindness of completely clarifying the systems of the great chariots [that is, great leaders] in his *Differentiating the Interpretable and the Definitive: The Essence of Eloquence,* the power of intelligence of present-day beings is very weak, and, therefore, all these beings involved in this period, like intellectually undeveloped children, cannot open even a portion of [Dzong-ka-ba's presentations which are] like vajra words [that is to say, words used in the Vajra Vehicle that are hard to fathom]. Having understood that these beings have become clueless, I will reveal to listeners with a very few words just those meanings—like a treasure beneath the ground—such that they

a *gzung don.*

b Ke-drup's *Opening the Eyes of the Fortunate,* 217.1-217.4; see also Cabezón, *A Dose of Emptiness,* 52. For his statement of the unique contribution, see p. 396.

> are like olives[a] sitting in the palm of their hand. Stay with your ears inclined!

Indeed, his presentation has a straightforward lucidity; we need only compare Ke-drup's final paragraph (see p. 409) with Ďzong-ka-ƀa's more opaque rendition of the same idea. Ďzong-ka-ƀa's, without Ďa-drin-rap-ďen's annotations (*Emptiness in Mind-Only,* 214-215), reads:

> *Objection:* This refutes apprehended-object and apprehending-subject related with conceptual mental consciousnesses, but it does not refute—through reasoning—apprehended-object and apprehending-subject related with non-conceptual consciousnesses that arise from stable predispositions. Therefore, how could this be feasible for entering into cognition-only?
>
> *Answer:* There is no fault, for when it is refuted through reasoning that blue's being the referent of a conceptual consciousness—conceiving the apprehended-object as another factuality—exists by way of its own character, it will be established that [a consciousness] apprehending blue to which blue's being the referent of a conceptual consciousness appears is mistaken with respect to its appearing object. This is because, when it appears, it appears as established by way of its own character. When this has been established, it has been established that blue does not exist as another substantial entity from the consciousness perceiving it [but instead is established as cognition-only].

Ke-drup's two chief contributions are (1) to identify clearly Ďzong-ka-ƀa's many unstated referents and (2) to introduce the vocabulary of apprehended-objects not being produced through the power of external objects. Let us summarize his points:

1. Forms and so forth appear to conceptual consciousnesses to be established by way of their own character as the referents of the conventions of entity and attribute.
2. A conceptual consciousness adheres to this mistaken appearance as being correct.
3. Reasoning refutes the correctness of this appearance and thus also the correctness of a conceptual consciousness's assenting to this appearance.
4. Objects also appear to sense consciousnesses to be established by way of their own character as the referents of the conventions of entity and attribute, and thus the correctness of this appearance to **non-conceptual**

---

[a] *skyu ru ra* (*āmalakī*). The term also is used for a sour medicinal fruit, *Emblica officinalis Linn.,* said to cure diseases of phlegm, bile, and blood; see Sarat Chandra Das, *A Tibetan-English Dictionary* (Calcutta: 1902; reprint, Delhi: Motilal Banarsidass, 1969, 1970; compact reprint, Kyoto, Japan: Rinsen Book Company, 1981), 103. The usage here is to indicate something that is perfectly clear in front of the eyes.

consciousnesses, such as sense consciousnesses, is also refuted.

5. Thereby, sense consciousnesses are shown to be mistaken with respect to their appearing objects, in that their objects seem to be established by way of their own character as the referents of the conventions of entity and attribute, whereas they are not.
6. Thereby, it is refuted that the apprehended-object is produced through the power of an external object. (That is to say, it is refuted that the images of objects apprehended in sense perception are produced through external objects impinging on consciousness; rather, they are produced through the activation of seeds of perception contained within the mind-basis-of-all.[a])
7. Thereby, it is also refuted that a sense object, such as a patch of blue, exists as an entity other than, or outside of, the sense consciousness that perceives it. (The one seed of perception contained within the mind-basis-of-all produces both the apprehended-object and the consciousness apprehending it, which, although they **appear** to be separate entities, are not.)

Except for the part about the apprehended-object not being produced through the power of an external object, all of the points are drawn from D̄zong-ka-b̄a's exposition but are stated much more clearly.

Ke-drup's central point is that if it is proven that a sense consciousness is mistaken in that its objects **appear** to be established by way of their own character as the referents of names and conceptual consciousnesses but are not actually so, it is entailed that the object being apprehended is not produced from an external object. This opinion is most likely based on D̄zong-ka-b̄a's statement (*Emptiness in Mind-Only,* 215):

> When it has been established [that a consciousness apprehending blue to which blue's being the referent of a conceptual consciousness appears is mistaken with respect to its appearing object], it has been established that blue does not exist as another substantial entity from the consciousness perceiving it [but instead is established as cognition-only].

They may be merely saying that if a perception has **any** element of error, then the apprehended-object is not generated by an external object in any way at all. However, it is likely that their view is not so simple; rather, because sense consciousnesses involve this **particular** type of error—their objects' appearing to be established by way of their own character as the referents of conceptual consciousnesses—it can be concluded that the apprehended-object is not generated by an external object in any way at all.

Despite the clarity of the progression of Ke-drup's argument, this connection between the two types of erroneous appearances of objects—as established by way of their own character as the referents of conceptual consciousnesses and

[a] *kun gzhi rnam shes, ālayavijñāna.*

as external objects—is still not clear. If, on the other hand, his point is that any consciousness that is mistaken with respect to its appearing object is necessarily not a separate entity from the object, then the connection between these two appearances need not be explicated; instead, we would be dealing with a general theory of perceptual error. This may be the case, but he does not go on to cite obvious examples, such as the appearance of a blue snow mountain as a reason for denying that a white snow mountain is involved in any part of the appearance. My guess is that his point revolves around an inextricable connection between objects' being external entities and being referents of thoughts and words by way of their own character. Ke-drup's commentary, while adding considerable clarity to Dzong-ka-b̄a's presentation, has not explicated this issue, which has come to the fore perhaps because he has made the other steps of the argument so clear.

The Second Dalai Lama

Gen-dün-gya-tso[a]—retrospectively called the Second Dalai Lama when his successor Sö-nam-gya-tso[b] received the name "Dalai" from the Mongolian chieftain Altan Khan—wrote a commentary, when almost twenty-four years old, on Dzong-ka-b̄a's *The Essence of Eloquence* that figures prominently in the extensive tradition of scholarship on Dzong-ka-b̄a's text. About the question of how one enters into realization of cognition-only through realizing that the imputational nature is empty of being established by way of its own character, he more boldly recasts Dzong-ka-b̄a's text, enhancing its import with more evocative vocabulary and phraseology. Based partly on Ke-drup's commentary, the Second Dalai Lama says:[387]

> When that phenomena ranging from forms through to exalted knowers of all aspects [that is, omniscient consciousnesses] are the foundations of the imputation of nominal conventions and the referents of conceptual consciousnesses is refuted as established by way of its own character, one realizes that all phenomena ranging from forms through to exalted knowers of all aspects are of the essence of mind-only without there being external objects. For:
>
>> The phenomena of forms and so forth appear to conceptual consciousnesses apprehending forms and so forth to be the referents of the conventions of entity and attribute from the side of the mode of subsistence of the intrinsic factuality of those forms and so forth.[c] When those phenomena are refuted

---

[a]   *dge 'dun rgya mtsho*, 1475-1542.

[b]   *bsod nams rgya mtsho*, 1543-1588. For more on "Dalai," see p. 14.

[c]   *gzugs sogs kyi chos rnams gzugs sogs 'dzin pa'i rtog pa la ngo bo dang khyad par gyi tha snyad kyi gzhir gzugs sogs rang gi dngos po'i gnas tshul gyi ngos nas snang ba.*

as being established that way, one thinks:

> The appearance[a] of forms and so forth—to conceptual consciousnesses—as [being] the referents of the conventions of entity and attribute does not manifest[b] by way of their likeness [or representation] being cast from the side of the mode of subsistence of the intrinsic factuality of those forms and so forth over to [the consciousness] but is an appearance of what has an essence of internal consciousness. Through the force of predispositions of verbalization, objects appear to be the referents of the conventions of entity and attribute in the aspect of external forms and so forth. [Given this appearance] mistaken conceptual consciousnesses merely adhere to [those objects] as established that way.

Thinking this, one enters into cognition-only, which is the emptiness of apprehended-objects and apprehending-subjects as other factualities....[c]

Objection: Even if this explanation of the mode of entry into cognition-only by way of the four examinations and four thorough knowledges refutes apprehended-object and apprehending-subject related with conceptual mental consciousnesses as other factualities, it does not refute, as other factualities, apprehended-object and apprehending-subject that appear to **sense** consciousnesses which arise from stable predispositions. Therefore, how could this be feasible for entering into cognition-only that is without external objects?

Answer: There is no fault because in dependence upon realizing that a form is not established by way of its own character as the referent of a conceptual consciousness apprehending a form, one will realize[d] that a form is only of the mere essence of consciousness without being a different substantial entity from a sense consciousness apprehending form. For:

1. In dependence upon realizing that a form is not established—from the side of the mode of subsistence of the intrinsic factuality

---

a *snang ba.*

b *shar ba.*

c In the ellipsis is the Second Dalai Lama's summary (*Lamp Illuminating the Meaning of [Ḏzong-ka-ḇa's] Thought,* 41b.5-42b.5) of the passage that Ḏzong-ka-ḇa cites from Asaṅga's *Summary of the Great Vehicle.*

d *rtogs par 'gyur;* Second Dalai Lama's *Lamp Illuminating the Meaning of (Ḏzong-ka-ḇa's) Thought,* 43a.2.

of the form itself—as the referent of a conceptual consciousness apprehending the form as an external object, one can realize that a sense consciousness apprehending a form to which that form appears to be the referent of a verbal convention is mistaken with respect to its appearing object.

2. If a sense consciousness apprehending a form is mistaken with respect to its appearing object, the form must not be established in accordance with how it appears to that [sense consciousness].
3. If a form is not established in accordance with how it appears to a sense consciousness apprehending it, the form must not be another substantial entity from the sense consciousness apprehending it.

The first half of the Second Dalai Lama's commentary is replete with richer vocabulary and specification of meaning. He begins by replacing Ḏzong-ka-ḇa's reference to refuting such an imputational nature as being "ultimately established" with its being "established by way of its own character," a synonym that is more evocative. Then, at the point where Ḏzong-ka-ḇa merely says that the phenomena ranging from forms through to omniscient consciousnesses "appear to a mental conceptual consciousness as the entities and the attributes of the objects verbalized," the Second Dalai Lama takes Ke-drup's reframing of this as "appear to a mental conceptual consciousness **as if established from the side of their own respective mode of subsistence** as the entities and the attributes of the objects verbalized" and expands it even more richly to "appear to conceptual consciousnesses apprehending forms and so forth to be the referents of the conventions of entity and attribute **from the side of the mode of subsistence of the intrinsic factuality of those forms and so forth.**" The shift in vocabulary brings even more emphasis to the point that the appearance of objects is polluted with the false sense that their own inner structure is such that they seem ready for verbal imputation.

The Second Dalai Lama then lucidly specifies what realization that phenomena do not exist this way means, both negatively and positively. Negatively, one realizes that this appearance "does not manifest by way of their likeness [or representation] being cast from the side of the mode of subsistence of the intrinsic factuality of those forms and so forth over to [the consciousness]." Positively, one realizes that this "is an appearance of what has an essence of internal consciousness—through the force of predispositions for verbalization—as the referents of the conventions of entity and attribute in the aspect of external forms and so forth." One realizes that internal predispositions, rather than external objects, are responsible for the appearance of objects as if they are established by way of their own character as the referents of names and of conceptual consciousnesses. Rather than objects casting a representation of themselves to the perceiving subject as being the referents of names and of conceptual consciousnesses, the appearance of their seeming to do this is fabricated by internal predispositions, called "predispositions of verbalization."[a] These are potencies infused in the mind through previous verbalization over the course of beginningless lifetimes. The Second Dalai Lama, like Ḏzong-ka-ḇa and Ke-drup, concludes that, with this type of penetrative reflections, one enters into, that is to say, realizes, cognition-only—the emptiness of a difference of entity between subject and object.

Next, the Second Dalai Lama addresses the objection, raised in *The Essence of Eloquence*, that Asaṅga's *Summary of the Great Vehicle* (the primary source for the above explanation) is concerned with an appearance to conceptual consciousnesses but not to sense consciousnesses, and thus speaks only to a narrow range of consciousnesses and cannot establish a general principle of cognition-only in terms of all consciousnesses, both conceptual and non-conceptual. His reframing of Ḏzong-ka-ḇa's answer appears to be based, to a large extent, on Ke-drup's commentary, but has a greater straightforwardness that brings considerable clarity to the argument. Whereas Ke-drup speaks of "refuting" or "negating," the Second Dalai Lama speaks, more positively, of "realizing"; let us juxtapose their commentaries. First, their respective general statements:

> *Ke-drup:* Just through negating this superimposition it will also be effortlessly refuted that apprehended-object and apprehending-subject related with external objects have an otherness of substantial entity.
>
> *Second Dalai Lama:* In dependence upon realizing that a form is not established by way of its own character as the referent of a conceptual consciousness apprehending a form, one will realize that a form is only of the mere essence of consciousness without being a different substantial entity from a sense consciousness apprehending form.

The first step in their reasoning:

> *Ke-drup:* When it is refuted through reasoning that forms and so forth exist in accordance with the mode of adherence that adheres to them as established by way of their own character as the referents, or foundations of reference, of the conventions of entity and attribute, their existence in accordance with the mode of appearance of sense consciousnesses to which such appears is also refuted. Thereby, it is established that sense consciousnesses are mistaken with respect to their appearing objects.
>
> *Second Dalai Lama:* In dependence upon realizing that a form is not established—from the side of the mode of subsistence of the intrinsic factuality of the form itself—as the referent of a conceptual consciousness apprehending the form as an external object, one can realize that a

---

[a] *mngon brjod kyi bag chags, abhilāpavāsanā.*

> sense consciousness apprehending a form to which that form appears to be the referent of a verbal convention is mistaken with respect to its appearing object.

The second step in their reasoning:

> *Ke-drup:* When this has been established, it is refuted that the apprehended-object is produced through the power of an external object.
>
> *Second Dalai Lama:* If a sense consciousness apprehending a form is mistaken with respect to its appearing object, the form must not be established in accordance with how it appears to that [sense consciousness].

Their conclusions:

> *Ke-drup:* Consequently, it is also refuted that blue and so forth exist as other substantial entities from the sense consciousnesses that perceive them.
>
> *Second Dalai Lama:* If a form is not established in accordance with how it appears to a sense consciousness apprehending it, the form must not be another substantial entity from the sense consciousness apprehending it.

An initial difference between the two expositions is that the Second Dalai Lama pointedly says that through realizing the first type of emptiness "one **can** realize that a sense consciousness apprehending a form to which that form appears to be the referent of a verbal convention is mistaken with respect to its appearing object." By using the word "can," he emphasizes that the first realization does not contain within it or imply the second. This qualification makes more explicit Ke-drup's suggestion of the same when he says, "Just through negating this superimposition it **will** also be effortlessly refuted that apprehended-object and apprehending-subject related with external objects have an otherness of substantial entity." The qualification also is consonant with Ḏzong-ka-ḇa's presentation of a **multi-staged** process of realization suggesting that the two types of emptiness might be realized serially, not simultaneously.

Another difference is that the Second Dalai Lama makes explicit the principle (at best implicit in Ke-drup's presentation) that if a sense consciousness is mistaken with respect to its appearing object, then what it apprehends does not exist in accordance with how it appears and that this necessitates that the form is not a different entity from the consciousness perceiving it. One can readily understand that in cases of perceptual error, such as in perceiving a white conch to be yellow due to a bile disorder (to use a traditional example), an inner condition has affected how an outer object appears, but it is not apparent **how** this results in the conclusion that an external conch is not at all involved in stimulating the perception. Still, the Second Dalai Lama has enunciated the principle clearly, even if the glue that holds it together is not apparent.

The connection between an object's being established by way of its own character as the referent of words and conceptual consciousnesses and its being a different entity from the consciousness apprehending it still seems to be forced. Consider, for instance, how the Second Dalai Lama intertwines the two topics by suddenly introducing the vocabulary of the appearance of externality into the discussion. Whereas Ḏzong-ka-ḇa merely says that phenomena "appear to a mental conceptual consciousness as the entities and the attributes of the objects verbalized," the Second Dalai Lama turns this into:

> an appearance **of what has an essence of internal consciousness—through the force of predispositions of verbalization**—as the referents of the conventions of entity and attribute **in the aspect of external forms and so forth.**

The changes are similar to a sudden qualification made by Ḏzong-ka-ḇa when later he (*Emptiness in Mind-Only,* 215) explains how refuting an appearance to conceptual consciousnesses applies to non-conceptual sense consciousnesses. There, he introduces the vocabulary of a difference of entity when he speaks of refuting that "blue's being the referent of a conceptual consciousness conceiving **the apprehended-object as a factuality other [than the consciousness apprehending it]** exists by way of its own character." This is a sudden switch because the context all along has not involved any mention of externality. Ḏzong-ka-ḇa, without explanation, has the conceptual consciousness apprehending the object as a different entity from itself.

In the same way, the Second Dalai Lama speaks of "an appearance **of what has an essence of internal consciousness—through the force of predispositions of verbalization**—as the referents of the conventions of entity and attribute **in the aspect of external forms and so forth,**" without saying how these phrases come to be justifiably added. He deliberately ties the two types of false appearances together, and why they must be associated is explained to some extent by a principle of perceptual error that itself, however, calls for more elaboration.

By subtle shifts of vocabulary, these scholars have tried to suggest **how** conceiving an object to be established by way of its own character as the referent of a conceptual consciousness also involves conceiving that it is a separate entity from the consciousness perceiving it. Stress has been put on the "out there" character of objects when it is viewed that, by way of their own nature, they are the referents of our thoughts and names. The natural tendency, upon being asked what such and such is, to point to the object or to say without any further reflection, "It **is** this and that," rather than to say, "This and that are imputed as that object," indicates that even appearances to our sense consciousnesses are infected with a false sense of the nature of those objects. This false appearance of the object's naturally being a basis of reference of thought and word carries with it a sense of being an external object.

Paṇ-chen Sö-nam-drak-ba

Difficult issues are presented in a genre of monastic textbook literature called "the general meaning,"[a] which are sometimes supplemented with more debate-oriented "decisive analyses."[b] In such texts issues are presented mostly in the format of debate, first refuting mistaken notions, then positing one's own system, and then dispelling objections to one's own system. In the first half of the sixteenth century, Paṇ-chen Sö-nam-drak-ba (1478-1554)—whose textbooks are used in the Lo-sel-ling College of Dre-bung Monastic University and in the Shar-dzay College of Gan-den Monastic University—wrote a general-meaning commentary on Dzong-ka-ba's *The Essence of Eloquence* entitled *Distinguishing Through Objections and Answers (Dzong-ka-ba's) "The Essence of Eloquence, Differentiating the Interpretable and Definitive Meanings of All the Scriptures": Garland of Blue Lotuses.*[c] Paṇ-chen Sö-nam-drak-ba maintains that, in dependence upon realizing that objects are not established by way of their own character as the referents of a conceptual consciousness, one **can** realize that a form and a sense consciousness apprehending it are not different substantial entities, that is to say, are mind-only.

He[388] frames his brief presentation around a response to an unattributed, mistaken notion that these two types of emptiness are held by different Indian scholars, not by the same scholars:

> *Statement of a [wrong] opinion:* The view of emptiness that is a negation of the imputational nature's establishment by way of its own character is a view asserted by Asaṅga and his [half] brother [Vasubandhu], and the view of emptiness that is a negation of apprehended-object and apprehending-subject as other substantial entities is the view of emptiness asserted by Dignāga and Dharmakīrti.
>
> *Response:* The association [of these views with] individual [scholars] is not good because Asaṅga and his [half] brother [Vasubandhu also] assert the latter view and Dignāga and Dharmakīrti [also] assert the former view.

Paṇ-chen Sö-nam-drak-ba proceeds to cite evidence that these four scholars assert both views, but, since Dzong-ka-ba treats this topic at length in *The*

---

a *spyi don.*

b *mtha' dpyod.*

c One of his recent followers reported that Paṇ-chen Sö-nam-drak-ba also wrote a "decisive analysis" entitled *Eliminating Qualms about Difficult Topics in (Dzong-ka-ba's) "The Essence of Eloquence"* (*legs bshad snying po'i dka' gnad dogs gcod*), but that despite considerable search it has not been found.

Essence of Eloquence (see *Emptiness in Mind-Only,* chapters 6-11), I will not cite Paṇ-chen Sö-nam-drak-b̄a's brief explanation here.

Then, like the exposition by the Second Dalai Lama, who was born three years before him and died twelve years before him, he reframes the issue by using the word "can" six times, whereas the Second Dalai Lama uses it only once:

> It follows that your root thesis is not correct because through the reasoning refuting that forms and so forth are established by way of their own character as the referents of conceptual consciousnesses apprehending them one enters into cognition-only refuting that apprehended-object and apprehending-subject are other substantial entities. This is because in dependence upon realizing that forms and so forth are not established by way of their own character as the referents of a conceptual consciousness apprehending them, one **can** realize that a form is not a different substantial entity from a sense consciousness apprehending it. This is because, in dependence upon that, one **can** realize that a sense consciousness apprehending a form is a mistaken consciousness. [The fact that, in dependence upon realizing that forms and so forth are not established by way of their own character as the referents of a conceptual consciousness apprehending them, one can realize that a sense consciousness apprehending a form is a mistaken consciousness] entails [that one can realize that a form is not a different substantial entity from a sense consciousness apprehending it] because if one **can** do this, one **can** realize what appears to that sense consciousness does not exist in accordance with how it appears and if one **can** do this, one **can** realize that apprehended-object and apprehending-subject are not other substantial entities.

Paṇ-chen Sö-nam-drak-b̄a brings all the more emphasis to the point that the first realization **does not contain within it** or **imply** the second. Again, the word "can" is consonant with D̄zong-ka-b̄a's presentation of a multi-staged process of realization and makes more explicit Ke-drup's suggestion of serial realization through his usage of the future tense when he says, "Just through negating this superimposition it **will** also be effortlessly refuted that apprehended-object and apprehending-subject related with external objects have an otherness of substantial entity."[a]

[a] In his *General-Meaning Commentary,* Jay-d̄zün Chö-ḡyi-gyel-tsen (1469-1546) of the Jay College of S̄e-ra Monastic University often refines or refutes the views of his fellow student, Paṇ-chen Sö-nam-drak-b̄a. On this issue, he presents only a slight refinement of the argument. The material (34b.4-35a.1) is presented in the format of a statement of an erroneous opinion and his response to it:

> *Statement of a [wrong] opinion*: It follows that the explanation that one enters into cognition-only in dependence upon realizing that a form is not established by way of its own character as the referent of a conceptual consciousness

Jam-yang-shay-b̄a

Born in the Am-do province of Tibet in 1648, Jam-ȳang-shay-b̄a-nga-w̄ang-d̄zön-drü,[a] commonly known as Jam-ȳang-shay-b̄a, went to Central Tibet at age twenty-one for studies at the Go-mang College of Dre-b̄ung Monastic University on the outskirts of Hla-s̄a, where eventually textbooks that he authored became the standard syllabus.[389] At age sixty-two he returned to Am-do, where he founded, in 1710, a monastic university called D̄ra-s̄hi-kyil. Among the authors of the major textbooks for the three great monastic universities near Hla-s̄a, he composed the most extensive commentary on the Mind-Only section of D̄zong-ka-b̄a's *The Essence of Eloquence,* based to a great degree on the textbook by his predecessor Gung-ru Chö-jung, which he refined. His text, entitled *Decisive Analysis of (D̄zong-ka-b̄a's) "Differentiating the Interpretable and the Definitive," Store-House of White Lapis-Lazuli of Scripture and Reasoning Free from Error, Fulfilling the Hopes of the Fortunate,*[390] is limited to the Mind-Only section and is written in the sub-genre of monastic textbooks, mentioned above, called a "decisive analysis" or "critical analysis," which often is supplementary to a "general meaning" commentary and is more analytic. Jam-ȳang-shay-b̄a, however, did not write separate "general meaning" texts, and thus his

---

apprehending it is not correct, because (1) in order to enter into cognition-only it is necessary to realize that a form is empty of [being] another substantial entity from a sense consciousness apprehending it and (2) realizing that a form is not established by way of its own character as the referent of a conceptual consciousness apprehending it does not entail realizing that a form does not exist as another substantial entity from a sense consciousness apprehending form.

Response: That is incorrect because:

- in dependence upon realizing that a form is not established by way of its own character as the referent of a conceptual consciousness apprehending it, there arises the realization that a consciousness—to which the form and the [consciousness] apprehending it appear as other substantial entities—is a mistaken consciousness, and
- a person who realizes that a consciousness to which a form and the [consciousness] apprehending it appear as other substantial entities is a mistaken consciousness necessarily is a person who realizes that a form is empty of [being] another substantial entity from a sense consciousness apprehending form.

In order to avoid having to hold that one consciousness has two distinct realizations—(1) realizing that a form is not established by way of its own character as the referent of a conceptual consciousness apprehending it and (2) realizing that a form is empty of (being) another substantial entity from a sense consciousness apprehending form, Jay-d̄zün Chö-ḡyi-gyel-tsen speaks of the **person** as having both realizations. However, he does not explain whether this means that the two realizations occur simultaneously. Typical of his text, he leaves the reader to speculate on his meaning, which probably is not that, when the first is realized explicitly, the second is realized implicitly.

[a] *'jam dbyangs bzhad pa ngag dbang brtson grus,* 1648-1721.

commentaries in the genre of "decisive analysis" tend, stylistically, to fill both functions. Scholars of the colleges that use his textbooks—Go-mang, D̄ra-s̄hi-kyil, and various other Tibetan and Mongolian colleges—explain that D̄zong-ka-b̄a's own texts are used as the "general meaning" textbooks.

Since his analysis is thoroughgoing, let us cite the relevant portions as an overview of the issues to set the stage for turning to a twentieth-century oral commentary. First, he reframes the last part of the objection—the part that directly concerns us here—as:[391]

> *Objection:* Moreover, it follows that the fact that factors imputed in the manner of entity and attribute are not established by way of their own character is not the selflessness of phenomena that is the object observed by [the path] purifying the obstructions to omniscience. This is because it does not contain the meaning of cognition-only that is the negation of apprehended-object and apprehending-subject as different substantial entities.

He begins his answer to the entire objection, not just the part cited, with:[392]

> *Response:* It follows that it is not correct that the emptiness—of factors imputed in the manner of entity and attribute—as established by way of their own character is already validated by the Hearer Schools [that is, the Great Exposition School and the Sūtra School] and that this mode of emptiness does not have the meaning of[393] cognition-only because:
>
> - Such an emptiness is described in the *Sūtra Unraveling the Thought* as the final object observed by the path of purification purifying the obstructions to omniscience.
> - The path realizing this is described in Asaṅga's *Grounds of Bodhisattvas* as the middle path of which there is none higher.
> - Asaṅga's *Summary of the Great Vehicle* explains that in dependence upon this mode of emptiness one enters into cognition-only.

Jam-ȳang-shay-b̄a's reasoning is that, since such an emptiness is described in the *Sūtra Unraveling the Thought* as the object of meditation for purifying the obstructions to omniscience, it could not be taught in the Low Vehicle schools, since those schools do not posit a path leading to the **simultaneous** cognition of all objects of knowledge—both emptinesses and the phenomena they qualify. Those schools only speak of a Buddha as having an all-knowingness in the sense of serially realizing anything the Buddha wishes to know.[394] He also holds that such an emptiness has the meaning of cognition-only (meaning a denial of external objects) because Asaṅga's *Summary of the Great Vehicle* relates this emptiness with cognition-only. He thereby suggests that it is necessary to read the "Chapter on Suchness" in Asaṅga's *Grounds of Bodhisattvas* together with his *Summary of the Great Vehicle* in order not to miss the import of Asaṅga's own association of these two types of emptinesses.

Jam-ȳang-shay-b̄a proceeds to explain in considerable detail (which I will omit here)[a] that the Proponents of Sūtra have not already realized this emptiness. Then he explains how, upon realizing that phenomena are not established by way of their own character as the referents of a conceptual consciousness, one enters, or realizes, cognition-only. First he indicates that:

- A form's emptiness of being established by way of its own character as the referent of a conceptual consciousness and the emptiness—of a form and a valid consciousness cognizing it—as being other substantial entities are similarly the subtle selflessness of phenomena, but
- They differ in the sense that the former is easier to realize and the latter is more difficult to realize.

He thereby draws out the implications of the Second Dalai Lama's statement that in dependence upon realizing the first emptiness, the second **can** be realized, the suggestion being that the second realization is separate from the first and in a serial order.

To back up the claim that realization of the first type of emptiness leads to realizing the second, Jam-ȳang-shay-b̄a cites supporting evidence from Ke-drup that, before meditating on a reasoning proving emptiness, in the important step of ascertaining the false status of phenomena it is easier to get a sense of the mode of apprehension in conceiving that a form, for instance, is established by way of its own character as the referent of a conceptual consciousness than it is to get a sense of the mode of appearance—to a sense consciousness—that object and subject are different entities. However, he does not accept, as a consequence of this difference in ease of realization, that the first type of emptiness is more coarse than the second.

In Jam-ȳang-shay-b̄a's own words:[395]

> ***First: Refutation of a Mistaken Opinion***
>
> *Statement of [wrong] opinion:* It follows that the two emptinesses, a form's emptiness of being established by way of its own character as the referent of a conceptual consciousness and the emptiness—of a form and a valid consciousness cognizing it—of being other substantial entities differ in terms of coarseness and subtlety because they necessarily differ in terms of ease and difficulty of realization.
>
> *Response:* [That they differ in terms of ease and difficulty of realization] does not entail [that they differ in terms of coarseness and subtlety. However] the reason[—that they differ in the sense that the former is easier to realize and the latter is more difficult to realize—]is confirmed because the former is easier to realize and the latter is more

[a] See *Absorption*, #78, 81, 123, 124.

difficult to realize than it. This is because in dependence upon realizing that a form is not established by way of its own character as the referent of a conceptual consciousness, one can realize that a sense consciousness to which a form appears to be established by way of its own character as the referent of a conceptual consciousness is mistaken with respect to its mode of appearance and, in dependence upon this, one can realize that a form and a valid consciousness cognizing it do not exist as other substantial entities. This is because Ḏzong-ka-ḇa's *The Essence of Eloquence* (*Emptiness in Mind-Only,* 212-213) says:

> When that phenomena ranging from forms through to exalted knowers of all aspects [that is, omniscient consciousnesses] are the foundations of the imputation of nominal conventions and the referents of conceptual consciousnesses is refuted as ultimately established, one enters into cognition-only which is the non-dualism of apprehended-object and apprehending-subject. In doing this, one thinks:
>
>> In dependence upon a verbalizing name [such as "pot"], the verbalized meaning [such as that which is bulbous, flat-bottomed, and capable of holding fluid], and the relationship between the name and the meaning, [the phenomena ranging from forms through to omniscient consciousnesses] appear to a mental conceptual consciousness [to be established by way of their own subsistence] as the entities and the attributes of the objects verbalized. Objects conceived in accordance with such appearance [to be separate entities from their respective conceptual consciousnesses] do not exist, and hence unmistaken [consciousnesses] apprehending such also do not exist.

If one accepted [that the two emptinesses, a form's emptiness of being established by way of its own character as the referent of a conceptual consciousness and the emptiness—of a form and a valid consciousness cognizing it—of being other substantial entities differ in terms of coarseness and subtlety], then it would [absurdly] follow that form's emptiness of being established by way of its own character as the referent of a conceptual consciousness would be a coarse selflessness of phenomena and the emptiness of duality would be a subtle selflessness of phenomena. This cannot be accepted because both are subtle selflessnesses of phenomena....Therefore, those two differ in terms of ease and difficulty of realization because (1) it is more difficult to reflect on [or get a sense of] the mode of appearance of apprehended-object and apprehending-subject as other substantial entities to a sense consciousness than [to get a sense of] the mode of conception in the conception that form is established by way of its own character as the referent of a conceptual consciousness and (2) not only can the object of negation not be refuted until how it [seems to] exist for the mind is identified but also the more easily appearing object of negation is easier to refute and the more difficult to appear is more difficult to refute. The first [reason—that it is more difficult to reflect on, or get a sense of, the mode of appearance of apprehended-object and apprehending-subject as other substantial entities to a sense consciousness than (to get a sense of) the mode of conception in the conception that form is established by way of its own character as the referent of a conceptual consciousness—]is confirmed because Ke-drup's *Opening the Eyes of the Fortunate* says:[396]

> It is more difficult for the object of negation as it appears to a sense consciousness to appear as an object of awareness than for the object of negation as it is adhered to by a conceptual consciousness to appear as an object of awareness....[a]

The second [reason—that not only can the object of negation not be refuted until how it exists for the mind is identified but also the more

---

[a] When Jam-ȳang-shay-b̄a's citation is put in context, it is seen to be forced, for Ke-drup (*Opening the Eyes of the Fortunate,* 222.1; see also José Ignacio Cabezón, *A Dose of Emptiness* [Albany, N.Y.: State University of New York Press, 1992], 55-56) says:

> Through refuting that forms and so forth are established by way of their own character as referents of conventions imputing entity and attribute, the self of phenomena is negated. Concerning this, it is more difficult for the object of negation as it appears to a sense consciousness to appear as an object of awareness than for the object of negation as it is adhered to by a conceptual consciousness to appear as an object of awareness. Hence, if that mode of appearance [to a sense consciousness] is identified first, it makes a great difference with respect to knowing the mode of refuting establishment in accordance with how a conceptual consciousness adheres to [objects'] being established that way.

Jam-ȳang-shay-b̄a has Ke-drup speaking about two types of object of negation and seemingly recommending identifying the easier before the more difficult, whereas Ke-drup appears to be speaking only about the appearance of objects as established by way of their own character as the referents of words and conceptual consciousnesses and recommends identifying the more difficult. Still, Jik-may-dam-chö-gya-tso (*Port of Entry,* 613.3) takes Ke-drup's last two sentences as meaning:

> For realizing that [objects] are not established by way of their own character as the referents of their respective conceptual consciousnesses, it is very important to identify the mode of appearance of subject and object as other substantial entities to sense consciousnesses.

easily appearing object of negation is easier to refute and the more difficult to appear is more difficult to refute—]is confirmed because it is like, for example, the fact that due to differences in the ease or difficulty of seeing a target, it comes to be easier or more difficult to shoot an arrow. Shāntideva's *Engaging in the Bodhisattva Deeds* says:[a]

> Without contacting the imputed existent
> Its non-existence is not apprehended.

Also, Ke-drup's *Opening the Eyes of the Fortunate* says:[397]

> Initially, it is necessary to ascertain just what sort of object is to be negated—through the elimination of which suchness must be ascertained—because without the appearance of the generality of the object of negation, the generality of the negation that is the negative of it does not appear.

There are a great many such statements in the speech of the foremost father [D̄zong-ka-b̄a] and his spiritual sons [Gyel-tsap and Ke-drup].

Jam-ȳang-shay-b̄a makes the distinction that, although the two emptinesses are equally subtle, the first is easier to realize than the second. This position is controversial, since the meaning of coarse and subtle levels of emptiness is usually explained as referring to difficulty and ease of realization, and he does not delineate in what sense they are equally subtle despite differing in ease of realization. Simply put, it is likely that, if the one is realized **before** the other, it must be easier to realize than the other. I can appreciate, however, why he has not split the hair this way, since there is no Indian source for making one coarser than the other and since there are sources indicating their serial realization.

Jam-ȳang-shay-b̄a supports his position with what he takes to be Ke-drup's statement that it is easier to get a sense of the mode of apprehension in conceiving that an object is established by way of its own character as the referent of a conceptual consciousness than it is to get a sense of the mode of appearance—to a sense consciousness—that object and subject are different entities. He thereby ancillarily stresses the importance of ascertaining the object of negation before beginning to meditate on emptiness.

Having refuted the wrong opinion that the two types of emptiness are not associated, he sets forth his estimation of D̄zong-ka-b̄a's own system[398] and then considers the objection that this does not involve cognition-only.[399] These lengthy sections, which liberally borrow from the commentaries by the Second Dalai Lama and Gung-ru Chö-jung[400] (his predecessor as textbook author of the Go-mang tradition), set the issues in clear relief:

[a] *byang chub sems dpa'i spyod pa la 'jug pa, bodhisattvacaryāvatāra,* IX.140. The Sanskrit, as found in *Bodhicaryāvatāra,* ed. Vidhushekhara Bhattacharya, Bibliotheca Indica vol. 280 (Calcutta: Asiatic Society, 1960), 221, is: *kalpitam bhāvamaspṛṣṭvā tadabhāvo na gṛhyate.*

Second: Our Own System

When it is refuted that forms and so forth are established by way of their own character as the referents or foundations of reference of names and conventions, one realizes that forms and so forth are of the essence of internal consciousness without existing in accordance with their appearance as concrete[a] external objects, distant and cut off. For:

> Forms and so forth appear to conceptual consciousnesses apprehending them to be the referents of the conventions of entity and attribute from the side of the level of subsistence of the entities of those forms and so forth themselves,[b] and when[401] those are refuted and thus negated as being established that way, there arises ascertainment that the appearance[c] of forms and so forth—to conceptual consciousnesses—as [being] the referents of the conventions of entity and attribute does not manifest[d] by way of their likeness [or representation] being cast from the side of the level of the mode of subsistence of the forms and so forth. In dependence upon that, one thinks, "Conceptual consciousnesses are mistaken with respect to the fact that—through the force of predispositions for verbalization—what has an essence of internal consciousness [falsely] appears as the referents of the conventions of entity and attribute in the aspect of external forms and so forth, and hence [those conceptual consciousnesses] merely adhere to such." Thinking this, one enters into cognition-only, which is the absence of duality between apprehended-objects and apprehending-subjects, that is, the absence of apprehended-objects and apprehending-subjects being other factualities.

This is because Asaṅga's *Summary of the Great Vehicle* and so forth explain a mode of entry into cognition[-only] by way of the four examinations and the four knowledges. For Dzong-ka-ba's *The Essence of Eloquence* (*Emptiness in Mind-Only,* 212-213) says:

> ...one enters into cognition-only which is the non-dualism of apprehended-object and apprehending-subject. In doing this, one thinks:
>
> > In dependence upon a verbalizing name [such as "pot"], the verbalized meaning [such as that which is

a *ling po.*

b *gzugs sogs rang gi ngo bo'i gnas tshod gyi ngos nas snang ba.*

c *snang ba.*

d *shar ba.*

> bulbous, flat-bottomed, and capable of holding fluid], and the relationship between the name and the meaning, [the phenomena ranging from forms through to omniscient consciousnesses] appear to a mental conceptual consciousness [to be established by way of their own subsistence] as the entities and the attributes of the objects verbalized. Objects conceived in accordance with such appearance [to be separate entities from their respective conceptual consciousnesses] do not exist, and hence unmistaken [consciousnesses] apprehending such also do not exist.

And (*Emptiness in Mind-Only,* 219):

> The setting out of the four examinations and the four thorough knowledges in Asaṅga's *Grounds of Bodhisattvas, Summary of the Great Vehicle, Summary of Manifest Knowledge,* and so forth is said to be the excellent door of entry to cognition-only—the means of settling the view of cognition—[and also] the antidote to the obstructions to omniscience [which consist of] the conceptuality that serves as the basis of even the afflictive emotions.

And Ke-drup's *Opening the Eyes of the Fortunate* says:[402]

> Nevertheless, if one does not know:
>
> - how entity and attribute are imputed upon taking an other-powered nature as the foundation of the imputation
> - how to refute that such an imputational nature is established by way of its own character, and
> - how to posit the selflessness of phenomena which is the negation [of that],
>
> one cannot know even a portion of the presentations, extensively explained in this system, of:
>
> - the full mode of positing the selflessness of phenomena
> - the four thorough knowledges and four examinations
> - the mode of entry into cognition-only by way of those, and
> - how the Perfection of Wisdom Sūtras teach [cognition-only] as the antidote to the ten distracted conceptualizations.

This citation from Ke-drup emphasizes the importance of comprehending the connection between the two types of emptiness, since otherwise many facets of the Yogic Practice, or Mind-Only, system will be impenetrable.[a]

Summation

With one voice, all these scholars stress the importance of the fact that this two-fold false appearance occurs also to sense consciousnesses and thus is not just a fabrication by current conceptuality. It is part of the stuff of ordinary appearance, assent to which draws beings into afflictive emotions. Jam-ȳang-shay-b̄a, while drawing major portions of his exposition from the Second Dalai Lama's commentary and Gung-ru Chö-jung, adds a well-supported presentation of the **serial** realization of the two types of emptiness. Nevertheless, he too does not address just **how** the appearance of an object as established by way of its own character as the referent of terms and conceptual consciousnesses necessarily involves an appearance of that object as a different entity from the consciousness apprehending it.

A Contemporary Oral Commentary: Ken-sur Ye-shay-tup-d̄en

Another level of scholarship that takes place in the debating courtyard of Tibetan monastic universities but only occasionally finds its way into print provides further insights into the connection between the two false appearances and the two emptinesses. When the late Ken-sur Ye-s̄hay-tup-d̄en,[b] abbot of the L̄o-s̄el-l̄ing College of Dre-b̄ung Monastic University in the 1970s at its resettlement in Karnataka State in India, taught at the University of Virginia in 1982-1983, I had an opportunity to study with him the entire text of D̄zong-ka-b̄a's *The Essence of Eloquence* as well as the commentary on it by the textbook author of his L̄o-s̄el-l̄ing College, Paṇ-chen S̄ö-nam-drak-b̄a, and the commentaries on the Mind-Only sections by the original textbook author of S̄e-ra Jay College, B̄el-jor-hlün-drup, and by A-ku L̄o-drö-gya-tso, a commentator in the Go-Mang tradition. Several times during the course of our study he laid out an intriguingly cogent presentation addressing this important issue. Distilling its essence, I render it in my own words this way:

---

[a] For A-ku L̄o-drö-gya-tso's brief presentation of the relationship between the two types of emptiness in which he speaks of four modes of appearances and four seeds, see 219ff. He, too, does not address in a satisfying way the **necessary** connection between the two false appearances.

[b] *mkhan zur ye shes thub bstan,* d. 1988. For his exposition of facets of the Middle Way School, see Anne Carolyn Klein, *Path to the Middle: The Spoken Scholarship of Kensur Yeshey Tupden* (Albany, N.Y.: State University of New York Press, 1994).

When a form appears, whether it be to a sense consciousness or to the mental consciousness, it seems to be established by way of its own character as the referent of our words and thoughts about it. Right along with the appearance of the form is an appearance that the form (1) is the referent of our mental conceptions about it and (2) is the referent of our terms expressing it. To us it seems that the form's being the referent of our mental conceptions and being the referent of our terms expressing it subsist right in the form's nature—that is to say, are established within the character of the form—whereas they are not.

Thus, we must learn to discriminate between the complex appearance that is the actual form and the simple, abstract appearance of that form that, due to our beginningless usage of words, appears together with the appearance of the form. We must understand that the abstracted appearance does not subsist in the character of the form—that it is not established in the object by way of the object's own character.

There are two levels of referents of our thoughts and of our terms; both are abstractions, but one of them appears only to conceptual consciousnesses, whereas the other also appears to sense consciousnesses. The first is a conceptual image of the object, which a Proponent of Sūtra (lower than a Proponent of Mind-Only) can distinguish from the object itself, but the second is an abstraction of the object that appears even to sense consciousnesses due to predispositions established by beginningless verbalization; it is a superimposition, not something subsisting in the nature of the object even though it seems to do so. A Proponent of Sūtra cannot distinguish between the appearance of a form to a sense consciousness and the abstract image of it that also appears to the same sense consciousness. The ability to make this distinction constitutes the prime difference between a Proponent of Mind-Only and a Proponent of Sūtra.

A Proponent of Sūtra does not realize that this second type of abstracted image—which is the main referent of a conceptual consciousness apprehending form and the main referent of the term "form"—is not established by way of its own character, since a Proponent of Sūtra confuses the abstract image with the object itself. Also, since the form itself is established by way of its own character, the Proponent of Sūtra comes to hold that the abstracted image that appears even to a sense consciousness is established by way of its own character. This is how a Proponent of Sūtra comes to hold that a form is established by way of its own character as the referent of a conceptual consciousness and of terminology.

Due to our predispositions, we live in a world overlain with abstract images—simplified versions of objects—that are the referents of our thoughts and terms. Even if these referents appear to our sense consciousnesses, they do not subsist in the very thingness of those objects, which therefore are called "inexpressible things."[a] Thus, the objects that are the referents of our conceptions and of our terms are quite different from the actual objects.

A Proponent of Sūtra can realize that the conceptual image, or meaning-generality,[b] of an object that appears to a conceptual consciousness and is also a referent of thoughts and terms is not established by way of its own character but does not realize that there is an abstracted image appearing both to a conceptual consciousness and to a non-conceptual consciousness such as an eye consciousness. Wanting persons to realize this, Buddha taught that imputational natures are natureless in terms of character—that such referents are not established by way of their own character.

Since in naming objects we have a sense of ourselves—the namers or users of names—on one side and the object named on the other side, there is a sense of a difference of entity between namer and named that goes along with the affixing of names. Thus, when objects appear to be established by way of their own character as the referents of conceptual consciousnesses, we have a sense that the consciousness is on one side and the object named is on the other—a difference of entity between the apprehending-subject and the apprehending-object. Since the elements of naming appear this way, when it is refuted that objects are established by way of their own character as the referents of conceptual consciousnesses, it also comes to be refuted that subject and object are established as separate entities.

When we name, the consciousness is on the side of the namer, and the object named is on an opposite side, thus yielding a sense of a split, a difference of entity, between subject and object. Hence, when one refutes that objects are established by way of their own character as referents of names or conceptual consciousnesses, one comes to refute that subject and object are different entities. This is because, for one who does not know emptiness, the naming activity carries with it a sense of difference of entity between subject and object.

Ken-sur Ye-s̄hay-tup-d̄en's exposition ties together the two false appearances and two emptinesses intimately by emphasizing the bifurcation that accompanies naming and conceptualizing. He also goes so far as to maintain that an explicit realization of the first type of emptiness implicitly contains within it realization of the emptiness of external objects. His explanation thereby goes a step beyond the progressive realization that D̄zong-ka-b̄a, Ke-drup, and the Second Dalai Lama suggest but do not elucidate and Jam-ȳang-shay-b̄a

---

a *brjod du med pa'i dngos po.*

b *don spyi, arthasāmānya.*

elaborates. His innovation, based on understanding the difficulty of explicating such a serial realization, indicates the dynamic creativity present among communities of Tibetan scholars.

Though undoubtedly not the final word on the topic, Ken-sur Ye-s̄hay-tup-d̄en's explanation is provocative and helpful, illustrating the danger of limiting the study of Buddhism in general and Tibetan Buddhism in particular to texts. It testifies to the importance of taking advantage of opportunities to consult oral traditions, available to those interested in Tibetan culture due to the diaspora that began in 1959.

20. Does Asaṅga Associate the Two Types of Emptiness?

Now that we have considered explanations—of Ḏzong-ka-ḇa's pregnant but cryptic linking of these two topics—that were formulated by his followers over a period of five centuries, let us return to *The Essence of Eloquence* for his wrap-up of the topic.

Having presented the manner of entry into cognition-only through the four thorough examinations and the four thorough knowledges, he proceeds to consider peripherally related objections concerning self-cognizing consciousnesses (*Emptiness in Mind-Only,* 214-217) and the appearance to non-conceptual consciousnesses of being referents of names and conceptual consciousnesses (*Emptiness in Mind-Only,* 217). He demonstrates that the false appearance of phenomena as if established by way of their own character as the referents of conceptual consciousnesses does not appear to self-cognizing consciousnesses and that even though blue's being the referent of a conceptual consciousness is only posited through the force of conceptuality, it nevertheless appears to an eye consciousness devoid of conceptuality. As these points are not directly related to our present topic, I will pass on to his conclusion (*Emptiness in Mind-Only,* 217), in which he shows, through a multifaceted argument, that the emptiness of such an imputational nature implies an absence of external objects:

> Therefore, it is also not that a negation of an otherness of substantial entity between apprehended-object and apprehending-subject is absent in the statements in the *Sūtra Unraveling the Thought* that the emptiness of imputational factors imputed in the manner of entities and attributes is the thoroughly established nature.

If we drop the double negative, his meaning is that even when the *Sūtra Unraveling the Thought* explicitly speaks only of the emptiness of the imputational nature, these very statements contain a refutation of subject and object as different entities. He (*Emptiness in Mind-Only,* 217) adds:

> ...in that sūtra on the occasion of [discussing] calm abiding [in the "Questions of Maitreya Chapter"], a refutation of external objects is clearly set forth.[a]

Not only is an emptiness of difference of entity between subject and object **implicitly** set forth in the seventh chapter of the *Sūtra Unraveling the Thought,* the "Questions of Paramārthasamudgata," but also this type of emptiness is "clearly," or explicitly, set forth in the eighth, the "Questions of Maitreya."

---

[a] See *Absorption,* #52, 53.

Let us pursue Ḏzong-ka-ḇa's point by citing the passage in the "Questions of Maitreya Chapter" of the *Sūtra Unraveling the Thought* (as it is found in Asaṅga's *Summary of the Great Vehicle*),[a] but first let us place the topic in the context of other related points in *The Essence of Eloquence.* Ḏzong-ka-ḇa's remark harks back to an earlier discussion in which he speaks of this passage in the *Sūtra Unraveling the Thought* as being cited in Asaṅga's *Summary of the Great Vehicle.* He (*Emptiness in Mind-Only,* 156-157) refers to:

> ...the proof of no external objects in Asaṅga's *Summary of the Great Vehicle*—that is made within citing the *Sūtra Unraveling the Thought*—and thereupon the explanation of external and internal objects and subjects [which are different substantial entities] as imputational factors.

He does not quote the actual passage in Asaṅga's *Summary of the Great Vehicle,* but, as will be seen below, it is easy to locate. We need also to recall Ḏzong-ka-ḇa's statement (*Emptiness in Mind-Only,* 200-201) that Asaṅga's *Summary of the Great Vehicle* associates the two types of emptiness:

> In Asaṅga's *Grounds of Bodhisattvas,* this mode of emptiness [set forth in the *Sūtra Unraveling the Thought*] is explained as the object observed by the exalted wisdom purifying the obstructions to omniscience and as the middle path abandoning the two extremes of which there is none higher, and his *Summary of the Great Vehicle* says that entry by way of this [mode of emptiness] is entry into cognition-only.

The hinge of Ḏzong-ka-ḇa's point that Asaṅga's *Summary of the Great Vehicle* associates the two types of emptiness is not the mere fact that Asaṅga uses the term "cognition-only" but that the *Summary of the Great Vehicle* clearly explains that this term means no external objects, as will be detailed below. For Ḏzong-ka-ḇa, textual evidence shows that it means mind-only and not "representation-only," if the latter necessitates that external objects cast a representation to the perceiving consciousness.[b]

The reason why he emphasizes the teaching of no external objects in Asaṅga's *Summary of the Great Vehicle* is that the "Chapter on Suchness" in Asaṅga's *Grounds of Bodhisattvas* does not speak of a lack of externality—an astounding omission if there is a continuity of view between the two texts. Ḏzong-ka-ḇa, however, relies on a linguistic analysis of similar vocabulary in the two texts—the threefold reasoning, the four thorough examinations, and

---

a I cite the sūtra "as it is found in Asaṅga's *Summary of the Great Vehicle*" because I wish to establish that external objects are refuted in Asaṅga's *Summary.* Since I hold that it can be shown that the sūtra obviously refutes external objects, Asaṅga's citation of the passage is most pertinent. Also, his version differs, as will be seen, from that in the Peking edition.

b An entirely different meaning of "representation-only" could be that objects are representations of consciousness itself.

the four thorough knowledges—to show the consonance of view between the *Grounds of Bodhisattvas* and the *Summary of the Great Vehicle* and thus the necessity to read into the former the teaching of no external objects found in the latter.

In a later comment at the end of this section in *The Essence of Eloquence* (*Emptiness in Mind-Only,* 219), he makes the point that Asaṅga consistently propounds in three works that realization of cognition-only, which Ḏzong-ka-ḇa takes to mean an emptiness of external objects, is entered by way of realizing the emptiness of factors imputed in the manner of entity and attributes:

> The setting out of the four examinations and the four thorough knowledges in Asaṅga's *Grounds of Bodhisattvas, Summary of the Great Vehicle, Summary of Manifest Knowledge,* and so forth are said to be the excellent door of entry to cognition-only—the means of settling the view of cognition—[and also] the antidote to the obstructions to omniscience [which consist of] the conceptuality that serves as the basis of even the afflictive emotions.

He (*Emptiness in Mind-Only,* 219) finishes his presentation by emphasizing its importance:

> To understand the meaning of these, it appears to be necessary to understand from the level of subtle detail the reasonings refuting the imputational factor and the superimposition that are objects of negation discussed in the *Sūtra Unraveling the Thought.* In particular, it appears to be necessary to know how through those reasonings an otherness of substantial entity of apprehended-object and apprehending-subject is refuted, whereupon there is entry into cognition-only. Having seen that [many] nevertheless have not even involved themselves in analyzing these, [I] have indicated a mere door of analysis for the intelligent.

It is not sufficient merely to study the absence of external objects, for that understanding will be deepened by realizing the emptiness of imputation in the manner of entity and attribute and how it comes to refute external objects.

From these statements it is clear that, for Ḏzong-ka-ḇa, Asaṅga's *Summary of the Great Vehicle* is the source forcing association of these two types of emptiness. Since he only mentions these texts and does not actually cite the relevant passages, let us turn to the passages in Asaṅga's texts to which he is referring.

Ḏzong-ka-ḇa's References

Let us first cite the passages in Asaṅga's *Summary of the Great Vehicle* to which Ḏzong-ka-ḇa (*Emptiness in Mind-Only,* 156) refers when he speaks of:

> ...the proof of no external objects in Asaṅga's *Summary of the Great Vehicle*—that is made within citing the *Sūtra Unraveling the*

> *Thought*—and thereupon the explanation of external and internal objects and subjects [which are different substantial entities] as imputational factors.

The second chapter of Asaṅga's *Summary of the Great Vehicle,* entitled "The Character of Objects of Knowledge,"[a] begins with a discussion of the three characters[b]—the other-powered character,[c] the imputational character,[d] and the thoroughly established character.[e] Under the heading of the other-powered character, it lists fifteen "cognitions,"[f] which are categories of phenomena, and later identifies the phenomena included in each category. Asaṅga says:[403]

> Moreover, what are they? Cognitions of the body [the five senses], cognitions of the embodied [the afflicted mentality], cognitions of the enjoyer [the mind constituent, that is, the mental consciousness], cognitions of what is used by those [the six objects—forms, sounds, odors, tastes, tangible objects, and phenomena], cognitions making use of those [the six consciousnesses], cognitions of time, cognitions of enumeration [numbering], cognitions of location [the world of the environment], cognitions of conventions [the four conventions—the seen, the heard, the known, and the understood], cognitions of the specifics of self and others [perceptions of self and other], cognitions of good transmigrations [humans and gods], cognitions of bad transmigrations [animals, hungry ghosts, and hell-beings], cognitions of death, and cognitions of birth. Concerning this, those that are the cognitions of body, the embodied, and the enjoyer as well as that which is cognition of what is used by those, that which is cognition making use of those, and those which are the cognitions of time, enumeration, location, and conventions arise from predisposing seeds [infused by] verbalization. Those that are the cognitions of the specifics of self and others arise from predisposing seeds [infused by] the view of self. Those that are the cognitions of the good transmigrations, bad transmigrations, death, and birth arise from predisposing seeds [infused by] the branches of cyclic existence.

In list form, the fifteen are:[404]

1. Cognitions of the body: the five sense powers
2. Cognitions of the embodied: the afflicted mentality

---

[a] *shes bya'i mtshan nyid, jñeyalakṣaṇa.*
[b] *mtshan nyid gsum, trilakṣaṇa.*
[c] *gzhan dbang gi mtshan nyid, paratantralakṣaṇa.*
[d] *kun btags kyi mtshan nyid, parikalpitalakṣaṇa.*
[e] *yongs grub kyi mtshan nyid, pariniṣpannalakṣaṇa.*
[f] *rnam rig, vijñapti.*

3. Cognitions of the enjoyer: the mind constituent, that is, the mental consciousness
4. Cognitions of what is used by those: the six objects
5. Cognitions of what uses those: the six consciousnesses
6. Cognitions of time: the continuity of cyclic existence
7. Cognitions of enumeration: numbering
8. Cognitions of location: the world of the environment
9. Cognitions of conventions: the four conventions—the seen,[a] the heard,[b] the known,[c] and the understood[d]
10. & 11. Cognitions of the specifics of self and others: perceptions of self and other
12. Cognitions of good transmigrations: humans and gods
13. Cognitions of bad transmigrations: animals, hungry ghosts, and hell-beings
14. Cognitions of death
15. Cognitions of birth.

Asaṅga[e] identifies that:

- The first nine arise from latent predispositions of verbalization, also called predispositions of verbal repetition,[f] these being predispositions that cause generation of conceptual consciousnesses designating various conventions.[405]
- The tenth and the eleventh arise from latent predispositions of the view of self, also called predispositions of the view of the transitory collection,[g] these being predispositions that cause generation of an awareness in which the afflicted intellect views the mind-basis-of-all and thinks, "I."
- The twelfth through the fifteenth arise from latent predispositions of the causal branches of existence, also called predispositions of maturation,[h] these being predispositions that generate effects of maturation in the form of an entire lifetime, such as the sense-spheres of happy transmigrations and of bad transmigrations.

These fifteen cognitions include all other-powered natures, impermanent phenomena produced in dependence upon the power of other causes and conditions, specifically these latent predispositions, as well as uncompounded phenomena.[406] This provides an account of **how** the appearances of objects occur—

---

a *dṛṣṭa.*
b *śruta.*
c *vijñāta.*
d *mata.*
e For a discussion of the three, or four, types of predispositions, see p. 219ff.
f *zlos pa'i bag chags.*
g *'jig tshogs la lta ba'i bag chags.*
h *rnam smin gyi bag chags.*

that is, through activation of seeds of perception deposited in consciousness from earlier (and therefore beginningless) perceptions.[a]

Asaṅga proceeds to identify that the imputational character is the appearance of those mere-cognitions as just (external) objects and then that the thoroughly established character is just the utter non-existence of the character of being (external) objects in other-powered characters.[407] That Asaṅga is speaking about the absence of **external** objects, and not objects in general, is clear from a question that he poses and his answer to it:[408]

> What examples are there for these cognitions' being called "cognition-only" due to there being no objects? One is to view dreams and so forth as examples.

Dreams are commonly known to lack actual external objects, and thus Asaṅga uses dreams as examples for these categories of phenomena being "cognition-only." He continues:

> For example, in dreams, without there being any objects, just consciousness itself appears in the aspects of various objects—forms, sounds, odors, tastes, tangible objects, houses, forests, ground, mountains, and so forth. Through this example everything is also to be understood as just cognition-only. Through "and so forth" [in the statement above that one is to view dreams **and so forth** as examples] a magician's illusions, mirages, and objects seen by those with eye disease are to be known as examples.

Asaṅga clearly says that the objectlessness of dreams is to be carried over to all situations: "Through this example everything is also to be understood as just cognition-only."

Later in the same chapter in the *Summary of the Great Vehicle* when Asaṅga speaks about the usage of a magician's illusions and so forth as examples for other-powered natures, he says that these are used to show how, without an object, a consciousness nevertheless is still produced:[409]

> Why are other-powered entities indicated as like [a magician's] illusions as mentioned before? In order to overcome others' erroneous doubts with respect to other-powered entities.
>
> How do others have erroneous doubts with regard to other-powered entities? It is thus: In order to overcome the doubt of others wondering how a non-existent could serve as an object of activity [of consciousness], other-powered entities are taught as just like [a magician's] illusions. In order to overcome doubt wondering how minds and mental factors arise without objects, other-powered entities are

[a] For a discussion of how these types of predispositions function in a theory of perception, see 217ff.

> taught as just like mirages. In order to overcome doubt wondering how, if there are no objects, one gets involved in activities of desire and non-desire, other-powered entities are taught as just like dreams. In order to overcome doubt wondering how, if there are no objects, one could accomplish the wanted effects of virtuous actions and the unwanted effects of non-virtuous actions, other-powered entities are taught as just like reflections. In order to overcome doubt wondering how, if there are no objects, the varieties of consciousness arise, other-powered entities are taught as just like hallucinations. In order to overcome doubt wondering how, if there are no objects, the varieties of expressions arise, other-powered entities are taught as just like echoes. In order to overcome doubt wondering how, if there are no objects, the objects of activities of correctly apprehensive meditative stabilization arise, other-powered entities are taught as just like a moon [reflected in] water. In order to overcome doubt wondering how, if there are no objects, Bodhisattvas whose minds are not distorted[a] are born in accordance with their thought to accomplish the aims of sentient beings, other-powered entities are taught as just like emanations.

Asaṅga exemplifies how, in general, consciousness, afflictive emotions, cause and effect of karma, verbalization, meditative stabilization, and so forth can occur without external objects.

Furthermore, that, for Asaṅga, "cognition-only," meaning a lack of external objects, is to be applied to all phenomena is clear in a question and answer that immediately follows the earlier passage. There, Asaṅga extends the dream analogy to the waking state:[410]

> *Question:* If, like dreams and so forth, the waking state also is reduced to just cognition-only in all respects, then just as, for example, with respect to dreams an awareness that a dream is just cognition-only arises, why does such not arise here [with respect to the waking state]?
>
> *Answer:* It does arise for those who have been awakened through knowledge of suchness. Just as, for example, this awareness [that a dream is just cognition-only] does not [usually] arise in a dream,[b]

---

[a] In the Peking edition (225.1.4) read *byang chub sems dpa' sems phyin ci* ***ma*** *log pa rnams* for *byang chub sems dpa' sems phyin ci log pa rnams* in accordance with Lamotte, *La Somme,* vol. 1, 38.

[b] The translation of this sentence follows the edition of Lamotte, *La Somme,* vol. 1, 26; see his n. 6.1. His edition reads: *dper na rmi lam la blo 'di mi 'byung gi sad pa la 'byung ba de bzhin du,* whereas the Peking edition reads *dper ni* [sic] *rmi lam gyi zhing ma sad pa la 'byung ba de bzhin du* and so forth. The Peking edition, also acceptable but not so straightforward, would be rendered, "Just as, for example, a dream land arises for the unawakened, [awareness of cognition-only] does not arise for those unawakened through knowledge of suchness but

> [awareness of cognition-only] does not arise for those who are not awakened through knowledge of suchness but does arise for those awakened through knowledge of suchness.

Asaṅga says that when persons know the suchness of phenomena, they view all that appears as cognition-only. He explains the usual absence of such understanding as due to lack of knowing suchness.

Asaṅga next raises the question of how those who do not know reality can infer it. In answer, he cites scripture and reasoning. For the first, he refers to a passage in the *Sūtra Unraveling the Thought* in the eighth chapter, the "Questions of Maitreya," at the point of discussing the one-pointed meditative state of calm abiding, this being the passage to which Ḏzong-ka-ḇa (*Emptiness in Mind-Only,* 217) refers when he says:

> ...in that sūtra on the occasion of [discussing] calm abiding [in the "Questions of Maitreya Chapter"], a refutation of external objects is clearly set forth.

Specifically, Maitreya asks Buddha whether a meditative object is the same entity as the mind or a different entity from it. Buddha's response is that it is not different and that, in fact, objects of observation[a] of consciousness, in general, are not different entities from consciousness. Asaṅga says:[411]

> How are those who are not awakened through knowledge of suchness to infer [that everything is] just cognition-only? It is to be inferred through scripture and reasoning. Concerning this, scriptures are, for instance, the statement by the Supramundane Victor in the *[Sūtra] on the Ten Grounds,*[412] "These three realms are mind-only," and the statement by the Supramundane Victor in the *Sūtra Unraveling the Thought* upon being questioned by the Bodhisattva Maitreya:[413]
>
> > "Supramundane Victor, is the image that is the object of activity of meditative stabilization different from the mind or not different?"
> >
> > The Supramundane Victor spoke, "Maitreya, it is said to be not different. Why? I explain that consciousness is distinguished by [the fact that its] object of observation[b] is just cognition-only."
> >
> > "Supramundane Victor, if the image that is the object of activity of meditative stabilization is not different from the mind, how does the mind itself apprehend the mind itself?"
> >
> > "Maitreya, although no phenomenon apprehends any

does arise for those awakened through knowledge of suchness."

a *dmigs pa, ālambana.*

b *dmigs pa, ālambana.*

> phenomenon, the mind which is generated that way appears as such. For example, with form acting as a condition, form itself is seen [in a mirror], but one thinks, 'I see an image.' In that, the form and the appearance of the image appear as different factualities.[a] Likewise, the mind generated in that way also appears to be a different factuality from that."[b]

These scriptures also indicate a reasoning as follows. When the mind is set in equipoise, whatever images of objects of knowledge—foulness and so forth—are seen as [cases of] seeing the mind; the foulness and so forth do not exist as other factualities. Through this reasoning it is suitable for a Bodhisattva to infer that all cognitions [that is, all fifteen categories of phenomena given above] are just cognition-only.

Buddha extends the discussion to consciousness **in general** and does not just limit it to consciousness in meditation. Also, Asaṅga takes Buddha's other statements specifically about a consciousness of meditation as "reasoning" for settling that all fifteen cognitions, or categories of existents, are cognition-only. Hence, the obvious intention is to make an extension of something that is true in the meditative situation to all conscious experience.

Asaṅga (as cited above) even calls this "seeing the mind"; specifically, he says that meditative images, such as of the foulness of the body when meditating in order to overcome lust, do not exist as other factualities, and then he calls for extending this reasoning to all existents: "Through this reasoning it is

---

[a] *don tha dad pa.*

[b] With respect to the rendition of the example, the Peking edition of the *Sūtra Unraveling the Thought* (Peking 774, vol. 29, 14.1.3-14.1.7) differs considerably from the Peking edition of Asaṅga's citation of the sūtra; therefore, let us cite it, along with an additional question and answer from the sūtra that, even though not cited by Asaṅga, confirms the points made above (for Lamotte's remarks on the difference in texts, see *La Somme,* vol. 1, 27):

> "Maitreya, it is thus: For example, although form itself is seen in a very clean mirror in dependence upon a form, one thinks, 'I see an image.' In that, the form and the appearance of the image appear as different factualities. Likewise, the mind generated in that way and the object of activity of meditative stabilization called an image also appear to be different factualities."
>
> "Supramundane Victor, are the appearances of forms and so forth of sentient beings, which abide in the nature of images of the mind, not different from the mind?"
>
> He said, "Maitreya, they are said to be not different. With respect to those images, childish beings with distorted awareness do not know cognition-only just as it is in reality, due to which they consider [them] wrongly."

In this version, the progression of first establishing the sameness of entity of subject and object in meditative situations and then extending this understanding to all appearances of forms and so forth is even clearer.

suitable for a Bodhisattva to infer that all cognitions are just cognition-only." Therefore, it is clear that in the second chapter of the *Summary of the Great Vehicle,* Asaṅga is speaking of the absence of external objects, cognition-only, which in Ge-luk-b̄a vocabulary is called a non-difference of entity between subject and object.

These passages in Asaṅga's *Summary of the Great Vehicle* that set forth a doctrine of no external objects are undoubtedly those to which D̄zong-ka-b̄a (*Emptiness in Mind-Only,* 156-157) refers when he speaks of:

> ...the proof of no external objects in Asaṅga's *Summary of the Great Vehicle*—that is made within citing the *Sūtra Unraveling the Thought*—and thereupon the explanation of external and internal objects and subjects [which are different substantial entities] as imputational factors.

Later in the same chapter[414] of the *Summary of the Great Vehicle,* Asaṅga sets forth the triple reasoning[a] refuting that objects are established in accordance with such an imputational nature. In the third chapter, entitled "Entry Into the Character of Objects of Knowledge,"[b] he describes the four thorough examinations and four thorough knowledges, at the conclusion of which he says:[415]

> Therefore, when they apprehend these as just exhausted as only mental verbalization and when they do not apprehend meanings together with names involving imputation in the manner of entities and attributes nor [anything][416] involving [imputation] in the manner of entity and attribute as having a factual character, [they attain] the four thorough examinations and the four thorough knowledges just as they are in reality. Through these, they enter into cognition-only concerning those mental conceptual consciousnesses to which letters and meanings appear.

This passage is undoubtedly D̄zong-ka-b̄a's reference when he (*Emptiness in Mind-Only,* 200) says:

> ...and his *Summary of the Great Vehicle* says that entry by way of this [mode of emptiness] is entry into cognition-only.

By identifying D̄zong-ka-b̄a's references, we have seen that his brief and seemingly cryptic argument is a result of considerable textual analysis of Indian sources.

Summation

The fulcrum of D̄zong-ka-b̄a's argument is that the threefold reasoning, the

---

a See pp. 401ff. and 466ff.

b *shes bya'i mtshan nyid la 'jug pa, jñeyalakṣaṇapraveśa.*

four thorough examinations, and the four thorough knowledges that Asaṅga describes in the "Chapter on Suchness" in the *Grounds of Bodhisattvas* are in harmony with the presentation of these in his *Summary of the Great Vehicle.* From this, he concludes that, since the latter manifestly involves a proof of no external objects, the former must also, even though such explicit vocabulary is lacking.

As detailed above, there is solid textual support for Ḏzong-ka-ḇa's conclusion that the two types of emptinesses are intimately related in Asaṅga's *Summary of the Great Vehicle* itself. His further point that this emptiness of externality holds also for the *Grounds of Bodhisattvas* is founded on a linguistic analysis of similarities between the two texts—both have similar presentations of the threefold reasoning, the four thorough examinations, and the four thorough knowledges. Based on such consonance between the two texts and on the fact that the *Summary of the Great Vehicle* views these sets of doctrines as providing entry into cognition-only which it explicitly associates with refuting external objects, he concludes that the *Grounds of Bodhisattvas* should also be read as refuting external objects. Ḏzong-ka-ḇa himself only gives a skeletal outline of the textual support, but we have easily located the relevant passages. At minimum, he has established well that, at least in his *Summary of the Great Vehicle* Asaṅga, the foremost proponent of the early Yogic Practice School, holds a view of mind-only, meaning no external objects.

More questionable is Ḏzong-ka-ḇa's treatment of Asaṅga's presentation of emptiness in his *Grounds of Bodhisattvas* in the light of his presentation in the *Summary of the Great Vehicle.* He sees a harmonious relationship between the emptiness of external objects and the emptiness of imputation in the manner of entity and attribute even in Asaṅga's *Grounds of Bodhisattvas,* where the former type is not even mentioned. He justifies this association of the two texts through noticing the parallelism of basic vocabulary, and Tibetan scholars such as Ke-drup, the Second Dalai Lama, Paṇ-chen S̄ö-nam-drak-ḇa, and Jam-ȳang-shay-ḇa explicate reasons behind the harmonious connection. The exposition of the **reasons behind** the intimate connection between the two types of emptiness is a Tibetan development continuing to the present, as exemplified by Ken-sur Ye-s̄hay-tup-ḏen's interpretation that emphasizes the bifurcation of namer and named, and thus subject and object.

The assertion itself of a connection between the two types of emptiness is clearly evident in a textual analysis of Asaṅga's *Summary of the Great Vehicle* and is not a later development, but the question of whether Ḏzong-ka-ḇa's extension of this perspective to the *Grounds of Bodhisattvas* is justified remains. To highlight this issue, let us turn to the analyses of the relationship between these two texts by Lambert Schmithausen and Janice Dean Willis, who have presented the opinion that in the early Yogic Practice School mind-only, meaning no external objects or a lack of difference of entity between subject and object, is not taught. Based on historical and linguistic analysis, Schmithausen nuances and Willis disagrees with how later adherents to the Yogic Practice School and Proponents of the Middle as well as major French scholars, such as Étienne Lamotte, Sylvain Lévi, Louis de la Vallée Poussin, and so forth, read the works attributed to Asaṅga, Vasubandhu, and Sthiramati. They thereby present a different view of the early Yogic Practice School.

21. Nominalism in the *Grounds of Bodhisattvas*

At first reading, Ḏzong-ka-ḇa's interpretation of the view of emptiness in the *Grounds of Bodhisattvas* seems to differ sharply from that of Lambert Schmithausen,[417] but there may be a way of bringing the two explanations together despite their differences. Let us first present Schmithausen's view.

According to Schmithausen, the idealistic philosophy of the later Yogic Practice School and its basic terms, *vijñaptimātra* (cognition-only) and *cittamātra* (mind-only), are not yet traceable in the *Grounds of Yogic Practice*,[a] which is attributed by the tradition to Asaṅga but, according to him, is actually a compilation of earlier teachings. Rather, some portions of the *Grounds of Yogic Practice*—especially the *Grounds of Bodhisattvas*—as well as the *Compendium of Ascertainments*[b] evince a kind of nominalistic philosophy according to which finite entities are mere denominations.[c] According to Schmithausen, this is a stage preparing the way for the idealism of the Yogic Practice School, but not yet itself idealism. He says:[418]

> As I have tried to prove in another article, the oldest materials of the Yogācāra school have been collected in the voluminous *Yogācārabhūmi*. In this text, as far as I can see, the idealistic-spiritualistic philosophy of the later Yogācāras and its characteristic terms, *vijñaptimātra* and *cittamātra*, are not yet traceable....In most of its parts, the *Yogācārabhūmi* obviously presupposes the realistic ontology of the traditional schools of Hīnayāna Buddhism which merely deny the existence of a substantial Self (*ātman*) whereas the reality of insubstantial entities (*dharma*), mental *as well as material ones*, is not questioned. There are, however, some portions of the *Yogācārabhūmi*—especially the chapters *Bodhisattvabhūmi* and *Bodhisattvabhūmiviniścaya*—where we meet with a kind of nominalistic philosophy according to which finite entities are mere denominations (*prajñaptimātra*)....They may be stages preparing Yogācāra idealism, but they are not yet idealism itself.

Schmithausen sees a transitional movement from this nominalism to complete idealism in a passage concerned solely with meditative objects in the *Grounds of Hearers*[d] chapter of the *Grounds of Yogic Practice*. The **full** transition to idealism is effected in the eighth chapter of the *Sūtra Unraveling the Thought* in the passage first about meditative objects and then objects in general (see p. 440) where a full-blown idealism, generalized from the practice situation, is presented. Schmithausen sees the *Sūtra Unraveling the Thought* (especially the

a *rnal sbyor spyod pa'i sa, yogācārabhūmi;* Peking 5536-5538, vols. 109-110.

b *gtan la dbab pa sdu ba, viniścayasaṃgrahaṇī;* Peking 5539, vols. 110-111.

c *btags pa tsam, prajñaptimātra.*

d *nyan thos kyi sa, śrāvakabhūmi;* Peking 5537, vol. 110.

eighth chapter) as being completed after a pre-Asaṅga version of the *Grounds of Yogic Practice.*[a] He says:[419]

> However, in the *Śrāvakabhūmi* chapter the *Yogācārabhūmi* quotes an unknown Sūtra in which the purely *ideal* character of the object visualized by the meditating Yogin—for example repulsive things like decaying corpses—is at least seen as one possibility....It is, however, quite obvious that our text, by considering the possibility that *some* objects (viz., those perceived in visionary meditation) do not possess any reality apart from the subject's perception or visualizing recollection, does *not* yet propound universal idealism. The reality of *ordinary* objects is not called in question.
>
> This is different in the case of the *Saṃdhinirmocanasūtra* [that is, the *Sūtra Unraveling the Thought*] which seems to be the oldest, at least the oldest extant, Yogācāra text that clearly expresses universal idealism. The *Saṃdhinirmocanasūtra* is obviously earlier than the Yogācāra treatises ascribed to "Maitreya-(nātha)" and Asaṅga. It must have been completed even before the completion or final redaction of the *Yogācārabhūmi.* But it contains many materials which clearly represent a later stage of development than most parts of the

---

[a] See also Lambert Schmithausen, *Ālayavijñāna: On the Origin and the Early Development of a Central Concept of Yogācāra Philosophy,* Studia Philologica Buddhica Monograph Series IVa (Tokyo: International Institute for Buddhist Studies, 1987), Part I, 12-13. There he says:

> The *Saṃdhinirmocanasūtra* seems rather to presuppose some of the peculiar concepts and doctrines of the *Basic Section* of the *Yogācārabhūmi*....Therefore, the *Saṃdhinirmocanasūtra,* at least the portions concerned with the new kind of *vijñāna* distinguished from the ordinary six, was most probably composed before the *Viniścayasaṃgrahaṇī* but after the *Basic Section* of the *Yogācārabhūmi.*

That even within a traditional account there could be a pre-Asaṅga version of the *Grounds of Yogic Practice* is suggested by Bu-dön's (*bu ston*) relating that Asaṅga heard this treatise during his magical visit to Maitreya's heaven; see E. Obermiller, *History of Buddhism (Chos-ḥbyung) by Bu-ston* (Heidelberg: Heft, 1932; Tokyo: Suzuki Research Foundation, n.d.), 139. Bu-dön also says, on the next page, that Asaṅga composed the work upon his return to this world. The sequence suggests Asaṅga's revision of an already existent work.

In agreement with the order of a list of Asaṅga's works in Tāranātha's history (Lama Chimpa and Alaka Chattopadhyaya, *Tāranātha's History of Buddhism in India* [Simla, India: Indian Institute of Advanced Study, 1970; reprint, Delhi: Motilal Banarsidass, 1990], 160-161), Janice D. Willis (*On Knowing Reality: The Tattvārtha Chapter of Asaṅga's Bodhisattvabhūmi* [New York: Columbia University Press, 1979; reprint, Delhi: Motilal Banarsidass, 1982], 10) speaks of Asaṅga's composition of the *Grounds of Yogic Practice* after the *Summary of Manifest Knowledge* and the *Summary of the Great Vehicle* but notes (*On Knowing Reality,* 53 n. 43) that the *Summary of Manifest Knowledge* is "said to be an abridgment of the first two sections of the *Yogācārabhūmi.*" This contrary evidence is found in Bu-dön (Obermiller, *History of Buddhism,* 140), whose chronology seems more likely.

> *Yogācārabhūmi,* esp. than the *Bodhisattvabhūmi* and the *Śrāvakabhūmi.* This is especially true for the eighth chapter of the *Saṃdhinirmocana-sūtra* in which the question is raised whether the images which are the objects of meditation (*samādhigocarapratibimba*) are different from the mind (*citta*) or not. The answer is that they are *not* different from the mind because they are nothing but cognition (*vijñaptimātra*)....the mind is characterized by [the fact that its] object is nothing but cognition, that its object has no existence apart from the subjective act or event of cognition. Thus, the *Saṃdhinirmocanasūtra* seems to be the first text to use, in an idealistic sense, the expression *vijñaptimātra* which was to become the most used and most typical term of Yogācāra idealism.
>
> Moreover, already in the *Saṃdhinirmocanasūtra* the use of the term is not limited to objects of meditation. Like the Abhidharmic theory of which it seems to be a transformation, the statement that mind (*vijñāna*) is characterized by the fact that its object is nothing but cognition contains no restriction. Accordingly, the following paragraph of the text raises the question whether the statement is valid also for *ordinary* objects. This question is answered in the affirmative: even the ordinary objects are not different from the mind, are nothing but cognition (*vijñaptimātra*).

As Schmithausen says, in this passage in the *Sūtra Unraveling the Thought,* the statement that mind (*vijñāna*) is characterized by the fact that its object is nothing but cognition contains no restriction; it applies to all consciousnesses and their objects of apprehension. As I also did in my analysis given earlier, he places that statement in the additional context of the question about whether such is true of ordinary objects, the answer being that it is.

Janice D. Willis, on the other hand, attempts to explain away the extension of idealism to ordinary objects by showing that this is a generalization from meditative practice and thus not philosophically reliable. In her doctoral dissertation, Willis, based on the writings of Ueda, Schmithausen, and Wayman, presents an analysis of and translation of the "Chapter on Suchness" in Asaṅga's *Grounds of Bodhisattvas.* The basic position in Willis's *On Knowing Reality* is that, in order to avoid mis-identifying Asaṅga and his half brother Vasubandhu as setting forth a doctrine denying the existence of external objects, we must discern two periods of development in the Yogic Practice School—an earlier non-idealist one associated with Maitreya, Asaṅga, Vasubandhu, and Sthiramati and a later idealist one associated with Dharmapāla and so forth. Willis says:[420]

> Assessments which claim to characterize the whole of Yogācāra thought as being uniformly "idealistic" take little notice of the fact that historically—and according to the texts themselves—there existed at least two varying streams of Yogācāra thought, viz., (1) what may be

> called an "original" thread propounded by Maitreya, Asaṅga, Vasubandhu, and Sthiramati; and (2) a "later" thread which found expression notably through such doctors as Dharmapāla and Hsüan-tsang.[a]

The reason behind the not merely temporal but ideological division is that significant usage of key idealist vocabulary is not to be found in the works of the earlier proponents of the Yogic Practice School. She says:[421]

> My contention is that while later Yogācārins like Dharmapāla (6th century) employ key terms associated with the school in a way that seems to deny the existence of external entities altogether, the earliest doctors of the school—Asaṅga, Vasubandhu, and Sthiramati—do not.

From this perspective she renders the passage in question in the *Sūtra Unraveling the Thought* differently:[422]

> Maitreya asked: Lord, are those images cognized in meditation different from that mind (which cognizes them) or are they not different? The Lord answered: Maitreya, they are not different. And why? Because those images are nothing but conceptualization (*vijñaptimātra*). Maitreya, I have explained that the meditative object (*ālambana*) of consciousness (*vijñāna*) is comprised of (*prabhāvita*) nothing but conceptualization (*vijñaptimātra*).

Willis understands the passage as limited in meaning just to meditative images, translating *ālambana* (*dmigs pa*) as "meditative object," even though it usually means "object support," "object of observation," or "object" without a necessary connotation of "meditative."

In contrast to Willis's interpretation, Étienne Lamotte, translator of the *Mahāyānasaṃgraha* into French as *La Somme du grand véhicule d'Asaṅga,* renders the word in the general sense:[423]

> Maitreya demandait: "Bhagavat, les images (*pratibimba*) perdues en concentration (*samādhigocara*) sont-elles différentes (*bhinna*) ou non-différente de la pensée (*citta*) qui les perḍoit?"—Bhagavat repond: "Maitreya, elles ne sont pas differéntes de la pensée. Pourquoi? Parce que ces images ne sont rien qu'idée (*vijñaptimātra*). J'ai dit que l'object de la connaissance (*vijñānālambana*) est formé (*prabhāvita*) par une idée sans plus, [donce qu'il n'y a pas d'objet extérieur]."

Lamotte translates the term *vijñānālambana* at face value as "l'object de la connaissance" ("object of consciousness"), not limiting its meaning to meditative objects. Willis, on the other hand, based on her estimation that this passage is limited in its discussion to meditative objects, suggests that Asaṅga's citation of

[a] Willis's source here is Yoshifumi Ueda; see Appendix 2, p. 520ff.

the statement from the *Sūtra on the Ten Grounds,*[424] "These three realms [the realms of desire, corporeal matter, and immateriality] are nothing but mind" (brackets hers) (*cittamātram idaṃ yad idaṃ traidhātukaṃ*), is thereby put in context, that is, is also limited to the meditative or practical situation. Willis says:[425]

> It is significant that this quotation, focusing as it does on the nature of the *meditative image,* is found in Asaṅga's *Mahāyānasaṃgraha* immediately following another quotation there, namely, the famous phrase from the *Daśabhūmika* alluded to earlier. Clearly, for Asaṅga the terms *cittamātra* and *vijñaptimātra* function preeminently within discourses pertaining to actual meditative instruction and practice.

Schmithausen, however, does not dismiss the importance of the sūtra's extension of the idealist position to all objects; he says:[426]

> As we have seen, the *Saṃdhinirmocanasūtra* starts from the ideality of meditation-objects (which has already been articulated in the sūtra quoted in the *Śrāvakabhūmi*) and then simply extends this fact to ordinary objects, without justifying this procedure by any rational argument. Thus, the result of our reexamination of the oldest materials of the Yogācāra school clearly speaks in favour of the theory that Yogācāra idealism primarily resulted from a *generalization* of a fact observed in the case of meditation-objects, that is in the context of *spiritual practice.*

To explain the reason behind the generalization, Schmithausen points to the fact that in meditative equipoise the entire world of objects disappears, leaving only emptiness, and that idealism is more compatible with this experience than a realistic worldview:[427]

> Thus, the generalization of the ideality of meditation-objects into universal idealism was motivated by the urge of making more plausible the spiritual practice of eliminating all objective phenomena by supplying it with a corresponding metaphysical basis.

That Schmithausen, unlike Willis, does not back off of this generalization is clear from his statement that the generalization found in the *Sūtra Unraveling the Thought* constitutes a definite and final step in the progression to the idealist position:[428]

> Compared with this semi-realistic illusionism of the *Bodhisattvabhūmiviniścaya,* at least in the context of the metaphysical foundation of the spiritual practice described above, the frank idealism of the *Saṃdhinirmocanasūtra* constitutes a decisive advance.

He states that this theory of an extension of idealism from meditative, spiritual experience is a conclusion of his research:[429]

> ...the thesis of universal idealism originated from the *generalization* of a situation observed in the case of objects visualized in meditative concentration, that is, in the context of *spiritual practice.*

Schmithausen makes the important point that practical insights in meditation sometimes lead to metaphysical doctrines.

Similarly, he does not dismiss a statement of mind-only in the *Bhadrapālasūtra;* rather, he sees it as harmonious with what he calls "complete emptiness":[430]

> The reduction of objects to the mind is thus merely a preliminary step towards the intuition of complete Emptiness.

Even though Schmithausen says,[431] "This ideality of the meditation-images, however, has to be extended to *all* phenomena..." and explains that the extension was "motivated by the urge of making more plausible the spiritual practice of eliminating all objective phenomena by supplying it with a corresponding metaphysical basis,"[432] Willis, recognizing the demands of consistency with her basic position that Asaṅga did not hold a view of idealism (even in the sense that an object is of the same entity as the consciousness apprehending it),[a] disregards this extension. Her point here is not that "mind-only" refers merely to imagined objects of meditation; rather, she maintains that even though the texts, based on such meditative experience, extend this insight to all phenomena, the extension simply cannot be taken as a philosophical assertion. Willis notes at this point:[433]

> While the final paragraph of this quotation [from Schmithausen] shows that the *Bhadrapālasūtra* does go on to "extend" the notion of *cittamātra* to all phenomena, Schmithausen, 247, duly notes that its "thesis of universal idealism originated from the *generalization* of a situation observed in the case of objects visualized in meditative concentration, that is, in the context of *spiritual* practice."

Why a generalization stemming from insight gained in spiritual practice and extended to all phenomena must be disregarded is unclear. One would think that, in a spiritual system with a clear soteriological orientation dependent on meditation, such extensions would be highly regarded.

Schmithausen, on the other hand, sees a consonance between practice and philosophy. Giving a possible reason behind this movement to idealism, he points to the need for a fully consistent philosophical theory much like the Hīnayāna Abhidharma. He says:[434]

---

[a] For a short discussion of the compatibility of emptiness and idealism, see *Emptiness in Mind-Only,* 37-38.

> It was probably the influence of the Hīnayānistic heritage that induced the Yogācāras to transform the exceptional position that mind possessed in the context of *spiritual* practices into a positive ***ontological*** pre-eminence over the objects, and to rebuild, on this level of idealism, a detailed system fully equivalent to that of the Hīnayānistic Abhidharma.

Schmithausen sees a harmony between practical, meditational insight and the metaphysics of idealism in the Yogic Practice School, the former motivating the latter.

Schmithausen's point that texts proceed sometimes from philosophy to practice and sometimes from practice to philosophy is important. Often the fundamental appeal is made, not to philosophical correctness, but to a fact of practice, a fact of insight, after which this is used as a basis of logical or philosophical extension. This is not to say that insight from practice will not be seen as certified by logic and philosophy; rather, sometimes the **style** is to proceed from practical insight to larger ontological issues. Though logic also appeals to experience, here the appeal is to a special type of experience in meditation, thereby stressing the importance of practical insight. The frequently emphasized dedication to reason that is found in Buddhism in general and in texts of Ge-luk-b̄a scholasticism in particular should, therefore, not blind one to noticing that many appeals, even in Ge-luk-b̄a religious life, are made based on spiritual experience. That experience, like ordinary experience, can be used as a basis for logical extensions or generalizations. Schmithausen's point is extremely well taken.

Summary of the Great Vehicle. In this article, Schmithausen does not speak to the question of Asaṅga's view as presented in his *Summary of the Great Vehicle,* but since Asaṅga quotes the very passage in the *Sūtra Unraveling the Thought* that Schmithausen describes as teaching idealism, Schmithausen most likely would agree with D̄zong-ka-b̄a that Asaṅga—the chief proponent of the early Yogic Practice School—taught idealism at least in the *Summary of the Great Vehicle.* Indeed, that in Asaṅga's *Summary of the Great Vehicle* the meaning of "cognition-only" involves a non-difference of entity between subject and object can be established through examining the contents of the first three chapters of the *Summary of the Great Vehicle.* The first chapter, "The Support of Objects of Knowledge,"[a] is largely concerned with the mind-basis-of-all, which (as Willis admits)[435] is in the "'ontological psychological' model for explaining the bifurcation of apparent reality into a subject and an object." The chapter presents the nature, function, and so forth of the basis-of-all in its capacities as a consciousness and as the seeds that give rise to the appearances of

---

[a] *shes bya'i gnas, jñeyāśraya.* Lamotte translates this as "le support du connaissable" (*La Somme du grand véhicule d'Asaṅga,* reprint, 2 vols., Publications de l'Institute Orientaliste de Louvain 8 [Louvain: Université de Louvain, 1973], vol. 2, 12).

objects and consciousnesses knowing those objects. The second chapter then divides all knowables into fifteen categories (see p. 436) and proceeds to consider their nature, first through the *Sūtra on the Ten Grounds* and then the *Sūtra Unraveling the Thought* as discussed above, establishing mind-only in the sense of there being no objects, which can be understood to mean no external objects. When that section of the *Sūtra Unraveling the Thought* is examined, it is seen, as detailed above (p. 440ff.), that there is a deliberate extension from meditative objects to all objects. Given the explicit extension to the objects of the ordinary world, Willis's restriction of the meaning merely to meditative objects is unjustified. Also, the explicit mention in that passage in the *Sūtra Unraveling the Thought* that the mind sees the mind defies any other interpretation but that external objects are being refuted.

Also, later in the same chapter in the *Summary of the Great Vehicle,* when Asaṅga speaks about the usage of a magician's illusions and so forth as examples for other-powered natures, he says that these examples are used to show how without an object a consciousness nevertheless is still produced (see p. 438). Thus, the teaching of idealism in the *Summary of the Great Vehicle* is clear, and we can presume harmony between Ḏzong-ka-b̄a and Schmithausen with regard to it. However, Schmithausen would not accept Ḏzong-ka-b̄a's reasoning that, given the similarity of vocabulary between the *Grounds of Bodhisattvas* (which Schmithausen takes as attributed to Asaṅga but representing a compilation of earlier, non-homogeneous material) and Asaṅga's own *Summary of the Great Vehicle,* we should conclude that just as the latter text refutes external objects and establishes idealism, so does the *Grounds of Bodhisattvas.*

According to what I surmise to be Schmithausen's position, since the *Sūtra Unraveling the Thought* (especially the eighth chapter) was completed after the composition of the pre-Asaṅga version of the *Grounds of Bodhisattvas,* Asaṅga's citation—in his *Summary of the Great Vehicle*—of the passage in the eighth chapter of the *Sūtra Unraveling the Thought* that presents a full-blown idealism cannot be used retroactively to contextualize the thought of the "Chapter on Suchness" of the *Grounds of Bodhisattvas.* According to Schmithausen's speculative chronology, the *Sūtra Unraveling the Thought* took its final form **after** the composition (but not by Asaṅga) of the *Grounds of Bodhisattvas;* later still, Asaṅga composed the *Summary of the Great Vehicle.*[a]

Thus, for Schmithausen, Ḏzong-ka-b̄a's interpretation of the view of emptiness—as presented in the "Chapter on Suchness" in the *Grounds of Bodhisattvas*—in the light of the description of emptiness in Asaṅga's *Summary of the Great Vehicle* that explicitly speaks of mind-only and related topics, is unwarrantedly founded on an assumption of a lack of historical development. For him, Ḏzong-ka-b̄a would be making the mistaken presuppositions that sūtras were composed prior to treatises and that Asaṅga, with Maitreya in the background, was the author of the *Grounds of Bodhisattvas.*

[a] See p. 446, footnote a.

We can surmise that Schmithausen's interpretation is that the two texts—the first being the *Grounds of Bodhisattvas,* which was attributed to Asaṅga but was actually a pre-existent compilation foundational to his school, and the second being his own *Summary of the Great Vehicle*—represent a change of view. Whereas Ḏzong-ka-ḇa's procedure is philological in the sense of relying on similarities of vocabulary between the two texts, Schmithausen's is "a strictly *historico-philological method.*"[436] Schmithausen's emphasis on historical development of strata of material even within a text provides a more plausible explanation for the absence of the vocabulary of the lack of external objects in the "Chapter on Suchness" of the *Grounds of Bodhisattvas,* an astounding omission if there is a seamless connection between it and Asaṅga's *Summary of the Great Vehicle.*

Just as Ḏzong-ka-ḇa forges a consistency between the two texts by superimposing the view of the latter (Asaṅga's *Summary of the Great Vehicle*) on the former (the *Grounds of Bodhisattvas*), Willis also forges consistency between the two texts, but by superimposing the view of the former on the latter. Recognizing the demands for a consistent rendition, she rewrites the passage from the eighth chapter of the *Sūtra Unraveling the Thought* so that it does not teach idealism (despite Schmithausen's and Lamotte's reading as well as the demands of the context of both the sūtra and the first three chapters of the *Summary of the Great Vehicle*). Schmithausen, on the other hand, sees a historical progression from the assertion of a type of nominalism in the *Grounds of Bodhisattvas* to the assertion of idealism in the eighth chapter of the *Sūtra Unraveling the Thought,* but he certainly would not be swayed by Ḏzong-ka-ḇa's presentation of textual similarities between the *Grounds of Bodhisattvas* and Asaṅga's *Summary of the Great Vehicle* that tie these two together in a harmonious way.

Conceived this way, Ḏzong-ka-ḇa's exposition can be seen as detailing a certain harmony between Asaṅga's presentations of emptiness in the *Summary of the Great Vehicle* and in the final form of the *Grounds of Bodhisattvas.* Schmithausen's exposition, on the other hand, offers a perspective on possible evolution of positions in the *Grounds of Bodhisattvas* to those of the *Summary of the Great Vehicle.* Together, the two explanations offer a more rounded picture, since just as Ḏzong-ka-ḇa does not entertain even the notion of a historical development between the two texts or within the *Grounds of Bodhisattvas,* Schmithausen does not consider the possible continuity of view between the *Summary of the Great Vehicle* and the final form of the *Grounds of Bodhisattvas* to which Asaṅga's name was attached.[a] Seen this way, the interpretations of

[a] Schmithausen (*Ālayavijñāna,* 13) appears to be neutral on the question of whether Asaṅga was the compiler of the *Yogācārabhūmi.* Willis (*On Knowing Reality,* 3) notes that "the sage Dharmakṣema saw it proper to translate the *Bodhisattvabhūmi* into Chinese in 418 AD, very soon after its composition" and that thus it seems unlikely that a legend of authorship would have developed so quickly if Asaṅga had nothing to do with the text.

both Dzong-ka-ba and Schmithausen contribute to our understanding of the early Yogic Practice School.

Conclusion

The Ge-luk-ba order of Tibetan Buddhism, despite many sub-differences in exposition, uniformly puts forward a careful, textually based argument that the style of reasoning and the stages of realization in the "Chapter on Suchness" of Asaṅga's *Grounds of Bodhisattvas* resonate with similar presentations in Asaṅga's *Summary of the Great Vehicle*, where it can be seen that Asaṅga is refuting external objects. The argument, though presented in skeletal form, is seen to be carefully framed when its references and implications are supplied. It provides a framework for critical examination of current reassessments of the view of emptiness in the early Yogic Practice School in that it demonstrates clearly the mind-only character of Asaṅga's *Summary of the Great Vehicle* and thus of the early Yogic Practice School beginning with him. (As Schmithausen has shown, pre-Asaṅga is a different matter.)

However, it seems to me that the extension—by Dzong-ka-ba and his followers—of this position to what might be seen as older materials in the "Chapter on Suchness" of the *Grounds of Bodhisattvas* is forced, given the insuperable difficulties presented by that text's lack of discussion of the non-existence of external objects; also, Lambert Schmithausen has supplied a possible chronology that provides the framework for a historical development of a more nominalistic view in older materials of the *Grounds of Bodhisattvas* to a full-blown idealism in Asaṅga's *Summary of the Great Vehicle*. Dzong-ka-ba's pointing out the similarity of the vocabulary of the threefold reasoning, of the four thorough examinations, and of the four thorough knowledges in the two texts contributes greatly to understanding that there are continuities between the two texts and explains how Asaṅga's name could have been put to the final redaction of the *Grounds of Bodhisattvas*. However, it does not adequately explain the absence of key mind-only vocabulary in the *Grounds of Bodhisattvas*. This is more plausibly explained by viewing the *Grounds of Bodhisattvas* not as the work of a single author but as a compilation of materials pre-dating Asaṅga at which time a full-blown idealism had not yet developed. That Asaṅga could, without self-contradiction, put his name (or that the tradition could put his name) to the final version of the text despite the absence of the peculiarly mind-only vocabulary that is found in his *Summary of the Great Vehicle* may be explained by a wish not to revise too heavily an inherited text. Also, in his *Summary of the Great Vehicle*, Asaṅga may have been self-consciously seeking consistency with an earlier description of the view of emptiness by using much of its terminology but within a framework of explicitly introducing the notion of mind-only.

Though the model of historical development of a system or of a particular author's view within a single lifetime is not foreign to Tibetan scholarship, it does not provide the paradigm motivating the main thrust of scholastic activity. (The possibility that certain chapters of a sūtra were composed after others is simply not entertained, since the tradition holds that all true sūtras are the word of Shākyamuni Buddha.) Rather, in Tibetan scholarship as a whole and Ge-luk-b̄a in particular, comparison of systems on a philosophical level is the principal thrust, and thus grouping of views convenient to a comparative study of tenets can and does obscure historical developments. It strikes me that there is considerable benefit in juxtaposing D̄zong-ka-b̄a's linguistic-doctrinal perspective with Schmithausen's linguistic-historical perspective—both scholars sifting through linguistic clues, the former finding philosophical resonances between texts and the latter finding strata of material within and between texts. What emerges is a fuller picture of the early Yogic Practice School.

PART SIX: *UNDERMINING ERROR*

22. Reasoning against Illusion

Path

Emerging from the descriptions of the three natures teamed with the three non-natures and the descriptions of the paths of persons of the three capacities[a] is a perspective that beings are not familiar with their own nature and that training is required to overcome the obstacles preventing profound recognitions from being manifested. In Buddhist literature, the process of training is called the "path," the Sanskrit for which is *mārga;* it has many meanings:[437]

> way, road, path, course, passage, tract passed over; reach, range; scar, mark; path or course of a planet; search, inquiry, investigation; canal, channel, passage; means, way; right way or course, proper course; mode, manner, method, course; style, direction; custom, usage, practice...[b]

The goal-directed nature of many of these terms is reflected in the verbal root *mārg,* which means to seek, seek for; to hunt after, chase; to strive to attain, strive after; to solicit, beg, ask for; to ask in marriage; to seek through, to trace out; to go, and to move.[438]

In Ge-luk-b̄a colleges, the study of spiritual paths is supplemented by short texts called "grounds and paths,"[c] used to structure in a technical but more accessible format the complex presentations found in Indian texts, especially Maitreya's *Ornament for Clear Realization.* A straight reading of such a text can be an exercise in boredom, but with the oral commentary of a teacher who is versed in a lineage of exegesis, the technical vocabulary can come to life in a vivid realm of imagination much like a novel about a mythic land. As we have seen, such stimulation of the metaphysical imagination is at the heart of the process of study in this tradition. Whereas it may seem dry and sterile to those for whose minds the terminology has not been enlivened through evocative commentary, the same technical vocabulary—for those who have undergone this process—reverberates with meaning and epiphanies of new connections. Exploration of the elaborate architecture of the path itself becomes an important phase of the path, not to the exclusion of actually generating these path-states in meditation, but as an important part of creating a worldview that itself

---

[a] See p. 162ff.

[b] Also: hunting or tracing out game; a title or head in law, ground for litigation; high style of acting, dancing, and singing; hinting or indicating how anything is to happen; section; anus, musk; a certain month; and a name of viṣṇu.

[c] *sa lam;* for a translation of a text in this genre, see Jules Brooks Levinson, "The Metaphors of Liberation: A Study of Grounds and Paths according to the Middle Way Schools" (Ann Arbor, Mich.: University Microfilms, 1994).

exerts a transformative force on the mind. It also often serves as a substitute for meditative implementation, but, even in such a context, its power is not to be belittled just because its substitution for meditation contradicts the system's own dictum that meditation is the goal.

In Ḡön-chok-jik-may-w̄ang-b̄o's *Presentation of the Grounds and the Paths,* the Tibetan term for path, *lam* (no connection with "lama" which is spelled *bla ma*), is said to refer to something that opens the way to higher states:[439]

> The definition of a path is an exalted knower—of one who has entered the path[a]—that serves to open a passageway allowing the opportunity of progressing to the enlightenment that is its own fruit.

Den-ma L̄o-chö Rin-b̄o-chay brings the stilted language of the monastic textbook to life:[440]

> For instance, opening a door reveals a passageway, allows a passageway. Or, in another way, if you are driving a car and there is a large boulder in the road, you would have to break it up into pieces and get it aside, thus opening up a passageway.

Paths allow passage by removing obstacles. They also are tracks set down by earlier practitioners; Den-ma L̄o-chö Rin-b̄o-chay contextualizes the vocabulary in everyday experience:

> What is a path? In the world we call the tracks[b] of someone who went before and which serve as a way to be followed by those afterwards a "path." We know many kinds of paths—a road such as is used by cars, the tracks used by a train, a footpath one might follow when walking in the mountains. The term "path" is used here in a similar manner. We call paths those ways of proceeding of the Buddhas, Bodhisattvas, and Superiors of the past—the kinds of thought they generated—which is how those who wish to generate such realizations in the present and the future must proceed.

In addition to removing obstacles and opening a way, "path" has the connotation of a tradition, the tracks worn into the ground by the passage of predecessors (which is a reflection of the meaning of *mārga* as "scar" or "mark," given above).

Ḡön-chok-jik-may-w̄ang-b̄o[441] lists the equivalents of "path" and an etymology:

---

[a] This is a necessary qualification in order to eliminate similar experiences by those who have not reached a level of a formal path, that is to say, any of the five paths of accumulation, preparation, seeing, meditation, or no more learning.

[b] *shul.*

> Path of liberation,[a] exalted knower,[b] exalted wisdom,[c] clear realizer,[d] mother,[e] and vehicle[f] are mutually inclusive synonyms. They are called "paths" because they cause one to progress to the status of liberation.

Den-ma Lo-chö Rin-bo-chay explains:

> A path of liberation is so called because it is a path that allows progress to liberation. An exalted knower is so called because it is unmistaken knowledge of a method for proceeding to that enlightenment which is one's own object of attainment. Exalted wisdom and clear realizer are the same. A path is called a mother because it produces or gives birth to that superior person which is its own effect. It is called a vehicle [or platform] because it is like a ladder.... All of these are called paths because they cause progress to the state of liberation. The word "liberation" here refers to both the liberation of a Foe Destroyer and the great liberation of a Buddha.

Paths are goal-directed—leading to, producing, and ascending to a higher state.

Paths are also called "grounds" or "earths"[g] in the sense that they serve as **bases**[h] of high qualities of mind just as the earth serves as the basis of myriad activities. Den-ma Lo-chö Rin-bo-chay elaborates:

> A ground acts as a basis of the many qualities that are its fruit.... Just as the ground [or earth] acts as a basis of orchards, forests, and so forth, so these consciousnesses act as the basis of many qualities of those who have entered the path; therefore, they are called grounds.... A ground serves as a basis not only for producing that which has not been produced but also for maintaining what has been produced as well as causing non-degeneration of what has been produced.

The term "ground,"[i] which seems so awkward and forced in the context of a discussion of spiritual paths in English, is explained by Den-ma Lo-chö Rin-bo-chay as employed because of its familiarity and ease of understanding:

> The reason why the paths of the three vehicles are called grounds is that they serve as bases of one's generating higher qualities in one's own mental continuum. If, in the imputation of a name, one employs

---

a *thar lam.*

b *mkhyen pa.*

c *ye shes, jñāna.*

d *mngon rtogs, abhisamaya.*

e *yum, mātṛ.*

f *theg pa, yāna.*

g *sa, bhūmi.*

h *gzhi.*

i Or the French *terre* used by David S. Ruegg.

> a term from common usage, then it is easily remembered and used. The term "ground" is known well, for if we are going, wandering, lying down, or sitting, our activities are involved with the ground [or earth]. Thus, through skill in means—using a term that is easy to understand—the term "ground" is used. The reason for designating the paths of the three vehicles as grounds is from the viewpoint of a similarity of function.

Given the descriptions of spiritual practices as **paths** that are the tracks of predecessors leading to salutary aims, as **vehicles** or **platforms** reaching higher states, as **mothers** giving birth to high qualities, and as **grounds** that are the bases of growing favorable states of mind, it is clear from these metaphors that soteriological activities are viewed as goal-directed. Even in tantra, as described by D̄zong-ka-b̄a and his followers,[442] despite the fact that the tantric system is said to use the fruit (or goal) as the path in that a Buddha's abode, body, resources, and altruistic activities are mimicked in the practice of deity yoga (that is, the yoga of imitating an ideal being), it is emphasized that one is merely **mimicking** Buddhahood in order more effectively to induce it.[a]

Paths are what make advancement possible; they allow passage forward by removing obstacles—a withdrawal of the mind from counterproductive obstacle-making behavior and thereby an expansion of the mind to a new horizon. Let us apply this perspective to the practices of the beings of the three capacities discussed in chapter 11:

- On the levels of a being of the low and the middling within the small capacity, the path of realizing and meditating on the facts (1) that the present situation as a human endowed with pleasurable features is valuable and (2) that one will not stay long in this situation and could be impelled by past karma into unfortunate lifetimes as an animal, hungry ghost, or hell-being causes withdrawal of attachment to the temporary appearances of this lifetime and expands one's horizon of attention and concern to the future lifetimes.
- Having become a being of the great within the small capacity, the path of realizing and meditating on the entire spectrum of cyclic existence—both favorable and unfavorable lives—as bound within the confines of karma, driven by afflictive emotions, causes withdrawal of attachment to the temporary appearances of all types of lifetimes in cyclic existence and expands one's horizon of attention and concern to the process of misconception that is at the root of the afflictive emotions that impel the process of cyclic existence.

[a] This does not seem to be the case in certain N̄ying-ma and certain East Asian teachings, in which it is more that one is uncovering an enlightenment already primordially present.

- Having become a being of middling capacity through such meditation on the whole scope of suffering and on impermanence and selflessness, one infers—from the unflinching knowledge of one's own situation gained earlier—the plight of all sentient beings; the path of realizing and meditating on this causes withdrawal from self-centeredness and expands one's attention and concern to include the whole scope of the types and varieties of sentient beings.

These three levels of path hold practitioners back from a series of increasingly subtle, counterproductive attitudes and rescue them to a series of more salutary concerns. The stages progress from short-term self-orientation to long-term self-orientation and then to other-orientation—each stage requiring a profoundly ethical transformation. For even the self-oriented stages are built on practices that are aimed at not harming others and culminate eventually, as a being of great capacity, in a commitment to helping others.

Each of these phases of withdrawal is from a mental perspective characterized by multiplicity and a fracturing of attention—being sunk in attachment to the manifold appearances and purposes of the presently appearing world and of future lifetimes and being sunk in the inequality of self-cherishing. Carl Jung speaks to this fractured state and the attempt by religions to re-gather this energy:[443]

> To be like a child means to possess a treasury of accumulated libido which can constantly stream forth. The libido of the child flows into things; in this way he gains the world, then by degrees loses himself in the world (to use the language of religion) through a gradual over-valuation of things. The growing dependence on things entails the necessity of sacrifice, that is, withdrawal of libido, the severance of ties. The intuitive teachings of religion seek by this means to gather the energy together again; indeed, religion portrays this process of re-collection in its symbols.

In Buddhism, the over-valuation of objects that the ordinary consciousness suffers is reversed both through its symbols—such as the central image of the contemplative Buddha withdrawn into internal contemplation—and rituals of severance of ties to the world and also through a series of increasingly re-collective meditatively reflective exercises.

The meditations causing withdrawal of energy from these counterproductive states are realizations of qualities that are **universal** or at least applicable to broad categories of objects:

- The nature of suffering of **all** the bad transmigrations as animals, hungry ghosts, and hell-beings and then of **all** transmigrations in general
- The nature of impermanence that pervades **all** commonly experienced phenomena

- The nature of the thoroughly established nature that pervades **all** phenomena
- The suitability of concern for **all** other beings.

These meditations, the basic structure of which is constituted by withdrawal of a certain type of involvement and expansion of another, higher level with more homogeneous involvement, are consonant with the practice in Highest Yoga Tantra of withdrawing all of the winds (energies) that support the grosser levels of consciousness so that the meditator can expand consciously controlled usefulness to the level of the fundamental innate mind of clear light. The mind of clear light, in turn, is viewed as the stuff of appearances—**all** appearances being viewed as the manifestation,[a] the sport,[b] of the mind of clear light. The mind of clear light is viewed as the **universal** substrate of appearance on this expanded level of awareness that is beyond self-centeredness and is a constant expression of the equality of self and other.[c]

In this way, the paths of the beings of the three capacities—by withdrawing energy (wind) and applying realization of universal qualities—can be seen as consonant with and leading to manifesting the mind of clear light. Ascent over these levels is effected by a process that expands common perspectives beyond their usual range. The common concern for one's own present happiness is expanded to future lives; the common concern for happiness is expanded to a type of happiness that is beyond the vicissitudes of the rapidly changing nature of cyclic existence; the common concern for relatives and close friends is expanded to all beings, seen as close by virtue of similarity in type in that both oneself and others equally want happiness and do not want suffering and by virtue of having been friends in former lifetimes. Similarly, the common nature of mind—its luminous and cognitive essence—is expanded in the sense that it becomes a primary focus of attention whereby it, rather than its contents, becomes the dominant factor of experience such that it can be seen as the stuff of all appearances. The earlier practices lead to the later, in that the radical withdrawal of the winds that operate the grosser levels of consciousnesses could not be effected without the withdrawals brought about by the preceding practices; the practitioner's attached involvement with appearances would be too firm to allow conscious stoppage of these levels of mind.

To withdraw from appearances, it is necessary to come to disbelieve in their veracity, this being why Tibetan colleges put great emphasis on multiple approaches for **reasoned** understanding of the thoroughly established nature, emptiness. The underpinnings of habitual assent to the deceptive allure of the

---

a *rnam 'gyur.*

b *rol pa, līla.*

c See the final chapter, "Union of the Old and New Translation Schools," in H.H. the Dalai Lama, Tenzin Gyatso, *Kindness, Clarity, and Insight* (Ithaca, N.Y.: Snow Lion, 1984), 200-224, especially 210-221.

concreteness of objects' being established by way of their own character as the referents of their respective conceptual consciousnesses are challenged through argumentation internalized in meditation such that the reasonings themselves rise above mere verbiage with shattering import. It is clear that these approaches are meant not as superficial exercises in sophistry but as disturbing and finally destroying the process of assent to the appearance of other-powered natures in the guise of the imputational nature. The psychology of cyclic existence and of finitude is put under assault.

Reasoning

According to Jik-may-dam-chö-gya-tso,[444] there are two types of objects of negation—those by the path and those by reasoning. The objects of negation by the path are the afflictive obstructions and obstructions to omniscience, and the way the path negates them is to stop them such that they are not fit to be produced again; the path does not refute that they exist. He says that, if this were not so—that is, if the afflictive obstructions and obstructions to omniscience actually did not exist—sentient beings would be released without striving, and the hard work of cultivating the path would be senseless.

The objects of reasoned negation, on the other hand, are of two types—existent and non-existent. The negation, or stoppage, of a consciousness conceiving a self of phenomena is by way of uprooting belief in the referent object of a consciousness conceiving a self of phenomena; something that exists, an erroneous consciousness, needs to be stopped. However, the refutation of the self of phenomena is a matter of refuting that it exists; one must come to understand that it never existed. Of these two, the latter is considered to be the principal object of negation, since it is through refuting it that an erroneous consciousness misconceiving the status of phenomena is undermined.

Consciousnesses engaged in the superimposition of the imputational nature are either artificial[a] (that is, intellectually acquired) or innate.[b] The former are delusive consciousnesses that have as their basis the reasonings and/or the scriptures of a mistaken system. No matter how ingrained or habitual these become or no matter how much one becomes unaware or unconscious of them, as long as the initial impetus comes from reasonings and/or scriptures, the mistakenly conceiving consciousness is called "artificial," or, more literally, "imputed." The innate, on the other hand, is not dependent on reasoning and scripture or on training in a mistaken system or even on learning language and thus exists even among babies, animals, insects, and so forth. The innate superimposition is one that beings engage in without stimulus from formal systems of any sort but, nevertheless, is supported by certain systems, both non-Buddhist and Low Vehicle Buddhist schools. The conceptual error cannot be

---

a *kun btags, parikalpita.*

b *lhan skyes, sahaja.*

one that requires education for its inception or one that would be either obviously silly or refutable by reasoning in the Low Vehicle schools of tenets; Great Vehicle reasoning is required to refute it.

The *Sūtra Unraveling the Thought* itself (*Emptiness in Mind-Only,* 207) does not offer any reasonings establishing selflessness; it merely declares selflessness to be the truth. The reasonings are provided by Indian scholar-yogis, namely, Asaṅga, Vasubandhu, Dignāga, and Dharmakīrti. Eleven reasonings—gleaned mainly from Jam-ȳang-shay-ba's *Great Exposition of Tenets,* Nga-w̄ang-b̄el-den's *Annotations,* and Jik-may-dam-chö-gya-tso's *Port of Entry*[a]—are explained below. The first two reasonings explicitly prove that objects are not established by way of their own character as the referents of their respective consciousnesses and as the objects verbalized by respective names, whereas the last nine explicitly prove that apprehended-object and apprehending-subject are not different entities.[b]

1. Threefold Reasoning

In his *Grounds of Bodhisattvas, Compendium of Ascertainments,* and *Summary of the Great Vehicle,* Asaṅga presents similar threefold reasonings built around the relationship between an object and its names. Since this has been discussed above (p. 401ff.) and in *Emptiness in Mind-Only* (207-210, 324-326), let us briefly consider here the presentation of this reasoning in the root text of

---

[a] Jik-may-dam-chö-gya-tso's *Port of Entry,* 632.1-666.5. For the part in which Jik-may-dam-chö-gya-tso (*Port of Entry,* 650.4-655.2) responds to J̄ang-ḡya's position that the reasoning of simultaneous certification does not prove a mere negative, see p. 250ff.

[b] D̄zong-ka-b̄a (*Emptiness in Mind-Only,* 218) briefly refers to the reasonings refuting "apprehended-object and apprehending-subject related with externality," mentioning four:

1. In Asaṅga's *Summary of the Great Vehicle,* the reasonings of dreams, reflections, and so forth
2. In Vasubandhu's *The Twenty,* the reasoning refuting partless particles
3. By Dharmakīrti [in his *Commentary on (Dignāga's) "Compilation of Prime Cognition"*], the reasoning refuting that the character of an apprehending-subject is produced from the apprehended-object and is similar to the apprehended-object
4. By Dignāga [in his *Examination of Objects of Observation*], the reasoning refuting that an aggregation of particles or an [individual] minute particle is the apprehended-object.

Jik-may-dam-chö-gya-tso (*Port of Entry,* 641.2) calls for analysis of:

- why, from among the four reasonings given in Asaṅga's *Summary of the Great Vehicle,* D̄zong-ka-b̄a mentions the second (item 1 in D̄zong-ka-b̄a's list and item 4 in the current exposition)
- why he lists Dharmakīrti first and Dignāga second, out of temporal order.

That Jik-may-dam-chö-gya-tso calls for analysis of these points means that he could not figure out why D̄zong-ka-b̄a does these, and neither can I.

Jam-ȳang-shay-b̄a's *Great Exposition of Tenets* together with the commentaries by the Am-do scholar L̄o-sang-ḡön-chok[a] and the Kalkha Mongolian scholar Nga-w̄ang-b̄el-den. First, Jam-ȳang-shay-b̄a's cryptic, code-like stanza without bracketed additions:[445]

> Because an awareness does not exist prior, the nature of that—
> contradictory.
> Because that has many names, one object many essences—
> contradictory.
> Because there is no limitation that a name is used for one object,
> Essences mixed—contradictory.

Now, with bracketed additions:

> Because an awareness [knowing that a bulbous object is called "pot"] does not exist prior [to learning the name "pot," that the name "pot" exists in] the nature of that [bulbous object] is contradictory.
> Because that [bulbous object] has many names, one object [would have] many essences, [but that is] contradictory.
> Because there is no limitation that a name is used for [only] one object,
> [Various] essences [would be] mixed, [but that is] contradictory.

In his word-commentary on that stanza, L̄o-sang-ḡön-chok makes the reasoning accessible:[446]

> With respect to how selflessness is proven:
>
> - If a bulbous thing were established by way of its own mode of subsistence as a basis of the convention "pot," it would necessarily not depend on learning the language for it. Therefore, because the awareness that [it is called "pot"] does not exist prior to designating it [as "pot," that is to say, learning the name "pot"], it is contradictory for [the name] to exist independently in the nature of that [object].
> - Because [one object] has many names, the fact that one object would be many different, mutually unrelated essences is a contradiction [because there is only one object].
> - There is no limitation that a name is used for just one object. Therefore, when a name is used for two objects, and so forth, that are contradictory, the essences of those contradictory objects would be mixed, or one. This is contradictory [with the fact that there is more than one].

---

a *blo bzang dkon mchog.*

Nga-w̄ang-b̄el-den revealingly frames his own commentary around the absurdities involved in asserting that objects are established by way of their own character as the referents of words and conceptual consciousnesses:

- It [absurdly] follows with respect to the subject, a bulbous thing, that—prior to designating it with a name for pot—there exists an awareness thinking "Pot," with regard to it because [according to you] it is established through the force of its own mode of subsistence as a foundation of a convention for pot. There is entailment because, if it were established that way, a bulbous thing's being a foundation of a convention for pot would not be posited through the force of language, due to which a linguistic awareness also would be generated without depending on [learning] language [for it]. It cannot be accepted [that with respect to a bulbous thing—prior to designating it with a name for pot—there exists an awareness thinking "Pot," with regard to it] because it is manifestly established that it is necessary to make a linguistic connection for pot in one who does not know any language for pot. In that case, since the generation of an awareness thinking "Pot" does not exist prior to designating a name for pot, it is contradictory for the linguistic referentiality[a] "pot" to exist in the essence or the mode of abiding of a bulbous thing.
- It [absurdly] follows that the subject, the Lord of the Heaven of the Thirty-three, is plural because [according to you] many names—such as Shakra, the god Indra, Grāmaghātaka, and so forth—are affixed for him through the force of the object itself,[b] since he is established by way of his own character as the referent of those names. If those names were affixed through the force of the object itself, then what appears to a conceptual consciousness would have to abide [that is, exist] in the object itself in accordance with how it appears, and hence that object would have to be plural.[c]
- It [absurdly] follows that the subject, two Upaguptas, one in the east and one in the west, are one because the name "Upagupta" is affixed to them through the force of the objects themselves, since [according to you] they are established—through their own mode of abiding—as the referent of that [name]. If the name "Upagupta" were established through the force of the objects themselves, then since (1) what appears to a conceptual

a *brda byas pa.*

b *dngos dbang gis 'jug pa.*

c Since the names appear in different aspects to conceptual consciousnesses, there would have to be correspondingly plural objects.

> consciousness would have to abide [that is, exist] in the object itself in accordance with how it appears and (2) a conceptual consciousness thinking "Both of them are Upagupta," perceives their natures as mixed, those [two persons] would have to be mixed.

It needs to be stressed that these scholars identify the innate superimposition, which is being refuted, as the conception that other-powered natures are established by way of their own character as factors imputed in the manner of entity and attribute. The innate erroneous conception is not that the name is the object or that the object is its name, and so forth, since even the Low Vehicle schools realize that such is not the case, and it is obvious that anyone endowed with common sense can understand that saying, "Gold," does not produce gold. Rather, what is being refuted is the conception that objects' being the referents of terms and of conceptual consciousnesses is established by way of their own character. A **consequence** of such would be that a person who had not learned the name of an object would know its name merely from seeing the object, and so forth. The absurdity of these consequences is the **reason** refuting that objects are established by way of their own character as the referents of conceptual consciousnesses. The reasons should not be confused with the status of objects that the reasons refute.

Also, what is being refuted is not merely that objects are the referents of a conceptual consciousness or that objects are the referents of terms. For objects are indeed the referents of a conceptual consciousness and of terms. Put more simply, we can think about objects, and terms can indeed refer to objects. Hence, what is being refuted is that objects are **established by way of their own character** as the referents of conceptual consciousnesses and of terms expressing them. That objects are established this way is refuted by way of necessary consequences that common experience shows to be absurd.

To repeat: Neither the conclusion nor the reasoning is aimed at negating the sense that objects are words; that is a grosser mistake than the one being considered here. The three reasonings that appear in Asaṅga's texts:

- that the names of objects absurdly would be known without learning them
- that many names absurdly would not be used for one object
- that a certain name absurdly would be restricted to just one object

prove a conclusion or thesis that does not consist of the reasons. Rather, those are the **reasons**; what is being refuted **through them** is that objects exist by way of their own mode of subsistence as the referents of words and thoughts.

2. Reasoning Of Four Thorough Examinations

Ḏzong-ka-ḇa (*Emptiness in Mind-Only,* 213-214) cites Asaṅga's *Summary of the Great Vehicle* for another reasoning, the four thorough examinations (see p. 404ff.), which is so dependent on the same threefold analysis that it hardly deserves to be called a separate reasoning. About it, Jam-ȳang-shay-b̄a says in an incredibly cryptic way in his root text:[447]

> Because when investigating by way of the four thorough examinations in that way, it does not exist in that.

L̄o-sang-ḡön-chok explains:[448]

> The four thorough examinations are examination into names, examination into objects, examination into imputing entities, and examination into imputing attributes. Further, if names referred to those objects by way of their own nature or if those objects were established by way of their own character as referents of those names, when one analyzes as before [in the threefold analysis which reveals that knowledge of names] would have to be independent [of any instruction in language] and so forth, then because of not existing [in that way], a mode of being factually other than the mind does not exist in those referents.

3. Reasoning Of Discordant Perception Of Objects

The remaining reasonings explicitly prove that apprehended-object and apprehending-subject are not different entities. In his *Summary of the Great Vehicle,*[449] Asaṅga states the reasoning of the generation of discordant consciousnesses with respect to one thing, such as when hungry ghosts, animals, humans, and gods look at a bowl full of fluid. In accordance with their own karma, hungry ghosts see pus; animals such as fish see an abode; humans see water; and gods see ambrosia. From this fact, it is concluded that external objects do not exist.

Jam-ȳang-shay-b̄a presents the reasoning:[450]

> *[Correct position:]* There are no external objects because consciousnesses that perceive external objects are mistaken with respect to their appearing objects[a] [as, for example, is the case with dream-appearances].[451]
>
> *Objection:* The reason is not established.
>
> *Reply:* Then, because [according to you] the reason is not established, it [absurdly] follows that it is suitable to make assertions in accordance with how [objects] appear to sense consciousnesses of the

[a] Jik-may-dam-chö-gya-tso (*Port of Entry,* 635.5) adds:

If a consciousness that perceives something as an external object is mistaken with respect to its appearing object, then that thing is necessarily not established as an external object, because, if something is established as an external object, it must cast its aspect [that is, representation] to the sense consciousness to which it appears and, in that case, the sense consciousness must be generated into having its aspect [that is, representation] in accordance with how it casts the aspect [that is, representation].

short-sighted [that is, of those who have not realized emptiness] which have not been polluted by superficial causes of error.[a]

If you accept [that it is suitable to make assertions in accordance with how objects appear to sense consciousnesses of the short-sighted which have not been polluted by superficial causes of error], then, because you accept such, it [absurdly] follows that, even with respect to one object such as a bowl filled with what is wet and moistening,[b] when, due to the proprietary condition of very powerful karma, it appears to certain gods, humans, and hungry ghosts respectively as ambrosia, water, and pus and blood, those are established in accordance with how they appear to the eye consciousnesses of each of them.

If you accept this, it [absurdly] follows that on that spot where there is a bowl full of what is wet and moistening (1) there exists a bowl full of ambrosia and (2) water and so forth do not exist because [according to you] (1) there is establishment in accordance with the mode of appearance to such an eye consciousness of a god and (2) to such an eye consciousness of a god ambrosia appears but water, pus and blood, and so forth do not appear. You have asserted the first reason. The second reason [that is, that to such an eye consciousness of a god ambrosia appears but water, pus and blood, and so forth do not appear] is established because [a god] is a person having such karma; this is because such exists.

If it is accepted [that on that spot where there is a bowl full of what is wet and moistening (1) there exists a bowl full of ambrosia but (2) water and so forth do not exist], it [absurdly] follows that on that place there is a bowl full of water but not ambrosia, pus and blood, and so forth, because [according to you] (1) there is establishment in accordance with the mode of appearance to such an eye consciousness of a human and (2) to the eye consciousness of such a human the other two do not appear. The first reason has been asserted. The

---

[a] Four types of consciousnesses affected by superficial causes of error are enumerated:

- cause of error existing in the object: a consciousness perceiving a circle of fire due to a firebrand being twirled quickly
- cause of error existing in the basis: an eye consciousness that sees a single moon as double due to a fault in the eye
- cause of error existing in the abode: an eye consciousness that sees trees as moving when a person is riding in a boat (causing stationary objects on the shore to appear to move)
- cause of error existing in the immediately preceding condition: an eye consciousness that sees everything as red when a person is overcome by anger.

See Lati Rinbochay and Elizabeth Napper, *Mind in Tibetan Buddhism* (London: Rider, 1980; Ithaca, N.Y.: Snow Lion, 1980), 51-52.

[b] That which is wet and moistening (*rlan zhing gsher ba*) is the definition of water—"water" here referring to all fluids.

second reason [that is, that to the eye consciousness of such a human the other two do not appear] is established because [that person] is a human having such karma; this is because such a human exists. If it is accepted [that on that place there is a bowl full of water but not ambrosia, pus and blood, and so forth], you have explicitly contradicted yourself.

Reasonings with respect to hungry ghosts, animals, and so forth are to be applied similarly. Therefore, it follows that external objects are not established because the different modes of mental appearance even with respect to one thing as an object only appear [to inflict] manifold damage [to an assertion of external objects]. Asaṅga's *Summary of the Great Vehicle* says:[452]

> In accordance with their respective type
> As hungry ghosts, animals, humans, and gods,
> The thing is one [but their] minds are different.
> Hence, it is expressed that [external] objects are not established.

One might think that it would be much easier just to posit an external object, but Jam-ȳang-shay-b̄a's maneuverings to attempt to present how the Consequence School could posit a coherent external object fall short of being convincing. In his *Great Exposition of the Middle,*[453] he says that the bowl of fluid has a factor[a] of ambrosia (which gods see), a factor of pus and blood (which hungry ghosts see), and a factor of water (which humans see). This astounding presentation engenders appreciation of the perhaps insuperable difficulties in asserting external objects while recognizing the multiple ways that objects are seen.

4. Reasoning Presenting Examples For Consciousness Of Objects Despite Absence Of External Objects

In his *Summary of the Great Vehicle,* Asaṅga draws parallels between the lack of external objects in states such as dreams and other types of unusual consciousness, citing these as reasons for the non-establishment of external objects (see p. 438ff.). Also, to show how there could be perception of objects despite the absence of external objects, Asaṅga[454] cites four examples—reflection on past and future objects, dream-objects, appearances of falling hairs to a person afflicted with an eye disease, special meditative objects of reflection such as an area filled with the corpses, or skeletons, that one had used over lifetimes in cyclic existence. Jam-ȳang-shay-b̄a presents the reasoning:[455]

---

a *cha shas.*

With respect to this, a Hearer Sectarian asks: What examples are there for external objects not being established but there being appearances as objects of observation of consciousness?

Reply: Although external objects, like the horns of a rabbit, are utterly not established, there are many examples of how [external objects] appear as objects of observation of [consciousness] because the following are examples of this:

1. The appearance of past and future [objects] to awarenesses at the present time
2. Similarly, the appearance—in a dream of a person sleeping in a small room—of a herd of elephants intermingling
3. Despite the appearance of falling hairs to someone with an eye disease, the non-establishment of such in accordance with how it appears
4. Despite the appearance of an area filled with corpses in a meditative stabilization on ugliness, the non-establishment of such in accordance with how it appears.

This is because Asaṅga's *Summary of the Great Vehicle* says:[456]

> Since in cases of the past and so forth, dreams,
> And the two types of reflections[a]
> [External] objects of observation do not exist,
> It is suitable for there to be observation of [objects despite the absence of external objects].

5. Reasoning That Without External Objects, Either Release Would Be Impossible, Or Sentient Beings Would Be Released Without Striving

Asaṅga's *Summary of the Great Vehicle*,[457] based on the fact that a wisdom consciousness does not see forms and so forth, argues that, if external objects did exist, then a Buddha's wisdom would not exist. Jam-ȳang-shay-b̄a presents the reasoning:[458]

External objects are refuted through the consequence that, if external

[a] The two types of reflections are identified as reflections in a mirror and reflections, or images, that appear in meditation on the ugliness of the body and the like; see Nga-w̄ang-b̄el-den's *Annotations for (Jam-ȳang-shay-b̄a's) "Great Exposition of Tenets," dngos,* 121.2, and Jik-may-dam-chö-gya-tso's *Port of Entry,* 633.1. S̄er-s̄hül (*Notes,* 50a.3) identifies them similarly in dependence upon Vasubandhu's commentary (Peking 5551, vol. 112) and Asvabhāva's commentary (Peking 5552, vol. 113); he questions Jam-ȳang-shay-b̄a's identification of them as an appearance of falling hairs and the appearance of skeletons to meditative stabilization on ugliness, the problem being with the first of these.

objects existed, non-conceptual exalted wisdom and Buddhahood would not exist. Asaṅga's *Summary of the Great Vehicle*[459] says:

> If objects were established as [external] objects,
> Non-conceptual exalted wisdom would not exist.[a]
> Due to its not existing, it would not be feasible
> For there to be attainment of Buddhahood.

Jik-may-dam-chö-gya-tso[460] re-frames the reasoning to indicate that either no one could be liberated or everyone would be liberated:

> If external objects existed, either sentient beings would be released without striving, or, despite striving, sentient beings would not be released. There is entailment because:
>
> - If external objects existed, such would have to be established as the mode of subsistence of things, and, in that case, it would absurdly follow that common beings directly perceive the mode of subsistence of things.
> - A Superior's exalted wisdom that realizes the non-duality of apprehended-object and apprehending-subject would not exist.

6. Reasoning Of Yogic Power Over Appearances And The Non-Appearance Of External Objects To Exalted Wisdom

Asaṅga's *Summary of the Great Vehicle*[461] points to the facts that:[462]

1. In special states of yogic mental control, earth appears as water, or the like, in accordance with whatever is imagined.
2. Yogis who have attained calm abiding and special insight perceive objects in accordance with their contemplation of all phenomena as of the nature of mind and do not perceive external objects.
3. If external objects existed, they would have to appear to non-conceptual exalted wisdom, but such do not appear.

From these facts, it is concluded that external objects do not exist. Jam-ȳang-shay-b̄a presents the reasoning:[463]

> External objects are refuted by the fact that Bodhisattvas who have attained dominion and those who have attained the dominion of familiarization with meditative stabilization perceive [objects] in accordance with their interest and are refuted through the fact that among the objects of non-conceptual exalted wisdom external objects do not appear, and so forth. Asaṅga's *Summary of the Great Vehicle* says:[464]

---

[a] Jik-may-dam-chö-gya-tso (*Port of Entry*, 633.1) prefers *mi rtog ye shes yod mi 'gyur* to *shes pa rtog pa med mi 'gyur.*

Bodhisattvas who have attained dominion
And yogis as well observe
Phenomena such as [all-pervasive] earth and so forth
Through the force of their imagination.

Whoever is endowed with intelligence[a]
And has attained calm and the accomplishment [of special insight][465]
Perceives objects in the way
That all phenomena are contemplated [as of the nature of mind].[466]

Moreover since, when non-conceptual exalted wisdom
Is active, there is no appearance of any [external] objects,
It should be understood that [external] objects do not exist.
Since they do not exist, cognition does not exist.

The last line seems to suggest that even cognition, or consciousness, does not truly exist. In order to avoid this reading, Nga-w̄ang-b̄el-den[467] creatively forces the line to mean that, when cognition-only is realized, a consciousness that takes things to be external objects also does not exist:

> Since external objects do not exist, in cognition-only the taking of things to be [external] objects also does not exist.

As L̄o-sang-ḡön-chok[468] says later at the end of expanding on Jam-ȳang-shay-b̄a's clear summation of several of the reasonings:[b]

> [Proponents of Mind-Only assert that there are no external objects]:
>
> - because objects such as forms, and so forth, do not appear to the uncontaminated exalted wisdom consciousnesses of Superiors
> - because when the three—gods, humans, and hungry ghosts—see a

---

[a] That is, Bodhisattvas; see Jik-may-dam-chö-gya-tso's *Port of Entry,* 633.2.

[b] This is in commentary on the root text of Jam-ȳang-shay-b̄a's *Great Exposition of Tenets* (*nga,* 48a.6):

> Because [no external objects appear] to exalted wisdom consciousnesses, because with respect to one thing there are many mental consciousnesses,
> Because the pleasant and unpleasant [arise together], because appearances [are controlled by] yogis, and so forth,
> And because [the appearance of external objects] is similar to dreams, and so forth, there are no [external] objects, and that they are just mind is true.
> Since objects are not [established by way of their own character] as the referents of conceptual consciousnesses, their appearance as that to non-conceptual consciousnesses
> Is mistaken, whereby it is refuted that those [objects] and [consciousnesses] are different substantial entities.

thing, for instance, water, many mental awarenesses arise in which ambrosia, water, or pus appears in accordance with their own karma

- because when one person is simultaneously seen by enemies and friends, the pleasant and unpleasant arise together
- because earth appears as water in accordance with whatever is imagined in yogic appearance
- because [the appearance of objects] is similar to dream [objects], and so forth.

Since external objects do not exist, the abiding of all phenomena as the nature of the internal mind is true.

When those objects, that is, all phenomena, are seen as not existing by the force of their own measure of subsistence as the referents of a conceptual consciousness, then, through knowing that even to a non-conceptual sense consciousness, there are appearances [of objects] as being established by way of their own character as the referents of conceptual consciousnesses, one understands that those [appearances] are false. Thereby it comes to be refuted that the two—those [consciousnesses] and objects—are different substantial entities.

In accordance with the statement, "An apprehender without an apprehended-object is not seen," it should be known how, when an object's establishment as an external object is taken as one's object of negation, the subject's being a mind that realizes an external object must also be taken as the object of negation.[a]

7. Reasoning Of Impossibility Of Building Blocks

In his *The Twenty,* Vasubandhu attacks the possible building blocks of external objects—partless particles[b]—by considering that they are surrounded by other

---

[a] Contrary to such a maneuver, Šhay-rap-gyel-tsen (*Ocean of Definitive Meaning,* 218.3) takes the line of Asaṅga's *Summary of the Great Vehicle* at face value, concluding that there is a step beyond mind-only:

> These statements, and so forth, that cognition does not exist are very contradictory with the assertion that Proponents of Mind-Only ultimately assert that consciousness is true [that is, truly established].

See p. 304.

[b] A reasoning refuting partless particles is also found in the third chapter of Dharmakīrti's *Commentary on (Dignāga's) "Compilation of Prime Cognition"* and in Dharmakīrti's *Ascertainment of Prime Cognition;* see Jik-may-dam-chö-gya-tso's *Port of Entry,* 633.4 and 637.4. Jik-may-dam-chö-gya-tso (638.1) also gives similar reasonings from Shāntarakṣhita *Ornament for the Middle* and Kamalashīla's *Illumination of the Middle* and cautions, "Although reasonings refuting partless particles appear frequently in the great texts, they sometimes are and sometimes are not explicitly set forth as refutations of external objects."

particles and thus have sides (and hence parts) facing those other particles. Jam-ȳang-shay-b̄a[469] renders the debate as follows:

> *Challenge:* It follows that external objects do not exist because not even a single partless particle—which you Proponents of Truly Existent External Objects assert to be the building blocks of external objects—exists. This is because, when those minute particles that are the smallest of particles also are examined, they have parts. It follows that the reason is so because a single minute particle is surrounded by six minute particles—in the four directions, above, and below—and thus the central particle has six parts relative to where it is surrounded by the six minute particles.
>
> *Objection:* The reason, that is, that a single minute particle is surrounded by six minute particles—in the four directions, above, and below—and thus the central particle has six parts relative to where it is surrounded by the six minute particles, is not proven.
>
> *Reply:* Because you say that the reason is not proven, it absurdly follows that the side of the central minute particle that faces the east also faces the particles in the south, the west, and so forth. If you accept that the side of the central minute particle that faces the east also faces the particles in the south, the west, and so forth, then, because you accept this, it absurdly follows that, on the area of the one minute particle in the east, the remaining five particles also exist. If you accept that, on the area of the one minute particle in the east, the remaining five particles also exist, then, because you accept this, it absurdly follows that the mass of howsoever many particles aggregate is equal in measure only to a single minute particle. If you accept that the mass of howsoever many particles aggregate is equal in measure only to a single minute particle, it absurdly follows that even Mount Meru is the same size as a single particle. Vasubandhu's *The Twenty* says:[a]
>
> > How is it not so established? Because:
> >
> > Due to simultaneous conjunction with six [particles]
> > A particle has six parts.
> > Also, if the six were in the same place,
> > Even a mass would be of the size of a particle.

Vasubandhu's own commentary on the first two lines is:

> When a particle is simultaneously in conjunction with six particles from the six directions, it comes to have six parts, because the others are not in the place one occupies.

---

[a] The introductory line is from the Vasubandhu's own commentary prior to stanza twelve.

And his commentary on the last two lines is:

> If just the place occupied by the one particle were the place occupied by all six, then, because all would occupy the same place, the entire mass would have the size of a particle. Since they mutually would not differ from each other, no mass at all would be seen.

8. Reasoning Refuting Aggregations Of Particles and Single Particles As Observed-Object-Conditions

In his *Examination of Objects of Observation,*[470] Vasubandhu's student Dignāga employs a reasoning examining what kind of object could possibly impinge upon the consciousness, generating it into its likeness. In technical vocabulary, this is called an observed-object-condition because it is the object observed that serves as a condition, or cause, generating the consciousness.

An eye consciousness, for instance, has three conditions which are its causes. In relation to an eye consciousness that apprehends a patch of blue, these three, according to the proponents of external objects, are:

- the uncommon proprietary condition[a]—the eye sense power;[b] it gives the consciousness the power, or ability, to perceive colors and shapes
- the immediately preceding condition[c]—the immediately preceding moment of consciousness; it ceases just before the new eye consciousness and causes it to be a conscious entity
- the observed-object condition[d]—the patch of blue; it is the object of that eye consciousness and causes the consciousness to contain a representation of blue.

In the first two stanzas of his eight-stanza text, Dignāga refutes the two possibilities for an observed-object condition which is an external object—an individual minute particle or an aggregation of particles. Jam-ȳang-shay-b̄a[471] frames the reasoning around a multi-staged debate:

> *Proponent of External Objects:* An external form is an actual observed-object-condition of an eye sense consciousness because (1) an aspect similar to it, that is, a representation, appears to that eye sense consciousness and (2) it is a direct cause of that eye sense consciousness.
>
> *Proponent of Mind-Only:* Do you propound such within holding that external **partless minute** particles are the bases of formation of external objects, or do you propound such within holding **gross** external

a *thun mong ma yin pa'i bdag rkyen, asādhāraṇādhipatipratyaya.*

b *mig gi dbang po, cakṣurindriya.*

c *de ma thag rkyen, samanantarapratyaya.*

d *dmigs rkyen, ālaṃbanapratyaya.*

objects to be the bases of formation? In accordance with the first, since aspects similar to minute particles do not appear to sense consciousnesses, you should state as your reason why an external form is an actual observed-object-condition of an eye sense consciousness merely "because it is the direct cause of that eye sense consciousness." In accordance with the second, since a gross object is not the direct cause, you should say, "because an aspect similar to it appears to that eye sense consciousness."

Proponent of External Objects: It is in accordance with the first reason.

Proponent of Mind-Only: It follows that something's being a direct cause of an eye sense direct perception is not a correct reason proving that it is an observed-object-condition of an eye sense direct perception because, even if it was allowed that external minute particles are direct causes of an eye sense direct perception, those external small particles are not observed-object-conditions of an eye sense direct perception. This is because an aspect of a minute particle does not appear to an eye sense direct perception. This is like, for example, the fact that, although an eye sense power is a direct cause of an eye sense direct perception, it is not an observed-object-condition.

Proponent of External Objects: It is in accordance with the second reason.

Proponent of Mind-Only: It follows that the fact that an aspect similar to it appears to an eye sense direct perception is not a correct reason proving that a gross external object is an observed-object-condition of an eye sense direct perception because, even though there is an appearance in the manner of an aspect of external form to an eye sense direct perception, an eye sense direct perception is not produced from it. This is like, for example, the fact that, although the aspect of a double moon appears to a sense consciousness perceiving a double moon, a double moon is not its producer and its observed-object-condition. There is entailment because it is explained in [the division of the scriptures called] Manifest Knowledge that an observed-object-condition of a consciousness is a condition causing that consciousness.

Hence, neither of the two, subtle or gross external objects, are observed-object-conditions of sense direct perceptions because each of those two does not fulfill the branches, or reasons, for positing an observed-object-condition. This is because small external particles do not fulfill the requirement of their aspect **appearing** to a sense direct perception and gross external objects do not fulfill the requirement of **producing** a sense direct perception.

Dignāga's *Examination of Objects of Observation* itself says:

> Minute particles might be
> Causes of sense cognitions,
> But since those [minute particles] do not appear, their objects
> Are not small particles, just as the sense powers [are not observed-object-conditions].
>
> In any case, that perception is not [produced] from that [aggregation of particles]
> Because [an aggregation] does not substantially exist, like a double moon.
> Thus even both external [objects—single particles and aggregations—]
> Are not fit to be objects of an awareness.[a]

From this viewpoint, Dignāga refutes that objects such as patches of color are observed-object-conditions. B̄el-jor-hlün-drup[472] explains that, nevertheless, Dignāga still uses the term "observed-object-condition" to refer to an internal capacity that is within a previous moment of consciousness[b] to generate a direct perception apprehending blue, for instance, into having the aspect of blue. He also uses the same term for the object, blue, that is simultaneous with an eye consciousness apprehending blue and is the same entity as that consciousness, not in the sense of being an actual condition generating the consciousness but of merely being a fully qualified appearance. Through making these distinctions, Ge-luk-b̄a scholars view Dignāga as at once refuting observed-object-conditions that are external objects, but still employing the vocabulary of observed-object-conditions.[c]

9. Reasoning Disproving That An Object Produces A Similar Consciousness

In his *Commentary on (Dignāga's) "Compilation of Prime Cognition"* and in his *Ascertainment of Prime Cognition*,[473] Dignāga's follower but not direct student Dharmakīrti likewise refutes external objects by way of demonstrating that an apprehended-object does not produce an apprehending-subject similar to it. He challenges the position that an external object impinges on a consciousness making it similar to the object in a three-staged argument:

- The first examines whether mere similarity is sufficient to draw the conclusion that such an external object exists.

---

[a] Jik-may-dam-chö-gya-tso (*Port of Entry*, 639.3) cites a similar reasoning in Dignāga's *Compilation of Prime Cognition.*

[b] This is the immediately preceding condition.

[c] See Appendix 1 (p. 506ff.) for a discussion of Alex Wayman's conclusion that Dignāga indeed asserts that there are external objects.

- The second concerns what sort of similar object might impinge on a consciousness, that is, a single particle or an aggregation of particles.
- The third concerns production from what is similar.

Dharmakīrti first refutes the notion that external objects must exist by reason that consciousnesses are similar to objects. He simply points out a consciousness perceiving a double moon appears in an aspect similar to a double moon, but a double moon is known not to exist. Thus mere similarity is not sufficient to show that such an external object exists. As Jam-ȳang-shay-b̄a[474] renders the first steps of the argument:

> *Proponent of Mind-Only:* What are consciousnesses knowing external objects in your frequent mention of "consciousnesses knowing external objects"?
>
> *Proponent of External Objects:* Those that individually know and directly perceive blue, yellow, and so forth.
>
> *Proponent of Mind-Only:* What is the reason why direct preceptions apprehending blue, yellow, and so forth are knowers of external objects?
>
> *Proponent of External Objects:* From the fact that an awareness is similar to an external object, it is posited as knowing that.
>
> *Proponent of Mind-Only:* It follows that it is not feasible for similarity with something to be a means of positing a consciousness as realizing an external object because the entailment [that is, that whatever is an awareness similar to an external object is necessarily posited as knowing that object] is mistaken; for example, although a consciousness appears similar to a double moon, it does not realize a double moon.

In the second stage of the argument Dharmakīrti examines whether the representation of consciousness is cast from minute particles or a gross object. It is obvious that minute particles do not cast their representation to consciousness, since what a sense consciousness perceives is a gross object and, furthermore, single particles do not have the capacity to cast a representation of a gross object. The likely possibility is that a gross object that has parts is what casts its representation to consciousness; however, gross objects have to be composed of particles, and such particles have not been shown to exist. As Jam-ȳang-shay-b̄a frames these steps in the argument:

> *Proponent of Mind-Only:* Furthermore, it follows that an awareness is not similar to an external object because (1) it is not similar to a subtle external object and (2) it is not similar to a gross external object. If you say that the first reason, that is, that it is not similar to a subtle external object, is not proven, it follows that those small particles do not explicitly cast aspects similar to themselves to an unmistaken sense

consciousness because (1) an aspect of only a gross object appears to a sense consciousness and (2) particles do not have the capacity to make an unmistaken awareness into being similar to the appearance of a gross object, as is the case, for example, with the fact that a round shape does not cast the aspect of longness to an awareness that is unmistaken with respect to a round shape.

If you say that the second reason, that is, that an awareness is not similar to a gross external object, is not proven, it follows that it is not similar to a partless gross external object because such does not occur. The reason is easy to prove [since a **gross** object could not be partless].

Proponent of External Objects: An awareness is similar to a gross external object that has parts.

Proponent of Mind-Only: It follows that this also is not feasible because—without particles that are external objects—gross objects that are composed of them do not occur. Therefore, it follows that those direct perceptions do not certify things that are external objects because neither gross nor subtle external objects place their aspects [that is, representations] in consciousness.

The third and last phase of the reasoning allows, for the sake of argument, that the consciousness is indeed similar to the object but questions the proof for external objects—this being that the object is similar and produces the consciousness. Dharmakīrti draws the absurd conclusion that then the second moment of an eye consciousness experiencing blue would have to experience the consciousness that is its immediately preceding condition, since it fulfills the two qualities of:

- being similar (in the sense that both the second moment of an eye consciousness perceiving blue and the consciousness that is the immediately preceding condition contain a representation of blue)
- being produced from it (in the sense that the consciousness that is the immediately preceding condition is a cause of the consciousness).

Such an eye consciousness absurdly would never have a chance to apprehend blue since it would have as its object the preceding moment of consciousness that produces it. Dharmakīrti thereby challenges the proofs for the existence of external objects. In Jam-ȳang-shay-b̄a's rendering of this part of the argument:

Proponent of Mind-Only: Even if it were allowed that direct perceptions are similar to external objects, it follows that it cannot be proven that external objects are entities experienced as apprehended-objects because the proof for this is mistaken.

Proponent of External Objects: It is not established that the proof for this is mistaken because an awareness is arisen—in the sense of being produced—from an object that is similar to it and that which is similar has the character of being experienced upon being taken as the apprehended-object.

Proponent of Mind-Only: Then, it absurdly follows that a consciousness apprehending blue experiences its immediately preceding condition—a previous consciousness apprehending blue—upon taking it as its apprehended-object because it is produced from that previous consciousness of blue and is similar to it. You have asserted the entailment. It follows that it is similar because it is similar in having the aspect of the object blue. If it is accepted that a consciousness apprehending blue experiences its immediately preceding condition—a previous consciousness apprehending blue—upon taking it as its apprehended-object, then, because such is asserted, it absurdly follows that moving out to external objects does not occur since a consciousness would always be involved with experiencing the consciousness that is the immediately preceding condition producing it and would not have a chance to realize anything else.

10. Reasoning Of Discordant Experience

Dharmakīrti also uses the reasoning that it is impossible for an external object to have a plurality of contradictory natures. For instance, when a patch of blue is simultaneously seen by two people, an aspect of unpleasantness could arise in the sense consciousness of one of them, whereas an aspect of pleasantness could arise in the sense consciousness of the other. Dharmakīrti's *Commentary on (Dignāga's) "Compilation of Prime Cognition"* [475] says:

> Even if there were external objects,
> How could experience [be explained],
> Because there would be the fallacy
> That a limited entity would by its own nature have many contrary [natures].

B̄el-jor-hlün-drup[476] explains the two lines clearly:

> If blue cast an aspect similar to itself to a direct perception apprehending blue as beautiful, blue would have to be beautiful, and if blue cast an aspect similar to itself to a direct perception apprehending blue as not beautiful, blue would have to not be beautiful. However, blue does not have contrary natures.

11. Reasoning Of The Certainty Of Simultaneous Certification

As mentioned earlier (p. 257), Jik-may-dam-chö-gya-tso points out that D̄zong-ka-b̄a (*Emptiness in Mind-Only,* 218) does not even put the reasoning of the certainty of simultaneous certification[a] in his list of reasonings proving the emptiness of difference of entity of subject and object. He says no more than that this omission calls for analysis; however, I would speculate that Ḏzong-ka-ḇa does not include it because it appears only in the works of Dharmakīrti and is not mentioned by Maitreya, Asaṅga, Vasubandhu, and Dignāga. Nevertheless, Ge-luk-ḇa scholars are particularly fond of this reasoning and often make the unfounded claim that the emptiness of difference of entity of subject and object cannot be presented without it. I call their assertion "unfounded" because the assertion of self-cognizing consciousness is central to the argument, and, as J̄ang-ḡya says,[477] Asaṅga is unclear as to whether he asserts self-cognizing consciousness or not, and such lack of clarity would be inexplicable from the founder of the school, if this reasoning were indeed crucial to the establishment of mind-only.

Still, Ge-luk-ḇa scholars are fascinated with this reasoning as a means of delineating that apprehended-object and apprehending-subject are not different entities, and thus I include it here. Jik-may-dam-chö-gya-tso[478] begins a presentation of it by citing the source verses in Dharmakīrti's *Commentary on (Dignāga's) "Compilation of Prime Cognition"*:

> Since [the object] certainly is concurrently
> [Observed] simultaneously with the awareness,
> By what means is the object
> Established as just other than it?

and in his *Ascertainment of Prime Cognition:*

> Because of the certainty of simultaneous observation,
> Blue and an awareness of it are not other.

When the reasoning is explained (as it will be below), it appears, at first reading, to be excessively complicated, but it revolves around three basic notions:

- Whatever exists is necessarily certified through being observed by valid cognition.
- Whenever an object, such as a patch of blue, is observed by a valid cognition, the valid cognition that certifies it is also simultaneously certified through being observed by a self-cognizing consciousness.
- Whatever are necessarily simultaneously observed by valid cognition are not separate entities but one entity.

---

[a] *lhan cig dmigs nges;* literally, "simultaneous observation." S̄er-s̄hül Ge-s̄hay L̄o-sang-pün-tsok (*Notes,* 17a.6) says that the meaning of simultaneous observation can be taken either as simultaneous observation (of object and subject) by valid cognitions or as simultaneous production, abiding, and disintegration. It seems to me that the former meaning is predominant.

Let us cite in full how Jik-may-dam-chö-gya-tso unpacks the steps of argument:

> The statement of the reasoning is:
>
> > The subjects, a valid cognition apprehending blue and the blue that appears to it, do not exist as separate entities because of the certainty of being observed [that is, certified] simultaneously—for example, like sound and object of hearing.

Sound and object of hearing are equivalent, and thus when one is observed with valid cognition, the other is also observed. In the same way, the Proponents of Mind-Only hold that a patch of blue and the valid cognition apprehending it are necessarily observed by valid cognitions (an eye consciousness and a self-cognizing consciousness that accompanies the eye consciousness, respectively) and thus could not be separate entities. Jik-may-dam-chö-gya-tso continues:

> The opponents of this [reasoning] are the Proponents of the Great Exposition and of the Sūtra School. The Proponents of Cognition state this to those who adhere to blue and the valid cognition apprehending blue as separate substantial entities due to their appearing to be separate substantial entities.
>
> The proof of the presence of the reason in the subject [that is, that a valid cognition apprehending blue and the blue that appears to it are certainly observed simultaneously] is:
>
> > The subjects, a valid cognition apprehending blue and the blue that appears to it, are certainly observed simultaneously because, when any person[a] in any place at any time observes the one with valid cognition, that person at that place and at that time necessarily also observes the other with valid cognition.
> >
> > *Objection:* The reason is not established.
> >
> > *Answer:* It follows that such is necessary because:
> >
> > - when that person at that place and at that time observes blue with valid cognition, there is a valid cognition observing the valid cognition apprehending blue, and
> > - it is not reasonable that such a valid cognition is produced **after** that person observes blue with valid cognition at that place and at that time.

[a] Jik-may-dam-chö-gya-tso uses "person" instead of "consciousness" because, as in the case of apprehending blue with an eye consciousness, it is not just one consciousness that observes both blue and the eye consciousness. Rather, the eye consciousness observes blue, and a self-cognizing consciousness—that exists together with and is the same entity as the eye consciousness but is not the eye consciousness itself—observes the eye consciousness.

> *Objection:* The first reason is not established.
>
> *Answer:* With respect to the subject, the valid cognition apprehending blue when that person at that place and at that time observes blue with valid cognition, it follows that there exists a valid cognition observing it because it is observed by valid cognition.

The point is that there must be a valid cognition observing anything that exists simply because it exists, for the definition of an existent is: that which is observed by valid cognition.

> *Objection:* The second reason is not established. [That is to say, it **is** reasonable that such a valid cognition is produced **after** that person observes blue with valid cognition at that place and at that time.]
>
> *Answer:* If such a valid cognition were produced after that person observes blue with valid cognition at that place and at that time, then an other-cognizing consciousness that observes it also would have to be produced after it, due to which the number of consciousnesses required would be limitless.[a]

Now the exposition turns to the heart of the issue:

> The proof of the [original] positive entailment [that is, if, when any person in any place at any time observes the object with valid cognition, that person at that place and at that time necessarily also observes this consciousness with valid cognition, it is entailed that those two are certainly observed simultaneously] is:
>
> With respect to a valid cognition apprehending blue and the blue that appears to it, it follows that the relationship of mutual existence—that is, if they mutually exist at the same time, they must exist and, if they mutually do not exist at the same time, they must not exist—is established. This is because the relationship of entailment—that, if they mutually are observed by valid cognition at the same time, they must be observed—is established because they are certainly observed simultaneously. You have asserted the reason.
>
> If that is accepted, it follows that a valid cognition apprehending blue and the blue that appears to it are related as one entity because of being related and existing simultaneously.
>
> *Objection:* It is not established that a valid cognition

[a] It is likely that concern over such a regress causes the Indian master Dharmapāla to posit one more simultaneous self-cognizing consciousness but to cut the process there.

apprehending blue and the blue that appears to it exist simultaneously.

Answer: It [absurdly] follows that there is a time when blue is established, but the existence of blue is not established.

The absurdity from which the reasoning stems, so to speak, is embodied in opposite form in the first of the three pivots of the argument mentioned above:

- Whatever exists is necessarily certified through being observed by valid cognition.
- Whenever an object, such as a patch of blue, is observed by a valid cognition, the valid cognition that certifies it is also simultaneously certified through being observed by a self-cognizing consciousness.
- Whatever are necessarily simultaneously observed by valid cognition are not separate entities but one entity.

Handling Challenges To Mind-Only

Jik-may-dam-chö-gya-tso[479] briefly addresses thorny issues in a system of no external objects, the "answers" to which, while not satisfying, are provocative. Basic propositions of the system are that a patch of blue, for instance, is not a different entity from the eye consciousness apprehending it, and yet the consciousnesses of persons are different entities, whereby solipsism is avoided. Slippery distinctions are made in order to protect the system.

1. Are shared objects of perception possible?

If both the appearance of an object such as a patch of blue and the perception of it are due to a single seed residing in an individual's mind-basis-of-all and not due to an object impinging on the person's consciousness, how could it be said that two persons perceive the same object? (If shared objects of perception do not occur, a presentation of worldly activities would be totally impossible.)

The slippery answer is to first make an all-encompassing claim that there are shared objects of perception and then back it with a hair-splitting distinction in order to preserve the doctrine of mind-only:

1. Even though, when two persons look at a patch of blue, the factor that appears to one of them does not appear to the other, it is not contradictory that there is a shared object of perception.
2. For the blue that is the common object of perception is not one substantial entity with the consciousness of either of the two persons, but it is one substantial entity with the consciousness apprehending it.

If the blue that is the common object of perception was one substantial entity with both of the two consciousnesses, there would absurdly be two common objects of perception, in which case the object would not be common. However, if the blue that is the common object of perception was not one substantial entity with any consciousness, the doctrine of the sameness of entity of object and subject would be lost. Maneuvering to avoid these consequences, Jik-may-dam-chö-gya-tso has the Proponent of Mind-Only School make the general claim that the blue that is the common object of perception is one substantial entity with "the consciousness apprehending it," as if there was some such general consciousness.

2. Could two persons look at a third person's body?

There would seem to the fault that, when two persons perceive a third person's body, that body would have to be one entity with each of their eye consciousnesses, and hence the third person would absurdly have two bodies. Jik-may-dam-chö-gya-tso again first has the Proponent of Mind-Only School state an all-encompassing claim and then make a slippery distinction in order to preserve the doctrine of mind-only:

- Each body that is the **un**shared basis of appearance for the two observers and the body that is the common basis of appearance are actual bodies.
- However, when two persons look, for instance, at Upagupta's body, that shared body is Upagupta's body, but the other two, aside from having the **aspect** of Upagupta's body, are not his actual body, since otherwise there would be three bodies of Upagupta included in the continuums of three different personal continuums.

It is difficult to determine what the word "aspect"[a] means. Obviously, it does not mean a representation of an external object, and also it does not mean a particular feature. Rather, it seems to be a nonsense word used to gloss over a problem.

3. Is a clairvoyant consciousness the mind it knows?

Even more onerous is the problem that there seemingly is the fault that a clairvoyant consciousness directly knowing another's consciousness would have to be the same substantial entity as that person's mind. This would entail solipsism with its faults, such as that when Shākyamuni became enlightened, everyone did, or since we are not enlightened, he did not. The answer to this seemingly insuperable dilemma is twofold—again make use of the word "aspect" and posit a mode of appearance of objects other than by way of seeds of perception:

- Since an **aspect** of the other person's consciousness appears to a clairvoyant consciousness **through the force of a meditative stabilization that is a union of calm abiding and special insight**, the clairvoyant consciousness does not have to be the same substantial entity as the mind that it perceives.

---

[a] *rnam pa.*

Although objects that appear through the activation of seeds of perception have to be the same entity as the consciousness perceiving them, objects (such as another person's mind) that appear through the force of meditative cultivation do not have to be the same entity as the perceiver's mind.

4. Is an omniscient consciousness miserable?

In a similar way, there would seem to be the fault that an omniscient consciousness would have to be the same entity as all the objects it knows, including true sufferings, and thus would itself be a true suffering. The solution is to posit yet another way through which objects can appear to a consciousness:

- Since a Buddha cognizes all phenomena **through the force of having completed the two collections of merit and wisdom**, an omniscient consciousness does not have to be the same entity as the true sufferings that it perceives.

From these last two points, it can be seen that, according to this system of exegesis, mind-only allows for other minds and does not restrict the possibilities of perception to the activation of predispositions—objects are also perceived through the force of meditative stabilization and through the force of having completed the two collections. (See Appendix 2, p. 520ff., for a different set of conclusions drawn by Yoshifumi Ueda.) The goal is to gain a state of perception through the force of having brought to completion the collections of merit and wisdom.

23. Dread of Reality

This highly developed Tibetan tradition presents an intricately formulated series of paths, the very orderliness of which gives an impression of smooth, methodical progress.[a] The elegance of the architecture of the system suggests that with the will to perform a graded series of practices, like following a map to a city, enlightenment is sure to be found. However, the religion—as it is meant to be in its ideal form—exists in a not so orderly world, in which even the basic postures and goals of the system become distorted. For instance:

- Consider the Great Vehicle doctrine that the process of completely removing obstructions to highest enlightenment takes three periods of countless great eons, with "countless" referring to an extremely long period of time—a Tibetan scholar saying that it is a one with fifty-nine zeros, not years but great eons. The long period of time that full enlightenment takes is said to indicate the enormity of the task and to encourage a profound level of effort; also, if we consider a practitioner's imagination of path-cultivation projected into such a long period of time, the imaginary extension of the field of reference of insight and practice must have beneficial effects on levels of the unconscious mind by disturbing thresholds of anger, and so forth. On the down-side, however, the extremely long period of time also is used by the culture as a technique to distance enlightenment, to provide an excuse for why enlightenment is not being achieved.

- Consider that even the stage of release from cyclic existence which is said in so-called "Lesser Vehicle" presentations to take a minimum of three years is described in Great Vehicle sūtra systems as taking two periods of countless eons. Is this like the Great Exposition School's presentation of six types of Foe Destroyers, five of which slip back from their attainment? The five fancy that they have attained liberation from cyclic existence but have not—the suggestion perhaps being that liberation is questionable. That the Great Vehicle, in turn, distances even liberation from cyclic existence such that it takes two periods of countless great eons makes one wonder whether, over the course of centuries, many practitioners found that even the lower level of enlightenment was not achievable and thus they presented it as being gained only after an incredibly long period of time, creating a fantasy of future attainment in order to preserve the socioeconomic advantages that had developed despite its failure to produce final results.

- Consider the doctrine that, although all beings have the Buddha nature, there is no time when all beings will be enlightened. Many reasons are cited

---

[a] See p. 55ff., but especially the vast literature on the stages of the path, such as Dzong-ka-ba's *Great Exposition of the Stages of the Path to Enlightenment.*

for adopting this posture, ranging from the infinite number of beings to become enlightened—since an infinite number cannot become reduced when a person becomes enlightened—to the structural need for Complete Enjoyment Bodies to have persons to whom to preach. Adopting a suspicious attitude, however, we could ask whether this doctrine indicates a failure to imagine a situation in which one's own afflictive emotions have been entirely removed.

- Consider the doctrine that there are beings "whose wholesome roots are eradicated" either temporarily or forever. The continual existence of unenlightened beings might be an unconscious projection of one's own recalcitrant afflictive emotions onto other beings. (Even though it strikes me as arrogant and facile to come to such a decision that this is all that is behind these doctrines, it is provocative to entertain the issue.)

- Consider the possibly cynical reformulation of doctrine in the Great Vehicle in which Shākyamuni Buddha's own enlightenment is distanced into the extremely remote past—his activities in India becoming merely a display by an already enlightened being of how to do so, for the benefit of his potential followers. The removal of even the founder's enlightenment from the scope of this world system's history perhaps contributes to an apologetic aimed at mitigating present practitioners' lack of progress on the path of self-liberation.

- Consider the identification—in the Tibetan cultural region—of children as "tulkus,"[a] Emanation Bodies of Buddhas. What could be more contrary to a religious system of self-help than to appoint enlightenment to children too young to have made serious effort at spiritual development? By adopting a system of appointment that flies in the face of its own doctrine of the necessity of individual effort, the culture seems to be excusing itself from having achieved spiritual progress. From this perspective, the elaborate path-structure can be seen as so distancing enlightenment into the unreachable future that high levels of attainment are viewed as being far beyond the reach of even serious practitioners. Also, when children are appointed to these high ranks, the populace is put in a decidedly inferior position as submissive tools in the hands of those who make the designations (and who also thereby manipulate the child-appointees). Is the hierarchy of soteriological attainments that the religious system teaches unscrupulously used to rigidify a social, economic, and political order by placing the populace in a position of unquestioning servitude? (The corrupting influence of co-opting lofty spiritual attainments for governmental, economic, and sociological purposes would seem to be so great that religious institutions would be reduced to being mere legitimators of political power, but it is

---

[a] *sprul sku, nirmāṇakāya.*

clear that this has not swamped the practice of religion in the Tibetan cultural region, most likely because of its dedication to the strong, even extreme, expression of a multiplicity of aspects—diversity being its means of balance.)

- Consider that another consequence of institutional identification of Buddhas from birth is that the religious organization turns away from its basic doctrine of self-help to a system of other-help, namely, descent of the divine as lama-saviors who, inscrutably, are endowed with special blessings. Practitioners become seekers of blessings rather than contemplators working at changing the ideational structure of their minds (1) by reflecting on the nature of cyclic existence as taught through the production-non-nature, the illusion of over-concretized existence as taught through the character-non-nature, and the final nature of phenomena as taught through the ultimate-non-nature and (2) by applying themselves to meditation revealing the closeness of other sentient beings, and so forth. The very inability of the widespread appointment of enlightenment to bear analysis contradicts the basic tenet to analyze and, in its demands for allegiance, either fosters fanatic attachment to leaders and cultic spirits or, in the more critical, breeds cynicism.
- Consider that the structure of the educational system removes the cream of the crop of intellectuals from society, putting them into celibate institutions that concentrate much of their mental energy on issues of personal transformation. The individual development that dominates the concerns of the path-structure itself—no matter how much it calls for altruistic concern—becomes the focus of intellectuals to the point where challenges to the socioeconomic structure are not even seen as means for betterment. The arena of discourse is so confined to individual development that the social and political structure is left intact. Were one to adopt a paranoiac view of history as a grand scheme of ever greedy "haves," what better way to clear the streets than to put all the thinkers in monasteries endlessly debating with each other about a grand scheme of individually achieved utopianism?
- Consider also that the culture causes the non-celibate populace to feel inferior to those in monasteries simply because they are not monks or nuns. In Tibet, either one is of the cloth or has a family—there is little in-between when it comes to religious practice (although this is changing with the increasing numbers of disrobed tulkus who still claim their status as exalted beings). The general culture at times seems to recognize only the form of monasticism and not the content of internal practice, which it seems the unencumbered layperson, if not also the encumbered, might be able to manage despite the obvious disadvantages of lay life.

- Consider that the exclusionary nature of the threefold typology of religious practitioners (discussed in chap. 11) is commandeered in this process. Socially, it justifies recruitment of new members into the only system that can actually function as a religion. Economically, it justifies the receipt of offerings, acquisition of land, and so forth. Politically, it forces attention away from re-structuring the political and social system by confining energy to the process of individual, internal development. Witness Buddhism's well-known ability to live with almost any system of government.
- Consider the culture's affirmation of parochial bias—regional and so forth—which has far-reaching implications. Contrary to both reason and compassion (the hallmarks of the system), the persistent strength of provincial prejudice suggests that the culture does not value and does not view the path-structure as adequate. The traditional rationalization of powerful college affiliations within the large monastic universities that evoke discriminatory and exclusionary adherence to one's college is that it draws attention and energy to study of the college's particular textbooks and to self-cultivation. However, the rationalization may mask an admission that the path-system so carefully laid out as a harmonious process indeed does not fit together when implemented in practice.

These several points may suggest that reason, based on harmony and non-contradiction, is not all-important (despite claims to the opposite) and that the linear progression of a path removing obstacles and taking one forward to the city of nirvāṇa does not capture the entire scope of the soteriological process. The implication is that mere acquisition of more knowledge is not sufficient. The neatly ordered path-structure communicates few of the dangers with which mental transformation is fraught—the harrowing readjustments of perceptions and priorities, the stagnation brought on by psychological blockages, and the counterproductive illusions generated by misunderstandings and preliminary experiences. These difficulties, coupled with humanity's penchant to employ anything and everything in its corruptions, pave the way for cultural distortions (which certainly are not limited to Tibet).[a]

Still, the systemization of the Buddhist path that Tibetan orders present performs many functions—it provides a basic handbook for practitioners; it explicates spiritual experience by providing a map of its levels; it offers a structure for theoretic discourse the impetus for which comes from actual experience but also from demands of coherence, elegance of system, and an over-riding agenda of providing a comprehensive worldview. It also serves socioeconomic purposes of providing favored group identification, isolating the "ins" from the "outs." These inter-penetrating layers are often at cross-purposes such that a

[a] During my prep school and college days, I was introduced to cynicism and relativistic nihilism, but I have not found writing about such distortions to be of particular interest. What came to fascinate me is the possibility of the genuine, albeit with a critical eye.

message of universal compassion, for instance, becomes wrapped in a package of prejudiced parochialism.

In order to bring to the fore the fractious aspects of practice of the path, in this chapter I will briefly examine Rudolph Otto's[a] radically different presentation of what it means to be religious—his description of the *mysterium tremendum*—in order to provide a mirror in which similar presentations **within** this Tibetan tradition can be seen.[b] This will put the compellingly beautiful, symmetrical structure of the path in the asymmetrical perspective of actual experience. This juxtaposition yields hints that soteriological experience even in this so neatly ordered, harmonious system may be a matter of acquiring (or uncovering) perspectives that at first are dramatically and fractiously "other" but, with acculturation, are felt as being one's own basic nature.

Otto's "Mysterium Tremendum"

I find that Rudolph Otto's work, though treating experience of the sacred within a theistic context, provides a means of unmasking facets of the **experience** of the practice of this Buddhist system. The seemingly great difference between the two systems has challenged me to notice descriptions of the emotionally harrowing nature of soteriological experience that are indeed to be found in Tibetan traditions but are buried, so to speak, under the format of a grand design of spiritual development that easily fosters a sense that, with the proper will, the implementation of certain practices yields a predictable series of results. Let us first consider Otto's position in some detail, citing his text to a degree sufficient to get its flavor.

He describes religious experience as being of the "*mysterium*"—"that which is hidden and esoteric, that which is beyond conception or understanding, extraordinary and unfamiliar"[480]—under five headings: awefulness, overpoweringness, energy or urgency, wholly otherness, and fascination.[c] "Awefulness" is analogous to fear but "wholly distinct from being afraid,"[481] a "terror fraught with an inward shuddering such as not even the most menacing and

[a] Rudolph Otto, *The Idea of the Holy*, trans. John W. Harvey (London: Oxford University Press, 1923); see especially chap. 4, "Mysterium Tremendum," and chap. 5, "The Analysis of '*Mysterium*.'" See Donald S. Lopez Jr., "Approaching the numinous: Rudolf Otto and Tibetan Tantra," *Philosophy East and West* 29, no. 4 (1979):467-476; Lopez sharply contrasts Otto's view of the holy with the Ge-luk-b̄a emphasis on the compatibility between reason and profound religious experience. Although I agree with Lopez on the theoretical level, my agenda here is different—I am using Otto's presentation to get at the awe-inspiring (and even dreadful) experience of the path, which, to a great extent, is hidden by the Ge-luk-b̄a emphasis on reasoning.

[b] An earlier version of this material appeared in "A Tibetan Perspective on the Nature of Spiritual Experience," in *Paths to Liberation*, ed. Robert E. Buswell and Robert Gimello (Honolulu: University of Hawaii Press, 1992), 182-217.

[c] These are the section headings of chapters 4 and 5 of his *The Idea of the Holy*.

overpowering created things can instill,"[482] "the feeling of personal nothingness and submergence before the awe-inspiring object directly experienced."[483] Similarly, about "overpoweringness" he says:

> Thus, in contrast to "the overpowering" of which we are conscious as an object over against the self, there is the feeling of one's own submergence, of being but "dust and ashes" and nothingness. And this forms the numinous raw material for the feeling of religious humility.[484]

And:

> For one of the chiefest and most general features of mysticism is just this *self-depreciation* (so plainly parallel to the case of Abraham), the estimation of the self, of the personal "I," as something not perfectly or essentially real, or even as mere nullity, a self-depreciation which comes to demand its own fulfillment in practice in rejecting the delusion of selfhood, and so makes for the annihilation of the self. And on the other hand mysticism leads to a valuation of the transcendent object of its reference as that which through plenitude of being stands supreme and absolute, so that the finite self contrasted with it becomes conscious even in its nullity that "I am naught, Thou art all."[485]

Otto describes the third attribute of the *mysterium,* energy or urgency, as "a force that knows not stint or stay, which is urgent, active, compelling, and alive."[486] The *mysterium* is also characterized by being the "wholly other":

> that which is quite beyond the sphere of the usual, the intelligible, and the familiar, which therefore falls quite outside the limits of the "canny," and is contrasted with it, filling the mind with blank wonder and astonishment.[487]

And:

> The truly "mysterious" object is beyond our apprehension and comprehension, not only because our knowledge has certain irremovable limits, but because in it we come upon something inherently "wholly other," whose kind and character are incommensurable with our own, and before which we therefore recoil in a wonder that strikes us chill and numb.[488]

And:

> Mysticism continues to its extreme point this contrasting of the numinous object (the numen), as the "wholly other," with ordinary experience. Not content with contrasting it with all that is of nature or this world, mysticism concludes by contrasting it with Being itself and all

> that "is," and finally actually calls it "that which is nothing." By this "nothing" is meant not only that of which nothing can be predicated, but that which is absolutely and intrinsically other than and opposite of everything that is and can be thought. But while exaggerating to the point of paradox this ***negation*** and contrast—the only means open to conceptual thought to apprehend the ***mysterium***—mysticism at the same time retains the ***positive quality*** of the "wholly other" as a very living factor in its over-brimming religious emotion.
>
> But what is true of the strange "nothingness" of our mystics holds good equally of the *sūnyam,* the "void" and "emptiness" of the Buddhist mystics. This aspiration for the "void" and for becoming void, no less than the aspiration of our western mystics for "nothing" and for becoming nothing, must seem a kind of lunacy to anyone who has no inner sympathy for the esoteric language and ideograms of mysticism, and lacks the matrix from which these come necessarily to birth.[489]

About the fifth and final characteristic, fascination, Otto says:

> Possession of and by the numen becomes an end in itself; it begins to be sought for its own sake; and the wildest and most artificial methods of asceticism are put into practice to attain it....the ***mysterium*** is experienced in its essential, positive, and specific character, as something that bestows upon man a beatitude beyond compare, but one whose real nature he can neither proclaim in speech nor conceive in thought, but may know only by a direct and living experience. It is a bliss which embraces all those blessings that are indicated or suggested in positive fashion by any "doctrine of salvation," and it quickens all of them through and through...[490]

And:

> ...what we have here to point out is the unutterableness of what has been yet genuinely experienced, and how such an experience may pass into blissful excitement, rapture, and exaltation verging often on the bizarre and the abnormal.[491]

For Otto, the sacred is overpowering, charged with energy, awe-inspiring, and shocking/fascinating. His description finds so little resonance with the Indo-Tibetan presentation of the threefold typology of religious practitioners and the structure of the religious path that we could easily be drawn into concluding that his theistic perspective makes comparison impossible.

However, such language is not entirely lacking in the Tibetan cultural region; there are similar but not so prominent explanations that run counter to the seeming ease and fluidity of the steps in the Buddhist structure of the spiritual path. For instance, with regard to approaching realization of emptiness as it is described in the Consequence School, the late eighteenth- and early nineteenth-century Mongolian scholar Ḏen-dar-lha-ram-ba[a] describes a stage of fear that is eventually overcome through training:[492]

> An object that appears to a non-conceptual [sense] consciousness is the object conceived to exist inherently by a conceptual consciousness [in the sense that a conceptual consciousness assents to the object's appearance of inherent existence]. Therefore, related with this object are (1) the appearance of existing from its own side which is to be refuted and (2) the mere appearance [of the object] which is not to be refuted. [However] before attaining the view [of the absence of inherent existence] these two appear confused as one. When the view is found, these two [the appearance of existing from its own side and the mere appearance] are discriminated, and it is well renowned in the words of the wise that it is an important essential that the mere appearance is not refuted. When mountains, fences, houses, and so forth appear to ordinary beings, they appear in all respects to exist from their own side. Therefore, one should meditate until, destroying this mode of appearance, it is cancelled in all respects for one's mind, and the fear, "Now there is nothing left over," is generated.
>
> The generation of such fear is extremely rare. Ke-drup's *Opening the Eyes of the Fortunate* says:
>
>> If even arrival at the point of actual generation of fear and fright of the profound emptiness is extremely rare, what need is there to say that arrival at an actual ascertainment, which is an understanding of an emptiness through experience, is almost non-existent!
>
> Therefore, greatly superior to the present-day philosophers to whom not even an image of the mode of [an object's] existing from its own side has appeared are those in earlier times who overextended what is refuted [in the view of selflessness and held that objects themselves are refuted].
>
> There are reasons for not being frightened about emptiness. On the one hand, the stupid who do not know either the term or the meaning of emptiness are not frightened because they do not know any of its disadvantages or advantages. For example, the stupid who do not know about how one can fall from a horse are brave to mount a wild horse. On the other hand, those who perceive emptiness directly do not fear it because they lack the cause of fear, that is, the conception of inherent existence which is abandoned through seeing [the

[a] *bstan dar lha ram pa,* b. 1759.

> truth], like a being who has learned well the ways of controlling a wild horse.
>
> Then, who fears [emptiness]? It is suitable for fear to be generated in those who have understood emptiness a little and are investigating whether such and such a phenomenon exists or not. For suddenly the phenomenon appears to their minds to be totally non-existent. An example is a person who has understood a little but not completely how to mount a wild horse.

Emptiness **seems** to be incompatible with appearance in that when one understands it a little, objects no longer seem positable. Emptiness becomes a threat, like a wild horse—the analogy resonating with Otto's description of the sacred as overpowering, charged with energy, awe-inspiring, and shocking/fascinating. Indeed, meditators must bring their analysis of objects to a point of fright; otherwise, the implications of emptiness—realization of which is diametrically opposed to the ingrained assent to a false status of objects on which all emotional turmoil is built—are missed. However, with acculturation, like acquiring skill with horses, the fear is removed, for one becomes able to make the distinction between the appearance that is negated—the object's seeming to be established by way of its own character as the referent of words and conceptual consciousness—and the mere appearance of the object itself which is not negated. The problem, therefore, is not with emptiness; it is with the untrained mind's perception of it as negating appearance—oneself and everything else.

In addition, even though the logical presentation of the threefold typology of practices may make it seem as if the progression from one level to another is a smooth process of gradual acquisition of a new outlook, the very structure of the three tiers suggests that the soteriological experiences of each succeeding level are not accessible and are even foreign to those on a lower level. The upper levels are **outside** the experience of those on lower levels—they are dramatically **other**. One may study about the upper levels, but **being** a person of a higher level is outside of one's experience. A realistic appraisal of one's own motivation, in the face of carefully considering this typology, yields a self-identification as **very** low on the scale; the typology gives practitioners both a means to assess accurately their present condition and goals to strive toward. The typology itself thereby exerts an influence on practitioners, beckoning toward the development of a more profound perspective but also making it clear that those levels are foreign.

On the other hand, the usage of **common** concerns—first with one's own suffering and then with familial responsibility—as means to deepen and then broaden one's perspective suggests that the seeds of the higher levels are **common** to all. Seen in this light, the higher attitudes are present in a **common** seed-form which, through repeated training, can be extended in a process of development, but they are profoundly **other**, in the sense that they are outside present manifestation, their implications being unbearable to the present personality structure.

Similarly, with respect to the manifestation of the mind of clear light, the fact that this awesomeness is one's own final nature suggests that the otherness and fear associated with its manifestation are not part of its nature but are due to the shallowness of untrained beings. As was mentioned earlier (p. 24), much of the Ge-luk-ba system of spiritual education, framed around the practices of beings of the three capacities, indeed can be viewed as aimed at overcoming this fear of one's own most basic nature. The strangeness of our own nature is a function of misconception, in this case of the basic nature of the mind, specifically the sense that afflictive emotions subsist in the nature of the mind. As the Zen master Enni (1202-1280) indicates, the source of suffering is the misidentification of afflictive emotions as the very nature of the mind:[493]

> Those injured by this spirit of the afflictions, believing that their deluded thoughts are the original mind and taking delight in the seeds of desire, revolve through the four [kinds of] rebirth in the three evil [destinies].

Ge-luk-ba texts similarly stress that beings are so identified with their own afflictive emotions that when their own basis starts to manifest, the fright of annihilation is generated. According to descriptions in Highest Yoga Tantra, when the fundamental innate mind of clear light dawns, it **seems** to leave no room for appearances, even annihilating oneself and thus generating fright. As a remedy, Ge-luk-ba scholars call for **reasoned** affirmation of the basic purity of the mind, this being within the frequently reiterated context that well-reasoned faith is far stronger than unreasoned faith. However, this dictum may not take into account the power and effectiveness of faith that is built, not on reasoning, but on inklings, on glimpses; such faith is a central element in leading a practitioner, consciously and unconsciously, to profound experience. As the Sixth Patriarch Hui-Neng says in the *Platform Sūtra,* "Don't doubt that your own mind is Buddha."

The Fundamental Innate Mind Of Clear Light In Highest Yoga Tantra

Since the final aim of the spiritual path as presented in the Tibetan cultural region is to manifest this most subtle level of mind and to remain within it—all the while manifesting dualistically in order to be of service to others—let us consider the fundamental innate mind of clear light in detail so that its significance and relationship to the broad spectrum of paths presented earlier can be discussed.

The mind of clear light is identified as the eighth in a series of increasingly subtle experiences that pervade conscious life.[494] It manifests at periods when the grosser levels of consciousness cease either intentionally—as in profound states of meditation—or naturally, as in the process of death, going to sleep, ending a dream, fainting, and orgasm.[a] Prior to its manifestation, there are several stages during which a practitioner experiences increasingly subtler levels of mind.

Through meditative focusing on sensitive parts of the body, the winds,[b] or currents of energy, that serve as foundations for various levels of consciousness are gradually withdrawn, in the process of which one first has a visual experience of seeing an appearance like a mirage. Then, as the withdrawal is more and more successful, one successively "sees" an appearance like billowing smoke, an appearance like fireflies within smoke, an appearance like a sputtering butter-lamp when little wax is left, and then that of a steady candle flame. Then, with the withdrawal of conceptual consciousnesses,[c] a more dramatic phase begins, at which point profound levels of consciousness that are at the core of experience manifest.

The first subtle level of consciousness to manifest is the mind of vivid whiteness called "appearance." It is described as like a clear night sky filled with moonlight, not the moon shining in empty space but space filled with white light. All coarse conceptuality has ceased, and nothing appears except this slightly dualistic vivid white appearance, which is one's consciousness itself appearing as an omnipresent, huge, white, vivid vastness. When that mind ceases, a more subtle mind of vivid redness or orangeness called "increase" dawns; this state is compared to a clear sky filled with sunlight, again not the sun shining in

[a] The traditional way of explaining the process of proceeding from grosser to subtler states is in the context of dying. The explanation—in Highest Yoga Tantra—of the stages of dying and the physiological reasons behind them is based on a complicated theory of winds that serve as foundations for various levels of consciousness. Upon the serial collapse of the ability of these "winds" to serve as bases of consciousness, the events of death—internal and external—unfold. The same experiences also can be induced by consciously withdrawing the winds in the practice of Highest Yoga Tantra.

[b] *rlung, prāṇa.*

[c] In the Guhyasamāja system of Highest Yoga Tantra as presented in Nāgārjuna's *Five Stages* (*rim pa lnga pa, pañcakrama;* Peking 2667, vol. 61), conceptual consciousnesses are detailed as of eighty types, divided into three classes. The first group of thirty-three is composed of conceptual consciousnesses that involve a strong movement of "wind" to their objects. They include conceptions such as fear, attachment, hunger, thirst, compassion, acquisitiveness, and jealousy. The second group of forty conceptions is composed of conceptual consciousnesses that involve a medium movement of "wind" to their objects—conceptions such as joy, amazement, generosity, desiring to kiss, heroism, non-gentleness, and crookedness. The third group of seven conceptions involve a weak movement of "wind" to their objects—forgetfulness, mistake as in apprehending water in a mirage, catatonia, depression, laziness, doubt, and equal desire and hatred. Although the difference between the first two groups is not obvious (at least to me), it is clear that in the third group the mind is strongly withdrawn; the three represent, on the ordinary level of consciousness, increasingly less dualistic perception.

the sky but space filled with red or orange light. Nothing appears except this even less dualistic vivid red or orange appearance, which is one's consciousness itself, appearing as an omnipresent, huge, orange or red, vivid vastness. The consciousness remains in this state for a period, and then when this mind ceases, a still more subtle mind of vivid blackness called "near-attainment" dawns; it is so called because one is close to manifesting the mind of clear light. The mind of black near-attainment is compared to a moonless, very black sky just after dusk when no stars shine. Nothing appears except this still less dualistic, vivid, black appearance which is one's consciousness, appearing as an omnipresent, huge, black, thick, vivid vastness. During the first part of this phase of utter blackness, one remains conscious but then, in a second phase, becomes unconscious in thick blackness.

Then, when the mind of black near-attainment ceases, the three "pollutants"[a] of the white, red/orange, and black appearances have been entirely cleared away, whereupon the mind of clear light dawns. This is the most subtle level of consciousness; it is compared to the sky's own natural cast without the "pollutions" of moonlight, sunlight, or darkness—the fundamental innate mind of clear light.[b]

In this way, the process of manifesting the most subtle level of mind involves passage through eight steps which are appearances of:

1. mirage
2. smoke
3. fireflies
4. flame of a lamp
5. vivid white mind-sky
6. vivid red or orange mind-sky
7. vivid black mind-sky
8. clear light.

It is said that these deeper, more subtle levels of mind manifest not only in this order during the process of dying but also in **reverse** order when taking rebirth. Similarly, when going to sleep, they manifest in the forward order, just as in the process of dying but more briefly, and they manifest in reverse order when awakening. Correspondingly, they manifest in reverse order when a dream begins and in forward order when a dream ends. They also are said to manifest in forward and reverse orders during sneezing, fainting, and orgasm. Thus, a life is spent in the midst of thousands of small "deaths" and "rebirths."

Since untrained beings are identified with superficial states, the manifestation of deeper states brings out a fear of annihilation. This description recalls Carl Jung's recounting of a Swiss mystic who, upon the dawning of great illumination, bashed his face into a large rock in front of him. The fear-inspiring

a *bslod byed.*

b *gnyug ma lhan cig skyes pa'i 'od gsal gyi sems.*

aspect of its manifestation accords with the often described awesomeness and sense of otherness that not only Rudolph Otto but much of world culture associates with types of profound religious experience.

In both the practices of the being of three capacities and the practices of Highest Yoga Tantra, energies are withdrawn, and elements common to the ordinary mind are emphasized and expanded, but, despite the commonness of the expanse in the process, the experience of such withdrawal and expansion is fraught with uneasiness (except apparently for a few gifted persons).[a] Attempts to expand common attitudes of concern for one's own welfare and concern for friends to larger perspectives are characterized with a sense of alienness because of the attachments that must be overcome in order to open the way for such new perspectives, and similarly the manifestation of the mind of clear light—the inner nature of all conscious experience—can evoke such a great sense of alienness that it is feared as a force annihilating oneself, this being because of self-identification with mental and physical factors that are contrary to one's own nature. Thus, soteriological experience on many levels evokes a sense of dread—of the loss of directionality that pursuit of temporary pleasures affords, of the loss of permanence, of the loss of a solidly existent sense of self, and of the loss of one's very being—facing what is awesomely other than one's present, limited perspective. Nevertheless, the very same insights, after acculturation by means of paths of practice, are perceived as like finding a lost treasure. As the Fifth Dalai Lama says about the experience of realizing emptiness:[495]

> This initial generation of the Middle Way view is not actual special insight; however, like a moon on the second day of the month, it is a slight finding of the view. At that time, if you have no predispositions for emptiness from a former life, it seems that a thing which was in the hand has suddenly been lost. If you have predispositions, it seems that a lost jewel which had been in the hand has suddenly been found.

What is experienced with a sense of loss at an early stage is later re-experienced with a sense of finding a treasure that had been lost.

The frequent descriptions in the literature of Tibet's Old Translation School of Ñying-ma, as well as in East Asian Buddhism, of identifying one's own actual nature, one's own face, suggest that the sense of at-homeness, of "being set on mama's lap," reveals religion not as something separate but as eventually most familiar.[b] The joy and sense of at-homeness that a child feels

---

[a] About sudden enlightenment in the Ñying-ma school, see Khetsun Sangpo, *Tantric Practice in Nyingma* (London: Rider, 1982; reprint, Ithaca, N.Y.: Snow Lion, 1983), 187-193.

[b] In a different context, Wilfred Cantwell Smith has said that religion is, in a sense, most common, its isolated separateness being a fabrication of our current secularism. In his presidential address at the 1983 annual meeting of the American Academy of Religion, Smith said:

when (in a happy mood) he or she is set on mama's lap is an analog to highly developed yogis' sense of joyful naturalness when they identify in experience their own basic nature. The fundamental innate mind of clear light, when experienced by one who has overcome the initial, distorted fear and sense of annihilation, is most familiar, most comforting, most **common**, most ordinary. One might even think that such an experience is not religious because of not having the quality of separateness and awe, but as we have seen, soteriological experience in this tradition is an acculturation to a state that is foreign only because of the afflicted state of the practitioner. The experience of the fundamental innate mind of clear light as the "standard everyday" stuff of basic mind indicates that this most profound of religious experiences in Indian and Tibetan tantrism is not of a realm of the sacred that is radically other; rather, it is one's own nature that is immanent in all consciousness but is transcendent until its manifestation. When manifested, it loses the distance of transcendence much as is done in the Vedānta dictum "*Tat tvam asi,*" ("You are that,") in which an identification of oneself with ultimate reality, Brahman, is made.[a] The diseased

---

> For the fact is that reasonably well-informed perceptive awareness of the history of our planet over the past thirty or so millennia makes clear that modern Western secularism is an aberration; and that its attempt to interpret religion as some sort of extra in human life is dogmatic, is ideological eisegesis. The notion that human nature and truth are fundamentally secular, are the norm, from which most human beings have, whether for good or other reason, deviated, is sheer projection.
>
> By this I do *not* mean that humanity is, rather, fundamentally *homo religiosus.* That is an error that further illustrates my thesis, by its perpetuating the idiosyncratic outlook that the Modern West has defensively constructed. It took us some time to detect this. The concept "religion" has itself been developed by Western secularism as naming something that is supposedly over and above the standard everyday. Religion is in fact not something special, the historian can now see; it is secularism that is odd. "Religion" is a secularist notion, a conceptual element in that particular worldview—but a misleading one, setting up a dichotomy that secularists need in order to justify their own separate peculiarity, but normal people do not and cannot. The dichotomy is retained, in inverted form, in that phrase *homo religiosus.* Actually, there is rather just plain *homo sapiens,* and then a minority of those not quite *sapientes* enough to have sensed what kind of universe we live in and what kind of being we are.

See "The Modern West in the History of Religion," *Journal of the American Academy of Religion* 52, no. 1 (March 1984):9.

Admittedly, Smith is not making the points that I am making, but it strikes me that once it is held that religion is not separate, its non-separateness must be grounded in a reality that is at the very root of existence, as is the case with the fundamental innate mind of clear light. Smith's point is not just that at a different cultural period religion was not separated out; he is suggesting that this is the case *in fact*—that religion is rooted in "what kind of universe we live in and what kind of being we are."

[a] For a lucid exposition of this, see Śri Sureśvarācārya, *Naiṣkarmyasiddhi,* trans. S. S. Radhavachar (Mysore: University of Mysore, 1965).

nature of oneself and the distance of Brahman, the ultimate, are canceled in the immediacy and closeness ("at-homeness") of recognizing one's own final nature.

Such non-alienness is not limited to mature experience of the fundamental innate mind of clear light, for, as explained earlier, the practices of the beings of the three levels of capacity, though extensions of common experiences, pass through a phase of alienness but then culminate in a sense of familiarity, resulting from cultivation of the path. The path is the bridge between an original common endowment and a final expansion of such experience to a universal level; it opens a passageway by removing the obstacles—the inability to stand the implications of these profound states. This need for acculturation is reflected in the frequently repeated Tibetan oral teaching that "meditation" (*sgom*) is actually "familiarization" (*khoms*),[a] a matter of getting used to, or adjusting one's mind to, the implications of profound realizations.[b] Specifically, with respect to the mind of clear light, the experience of this basic state as alien and dreadful is only relative to clinging to distorted notions about one's own nature. It is a function of a temporary inadequacy of the mind perceiving it, a failure that, according to this system, can be overcome through meditative cultivation of the path.

The fact of this final at-homeness, as well as the system's presentation of the compatibility of reason and experience of the sacred, could cause us to ignore the awe-inspiring, horrific, sometimes stultifying clashes with what seems to be one's own basic personality due to mis-identifying the afflictive emotions as being the very fabric of the mind. However, the experience of the sacred (the "sacred," as per the above discussion, includes not just the experience of the fundamental innate mind of clear light but also the path-experiences of beings of all three capacities) as dreadful, as so shattering that one cannot stand it, is not to be discounted. For when the sacred—these common experiences in their expanded meaning—impinge on a consciousness not yet ready for them, they are indeed dreadful, fraught with implications undermining and threatening distorted postures of personality. To appreciate the significance of the path, we must realize that initial contemplations of

- the plight of transmigrations as animals, hungry ghosts, and hell-beings
- the plight of cyclic existence in general
- the needs of the endless number of sentient beings
- the implications of the basic nature of the mind

are upsetting because they are in such great opposition to ingrained attitudes. When done effectively (and the various traditions supply many techniques to

[a] This is a play on words, since the first is pronounced "gom" and the second, "kom"; the change is slight.

[b] That the term "forbearance" (*bzod pa, kṣānti*) is used for levels of the path indicates an overcoming of non-facility with profound doctrine.

accomplish this, the very diversity of which should not be lost in exclusivistic allegiance to one), the impact of such contemplations on the pursuit of present and superficial pleasures as well as on the pursuit of self-centered goals—which are so central to ordinary perspectives—is indeed devastating in its demand for rearrangement of the personality.

Attachment is built on bias, and the extension of more homogeneous attitudes requires a dramatic withdrawal of the energy of attachment. Thus, even though the awe-inspiring nature of the path is relative to attachment to biased states—namely, to viewing the afflictive emotions as the basic nature of the mind—it should not be ignored in favor of the comfortably ordered layout of stages which communicate little of the pain and clash between intimately held attachments and higher attitudes. Only when we see these implications can we place the path in the context of its liberative task. All three phases of experience of the sacred—dreadful, overcoming obstacles, and totally "at-home"—need to be emphasized in order to convey a basic picture of the path. From this perspective we see the enormity and momentousness of this religious endeavor.

Appendix 1: Is Representation-Only Compatible with External Objects?

In his article "Yogācāra and the Buddhist Logicians,"[496] Alex Wayman of Columbia University seeks to prove a basic thesis, which, in my own words, is:

> In the early Yogic Practice School—that is, from Asaṅga to Vasubandhu and his commentator Sthiramati—there is no denial of the external object, but rather a stress on its mis-reported nature.

He holds that the evidence cited by others as supporting the view that external objects are denied can be explained elsewise. In the process, he presents four propositions:

1. If sense objects are consciousness-supports,[a] then external objects exist.
2. If different beings see the same object differently, then external objects exist.
3. Refutations of external objects in the early Yogic Practice School are limited to the meditative situation.
4. If atomic particles exist, then external objects exist.

Wayman[497] embarks on the demanding task of re-interpreting a wide range of passages usually considered to be presenting an idealist view:

> The present writer found in the course of his studies over the years that the philosophical position of these texts that emerged while he read the texts of Asaṅga and his followers did not bear out the standard survey explanation of the Yogācāra position....I allude to the unqualified denial of an external object, attributed to this school. Of course, if indeed the Yogācāra school denies the reality of an external object, it would hardly be possible to find its position attractive to the Buddhist logicians who were to follow, since Dignāga and his successors, especially Dharmakīrti, do not deny an external object; rather they call it a *svalakṣaṇa* (the "particular") and even sometimes describe it as *Paramārtha-sat* ("absolute existence"), to underscore the reality of this object of direct perception (*pratyakṣa*).

Basically, Wayman seeks to present the notion that Vasubandhu and his student Dignāga harmoniously hold that external objects exist. He does this by examining multiple usages of the term *ālambana,* "consciousness-support," or, as I translate it, "object of observation." (Ge-luk-b̄a scholars hold that Vasubandhu in his Yogic Practice works and Dignāga harmoniously assert the non-existence of external objects.)

---

[a] *dmigs pa, ālambana.*

1. Wayman: If Sense Objects Are Consciousness-Supports, Then External Objects Exist

Wayman makes the case that, since Sthiramati, in commentary on Vasubandhu, makes reference to a sense object as an object of observation, it is clear that external objects are not being refuted. He first cites Sthiramati:[498]

> A consciousness-support is a sense object of a thought (*citta*) and a mental (*caitta*)[a]; furthermore, it is of six kinds, from form (*rūpa*) up to natures (*dharma*).

Then he says:

> Notice that there is no denial of an *ālambana* in the meaning of a sense object.

Wayman's argument seems to be that, if sense objects,[b] that is to say, objects of any of the six consciousnesses, are consciousness-supports, then external objects are not refuted. However, since, as will be seen below in item 3, he holds that in the meditative situation consciousness-supports are not external objects, his meaning must be that, if a consciousness-support **generates** a consciousness, then the consciousness-support (that is, object) is an external object.

Ge-luk-b̄a scholars agree with this reframing of his argument, and thus they are particularly concerned with those instances when supposed Proponents of Mind-Only speak not just of consciousness-supports (or, in my terms, objects of observation) but of object-of-observation-conditions.[c] For here the term "condition," or cause, is openly being used, and they hold that:

- An object, such as a patch of blue, cannot be an object-of-observation-**condition** without being a cause of the eye consciousness apprehending it.
- If it causes the consciousness, it must be a separate entity from the consciousness—the dictum being that causes and their respective effects are separate entities, thereby contradicting the view that a path of blue and the eye consciousness apprehending it are the same substantial entity.

To avoid having to posit such an egregious self-contradiction in the Mind-Only School and yet maintain sameness of entity of object and subject, Ge-luk-b̄a scholars hold that in the Mind-Only School:

- the **actual** object-of-observation-condition is the internal predisposition

---

[a] In my terminology, these two would be "minds and mental factors."

[b] Since Wayman is explaining Sthiramati's line, which refers to six types of objects, he obviously is not referring to objects of the five sense consciousnesses as opposed to those exclusively of the mental consciousness, but is including the objects of all consciousnesses in "sense objects."

[c] *dmigs rkyen, ālambanapratyaya.*

that causes the appearance of the object, whereas

- the object, the patch of blue, is merely an **imputed** object-of-observation-condition,[a] called an **appearing** object-of-observation-condition.[b]

In Ge-luk-b̄a scholarship the position of the Mind-Only School on object-of-observation-conditions is typically contrasted with that of the Sūtra School:[499]

> The Chittamātra presentation differs significantly. In the latter's system, not objects but latent predispositions are posited as the observed object condition for both sense and mental direct perceivers. Thus, as the observed object condition of either a sense or mental direct perceiver apprehending a form the Chittamātrins posit a predisposition which exists with the immediately preceding condition of that consciousness and causes it to be generated as having the aspect of blue. The form which is apprehended by that sense of mental direct perceiver is called an *appearing* observed object condition. It is an observed object condition but not an actual one, called such because although it appears to the consciousness it does not produce it.
>
> In the Chittamātra system, a form and the sense of mental direct perceiver apprehending it are one substantial entity and thus simultaneous, whereas an observed object condition must be a *cause* of a consciousness; whatever is a cause of something must be a different substantial entity from it and in a relationship of temporal sequence. If there were such an observed object condition, external objects would be entailed—this being impossible in the Chittamātra or Mind-Only system. In fact, the Sautrāntikas point to the existence of observed object conditions as establishing the existence of external objects.

In this explanation, the term "condition," or cause, is explained away as merely being "an imputed condition."

From the footwork that is necessary to avoid the implications of the usage of the term "object-of-observation-condition," one can see that Wayman has hit on a sensitive topic. (For more discussion, see item 4 below.)

2. Wayman: If Different Beings See The Same Object Differently, Then External Objects Exist

Next Wayman turns to Vasubandhu's *The Twenty,* verse 3, in which there is reference to different beings—hungry ghosts and so forth—encountering a stream but seeing it differently due to their predispositions (see p. 470ff.). He sees this as reasoning showing not that there are no external objects but that, due to their karma, beings of different types superimpose different types of

---

a *dmigs rkyen btags pa pa.*

b *snang ba'i dmigs rkyen.*

fabrications on a basic external object. Wayman makes the point that often external objects are taught to be disregarded, not to be regarded as non-existent.

His position is based on the commonsense notion that, if various beings are looking at the same object and seeing it differently, then there is one basic object that they are seeing. The positing of such an external object is similar to John Locke's[a] "substance" composed of extension, solidity, and number and devoid of secondary qualities such as color, taste, and sound. Indeed, Wayman's calling attention to the common conclusion that multiple perception of one object means there is one object requires addressing if meaningful interaction among beings even of the same type is to be maintained. Again, the maneuverings of Ge-luk-b̄a scholars on this issue (see p. 488) suggest that Wayman has put his finger on a sensitive issue. The same is true of Wayman's own attempt[500] when he takes a passage from Dharmottara that describes color as ultimately existent but shape as conventionally existent as an affirmation of the position that a basic thing (color) constitutes the external object whereas another important factor (shape) is merely "in the mind." In this case, we are left with an external object that is amorphous color.

As further evidence, Wayman turns to the opinion of Jñānagarbha, generally considered to be of a different school of thought from Vasubandhu and a follower of Bhāvaviveka who posits the existence of external objects. I doubt that Wayman is suggesting that Vasubandhu must assert whatever Jñānagarbha asserts; rather, it is more likely that he means to point out that there is such a view and that we need to consider whether Vasubandhu holds this view:[501]

> Jñānagarbha's commentary on the Maitreya chapter of the *Saṃdhinirmocanasūtra* illustrates the mis-reported nature of the external object with the standard example of the stream of water which animals, hungry ghosts, men, and gods all see differently, the hungry ghosts seeing it full of pus, the gods seeing it as lapis lazuli, and so on. The stream itself is not denied. What those remarks mean is that the consciousness shared by a particular destiny (*gati*), say men, or hungry ghosts, agrees on a particular fabrication attributed to an external, and that the external is not the way it was represented. Hence, the point is not to deny an external object, but rather to affirm the representation of it as a group fabrication; and so the common denial of an external object means in these terms that there is no object of which the representation is a faithful copy. In short, Vasubandhu could well argue that his representation-only is the correct way to speak of the nature of consciousness in the light of the Buddhist teaching of five or six destinies (*gati*), with the position that the object is the same for all sentient beings: they only see it differently on account of the destiny.

[a] 1632–1704.

Having put forth the proposition that Vasubandhu "could" be accepting external objects, Wayman should proceed to show that indeed Vasubandhu does hold this opinion through citing textual evidence. However, he makes the leap to assume that this indeed **is** Vasubandhu's opinion:[502]

> Once we take this as Vasubandhu's position, it becomes more reasonable to assume a possible consistency with Dignāga's *ālambanaparīkṣā,* since this work indeed admits an *ālambana.*

Dignāga's presentation is treated in item 4 below.

3. Wayman: Refutations Of External Objects In The Early Yogic Practice School Are Limited To The Meditative Situation

Wayman proceeds to show that Vasubandhu uses the term *ālambana* in his *The Thirty,* verse 28, without denying its existence, but with a different meaning. In this context, instead of translating the term as "consciousness-support" as he did before, he now translates it as "meditative object" to indicate that what is being denied in his case is an external meditative object:[503]

> It is also well to notice that Vasubandhu treats the transcendental experience, since Dignāga also admits a *yogipratyakṣa.* Thus toward the end of the *Triṃsikā* (verse 28):
>
>> When perception (*vijñāna*) does not perceptively reach the meditative object (*ālambana*), it abides in the state of perception-only (*vijñāna-mātra*), which lacks an apprehendable by reason of not apprehending that meditative object.
>
> Here again Vasubandhu clarifies that he does not deny the *ālambana.* The state of *vijñāna-mātra* is reached when *vijñāna* does not apprehend the *ālambana.* Subject and object have become one in *saṃādhi*...

Wayman tries to make a case for a harmony between Vasubandhu's:

- accepting "consciousness-supports" that generate consciousnesses, but
- denying external "meditative objects" in certain concentrative states

and Asaṅga's citing the passage from the Maitreya chapter of the *Sūtra Unraveling the Thought,* which we have considered at length earlier (see p. 440ff.). He seeks to show that in, for example, the Maitreya chapter of the *Sūtra Unraveling the Thought,* Asaṅga's *Summary of the Great Vehicle,* and Vasubandhu's *The Twenty* and *The Thirty,* external objects are refuted only in the context of meditation.

Unlike Schmithausen and Lamotte but like his student Willis,[a] Wayman[504] limits the meaning of the denial of *ālambana* to meditative situations:

> ...and Vasubandhu's verse is consistent with Asaṅga's citation of the *Saṃdhinirmocanasūtra* (Maitreya chapter) in his *Mahāyānasaṃgraha:*
>
> > Lord, is that image which is *saṃādhi*-domain different from that mind (which perceives) or is it the same? The lord answered: Maitreya, it is not different. And why? Because that image amounts to representation-only (*vijñaptimātra*). Maitreya, I have explained that the meditative object (*ālambana*) of perception (*vijñāna*) is distinguished (*vibhakta*) by representation-only (*vijñaptimātra*).
>
> This passage again clarifies that there is no denial of the *ālambana* even in the successful *samādhi* situation.

Wayman interprets "representation-only" here as negating external objects only within the meditative context.

Later, Wayman[505] considers the *Descent into Laṅkā Sūtra,* suggesting that, although the Yogic Practice School could not adopt Chandrakīrti's approach of considering the sūtra to teach no external objects in a provisional sense, the meaning of the sūtra should be limited to meditative situations. For in a meditative context external objects are to be disregarded, not refuted as existing in general. Wayman finds evidence for this in Sthiramati's statement:[506]

> The halting of thought on such a single area of thought as "Mind-only is the three worlds; they are nothing but the mind," constitutes calming (of the mind) (*śamatha*).

The dictum that the three realms—Desire Realm, Form Real, Formless Realm—are mind-only is reduced (in Wayman's interpretation) to a technique to keep the mind from being distracted to other, exterior objects.

Wayman finds support for this view in Maitreya's *Ornament for the Great Vehicle Sūtras,* since the term *cittamātra* is used in a passage about the four levels (see p. 240) of the path of preparation:[507]

> In these meditative passages, it could be argued, the sense of *mātra* in *cittamātra,* i.e., "only," as excluding external objects, is not to do away with external objects, but to disregard them, since this situation of *samādhi* is purely an interior movement.

Wayman's saying that such "could" be argued suggests that even he can hardly overlook that meditative situations are used to **realize** the philosophical view, and hence the fact that "mind-only" is used in a meditative context on occasion does not suggest that all other usages of it, such as in the *Descent into Laṅkā*

[a] See p. 447ff. and Appendix 3 (p. 525ff.)

Sūtra, should be re-read as somehow indicating only a technique for avoiding distraction. Rather, the more likely reading is that the Yogic Practice School holds that mind-only needs to be realized and that this realization needs to be deeply absorbed in the mental continuum through prolonged meditation.

Wayman next notes that Prajñākaragupta, in his commentary on Dharmakīrti's *Commentary on (Dignāga's) "Compilation of Prime Cognition,"* seems to say that for the Buddhist logicians a mind-basis-of-all[a] is not pertinent to discussions of direct perception and inference but is for the topic of karma. Wayman says:[508]

> Prajñākaragupta apparently means that the Buddhist logicians treat the problem of perception and inference without bringing in the notion of *ālayavijñāna;* and for all that, not necessarily rejecting it in terms of the *karma* theory.

Wayman's point in bringing up this topic is never made explicit. However, because he[509] refers to Gön-chok-jik-may-wang-bo's presentation that:

- for the Mind-Only School Following Scripture, the mind-basis-of-all is that which is the person,[b] but
- for the Mind-Only School Following Reasoning, the mental consciousness is that which is the person,

his point probably is that the mind-basis-of-all is not central to the tenets of the Yogic Practice School, since one branch of the school does not, at minimum, put as much emphasis on it. However, in Gön-chok-jik-may-wang-bo's presentation, the Mind-Only School Following Reasoning denies the existence of a separate eighth consciousness called a mind-basis-of-all and yet asserts that there are no external objects; it does this by holding that predispositions for the appearance of objects are infused in the mental consciousness. For him, a system could deny a mind-basis-of-all and still refute external objects.

Wayman, in summarizing his argument, refers to a conversation with Professor Masaaki Hattori on the topic:[510]

> I mentioned that I had failed to find any denial of an external object when I read the mirror simile passage in the Maitreya chapter of the *Saṃdhinirmocanasūtra* and as it was taken over by Asaṅga in his *Mahāyānasaṃgraha* along with Vasubandhu's comment; or when I read the extensive material on that simile passage in Yüan-ts'e's [that is, Wonch'uk's] great commentary on the *Saṃdhinirmocana* that was translated into Tibetan; or when I read Jñānagarbha's commentary on the Maitreya chapter. It seemed to me that these authors took the

a *kun shes rnam par shes pa, ālayavijñāna.*

b *mtshan gzhi.* See Geshe Lhundup Sopa and Jeffrey Hopkins, *Cutting through Appearances: The Practice and Theory of Tibetan Buddhism* (Ithaca, N.Y.: Snow Lion, 1989), 267.

> external entity for granted, but were silent about it because the sūtra itself was concerned with the *saṃādhi* image, which is not derived from the reflex in consciousness of an external object. Dr. Hattori agreed with me that the *Saṃdhinirmocana* there was silent about an external rather than in denial of it. But he added: the later Yogācāra school stems from the Vijñaptimātratā after Vasubandhu, and in this developed school there is definitely a denial of the external object. I am pleased to mention this agreement on the thesis I have been advancing in this paper, since my own considerations of the Yogācāra in comparison with the Buddhist logicians go up to Vasubandhu and his commentator Sthiramati; and so far, anyway, there is no denial of the external object, but rather a stress on its mis-reported nature.

Since Wayman says, "It seemed to me that these authors took the external entity for granted, but were silent about it...," we can assume that his view is that the later Yogic Practice School (and the bulk of contemporary scholarship) mistook this silence and mistakenly assumed a denial of external objects.

Wayman finds confirmation for his view—that the denial of external objects is limited to the meditative situation—in a line from Ḏzong-ka-ḇa's *The Essence of Eloquence.* Wayman says:[511]

> After writing the forgoing, I found a corroboration from a work of Tsoṅ-kha-pa, founder of the Gelugpa sect of Tibetan Buddhism. He said, referring to the *Saṃdhinirmocanasūtra,* "In that sūtra it is clearly stated that the denial of an external is in the phase of calming (the mind)."

Wayman's reading of the passage[a] is entirely upside-down; the passage actually demonstrates, not that Ḏzong-ka-ḇa finds the refutation of external objects in the *Sūtra Unraveling the Thought* to be limited to the meditative situation, but that external objects are refuted in general. The passage (*Emptiness in Mind-Only,* 217) actually says:

> Therefore, it is also not that a negation of an otherness of substantial entity between apprehended-object and apprehending-subject is absent in the statements in the *Sūtra Unraveling the Thought* that the emptiness of imputational factors imputed in the manner of entities and attributes is the thoroughly established nature. [Not only that, but also,] in that sūtra on the occasion of [discussing] calm abiding [in the "Questions of Maitreya Chapter"], a refutation of external objects is clearly set forth.

Ḏzong-ka-ḇa is concluding that the refutation—found in the Questions of

---

[a] *mdo de las zhi gnas kyi skabs su ni phyi rol dgag pa gsal bar gsungs so:* see *Emptiness in Mind-Only,* 315.

Paramārthasamudgata Chapter of the *Sūtra Unraveling the Thought*—of the establishment of objects by way of their own character as the referents of words and of conceptual consciousnesses involves a refutation of external objects and that, in addition, in the Questions of Maitreya Chapter of the same sūtra a refutation of external objects is "clearly," that is, explicitly, set forth.[a]

The Second Dalai Lama's summation[512] of the meaning of this passage confirms this reading:

> Therefore, the meaning of cognition-only, which is a negation of an otherness in substantial entity between apprehended-object and apprehending-subject, also is complete in a very good manner in the emptiness—of imputation of entity and attribute—of [being] established by way of its own character.[513]

Dzong-ka-ba himself says at the end of this section (*Emptiness in Mind-Only,* 219) that the reasonings establishing the emptiness of the imputational nature also refute that subject and object are different entities:

> To understand the meaning of these, it appears to be necessary to understand from the level of subtle detail the reasonings refuting the imputational factor and the superimposition that are objects of negation discussed in the *Sūtra Unraveling the Thought.* In particular, it appears to be necessary to know how through those reasonings an otherness of substantial entity of apprehended-object and apprehending-subject is refuted, whereupon there is entry into cognition-only.

Wayman has missed the meaning of the passage; he cites, as a proof, a passage from Dzong-ka-ba that says the opposite.

Wayman[514] next considers the term *vijñaptimātra* (*rnam par rig pa tsam*), which he translates as "representation-only" and I translate as "cognition-only,"[b] in Vasubandhu's *The Twenty.* As before with instances of the denial of *ālambana,* he wants to limit the meaning of *vijñaptimātra* to the meditative situation. Despite his own gloss of "only" as a negation of external objects, he limits the scope of the passage to the meditative situation. Examining the term "negation," he decides that, from between the two types of negations—simple (non-affirming) negations and qualified (affirming) negations—the negation of external objects here is a "qualified negation," that is, limited strictly to the meditative situation:[515]

> However, even granted that the *Saṃdhinirmocanasūtra,* the basic scripture of Yogācāra, did not deny an external object except for in the *samādhi* situation, it should be acknowledged that various scholars

---

[a] For a thorough discussion of this topic, see Part 5 (p. 393ff., especially pp. 433-442); and *Absorption,* #52, 53.

[b] For other translations, see p. 38, footnote b.

> have understood Vasubandhu's *Viṃśatikā Vijñaptimātrasiddhi* to have denied an external object without reference to the *samādhi* situation. But the opening gloss, which seems to indicate such a denial, can be understood differently. Explaining the term "representation-only" (*vijñaptimātra*), it defines the "only" this way: *mātram ity arthapratiṣedhārthaṃ* ("only" means negation of an object). Here the word *artha* is properly taken as "external object." The word *pratiṣedha* is known in Indian logic, including Buddhist logic, to have two kinds, "simple negation" (*prasajya-pratiṣedha*) and "qualified negation" (*paryudāsa*). The interpretation that this treatise of Vasubandhu's has denied an external object without qualifications opts for the "simple negation." In the light of passages previously cited from his two treatises, it is reasonable to opt for the "qualified negation." It is qualified because for the ordinary situation of life Vasubandhu indicates that the representation differs for the various destinies of men, hungry ghosts, etc.; and because for the special case of the yogin, "representation-only" concerns the *samādhi* situation.

An affirming negation or "qualified negation" is one that implies something **in place of its object of negation** as in the case of the corpulent Devadatta's not eating during the day implying in place of eating during the day that he eats at night; therefore, it appears that Wayman has missed the basic meaning of such a negation. For the object of negation here is not **no external objects** but **external objects.**[a]

Still, we need to consider Wayman's point that—in order to achieve textual consistency with the presentation in *The Twenty* of what various beings see when they view water—this gloss must be limited in its refutation to the meditative situation. As will be remembered, Wayman takes the section about the various appearances to various types of beings as indicating that there is a basic external object onto which, due to karma, beings add their own "representation." Thus, Wayman's point here more properly is that the negation must be limited because later parts of the same text must be read as indicating the existence of external objects, thereby forcing interpretation of the negation of external objects at the beginning as being limited to the meditative situation.

To review the first three parts of Wayman's argument: He has clearly indicated that the term *ālambana* is used in the literature of the Yogic Practice School. From this, he draws the conclusion that, for the early Yogic Practice School, external objects exist. He has indicated a plausible way of interpreting the emphasis on "representation-only" in the school through suggesting that, as in the case of Jñānagarbha, it could indicate the tremendous contribution from the subject's side to the appearance of the object, on karmically determined individual and group levels. We should note that, although Wayman

[a] For a discussion of types of negations, see 242ff.

mis-translates the term *ālambana* in the passage from the *Sūtra Unraveling the Thought* as "meditative object," his interpretation does not necessarily hinge on this, for—even if we use the wider meaning of *ālambana* as referring to objects of consciousness in general with the result that the passage is saying, "All consciousness is distinguished by the fact that its object of observation (or consciousness-support) is representation-only," the latter term (in Wayman's interpretation) does not have to mean that there are no external objects but could mean only that there is a powerful subjective overlay, as he contends. Both Wayman and Willis (see Appendix 3) limit the denial of external objects to the meditative situation, and when "representation-only" (Wayman's translation for *vijñaptimātra*) or "conceptualization-only" (one of Ueda's[a] and Willis's translations for the same) is applied to all objects, both Wayman and Willis deny that it means that there are no external objects.

We must note that, although Wayman and Willis unwarrantedly restrict the meaning of the passage from the Maitreya chapter of the *Sūtra Unraveling the Thought* to meditative objects, both present arguments that do not revolve around this fallacious restriction of the meaning of the passage. Both reform the meaning of "cognition-only," or "representation-only," so that in other situations it allows external objects. Wayman includes as evidence the undisputed fact that scholars of even the early Yogic Practice School use the term "consciousness-support" in a positive way, indicating that consciousness-supports are not denied in all respects (although the actual issue is whether objects of object-of-observation-**conditions** exist). Wayman draws the conclusion that there still is an external object upon which karmically controlled factors superimpose qualities not residing in the external object.

4. Wayman: If Atomic Particles Exist, Then External Objects Exist

Having made a case for a possible consistent advocacy of external objects in works of Vasubandhu and Asaṅga, Wayman proceeds to analyze Dignāga's *Examination of Objects of Observation,* since this text is widely seen as refuting external objects that serve as objects of observation generating consciousnesses (see p. 478ff.). His task is to show that this text actually does not refute "consciousness-supports" and hence that it does not refute external objects. The brunt of his argument is that the Buddhist logicians (Dignāga and his followers, especially Dharmakīrti) are considered also to be of the Yogic Practice School and yet do not assert an absence of external objects, as is evident in their assertion of atomic particles.

By Wayman's reasoning, if there are consciousness-supports, there must be external objects. Indeed, as mentioned above, even in Ge-luk-b̄a treatises on the

[a] See Appendix 2 (p. 520ff.).

topic, if there are consciousness-supports that are causes **producing** consciousness—these being called object-of-observation-condition—then, since the consciousness produced must be an effect of the consciousness-support, it must be a different entity from that consciousness-support and hence must be an external object. Thus, Wayman has indeed gone right to the heart of the matter. Even though again he does not make a distinction between object of observation (*dmigs pa, ālambana*) and observed-object-condition (*dmigs rkyen, ālambanapratyaya*) which would be useful in his own interpretation of the Maitreya chapter of the *Sūtra Unraveling the Thought,* Dignāga himself employs the term *ālambana* even in his title to refer to *ālambanapratyaya.*

Wayman offers[516] a translation of the eight stanzas that constitute Dignāga's text and concludes from his reading of them that a form of nominalism, not idealism, is being presented. He argues that, since the real is necessarily causal, the atomic object must be causal, and this requires external objects:[517]

> So far I detect no divergence from that part of Vasubandhu's two treatises, Asaṅga's citation of the *Mahāyānasaṃgraha,* and Sthiramati's passage, as presented above. In this kind of nominalism (though called "idealism" in Indian Philosophy surveys), what is real is the atomic object, called in other logic texts the *svalakṣaṇa,* and the real is causal and has the sense organ as a cooperating capacity. On top of this the mind adds the "form," more comprehensible by the word "shape," meaning that the aggregation of atoms was not what caused the perception: this aggregation is a representational-only (*vijñāna-mātra*) of a consciousness-support (*ālambana*) and makes up a picture in the mind, which the mind attributes to the external world. It is impossible that this picture or aggregation could exist in the external world, since it is representation-only. The vulgar interpretation—that this denies external objects—is nonsense. It fails to get Vasubandhu's point, or Dignāga's either.

Wayman's general position is clear:

- Even in the early Yogic Practice School there are external objects.
- What the mind adds to an object is considerable; this addition is what is called representation-only and does not entail a denial of external objects.

In this case, his evidence is that other logic texts assert specifically characterized objects (*svalakṣaṇa*), which Wayman limits to meaning atomic particles. Though his identification is too narrow (since, at minimum, moments of consciousness are also included, if not also aggregations of particles and continuums of moments of consciousness that are able to perform functions), he raises the vital question of whether in a system that denies external objects there can be atomic particles. Ḏzong-ka-ḇa himself finesses the problem of how a mind-only system could also speak of forms; he does this by holding that, according to the Mind-Only School, **upon analysis** there are no forms.[518] However, subsequent Ge-luk-b̄a scholars write this statement off as an early repetition of an older tradition and not D̄zong-ka-b̄a's final position. They hold that the doctrine of mind-only does not militate against forms and their constituent particles as long as these appearances are of the same entity as the consciousness apprehending them.

From these maneuverings within Ge-luk-b̄a scholarship, it can be seen that Wayman again has hit on a sensitive issue. Dignāga himself, in the sixth and seventh stanzas of the *Examination of Objects of Observation*, after refuting the possibility of an external object-of-observation-condition (see 478ff.), is compelled to explain why objects of sense consciousnesses are called object-of-observation-conditions even though there are no external objects. His commentary begins:

> Therefore, it is logical that the objects of sense awarenesses are not external.
>
> > The entity of an internal object of knowing
> > Which appears as if external is the **object**.
>
> While there are no external objects, an appearance—as if external—that only exists internally is the object-of-observation-condition.
>
> > This is because of being the entity of consciousness
> > [And] because it is also just a **condition** of it.
>
> Due to being endowed with two features—since an internal consciousness appears as an [external] **object** and it is **produced** from it—that which only exists internally is the object-of-observation-condition.
>
> *Objection:* Even if it is allowed that the appearance is [the object] in that way, how is [the appearance]—which is generated simultaneously [with the consciousness] and is a factor of that [consciousness]—a condition [producing the consciousness]?
>
> *Answer:* Though simultaneous, [the object and the perceiving consciousness] are ineluctable, and hence it is a condition.
>
> Though [the object and the perceiving consciousness] are simultaneous, they are ineluctable, and hence [the object] is a condition in the context of production from other.

As Nga-w̄ang-b̄el-den[519] explains, even though the patch of blue that appears to a sense consciousness is a factor that is of the entity of that very sense consciousness, the term "condition" is used for it to refer to the ineluctability of the concomitance of the patch of blue and a sense consciousness perceiving it—if the one exists, then the other exists.[a]

---

[a] Having explained how the term "condition" can be used for an object that is

Since even Dignāga explains away difficulties with positing observed-object-conditions without external objects, it seems that Wayman, despite identifying sensitive issues, is on shaky ground in trying to claim that Dignāga himself asserts external objects. Still, Wayman's presentation suggests an elegant way by which we could reformulate what Ge-luk-b̄a scholars take to be three different strata of views within the works of Dharmakīrti. They commonly hold that Dharmakīrti's *Commentary on (Dignāga's) "Compilation of Prime Cognition"* contains:

- portions that present external objects and hence the system of the Sūtra School Following Reasoning
- portions that present no external objects and hence the system of the Mind-Only School
- portions that present topics without qualification of either external objects or denial of external objects and hence a system common to the Sūtra School Following Reasoning and the Mind-Only School.

If we adopted Wayman's position that Dignāga and Dharmakīrti are not denying external objects and are merely pointing to the non-existence of mentally dependent representations in the external world, we could view their works as being under the rubric of a single view, rather than three. However, it would be difficult to explain why Dignāga explains away the usage of the term "observed-object-condition" and does not just say that there actually are external objects that produce consciousnesses. Also, it would be difficult to explain reasonings found in Dharmakīrti's works such as those described earlier (p. 480ff.).

---

simultaneous with the subject perceiving, Dignāga offers an alternative explanation of the observed-object-condition that is built around seriality:

> Because of positing [aspects of objects in consciousnesses], potencies are [conditions] serially.

As Nga-w̄ang-b̄el-den (*Annotations, dngos,* 208.6) explains the line:

> Potencies with former consciousnesses to generate later consciousnesses into having the aspects of [their] objects are serially the observed-object-conditions of later consciousnesses because of being conditions positing aspects in those [consciousnesses].

Taken this way, Dignāga's own commentary on the above line seems to read:

> [The observed-object-condition] is also serial: With respect to appearances as [external] objects, the potencies generating effects concordance with them act as supports of consciousness, and hence there is no contradiction [in calling those potencies "conditions."]

Appendix 2: Is Idealism Compatible with Seeing Things as They Are?

In his article "Two Main Streams of Thought in Yogācāra Philosophy," Yoshifumi Ueda[520] of Nagoya University argues that Asaṅga's and Vasubandhu's texts do not evince idealism. Presenting a nuanced view that *vijñaptimātratā* in their texts means "consciousness-only," which he says actually indicates "conceptualization-only," Ueda makes the case that the later, idealist Hsüan-tsang/Dharmapāla transmission to China is unfounded.

Ueda[521] recognizes two strains of the Yogic Practice School and declares that this is nothing new to Japanese scholarship even though it seems to be so in current Western and Indian scholarship:

> In the tradition of Buddhism which has been transmitted to China and Japan, we can see two basically different streams of thought in the Yogācāra philosophy. Although this fact is well-known among Japanese scholars, it does not seem to be widely known among American, European, and Indian scholars. In order to understand correctly the Yogācāra philosophy, however, the clear understanding of these two streams of thought, their mutual differences, and their relation to the theories of Maitreya, Asaṅga, and Vasubandhu is indispensable.

Ueda identifies the earlier, true stream with the translations by Paramārtha and so forth and the later stream as constituted by the translations by Hsüan-tsang, especially his systematic presentation of the views of Dharmapāla. He[522] says that Hsüan-tsang is the dividing line between the two streams:

> One of these two streams was introduced into China by Hsüan-tsang. Although the thought of this stream can be known through the works of Maitreya, Asaṅga, and Vasubandhu as translated by Hsüan-tsang, it can be known in its most all-inclusive and systematic form in the *Ch'eng wei shih lun* of Dharmapāla....The other stream of thought, represented by the works of Maitreya, Asaṅga, and Vasubandhu as translated by Buddhaśānta, Bodhiruci, Paramārtha, Dharmagupta, Prabhākaramitra, and others, was introduced into China before the time of Hsüan-tsang.

Ueda[523] sees American, European, and Indian studies of the Yogic Practice School not only as ignorant of these two streams of interpretation but also as not agreeing with either, resulting in confusion:

> As the studies of the Yogācāra philosophy by Western and Indian scholars have been lacking in knowledge of these two streams of thought, their interpretations of the central problems of the Yogācāra

> philosophy have been ambiguous and often erroneous and do not show a clear understanding of it. Their understanding of the Yogācāra philosophy is not in accord with the theory of either one of these two streams of thought. And, because the differences between their interpretations and the two streams of thought are not clear, one cannot find a clear-cut understanding of the theories of Maitreya, Asaṅga, and Vasubandhu.
>
> It is my aim in this paper to present the differences of interpretation of these two streams of thought relating to the theories of Maitreya, Asaṅga, and Vasubandhu which were transmitted to China and to examine the question of which of the two streams is faithful to the thought of Maitreya, Asaṅga, and Vasubandhu.

Ueda seeks to show that the earlier of the two streams of transmission of the philosophy of the Yogic Practice School to China is the more accurate.

He demonstrates the incorrectness of the idealist Hsüan-tsang/Dharmapāla transmission through discussing their unfounded interpretation of the term *pariṇāma* in Vasubandhu's *The Thirty* as an evolution of consciousness into subject and object portions:[524]

> Thus, according to Dharmapāla, "evolution" means that the mind or consciousness, and its concomitant psychic activities, appear in the form of the seer and the seen, and that "the perceiver or knower," in the 17th *kārikā,* is the seeing part and "that to be perceived or known" is the seen part. All the objects, such as trees, mountains, birds, etc., which are considered by an ordinary man really to exist outside our consciousness are expounded to be none other than the seen part of the consciousness (*vijñāna*).

Ueda holds that whereas *pariṇāma* meant just "consciousness" for Vasubandhu, Dharmapāla has twisted the term to refer to the development of consciousness into subject and object portions, an outright idealism:[525]

> Thus, we would have to conclude that the word *pariṇāma,* capable of having the meaning of *vijñāna* according to Vasubandhu and not capable of having this meaning according to Dharmapāla, has a different meaning in each case.

And:[526]

> It is needless to say that this interpretation of *pariṇāma* by Dharmapāla cannot be found in the *Viṃśatikā.* Moreover, no other text of Vasubandhu mentions the fact that the *vijñāna* is evolved into seeing and seen parts. Therefore, this interpretation by Dharmapāla, based on the *Triṃśikā,* could not be said to be faithful to Vasubandhu since it is nothing more than an addition to Vasubandhu's *Triṃśikā* by

Dharmapāla himself. This will become clearer in comparing Dharmapāla's commentary to the *Triṁśikā* with that of Sthiramati. Sthiramati, unlike Dharmapāla, has given a commentary which is faithful to Vasubandhu's *Triṁśikā*.

Ueda avers that when Vasubandhu speaks of "consciousness-only," he is referring to the relation between subject and object **in the case of an unenlightened being**. For such persons, the object with which such a being ignorantly deals actually is merely a conceptualized object, a name, a concept that is mistaken to be the actual object. He says:[527]

> The same idea is expressed in the 17th verse [of the *Thirty*]: "This *vijñānapariṇāma* is *vikalpa*. Anything which is discriminated or conceptualized by the *vikalpa* does not really exist. Therefore the whole world (which is discriminated or conceptualized by it) is consciousness-only" (17th verse). *Vikalpa* or *vijñānapariṇāma* refers to the consciousness of an ordinary man, i.e., a man who is not yet enlightened. The object which is known through this *vijñānapariṇāma* is not a thing as it really is, but rather a conceptualized thing. In other words, this mind does not grasp the object as it really is, but rather as a concept or name. In truth, he does not take real existence itself as the object, but instead takes the concept as the object and thinks that he is taking real existence as the object, not realizing what he has done. In Vasubandhu's words, he is not abiding in *vijñaptimātratā* (all that which is seen by *vijñāna* is none other than the seeing *vijñāna*).

For the enlightened being, however, this overload of the object from the subject's side is understood for what it is, and all conceptual consciousnesses are viewed as infected with such subjective overlay:[528]

> For one who has not realized what is expressed in the above-quoted 17th and 20th verses (the objects of *vikalpa* are all consciousness-only [*vijñaptimātratā*]), that is, for one whose mind is *vijñāna*, the object known is a conceptualized thing, and not the object as it really exists.

An enlightened being sees objects as they actually are, without the subjective overlay. The actual object is not of the same entity as the mind perceiving it, since we are, at this point, beyond mind:[529]

> When the mind sees the mountain as it really is, it does not see the mountain as its object, and accordingly, the object (the mountain) must become identified with the subject (the mind). In other words, the dichotomy between subject and object must be extinguished, for there is no object except the mind (the seer). And this self-identity of the seer with itself, by the extinction of the object, must at the same time be the self-identity of the seen because a thing (the mountain) is

> seen by the mind as it really is. Here the mountain is seen from within, or by itself without the seer outside it. This negation of the seer which stands in opposition to the seen is called no-mind (*acitta*) in the 29th verse, and the negation of the object (the seen) is called nothing-grasped (*anupalambha*).

The idealist description of perception found in Vasubandhu's writings, therefore, is limited to the pre-enlightenment state, where seemingly all perception is conceptual:[530]

> Thus we can see that the standpoint of the philosophy of the consciousness-only is reality itself. A Yogācāra philosopher stands on the reality of himself as well as of everything. In contrast to this, the standpoint of those who do not stand on the consciousness-only (*vijñaptimātratā*) should be called ideal or conceptual. While the former deals with reality, the latter deals with conceptualized things. When a man can truly say that all this (which is seen by *vikalpa*) is consciousness-only, he means that his thinking is no longer conceptualizing thinking or objectifying thinking (i.e., *vikalpa*); his thinking belongs to that kind of thinking which is called *prajñā* or *nirvikalpa jñāna* in Buddhist terminology.
>
> We have roughly examined the meaning of *vijñaptimātratā* in Vasubandhu and Sthiramati. This is identical with Paramārtha's understanding of *vijñaptimātratā*. I think that there will be no need to comment further on how far the meaning of consciousness-only according to Dharmapāla is from that of these earlier philosophers of the Yogācāra School. One may be called a kind of idealism; the other should be called a theory of reality. In the latter, what is meant by the word "consciousness-only" is not different from that to which the word "no-mind" (*acitta*) points.

According to Ueda, "consciousness-only" (*vijñaptimātratā*) comes to have a double meaning in Vasubandhu's works. In the first meaning, it refers to the fact that for ordinary, ignorant beings the objects of their consciousnesses are only conceptualizations and not the actual objects. In the second meaning, for an enlightened being, "consciousness-only" means, not idealism, but reality, no-mind beyond such distinctions, non-conceptual realization.

Remarks

Even if Vasubandhu does not speak of an evolution of consciousness into seer and seen portions, he could still be presenting idealism in the sense of a sameness of entity of subject and object. Among idealisms, we must differentiate between what Dharmapāla added and the basic idealism already present in

Vasubandhu's *The Twenty.* It seems to me that Ueda's description of the enlightened being's mode of perception[531] is idealist even if he does not call it so:

> And this self-identity of the seer with itself, by the extinction of the object, must at the same time be the self-identity of the seen because a thing (the mountain) is seen by the mind as it really is. Here the mountain is seen from within, or by itself without the seer outside it.

Ueda's non-idealist interpretation stems from the fact that even at Buddhahood objects are perceived. When he[532] speaks of the Yogic Practitioner as standing on the reality of everything, this is reminiscent of Ge-luk-b̄a teachings that, despite the fact that at Buddhahood all seeds have been destroyed or fully activated, there nevertheless is perception of objects through the force of having completed the collections of merit and wisdom.[a] The claim of this additional mode of the perception of objects is aimed at explaining how objects could still be perceived at Buddhahood, absent the seeds that usually give rise to perception of objects. Indeed, the uneasiness of merely adding an additional mode of perception gives credence to Ueda's view of a mode of perception beyond mind-only. Even if the object of the path of seeing could be the absence of the difference of entity between subject and object, the perception of objects in the context of Buddhahood's lacking the usual source of the perception of objects is not adequately explained merely by declaring that there is this different mode of perception, without undermining idealism as the final position. Perhaps S̄hay-rap-gyel-tsen's presentation of conventional and ultimate levels of mind-only offers a way to retain a more refined idealism.

Still, there is a possible harmony between Ueda and D̄zong-ka-b̄a, since both see the error as mistaking the "conceptualized object" for the actual object, provided this is understood as conceiving that objects are established by way of their own character as the referents of conceptual consciousnesses apprehending them and of the terms expressing them. Perhaps the non-conceptual realization of which Ueda speaks refers here to perception without the overlay of the false appearance of objects as if they are established by way of their own character as the referent of conceptual consciousness and terms.

---

[a] See p. 217ff. and especially pp. 224 and 489.

Appendix 3: Is Emptiness Compatible with Idealism?

Willis: Emptiness And Idealism Are Incompatible

In her *On Knowing Reality,*[533] Janice D. Willis of Wesleyan University presents an argument that the early Yogic Practice School did not propound a doctrine of mind-only. She views Asaṅga as presenting a clarification of the doctrine of *śūnyatā*—emptiness or voidness—in which nominalism, not a denial of external objects, is central. She says:[534]

> Modern-day Buddhist scholars almost unanimously characterize the Yogācāra as being a school of Buddhist idealism, but to view it solely in this way distorts the true sense of Asaṅga's teaching. Asaṅga's words were aimed at correcting the mistaken views held by many Buddhist adherents of his day concerning the true meaning of the Mahāyāna scriptures. To be sure, the single, most misunderstood doctrine taught by these texts was that of *śūnyatā,* "voidness" or "emptiness."

And:[535]

> At any rate, all this terminology most often associated with treatments of the Yogācāra is conspicuously absent from Asaṅga's *Tattvārtha* chapter. Instead, the chapter presents a kind of nominalistic philosophy wherein the key terms are *vastu* and *prajñapti* ("given thing" or "basis of the name" and "designation," respectively).

Willis views as one of Asaṅga's contributions his presentation of emptiness as a positive existent:[536]

> He has affirmed śūnyatā as the ***positive,*** underlying principle and formal ***structure*** of all relative existence. In a passage from the *Tattva* chapter, Asaṅga writes:
>
> > Now how is voidness rightly conceptualized? Wherever and in whatever place something is not, one rightly observes that [place] to be void of that [thing]. Moreover, whatever remains in that place one knows as it really is, that "here there is an existent."
>
> When all false dualities, of subject and object, of designations and bases of designations, are abandoned, voidness—as the ***ultimate mode*** of all relative existence—remains.

Based on her interpretation of that passage, Willis says:[537]

> On the other hand, designations are not to be regarded as being completely devoid of essential nature since, in truth, they do possess the essential nature of śūnyatā, which is, for Asaṅga, an existent.

It is clear that, for Willis, emptiness and idealism (even in this limited sense of denying external objects and not implying solipsism) are mutually exclusive in the sense that, if a school asserts one, it cannot assert the other. For her, an assertion of emptiness is itself a sign that the idealist position is not asserted:[538]

> If, as I have argued, Asaṅga's main concern in the *Tattva* chapter is to clarify the doctrine of śūnyatā, why is it that the school he founded is viewed—almost unanimously—as solely advocating an absolutist idealism?

Response: The Need To Distinguish Between Absolute Idealism And Idealism—Emptiness Does Not Negate Idealism

Types of idealism need to be distinguished; I use the term "idealism" only to mean the absence of external objects, more specifically that an object such as blue does not exist as a separate entity from a consciousness apprehending blue and that a consciousness apprehending blue does not exist as a separate entity from that blue. This is sometimes called subjective idealism in European and American philosophy. (It is important to note that subjective idealism in this Buddhist system does not entail that all objects are the same entity as **one particular** subject and does not entail solipsism—there are other consciousnesses and their percepts.)

Such idealism also does not necessitate the positing of a permanent, pure consciousness that is the ultimate truth, or absolute reality. Willis has overloaded idealism with notions that it necessarily entails the assertion of a permanent pure consciousness as the ultimate truth and then has mistakenly proposed that Asaṅga in these texts does not propound idealism, since it is clear that for him emptiness is the ultimate truth. Willis is right that for Asaṅga emptiness is the ultimate truth, for when he speaks about the path of seeing, for instance, he says not that a meditator sees just mind but that a meditator sees emptiness.[a] His *Summary of the Great Vehicle*[b] says, "A non-conceptual consciousness is like

---

[a] The material here repeats part of the presentation by Gung-tang (*Difficult Points,* 132.6), given earlier (p. 240ff.).

[b] Étienne Lamotte, *La Somme du grand véhicule d'Asaṅga,* reprint, 2 vols., Publications de l'Institute Orientaliste de Louvain 8 (Louvain: Université de Louvain, 1973), vol. 1, 78 (VIII.16), and vol. 2, 244-245; and John P. Keenan, *The Summary of the Great Vehicle by Bodhisattva Asaṅga: Translated from the Chinese of Paramārtha* (Berkeley, Calif.: Numata Center for Buddhist Translation and Research, 1992), 96-97. For Shay-rap-gyel-tsen's opinion that such passages indicate that Asaṅga's *Summary of the Great Vehicle* denies that mind truly exists, see p. 303ff.

the eyes of a person that have been closed." Since nothing but an absence—which is other-powered natures' emptiness of the imputational nature—appears, such a non-conceptual consciousness of meditative equipoise is said to be "without appearance."[a] No conventional phenomenon, such as the luminous and cognitive nature of the mind, appears, and thus non-conceptual realization is compared to closed eyes. Willis's mistake comes in mis-identifying what idealism entails, mistakenly turning it into absolute idealism, which would indeed entail that on the path of seeing a yogi would have to realize just mind.

Willis points out with considerable clarity that the object of non-conceptual wisdom is not mind but emptiness. Though she uses this point to show that mind-only is not a final doctrine, Ge-luk-ba scholars hold that the very emptiness of a difference of entity between subject and object is the ultimate truth, the object of direct perception on the path of seeing, and so forth. According to standard Ge-luk-ba presentations of the path structure in the Mind-Only School,[539] the emptiness that is directly seen on the path of seeing and the path of meditation is the absence of a difference of entity between subject and object or the absence of objects' being established by way of their own character as the referents of their respective conceptual consciousnesses and respective terminology. Thus, emptiness so defined does not cancel out mind-only; it is in accord with mind-only. Emptiness is the very absence of a difference of entity between subject and object upon which such idealism depends. Hence, Willis's frequently mentioned point that idealism and emptiness could not go together in one system is unfounded, at least in terms of Ge-luk-ba scholarship.

The passage (cited above, p. 525) that Willis sees as speaking of emptiness remaining and its existing does not seem to be limited to this. As can be seen from the earlier extensive analysis (pp. 329-346) of similar statements in Asaṅga's *Grounds of Bodhisattvas,* Maitreya's *Differentiation of the Middle and the Extremes,* and Asaṅga's *Summary of Manifest Knowledge:*

- The first explicitly says that other-powered natures remain.
- The second explicitly says that other-powered natures and emptiness remain.
- The third explicitly says that emptiness remains.

Jik-may-dam-chö-gya-tso draws the cogent conclusion that in the explicit teaching at this point in the *Grounds of Bodhisattvas* nothing other than other-powered natures is presented as what remains, whereas in general this type of passage in Asaṅga's Five Treatises on the Grounds teaches that thoroughly established natures are also among the remainder. Willis,[540] however, unjustifiably takes the remainder mentioned in Asaṅga's *Grounds of Bodhisattvas* only to be emptiness.

Even though the point of the passage that she cites is not concerned solely

[a] *snang med*

with the existence of emptiness, Asaṅga does frequently say that, if other-powered natures do not exist (this being how he takes the proposition by the Proponents of Non-Nature that all phenomena only conventionally exist), the thoroughly established nature—emptiness—would not exist. Hence, we can draw the conclusion that, for Asaṅga, emptiness does exist, as Willis says. Moreover, it seems that, even according to the Middle Way School, emptiness must exist, since emptiness is included in the long lists of phenomena that repeatedly appear in Perfection of Wisdom Sūtras, and these sūtras say that all phenomena[a] conventionally exist.

Nevertheless, Willis's conclusion that, just because emptiness exists, it must be positive is unwarranted. Not only are there negatives,[b] but also there are negatives that do not imply anything in place of their objects of negation.[c] Still, neither Willis's unfounded restriction of the import of that particular passage to emptiness nor the unwarranted assumption that whatever exists is necessarily positive diminishes her points that:

- Emptiness is an underlying structure of all phenomena.
- Asaṅga seeks to correct the wayward views of those who misunderstand the doctrine of emptiness in the Perfection of Wisdom Sūtras.

Willis: Idealism Is An Expedient Device In The Early Yogic Practice School

Willis does not claim that Asaṅga taught idealism in no sense at all; rather, according to her,[541] he adopted several techniques in response to historical necessity resulting from Nāgārjuna's radical critique of phenomena:

> Unfortunately, however, Nāgārjuna's negative approach resulted in many followers' misunderstanding of the meaning of śūnyatā as unqualified nihilism. It was largely to correct this misunderstanding of the meaning of śūnyatā that Asaṅga wrote his philosophical works, a key representation of which is the *Tattva* chapter.
>
> In order to accomplish the task of clarifying the chief Mahāyāna doctrine in a balanced, intelligible, and less frightening way, Asaṅga employed a number of methods (*upāya*). One was the invention of an "ontological psychological" model for explaining the bifurcation of apparent reality into a subject and an object....Another was what might be called a nominalist approach. This approach figures prominently in the *Tattva* chapter. Yet another was the extremely important introduction of a new schema in which the model of the so-called

a *chos, dharma.*

b *dgag pa, pratiṣedha;* see the discussion of negatives, p. 242ff.

c *med dgag, prasajyapratiṣedha.*

three natures (*trisvabhāvas* or *trilakṣaṇa*) is used to extend and supplement the older Mahāyāna formula of the "two truths."

According to Willis,[542] unlike the nominalist teachings to be found in the *Tattva* chapter, Asaṅga's seeming teachings of idealism, such as his presentation of a mind-basis-of-all, are to be seen as helpful techniques used by him to aid certain trainees—provisional teachings in preparation for the final teaching:

> As previously mentioned, one of Asaṅga's expedient devices (*upāya*) was the explication of an "ontological psychological" model for detailing the evolution of consciousness that creates the seeming reality of the subject-object duality. Central to this model was the notion of the *ālayavijñāna* ("store-consciousness" or "underlying awareness")....This model has led many Buddhologists to conclude that the Yogācāra considered the *ālayavijñāna* the ultimate reality....However, to suppose that Asaṅga intended the *ālayavijñāna* as a synonym for ultimate reality is to disregard his own (as well as Vasubandhu's and Sthiramati's) statements to the contrary.

Instead of arguing that Asaṅga and Vasubandhu accept the mind-basis-of-all (*kun gzhi rnam par shes pa, ālayavijñāna*) but do not hold it to be the ultimate reality and thereby opposing those Buddhologists who hold the mind-basis-of-all to be the ultimate reality, Willis suggests that, because these three masters speak of emptiness, they could not also hold idealism.

Moreover, she explicitly says:[543]

> Again, given the fact that—at least in the *Tattva* chapter—Asaṅga clearly posits *voidness,* not mind, as the only absolute in the final analysis, how is it that this [idealism] remains the generally accepted assessment of the Yogācāra?

Her reasoning is that Asaṅga teaches the mind-basis-of-all not with the status of a metaphysical proposition but merely in response to queries as to how the false notion that subjects and objects exist in their own right comes into being. As supporting evidence from Asaṅga's own works, Willis[544] cites the fact that for Asaṅga consciousness is impermanent, suffering, and without self, and the mind-basis-of-all is a consciousness.

Her reasoning again seems to be that, if the mind-basis-of-all and its concomitant idealism actually do exist, then the mind-basis-of-all must be an absolute reality—permanent, pure, and self. For her, Asaṅga's doctrine of emptiness—selflessness—negates idealism, and thus idealism could not be a final doctrine. According to Willis, there clearly is no way that idealism could coexist with Asaṅga's doctrine of emptiness. However, once it is shown that emptiness and idealism are indeed compatible within emptiness being permanent and the mind-basis-of-all being impermanent, Willis's argument that Asaṅga could not have taught the mind-basis-of-all in any other way than provisionally because he also teaches that it is impermanent is unfounded.

Response: The Absence Of Supporting Documentation In These Texts For Holding That The Teaching Of An *Ālayavijñāna* And So Forth Are Merely Provisional

Given that Asaṅga and Vasubandhu are interested in positing Buddha's thought behind his teaching non-final doctrines, it is inexplicable why, if they use the "ontological psychological" model only provisionally as Willis claims, they never posit Buddha's thought, or their own thought, behind such teaching. Asaṅga is particularly concerned with spelling out the meaning in Buddha's thought, that is, where Buddha was coming from when he taught what is not literally acceptable. For instance, the *Grounds of Bodhisattvas* (*Emptiness in Mind-Only,* 146) says:[545]

> Therefore, some persons [that is, only Consequentialists], who have heard sūtras that are difficult to understand, profound, imbued with the Great Vehicle, endowed with the profound emptiness, and taught with a meaning in [Buddha's] thought [that is other than the literal reading] do not know, just as it is, the real meaning that is expounded.

Also, in his *Summary of the Great Vehicle,* Asaṅga categorizes ways of approaching non-literal doctrines:[546]

> Furthermore, through the four thoughts and the four intentions,[a] all of Buddha's speech is understood....

Also, Vasubandhu's *The Twenty* (*Emptiness in Mind-Only,* 235) says:

> That form-sense-spheres and so forth exist [as external objects]
> Was said through the force of a thought behind it
> With regard to beings tamed by that,
> Like [the teaching of] spontaneously arisen sentient beings [as substantially established or permanent].

Furthermore, about Vasubandhu's reasons for composing *The Thirty,* Sthiramati (*Emptiness in Mind-Only,* 187) says in his commentary:

> Or, in another way, [this] work [that is, *The Thirty*] was initiated in order to refute two types of proponents: some [that is, Proponents of the Great Exposition and Proponents of Sūtra] who single-pointedly think that, like consciousness, objects of knowledge also [exist] just substantially and (2) others [that is, Proponents of Non-Nature] who

[a] *dgongs pa* (*abhiprāya*) and *ldem dgongs* (*abhisaṃdhi*). For discussion of these, see *Absorption,* chap. 19.

> single-pointedly think that, like objects of knowledge, consciousness also exists just conventionally but does not exist ultimately.

Moreover, Vasubandhu, in his *Principles of Explanation* (*Emptiness in Mind-Only,* 240), first establishes that the Perfection of Wisdom Sūtras speak of practice and so forth, and then he speaks of the internal contradictions that would result if the same sūtras' teachings of naturelessness were taken literally:

> The Perfection of Wisdom [Sūtras] indicate many times, for instance, that all phenomena are natureless and so forth. However, they say that those who wish to enter into the flawlessness of Bodhisattvas [should train in the Perfection of Wisdom] and...they also teach the individual disclosure of all ill deeds, and so forth. If the words of naturelessness and so forth [in the Mother Sūtras] were of only literal meaning, they would contradict all of these. As there would be nothing to be adopted [in practice], it would not be suitable to adopt [a practice] within thinking, "From this cause such and such will arise." Or, one would wonder what thing to be adopted exists to be adopted. Therefore, those words [speaking of naturelessness] definitely should not be taken as of literal meaning. Then, as what? As having another thought [behind them].

These passage illustrate Asaṅga's and Vasubandhu's concern with positing the thought behind teachings and of refuting those who take those teachings as literal. Thus, since they themselves at least sometimes teach a doctrine of no external objects (such as in Asaṅga's teaching of a mind-basis-of-all and Vasubandhu's analyzing away partless particles as the building blocks of external objects), it strains credulity that they would never explain the thought behind these teachings or the faults of taking such literally. Given Asaṅga's and Vasubandhu's interest in strategies of interpretation, it is hard to fathom that they themselves would not address this issue if, as Willis claims, they did teach idealism merely as an expedient means. However, if we take their teaching of these doctrines as literal, the absence of their identifying any thought behind them is consistent and sensible.

Willis: The Proponents Of The Middle Way School Did Not Consider The "Mind-Only" Source Quotes To Teach Mind-Only

Willis[547] posits a threefold usage of such terms as *cittamātra* and *vijñaptimātra:* (1) as a description of meditative insights limited to the sphere of practice, (2) as provisionally prescriptive for beings too attached to material things, and (3) as descriptive of the causation of an ordinary being's suffering:

> And finally, even within the "early" Yogācāra, i.e., within the works of Asaṅga and Vasubandhu, *cittamātra* (and its companion term *vijñaptimātra*) seems to have had at least three distinct, intentional uses, depending upon whether those doctors were addressing themselves to (1) technical information concerning the meditative experience per se, that is, to specific meditative contexts and practice; (2) common sense, prescriptive advice for ordinary beings overly attached to materiality (where it may be said to have had a "provisional meaning," marking a sort of intermediate stage in terms of general practice); or (3) the philosophical analysis and description of the cause of ordinary beings' suffering.

Willis analyzes the usage of the term *cittamātra* (mind-only) in the ***Sūtra on the Ten Grounds***[548] and ***Descent into Laṅkā Sūtra***[549] as well as the usage of the term *vijñaptimātra* (cognition-only) in the eighth chapter of the ***Saṃdhinirmocanasūtra***[550] and in Vasubandhu's *Viṃśatikā* and *Triṃśikā*.[551] With regard to *cittamātra* in the ***Sūtra on the Ten Grounds,*** she argues that the early masters of the Yogic Practice School did not take the proclamation *cittamātram idaṃ yad idaṃ traidhātukaṃ,* "These three realms [the realms of desire, corporeal matter, and immateriality] are nothing but mind" (brackets hers), as indicating idealism. Rather, according to her, by looking into the context of the passage, one can determine that idealism is not intended. She points out that Mādhyamika doctrinalists do not take the passage as denying external objects but take it as emphasizing[552] "...that mere mind (or thought) conventionally (*saṃvṛtitas*) creates the external entities." She admits that those same Proponents of the Middle Way School held that **for the Yogic Practice School** the passage does mean "...the denial of external entities," but she holds that, according to the Yogic Practice School itself, the passage does not mean a denial of external objects. (Schmithausen, who found this phrase in the *Bhadrapāla* in the context of visionary meditation, sees this idealism as extended to **all** phenomena, but Willis disregards this extension; see p. 450).

Willis next considers the usage of the term *vijñaptimātra* in the eighth chapter of the ***Sūtra Unraveling the Thought,*** as was discussed above (p. 448). Her argument that the term *cittamātra* in Asaṅga's explanation of that passage (as cited in his *Summary of the Great Vehicle*) does not mean the non-existence of external objects hinges only partly on her estimation of what the ***Sūtra Unraveling the Thought,*** quoted by Asaṅga, is saying. For she also uses the ***Descent into Laṅkā Sūtra*** to establish the provisional meaning of *cittamātra* for Asaṅga. Though Willis recognizes the many idealistic statements in that sūtra, she refers to the opinion of[553]

> ...the great Tsoṅ-kha-pa who referred to the *Laṅkāvatāra* as a sūtra of "provisional" or "indirect" meaning (*neyārtha*) requiring further interpretation (as opposed to one of "final" or "definitive" meaning,

nītārtha). To bear out his assessment of the *Laṅkāvatāra*, Tsoṅ-kha-pa cites a verse drawn from that text:

> In the way that a physician offers a medicine to one patient and a medicine to another patient, in that way the Buddhas teach mind-only for the sentient beings.

Response: The Need To Distinguish Between Ḏzong-ka-ḇa's Assertions About Chandrakīrti And Asaṅga

In the chapter on the Consequence School in *The Essence of Eloquence*, Ḏzong-ka-ḇa[554] cites this passage in the *Descent into Laṅkā Sūtra* from Chandrakīrti's quotation of it in his autocommentary on the *Supplement to (Nāgārjuna's) "Treatise on the Middle"*:[555]

> *Question:* What are the sūtra passages of such type?
>
> *Answer:* In the teaching of the three natures—called imputational natures, other-powered natures, and thoroughly established natures—in [Chapters 6 and 7 of] the *Sūtra Unraveling the Thought*, [it is said that] imputational natures are just non-existent and other-powered natures[a] are just existent. Likewise, [speaking of the mind-basis-of-all] it says [in Chapter 5]:[556]

---

[a] Notice that Chandrakīrti does not say that the *Sūtra Unraveling the Thought* describes thoroughly established natures as "existent," that is, existent by way of their own character, whereas Ḏzong-ka-ḇa repeatedly does. In his *Explanation of (Chandrakīrti's) "Supplement to (Nāgārjuna's) 'Treatise on the Middle,'"* Ḏzong-ka-ḇa explains this away as being in deference to the centrality of other-powered natures:

> Although in that *Sūtra* [*Unraveling the Thought*] it is said that both other-powered natures and thoroughly established natures are established by way of their own character, in his commentary [on the *Supplement*, Chandrakīrti] speaks of nothing beyond just other-powered natures. This is because the main bases of debate by the Proponents of Mind-Only and the Proponents of the Middle about truly existing or not truly existing are other-powered natures, since the bases of imputation of imputational natures are other-powered natures and thoroughly established natures also must be posited in dependence upon other-powered natures.

See Jik-may-dam-chö-gya-tso (*Port of Entry*, 438.5).

The passage to which Ḏzong-ka-ḇa most likely is referring when he says that the *Sūtra Unraveling the Thought* itself (*Emptiness in Mind-Only*, 96) explains that thoroughly established natures are established by way of their own character is:

> If the other-powered character and the thoroughly established character exist [by way of their own character], the imputational character is known [that is, is possible]. However, those who perceive the other-powered character and the thoroughly established character as without character [that is to say, as not being established by way of their own character] also deprecate the imputational character.

If the appropriating consciousness,[a] profound and subtle,
Having all the seeds [of the afflicted class and purified
class],[557] flowing like the continuum of a river [on all occasions of cyclic existence],[558]
Were considered to be a self, it would be unsuitable.
Thus I do not teach this to children.[b]

And so forth.[c] These [sūtra passages of such type as that in the *Descent into Laṅkā Sūtra,* cited earlier in my commentary, teaching no external objects:

(Objects) do not exist as external objects as perceived

---

[a] This is the consciousness that appropriates, or takes, the body of the next life and also holds (or maintains) the body until death; see Ser-shül (*Notes,* 50a.2) for sources in the *Sūtra Unraveling the Thought* and so forth.

[b] As Ser-shül (*Notes,* 50a.6) expands on the last two lines:

Thinking that since, when a mind-basis-of-all, which is the basis [of the connection] of actions and their effects and is an entity separate from the six collections of consciousness, is taught, it is possible to conceive and adhere to it as an internal person or self as imputed by Outsiders, and if that happens, it would not be suitable, I—the Subduer, the Supramundane Buddha—do not teach such a basis-of-all to unskilled children, that is, the two Hearer sects and so forth.

[c] Jik-may-dam-chö-gya-tso (*Port of Entry,* 437.6-438.3) identifies two teachings as included within "and so forth":

- The teaching of no external objects in chapter 8, called the "Questions of Maitreya," of the *Sūtra Unraveling the Thought* (Peking 774, vol. 29, 13.5.7-14.1.5); see p. 440ff.:

  "Supramundane Victor, is the image that is the object of activity of meditative stabilization different from the mind or not different?"

  The Supramundane Victor spoke, "Maitreya, it is said to be not different. Why? I explain that consciousness is distinguished by [the fact that its] object of observation is just cognition-only."

- The teaching of three final lineages in chapter 7 of the *Sūtra Unraveling the Thought* (Peking 744, vol. 29, 10.4.7):

  Though all the Buddhas exert themselves, those who have the lineage of a Hearer, proceeding solely to peacefulness, cannot attain highest, complete, perfect enlightenment upon being set in the essence of enlightenments. Why? It is thus: Because of having very slight compassion and being very afraid of suffering, they are only of naturally low lineage.

That the teaching of no external objects is included in "and so forth" is cogent because Chandrakīrti immediately cites a passage from the *Descent into Laṅkā Sūtra* that indicates that the teaching of no external objects requires interpretation. The justification for identifying the teaching of three final vehicles as included in "and so forth" is less apparent, although there is no question that Nāgārjuna pays particular attention to this in his *Compendium of Sūtra.*

The mind appears as various (objects through the power of
predispositions).
(Because the mind is generated) in the likeness of bodies (that
is, senses), enjoyments (that is, objects of senses), and
abodes (that is, physical sense organs and environments),
I have explained (that all phenomena are) mind-only.]

are clarified as just requiring interpretation by these [three] passages [in the *Descent into Laṅkā Sūtra*]:[a]

Just as a doctor gives medicines
To patients in accordance with their illness,
So Buddha speaks even of mind-only
To sentient beings in that way.

Ḏzong-ka-ḇa comments:

[Chandrakīrti] explains that four [types of passages in the *Sūtra Unraveling the Thought*] require interpretation:

1. The explanation [in the sixth and seventh chapters of the *Sūtra Unraveling the Thought*] that the first two natures do not exist by way of their own character and do exist by way of their own character [that is, that imputational natures do not exist by way of their own character and that other-powered natures exist by way of their own character]
2. The explanation [in the fifth chapter of the *Sūtra Unraveling the Thought*] of the basis-of-all

and those included within "and so forth" [in his commentary]:

3. The explanation [in the eighth chapter of the *Sūtra Unraveling the Thought*] of the non-existence of external objects
4. The explanation [in the fifth chapter of the *Sūtra Unraveling the Thought*] of the definiteness of [three] final lineages.

Since Ḏzong-ka-ḇa cites the passage from the *Descent into Laṅkā Sūtra* about a doctor distributing medicines in the context of explaining Chandrakīrti's views,

---

[a] Peking 775, vol. 29, 34.3.5, chap. 2; Daisetz Teitaro Suzuki, *The Lankavatara Sutra* (London: Routledge and Kegan Paul, 1932), 44 (123). Ḏzong-ka-ḇa cites the first of three passages from the *Descent into Laṅkā Sūtra* that Chandrakīrti quotes. The other two that Chandrakīrti cites are:

- Buddha's explanation of the teaching of a matrix of One Gone Thus endowed with Buddha qualities
- Buddha's explanation that his teaching is imbued with emptiness, "Mahāmati, this character of emptiness, non-production, non-duality, and absence of inherent existence which is contained in the sūtras of all Buddhas..."

he is not speaking about the opinion of Asaṅga (as author of the *Grounds of Bodhisattvas* and the *Summary of the Great Vehicle*), and thus Willis's citation of Ḏzong-ka-ḇa's opinion is out of context.

Indeed, it can be seen from the fact that Ḏzong-ka-ḇa strives to show that Asaṅga refutes external objects in both the Chapter on Suchness in the *Grounds of Bodhisattvas* and his *Summary of the Great Vehicle* (see chapters 18-21) that he certainly does not hold that, according to these works by Asaṅga, the idealist statements in the *Descent into Laṅkā Sūtra* require interpretation. If, because of the thoroughness of Ḏzong-ka-ḇa's scholarship, it is notable that he himself agrees with Chandrakīrti, then it is all the more important to note Ḏzong-ka-ḇa's estimation of Asaṅga's thought in the Chapter on Suchness of the *Grounds of Bodhisattvas* and in the *Summary of the Great Vehicle.* Furthermore, although Willis[559] recognizes that all doctrines taught in this sūtra are not necessarily accepted by Asaṅga and Vasubandhu, she makes no reference to Asaṅga's ever citing that passage in the *Descent into Laṅkā Sūtra.* Hence, it is unclear how this passage in a text that she describes as syncretic is indicative of Asaṅga's opinion in the *Summary of the Great Vehicle.*

It should be noted that within Ge-luk-ḇa scholarship, there is nothing strange about Asaṅga's holding one view yet evincing another in certain works (such as his *Commentary on (Maitreya's) Sublime Continuum of the Great Vehicle*) for the sake of aiding other beings. They heartily agree that Asaṅga taught mind-only, a mind-basis-of-all, and so forth merely for the sake of others, since, for them, he was really a proponent of the Middle Way Consequence School. However, unlike Willis, they do not hold that Asaṅga evinces any of this provisionality in the Chapter on Suchness in his *Grounds of Bodhisattvas* or in his *Summary of the Great Vehicle;* thus they hold that these **texts** set forth a view of no external objects.

Conclusion

It seems that Willis, not seeing the connection between the emptiness of external objects and the emptiness of factors imputed in the manner of entity and attributes, considers Asaṅga to be a Proponent of Non-Nature and applied this emptiness to texts (the *Grounds of Bodhisattvas* and the *Summary of the Great Vehicle*) that neither Ḏzong-ka-ḇa nor his followers saw as evincing anything but the idealist position, despite their being eager to prove that Asaṅga himself was not actually a Proponent of the Mind-Only School, as is evident in his *Commentary on (Maitreya's) Sublime Continuum of the Great Vehicle,* where he indicates that all sentient beings have the Buddha-nature.

Ge-luk-ḇa scholars explicate this idealism by way of contextual analysis that delineates the ultimate truth—both an emptiness of the establishment of objects by way of their own character as the referents of conceptual consciousnesses and an emptiness of a difference of entity between subject and object—

in even the early Yogic Practice School as consistent with idealism. Their skeletal analysis (fleshed out in chapters 18-20 by supplying and analyzing the references) cogently refutes the notion that an emptiness of a difference of entity between subject and object, or an emptiness of external objects, is not taught in Asaṅga's *Summary of the Great Vehicle;* however, as explained in chapter 21, Ḏzong-ka-ḇa's extension of this perspective to the Chapter on Suchness of Asaṅga's *Grounds of Bodhisattvas* appears to be unwarranted.

Willis's point that emptiness, and not mind, is the object realized in meditative equipoise on the paths of seeing and meditation is indeed well taken. This emptiness of the establishment of objects by way of their own character as the referents of conceptual consciousness is, however, harmonious with an emptiness of a difference of entity between subject and object (or an emptiness of external objects) and is thus consistent with idealism. The uniformity of the Ge-luk-ḇa position on this basic point, as presented in chapter 20, challenges the statement by E. Todd Fenner in a review of Janice Willis's *On Knowing Reality* that some Ge-luk-ḇa scholars hold a view similar to Willis's. Fenner says:[560]

> Most people view Yogācāra as a philosophy of idealism. While there have been some exceptions, some scholars pointing out that such a characterization may not be applicable to all Yogācārins, this view seems fairly entrenched. Speaking for myself, it is the view I was first taught. I didn't realize that it might be subject to modification until I began to study the subject with some Gelugpa teachers who held differently. Janice Willis, in her welcome book, joins the ranks of those who take exception, and argues a good case.

I, too, find Willis's book welcome and well written (especially in that one can sense the workings of a keen mind creatively forging consistency), but I nevertheless disagree with her basic argument. I suspect that Fenner shares her view that emptiness negates idealism and that this has caused him to hear Ge-luk-ḇa scholars' presentations that emptiness is the object realized in meditative equipoise as if they were saying that Asaṅga does not refute external objects. However, contrary to his claim, within Ge-luk-ḇa scholarship there is no support, not a shred of evidence, for the position that in the early Yogic Practice School beginning with Asaṅga there is no refutation of external objects. Every single textbook author of the major Ge-luk-ḇa monastic colleges tries to show how the two types of emptiness go together. Also, not satisfied with Asaṅga's statements indicating merely that these two go together, they work hard at showing **how** the one requires the other, **why** realization of the emptiness of imputation in the manner of entity and attribute leads to realization of the absence of external objects. As demonstrated earlier (p. 429ff.), even more interesting explanations are to be found in oral explanations.

Backnotes

Note to the Preface

1 Berkeley: University of California Press, 1999.

Notes to Part One, Chapter 2

2 *mngon rtogs rgyan, abhisamayālaṃkāra;* Peking 5184, vol. 88.

3 *'grel pa don gsal / shes rab kyi pha rol tu phyin pa'i man ngag gi bstan bcos mngon par rtogs pa'i rgyan ces bya ba'i 'grel pa, sphuṭārtha / abhisamayālaṃkāranāmaprajñāpāramitopadeśaśāstravṛtti;* Peking 5191, vol. 90.

4 *lam rim chen mo / skyes bu gsum gyi nyams su blang ba'i rim pa thams cad tshang bar ston pa'i byang chub lam gyi rim pa;* Peking 6001, vol. 152.

5 *byang chub lam gyi sgron ma, bodhipathapradīpa;* Peking 5343, vol. 103.

6 *byang chub sems dpa'i spyod pa la 'jug pa, bodhicāryāvatāra;* Peking 5272, vol. 99. Gyel-tsap's commentary is his *Explanation of (Shāntideva's) "Engaging in the Bodhisattva Deeds": Entrance of Conqueror Children* (*byang chub sems dpa'i spyod pa la 'jug pa'i rnam bshad rgyal sras 'jug ngogs*).

7 I have translated the first three sections of this work in two volumes of the Wisdom of Tibet Series: H.H. the Dalai Lama, Tsong-ka-pa, and Jeffrey Hopkins, *Tantra in Tibet* (London: George Allen and Unwin, 1977; reprint, with minor corrections, Ithaca, N.Y.: Snow Lion, 1987); and H.H. the Dalai Lama, Tsong-ka-pa, and Jeffrey Hopkins, *The Yoga of Tibet* (London: George Allen and Unwin, 1981); reprinted as *Deity Yoga*—my original title—with minor corrections (Ithaca, N.Y.: Snow Lion, 1987).

8 See H.H. the Dalai Lama, Tenzin Gyatso, *Kindness, Clarity, and Insight,* trans. and ed. Jeffrey Hopkins (Ithaca, N.Y.: Snow Lion, 1984), 142.

9 H.H. the Dalai Lama, Tenzin Gyatso, *The Buddhism of Tibet and the Key to the Middle Way,* trans. Jeffrey Hopkins (London: George Allen and Unwin, 1975), 55-56.

10 H.H. the Dalai Lama, Tenzin Gyatso, *The Buddhism of Tibet and The Key to the Middle Way,* 56.

11 *skye shi bar do'i rnam bzhag,* Collected Works (Leh: S. Tashigangpa, 1973), vol. 1, 466.2. Cited in Lati Rinbochay and Jeffrey Hopkins, *Death, Intermediate State, and Rebirth in Tibetan Buddhism* (London: Rider, 1980; Valois, N.Y.: Gabriel/Snow Lion, 1980; reprint, Ithaca, N.Y.: Snow Lion, 1985), 47.

12 See Elizabeth Napper, *Dependent-Arising and Emptiness* (London: Wisdom, 1989), 101-122, 176-181, 311-321.

Notes to Part Two, Chapter 3

13 *grub mtha'i rnam bzhag, *siddhāntavyavasthāpana.* Some of the material in this section appears in my "The Tibetan Genre of Doxography: Structuring a Worldview," in *Tibetan Literature,* ed. José Ignacio Cabezón and Roger Jackson (Ithaca, N.Y.: Snow Lion, 1996), 170-186.

14 *rtog ge 'bar ba, tarkajvālā.* This is Bhāvaviveka's commentary on his *Heart of the Middle* (*dbu ma snying po, madhyamakahṛdaya*). For a partial English translation of the latter (chap. III. 1-136), see Shōtarō Iida, *Reason and Emptiness* (Tokyo: Hokuseido, 1980).

15 See David Seyfort Ruegg, *The Literature of the Madhyamaka School of Philosophy in India* (Wiesbaden, Germany: Otto Harrassowitz, 1981), 61.

16 *de kho na nyid bsdud pa'i tshig le'ur byas pa, tattvasaṃgrahakārikā.* A translation into English is available in G. Jha, *The Tattvasaṃgraha of Śāntirakṣita with the Commentary of Kamalaśīla,* Gaekwad's Oriental Series, vols. 50 and 53 (Baroda, India: Oriental Institute, 1937-1939).

17 *theg pa mtha' dag gi don gsal bar byed pa grub pa'i mtha' rin po che'i mdzod.*

18 *grub mtha' kun shes nas mtha' bral grub pa zhes bya ba'i bstan bcos rnam par bshad pa legs bshad kyi rgya mtsho.*

19 *grub mtha'i rnam bshad rang gzhan grub mtha' kun dang zab don mchog tu gsal ba kun bzang zhing gi nyi ma lung rigs rgya mtsho skye dgu'i re ba kun skong/ grub mtha' chen mo.* For an English translation of the beginning of the chapter on the Consequence School, see Jeffrey Hopkins, *Meditation on Emptiness* (London: Wisdom, 1983; rev. ed., Boston: Wisdom, 1996), 579-697.

20 *grub pa'i mtha'i rnam par bzhag pa gsal bar bshad pa thub bstan lhun po'i mdzes rgyan.*

21 *grub mtha' thams cad kyi khungs dang 'dod tshul ston pa legs bshad shel gyi me long.*

22 *chos mngon pa'i mdzod, abhidharmakośa;* VI.4.

23 See Anne C. Klein, *Knowledge and Liberation: A Buddhist Epistemological Analysis in Support of Transformative Religious Experience: Tibetan Interpretations of Dignāga and Dharmakīrti* (Ithaca, N.Y.: Snow Lion, 1986), 19-22, 40-44.

24 Jam-ȳang-shay-b̄a's *Great Exposition of Tenets,* section *nga.*

25 See the tenets section of Geshe Lhundup Sopa and Jeffrey Hopkins, *Cutting through Appearances: The Practice and Theory of Tibetan Buddhism* (Ithaca, N.Y.: Snow Lion, 1989), 249-278.

26 J̄ang-ḡya's *Clear Exposition of the Presentation of Tenets,* 152-275.

27 For a list of these texts, see the bibliography.

28 *tshad ma kun las btus pa, pramāṇasamuccaya;* Peking 5700, vol. 130.

29 The latter is from B̄el-jor-hlün-drup's *Lamp for the Teaching,* 119.5.

30 Gung-tang's *Beginnings of a Commentary on the Difficult Points of (D̄zong-ka-b̄a's) "Differentiating the Interpretable and the Definitive": Quintessence of "The Essence of Eloquence" (drang nges rnam 'byed kyi dga' 'grel rtsom 'phro legs bshad snying po'i yang snying)*, 80.6-80.12 and 235.9ff. Gung-tang wrote two biographies of Ḡön-chok-jik-may-w̄ang-b̄o that are included in the latter's Collected Works; see the Bibliography.

31 Paraphrasing J̄ang-ḡya's *Clear Exposition of the Presentation of Tenets,* 176.11-176.14.

32 Paraphrasing ibid., 177.1-177.7.

33 Paraphrasing ibid., 175.12-175.15.

34 Paraphrasing ibid., 177.11-177.15.

35 Sopa and Hopkins, *Cutting through Appearances,* 260. The passage speaks of the "three characters" (*mtshan nyid gsum, trilakṣaṇa*), another term for the three natures.

36 See Louis de la Vallée Poussin, *Vijñaptimātratāsiddhi: La Siddhi de Hiuan-Tsang* (Paris: P. Geuthner, 1928-1929), 534; and Wei Tat, *Ch'eng wei-shih lun, The Doctrine of Mere-Consciousness* (Hong Kong: Ch'eng Wei-Shih Lun Publication Committee, c. 1973), 639.

37 J̄ang-ḡya's *Clear Exposition of the Presentation of Tenets,* 174.7; also Jam-ȳang-shay-b̄a's *Great Exposition of Tenets, nga,* 43a.3.

38 J̄ang-ḡya's *Clear Exposition of the Presentation of Tenets,* 174.14; also Jam-ȳang-shay-b̄a's *Great Exposition of Tenets, nga,* 43a.6.

39 Drawn from Nga-w̄ang-b̄el-den (*ngag dbang dpal ldan,* 1797-?), *Explanation of the Conventional and the Ultimate in the Four Systems of Tenets (grub mtha' bzhi'i lugs kyi kun rdzob dang don dam pa'i don rnam par bshad pa legs bshad dpyid kyi dpal mo'i glu dbyangs), dngos,* 31a.6.

Notes to Part Two, Chapter 4

40 See Louis de La Vallée Poussin, *L'Abhidharmakośa de Vasubandhu* (Paris: Geuthner, 1923-1931; reprint, Brussels: Institut Belge des Hautes Études Chinoises, 1971), 254 and 259, for the person as imputedly existent (*btags yod*) and as compounded, respectively.

41 See Jeffrey Hopkins, *Meditation on Emptiness* (London: Wisdom, 1983; rev. ed., Boston: Wisdom, 1996), 695-696.

42 Geshe Lhundup Sopa and Jeffrey Hopkins, *Cutting through Appearances: The Practice and Theory of Tibetan Buddhism* (Ithaca, N.Y.: Snow Lion, 1989), 264.

43 The material on the five lineages is drawn from J̄ang-ḡya's *Clear Exposition of the Presentation of Tenets,* 213.18-218.5.14; and Jam-ȳang-shay-b̄a's *Great Exposition of Tenets, nga,* 14b.3-20a.2.

44 Jam-ȳang-shay-b̄a's *Great Exposition of Tenets, nga,* 15a.4-15a.5 and 19a.3.

45 These are drawn from Nga-w̄ang-b̄el-den's *Explanation of the Conventional and the Ultimate in the Four Systems of Tenets, dngos,* 143.6, which lists them at the point of discussing activation of the Hearer lineage.

Notes to Part Two, Chapter 5

46 Gung-tang's *Difficult Points,* 18.10-22.9.

47 This section on the promise of composition is drawn from Gung-tang's *Difficult Points,* 16.16-18.9, and A-ku L̄o-drö-gya-tso's *Precious Lamp,* 8.1-8.6.

48 Gung-tang's *Difficult Points,* 22.9-23.5.

49 H.H. the Dalai Lama, Tenzin Gyatso, *Kindness, Clarity, and Insight,* trans. and ed. Jeffrey Hopkins (Ithaca, N.Y.: Snow Lion, 1984), 142-143.

50 The discussion of the homage to Mañjushrī is drawn from:

Unaffiliated

Second Dalai Lama's *Lamp Illuminating the Meaning of (D̄zong-ka-b̄a's) Thought,* 3a.5-3a.6.

Go-mang and D̄ra-s̄hi-kyil
Jam-ȳang-shay-b̄a's *Brief Decisive Analysis,* 476.4-476.5.
W̄el-mang Ḡön-chok-gyel-tsen's *Notes on (Ḡön-chok-jik-may-w̄ang-b̄o's) Lectures,* 384.4-385.1.
Gung-tang's *Annotations,* 2.1-4.1 (*ka*).
Gung-tang's *Difficult Points,* 2.16-3.11.
A-ku L̄o-drö-gya-tso's *Precious Lamp,* 4.1-4.6.
Pa-bong-ka-b̄a's *Brief Notes on Jo-ni Paṇḍita's Lectures,* 403.6-404.3.

S̄e-ra Jay
B̄el-jor-hlün-drup's *Lamp for the Teaching,* 4.3-4.4.
Jay-d̄zün Chö-ḡyi-gyel-tsen's *General-Meaning Commentary,* 2a.3-2b.1.
S̄er-s̄hül's *Notes,* 3a.5-3b.1.

51 This sentence and the next are drawn from Pa-bong-ka-b̄a's *Brief Notes on Jo-ni Paṇḍita's Lectures,* 403.6-404.2.

52 This material is drawn from S̄er-s̄hül's *Notes,* 3a.6-3b.1.

53 S̄er-s̄hül Ge-s̄hay L̄o-sang-pün-tsok's *Notes,* 3a.6-3b.1.

54 The last clause is from Pa-bong-ka-b̄a's *Brief Notes on Jo-ni Paṇḍita's Lectures,* 404.2: *gdul bya'i rgyud 'jam par mdzad pa'i gsung dbyangs.*

55 Jay-d̄zün Chö-ḡyi-gyel-tsen's *General-Meaning Commentary,* 2a.4-2b.1.

56 Gung-tang's *Difficult Points,* 2.16-3.10.

57 Oral teachings. Gung-tang's *Annotations* (2.1-3.1) was most likely his source.

58 Jay-d̄zün Chö-ḡyi-gyel-tsen's *General-Meaning Commentary,* 2a.5.

59 Gung-tang's *Difficult Points,* 3.2. He appears to be following his teacher Ḡön-chok-jik-may-w̄ang-b̄o, who reports that "some say that the expression is like a translator's homage" but indicates his preference for this second explanation that D̄zong-ka-b̄a pays homage to Mañjushrī as his teacher; see W̄el-mang Ḡön-chok-gyel-tsen's *Notes on (Ḡön-chok-jik-may-w̄ang-b̄o's) Lectures,* 384.6-385.1.

60 From D̄zong-ka-b̄a's text in H.H. the Dalai Lama, Tsong-ka-pa, and Jeffrey Hopkins, *Tantra in Tibet* (London: George Allen and Unwin, 1977; reprint, with minor corrections, Ithaca, N.Y.: Snow Lion, 1987), 84.

61 The Dalai Lama's introduction in ibid., 27. I have added the diacritics.

62 The Dalai Lama's introduction in ibid., 24. I have added diacritics.

63 Cited from my introduction to H.H. the Dalai Lama, Tenzin Gyatso, and Jeffrey Hopkins, *The Kālachakra Tantra: Rite of Initiation for the Stage of Generation* (London: Wisdom, 1985), 143-144. The source is Geshe Thupten Gyatso's condensation of Ke-drup's biography (unpublished manuscript), composed at my request.

64 W̄el-mang Ḡön-chok-gyel-tsen's *Notes on (Ḡön-chok-jik-may-w̄ang-b̄o's) Lectures,* 381.1.

65 A-ku L̄o-drö-gya-tso's *Precious Lamp,* 4.2.

66 As cited in ibid.

67 The discussion of the expression of worship to Shākyamuni Buddha is drawn from:

Unaffiliated
Second Dalai Lama's *Lamp Illuminating the Meaning,* 3a.6-4a.1.

Go-mang and D̄ra-s̄hi-kyil
W̄el-mang Ḡön-chok-gyel-tsen's *Notes on (Ḡön-chok-jik-may-w̄ang-b̄o's) Lectures,* 385.1-386.5.
Gung-tang's *Annotations,* 4.1-4.6 (*kha*).
Gung-tang's *Difficult Points,* 3.12-3.18.
A-ku L̄o-drö-gya-tso's *Precious Lamp,* 4.6-5.6.
Pa-bong-ka-b̄a's *Brief Notes on Jo-ni Paṇḍita's Lectures,* 403.6-404.3.

S̄e-ra Jay
B̄el-jor-hlün-drup's *Lamp for the Teaching,* 4.4-6.3.
Jay-d̄zün Chö-ḡyi-gyel-tsen's *General-Meaning Commentary,* 2b.1-3a.2.
S̄er-s̄hül's *Notes,* 3b.1-4a.5.
D̄a-drin-rap-d̄en's *Annotations,* 2.1-2.3.

68 A-ku L̄o-drö-gya-tso's *Precious Lamp,* 5.3.

69 Gung-tang's *Difficult Points,* 11.17-12.5.

70 Ibid., 10.3-10.14.

71 IV.34bc.

72 See *The Collected Works of C. G. Jung* (Princeton, N.J.: Princeton University Press, 1971, second printing 1974), vol. 8, 217-218 (this refers not to the page number but to the paragraph number used for coordination between editions).

73 See ibid., vol. 9.ii, 45-46.

74 Gung-tang's *Difficult Points,* 10.14-11.1.

75 III.76; see Leo M. Pruden, *Abhidharma-kośabhāṣyam,* 4 vols. (Berkeley, Calif.: Asian Humanities Press, 1988), vol. 2, 469.

76 Ibid., 7.5-7.10; A-ku L̄o-drö-gya-tso's

Precious Lamp, 5.2-5.3.

77 The sources for these origin stories are Prajñāvarman's *Commentary on (Udbhaṭasiddhasvāmin's) "Exalted Praise"* (*viśeṣastavaṭīkā*) and Chandrakīrti's *Supplement to (Nāgārjuna's) "Treatise on the Middle"* as cited in Nga-w̄ang-b̄el-den (*ngag dbang dpal ldan*), *Annotations for (Jam-ȳang-shay-b̄a's) "Great Exposition of Tenets," Freeing the Knots of the Difficult Points, Precious Jewel of Clear Thought* (*grub mtha' chen mo'i mchan 'grel dka' gnad mdud grol blo gsal gces nor*), *stod,* 32b.5ff. See Jeffrey Hopkins, *Meditation on Emptiness* (London: Wisdom, 1983; rev. ed., Boston: Wisdom, 1996), 320.

78 Gung-tang's *Difficult Points,* 8.7.

79 See Lati Rinbochay, Denma Lochö Rinbochay, Leah Zahler, and Jeffrey Hopkins, *Meditative States in Tibetan Buddhism* (London: Wisdom, 1983), 38-41.

80 Gung-tang's *Difficult Points,* 11.1ff.

81 Ibid., 11.9: *'dren pa mnyam med ston pa bcom ldan 'das.*

82 Ibid., 11.12.

83 Ibid., 12.6-12.9.

84 *sangs rgyas bcom ldan 'das la zab mo rten cing 'brel bar 'byung ba gsung ba'i sgo nas bstod pa legs par bshad pa'i snying po.* For English translations, see Geshe Wangyal, in *The Door of Liberation* (New York: Lotsawa, 1978), 117-125; and Robert Thurman, in *Life and Teachings of Tsong Khapa* (Dharmsala, India: Library of Tibetan Works and Archives, 1982), 99-107.

85 Gung-tang's *Difficult Points,* 12.11.

86 For the Sanskrit, see Louis de la Vallée Poussin, *Mūlamadhyamakakārikās de Nāgārjuna avec la Prasannapadā, commentaire de Candrakīrti,* Bibliotheca Buddhica, 4 (Osnabrück, Germany: Biblio Verlag, 1970), 11.12; for the Tibetan, see *dbu ma rtsa ba'i 'grel pa tshig gsal ba* (Dharmsala, India: Council of Religious and Cultural Affairs, 1968), 8.18.

87 Poussin, *Mūlamadhyamakakārikās de Nāgārjuna avec la Prasannapadā,* 12.1; *tshig gsal,* 9.1.

88 *theg pa chen po rgyud bla ma'i ṭīkka* (blockprint in the library of H.H. the Dalai Lama, no other data), 183a.6-183b.6. Gyel-tsap interprets Maitreya's title as meaning *Treatise on the Later Scriptures of the Great Vehicle;* see the beginning of his text.

89 The list is taken from *Meditation on Emptiness,* 210-211.

90 Gung-tang's *Difficult Points,* 13.3-13.8.

91 See his *How To Practice the Two Stages of the Path of the Glorious Kālachakra: Quick Entry to the Path of Great Bliss* (*dpal dus kyi 'khor lo'i lam rim pa gnyis ji ltar nyams su len pa'i tshul bde ba chen po'i lam du myur du 'jug pa*), Collected Works, vol. 1 (Delhi: Guru Deva, 1982), 123.5 (18a.5).

92 H.H. the Dalai Lama, Tsong-ka-pa, and Hopkins, *Tantra in Tibet,* 87.

93 Ibid., 89-90.

94 The Dalai Lama's introduction in ibid., 34-35.

95 H.H. the Dalai Lama, Tenzin Gyatso, *Kindness, Clarity, and Insight,* 47.

96 Gung-tang's *Difficult Points,* 13.16. For the equivalent in A-ku L̄o-drö-gya-tso's *Precious Lamp,* see 5.3-5.6.

Notes to Part Two, Chapter 6

97 Gung-tang's *Difficult Points,* 23.14-24.17.

98 Ibid., 36.14-39.16.

Notes to Part Three, Chapter 7

99 The discussion of Paramārthasamudgata's question in chapters 7-9 is drawn from:

Unaffiliated

- Second Dalai Lama's *Lamp Illuminating the Meaning,* 12.2-13.4.

Go-mang and D̄ra-s̄hi-kyil

- Gung-ru Chö-jung's *Garland of White Lotuses,* 4b.3-16b.1.
- Jam-ȳang-shay-b̄a's *Great Exposition of the Interpretable and the Definitive,* 26.2-41.1.
- Jam-ȳang-shay-b̄a's *Brief Decisive Analysis,* 486.3-494.3.
- W̄el-mang Ḡön-chok-gyel-tsen's *Notes on (Ḡön-chok-jik-may-w̄ang-b̄o's) Lectures,* 395.4-397.4.
- Gung-tang's *Annotations,* 13.4-16.1 (*tha* through *ma*).
- Gung-tang's *Difficult Points,* 75.13-96.8.
- Dön-drup-gyel-tsen's *Four Intertwined Commentaries,* 39.4-44.4.
- A-ku L̄o-drö-gya-tso's *Precious Lamp,* 50.3-69.3.
- Jik-may-dam-chö-gya-tso's *Port of Entry,* 132.1-158.5.
- Pa-bong-ka-b̄a's Brief Notes on J̄o-ni Paṇḍita's Lectures, 408.4-409.5.

L̄o-s̄el-l̄ing and S̄har-d̄zay

- Paṇ-chen S̄ö-nam-drak-b̄a's *Garland of Blue*

Lotuses, 10a.6-13a.6.

S̄e-ra Jay

B̄el-jor-hlün-drup's *Lamp for the Teaching,* 11.4-12.4.

Jay-d̄zün Chö-ḡyi-gyel-tsen's *General-Meaning Commentary,* 7a.2-10a.7.

D̄ra-d̄i Ge-s̄hay Rin-chen-dön-drup's *Ornament for the Thought,* 12.15-17.17.

S̄er-s̄hül's *Notes,* 13a.1-14b.1.

D̄a-drin-rap-d̄en's *Annotations,* 8.4-11.4.

S̄e-ra M̄ay

L̄o-sang-trin-lay-ye-s̄hay's *Summarized Meaning,* 155.9-156.3.

100 Wonch'uk's *Extensive Commentary,* Peking 5517, vol. 116, 128.4-130.2.3.

101 D̄ra-d̄i Ge-s̄hay Rin-chen-dön-drup's *Ornament for the Thought,* 13.6-16.13; he uses the four as the structure of his commentary. The four are also listed by A-ku L̄o-drö-gya-tso (*Precious Lamp,* 50.4).

102 Second Dalai Lama's *Lamp Illuminating the Meaning of (D̄zong-ka-b̄a's) Thought,* 12.4; see also Gung-ru Chö-jung's *Garland of White Lotuses,* 13a.5; Jam-ȳang-shay-b̄a's *Great Exposition of the Interpretable and the Definitive,* 37.6; and Jik-may-dam-chö-gya-tso's *Port of Entry,* 138.6-139.1.

103 Cited in Gung-tang's *Difficult Points* (95.4-95.7) from chap. 7 (Étienne Lamotte, *Saṃdhinirmocanasūtra: L'Explication des mystères* [Louvain: Université de Louvain, 1935], 67 [3]; and Dön-drup-gyel-tsen's *Four Intertwined Commentaries,* 6.6-7.1); a passage similar to it also appears in chap. 5, 34.5, in the *stog* Palace edition.

104 B̄el-jor-hlün-drup's *Lamp for the Teaching,* 12.1.

105 Gung-ru Chö-jung's *Garland of White Lotuses,* 4b.5-6a.2.

106 Jam-ȳang-shay-b̄a's *Great Exposition of the Interpretable and the Definitive,* 26.3-28.6; see also Jam-ȳang-shay-b̄a's *Brief Decisive Analysis* (488.1-488.4) for a less refined presentation of similar material. Jay-d̄zün Chö-ḡyi-gyel-tsen makes a similar but shorter objection in his *General-Meaning Commentary* (8a.4-9a.2).

107 See Jeffrey Hopkins, *Meditation on Emptiness* (London: Wisdom, 1983; rev. ed., Boston: Wisdom, 1996), 201-212.

108 As reported in Gung-tang's *Difficult Points,* 77.18-78.10.

109 Peking 5517, vol. 106, chap. 5, 128.5.7.

110 Ibid., 129.1.6 and 129.1.7.

111 Chap. 7; Lamotte, *Saṃdhinirmocana,* 69-70 [8] and 195; Dön-drup-gyel-tsen's *Four Intertwined Commentaries,* 8.4-9.1; and Powers, *Wisdom of Buddha,* 103.

112 Gung-tang's *Difficult Points,* 89.17.

113 Paṇ-chen S̄ö-nam-drak-b̄a's *Garland of Blue Lotuses,* 10a.6-11b.6.

Notes to Part Three, Chapter 8

114 Gung-tang's *Difficult Points,* 81.5-85.13.

115 Chap. 7; Étienne Lamotte, *Saṃdhinirmocanasūtra: L'Explication des mystères* (Louvain: Université de Louvain, 1935), 81 [25] and 203; Dön-drup-gyel-tsen's *Four Intertwined Commentaries,* 21.3-21.21.5; and John C. Powers, *Wisdom of Buddha: Saṁdhinirmocana Sūtra* (Berkeley, Calif.: Dharma, 1995), 131.

116 Chap. 4; Lamotte, *Saṃdhinirmocanasūtra,* 48 [1-6] and 178-180; and Powers, *Wisdom of Buddha,* 53-57.

117 Chap. 9; Lamotte, *Saṃdhinirmocanasūtra,* 147 [32] and 256; and Powers, *Wisdom of Buddha,* 269.

118 *mngon par 'byung ba'i mdo;* Peking 967, vol. 39.

119 Jik-may-dam-chö-gya-tso's *Port of Entry,* 155.5-156.2.

120 Ibid., 155.4.

121 From among the last four sentences, the first, second, and fourth are drawn from Gung-tang's *Annotations,* 14.4-14.6; the third is from A-ku L̄o-drö-gya-tso's *Precious Lamp,* 56.5.

122 Chap. 7; Lamotte, *Saṃdhinirmocanasūtra,* 71 [11] and 196-197; and Powers, *Wisdom of Buddha,* 107.

123 H.H. the Dalai Lama, Tenzin Gyatso, *Kindness, Clarity, and Insight,* trans. and ed. Jeffrey Hopkins (Ithaca, N.Y.: Snow Lion, 1984), 43.

124 See, for instance, Gung-ru Chö-jung's *Garland of White Lotuses,* 9a.3-9b.3; and Jam-ȳang-shay-b̄a's *Great Exposition of the Interpretable and the Definitive,* 33.6-34.4.

125 Jam-ȳang-shay-b̄a's *Great Exposition of the Interpretable and the Definitive,* 48.4.

126 Ibid., 48.3-48.6.

127 Jik-may-dam-chö-gya-tso's *Port of Entry,* 206.4-207.2.

Notes to Part Three, Chapter 9

128 In his *Extensive Explanation of*

(Chandrakīrti's) "Supplement to (Nāgārjuna's) 'Treatise on the Middle'": Illumination of the Thought (*dbu ma la 'jug pa'i rgya cher bshad pa dgongs pa rab gsal;* Peking 6143, vol. 154); see Tsong-ka-pa, Ken-sur Nga-wang-lek-den, and Jeffrey Hopkins, *Compassion in Tibetan Buddhism* (London: Rider, 1980; reprint, Ithaca, N.Y.: Snow Lion, 1980), 136.

129 *mdo sde sa bcu pa, daśabhūmika.* For a Sanskrit edition, see *Daśabhūmikasūtram,* P. L. Vaidya, ed. Buddhist Sanskrit Texts 7 (Darbhanga, India: Mithila Institute, 1967); for an English translation, see M. Honda, "An Annotated Translation of the 'Daśabhūmika,'" in *Studies in South, East and Central Asia,* ed. D. Sinor, Śatapiṭaka Series 74 (New Delhi: International Academy of Indian Culture, 1968), 115-276.

130 For an extensive list of references on the debate, see Elizabeth Napper, *Dependent-Arising and Emptiness* (London: Wisdom, 1989), 656 n. 36.

131 Gung-tang's *Difficult Points,* 35.11ff.

132 Gung-tang's *Annotations,* 9.5-9.6.

133 Gung-tang's *Difficult Points,* 35.11.

134 Ibid., 81.5-86.14.

135 A-ku Lo-drö-gya-tso's *Precious Lamp,* 57.2-57.3.

Notes to Part Three, Chapter 10

136 Peking 5517, vol. 106, 130.5.4ff. Jik-may-dam-chö-gya-tso (*Port of Entry,* 159.1-160.2) uses Wonch'uk's detailed breakdown of this section.

137 The headings in bold print are added to the sūtra. The first heading is taken from Wonch'uk's *Extensive Commentary,* Peking 5517, vol. 116, 130.2.4.

138 *rnam par gtan la dbab pa bsdu ba, viniścayasaṃgrahaṇī;* Peking 5539, vol. 111, 71.2.8; Tokyo *sde dge, sems tsam,* vol. 9 (*zi*), 8.4.5.

139 For other translations, see Stefan Anacker, *Seven Works of Vasubandhu* (Delhi: Motilal Banarsidass, 1984), 188; also Thomas A. Kochumuttom, *A Buddhist Doctrine of Experience* (Delhi: Motilal Banarsidass, 1982), 258.

140 Reported by the late Ken-sur Ye-shay-tup-den.

141 Chap. 7; Étienne Lamotte, *Saṃdhinirmocanasūtra: L'Explication des mystères* (Louvain: Université de Louvain, 1935), 75 [17-18] and 199; John C. Powers, *Wisdom of Buddha: Saṁdhinirmocana Sūtra* (Berkeley, Calif.: Dharma, 1995), 115-117.

142 Gung-ru Chö-jung's *Garland of White Lotuses,* 16b.4-17b.1.

143 Jam-yang-shay-ba's *Great Exposition of the Interpretable and the Definitive,* 43.1-43.4.

144 Peking 5517, vol. 106, 130.5.4ff.

145 See Jik-may-dam-chö-gya-tso's *Port of Entry,* 198.4; he identifies this explanation as from Wonch'uk's commentary.

146 Jik-may-dam-chö-gya-tso's *Port of Entry,* 198.6ff.

147 Ibid., 199.5.

148 Peking 5517, vol. 106; the final one is found at 106, 130.5.4. Jik-may-dam-chö-gya-tso's *Port of Entry,* 208.1.

149 Jik-may-dam-chö-gya-tso's *Port of Entry,* 208.3.

150 Ibid., 209.3.

151 Ibid., 209.5.

Notes to Part Three, Chapter 11

152 A-ku Lo-drö-gya-tso's *Precious Lamp,* 86.6.

153 Chap. 7; Étienne Lamotte, *Saṃdhinirmocanasūtra: L'Explication des mystères* (Louvain: Université de Louvain, 1935), 71-72 [11] and 196-197; Dön-drup-gyel-tsen's *Four Intertwined Commentaries,* 11.1-11.5; and John C. Powers, *Wisdom of Buddha: Saṁdhinirmocana Sūtra* (Berkeley, Calif.: Dharma, 1995), 107-108.

154 *bodhipathapradīpa, byang chub lam gyi sgron ma;* Peking 5343, vol. 103. For a Tibetan biography of Atisha, see Pabongka Rinpoche, *Liberation in Our Hands,* trans. Sera Mey Geshe Lobsang Tharchin with Artemus B. Engle (Howell, N.J.: Mahayana Sutra and Tantra Press, 1990), 31-57; also Pabongka Rinpoche, *Liberation in the Palm of Your Hand,* ed. Trijang Rinpoche, trans. Michael Richards (Boston: Wisdom, 1991), 45-71. An earlier version of my exposition on the three types of beings appeared in "A Tibetan Perspective on the Nature of Spiritual Experience," in *Paths to Liberation,* ed. Robert E. Buswell and Robert Gimello (Honolulu: University of Hawaii Press, 1992), 182-217.

155 Richard Sherbourne, *A Lamp for the Path and Commentary* (London: George Allen and Unwin, 1983), x-xii.

156 See, for instance, Ken-sur Nga-wang-lek-den's presentation in Kensur Lekden, *Meditations of a Tibetan Tantric Abbot,* trans. and ed. Jeffrey

Hopkins (Ithaca, N.Y.: Snow Lion, 2001).

157 Jam-ȳang-shay-b̄a's presentation is found in his textbook on Maitreya's *Ornament for Clear Realization* in the first chapter in a section supplementary to a presentation of the "openers of chariot-ways" (*shing rta srol 'byed*)—*Decisive Analysis of the Treatise (Maitreya's) "Ornament for Clear Realization": Precious Lamp Illuminating All of the Meaning of the Perfection of Wisdom* (*bstan gcos mngon par rtogs pa'i rgyan gyi mtha' dpyod shes rab kyi pha rol tu phyin pa'i don kun gsal ba'i rin chen sgron me*), Collected Works of 'Jam-dbyaṅs-bźad-pa'i-rdo-rje, vol. 7 (New Delhi: Ngawang Gelek Demo, 1973), 34.4-42.6; also (Sarnath, India: Guru Deva, 1965), 25.14-33.4. The running citations will be made to the Sarnath edition, since it is clearer.

158 Kensur Lekden, *Meditations of a Tibetan Tantric Abbot,* 25.

159 D̄zong-ka-b̄a's *Great Exposition of the Stages of the Path,* 58a.6 (Dharmsala, India: Tibetan Cultural Printing Press, 1964). See also the excellent translation in Tsong-kha-pa, *The Great Treatise on the Stages of the Path to Enlightenment,* vol. 1, trans. and ed. Joshua W. C. Cutler and Guy Newland (Ithaca, N.Y.: Snow Lion, 2000), 130.

160 Kensur Lekden, *Meditations of a Tibetan Tantric Abbot,* 25-26.

161 *sa lam gyi rnam bzhag theg gsum mdzes rgyan;* Collected Works of dkon-mchog-'jigs-med-dbang-po, vol. 7 (New Delhi: Ngawang Gelek Demo, 1972), 422.3. This work was used extensively in E. Obermiller, "The Doctrine of the Prajñā-pāramitā as Exposed in the Abhisamayālaṃkāra of Maitreya," *Acta Orientalia* (Leiden, Netherlands: Brill, 1932), 14ff.

162 Following Ḡön-chok-jik-may-w̄ang-b̄o's refinement.

163 Jam-ȳang-shay-b̄a's *Decisive Analysis of the Treatise (Maitreya's) "Ornament for Clear Realization,"* 27.5.

164 XXV.9; *ched du brjod pa'i tshom, udānavarga.* See W. Woodville Rockhill, *Udānavarga: A Collection of Verses from the Buddhist Canon* (London: Trübner & Co., 1883), 113. See also Gareth Sparham, *The Tibetan Dhammapada: Sayings of the Buddha* (London: Wisdom, 1986).

165 D̄zong-ka-b̄a's *Great Exposition,* 58b.3. See also Tsong-kha-pa, *The Great Treatise on the Stages of the Path,* 130.

166 Kensur Lekden, *Meditations of a Tibetan Tantric Abbot,* 27-28,

167 Unpublished transcript of lectures in Tibetan at the University of Virginia in 1978, trans. Jeffrey Hopkins and ed. Elizabeth Napper.

168 Ḡön-chok-jik-may-w̄ang-b̄o's *Presentation of the Grounds and Paths,* 423.3.

169 D̄zong-ka-b̄a's *Great Exposition,* 59a.6. See also Tsong-kha-pa, *The Great Treatise on the Stages of the Path,* 131.

170 This is drawn from Ken-sur Nga-w̄ang-lek-den's description of persons of great capacity in Tsong-ka-pa, Ken-sur Nga-w̄ang-lek-den, and Jeffrey Hopkins, *Compassion in Tibetan Buddhism,* 20.

171 Unpublished transcript of lectures in Tibetan at the University of Virginia in 1978, trans. Jeffrey Hopkins and ed. Elizabeth Napper.

172 Jam-ȳang-shay-b̄a's *Decisive Analysis of (Maitreya's) "Ornament for Clear Realization,"* 31.1-31.4.

173 Ibid., 30.4-30.8.

174 D̄zong-ka-b̄a's *Great Exposition,* 59b.2-60a.1. See also Tsong-kha-pa, *The Great Treatise on the Stages of the Path,* 132-133.

175 D̄zong-ka-b̄a's *Great Exposition,* 61a.6-61b.2. See also Tsong-kha-pa, *The Great Treatise on the Stages of the Path,* 135.

176 Jam-ȳang-shay-b̄a's *Great Exposition of the Interpretable and the Definitive,* 69.1.

177 Jik-may-dam-chö-gya-tso's *Port of Entry,* 182.3.

178 A-ku L̄o-drö-gya-tso's *Precious Lamp,* 87.4-93.3.

179 A-ku L̄o-drö-gya-tso's *Precious Lamp,* 92.2-93.3. His explanation is almost entirely drawn from Gung-tang's *Annotations,* 23.7-24.5 (Ngawang Gelek edition: 752.5-753.4).

180 See Étienne Lamotte, *La Somme du grand véhicule d'Asaṅga,* reprint, 2 vols., Publications de l'Institute Orientaliste de Louvain 8 (Louvain: Université de Louvain, 1973), vol. 1, 31 (II.15), and vol. 2, 107; and John P. Keenan, *The Summary of the Great Vehicle by Bodhisattva Asaṅga: Translated from the Chinese of Paramārtha* (Berkeley, Calif.: Numata Center for Buddhist Translation and Research, 1992), 46.

181 In A-ku L̄o-drö-gya-tso's *Precious Lamp* (92.3) read *rkyen* ***kyi*** for *rkyen* ***kyis*** in accordance with Gung-tang's *Annotations* (752.6). Lamotte (vol. 1, 31 [II.15]) reads *rkyen* ***gyi,*** not taking into account the extra suffix *da* on *rkyen.*

182 Ibid., 92.6.

Notes to Part Three, Chapter 12

183 Chap. 7; Étienne Lamotte, *Saṃdhinirmocanasūtra: L'Explication des mystères* (Louvain: Université de Louvain, 1935), 72-73 [12-13] and 197; Dön-drup-gyel-tsen's *Four Intertwined Commentaries,* 11.5-12.5; and John C. Powers, *Wisdom of Buddha: Saṁdhinirmocana Sūtra* (Berkeley, Calif.: Dharma, 1995), 109-111.

184 The exposition is based on the line of argument of Jam-ȳang-shay-b̄a's *Great Exposition of the Interpretable and the Definitive,* 49.1-59.3; Jam-ȳang-shay-b̄a is following Gung-ru Chö-jung's *Garland of White Lotuses,* 19a.3ff.

185 Gung-ru Chö-jung's *Garland of White Lotuses,* 19a.6-19b.5.

186 Jam-ȳang-shay-b̄a's *Great Exposition of the Interpretable and the Definitive,* 49.4-49.6.

187 Second Dalai Lama's *Lamp Illuminating the Meaning of [D̄zong-ka-b̄a's] Thought,* 16.2.

188 Gung-tang's *Difficult Points,* 107.16. See also Jik-may-dam-chö-gya-tso's *Port of Entry,* 173.1.

189 Jik-may-dam-chö-gya-tso's *Port of Entry,* 107.16: *skabs thob kyi kun btags.*

190 Ibid., 107.17: *kun btags spyi tsam.*

191 B̄el-jor-hlün-drup's *Lamp for the Teaching,* 14.3.

192 Paṇ-chen S̄ö-nam-drak-b̄a's *Garland of Blue Lotuses,* 27b.5.

193 Ibid., 28b.4-29a.4.

194 Recorded oral teaching.

195 Chap. 1; Lamotte, *Saṃdhinirmocanasūtra,* 36-37 [4] and 170-171; and Powers, *Wisdom of Buddha,* 15-17.

Notes to Part Three, Chapter 13

196 Such as Gung-ru Chö-jung (*Garland of White Lotuses,* 19a.6-19b.5) and Jam-ȳang-shay-b̄a (*Great Exposition of the Interpretable and the Definitive,* 49.4-49.6).

197 Jay-d̄zün Chö-ḡyi-gyel-tsen's *General-Meaning Commentary,* 11b.1.

198 As reported in A-ku L̄o-drö-gya-tso's *Precious Lamp,* 73.5 and 75.6-77.4

199 B̄el-jor-hlün-drup's *Lamp for the Teaching,* 14.5.

200 Gung-ru Chö-jung's *Garland of White Lotuses,* 25a.1-26b.3.

201 Jam-ȳang-shay-b̄a's *Great Exposition of the Interpretable and the Definitive,* 59.3-61.6. Jam-ȳang-shay-b̄a reframes Gung-ru Chö-jung's presentation of this topic, bringing to it greater clarity. See also Jam-ȳang-shay-b̄a's *Brief Decisive Analysis,* 502.1-503.5.

202 Gung-ru Chö-jung's *Garland of White Lotuses,* 25b.2ff; Jam-ȳang-shay-b̄a's *Great Exposition of the Interpretable and the Definitive,* 59.6.

203 Ke-drup's *Opening the Eyes of the Fortunate,* 238.5; see also José Ignacio Cabezón, *A Dose of Emptiness* (Albany, N.Y.: State University of New York Press, 1992), 68.

204 This sentence is drawn from Paṇ-chen S̄ö-nam-drak-b̄a's *Garland of Blue Lotuses,* 29b.2.

205 S̄er-s̄hül's *Notes,* 16a.2.

206 Ibid., 16b.6-17a.4.

207 Nga-w̄ang-b̄el-den's *Stating the Modes of Explanation in the Textbooks on the Middle and the Perfection of Wisdom in the L̄o-s̄el-ling and Go-mang Colleges: Festival for Those of Clear Intelligence* (*blo gsal gling dang bkra shis sgo mang grva tshang gi dbu phar gyi yig cha'i bshad tshul bkod pa blo gsal dga' ston*), Collected Works, vol. 3 (New Delhi: Guru Deva, 1983), 454.3-455.6.

208 See also Cabezón, *A Dose of Emptiness,* 57.

209 In the Guru Deva edition (225.4) read *kun slong rtog pa'**ang*** for *kun slong rtog pa'**am*** to accord with the previous reason clause.

210 This is in the second chapter of Asaṅga's *Summary of the Great Vehicle.*

211 Some of the material here is drawn from Jik-may-dam-chö-gya-tso's *Port of Entry* (550.1-564.4, especially 553.1-554.4), which gives an extensive delineation of this theory of perception at the point of D̄zong-ka-b̄a's mentioning (*Emptiness in Mind-Only,* 194-195) how crucial an understanding of the false manner of imputation of entities and attributes is for delineating emptiness in the Mind-Only School.

212 Jik-may-dam-chö-gya-tso's *Port of Entry,* 553.1.

213 Ibid., 665.3 and 666.3.

214 This paragraph is drawn from ibid., 551.1 and 555.6-557.4.

215 Ibid., 556.3.

216 Ibid., 557.1.

217 Ibid., 557.3.

218 B̄el-jor-hlün-drup's *Lamp for the Teaching,* 14.6-15.2.

219 Jam-ȳang-shay-b̄a's *Great Exposition of the Interpretable and the Definitive,* 63.3. See also Jik-may-dam-chö-gya-tso's *Port of Entry,* 171.2-

172.3.

220 Ḏra-ḏi Ge-s̄hay Rin-chen-dön-drup's *Ornament for the Thought,* 23.11.

221 Stanza 191 (VIII.16); see Karen Lang, *Āryadeva's Catuḥśataka: On the Bodhisattva's Cultivation of Merit and Knowledge,* Indiste Studier, 7 (Copenhagen: Akademisk Forlag, 1986), 83; and *Yogic Deeds of Bodhisattvas: Gyel-tsap on Āryadeva's Four Hundred,* commentary by Geshe Sonam Rinchen, trans. and ed. Ruth Sonam (Ithaca, N.Y.: Snow Lion, 1994), 194.

222 Chap. 7; Étienne Lamotte, *Saṃdhinirmocanasūtra: L'Explication des mystères* (Louvain: Université de Louvain, 1935), 69-70 [8] and 195; Dön-drup-gyel-tsen's *Four Intertwined Commentaries,* 8.4-9.1; John C. Powers, *Wisdom of Buddha: Saṁdhinirmocana Sūtra* (Berkeley, Calif.: Dharma, 1995), 103.

223 Ḏra-ḏi Ge-s̄hay Rin-chen-dön-drup's *Ornament for the Thought,* 24.12-24.16. See also Gung-tang's *Difficult Points* (114.11) within part of an opponent's statement that is unchallenged.

224 Jam-ȳang-shay-b̄a's *Great Exposition of the Interpretable and the Definitive,* 64.1.

225 See also Cabezón, *A Dose of Emptiness,* 42.

226 A-ku L̄o-drö-gya-tso's *Precious Lamp,* 83.5. His presentation is based on a less detailed presentation in Gung-ru Chö-jung's *Garland of White Lotuses* (28a.1-28a.5); Jam-ȳang-shay-b̄a, for no apparent reason, eliminated this part when he revised Gung-ru Chö-jung's textbook.

227 Gung-tang's *Difficult Points,* 121.16-122.12.

NOTES TO PART THREE, CHAPTER 14

228 For this section, see Jam-ȳang-shay-b̄a's *Great Exposition of the Interpretable and the Definitive,* 79.4-80.2; he is following Gung-ru Chö-jung's *Garland of White Lotuses,* 31a.2-31a.6.

229 Gung-tang's *Difficult Points,* 129.18.

230 Jam-ȳang-shay-b̄a's *Great Exposition of the Interpretable and the Definitive,* 80.3ff.

231 *ske tshang / ske'u tshang.* A-ku L̄o-drö-gya-tso's *Precious Lamp* (95.4) names him explicitly, whereas Gung-tang's *Annotations* (25.3) and *Difficult Points* (131.7) do not.

232 Jik-may-dam-chö-gya-tso's *Port of Entry,* 184.1-185.2.

233 Ḏa-drin-rap-ḏen's *Annotations,* 19.3-21.2. For a biography of Ḏa-drin-rap-ḏen, see B. Alan Wallace, trans. and ed., *The Life and Teachings of Geshé Rabten* (London: George Allen and Unwin, 1980).

234 Gung-tang's *Difficult Points,* 131.15-132.14; Gung-tang does not specify Ḡe-u-tsang as the opponent.

235 A-ku L̄o-drö-gya-tso's *Precious Lamp,* 96.1-97.5; he (95.4) specifies Ḡe-u-tsang as the opponent.

236 Gung-tang's *Difficult Points,* 132.6.

237 Ibid., 132.10. See also A-ku L̄o-drö-gya-tso's *Precious Lamp,* 96.5.

238 This appears to be largely based on a discussion of the four levels of the path of preparation; see Étienne Lamotte, *La Somme du grand véhicule d'Asaṅga,* reprint, 2 vols., Publications de l'Institute Orientaliste de Louvain 8 (Louvain: Université de Louvain, 1973), vol. 1, 54 (II1.13), and vol. 2, 170; and John P. Keenan, *The Summary of the Great Vehicle by Bodhisattva Asaṅga: Translated from the Chinese of Paramārtha* (Berkeley, Calif.: Numata Center for Buddhist Translation and Research, 1992), 68-69. However, the names for the three grounds do not appear there.

239 This elaboration of the three levels is drawn from A-ku L̄o-drö-gya-tso's *Precious Lamp,* 97.1-97.5.

240 Ibid., 96.3.

241 The presentation of positive and negative phenomena is adapted from Appendix 4 in Jeffrey Hopkins, *Meditation on Emptiness* (London: Wisdom, 1983; rev. ed., Boston: Wisdom, 1996), 721-727. Ḏzong-ka-b̄a gives a detailed presentation of negatives near the end of *The Essence of Eloquence* in the last part of the section on the Consequence School.

242 J̄ang-ḡya's *Clear Exposition of the Presentations of Tenets,* 250.10-255.11. J̄ang-ḡya raises this argument in the context of discussing Dharmakīrti's reasoning built around the certainty of simultaneous certification of subject and object, but it applies to all reasonings proving an absence of difference of entity of subject and object.

243 See ibid., 251.9, 255.9.

244 Jik-may-dam-chö-gya-tso's *Port of Entry,* 189.1.

245 A-ku L̄o-drö-gya-tso's *Precious Lamp,* 97.6.

246 Ibid., 207.4-215.4.

247 Jik-may-dam-chö-gya-tso's *Port of Entry,* 650.4-655.2.

248 In the section on the Autonomy School, Ye shes thabs mkhas edition, 140.9.

249 Jik-may-dam-chö-gya-tso's *Port of Entry,*

241.2, 266.1, and 468.1.

250 Geshe Lhundup Sopa and Jeffrey Hopkins, *Cutting through Appearances: The Practice and Theory of Tibetan Buddhism* (Ithaca, N.Y.: Snow Lion, 1989), 264.

251 Jik-may-dam-chö-gya-tso's *Port of Entry,* 666.4.

252 J̄ang-ḡya's *Clear Exposition of the Presentation of Tenets,* 193.10.

253 Jam-ȳang-shay-b̄a's *Great Exposition of the Interpretable and the Definitive,* 81.4-81.5.

254 Jik-may-dam-chö-gya-tso's *Port of Entry,* 185.6.

255 Gung-tang's *Difficult Points,* 151.6-152.13.

256 Chap. 3; Étienne Lamotte, *Saṃdhinirmocanasūtra: L'Explication des mystères* (Louvain: Université de Louvain, 1935), 43 [3] and 175; and John C. Powers, *Wisdom of Buddha: Saṁdhinirmocana Sūtra* (Berkeley, Calif.: Dharma, 1995), 37-38. I have lengthened Gung-tang's citation.

257 Chap. 3; Lamotte, *Saṃdhinirmocana,* 45 [5] and 177; and Powers, *Wisdom of the Buddha,* 43.

Notes to Part Three, Chapter 15

258 Étienne Lamotte, *Saṃdhinirmocanasūtra: L'Explication des mystères* (Louvain: Université de Louvain, 1935), 45 [5] and 177; and John C. Powers, *Wisdom of Buddha: Saṁdhinirmocana Sūtra* (Berkeley, Calif.: Dharma, 1995), 43.

259 D̄a-drin-rap-d̄en's *Annotations,* 22.4.

260 Jam-ȳang-shay-b̄a's *Great Exposition of the Interpretable and the Definitive,* 82.1.

261 Ibid., 83.2.

262 An earlier version of some of the material in this section appeared in an article, "Ultimate Reality in Tibetan Buddhism," *Buddhist-Christian Studies* 8 (1988):111-129.

263 A-ku L̄o-drö-gya-tso's *Precious Lamp,* 106.1. For the corresponding section in Jam-ȳang-shay-b̄a's *Great Exposition of the Interpretable and the Definitive,* see 83.6-84.3.

Notes to Part Four, Chapter 16

264 For something closely resembling this except for the important qualification of "ultimate" in ultimate qualities, see Gung-tang's *Difficult Points,* 137.5; *Annotations,* 19.7.

265 Gung-tang (*Difficult Points,* 138.5) cites this passage as quoted in S̄hay-rap-gyel-tsen's *Ocean of Definitive Meaning.*

266 S̄hay-rap-gyel-tsen's *Ocean of Definitive Meaning,* 39.4.

267 Ibid., 45.3.

268 Ibid., 45.4.

269 Ibid., 47.2.

270 Ibid., 106.4.

271 Ibid., 3.2.

272 Ibid., 54.1.

273 Ibid., 54.4-56.5.

274 Ibid., 69.2.

275 Ibid., 168.4.

276 Ibid., 155.4.

277 Ibid., 10.2.

278 Ibid., 155.2.

279 Paraphrasing A-ku L̄o-drö-gya-tso's *Precious Lamp,* 72.4-72.6. The description of their position is taken from W̄el-mang Ḡön-chok-gyel-tsen's *Notes on (Ḡön-chok-jik-may-w̄ang-b̄o's) Lectures,* 399.4-399.5.

280 S̄hay-rap-gyel-tsen's *Ocean of Definitive Meaning,* 206.6 (cursive edition).

281 As cited in Gung-tang's *Difficult Points,* 136.14; Gung-tang's *Annotations,* 19.4.

282 S̄hay-rap-gyel-tsen's *Ocean of Definitive Meaning,* 186.6.

283 Ibid., 187.1-188.3.

284 Ibid., 193.4.

285 Ibid., 189.3.

286 Ibid., 168.6.

287 Ibid., 176.2.

288 Ibid., 177.1.

289 Ibid., 172.1.

290 Ibid., 88.2.

291 Ibid., 176.2.

292 Gung-tang (*Difficult Points,* 136.16; *Annotations,* 19.4) appears to be paraphrasing S̄hay-rap-gyel-tsen's *The Fourth Council.* See, for instance, Cyrus R. Stearns, *The Buddha from Dol po: A Study of the Life and Thought of the Tibetan Master Dolpopa Sherab Gyaltsen* (Albany, N.Y.: State University of New York Press, 1999), 149-150, 154.

293 S̄hay-rap-gyel-tsen's *Ocean of Definitive Meaning,* 211.4.

294 Ibid., 57.5.

295 For *'dod pa* in the Gangtok edition, 58.6, read *rgod pa* in accordance with the 'dzam thang bsam 'grub nor bu'i gling edition, 32a.4.

296 Immediately following the preceding quote.

297 S̄hay-rap-gyel-tsen's *Ocean of Definitive*

Meaning, 209.6.
298 Ibid., 194.6.
299 *theg pa chen po'i mdo sde rgyan, mahāyānasūtrālaṃkāra;* VI.1; Peking 5521, vol. 108, 5.1.1; for the Sanskrit, see *Emptiness in Mind-Only*, 408, footnote b. For a translation into French, see Sylvain Lévi, *Mahāyānasūtrālaṃkāra: Exposé de la doctrine du grand véhicule selon le système Yogācāra* (Paris: Bibliothèque de l'École des Hautes Études, 1907, 1911; reprint, Shanghai: 1940), 22.
300 Shay-rap-gyel-tsen's *Ocean of Definitive Meaning*, 61.5.
301 Ibid., 218.6.
302 Ibid., 217.5.
303 Étienne Lamotte, *La Somme du grand véhicule d'Asaṅga*, reprint, 2 vols., Publications de l'Institute Orientaliste de Louvain 8 (Louvain: Université de Louvain, 1973), vol. 1, 52 (III.9), and vol. 2, 164-165; and John P. Keenan, *The Summary of the Great Vehicle by Bodhisattva Asaṅga: Translated from the Chinese of Paramārtha* (Berkeley, Calif.: Numata Center for Buddhist Translation and Research, 1992), 67.
304 Shay-rap-gyel-tsen's *Ocean of Definitive Meaning*, 210.3.
305 Ibid., 70.1.
306 Ibid., 98.2.
307 Ibid., 179.1.
308 Ibid., 75.6.
309 Ibid., 14.1.
310 Ibid., 33.3.
311 Gung-tang (*Difficult Points*, 136.16; *Annotations*, 19.4) cites this from Shay-rap-gyel-tsen's *The Fourth Council.*
312 Wel-mang Gön-chok-gyel-tsen's *Notes on (Gön-chok-jik-may-wang-bo's) Lectures*, 399.5.
313 *bar chad.*
314 Stearns, *The Buddha from Dol po*, 98.
315 In lectures on Maitreya's *Sublime Continuum of the Great Vehicle* in Bodh Gaya in 1982.
316 The Dalai Lama suggested this in lectures on Maitreya's *Sublime Continuum of the Great Vehicle* at Bodh Gaya in 1982.
317 *gsang chen rgyud sde bzhi'i sa lam gyi rnam bzhag rgyud gzhung gsal byed* (rgyud smad par khang edition, no other data), 52.1.
318 Ibid., 153.6.
319 Wel-mang Gön-chok-gyel-tsen's *Notes on (Gön-chok-jik-may-wang-bo's) Lectures*, 402.3.
320 Stanzas 96cd-99. Gung-tang cites only one line; Shay-rap-gyel-tsen (*Ocean of Definitive Meaning*, 22.3) cites stanzas 97-99. The bracketed material is from the commentary by Ju Mi-pam-gya-tso (*'ju mi-pham-rgya-mtsho*), *Annotations on (Maitreya's) "Great Vehicle Treatise, The Sublime Continuum": Sacred Word of Mi-pam* (*theg pa chen po rgyud bla ma'i bstan bcos kyi mchan 'grel mi pham zhal lung*) (Gangtok, Sikkim: Sonam Topgay Kazi, 1972), vol. *pa.* See Cyrus R. Stearns, *The Buddha from Dol po: A Study of the Life and Thought of the Tibetan Master Dolpopa Sherab Gyaltsen* (Albany, N.Y.: State University of New York Press, 1999), 156ff., for similar similes.
321 Stanzas 103-105.

Notes to Part Four, Chapter 17A

322 Shay-rap-gyel-tsen's *Ocean of Definitive Meaning*, 434.6.
323 Ye shes thabs mkhas edition, 275.14.
324 Jik-may-dam-chö-gya-tso's *Port of Entry*, 460.4.
325 Ibid., 460.6.
326 Ibid.
327 Shay-rap-gyel-tsen's *Ocean of Definitive Meaning*, 479.2.
328 Shay-rap-gyel-tsen's *Ocean of Definitive Meaning*, 481.4.
329 Shay-rap-gyel-tsen's *Ocean of Definitive Meaning*, 481.6.

Notes to Part Four, Chapter 17B

330 Shay-rap-gyel-tsen's *Ocean of Definitive Meaning*, 177.3.
331 Ibid., 191.1.
332 Ibid., 203.3.
333 Da-drin-rap-den's *Annotations*, 62.6.
334 A-ku Lo-drö-gya-tso's *Precious Lamp*, 188.6.
335 Jik-may-dam-chö-gya-tso's *Port of Entry*, 400.3-400.6.
336 Tāranātha's *The Essence of Other-Emptiness*, 503.1.
337 Shay-rap-gyel-tsen's *Ocean of Definitive Meaning*, 181.6.
338 Ibid., 201.2.
339 Daisetz Teitaro Suzuki, trans., *The Lankavatara Sutra* (London: Routledge and Kegan Paul, 1932), 67 (75).
340 Shay-rap-gyel-tsen's *Ocean of Definitive Meaning*, 194.1.
341 Ibid., 194.2-194.3.

342 Ibid., 194.3-194.5.

343 Ke-drup's *Opening the Eyes of the Fortunate,* 209.5; José Ignacio Cabezón, *A Dose of Emptiness* (Albany, N.Y.: State University of New York Press, 1992), 46-47.

Notes to Part Four, Chapter 17c

344 Jam-ȳang-shay-b̄a's *Great Exposition of the Interpretable and the Definitive,* 83.2.

345 S̄hay-rap-gyel-tsen's *Ocean of Definitive Meaning,* 68.6.

346 *bdag gi dbyings.*

347 S̄hay-rap-gyel-tsen's *Ocean of Definitive Meaning,* 82.4.

348 Ibid., 11.2. See also Cyrus R. Stearns, *The Buddha from Dol po: A Study of the Life and Thought of the Tibetan Master Dolpopa Sherab Gyaltsen* (Albany, N.Y.: State University of New York Press, 1999), 163.

349 S̄hay-rap-gyel-tsen's *Ocean of Definitive Meaning,* 65.2.

350 Ibid., 154.4.

351 Ibid., 190.2.

352 Ibid., 65.6.

353 Ibid., 66.6.

354 Ibid., 71.2.

355 Ibid., 70.6.

356 Ibid., 71.3.

357 Daisetz Teitaro Suzuki, trans., *The Lankavatara Sutra* (London: Routledge and Kegan Paul, 1932), 10 (44).

358 Ye shes thabs mkhas edition, 128.5.

359 Ibid., 273.4.

360 Peking 775, vol. 29, 39.5.2, chap. 2. See Jñānashrībhadra's commentary, Peking 5519, vol. 107, 112.3.7; Suzuki, *The Lankavatara Sutra,* 68.

361 Jik-may-dam-chö-gya-tso's *Port of Entry,* 454.6.

362 Ye shes thabs mkhas edition, 274.5.

363 Ibid., 276.9.

364 Jik-may-dam-chö-gya-tso's *Port of Entry,* 461.1.

365 Ye shes thabs mkhas edition, 274.14

366 Jik-may-dam-chö-gya-tso's *Port of Entry,* 458.6.

367 Ibid., 459.3.

368 Ibid., 459.4.

369 Ibid., 459.5.

370 Tāranātha's *The Essence of Other-Emptiness,* 512.

371 Ibid., 459.6.

Notes to Part Four, Chapter 17d

372 S̄hay-rap-gyel-tsen's *Ocean of Definitive Meaning,* 372.6.

373 Ibid., 172.1.

374 Ibid., 177.1.

375 Ibid., 337.6.

376 Ibid., 181.2.

377 Ibid., 178.1.

378 Ibid., 336.7.

379 See, for instance, ibid., 196.4ff., 205.2ff., 207.1ff.

Notes to Part Five, Chapter 18

380 Ke-drup's *Opening the Eyes of the Fortunate,* 217.1-217.4; see also José Ignacio Cabezón, *A Dose of Emptiness* (Albany, N.Y.: State University of New York Press, 1992), 52.

381 J̄ang-ḡya's *Presentation of Tenets,* 240.19.

382 In his "On the Problem of the Relation of Spiritual Practice and Philosophical Theory in Buddhism," in *German Scholars on India,* 235-250, Contributions to India Studies, vol. 2 (Bombay: Nachiketa, 1976).

383 In her *On Knowing Reality: The Tattvārtha Chapter of Asaṅga's Bodhisattvabhūmi* (New York: Columbia University Press, 1979; reprint, Delhi: Motilal Banarsidass, 1982). Others who have presented this view but are not mainly concerned with Asaṅga's *Grounds of Bodhisattvas* include Yoshifumi Ueda of Nagoya University in his "Two Main Streams of Thought in Yogācāra Philosophy," *Philosophy East and West* 17 (January-October 1967):155-165; and Alex Wayman of Columbia University in his "Yogācāra and the Buddhist Logicians," *Journal of the International Association of Buddhist Studies* 2, no. 1 (1979):65-78.

384 D̄a-drin-rap-d̄en's *Annotations,* 127.3.

385 Taken from Jeffrey Hopkins, *Meditation on Emptiness* (London: Wisdom, 1983; rev. ed., Boston: Wisdom, 1996), 371-372, with translation equivalents updated.

Notes to Part Five, Chapter 19

386 Ke-drup's *Opening the Eyes of the Fortunate,* 236.3-237.2; see also José Ignacio Cabezón, *A Dose of Emptiness* (Albany, N.Y.: State University of New York Press, 1992), 66.

387 Second Dalai Lama's *Lamp Illuminating the Meaning of (D̄zong-ka-b̄a's) Thought,* 41a.6-43a.4.

388 Paṇ-chen S̄ö-nam-drak-b̄a's *Garland of Blue Lotuses,* 13a.7-14a.4.

389 The biographical material is drawn from Jeffrey Hopkins, *Meditation on Emptiness* (London: Wisdom, 1983; rev. ed., Boston: Wisdom, 1996), 556-557.

390 *drang ba dang nges pa'i don rnam par 'byed pa'i mtha' dpyod 'khrul bral lung rigs bai ḍūr dkar po'i gan mdzod skal bzang re ba kun skong;* the edition cited is Buxaduor: n.d.

391 Jam-ȳang-shay-b̄a's *Great Exposition of the Interpretable and the Definitive,* 188.2.

392 Ibid., 188.3ff.

393 Read *tsam* ***gyi*** for *tsam* ***gyis,*** 188.4.

394 See Geshe Lhundup Sopa and Jeffrey Hopkins, *Cutting through Appearances: The Practice and Theory of Tibetan Buddhism* (Ithaca, N.Y.: Snow Lion, 1989), 205-206.

395 Jam-ȳang-shay-b̄a's *Great Exposition of the Interpretable and the Definitive,* 210.4-213.5.

396 Ke-drup's *Opening the Eyes of the Fortunate,* 222.2; see also Cabezón, *A Dose of Emptiness,* 55-56.

397 Ke-drup's *Opening the Eyes of the Fortunate,* 263.6; see also Cabezón, *A Dose of Emptiness,* 92.

398 Jam-ȳang-shay-b̄a's *Great Exposition of the Interpretable and the Definitive,* 213.5-215.3.

399 Ibid., 225.1-226.5.

400 Gung-ru Chö-jung's *Garland of White Lotuses,* 106a.2-109b.2. Jam-ȳang-shay-b̄a creatively condenses and expands on Gung-ru Chö-jung's exposition.

401 Read *khegs pa* ***na*** for *khegs pa* ***ni,*** 214.1.

402 Ke-drup's *Opening the Eyes of the Fortunate,* 218.6-219.2; see also Cabezón, *A Dose of Emptiness,* 53-54.

NOTES TO PART FIVE, CHAPTER 20

403 Étienne Lamotte, *La Somme du grand véhicule d'Asaṅga,* reprint, 2 vols., Publications de l'Institute Orientaliste de Louvain 8 (Louvain: Université de Louvain, 1973), vol. 1, 24-25, and vol. 2, 87-89; and John P. Keenan, *The Summary of the Great Vehicle by Bodhisattva Asaṅga: Translated from the Chinese of Paramārtha* (Berkeley, Calif.: Numata Center for Buddhist Translation and Research, 1992), 39.

404 The list is adopted from the doctoral dissertation of Joe B. Wilson, *The Meaning of Mind in the Mahāyāna Buddhist Philosophy of Mind-Only (Cittamātra): A Study of a Presentation by the Tibetan Scholar Gung-tang Jam-b̄ay-ȳang (gung-thang-'jam-pa'i-dbyangs) of Asaṅga's Theory of Mind-Basis-of-All (ālayavijñāna) and Related Topics in Buddhist Theories of Personal Continuity, Epistemology, and Hermeneutics* (Ann Arbor, Mich.: University Microfilms, 1984), 388. Wilson has fleshed out Asaṅga's identifications with material from Nga-w̄ang-b̄el-den, *Annotations for (Jam-ȳang-shay-b̄a's) "Great Exposition of Tenets"* (Sarnath, India: Pleasure of Elegant Sayings Printing Press, 1964), *dngos,* 119.2-7. Nga-w̄ang-b̄el-den reports that he is following Vasubandhu's commentary. The list can also be rendered as five or nine items, or as eleven items, as Lamotte (*La Somme,* vol. 2, 89) has done.

405 The identifications of the meanings of the names of the three types are drawn from Jik-may-dam-chö-gya-tso's *Port of Entry,* 552.5ff.

406 For the latter, see Jik-may-dam-chö-gya-tso's *Port of Entry,* 551.1-551.4.

407 The above has been a brief synopsis of Asaṅga's *Summary of the Great Vehicle.* See Lamotte, *La Somme,* vol. 1, 24-25 (II.1-3), and vol. 2, 87-90; and Keenan, *Summary,* 39-40.

408 Peking 5549, vol. 112, 222.2.2-222.2.4. Lamotte, *La Somme,* vol. 1, 26 (II.6), and vol. 2, 92; and Keenan, *Summary,* 40.

409 Peking 5549, vol. 112, 224.5.5-225.1.4. Lamotte, *La Somme,* vol. 1, 38-39 (II.27), and vol. 2, 122-124; and Keenan, *Summary,* 52-53.

410 Peking 5549, vol. 112, 222.2.5-222.2.6. Lamotte, *La Somme,* vol. 1, 26 (II.6), and vol. 2, 92-93; and Keenan, *Summary,* 40-41.

411 Peking 5549, vol. 112, 222.2.6-222.3.6. Lamotte, *La Somme,* vol. 1, 26-27 (II.7), and vol. 2, 93-96; and Keenan, *Summary,* 41.

412 *sa bcu pa, daśabhūmika;* chap. 6. Peking 574, vol. 25, 263.3.8.

413 Peking 774, vol. 29, 13.5.7-14.1.5. Except for the final exchange as noted below, the differences between the passage as cited by Asaṅga and as found in the Peking edition of the sūtra itself are minor.

414 Peking 5549, vol. 112, 224.3.7-224.4.2. Lamotte, *La Somme,* vol. 1, (II.24), and vol. 2, 118-119; and Keenan, *Summary,* 50-51.

415 Peking 5549, vol. 112, 227.3.1-227.3.5. Lamotte, *La Somme,* vol. 1, 51-52 (III.7), and vol. 2, 162; and Keenan, *Summary,* 66.

416 D̄a-drin-rap-d̄en's *Annotations,* 129.3.

Notes to Part Five, Chapter 21

417 See Lambert Schmithausen, "On the Problem of the Relation of Spiritual Practice and Philosophical Theory in Buddhism" in *German Scholars on India,* 235-250, Contributions to India Studies, 2 (Bombay: Nachiketa, 1976).

418 Ibid., 238. The discrepancies as to italicization of the titles of texts are found in the article itself.

419 Ibid., 239-240.

420 Janice D. Willis, *On Knowing Reality: The Tattvārtha Chapter of Asaṅga's Bodhisattvabhūmi* (New York: Columbia University Press, 1979; reprint, Delhi: Motilal Banarsidass, 1982), 21.

421 Ibid., 58 n. 74.

422 Ibid., 29.

423 Étienne Lamotte, *La Somme du grand véhicule d'Asaṅga,* reprint, 2 vols., Publications de l'Institute Orientaliste de Louvain 8 (Louvain: Université de Louvain, 1973), vol. 2, 93-94.

424 *mdo sde sa bcu pa, daśabhūmika;* Peking 761.31, vol. 25.

425 Willis, *On Knowing Reality,* 29.

426 Schmithausen, "On the Problem," 241.

427 Ibid., 242.

428 Ibid., 243; see also 244.

429 Ibid., 245.

430 Ibid., 248.

431 Ibid., 246.

432 Ibid., 242.

433 Willis, *On Knowing Reality,* 60 n. 90.

434 Schmithausen, "On the Problem," 248.

435 Willis, *On Knowing Reality,* 17.

436 Schmithausen, "On the Problem," 236.

Notes to Part Six, Chapter 22

437 Vaman Shivaram Apte, *Sanskrit-English Dictionary* (Poona, India: Prasad Prakashan, 1957), 1264-1265.

438 Ibid., 1264.

439 G̱ön-chok-jik-may-w̱ang-ḇo's *Presentation of the Grounds and the Paths,* 428.3.

440 Unpublished transcript of lectures in Tibetan at the University of Virginia in 1978, translated by Jeffrey Hopkins and ed. Elizabeth Napper.

441 G̱ön-chok-jik-may-w̱ang-ḇo's *Presentation of the Grounds and Paths,* 428.3.

442 See H.H. the Dalai Lama, Tsong-ka-pa, and Jeffrey Hopkins, *Tantra in Tibet* (London: George Allen and Unwin, 1977; reprint, Ithaca, N.Y.: Snow Lion, 1987).

443 *The Collected Works of C. G. Jung* (Princeton, N.J.: Princeton University Press, 1971, second printing 1974), vol. 6, 422.

444 Jik-may-dam-chö-gya-tso's *Port of Entry,* 545.4.

445 Jam-ȳang-shay-ḇa's *Great Exposition of Tenets, nga,* 44b.6.

446 Ḻo-sang-g̱ön-chok's *Clear Crystal Mirror,* 141.2.

447 Jam-ȳang-shay-ḇa's *Great Exposition of Tenets, nga,* 45b.4.

448 Ḻo-sang-g̱ön-chok's *Clear Crystal Mirror,* 142.1.

449 See Étienne Lamotte, *La Somme du grand véhicule d'Asaṅga,* reprint, 2 vols., Publications de l'Institute Orientaliste de Louvain 8 (Louvain: Université de Louvain, 1973), vol. 1, 78 (VIII.20), and vol. 2, 250-251; and John P. Keenan, *The Summary of the Great Vehicle by Bodhisattva Asaṅga: Translated from the Chinese of Paramārtha* (Berkeley, Calif.: Numata Center for Buddhist Translation and Research, 1992), 98.

450 Jam-ȳang-shay-ḇa's *Great Exposition of the Interpretable and the Definitive,* 246.6.

451 Jik-may-dam-chö-gya-tso's *Port of Entry,* 635.4.

452 See Lamotte, *La Somme,* vol. 1, 78 (VIII.20), and vol. 2, 250-251; and Keenan, *Summary,* 98.

453 Jam-ȳang-shay-ḇa's *Great Exposition of the Middle,* 649.4-650.1 (Ngawang Gelek edition).

454 See Lamotte, *La Somme,* vol. 1, 79 (VIII.20), and vol. 2, 251; and Keenan, *Summary,* 98.

455 Jam-ȳang-shay-ḇa's *Great Exposition of the Interpretable and the Definitive,* 248.2.

456 See Lamotte, *La Somme,* vol. 1, 78 (VIII.20), and vol. 2, 250-251; and Keenan, *Summary,* 98.

457 Ibid.

458 Jam-ȳang-shay-ḇa's *Great Exposition of the Interpretable and the Definitive,* 249.1.

459 See Lamotte, *La Somme,* vol. 1, 78 (VIII.20), and vol. 2, 250-251; and Keenan, *Summary,* 98.

460 Jik-may-dam-chö-gya-tso's *Port of Entry,* 636.2.

461 See Lamotte, *La Somme,* vol. 1, 79 (VIII.20), and vol. 2, 251; and Keenan, *Summary,* 98.

462 Paraphrasing Jik-may-dam-chö-gya-tso's *Port of Entry,* 636.3.

463 Jam-ȳang-shay-ḇa's *Great Exposition of the Interpretable and the Definitive,* 249.1.

464 See Lamotte, *La Somme,* vol. 1, 79 (VIII.20), and vol. 2, 251; and Keenan, *Summary,* 98.

465 Jik-may-dam-chö-gya-tso's *Port of Entry,* 633.2.

466 Ibid., 636.5.

467 Nga-w̄ang-b̄el-den's *Annotations for (Jam-ȳang-shay-b̄a's) "Great Exposition of Tenets," dngos,* 121.3; see also Jik-may-dam-chö-gya-tso's *Port of Entry,* 633.2.

468 L̄o-sang-ḡön-chok's *Crystal Mirror,* 146.3.

469 Jam-ȳang-shay-b̄a's *Great Exposition of the Interpretable and the Definitive,* 249.5.

470 *dmigs pa brtag pa, ālambanaparīkṣa;* Peking 5703, vol. 130, 73.2.5.

471 Paraphrasing Jam-ȳang-shay-b̄a's *Great Exposition of the Interpretable and the Definitive,* 260.2.

472 This paragraph is drawn from B̄el-jor-hlün-drup's *Lamp for the Teaching,* 93.5.

473 For the passages, see Jik-may-dam-chö-gya-tso's *Port of Entry,* 633.4.

474 Jam-ȳang-shay-b̄a's *Great Exposition of the Interpretable and the Definitive,* 257.2.

475 See Jik-may-dam-chö-gya-tso's *Port of Entry,* 636.6.

476 B̄el-jor-hlün-drup's *Lamp for the Teaching,* 92.4.

477 J̄ang-ḡya's *Clear Exposition of the Presentation of Tenets,* 193.10.

478 Jik-may-dam-chö-gya-tso's *Port of Entry,* 639.4-641.2; 647.2-650.4.

479 Ibid., 665.3-666.4.

Notes to Part Six, Chapter 23

480 Rudolph Otto, *The Idea of the Holy,* trans. John W. Harvey (London: Oxford University Press), 1923, 13.

481 Ibid.

482 Ibid., 14.

483 Ibid., 17.

484 Ibid., 20.

485 Ibid., 21.

486 Ibid., 24.

487 Ibid., 26.

488 Ibid., 28.

489 Ibid., 29.

490 Ibid., 33.

491 Ibid., 37.

492 *Presentation of the Lack of Being One or Many (gcig du bral gyi rnam gzhag legs bshad rgya mtsho las btus pa'i 'khrul spong bdud rtsi'i gzegs ma),* Collected gsung 'bum of Bstan-dar Lha-ram of A-lak-sha, vol. 1 (New Delhi: Lama Guru Deva, 1971), 425.1ff.

493 Carl Bielefeldt, "A Discussion of Seated Zen," in *Buddhism in Practice,* ed. Donald S. Lopez Jr. (Princeton, N.J.: Princeton University Press, 1995), 203.

494 The material on the levels of consciousness is drawn from Lati Rinbochay's and my translation of a text by Ȳang-j̄en-ga-way-l̄o-drö (*dbyangs can dga' ba'i blo gros*); see our *Death, Intermediate State, and Rebirth in Tibetan Buddhism* (London: Rider, 1980; Ithaca, N.Y.: Snow Lion, 1980).

495 Nga-w̄ang-l̄o-sang-gya-tso (*ngag dbang blo bzang rgya mtsho,* 1617-1682), *Instruction on the Stages of the Path to Enlightenment, Sacred Word of Mañjushrī* (*byang chub lam gyi rim pa'i khrid yig 'jam pa'i dbyangs kyi zhal lung*) (Thimphu, Bhutan: kun-bzang-stobs-rgyal, 1976), as found in Jeffrey Hopkins, trans., "Practice of Emptiness" (Dharmsala, India: Library of Tibetan Works and Archives, 1974), 17.

Notes to Appendix 1

496 Alex Wayman, "Yogācāra and the Buddhist Logicians," *Journal of the International Association of Buddhist Studies* 2, no. 1 (1979):65-78. See also his "The Yogācāra Idealism" (review article), *Philosophy East and West* 15, no. 1 (1965):65-73; and "A Defense of Yogācāra Buddhism," *Philosophy East and West* 46, no. 4 (1996):447-476.

497 Wayman, "Yogācāra and the Buddhist Logicians," 65.

498 Ibid., 67.

499 Lati Rinbochay in Lati Rinbochay and Elizabeth Napper, *Mind in Tibetan Buddhism* (London: Rider, 1980; Ithaca, N.Y.: Snow Lion, 1980), 70.

500 Wayman, "Yogācāra and the Buddhist Logicians," 71.

501 Ibid., 67.

502 Ibid., 68.

503 Ibid.

504 Ibid.

505 Ibid., 72.

506 Ibid., 73.

507 Ibid.

508 Ibid., 75.

509 Ibid., 73.

510 Ibid., 75-76; brackets mine.

[511] Ibid., 76.

[512] Second Dalai Lama's *Lamp Illuminating the Meaning of (Dzong-ka-ba's) Thought,* 44a.4.

[513] See also Gung-ru Chö-jung's *Garland of White Lotuses,* 10b.4; and Jam-yang-shay-ba's *Great Exposition of the Interpretable and the Definitive,* 35.4.

[514] Wayman, "Yogācāra and the Buddhist Logicians," 76.

[515] Ibid.

[516] Ibid., 69.

[517] Ibid., 70.

[518] See Gareth Sparham, *Ocean of Eloquence: Tsong kha pa's Commentary on the Yogācāra Doctrine of Mind* (Albany, N.Y.: State University of New York Press, 1993), 53; text 170-171. This is a translation and presentation of Dzong-ka-ba's *Extensive Commentary on the Difficult Points of the Mind-Basis-of-All and Afflicted Intellect: Ocean of Eloquence* (*yid dang kun gzhi'i dka' ba'i gnas rgya cher 'grel pa legs par bshad pa'i rgya mtsho*), written in his twenties.

[519] Nga-wang-bel-den's *Annotations, dngos,* 208.3.

NOTES TO APPENDIX 2

[520] Yoshifumi Ueda, "Two Main Streams of Thought in Yogācāra Philosophy," *Philosophy East and West* 17 (January-October 1967):155-165.

[521] Ibid., 155.

[522] Ibid.

[523] Ibid., 156.

[524] Ibid., 157.

[525] Ibid., 158.

[526] Ibid., 160.

[527] Ibid., 162.

[528] Ibid., 163.

[529] Ibid., 164.

[530] Ibid., 165.

[531] Ibid., 164.

[532] Ibid., 165.

NOTES TO APPENDIX 3

[533] Janice D. Willis, *On Knowing Reality: The Tattvārtha Chapter of Asaṅga's Bodhisattvabhūmi* (New York: Columbia University Press, 1979; reprint, Delhi: Motilal Banarsidass, 1982).

[534] Ibid., 13.

[535] Ibid., 36.

[536] Ibid., 18-19.

[537] Ibid., 44.

[538] Ibid., 20.

[539] For instance, see Geshe Lhundup Sopa and Jeffrey Hopkins, *Cutting through Appearances: The Practice and Theory of Tibetan Buddhism* (Ithaca, N.Y.: Snow Lion, 1989), 271-272.

[540] Willis, *On Knowing Reality,* 18, 168.

[541] Ibid., 17.

[542] Ibid., 223-24.

[543] Ibid., 21.

[544] Ibid., 24.

[545] Peking 5538, vol. 110, 144.5.1-144.5.5. For Willis's translation, see *On Knowing Reality,* 161.

[546] Peking 5549, vol. 112, 225.4.1. See Étienne Lamotte, *La Somme du grand véhicule d'Asaṅga,* reprint, 2 vols., Publications de l'Institute Orientaliste de Louvain 8 (Louvain: Université de Louvain, 1973), vol. 1, 41 (II.31), and vol. 2, 129; and John P. Keenan, *The Summary of the Great Vehicle by Bodhisattva Asaṅga: Translated from the Chinese of Paramārtha* (Berkeley, Calif.: Numata Center for Buddhist Translation and Research, 1992), 55.

[547] Willis, *On Knowing Reality,* 25-26.

[548] Ibid., 26-28.

[549] Ibid., 31-32.

[550] Ibid., 28-31.

[551] Ibid., 33-36.

[552] Ibid, 27.

[553] Ibid., 32.

[554] Ye shes thabs mkhas edition, 268.11.

[555] Peking 5263, vol. 98, 136.1.1ff.

[556] Peking 774, vol. 29, 8.2.2, chap. 5; Étienne Lamotte, *Saṃdhinirmocanasūtra: L'Explication des mystères* (Louvain: Université de Louvain 1935), 58 [7] and 203; John C. Powers, *Wisdom of Buddha: Saṁdhinirmocana Sūtra* (Berkeley, Calif.: Dharma, 1995), 77.

[557] Ser-shül's *Notes,* 50a.4.

[558] Ser-shül's *Notes,* 50a.5.

[559] Willis, *On Knowing Reality,* 32.

[560] E. Todd Fenner, "Review of Janice Willis's *On Knowing Reality,*" *Journal of the International Association of Buddhist Studies* 3, no. 1 (1980):117.

Bibliography

Sūtras and tantras are listed alphabetically by English title in the first section of the bibliography. Indian and Tibetan treatises are listed alphabetically by author in the second section; other works are listed alphabetically by author in the third section.

"P," standing for "Peking edition," refers to the *Tibetan Tripiṭaka* (Tokyo-Kyoto: Tibetan Tripiṭaka Research Foundation, 1956). "Toh" refers to the *Complete Catalogue of the Tibetan Buddhist Canon,* edited by Hukuji Ui (Sendai, Japan: Tohoku University, 1934), and *A Catalogue of the Tohuku University Collection of Tibetan Works on Buddhism,* edited by Yensho Kanakura (Sendai, Japan: Tohoku University, 1953). "Dharma" refers to the *sde dge* edition of the Tibetan canon published by Dharma—the *Nying-ma Edition of the sDe-dge bKa'-'gyur and bsTan-'gyur* (Oakland, Calif.: Dharma, 1980), which contains excellent references to editions, translations, and so forth. "Tokyo *sde dge*" refers to the *sDe dge Tibetan Tripiṭaka—bsTan hgyur Preserved at the Faculty of Letters, University of Tokyo,* edited by Z. Yamaguchi et al. (Tokyo: Tokyo University Press, 1977-1984). "Karmapa *sde dge*" refers to the *sde dge mtshal par bka' 'gyur: a facsimile edition of the 18th century redaction of Si tu chos kyi 'byung gnas prepared under the direction of H.H. the 16th rgyal dbang karma pa* (Delhi: Delhi Karmapae Chodhey Gyalwae Sungrab Partun Khang, 1977). "*stog* Palace" refers to the *Tog Palace Manuscript of the Tibetan Kanjur* (Leh, Ladakh: Smanrtsis Shesrig Dpemdzod, 1979). "Golden Reprint" refers to the *gser bris bstan 'gyur* (Sichuan, China: krung go'i mtho rim nang bstan slob gling gi bod brgyud nang bstan zhib 'jug khang, 1989). Works mentioned in the first or second sections are not repeated in the third section.

For an excellent bibliography of Yogācāra texts, see John C. Powers, *The Yogācāra School of Buddhism: A Bibliography,* American Theological Library Association Bibliography Series 27 (Metuchen, N.J., and London: American Theological Library Association and Scarecrow Press, 1991).

1. Sūtras and Tantras

Compilations of Indicative Verse
udānavarga
ched du brjod pa'i tshom
P992, vol. 39
English translation: W. Woodville Rockhill. *The Udānavarga: A Collection of Verses from the Buddhist Canon.* London: Trübner, 1883. Also: Gareth Sparham. *The Tibetan Dhammapada.* New Delhi: Mahayana Publications, 1983; rev. ed., London: Wisdom, 1986.

Condensed Perfection of Wisdom Sūtra
prajñāpāramitāsañcayagāthā
shes rab kyi pha rol tu phyin pa sdud pa tshigs su bcad pa
P735, vol. 21
Sanskrit: E. E. Obermiller. *Prajñāpāramitā-ratnaguṇa-sañcayagāthā.* Osnabrück, Germany: Biblio Verlag, 1970. Also: P. L. Vaidya. *Mahāyāna-sūtra-saṃgraha.* Part I. Buddhist Sanskrit Texts 17. Darbhanga, India: Mithila Institute, 1961.
English translation: Edward Conze. *The Perfection of Wisdom in Eight Thousand Lines & Its Verse Summary.* Bolinas, Calif.: Four Seasons Foundation, 1973.

Descent into Laṅkā Sūtra
laṅkāvatārasūtra
lang kar gshegs pa'i mdo

P775, vol. 29

Sanskrit: Bunyiu Nanjio. *Bibl. Otaniensis,* vol. 1. Kyoto: Otani University Press, 1923. Also: P. L. Vaidya. *Saddharmalaṅkāvatārasūtram.* Buddhist Sanskrit Texts 3. Darbhanga, India: Mithila Institute, 1963.

English translation: D. T. Suzuki. *The Lankavatara Sutra.* London: Routledge and Kegan Paul, 1932.

Eight Thousand Stanza Perfection of Wisdom Sūtra

aṣṭasāhasrikāprajñāpāramitā

shes rab kyi pha rol tu phyin pa brgyad stong pa

P734, vol. 21

Sanskrit: P. L. Vaidya. *Aṣṭasāhasrika Prajñāpāramitā, with Haribhadra's Commentary called Ālokā.* Buddhist Sanskrit Texts 4. Darbhanga, India: Mithila Institute, 1960.

English translation: E. Conze. *The Perfection of Wisdom in Eight Thousand Lines & Its Verse Summary.* Bolinas, Calif.: Four Seasons Foundation, 1973.

Great Drum Sūtra

mahābherīhārakaparivartasūtra

rnga bo che chen po'i le'u'i mdo

P888, vol. 35

Hevajra Tantra

hevajratantrarāja

kye'i rdo rje zhes bya ba rgyud kyi rgyal po

P10, vol. 1

English translation: D. L. Snellgrove. *Hevajra Tantra,* Parts 1 and 2. London: Oxford University Press, 1959. Also: G. W. Farrow and I. Menon. *The Concealed Essence of the Hevajra Tantra.* Delhi: Motilal Banarsidass, 1992.

Lion's Roar of Shrīmālādevī Sūtra

phags pa lha mo dpal phreng gi seng ge'i sgra zhes bya ba theg pa chen po'i mdo

āryaśrīmālādevīsiṃhanādanāmamahāyanasūtra

P760.48, vol. 24

English translation: A. Wayman and H. Wayman. *The Lion's Roar of Queen Śrīmālā.* New York: Columbia University Press, 1974.

Mahāparinirvāṇa Sūtra

'phags pa yongs su mya ngan las 'das pa chen po'i mdo

P787, vols. 30-31; translated by wang phab shun, dge ba'i blo gros, rgya mtsho'i sde

P788, vol. 31; translated by Jinamitra, Jñānagarbha, Lhay-da-ba (*lha'i zla ba*)

English translation from the Chinese: Kosho Yamamoto. *The Mahayana Mahaparinirvāṇa-sutra.* Ube, Japan: Karinbunko, 1973.

Matrix of One Gone Thus Sūtra

āryatathāgatagarbhanāmamahāyanasūtra

'phags pa de bzhin gshegs pa'i snying po zhes bya ba theg pa chen po'i mdo

P924, vol. 36

Ornament Illuminating Exalted Wisdom Sūtra

āryasarvabuddhaviṣayāvatārajñānālokāṃkāranāmamahāyanasūtra

'phags pa sangs rgyas thams cad kyi yul la 'jug pa'i ye shes snang ba rgyan gyi mdo ces bya ba theg pa chen po'i mdo

P768, vol. 28

Questions of King Dhāraṇīṣhvara Sūtra / Sūtra Teaching the Great Compassion of a One Gone Thus

āryatathāgatamahākaruṇānirdeśasūtra

de bzhin gshegs pa'i snying rje chen po bstan pa'i mdo / 'phags pa gzungs kyi dbang phyug rgyal pos zhus pa'i mdo

P814, vol. 32

Renunciation Sūtra

mngon par 'byung ba'i mdo

P967, vol. 39

Sūtra for Maudgalyāyana

āryāṅgulimālīyanāmamahāyanasūtra

sor mo'i phreng ba la phan pa zhes bya ba theg pa chen po'i mdo

P879, vol. 34

Sūtra of the Great Emptiness

stong pa nyid chen po'i mdo

[?]

Sūtra on the Ten Grounds

daśabhūmikasūtra

mdo sde sa bcu pa

P761.31, vol. 25

Sanskrit: *Daśabhūmikasūtram.* P. L. Vaidya, ed. Buddhist Sanskrit Texts 7. Darbhanga: Mithila Institute, 1967.

English translation: M. Honda. "An Annotated Translation of the 'Daśabhūmika.'" In D. Sinor, ed, *Studies in South, East and Central Asia,* Śatapitaka Series 74. New Delhi: International Academy of Indian Culture, 1968, 115-276.

Sūtra Unraveling the Thought

saṃdhinirmocanasūtra

dgongs pa nges par 'grel pa'i mdo

P774, vol. 29; Toh 106; Dharma, vol. 18; *The Tog Palace Edition of the Tibetan Kanjur,* vol. 63, 1-160 (Leh: Smanrtsis Shesrig Dpemzod, 1975-1978)

Tibetan text and French translation: Étienne Lamotte. *Saṃdhinirmocanasūtra: L'Explication des mystères.* Louvain: Université de Louvain, 1935.

English translation: John C. Powers. *Wisdom of Buddha: Saṁdhinirmocana Sūtra.* Berkeley: Dharma, 1995. Also: Thomas Cleary. *Buddhist Yoga: A Comprehensive Course.* Boston: Shambhala, 1995.

Teachings of Akṣhayamati Sūtra

akṣayamatinirdeśa

blo gros mi zad pas bstan pa

P842, vol. 34

Twenty-five Thousand Stanza Perfection of Wisdom Sūtra

pañcaviṃśatisāhasrikāprajñāpāramitā

shes rab kyi pha rol tu phyin pa stong phrag nyi shu lnga pa

P731, vol. 19

English translation (abridged): Edward Conze. *The Large Sūtra on the Perfection of Wisdom.* Berkeley: University of California Press, 1975.

2. *Other Sanskrit and Tibetan Works*

A-ku Ḹo-drö-gya-tso / Gung-tang Ḹo-drö-gya-tso (*a khu blo gros rgya mtsho / gung thang blo gros rgya mtsho;* 1851-1930)

Precious Lamp / Commentary on the Difficult Points of (Ḍzong-ka-ḇa's) "Treatise Differentiating Interpretable and the Definitive Meanings, The Essence of Eloquence": A Precious Lamp

drang ba dang nges pa'i don rnam par 'byed pa'i bstan bcos legs bshad snying po'i dka' 'grel rin chen sgron me

Delhi: Kesang Thabkhes, 1982.

Āryadeva (*'phags pa lha,* second to third century C.E.)

Compilation of the Essence of Wisdom

jñānasārasamuccaya

ye shes snying po kun las btus pa

P5251, vol. 95

Four Hundred / Treatise of Four Hundred Stanzas / Four Hundred Stanzas on the Yogic Deeds of Bodhisattvas
catuḥśatakaśāstrakārikā
bstan bcos bzhi brgya pa zhes bya ba'i tshig le'ur byas pa
P5246, vol. 95
Edited Tibetan and Sanskrit fragments along with English translation: Karen Lang. *Āryadeva's Catuḥśataka: On the Bodhisattva's Cultivation of Merit and Knowledge.* Indiste Studier, 7. Copenhagen: Akademisk Forlag, 1986.
English translation: Geshe Sonam Rinchen and Ruth Sonam. *Yogic Deeds of Bodhisattvas: Gyel-tsap on Āryadeva's Four Hundred.* Ithaca, N.Y.: Snow Lion, 1994.
Italian translation of the last half from the Chinese: Giuseppe Tucci. "Study Mahāyānici: La versione cinese del Catuḥśataka di Āryadeva, confronta col testo sanscrito e la traduzione tibetana." *Rivista degli Studi Orientali* 10 (1925):521-567.

Asaṅga (*thogs med,* fourth century)
Explanation of (Maitreya's) "Sublime Continuum of the Great Vehicle"
mahāynottaratantraśāstravyākhya
theg pa chen po'i rgyud bla ma'i bstan bcos kyi rnam par bshad pa
P5526, vol. 108
Sanskrit: E. H. Johnston (and T. Chowdhury). *The Ratnagotravibhāga Mahāyānottaratantraśāstra.* Patna, India: Bihar Research Society, 1950.
English translation: E. Obermiller. "Sublime Science of the Great Vehicle to Salvation." *Acta Orientalia* 9 (1931):81-306. Also: J. Takasaki. *A Study on the Ratnagotravibhāga.* Rome: Istituto Italiano per il Medio ed Estremo Oriente, 1966.

Five Treatises on the Grounds

1. *Grounds of Yogic Practice*
yogācārabhūmi
rnal 'byor spyod pa'i sa
P5536-5538, vols. 109-110
Grounds of Bodhisattvas
bodhisattvabhūmi
byang chub sems pa'i sa
P5538, vol. 110
Sanskrit: Unrai Wogihara. *Bodhisattvabhūmi: A Statement of the Whole Course of the Bodhisattva (Being the Fifteenth Section of Yogācārabhūmi).* Leipzig: 1908; Tokyo: Seigo Kenyūkai, 1930-1936. Also: Nalinaksha Dutt. *Bodhisattvabhumi (Being the XVth Section of Asangapada's Yogacarabhumi).* Tibetan Sanskrit Works Series 7. Patna, India: K. P. Jayaswal Research Institute, 1966.
English translation of the Chapter on Suchness, the fourth chapter of Part I which is the fifteenth volume of the *Grounds of Yogic Practice:* Janice D. Willis. *On Knowing Reality.* New York: Columbia University Press, 1979; reprint, Delhi: Motilal Banarsidass, 1979.

2. *Compendium of Ascertainments*
nirṇayasaṃgraha / viniścayasaṃgrahaṇī
rnam par gtan la dbab pa bsdu ba
P5539, vols. 110-111

3. *Compendium of Bases*
vastusaṃgraha
gzhi bsdu ba
P5540, vol. 111

4. *Compendium of Enumerations*
paryāyasaṃgraha
rnam grang bsdu ba
P5543, vol. 111

5. *Compendium of Explanations*
vivaraṇasaṃgraha
rnam par bshad pa bsdu ba
P5543, vol. 111
Grounds of Hearers
nyan sa
śrāvakabhūmi
P5537, vol. 110
Sanskrit: Karunesha Shukla. *Śrāvakabhūmi.* Tibetan Sanskrit Works Series 14. Patna, India: K. P. Jayaswal Research Institute, 1973.
Two Summaries
1. *Summary of Manifest Knowledge*
abhidharmasamuccaya
chos mngon pa kun btus
P5550, vol. 112
Sanskrit: Pralhad Pradhan. *Abhidharma Samuccaya of Asaṅga.* Visva-Bharati Series 12. Santiniketan, India: Visva-Bharati (Santiniketan Press), 1950.
French translation: Walpola Rahula. *La Compendium de la super-doctrine (philosophie) (Abhidharmasamuccaya) d'Asaṅga.* Paris: École Française d'Extrême-Orient, 1971.
2. *Summary of the Great Vehicle*
mahāyānasaṃgraha
theg pa chen po bsdus pa
P5549, vol. 112
French translation and Chinese and Tibetan texts: Étienne Lamotte. *La Somme du grand véhicule d'Asaṅga,* 2 vols. Publications de l'Institute Orientaliste de Louvain 8. Louvain: Université de Louvain, 1938; reprint, 1973.
English translation: John P. Keenan. *The Summary of the Great Vehicle by Bodhisattva Asaṅga: Translated from the Chinese of Paramārtha.* Berkeley, Calif.: Numata Center for Buddhist Translation and Research, 1992.
Atisha (*atiśa / atīśa,* 982-1054)
Lamp for the Path to Enlightenment
bodhipathapradīpa
byang chub lam gyi sgron ma
P5343, vol. 103
English translation with Atisha's autocommentary: Richard Sherbourne, S.J. *A Lamp for the Path and Commentary.* London: George Allen and Unwin, 1983.
English translation: *Atisha's Lamp for the Path: An Oral Teaching by Geshe Sonam Rinchen.* Trans. and ed. Ruth Sonam. Ithaca, N.Y.: Snow Lion, 1997.
B̄el-jor-hlün-drup, N̄yel-d̄ön (*dpal 'byor lhun grub, gnyal* [or *gnyan*] *ston,* 1427-1514)
Lamp for the Teaching / Commentary on the Difficult Points of (D̄zong-ka-b̄a's) "The Essence of Eloquence": Lamp for the Teaching
legs bshad snying po'i dka' 'grel bstan pa'i sgron me
Delhi: Rong-tha Mchog-sprul-rnam-pa-gnyis, 1969.
Bhāvaviveka (*legs ldan 'byed,* c. 500-570?)
Blaze of Reasoning / Commentary on the "Heart of the Middle": Blaze of Reasoning
madhyamakahṛdayavṛttitarkajvālā
dbu ma'i snying po'i 'grel pa rtog ge 'bar ba
P5256, vol. 96
Partial English translation (chap. 3, 1-136): Shōtarō Iida. *Reason and Emptiness.* Tokyo: Hokuseido, 1980.
Heart of the Middle
madhyamakahṛdayakārikā
dbu ma'i snying po'i tshig le'ur byas pa

P5255, vol. 96

Partial English translation (chap. 3. 1-136): Shōtarō Iida. *Reason and Emptiness.* Tokyo: Hokuseido, 1980.

Bodhibhadra (*byang chub bzang po*)

Connected Explanation of [Āryadeva's] "Compilation of the Essence of Wisdom"

jñānasārasamuccayanāmanibandhana

ye shes snying po kun las btus pa shes bya ba'i bshad sbyar

P5252, vol. 95

Bu-dön Rin-chen-drup (*bu ston rin chen grub,* 1290-1364)

Catalogue of the Translated Doctrine

chos bsgyur dkar chag

Collected Works of Bu-ston, vol. 26, 401-644; vol. 28, 343-574. New Delhi: International Academy of Indian Culture, 1966.

Buddhaguhya (*sangs rgyas gsang ba*)

Commentary on the "Concentration Continuation Tantra"

dhyānottarapaṭalaṭīkā

bsam gtan phyi ma rim par phye ba rgya cher bshad pa

P3495, vol. 78

Chandrakīrti (*candrakīrti, zla ba grags pa,* seventh century)

[Auto]commentary on the "Supplement to (Nāgārjuna's) 'Treatise on the Middle'"

madhaymakāvatārabhāṣya

dbu ma la 'jug pa'i bshad pa / dbu ma la 'jug pa'i rang 'grel

P5263, vol. 98. Also: Dharmsala, India: Council of Religious and Cultural Affairs, 1968.

Tibetan: Louis de la Vallée Poussin. *Madhyamakāvatāra par Candrakīrti.* Bibliotheca Buddhica, 9. Osnabrück, Germany: Biblio Verlag, 1970.

English translation: C. W. Huntington, Jr. *The Emptiness of Emptiness: An Introduction to Early Indian Mādhyamika,* 147-195. Honolulu: University of Hawaii Press, 1989.

French translation (up to chap. 6, stanza 165): Louis de la Vallée Poussin. *Muséon* 8 (1907):249-317; *Muséon* 11 (1910):271-358; *Muséon* 12 (1911):235-328.

German translation (chap. 6, 166-226): Helmut Tauscher. *Candrakīrti-Madhyamakāvatāraḥ und Madhyamakāvatārabhāṣyam.* Vienna: Wiener Studien zur Tibetologie und Buddhismuskunde, 1981.

Clear Words, Commentary on (Nāgārjuna's) "Treatise on the Middle"

mūlamadhyamakavṛttiprasannapadā

dbu ma rtsa ba'i 'grel pa tshig gsal ba

P5260, vol. 98. Also: Dharmsala, India: Tibetan Cultural Printing Press, 1968.

Sanskrit: Louis de la Vallée Poussin. *Mūlamadhyamakakārikās de Nāgārjuna avec la Prasannapadā commentaire de Candrakīrti.* Bibliotheca Buddhica, 4. Osnabrück, Germany: Biblio Verlag, 1970.

English translation (chap. 1, 25): T. Stcherbatsky. *Conception of Buddhist Nirvāṇa,* 77-222. Leningrad: Office of the Academy of Sciences of the USSR, 1927; rev. reprint, Delhi: Motilal Banarsidass, 1978.

English translation (chap. 2): Jeffrey Hopkins. "Analysis of Coming and Going." Dharmsala, India: Library of Tibetan Works and Archives, 1974.

Partial English translation: Mervyn Sprung. *Lucid Exposition of the Middle Way: The Essential Chapters from the Prasannapadā of Candrakīrti translated from the Sanskrit.* London: Routledge, 1979; Boulder, Colo.: Prajñā Press, 1979.

French translation (chapters 2-4, 6-9, 11, 23, 24, 26, 28): Jacques May. *Prasannapadā Madhyamaka-vṛtti, douze chapitres traduits du sanscrit et du tibétain.* Paris: Adrien-Maisonneuve, 1959.

French translation (chapters 18-22): J. W. de Jong. *Cinq chapitres de la Prasannapadā.* Paris: Geuthner, 1949.

French translation (chap. 17): É. Lamotte. "Le Traité de l'acte de Vasubandhu, Karmasiddhiprakaraṇa." *Mélanges Chinois et Bouddhiques* 4 (1936):265-288.

German translation (chap. 5, 12-26): Stanislaw Schayer. *Ausgewählte Kapitel aus der Prasannapadā.* Krakow: Naktadem Polskiej Akademji Umiejetnosci, 1931.
German translation (chap. 10): Stanislaw Schayer. "Feuer und Brennstoff." *Rocznik Orjentalistyczny* 7 (1931):26-52.
Supplement to (Nāgārjuna's) "Treatise on the Middle"
madhyamakāvatāra
dbu ma la 'jug pa
P5261, P5262, vol. 98
Tibetan: Louis de la Vallée Poussin. *Madhyamakāvatāra par Candrakīrti.* Bibliotheca Buddhica, 9. Osnabrück, Germany: Biblio Verlag, 1970.
English translation (chaps. 1-5): Jeffrey Hopkins. *Compassion in Tibetan Buddhism.* London: Rider, 1980; reprint, Ithaca, N.Y.: Snow Lion, 1980.
English translation (chap. 6): Stephen Batchelor. *Echoes of Voidness* by Geshé Rabten, 47-92. London: Wisdom, 1983.
See also references under Chandrakīrti's *[Auto]commentary on the "Supplement."*

Chim Jam-b̄ay-ȳang (*mchims 'jam pa'i dbyangs* or *mchims nam mkha' grags,* died 1289 / 1290)
Commentary on [Vasubandhu's] "Treasury of Manifest Knowledge": Ornament of Manifest Knowledge
chos mngon mdzod kyi tshig le'ur byas pa'i 'grel pa mngon pa'i rgyan
Buxaduor, India: Nang bstan shes rig 'dzin skyong slob gnyer khang, n.d.

D̄a-drin-rap-d̄en (*rta mgrin rab brtan, tre hor dge bshes,* 1920-1986)
Annotations / Annotations for the Difficult Points of (D̄zong-ka-b̄a's) "The Essence of Eloquence": Festival for the Unbiased Endowed with Clear Intelligence
drang nges rnam 'byed legs bshad snying po dka' gnad rnams mchan bur bkod pa gzur gnas blo gsal dga' ston
Delhi: Lhun-grub-chos-grags, 1978.

D̄ak-tsang S̄hay-rap-rin-chen (*stag tshang lo tsā ba shes rab rin chen,* born 1405)
Explanation of "Freedom from Extremes through Understanding All Tenets": Ocean of Eloquence
grub mtha' kun shes nas mtha' bral grub pa zhes bya ba'i bstan bcos rnam par bshad pa legs bshad kyi rgya mtsho
Thimphu, Bhutan: Kun-bzang-stobs rgyal, 1976

Damṣhṭasena (*damṣṭasena;* attributed so by D̄zong-ka-b̄a; some others identify Vasubandhu as the author)
[Commentary on] the Three Mothers, Conquest over Harm / Extensive Explanation of the Superior One Hundred Thousand Stanza, Twenty-five Thousand Stanza, and Eighteen Thousand Stanza Perfection of Wisdom Sūtras
āryaśatasāhasrikāpañcaviṃsatisāhasrikāaṣṭadaśasāhasrikāprajñāpāramitābṛhaṭṭīkā
yum gsum gnod 'joms / 'phags pa shes rab kyi pha rol tu phyin pa 'bum pa dang nyi khri lnga stong pa dang khri brgyad stong pa'i rgya cher bshad pa
P5206, vol. 93

D̄en-b̄a-dar-gyay, Ke-drup (*bstan pa dar rgyas, mkhas grub,* 1493-1568)
General Meaning of (D̄zong-ka-b̄a's) "Differentiating the Interpretable and the Definitive": Essence of Eloquence, Garland of White Lotuses
drang nges rnam 'byed kyi spyi don legs par bshad pa'i snying po padma dkar po'i 'phreng ba
Indian ed., n.d. [Photocopy provided by Geshe Lobsang Tharchin]. Also: *Supplementary Texts for the Study of the Perfection of Wisdom at Sera Mey Tibetan Monastic University,* vol. 1, 1-50. Bylakuppe, India: The Computer Center, Sera Mey, 1990.
Decisive Analysis of (D̄zong-ka-b̄a's) "Differentiating the Interpretable and the Definitive"
mkhas grub smra ba'i khyu mchog dge 'dun bstan dar ba chen po'i gsung drang nges rnam 'byed kyi mtha dpyod
Indian ed., n.d. [Photocopy provided by Geshe Lobsang Tharchin]. Also: *Supplementary Texts for the Study of the Perfection of Wisdom at Sera Mey Tibetan Monastic University,* vol. 1, 51-153. Bylakuppe, India: The Computer Center, Sera Mey, 1990.

Dharmakīrti (*chos kyi grags pa,* seventh century)

Seven Treatises on Valid Cognition
1. *Analysis of Relations*
sambandhaparīkṣā
'brel pa brtag pa
P5713, vol. 130
2. *Ascertainment of Prime Cognition*
pramāṇaviniścaya
tshad ma rnam par nges pa
P5710, vol. 130
3. *Commentary on (Dignāga's) "Compilation of Prime Cognition"*
pramāṇavārttikakārikā
tshad ma rnam 'grel gyi tshig le'ur byas pa
P5709, vol. 130. Also: Sarnath, India: Pleasure of Elegant Sayings Press, 1974.
Sanskrit: Dwarikadas Shastri. *Pramāṇavārttika of Āchārya Dharmakīrtti.* Varanasi, India: Bauddha Bharati, 1968.
English translation (chap. 2): Masatoshi Nagatomi, "A Study of Dharmakīrti's Pramāṇavarttika: An English Translation and Annotation of the Pramāṇavarttika, Book I." Ph.D. diss., Harvard University, 1957.
4. *Drop of Reasoning*
nyāyabinduprakaraṇa
rigs pa'i thigs pa zhes bya ba'i rab tu byed pa
P5711, vol. 130
English translation: Th. Stcherbatsky. *Buddhist Logic.* New York: Dover Publications, 1962.
5. *Drop of Reasons*
hetubindunāmaprakaraṇa
gtan tshigs kyi thigs pa zhes bya ba rab tu byed pa
P5712, vol. 130
6. *Principles of Debate*
vādanyāya
rtsod pa'i rigs pa
P5715, vol. 130
7. *Proof of Other Continuums*
saṃtānāntarasiddhināmaprakaraṇa
rgyud gzhan grub pa zhes bya ba'i rab tu byed pa
P5716, vol. 130

Dignāga (*phyogs kyi glangs po,* sixth century)
Compilation of Prime Cognition
pramāṇasamuccaya
tshad ma kun las btus pa
P5700, vol. 130
English translation (partial): M. Hattori. *Dignāga, On Perception.* Cambridge, Mass.: Harvard University Press, 1968.
Examination of Objects of Observation
ālambanaparīkṣa
dmigs pa brtag pa
P5703, vol. 130
Summary Meanings of the Eight Thousand Stanza Perfection of Wisdom Sūtra
prajñāpāramitāpiṇḍārtha / prajñāpāramitāsaṃgrahakārikā
brgyad stong don bsdus / shes rab kyi pha rol tu phyin ma bsdus pa'i tshig le'ur byas pa
P5207, vol. 94

Dön-drup-gyel-tsen (*don grub rgyal mtshan;* fl. late eighteenth- and early nineteenth centuries)
Four Intertwined Commentaries / Extensive Explanation of (Dzong-ka-ba's) "Treatise Differentiating the Interpretable and the Definitive, The Essence of Eloquence," Unique to Ge-luk-ba: Four Intertwined

Commentaries
dge ldan thun mon ma yin pa drang ba dang nges pa'i don rnam par phye ba'i bstan bcos legs bshad snying po'i rgya cher bshad pa drang nges bzhi 'dril
New Delhi: Chophel Legdan, 1975.

Ḏra-ḏi Ge-s̄hay Rin-chen-dön-drup (*rin chen don grub, pra sti dge bshes;* fl. mid-seventeenth century)
Ornament for the Thought / Ornament for the Thought of (Ḏzong-ka-ḇa's) "Interpretable and Definitive: The Essence of Eloquence"
drang nges legs bshad snying po'i dgongs rgyan
Bylakuppe, India: Sera Je Printing Press: 1989.

Drak-ḇa-shay-drup, J̄o-nay-wa (*grags pa bshad sgrub, co ne ba,* 1675-1748)
Condensed Essence of All Tenets
grub mtha' thams cad kyi snying po bsdus
in *rje btsun grags pa bshad sgrub kyi mdzad pa'i grub mtha', sa lam dang stong 'khor zhabs drung gi mdzad pa'i don bdun cu bcas bzhugs so.*
Bylakuppe, India: Sermey Printing Press, 1995.

Ḏzong-ka-ḇa L̄o-sang-drak-ḇa (*tsong kha pa blo bzang grags pa,* 1357-1419)
Explanation of (Nāgārjuna's) "Treatise on the Middle": Ocean of Reasoning / Great Commentary on (Nāgārjuna's) "Treatise on the Middle"
dbu ma rtsa ba'i tshig le'ur byas pa shes rab ces bya ba'i rnam bshad rigs pa'i rgya mtsho / rtsa shes ṭik chen
P6153, vol. 156. Also: Sarnath, India: Pleasure of Elegant Sayings Printing Press, n.d. Also: *rJe tsong kha pa'i gsung dbu ma'i lta ba'i skor,* vols. 1-2. Sarnath, India: Pleasure of Elegant Sayings Press, 1975. Also: Delhi: Ngawang Gelek, 1975. Also: Delhi: Guru Deva, 1979.
English translation (chap. 2): Jeffrey Hopkins. *Ocean of Reasoning.* Dharmsala, India: Library of Tibetan Works and Archives, 1974.
Extensive Commentary on the Difficult Points of the Mind-Basis-of-All and Afflicted Intellect: Ocean of Eloquence: Ocean of Eloquence
yid dang kun gzhi'i dka' ba'i gnas rgya cher 'grel pa legs par bshad pa'i rgya mtsho
P6149, vol. 154. Also: Delhi: Ngawang Gelek, 1975. Also: Delhi: Guru Deva, 1979.
English translation: Gareth Sparham. *Ocean of Eloquence: Tsong kha pa's Commentary on the Yogācāra Doctrine of Mind.* Albany, N.Y.: State University of New York Press, 1993.
Extensive Explanation of (Chandrakīrti's) "Supplement to (Nāgārjuna's) 'Treatise on the Middle'": Illumination of the Thought
dbu ma la 'jug pa'i rgya cher bshad pa dgongs pa rab gsal
P6143, vol. 154. Also: Sarnath, India: Pleasure of Elegant Sayings Press, 1973. Also: Delhi: Ngawang Gelek, 1975. Also: Delhi: Guru Deva, 1979.
English translation (chapters 1-5): Jeffrey Hopkins. *Compassion in Tibetan Buddhism,* 93-230. Ithaca, N.Y.: Snow Lion, 1980.
English translation (chap. 6, stanzas 1-7): Jeffrey Hopkins and Anne C. Klein. *Path to the Middle: Madhyamaka Philosophy in Tibet: The Oral Scholarship of Kensur Yeshay Tupden,* by Anne C. Klein, 147-183, 252-271. Albany, N.Y.: State University of New York Press, 1994.
Golden Rosary of Eloquence / Extensive Explanation of (Maitreya's) "Ornament for Clear Realization, Treatise of Quintessential Instructions on the Perfection of Wisdom" as Well as Its Commentaries: Golden Rosary of Eloquence
legs bshad gser 'phreng / shes rab kyi pha rol tu phyin pa'i man ngag gi bstan bcos mngon par rtogs pa'i rgyan 'grel pa dang bcas pa'i rgya cher bshad pa legs bshad gser gyi phreng ba
P6150, vols. 154-155. Also: Delhi: Ngawang Gelek, 1975. Also: Delhi: Guru Deva, 1979.
Great Exposition of Secret Mantra / The Stages of the Path to a Conqueror and Pervasive Master, a Great Vajradhara: Revealing All Secret Topics
sngags rim chen mo / rgyal ba khyab bdag rdo rje 'chang chen po'i lam gyi rim pa gsang ba kun gyi gnad rnam par phye ba
P6210, vol. 161. Also: Delhi: Ngawang Gelek, 1975. Also: Delhi: Guru Deva, 1979.
English translation (chap. 1): H.H. the Dalai Lama, Tsong-ka-pa, and Jeffrey Hopkins. *Tantra in*

Tibet. London: George Allen and Unwin, 1977; reprint, with minor corrections, Ithaca, N.Y.: Snow Lion, 1987.

English translation (chaps. 2-3): H.H. the Dalai Lama, Tsong-ka-pa, and Jeffrey Hopkins. *The Yoga of Tibet.* London: George Allen and Unwin, 1981; reprinted as *Deity Yoga.* Ithaca, N.Y.: Snow Lion, 1987.

Great Exposition of the Stages of the Path / Stages of the Path to Enlightenment Thoroughly Teaching All the Stages of Practice of the Three Types of Beings

lam rim chen mo / skyes bu gsum gyi nyams su blang ba'i rim pa thams cad tshang bar ston pa'i byang chub lam gyi rim pa

P6001, vol. 152. Also: Dharmsala, India: Tibetan Cultural Printing Press, 1964. Also: Delhi: Ngawang Gelek, 1975. Also: Delhi: Guru Deva, 1979.

English translation through the part on the nature of the three trainings: Tsong-kha-pa, *The Great Treatise on the Stages of the Path to Enlightenment,* vol. 1, trans. and ed. Joshua W. C. Cutler and Guy Newland. Ithaca, N.Y.: Snow Lion, 2000.

English translation of the part on the excessively broad object of negation: Elizabeth Napper. *Dependent-Arising and Emptiness,* 153-215. London: Wisdom, 1989.

English translation of the parts on calm abiding and special insight: Alex Wayman. *Calming the Mind and Discerning the Real,* 81-431. New York: Columbia University Press, 1978; reprint, New Delhi: Motilal Banarsidass, 1979.

Medium Exposition of the Stages of the Path / Small Exposition of the Stages of the Path to Enlightenment

lam rim 'bring / lam rim chung ngu / skyes bu gsum gyi nyams su blang ba'i byang chub lam gyi rim pa

P6002, vols. 152-153. Also: Dharmsala, India: Tibetan Cultural Printing Press, 1968. Also: Mundgod, India: dga' ldan shar rtse, n.d. (includes outline of topics by Trijang Rinbochay). Also: Delhi: Ngawang Gelek, 1975. Also: Delhi: Guru Deva, 1979.

English translation of the section on special insight: Robert Thurman. "The Middle Transcendent Insight." *Life and Teachings of Tsong Khapa,* 108-185. Dharmsala, India: Library of Tibetan Works and Archives, 1982.

English translation of the section on special insight: Jeffrey Hopkins. "Special Insight: From Dzong-ka-ba's *Middling Exposition of the Stages of the Path to Enlightenment Practiced by Persons of Three Capacities,* with supplementary headings by Trijang Rinbochay." Unpublished manuscript.

Praise of Dependent-Arising / Praise of the Supramundane Victor Buddha from the Approach of His Teaching the Profound Dependent-Arising: The Essence of Eloquence

rten 'brel bstod pa / sang rgyas bcom ldan 'das la zab mo rten cing 'brel bar 'byung ba gsung ba'i sgo nas bstod pa legs par bshad pa'i snying po

P6016, vol. 153. Also: Delhi: Ngawang Gelek, 1975. Also: Delhi: Guru Deva, 1979.

English translation: Geshe Wangyal. *The Door of Liberation,* 175-86. New York: Maurice Girodias Associates, 1973; reprint, New York: Lotsawa, 1978; rev. ed., Boston: Wisdom, 1995. Also: Robert Thurman. *Life and Teachings of Tsong Khapa,* 99-107. Dharmsala, India: Library of Tibetan Works and Archives, 1982.

Treatise Differentiating the Interpretable and the Definitive: The Essence of Eloquence

drang ba dang nges pa'i don rnam par phye ba'i bstan bcos legs bshad snying po

Editions: see the preface to my critical edition, *Emptiness in Mind-Only,* 355. Also: Ye shes thabs mkhas. *shar tsong kha pa blo bzang grags pas mdzad pa'i drang ba dang nges pa'i don rnam par phye ba'i bstan bcos legs bshad snying po.* Tā la'i bla ma'i 'phags bod, vol. 22. Varanasi, India: vāṇa dbus bod kyi ches mtho'i gtsug lag slob gnyer khang, 1997.

English translation: Prologue and Mind-Only section translated in this book. Also: Robert A. F. Thurman. *Tsong Khapa's Speech of Gold in the Essence of True Eloquence,* 185-385. Princeton, N.J.: Princeton University Press, 1984.

Chinese translation: Venerable Fa Zun. "Bian Liao Yi Bu Liao Yi Shuo Cang Lun." In *Xi Zang Fo Jiao Jiao Yi Lun Ji,* 2, 159-276. Taipei: Da Sheng Wen Hua Chu Ban She, 1979.

Gen-dün-drup, First Dalai Lama (*dge 'dun grub*, 1391-1474)

Commentary on [Guṇaprabha's] "Aphorisms on Discipline" / Essence of the Entire Discipline, Eloquent Holy Doctrine

legs par gsungs pa'i dam chos 'dul ba mtha' dag gi snying po

Collected Works of the First Dalai Lama dge-'dun-grub-pa. Gangtok, Sikkim: Dodrup Lama Sangye, 1978-1981.

Explanation of [Vasubandhu's] "Treasury of Manifest Knowledge": Illuminating the Path to Liberation

dam pa'i chos mngon pa'i mdzod kyi rnam par bshad pa thar lam gsal byed

Collected Works of the First Dalai Lama dge-'dun-grub-pa, vol. 3. Gangtok, Sikkim: Dodrup Lama, 1978-1981. Also: Buxaduor, India: n.p., 1967. Also: Sarnath, India: wa na mtho' slob dge ldan spyi las khang, 1973.

English translation (chapters 1-5): David Patt. *Elucidating the Path to Liberation.* Ann Arbor, Mich.: University Microfilms, 1994.

English translation (chap. 6): Harvey B. Aronson, "The Buddhist Path: A Translation of the Sixth Chapter of the First Dalai Lama's *Path of Liberation.*" *Tibet Journal* 5, no. 3 (1980):29-51; 5, no. 4 (1980):28-47; 12, no. 2 (1987):25-40; 12, no. 3 (1987):41-61.

Great Treatise on Valid Cognition: Adornment of Reasoning

tshad ma'i bstan bcos chen po rigs pa'i rgyan

Collected Works of the First Dalai Lama dge-'dun-grub-pa. Gangtok, Sikkim: Dodrup Lama, 1978-81.

Gen-dün-gya-tso, Second Dalai Lama (*dge 'dun rgya mtsho*, 1476-1542)

Lamp Illuminating the Meaning / Commentary on the Difficult Points of "Differentiating the Interpretable and the Definitive" from the Collected Works of the Foremost Holy Omniscient [Ḏzong-ka-ḇa]: Lamp Thoroughly Illuminating the Meaning of His Thought

rje btsun thams cad mkhyen pa'i gsung 'bum las drang nges rnam 'byed kyi dka' 'grel dgongs pa'i don rab tu gsal bar byed pa'i sgron me

n.d. [blockprint borrowed from the library of H.H. the Dalai Lama and photocopied] volume *'a*

Ḡön-chok-jik-may-w̄ang-ḇo (*dkon mchog 'jigs med dbang po*, 1728-1791)

Precious Garland of Tenets / Presentation of Tenets: A Precious Garland

grub pa'i mtha'i rnam par bzhag pa rin po che'i phreng ba

Tibetan: K. Mimaki. Le Grub mtha' rnam bzhag rin chen phreṅ ba de dkon mchog 'jigs med dbaṅ po (1728-1791), *Zinbun* [The Research Institute for Humanistic Studies, Kyoto University], 14 (1977):55-112. Also, Collected Works of dkon-mchog-'jigs-med-dbaṅ-po, vol. 6, 485-535. New Delhi: Ngawang Gelek Demo, 1972. Also: Xylograph in thirty-two folios from the Lessing collection of the rare book section of the University of Wisconsin Library, which is item 47 in Leonard Zwilling. *Tibetan Blockprints in the Department of Rare Books and Special Collections.* Madison, Wis.: University of Wisconsin-Madison Libraries, 1984. Also: Mundgod, India: blo gsal gling Press, 1980. Also: Dharmsala, India: Tibetan Cultural Printing Press, 1967. Also: Dharmsala, India: Teaching Training, n.d. Also: A blockprint edition in twenty-eight folios obtained in 1987 from Go-mang College in Hla-s̄a, printed on blocks that predate the Cultural Revolution.

English translation: Geshe Lhundup Sopa and Jeffrey Hopkins. *Practice and Theory of Tibetan Buddhism,* 48-145. New York: Grove, 1976; rev. ed., *Cutting through Appearances: Practice and Theory of Tibetan Buddhism,* 109-322. Ithaca, N.Y.: Snow Lion, 1989. Also: H. V. Guenther. *Buddhist Philosophy in Theory and Practice.* Baltimore, Md.: Penguin, 1972. Also, the chapters on the Autonomy School and the Consequence School: Shōtarō Iida. *Reason and Emptiness,* 27-51. Tokyo: Hokuseido, 1980.

Presentation of the Grounds and Paths: Beautiful Ornament of the Three Vehicles

sa lam gyi rnam bzhag theg gsum mdzes rgyan

Collected Works of dkon-mchog-'jigs-med-dbaṅ-po, vol. 7. New Delhi: Ngawang Gelek Demo, 1972.

English translation: Jeffrey Hopkins. *Presentation of the Grounds and Paths: Beautiful Ornament of the Three Vehicles.* Unpublished manuscript.

Oral commentary: Den-ma L̄o-chö Rin-b̄o-chay. *Commentary on (Ḡön-chok-jik-may-w̄ang-b̄o's) "Presentation of the Grounds and Paths: Beautiful Ornament of the Three Vehicles."* Trans. Jeffrey Hopkins and ed. Elizabeth Napper. Unpublished manuscript, 1978.

Guṇaprabha (*yon tan 'od*)

Aphorisms on Discipline

vinayasūtra

'dul ba'i mdo

P5619, vol. 123

Gung-ru Chö-jung / Gung-ru Chö-ḡyi-jung-n̄ay (*gung ru chos 'byung / gung ru chos kyi 'byung gnas;* fl. most likely in sixteenth century, since he refutes positions like those of Paṇ-chen S̄ö-nam-drak-b̄a and Jay-d̄zün Chö-ḡyi-gyel-tsen)

Garland of White Lotuses / Decisive Analysis of (D̄zong-ka-b̄a's) "Differentiating the Interpretable and the Definitive, The Essence of Eloquence": Garland of White Lotuses

drang ba dang nges pa'i rnam par 'byed pa legs bshad snying po zhes bya ba'i mtha' dpyod padma dkar po'i phreng ba

sku bum, Tibet: sku bum Monastery, n.d. [blockprint obtained by the author in 1988].

Gung-tang Ḡön-chok-d̄en-b̄ay-drön-may (*gung thang dkon mchog bstan pa'i sgron me,* 1762-1823)

Annotations / Beginnings of Annotations on (D̄zong-ka-b̄a's) "The Essence of Eloquence" on the Topic of Mind-Only: Illumination of a Hundred Mind-Only Texts

bstan bcos legs par bshad pa'i snying po las sems tsam skor gyi mchan 'grel rtsom 'phro rnam rig gzhung brgya'i snang ba

Collected Works of Guṅ-thaṅ Dkon-mchog-bstan-pa'i-sgron-me, vol. 1, 725-876. New Delhi: Ngawang Gelek Demo, 1975. Also: Go-mang, n.d. [ed. printed in India with fixed type].

Difficult Points / Beginnings of a Commentary on the Difficult Points of (D̄zong-ka-b̄a's) "Differentiating the Interpretable and the Definitive": Quintessence of "The Essence of Eloquence"

drang nges rnam 'byed kyi dka' 'grel rtsom 'phro legs bshad snying po'i yang snying

Collected Works of Guṅ-thaṅ Dkon-mchog-bstan-pa'i-sgron-me, vol. 1, 403-723. New Delhi: Ngawang Gelek Demo, 1975. Also: Sarnath, India: Guru Deva, 1965.

Biography of Ḡön-chok-jik-may-w̄ang-b̄o

dus gsum rgyal ba'i spyi gzugs rje btsun dkon mchog 'jigs med dbang po'i zhal snga nas kyi rnam par thar pa rgyal sras rgya mtsho'i jug ngogs

Collected Works of Dkon-mchog 'Jigs-med-dbaṅ-po, vol. 1, 1-555. New Delhi: Ngawang Gelek Demo, 1971. Also: Collected Works of Guṅ-thaṅ Dkon-mchog-bstan-pa'i-sgron-me, vol. 4, 185-701. New Delhi: Ngawang Gelek Demo, 1972.

Secret Biography of Ḡön-chok-jik-may-w̄ang-b̄o

rje btsun dkon mchog 'jigs med dbang po'i gangs ba'i rnam thar

Collected Works of Dkon-mchog 'Jigs-med-dbaṅ-po, vol. 1, 557-566. New Delhi: Ngawang Gelek Demo, 1971. Also: Collected Works of Guṅ-thaṅ Dkon-mchog-bstan-pa'i-sgron-me, vol. 4, 703-711. New Delhi: Ngawang Gelek Demo, 1972.

Gyel-tsap-dar-ma-rin-chen (*rgyal tshab dar ma rin chen,* 1364-1432)

Commentary on (Maitreya's) "Sublime Continuum of the Great Vehicle" / Commentary on (Maitreya's) "Treatise on the Later Scriptures of the Great Vehicle"

theg pa chen po rgyud bla ma'i ṭīkka

Collected Works of Rgyal-tshab Dar-ma-rin-chen, vol. 2 (entire). Delhi: Guru Deva, 1982. Also: Collected Works of Rgyal-tshab Dar-ma-rin-chen, vol. 2 (entire). Delhi: Ngawang Gelek Demo, 1981. Also: blockprint in the library of H.H. the Dalai Lama, no other data.

Explanation of (Shāntideva's) "Engaging in the Bodhisattva Deeds": Entrance of Conqueror Children

byang chub sems dpa'i spyod pa la 'jug pa'i rnam bshad rgyal sras 'jug ngogs

Collected Works of Rgyal-tshab Dar-ma-rin-chen, vol. 4, 3-331. Delhi: Guru Deva, 1982. Also: Collected Works of Rgyal-tshab Dar-ma-rin-chen, vol. 4. Delhi: Ngawang Gelek Demo, 1981. Also: Varanasi, India: Pleasure of Elegant Sayings Printing Press, 1973.

How to Practice the Two Stages of the Path of the Glorious Kālachakra: Quick Entry to the Path of Great Bliss

dpal dus kyi 'khor lo'i lam rim pa gnyis ji ltar nyams su len pa'i tshul bde ba chen po'i lam du myur du 'jug pa

Collected Works of Rgyal-tshab Dar-ma-rin-chen, vol. 1, 89-203. Delhi: Guru Deva, 1982. Also: Collected Works of Rgyal-tshab Dar-ma-rin-chen, vol. 1. Delhi: Ngawang Gelek Demo, 1981.

Haribhadra (*seng ge bzang po,* late eighth century)

Clear Meaning Commentary / Commentary on (Maitreya's) "Ornament for Clear Realization, Treatise of Quintessential Instructions on the Perfection of Wisdom"

sphuṭhārtha / abhisamayālaṃkāranāmaprajñāpāramitopadeśaśāstravṛtti

'grel pa don gsal / shes rab kyi pha rol tu phyin pa'i man ngag gi bstan bcos mngon par rtogs pa'i rgyan ces bya ba'i 'grel pa

P5191, vol. 90

Sanskrit: Unrai Wogihara. *Abhisamayālaṃkārālokā Prajñā-pāramitā-vyākhyā, The Work of Haribhadra.* 7 vols. Tokyo: Toyo Bunko, 1932-1935; reprint, Tokyo: Sankibo Buddhist Book Store, 1973.

Jam-ȳang-shay-b̄a Nga-w̄ang-d̄zön-drü (*'jam dbyangs bzhad pa ngag dbang brtson grus,* 1648-1722)

Brief Decisive Analysis of (D̄zong-ka-b̄a's) "Differentiating the Interpretable and the Definitive"

Collected Works of 'Jam-dbyaṅs-bźad-pa'i-rdo-rdo-rje, vol. 12, 473-456. New Delhi: Ngawang Gelek Demo, 1973.

Decisive Analysis of (Maitreya's) "Ornament for Clear Realization" / Decisive Analysis of the Treatise (Maitreya's) "Ornament for Clear Realization": Precious Lamp Illuminating All of the Meaning of the Perfection of Wisdom

bstan gcos mngon par rtogs pa'i rgyan gyi mtha' dpyod shes rab kyi pha rol tu phyin pa'i don kun gsal ba'i rin chen sgron me

Collected Works of 'Jam-dbyaṅs-bźad-pa'i-rdo-rdo-rje, vols. 7-8 (entire). New Delhi: Ngawang Gelek Demo, 1973. Also: Sarnath, India: Guru Deva, 1965.

Great Exposition of the Interpretable and the Definitive / Decisive Analysis of (D̄zong-ka-b̄a's) "Differentiating the Interpretable and the Definitive": Storehouse of White Lapis-Lazuli of Scripture and Reasoning Free from Error: Fulfilling the Hopes of the Fortunate

drang ba dang nges pa'i don rnam par 'byed pa'i mtha' dpyod 'khrul bral lung rigs bai dūr dkar pa'i gan mdzod skal bzang re ba kun skong

Edition cited: Buxaduor: n.d. Also: Collected Works of 'Jam-dbyaṅs-bźad-pa'i-rdo-rdo-rje, vol. 11, 3-288. New Delhi: Ngawang Gelek Demo, 1973. Also: dga' ldan pho phrang [blockprint obtained by the author in 1987].

Great Exposition of the Middle / Analysis of (Chandrakīrti's) "Supplement to (Nāgārjuna's) 'Treatise on the Middle'": Treasury of Scripture and Reasoning, Thoroughly Illuminating the Profound Meaning [of Emptiness], Entrance for the Fortunate

dbu ma chen mo / dbu ma 'jug pa'i mtha' dpyod lung rigs gter mdzod zab don kun gsal skal bzang 'jug ngogs

Edition cited: Buxaduor, India: Go-mang, 1967. Also: Collected Works of 'Jam-dbyaṅs-bźad-pa'i-rdo-rdo-rje, vol. 9 (entire). New Delhi: Ngawang Gelek Demo, 1973.

Great Exposition of Tenets / Explanation of "Tenets": Sun of the Land of Samantabhadra Brilliantly Illuminating All of Our Own and Others' Tenets and the Meaning of the Profound [Emptiness], Ocean of Scripture and Reasoning Fulfilling All Hopes of All Beings

grub mtha' chen mo / grub mtha'i rnam bshad rang gzhan grub mtha' kun dang zab don mchog tu gsal ba kun bzang zhing gi nyi ma lung rigs rgya mtsho skye dgu'i re ba kun skong

Edition cited: Musoorie, India: Dalama, 1962. Also: Collected Works of 'Jam-dbyaṅs-bźad-pa'i-rdo-rdo-rje, vol. 14 (entire). New Delhi: Ngawang Gelek Demo, 1973.

English translation (beginning of the chapter on the Consequence School): Jeffrey Hopkins. *Meditation on Emptiness,* 581-697. London: Wisdom, 1983; rev. ed., Boston: Wisdom, 1996.

Notes on (D̄zong-ka-b̄a's) "Differentiating the Interpretable and the Definitive"

'jam dbyangs bzhad pa'i rdo rjes mdzad pa'i drang nges rnam "byed kyi zin bris

Collected Works of 'Jam-dbyaṅs-bźad-pa'i-rdo-rdo-rje, vol. 11, 289-331. New Delhi: Ngawang Gelek Demo, 1973.

J̄ang-ḡya Röl-b̄ay-dor-jay (*lcang skya rol pa'i rdo rje,* 1717-1786)

Presentations of Tenets / Clear Exposition of the Presentations of Tenets: Beautiful Ornament for the Meru of the Subduer's Teaching

grub mtha'i rnam bzhag / grub pa'i mtha'i rnam par bzhag pa gsal bar bshad pa thub bstan lhun po'i mdzes rgyan

Edition cited: Varanasi, India: Pleasure of Elegant Sayings Printing Press, 1970. Also: Lokesh Chandra, ed. *Buddhist Philosophical Systems of Lcan-skya Rol-pahi Rdo-rje.* Śata-piṭaka Series (Indo-Asian Literatures), vol. 233. New Delhi: International Academy of Indian Culture, 1977. Also: An edition published by gam car phan bde legs bshad gling grva tshang dang rgyud rnying slar gso tshogs pa, 1982.

English translation of Sautrāntika chapter: Anne C. Klein. *Knowing, Naming, and Negation,* 115-196. Ithaca, N.Y.: Snow Lion, 1988. Commentary on this: Anne C. Klein. *Knowledge and Liberation: A Buddhist Epistemological Analysis in Support of Transformative Religious Experience: Tibetan Interpretations of Dignāga and Dharmakīrti.* Ithaca, N.Y.: Snow Lion, 1986.

English translation of Svātantrika chapter: Donald S. Lopez Jr. *A Study of Svātantrika,* 243-386. Ithaca, N.Y.: Snow Lion, 1986.

English translation of part of Prāsaṅgika chapter: Jeffrey Hopkins. *Emptiness Yoga: The Middle Way Consequence School,* 355-428. Ithaca, N.Y.: Snow Lion, 1983.

Jay-d̄zün Chö-ḡyi-gyel-tsen (*rje btsun chos kyi rgyal mtshan,* 1469-1546)

General-Meaning Commentary / General Meaning of (D̄zong-ka-b̄a's) "Differentiating the Interpretable and the Definitive": Eradicating Bad Disputation: A Precious Garland

drang nges rnam 'byed kyi spyi don rgol ngan tshar gcod rin po che'i phreng ba

Edition cited: Bylakuppe, India: Se-ra Byes Monastery, 1977. Also: Sarnath, India: Guru Deva, 1965. Also: Lhasa, Tibet: par pa dpal ldan, 1987.

Presentation of Tenets

grub mtha'i rnam gzhag

Buxaduor, India: n.p., 1960. Also: Bylakuppe, India: Se-ra Byes Monastery, 1977.

Jetāri

Differentiating the Sugata's Texts

sugatamatavibhaṅga

bde bar gzhegs pa'i gzhung rnam par 'byed pa

P5867, vol. 146

Jik-may-dam-chö-gya-tso (*'jigs med dam chos rgya mtsho*); poetic name Mi-pam-ȳang-j̄en-gye-b̄ay-dor-jay (*mi pham dbyangs can dgyes* [or *dges*] *pa'i rdo rje;* 1898-1946)

Port of Entry / Treatise Distinguishing All the Meanings of (D̄zong-ka-b̄a's) "The Essence of Eloquence": Illuminating the Differentiation of the Interpretable and the Definitive: Port of Entry to "The Essence of Eloquence"

drang ba dang nges pa'i don rnam par phye ba gsal bar byed pa legs bshad snying po'i don mtha' dag rnam par 'byed pa'i bstan bcos legs bshad snying po'i 'jug ngogs

bkra shis chos sde, India: 199-?.

Jin-b̄a-dar-gyay, Ga-jang (*sbyin pa dar rgyas, dga' byang*)

Brief Illumination of the Difficult Points of (D̄zong-ka-b̄a's) "Differentiating the Interpretable and the Definitive": Mirror Illuminating Eloquence

drang nges rnam 'byed kyi dka' gnad gsal bar byed pa bsdus don legs bshad gsal ba'i me long

Buxaduor, India: no other data.

Jñānashrībhadra

Commentary on the "Descent into Laṅkā Sūtra"

'phags pa langkar gshegs pa'i mdo

āryalaṅkāvatāravṛtti

P5519, vol. 107

Jñānavajra

'phags pa langkar gshegs pa zhes bya ba theg pa chen po'i mdo'i 'grel pa de bzhin gshegs pa'i snying po'i rgyan

āryalaṅkāvatāramahāyānasūtravṛttitathāgatahṛdayālaṃkāra
P5520, vol. 107
Ke-drup-ge-lek-b̄el-sang (*mkhas grub dge legs dpal bzang*, 1385-1438)
Compilation on Emptiness / Opening the Eyes of the Fortunate: Treatise Brilliantly Clarifying the Profound Emptiness
stong thun chen mo / zab mo stong pa nyid rab tu gsal bar byed pa'i bstan bcos skal bzang mig 'byed
Collected Works of the Lord Mkhas-grub rje dge-legs-dpal-bzaṅ-po, vol. 1, 179-702 (edition cited). New Delhi: Guru Deva, 1980. Also: Collected Works of Mkhas-grub dge-legs dpal, vol. 1, 125-482. New Delhi: Ngawang Gelek Demo, 1983. Also: New Delhi: n.p., 1972.
English translation: José Ignacio Cabezón. *A Dose of Emptiness: An Annotated Translation of the* stong thun chen mo *of mKhas grub dGe legs dpal bzang*, 21-388. Albany, N.Y.: State University of New York Press, 1992.
English translation of the chapter on the Mind-Only School: Jeffrey Hopkins. *Ke-drup's "Opening the Eyes of the Fortunate": The Mind-Only School.* Unpublished manuscript.
L̄o-sang-ḡön-chok (*blo bzang dkon mchog*)
Clear Crystal Mirror, Word-Commentary on the Root Text of (Jam-ȳang-shay-b̄a's) "Tenets"
grub mtha' rtsa ba'i tshig ṭik shel dkar me long: in *Three Commentaries on the* grub mtha' rtsa ba gdoṅ nga'i sgra dbyaṅs *of 'jam dbyaṅs-bẓad-pa'i-rdo-rje ṅag-dbaṅ-brtson-'grus*
Delhi: Chophel Legden, 1978
L̄o-sang-w̄ang-chuk (*blo bzang dbang phyug*, 1901-1979)
Notes on (D̄zong-ka-b̄a's) "Interpretable and Definitive, The Essence of Eloquence": Lamp for the Intelligent
dang nges legs par bshad pa'i snying po'i zin bris blo gsal sgron me: *Notes on the Art of Interpretation: A Lamp to Light the Mind*, being a commentary on Je Tsongkapa's *Essence of Good Explanation*
Bylakuppe, India: Sera Jey Tibetan Monastic University, 1993.
L̄ong-chen-rap-jam (*klong chen rab 'byams / klong chen dri med 'od zer*, 1308-1363)
Precious Treasury of Tenets: Illuminating the Meaning of All Vehicles
theg pa mtha' dag gi don gsal bar byed pa grub pa'i mtha' rin po che'i mdzod
Gangtok, Sikkim: Dodrup Chen Rinpoche, 1969[?].
Maitreya (*byams pa*)
Five Doctrines of Maitreya
1. *Sublime Continuum of the Great Vehicle / Treatise on the Later Scriptures of the Great Vehicle*
mahāyānottaratantraśāstra
theg pa chen po rgyud bla ma'i bstan bcos
P5525, vol. 108
Sanskrit: E. H. Johnston (and T. Chowdhury). *The Ratnagotravibhāga Mahāyānottaratantraśāstra.* Patna, India: Bihar Research Society, 1950.
English translation: E. Obermiller. "Sublime Science of the Great Vehicle to Salvation." *Acta Orientalia* 9 (1931):81-306. Also: J. Takasaki. *A Study on the Ratnagotravibhāga.* Rome: Istituto Italiano per il Medio ed Estremo Oriente, 1966.
2. *Differentiation of Phenomena and the Final Nature of Phenomena*
dharmadharmatāvibhaṅga
chos dang chos nyid rnam par 'byed pa
P5523, vol. 108
3. *Differentiation of the Middle and the Extremes*
madhyāntavibhaṅga
dbus dang mtha' rnam par 'byed pa
P5522, vol. 108
Sanskrit: Gadjin M. Nagao. *Madhyāntavibhāga-bhāṣya.* Tokyo: Suzuki Research Foundation, 1964. Also: Ramchandra Pandeya. *Madhyānta-vibhāga-śāstra.* Delhi: Motilal Banarsidass, 1971.
English translation: Stefan Anacker. *Seven Works of Vasubandhu.* Delhi: Motilal Banarsidass, 1984.

Also, of chapter 1: Thomas A. Kochumuttom. *A Buddhist Doctrine of Experience.* Delhi: Motilal Banarsidass, 1982. Also, of chapter 1: F. Th. Stcherbatsky. *Madhyāntavibhāga, Discourse on Discrimination between Middle and Extremes Ascribed to Bodhisattva Maitreya and Commented by Vasubandhu and Sthiramati.* Bibliotheca Buddhica, 30 (1936). Osnabrück, Germany: Biblio Verlag, 1970; reprint, Calcutta: Indian Studies Past and Present, 1971. Also, of chapter 1: David Lasar Friedmann. *Sthiramati, Madhyāntavibhāgaṭīkā: Analysis of the Middle Path and the Extremes.* Utrecht, Netherlands: Rijksuniversiteit te Leiden, 1937.

4. *Ornament for Clear Realization*
abhisamayālaṃkāra
mngon par rtogs pa'i rgyan
P5184, vol. 88
Sanskrit: Th. Stcherbatsky and E. Obermiller, eds. *Abhisamayālaṃkāra-Prajñāpāramitā-Updeśa-Śāstra.* Bibliotheca Buddhica, 23. Osnabrück, Germany: Biblio Verlag, 1970.
English translation: Edward Conze. *Abhisamayālaṃkāra.* Serie Orientale Rome. Rome: Istituto Italiano per il Medio ed Estremo Oriente, 1954.

5. *Ornament for the Great Vehicle Sūtras*
mahāyānasūtrālaṃkāra
theg pa chen po'i mdo sde rgyan gyi tshig le'ur byas pa
P5521, vol. 108
Sanskrit: Sitansusekhar Bagchi. *Mahāyāna-Sūtrālaṃkāraḥ of Asaṅga* [with Vasubandhu's commentary]. Buddhist Sanskrit Texts 13. Darbhanga, India: Mithila Institute, 1970.
Sanskrit text and translation into French: Sylvain Lévi. *Mahāyānasūtrālaṃkāra, exposé de la doctrine du grand véhicule selon le système Yogācāra.* 2 vols. Paris: Bibliothèque de l'École des Hautes Études, 1907, 1911.
Sanskrit text and translation into English: Surekha Vijay Limaye. *Mahāyānasūtrālaṃkāra by Asaṅga.* Bibliotheca Indo-Buddhica Series 94. Delhi: Sri Satguru, 1992.

Mi-pam-gya-tso, Ju (*mi pham rgya mtsho, 'ju*)

Annotations on (Maitreya's) "Great Vehicle Treatise, The Sublime Continuum": Sacred Word of Mi-pam
theg pa chen po rgyud bla ma'i bstan bcos kyi mchan 'grel mi pham zhal lung. Collected Writings of 'jam-mgon 'ju mi-pham-rgya-mtsho, vol. pa, 349-561.
Gangtok, Sikkim: Sonam Topgay Kazi, 1972.

Nāgārjuna (*klu sgrub,* first to second century C.E.)

Five Stages
pañcakrama
rim pa lnga pa
P2667, vol. 61
Sanskrit: Katsumi Mimaki and Tōru Tomabechi. *Pañcakrama.* Bibliotheca Codicum Asiaticorum 8. Tokyo: Centre for East Asian Cultural Studies for UNESCO, 1994.
English translation of the introductory stanzas: Alex Wayman, *Yoga of the Guhyasamājatantra.* Delhi: Motilal Banarsidass, 1977.

Six Collections of Reasoning

1. *Precious Garland of Advice for the King*
rājaparikathāratnāvalī
rgyal po la gtam bya ba rin po che'i phreng ba
P5658, vol. 129
Sanskrit, Tibetan, and Chinese: Michael Hahn. *Nāgārjuna's Ratnāvalī,* vol. 1. *The Basic Texts (Sanskrit, Tibetan, and Chinese).* Bonn: Indica et Tibetica Verlag, 1982.
English translation: Jeffrey Hopkins. *Buddhist Advice for Living and Liberation: Nāgārjuna's Precious Garland,* 94-164. Ithaca, N.Y.: Snow Lion, 1998. Supercedes that in: Nāgārjuna and the Seventh Dalai Lama. *The Precious Garland and the Song of the Four Mindfulnesses,* translated by Jeffrey Hopkins, 17-93. London: George Allen and Unwin, 1975; New York: Harper and Row, 1975; reprint, in H.H. the Dalai Lama, Tenzin Gyatso. *The Buddhism of Tibet.* London: George Allen and Unwin, 1983; reprint, Ithaca, N.Y.: Snow Lion, 1987.

English translation: John Dunne and Sara McClintock. *The Precious Garland: An Epistle to a King.* Boston: Wisdom, 1997.

English translation of chap. 1, 1-77: Giuseppe Tucci. "The *Ratnāvalī* of Nāgārjuna." *Journal of the Royal Asiatic Society* (1934):307-324; reprint, Giuseppe Tucci, *Opera Minora,* II. Rome: Giovanni Bardi Editore, 1971, 321-366. Chap. 2, 1-46; chap. 4, 1-100: Giuseppe Tucci. "The *Ratnāvalī* of Nāgārjuna." *Journal of the Royal Asiatic Society* (1936):237-252, 423-435.

Japanese translation: Uryūzu Ryushin. *Butten II, Sekai Koten Bungaku Zenshu,* 7 (July, 1965):349-372. Edited by Nakamura Hajime. Tokyo: Chikuma Shobō. Also: Uryūzu Ryushin. *Daijō Butten* 14 (1974):231-316. *Ryūju Ronshū.* Edited by Kajiyama Yuichi and Uryūzu Ryushin. Tokyo: Chūōkōronsha.

Danish translation: Christian Lindtner. *Nagarjuna, Juvelkaeden og andre skrifter.* Copenhagen: 1980.

2. *Refutation of Objections*
vigrahavyāvartanīkārikā
rtsod pa bzlog pa'i tshig le'ur byas pa
P5228, vol. 95

Sanskrit: E. H. Johnston. *The Ratnagotravibhāga Mahāyānottaratantraśāstra.* Patna, India: Bihar Research Society, 1950.

Edited Tibetan and Sanskrit: Christian Lindtner. *Nagarjuniana,* 70-86. Indiske Studier 4. Copenhagen: Akademisk Forlag, 1982.

English translation: K. Bhattacharya, E. H. Johnston, and A. Kunst. *The Dialectical Method of Nāgārjuna.* New Delhi: Motilal Banarsidass, 1978.

English translation from the Chinese: G. Tucci. *Pre-Diṅnāga Buddhist Texts on Logic from Chinese Sources.* Gaekwad's Oriental Series 49. Baroda, India: Oriental Institute, 1929.

French translation: S. Yamaguchi. "Traité de Nāgārjuna pour écarter les vaines discussion (Vigrahavyāvartanī) traduit et annoté." *Journal Asiatique* 215 (1929):1-86.

3. *Seventy Stanzas on Emptiness*
śūnyatāsaptatikārikā
stong pa nyid bdun cu pa'i tshig le'ur byas pa
P5227, vol. 95

Edited Tibetan and English translation: Christian Lindtner. *Nagarjuniana,* 34-69. Indiske Studier 4. Copenhagen: Akademisk Forlag, 1982.

English translation: David Ross Komito. *Nāgārjuna's "Seventy Stanzas": A Buddhist Psychology of Emptiness.* Ithaca, N.Y.: Snow Lion, 1987.

4. *Sixty Stanzas of Reasoning*
yuktiṣaṣṭikākārikā
rigs pa drug cu pa'i tshig le'ur byas pa
P5225, vol. 95

Edited Tibetan with Sanskrit fragments and English translation: Christian Lindtner. *Nagarjuniana,* 100-119. Indiske Studier 4. Copenhagen: Akademisk Forlag, 1982.

5. *Treatise Called the Finely Woven*
vaidalyasūtranāma
zhib mo rnam par 'thag pa zhes bya ba'i mdo
P5226, vol. 95

Tibetan text and English translation: Fermando Tola and Carmen Dragonetti. *Nāgārjuna's Refutation of Logic (Nyāya) Vaidalyaprakaraṇa.* Delhi: Motilal Banarsidass, 1995.

6. *Treatise on the Middle / Fundamental Treatise on the Middle, Called "Wisdom"*
madhyamakaśāstra / prajñānāmamūlamadhyamakakārikā
dbu ma'i bstan bcos / dbu ma rtsa ba'i tshig le'ur byas pa shes rab ces bya ba
P5224, vol. 95

Edited Sanskrit: J. W. de Jong. *Nāgārjuna, Mūlamadhyamakakārikāḥ.* Madras, India: Adyar Library and Research Centre, 1977; reprint, Wheaton, Ill.: Theosophical Publishing House, c. 1977. Also: Christian Lindtner. *Nāgārjuna's Filosofiske Vaerker,* 177-215. Indiske Studier 2.

Copenhagen: Akademisk Forlag, 1982.

English translation: Frederick Streng. *Emptiness: A Study in Religious Meaning.* Nashville, Tenn.: Abingdon Press, 1967. Also: Kenneth Inada. *Nāgārjuna: A Translation of His Mūlamadhyamakakārikā.* Tokyo: Hokuseido Press, 1970. Also: David J. Kalupahana. *Nāgārjuna: The Philosophy of the Middle Way.* Albany, N.Y.: State University of New York Press, 1986. Also: Jay L. Garfield. *The Fundamental Wisdom of the Middle Way.* New York: Oxford University Press, 1995.

Italian translation: R. Gnoli. *Nāgārjuna: Madhyamaka Kārikā, Le stanze del cammino di mezzo.* Enciclopedia di autori classici 61. Turin, Italy: P. Boringhieri, 1961.

Danish translation: Christian Lindtner. *Nāgārjuna's Filosofiske Vaerker,* 67-135. Indiske Studier 2. Copenhagen: Akademisk Forlag, 1982.

Nga-w̄ang-b̄el-den (*ngag dbang dpal ldan,* b. 1797), also known as B̄el-den-chö-jay (*dpal ldan chos rje*)

Annotations for (Jam-ȳang-shay-b̄a's) "Great Exposition of Tenets": Freeing the Knots of the Difficult Points, Precious Jewel of Clear Thought

grub mtha' chen mo'i mchan 'grel dka' gnad mdud grol blo gsal gces nor

Sarnath, India: Pleasure of Elegant Sayings Press, 1964. Also: Collected Works of Chos-rje ṅag-dbaṅ Dpal-ldan of Urga, vols. 4 (entire)-5, 1-401. Delhi: Guru Deva, 1983.

Explanation of the Conventional and the Ultimate in the Four Systems of Tenets

grub mtha' bzhi'i lugs kyi kun rdzob dang don dam pa'i don rnam par bshad pa legs bshad dpyid kyi dpal mo'i glu dbyangs

New Delhi: Guru Deva, 1972. Also: Collected Works of Chos-rje ṅag-dbaṅ Dpal-ldan of Urga, vol. 1, 3-273. Delhi: Mongolian Lama Gurudeva, 1983.

Presentation of the Grounds and Paths of the Four Great Secret Tantra Sets: Illumination of the Texts of Tantra

gsang chen rgyud sde bzhi'i sa lam gyi rnam bzhag rgyud gzhung gsal byed

rgyud smad par khang edition, no other data

Nga-w̄ang-ke-drup (*ngag dbang mkhas grub,* 1779-1838)

Presentation of Death, Intermediate State, and Rebirth

skye shi bar do'i rnam bzhag

Collected Works of Ṅag-dbaṅ-mkhas-grub, Kyai-rdor Mkhan-po of Urga, vol. 1, 459-474. Leh, Ladakh: S. Tashigangpa, 1973.

Nga-w̄ang-l̄o-sang-gya-tso (*ngag dbang blo bzang rgya mtsho,* Fifth Dalai Lama, 1617-1682)

Instructions on the Stages of the Path to Enlightenment: Sacred Word of Mañjushrī

byang chub lam gyi rim pa'i 'khrid yig 'jam pa'i dbyangs kyi zhal lung

Thimphu, Bhutan: kun bzang stobs rgyal, 1976.

English translation of the "Perfection of Wisdom Chapter": Jeffrey Hopkins. "Practice of Emptiness." Dharmsala: Library of Tibetan Works and Archives, 1974.

Pa-bong-ka-b̄a Jam-b̄a-d̄en-dzin-trin-lay-gya-tso (*pha bong kha pa byams pa bstan 'dzin 'phrin las rgya mtsho,* 1878-1941)

Presentation of the Interpretable and the Definitive, Brief Notes on the Occasion of Receiving Profound [Instruction from J̄o-ne Paṇḍita L̄o-sang-gya-tso in 1927] on (D̄zong-ka-b̄a's) "The Essence of Eloquence"

drang ba dang nges pa'i don rnam par bzhag pa legs par bshad pa'i snying po'i zab nos skabs kyi zin bris mdo tsam du bkod pa

Collected Works of Pha-boṅ-kha-pa-bstan-'dzin-'phrin-las-rgya-mtsho, vol. 4, 400-476. New Delhi: Chophel Legdan, 1973.

Paṇ-chen S̄ö-nam-drak-b̄a (*paṇ chen bsod nams grags pa,* 1478-1554)

Distinguishing through Objections and Answers (D̄zong-ka-b̄a's) "Differentiating the Interpretable and Definitive Meanings of All the Scriptures, The Essence of Eloquence": Garland of Blue Lotuses

gsung rab kun gyi drang ba dang nges pa'i don rnam par 'byed pa legs par bshad pa'i snying po brgal lan gyis rnam par 'byed pa utpa la'i phreng ba

Collected Works (gsuṅ 'bum) of Paṇ-chen Bsod-nams-grags-pa, vol. 5. Mundgod, India: Drepung Loseling Library Society, 1982.

Prajñāvarman (*shes rab go cha, pra dznyā wa rmaṃ*)

Commentary on (Udbhaṭasiddhasvāmin's) "Exalted Praise"

viśeṣastavanāmaṭīkā

khyad par du 'phags pa'i bstod pa'i rgya cher bshad pa

P2002, vol. 46

Puṇḍarīka, Kalkī (*rigs ldan pad ma dkar po*)

Great Commentary on the "Kālachakra Tantra": Stainless Light

vimālaprabhānāmamūlatantrānusāriṇīdvādaśasāhasrikālaghukālacakratantrarājaṭīkā

bsdus pa'i rgyud kyi rgyal po dus kyi 'khor lo'i 'grel bshad rtsa ba'i rgyud kyi rjes su 'jug pa stong phrag bcu gnyis pa dri ma med pa'i 'od ces bya ba

P2064, vol. 46

English translation of the first section: John Newman. "The Outer Wheel of Time: Vajrayāna Buddhist Cosmology in the Kālachakra Tantra." Ph.D. dissertation, University of Wisconsin.

Ratnākarashānti (*ratnākaraśānti, rin chen 'byung gnas zhi ba*)

Commentary on (Nāgārjuna's) "Compendium of Sūtra," Ornament Sparkling with Jewels

sūtrasamuccayabhāṣyaratnālokālaṃkāra

mdo kun las btus pa'i bshad pa rin po che'i snang ba'i rgyan

P5331, vol. 102

Ser-shül Ge-shay Lo-sang-pün-tsok (*blo bzang phun tshogs, ser shul dge bshes;* fl. in early twentieth century)

Notes / Notes on (Dzong-ka-ba's) "Differentiating the Interpretable and the Definitive": Lamp Illuminating the Profound Meaning

drang nges rnam 'byed kyi zin bris zab don gsal ba'i sgron me

Delhi: n.p., 1974.

Sha-mar Ge-dün-den-dzin-gya-tso (*zhwa dmar dge 'dun bstan 'dzin rgya mtsho,* 1852-1912)

Notes Concerning Difficult Points in (Dzong-ka-ba's) "Differentiating the Interpretable and the Definitive, The Essence of Eloquence": Victorious Clearing Away Mental Darkness

drang nges legs bshad snying po'i dka gnas las brtsams pa'i zin bris bcom ldan yid kyi mun sel

n.d. [mentioned in Jik-may-dam-chö-gya-tso's *Port of Entry*]

Shāntarakṣhita (*śāntarakṣita, zhi ba 'tsho,* eighth century)

Compendium of Principles

tattvasaṃgrahakārikā

de kho na nyid bsdud pa'i tshig le'ur byas pa

P5764, vol. 138

Sanskrit: Dwarikadas Shastri. *Tattvasaṅgraha of Ācārya Shāntarakṣita, with the Commentary "Pañjikā" of Shrī Kamalashīla.* Varanasi, India: Bauddha Bharati, 1968.

English translation: G. Jha. *The Tattvasaṃgraha of Śāntirakṣita, with the commentary of Kamalaśīla.* Gaekwad's Oriental Series 80 and 83. Baroda, India: Oriental Institute, 1937, 1939; reprint, Delhi: Motilal Barnarsidass, 1986.

Shāntideva (*zhi ba lha,* eighth century)

Engaging in the Bodhisattva Deeds

bodhi[sattva]caryāvatāra

byang chub sems dpa'i spyod pa la 'jug pa

P5272, vol. 99

Sanskrit: P. L. Vaidya. *Bodhicaryāvatāra.* Buddhist Sanskrit Texts 12. Darbhanga, India: Mithila Institute, 1988.

Sanskrit and Tibetan: Vidhushekara Bhattacharya. *Bodhicaryāvatāra.* Bibliotheca Indica, 280. Calcutta: Asiatic Society, 1960.

Sanskrit and Tibetan with Hindi translation: Rāmaśaṁkara Tripāthī, ed. *Bodhicaryāvatāra.* Baudha-Himālaya-Granthamālā, 8. Leh, Ladākh: Central Institute of Buddhist Studies, 1989.

English translation: Stephen Batchelor. *A Guide to the Bodhisattva's Way of Life.* Dharmsala, India: Library of Tibetan Works and Archives, 1979. Also: Marion Matics. *Entering the Path of Enlightenment.* New York: Macmillan, 1970. Also: Kate Crosby and Andrew Skilton. *The*

Bodhicaryāvatāra. Oxford: Oxford University Press, 1996. Also: Padmakara Translation Group. *The Way of the Bodhisattva.* Boston: Shambhala, 1997. Also: Vesna A. Wallace and B. Alan Wallace. *A Guide to the Bodhisattva Way of Life.* Ithaca, N.Y.: Snow Lion, 1997.

Contemporary commentary by H.H. the Dalai Lama, Tenzin Gyatso. *Transcendent Wisdom.* Ithaca, N.Y.: Snow Lion, 1988. Also: H.H. the Dalai Lama, Tenzin Gyatso. *A Flash of Lightning in the Dark of the Night.* Boston: Shambhala, 1994.

Shay-rap-gyel-tsen (*shes rab rgyal mtshan, dol po pa,* 1292-1361)

The Mountain Doctrine: Ocean of Definitive Meaning

ri chos nges don rgya mtsho

Gangtok, Sikkim: Dodrup Sangyey Lama, 1976.

Also: 'dzam thang bsam 'grub nor bu'i gling, n.d.

Also: Matthew Kapstein. *The 'Dzam-thang Edition of the Collected Works of Kun-mkhyen Dol-po-pa Shes-rab-rgyal-mtshan: Introduction and Catalogue,* vol. 2, 25-707. Delhi: Shedrup Books, 1992.

Also: Beijing: mi rigs dpe skrun khang, 1998.

Condensed English translation: Jeffrey Hopkins. *The Mountain Doctrine: Ocean of Definitive Meaning.* Unpublished manuscript.

The Great Calculation of the Doctrine, Which Has the Significance of a Fourth Council

bka' bsdu bzhi pa'i don bstan rtsis chen po

Matthew Kapstein. *The 'Dzam-thang Edition of the Collected Works of Kun-mkhyen Dol-po-pa Shes-rab-rgyal-mtshan: Introduction and Catalogue,* vol. 5, 207-252. Delhi: Shedrup Books, 1992.

English translation: Cyrus R. Stearns. *The Buddha from Dol po: A Study of the Life and Thought of the Tibetan Master Dolpopa Sherab Gyaltsen,* 127-173. Albany, N.Y.: State University of New York Press, 1999.

Sthiramati (*blo gros brtan pa,* fl. late fourth century)

Explanation of (Vasubandhu's) "Commentary on (Maitreya's) 'Differentiation of the Middle and the Extremes'"

madhyāntavibhāgaṭīkā

dbus dang mtha' rnam par 'byed pa'i 'grel bshad / dbus mtha'i 'grel bshad

P5334, vol. 109

Sanskrit: Ramchandra Pandeya ed. *Madhyānta-vibhāga-śāstra.* Delhi: Motilal Banarsidass, 1971.

English translation (chap. 1): F. Th. Stcherbatsky. *Madhyāntavibhāga, Discourse on Discrimination between Middle and Extremes Ascribed to Bodhisattva Maitreya and Commented by Vasubandhu and Sthiramati.* Bibliotheca Buddhica, 30 (1936). Osnabrück, Germany: Biblio Verlag, 1970; reprint, Calcutta: Indian Studies Past and Present, 1971.

English translation (chap. 1): David Lasar Friedmann. *Sthiramati, Madhyānta-vibhāgaṭīkā: Analysis of the Middle Path and the Extremes.* Utrecht, Netherlands: Rijksuniversiteit te Leiden, 1937.

Explanation of (Vasubandhu's) "The Thirty"

triṃśikābhāṣya

sum cu pa'i bshad pa

P5565, vol. 113

Sanskrit: Sylvain Lévi. *Vijñaptimātratāsiddhi / Deux traités de Vasubandhu: Viṃśatikā (La Vingtaine) et Triṃsikā (La Trentaine).* Bibliothèque de l'École des Hautes Études, 245. Paris: Libraire Honoré Champion, 1925.

Tibetan: Enga Teramoto. *Sthiramati's Triṃçikābhāṣyaṃ (Sum-cu-paḥi ḥGrel-pa): A Tibetan Text.* Kyoto: Association for Linguistic Study of Sacred Scriptures, 1933.

Explanation of (Vasubandhu's) "Commentary of (Maitreya's) 'Ornament for the Great Vehicle Sūtras'"

sūtrālaṃkārāvṛttibhāṣya

mdo sde'i rgyan gyi 'grel bshad

P5531, vol. 108

Tāranātha (1575-1634)

The Essence of Other-Emptiness

gzhan stong snying po

Collected Works of Jo-naṅ rJe-btsun Tāranātha, vol. 4, 491-514. Leh, Ladakh: Smanrtsis Shesrig

Dpemzod, 1985
English translation: Jeffrey Hopkins, in collaboration with Lama Lodrö Namgyel. *The Essence of Other-Emptiness.* Unpublished manuscript.
Tsay-den-hla-ram-ba (*tshe brtan lha rams pa*); for his three texts, see p. 202, footnote d.
Tso-na-wa Shay-rap-sang-bo (*mtsho sna ba shes rab bzang po*)
Explanation of the Root Text of [Guṇaprabha's] "Aphorisms on Discipline": Clear Light of the Moon, Ocean of Scriptural Eloquence
'dul ba mdo rtsa ba'i rnam bshad nyi ma'i 'od zer legs bshad lung gi rgya mtsho; 'dul ṭik nyi ma'i 'od zer
Buxaduor: blo bzang 'gyur med, 1966.
Tu-gen Lo-sang-chö-gyi-nyi-ma (*thu'u bkvan blo bzang chos kyi nyi ma,* 1737-1802)
Mirror of Eloquence Showing the Sources and Assertions of All Systems of Tenets
grub mtha' thams cad kyi khungs dang 'dod tshul ston pa legs bshad shel gyi me long
Sarnath, India: Chhos Je Lama, 1963. Also: Gansu, China: kan su'u mi rigs dpe skrun khang, 1984.
Vajragarbha (*rdo rje snying po*)
Extensive Commentary on the "Condensed Meaning of the Hevajra Tantra"
hevajrapiṇḍārthaṭīkā
kye'i rdo rje bsdus pa'i don gyi rgya cher 'grel pa
P2310, vol. 53
English translation of the tantra itself: *Hevajra Tantra,* Parts I and II. Ed. and trans. D. L. Snellgrove. London: Oxford University Press, 1959
Vajrapāṇi (*phyag na rdo rje*)
Meaning Commentary on the "Chakrasaṃvara Tantra"
lakṣābhidhanāduddhṛtalaghutantrapiṇḍārthavivaraṇa
mngon par brjod pa 'bum pa las phyung ba nyung ngu'i rgyud kyi bsdus pa'i don rnam par bshad pa
P2117. vol. 48
Vasubandhu (*dbyig gnyen,* fl. 360)
Commentary on (Asaṅga's) "Summary of the Great Vehicle"
mahāyānasaṃgrahabhāṣya
theg pa chen po bsdus pa'i 'grel pa
P5551, vol. 112
Commentary on (Maitreya's) "Differentiation of the Middle and the Extremes"
madhyāntavibhāgaṭīkā
dbus dang mtha' rnam par 'byed pa'i 'grel pa / dbus mtha'i 'grel pa
P5528, vol. 108
Sanskrit: Gadjin M. Nagao. *Madhyāntavibhāga-bhāṣya.* Tokyo: Suzuki Research Foundation, 1964. Also: Ramchandra Pandeya. *Madhyānta-vibhāga-śāstra.* Delhi: Motilal Banarsidass, 1971.
English translation: Stefan Anacker. *Seven Works of Vasubandhu.* Delhi: Motilal Banarsidass, 1984. Also: Thomas A. Kochumuttom. *A Buddhist Doctrine of Experience.* Delhi: Motilal Banarsidass, 1982. Also, of chapter 1: F. Th. Stcherbatsky. *Madhyāntavibhāga: Discourse on Discrimination between Middle and Extremes Ascribed to Bodhisattva Maitreya and Commented by Vasubandhu and Sthiramati.* Bibliotheca Buddhica, 30 (1936). Osnabrück, Germany: Biblio Verlag, 1970; reprint, Calcutta: Indian Studies Past and Present, 1971. Also, of chapter 1: David Lasar Friedmann, *Sthiramati, Madhyāntavibhāgaṭīkā: Analysis of the Middle Path and the Extremes.* Utrecht, Netherlands: Rijksuniversiteit te Leiden, 1937.
Explanation of (Maitreya's) "Ornament for the Great Vehicle Sūtras"
sūtrālaṃkārābhāṣya
mdo sde'i rgyan gyi bshad pa
P5527, vol. 108
Sanskrit: S. Bagchi. *Mahāyāna-Sūtrālaṃkāra of Asaṅga* [with Vasubandhu's commentary]. Buddhist Sanskrit Texts 13. Darbhanga, India: Mithila Institute, 1970.

Sanskrit and translation into French: Sylvain Lévi. *Mahāyānasūtrālaṃkāra, exposé de la doctrine du grand véhicule selon le système Yogācāra.* 2 vols. Paris: Libraire Honoré Champion, 1907, 1911.

Principles of Explanation
vyākyhayukti
rnam par bshad pa'i rigs pa
P5562, vol. 113

Treasury of Manifest Knowledge
abhidharmakośakārikā
chos mngon pa'i mdzod kyi tshig le'ur byas pa
P5590, vol. 115

Sanskrit: Swami Dwarikadas Shastri. *Abhidharmakośa & Bhāṣya of Ācārya Vasubandhu with Sphuṭārtha Commentary of Ācārya Yaśomitra.* Bauddha Bharati Series 5. Banaras, India: Bauddha Bharati, 1970. Also: P. Pradhan. *Abhidharmakośabhāṣyam of Vasubandhu.* Patna, India: Jayaswal Research Institute, 1975.

French translation: Louis de la Vallée Poussin. *L'Abhidharmakośa de Vasubandhu.* 6 vols. Brussels: Institut Belge des Hautes Études Chinoises, 1971.

English translation of the French: Leo M. Pruden. *Abhidharmakośabhāṣyam.* 4 vols. Berkeley, Calif.: Asian Humanities Press, 1988.

The Thirty / Treatise on Cognition-Only in Thirty Stanzas
triṃśikākārikā / sarvavijñānamātradeśakatriṃśakakārikā
sum cu pa'i tshig le'ur byas pa / thams cad rnam rig tsam du ston pa sum cu pa'i tshig le'ur byas pa
P5556, vol. 113

Sanskrit: Sylvain Lévi. *Vijñaptimātratāsiddhi / Deux traités de Vasubandhu: Viṃśatikā (La Vingtaine) et Triṃsikā (La Trentaine).* Bibliotheque de l'École des Hautes Études. Paris: Libraire Honoré Champion, 1925. Also: K. N. Chatterjee. *Vijñapti-Mātratā-Siddhi (with Sthiramati's Commentary).* Varanasi, India: Kishor Vidya Niketan, 1980.

English translation: Stefan Anacker. *Seven Works of Vasubandhu.* Delhi: Motilal Banarsidass, 1984. Also: Thomas A. Kochumuttom. *A Buddhist Doctrine of Experience.* Delhi: Motilal Banarsidass, 1982.

The Twenty
viṃśatikā / viṃśikākārikā
nyi shu pa'i tshig le'ur byas pa
P5557, vol. 113

Sanskrit: Sylvain Lévi. *Vijñaptimātratāsiddhi / Deux traités de Vasubandhu: Viṃśatikā (La Vigtaine) et Triṃsikā (La Trentaine).* Bibliotheque de l'École des Hautes Études. Paris: Libraire Honoré Champion, 1925.

English translation: Stefan Anacker. *Seven Works of Vasubandhu.* Delhi: Motilal Banarsidass, 1984. Also: Thomas A. Kochumuttom. *A Buddhist Doctrine of Experience.* Delhi: Motilal Banarsidass, 1982.

English translation (stanzas 1-10): Gregory A. Hillis. *An Introduction and Translation of Vinitadeva's Explanation of the First Ten Stanzas of [Vasubandhu's] Commentary on His "Twenty Stanzas," with Appended Glossary of Technical Terms.* Ann Arbor, Mich.: University Microfilms, 1993.

Vinītadeva (*dul ba'i lha*)

Explanation of (Vasubandhu's) [Auto] Commentary on "The Thirty"
sum cu pa'i 'grel bshad
triṃśikāṭīkā
P5571, vol. 114

W̄el-mang Ḡön-chok-gyel-tsen (*dbal mang dkon mchog rgyal mtshan,* 1764-1853)

Notes on (Ḡön-chok-jik-may-w̄ang-b̄o's) Lectures / Notes on (Ḡön-chok-jik-may-w̄ang-b̄o's) Lectures on (D̄zong-ka-b̄a's) "The Essence of Eloquence": Stream of the Speech of the Omniscient: Offering for Purification

legs bshad snying po'i gsung bshad zin bris su bkod pa kun mkhyen gsung gi chu rgyun dag byed mchod yon

Collected Works of Dbal-maṅ Dkon-mchog-rgyal-mtshan, vol. 2, 376-464. New Delhi: Gyeltan Gelek Namgyal, 1974.

Wonch'uk (Tib. *rdzogs gsal / wen tshig / wen tshegs / wanydzeg,* Chin. *Yüan-ts'e,* 613-696)

Extensive Commentary on the "Sūtra Unraveling the Thought"

'phags pa dgongs pa nges par 'grel pa'i mdo'i rgya cher 'grel pa

P5517, vol. 116

Chinese edition: *Dai-nihon Zokuzōkyō, hsü tsang ching,* 134.d-535.a. Hong Kong Reprint, 1922. Also: *Da Zang Jing,* vol. 34, 581-952, vol. 35, 1-100. Taipei: Xin Wen Fong, 1977. Reconstruction of the first portion of the eighth fascicle and all of the tenth fascicle: Inaba Shōju. *Enjiki Gejinmikkyōsho Sanitsububan no kanbunyaku.* Kyoto: Hōzōkan, 1949.

Ȳang-j̄en-ga-way-l̄o-drö, A-kya-yong-dzin (*dbyangs can dga' ba'i blo gros, a khya yongs 'dzin,* c. 1750)

Lamp Thoroughly Illuminating the Presentation of the Three Basic Bodies

gzhi'i sku gsum gyi rnam gzhag rab gsal sgron me

Collected Works of A-kya Yongs-'dzin, vol. 1. New Delhi: Lama Guru Deva 1971. Also: Delhi: Dalama, Iron Dog year. Also: Nang-bstan-shes-rig-'dzin-skyong slob-gnyer-khang, n.d.

English translation: Lati Rinbochay and Jeffrey Hopkins. *Death, Intermediate State and Rebirth in Tibetan Buddhism.* London: Rider, 1980; Ithaca, N.Y.: Snow Lion, 1980.

Presentation of the Grounds and Paths of Mantra according to the Superior Nāgārjuna's System of the Glorious Guhyasamāja: Eloquence Serving as a Port for the Fortunate

dpal gsang ba 'dus pa 'phags lugs dang mthun pa'i sngags kyi sa lam rnam gzhag legs bshad skal bzang 'jug ngogs

Collected Works of A-kya Yoṅs-ḥdzin, vol. 1, 452-497. New Delhi, Lama Guru Deva, 1971.

3. Other Works

Apte, Vaman Shivaram. *Sanskrit-English Dictionary.* Poona, India: Prasad Prakashan, 1957.

Beal, Samuel. *Buddhist Records of the Western World: Translated from the Chinese of Hiuen Tsiang (A.D. 629).* London: Kegan Paul, Trench, and Trübner, 1884; reprint, New York: Paragon, 1968; reprint, Delhi: Motilal Banarsidass, 1981.

Bielefeldt, Carl. "A Discussion of Seated Zen." In *Buddhism in Practice,* edited by Donald S. Lopez Jr., 197-206. Princeton Readings in Religions. Princeton, N.J.: Princeton University Press, 1995.

Buswell, Robert E., and Robert Gimello, eds. *Paths to Liberation.* Honolulu: University of Hawaii Press, 1992.

Chan, Victor. *Tibet Handbook: A Pilgrimage Guide.* Chico, Calif.: Moon, 1994.

Chan, Wing-tsit. "The Thirty Verses on the Mind-Only Doctrine." In *A Sourcebook in Indian Philosophy,* edited by S. Radhakrishnan and C. A. Moore, 333-337. Princeton, N.J.: Princeton University Press, 1957.

Chimpa, Lama, and Alaka Chattopadhyaya. *Tāranātha's History of Buddhism in India.* Simla, India: Indian Institute of Advanced Study, 1970; reprint, Delhi: Motilal Banarsidass, 1990.

Cleary, Thomas. *Buddhist Yoga: A Comprehensive Course.* Boston: Shambhala, 1995.

Conze, E. *The Perfection of Wisdom in Eight Thousand Lines & Its Verse Summary.* Bolinas, Calif.: Four Seasons Foundation, 1973.

Cozort, Daniel. *Unique Tenets of the Middle Way Consequence School.* Ithaca, N.Y.: Snow Lion, 1998.

Cutler, Joshua W. C. and Guy Newland. *The Great Treatise on the Stages of the Path to Enlightenment.* Ithaca, N.Y.: Snow Lion, 2000.

Dondup, K. *The Water-Horse and Other Years: A History of 17th and 18th Century Tibet.* Dharmsala, India: Library of Tibetan Works and Archives, 1984.

Fenner, E. Todd. "Review of Janice Willis's *On Knowing Reality.*" *Journal of the International Association of Buddhist Studies* 3, no. 1 (1980):117-119.

Grupper, Samuel M. "Manchu Patronage and Tibetan Buddhism during the First Half of the Ch'ing Dynasty." *Journal of the Tibet Society* 4 (1984):47-75.

H.H. the Dalai Lama, Tenzin Gyatso. *The Buddhism of Tibet and the Key to the Middle Way.* Translated by Jeffrey Hopkins. London: George Allen and Unwin, 1975. Reprinted in a combined volume, *The Buddhism of Tibet.* London: George Allen and Unwin, 1983; reprint, Ithaca, N.Y.: Snow Lion, 1987.

———. *Kindness, Clarity, and Insight.* Translated and edited by Jeffrey Hopkins; coedited by Elizabeth Napper. Ithaca, N.Y.: Snow Lion, 1984.

H.H. the Dalai Lama, Tenzin Gyatso, and Jeffrey Hopkins. *The Kālachakra Tantra: Rite of Initiation for the Stage of Generation.* Translated and introduced by Jeffrey Hopkins. London: Wisdom, 1985; 2d rev. ed., 1989.

Hall, Bruce Cameron. "The Meaning of Vijñapti in Vasubandhu's Concept of Mind." *Journal of the International Association of Buddhist Studies* 9, no. 1 (1986):7-23.

Hick, John. "Religion as 'Skilful Means': A Hint from Buddhism." Unpublished manuscript.

Hookham, S. K. *The Buddha Within: Tathāgatagarbha Doctrine according to the Shentong Interpretation of the Ratnagotravibhāga.* Albany, N.Y.: State University of New York Press, 1991.

Hopkins, Jeffrey. *Emptiness in the Mind-Only School of Buddhism.* Berkeley: University of California Press, 1999.

———. "A Tibetan Contribution on the Question of Mind-Only in the Early Yogic Practice School." *Journal of Indian Philosophy* 20 (1992):275-343.

———. "A Tibetan Delineation of Different Views of Emptiness in the Indian Middle Way School: Dzong-ka-ba's Two Interpretations of the *Locus Classicus* in Chandrakīrti's *Clear Words* Showing Bhāvaviveka's Assertion of Commonly Appearing Subjects and Inherent Existence." *Tibet Journal* 14, no. 1 (1989):10-43.

———. "The Tibetan Genre of Doxography: Structuring a Worldview." In *Tibetan Literature,* edited by José Ignacio Cabezón and Roger Jackson, 170-186. Ithaca, N.Y.: Snow Lion, 1996.

———. "Ultimate Reality in Tibetan Buddhism." *Buddhist-Christian Studies* 8 (1988):111-129.

———. "The Wanderer: An Anglo-Saxon Poem." *Virginia Quarterly* 53, no. 2 (1977):284-287.

Jackson, David. *Enlightenment by a Single Means.* Vienna: Verlag der Österreichischen Akademie der Wissenschaften, 1994.

Jung, Carl G. *The Collected Works of C. G. Jung.* Princeton, N.J.: Princeton University Press, 1971; second printing, 1974.

Kämpfe, Hans-Rainer. *Ñi ma'i 'od zer / Naran-u gerel: Die Biographie des 2. Pekinger Lcaṅ skya-Qutuqtu Rol pa'i rdo rje (1717-1786).* Monumenta Tibetica Historica, 2 (1). Sankt Augustin: Wissenschaftsverlag, 1976.

Kapstein, Matthew. "From Kun-mkhyen Dol-po-pa to 'Ba'-mda' Dge-legs: Three Jo-nang-pa Masters on the Interpretation of the *Prajñāpāramitā.*" In *Tibetan Studies: Proceedings of the 7th Seminar of the International Association for Tibetan Studies, Graz 1995,* vol. 1, 457-475, edited by Helmut Krassser, Michael Torsten Much, Ernst Steinkellner, and Helmut Tauscher. Vienna: Verlag der österreichischen akademie der wissenschaften, 1997.

Klein, Anne C. *Knowing, Naming, and Negation.* Ithaca, N.Y.: Snow Lion, 1988.

———. *Meeting the Great Bliss Queen: Buddhists, Feminists, and the Art of the Self.* Boston: Beacon Press, 1994.

Lati Rinbochay and Elizabeth Napper. *Mind in Tibetan Buddhism.* London: Rider, 1980; Ithaca, N.Y.: Snow Lion, 1980.

Lati Rinbochay, Denma Lochö Rinbochay, Leah Zahler, and Jeffrey Hopkins. *Meditative States in Tibetan Buddhism.* London: Wisdom, 1983; rev. ed., Boston: Wisdom, 1997.

Lekden, Kensur. *Meditations of a Tibetan Tantric Abbot.* Translated and edited by Jeffrey Hopkins. Ithaca, N.Y.: Snow Lion, 2001.

Lessing, Ferdinand D. *Yung-Ho-Kung: An Iconography of the Lamaist Cathedral in Peking.* Stockholm: Elanders Boktryckeri Aktiebolag, 1942.

Levinson, Jules Brooks. "The Metaphors of Liberation: A Study of Grounds and Paths according to the Middle Way Schools." Ann Arbor, Mich.: University Microfilms, 1994.

Lopez, Donald S., Jr. "Approaching the Numinous: Rudolf Otto and Tibetan Tantra." *Philosophy East and West* 29, no. 4 (October 1979):467-476.

Mimaki, Katsumi. *Blo gsal grub mtha'.* Kyoto: Université de Kyoto, 1982.
———. "The *Blo gsal grub mtha'* and the Mādhyamika Classification in Tibetan *grub mtha'* Literature." In *Contributions on Tibetan and Buddhist Religion and Philosophy,* edited by Ernst Steinkellner and Helmut Tauscher, 161-167. Vienna: Arbeitskreis für tibetische und buddhistische Studien, 1983.
Nagao, Gadjin M. "What Remains in Śūnyatā? A Yogācāra Interpretation of Emptiness." In *Mahāyāna Buddhist Meditation, Theory and Practice,* edited by Minoru Kiyota, 66-82. Honolulu: University of Hawaii Press, 1978; reprinted in *Mādhyamika and Yogācāra: A Study of Mahāyāna Philosophies,* translated by Leslie S. Kawamura, 51-60. Albany, N.Y.: State University of New York Press, 1991.
Napper, Elizabeth. *Dependent-Arising and Emptiness.* London: Wisdom, 1989.
Obermiller, E. *History of Buddhism (Chos-ḥbyung) by Bu-ston.* Heidelberg: Heft, 1932; reprint, Tokyo: Suzuki Research Foundation, n.d.
———. "The Doctrine of the Prajñā-pāramitā as Exposed in the Abhisamayālaṃkāra of Maitreya." *Acta Orientalia.* Leiden, Netherlands: Brill, 1932.
Perdue, Daniel E. *Debate in Tibetan Buddhism.* Ithaca, N.Y.: Snow Lion, 1992.
Poussin, Louis de la Vallée. *Vijñaptimātratāsiddhi: La Siddhi de Hiuan-Tsang.* Paris: P. Geuthner, 1928-1929.
Powers, John C. *The Concept of the Ultimate (don dam pa, paramārtha) in the Saṃdhinirmocana-sūtra: Analysis, Translation and Notes.* Ann Arbor, Mich.: University Microfilms, 1991.
———. *Hermeneutics and Tradition in the Saṃdhinirmocana-sūtra.* Leiden, Netherlands: E. J. Brill, 1993.
———. *The Yogācāra School of Buddhism: A Bibliography.* American Theological Library Association Bibliography Series 27. Metuchen, N.J., and London: American Theological Library Association and Scarecrow Press, 1991.
Radhakrishnan, S., and C. A. Moore, eds. *A Sourcebook in Indian Philosophy.* Princeton, N.J.: Princeton University Press, 1957.
Roerich, George N. *The Blue Annals.* Delhi: Motilal Banarsidass, 1976.
Ruegg, David Seyfort. "The Jo Naṅ Pas: A School of Buddhist Ontologists according to the *Grub mtha' sel gyi me loṅ.*" *Journal of the American Oriental Society* 83, no. 1 (1963):73-91.
———. *The Literature of the Madhyamaka School of Philosophy in India.* Wiesbaden, Germany: Otto Harrassowitz, 1981.
———. *La Théorie du Tathāgathagarbha et du Gotra: Études sur la sotériologie et la gnoséologie du bouddhisme.* Paris: École Française d'Extrême-Orient, 1969.
———. *Le Traité du Tathāgatagarbha de Bu-ston rin-chen-grub.* Paris: École Française d'Extrême-Orient, 1973.
Sangpo, Khetsun. *Tantric Practice in Nyingma.* Translated and edited by Jeffrey Hopkins. London: Rider, 1982; reprint, Ithaca, N.Y.: Snow Lion, 1983.
della Santina, Peter. *Madhyamaka Schools in India.* Delhi: Motilal Banarsidass, 1986.
Schmithausen, Lambert. *Ālayavijñāna: On the Origin and the Early Development of a Central Concept of Yogācāra Philosophy.* Studia Philologica Buddhica Monograph Series IVa, Part I. Tokyo: International Institute for Buddhist Studies, 1987.
———. "On the Problem of the Relation of Spiritual Practice and Philosophical Theory in Buddhism." In *German Scholars on India,* edited by Alfred Würfel and Magdalene Duckwitz, 235-250. Contributions to India Studies, 2. Bombay: Nachiketa, 1976.
Sherbourne, Richard, S.J. *A Lamp for the Path and Commentary.* London: George Allen and Unwin, 1983.
Smart, Ninian. "Soteriology." In *Encyclopedia of Religion,* edited by Mircea Eliade, 13:418-426. New York: Macmillan, 1986.
Smith, E. Gene. "Introduction." In The Collected Works of Thu'u-bkwan Blo-bzang-chos-kyi-nyi-ma, 1:2-12. Delhi: N. Gelek Demo, 1969.
———. *University of Washington Tibetan Catalogue.* 2 vols. Seattle: University of Washington Press, 1969.
Smith, Wilfred Cantwell. "The Modern West in the History of Religion." *Journal of the American Academy of Religion* 52, no. 1 (March 1984):3-18.

Snellgrove, David L., and Hugh Richardson. *Cultural History of Tibet.* New York: Praeger, 1968.

Sponberg, Alan. "The Trisvabhāva Doctrine in India and China: A Study of Three Exegetical Models." *Bukkyō Bunka Kenkyū-jo Kiyō* 21 (1982):97-119.

Stearns, Cyrus R. *The Buddha from Dol po: A Study of the Life and Thought of the Tibetan Master Dolpopa Sherab Gyaltsen,* 127-173. Albany, N.Y.: State University of New York Press, 1999.

———. "Dol-po-pa Shes-rab-rgyal-mtshan and the Genesis of the *gzhan-stong* Position in Tibet." *Asiatische Studien/Études Asiatiques* 59, no. 4 (1995):829-852.

Sureśvarācārya, Śri. *Naiṣkarmyasiddhi.* Translated by S. S. Radhavachar. Mysore: University of Mysore, 1965.

Ueda, Yoshifumi. "Two Main Streams of Thought in Yogācāra Philosophy." *Philosophy East and West* 17 (January-October 1967):155-165.

Urban, Hugh B., and Paul J. Griffiths. "What Else Remains in Śūnyatā? An Investigation of Terms for Mental Imagery in the Madhyāntavibhāga-Corpus." *Journal of the International Association of Buddhist Studies* 17, no. 1 (1994):1-25.

Van der Kuijp, Leonard W. J. "Apropos of a Recent Contribution to the History of Central Way Philosophy in Tibet: *Tsong Khapa's Speech of Gold.*" *Berliner Indologische Studien* 1 (1985):47-74.

Wallace, B. Alan. *The Life and Teachings of Geshé Rabten.* London: George Allen and Unwin, 1980.

Wayman, Alex, and H. Wayman. *The Lion's Roar of Queen Śrīmālā.* New York: Columbia University Press, 1974.

Wayman, Alex. "A Defense of Yogācāra Buddhism." *Philosophy East and West* 46, no. 4 (1996):447-476.

———. "The Yogācāra Idealism." *Philosophy East and West* 15, no. 1 (1965):65-73.

———. "Yogācāra and the Buddhist Logicians." *Journal of the International Association of Buddhist Studies* 2, no. 1 (1979):65-78.

Wei Tat. *Ch'eng wei-shih lun, The Doctrine of Mere-Consciousness.* Hong Kong: Ch'eng Wei-Shih Lun Publication Committee, c. 1973.

White, David. "Why Gurus Are Heavy." *Numen* 33 (1984):40-73.

Willis, Janice D. *On Knowing Reality: The Tattvārtha Chapter of Asaṅga's Bodhisattvabhūmi.* New York: Columbia University Press, 1979; reprint, Delhi: Motilal Banarsidass, 1982.

Wilson, Joe B. *The Meaning of Mind in the Mahāyāna Buddhist Philosophy of Mind-Only (Cittamātra): A Study of a Presentation by the Tibetan Scholar Gung-tang Jam-ḃay-ẏang (gung-thang-'jam-pa'i-dbyangs) of Asaṅga's Theory of Mind-Basis-of-All (ālayavijñāna) and Related Topics in Buddhist Theories of Personal Continuity, Epistemology, and Hermeneutics.* Ann Arbor, Mich.: University Microfilms, 1984.

Wylie, Turrell. "A Standard System of Tibetan Transcription." *Harvard Journal of Asiatic Studies* 22 (1959):261-267.

Yotsuya, Kodo. *The Critique of Svatantra Reasoning by Candrakīrti and Tsong-kha-pa: A Study of Philosophical Proof According to Two Prāsaṅgika Madhyamaka Traditions of India and Tibet.* Tibetan and Indo-Tibetan Studies 8. Stuttgart: Franz Steiner Verlag, 1999.

Index

Compositor: Jeffrey Hopkins
Text: 10.5/12.3 DHop
Display: DHop
Printer and Binder: Maple-Vail Manufacturing Group

Carleton College Library
One North College Street
Northfield, MN 55057-4097

WITHDRAWN